Hans-Jörg Schek   Felix Saltor
Isidro Ramos   Gustavo Alonso   (Eds.)

Advances in Database Technology – EDBT'98

6th International Conference
on Extending Database Technology
Valencia, Spain, March 23-27, 1998
Proceedings

Springer

Series Editors

Gerhard Goos, Karlsruhe University, Germany
Juris Hartmanis, Cornell University, NY, USA
Jan van Leeuwen, Utrecht University, The Netherlands

Volume Editors

Hans-Jörg Schek
Gustavo Alonso
ETH Zürich, Institute of Information Systems, ETH Zentrum
CH-8092 Zürich, Switzerland
E-mail: {schek,alonso}@inf.ethz.ch

Felix Saltor
Universitat Politècnica de Catalunya
Departament de Llengutges i Sistemes Informàtics
UPC Campus Nord, Dept. LSI, C5/C6
Jordi Girona Salgado, 1-3, E-08034 Barcelona, Catalonia, Spain
E-mail: saltor@lsi.upc.es

Isidro Ramos
Departamento de Sistema Informáticos y Computación
Universidad Politècnica de València
Camino de Vera s/n, Apdo. 22.012, E-46020 València, Spain
E-mail: iramos@dsic.upv.es

Cataloging-in-Publication data applied for

Die Deutsche Bibliothek - CIP-Einheitsaufnahme

Advances in database technology : proceedings / EDBT '98, 6th
International Conference on Extending Database Technology,
Valencia, Spain, March 23 - 27, 1998. Hans-Jörg Schek ... (ed.). -
Berlin ; Heidelberg ; New York ; Barcelona ; Budapest ; Hong Kong
; London ; Milan ; Paris ; Santa Clara ; Singapore ; Tokyo : Springer,
1998
  (Lecture notes in computer science ; Vol. 1377)
  ISBN 3-540-64264-1

CR Subject Classification (1991): H.2, H.4, H.3, H.5, I.2.5, D.2

ISSN 0302-9743
ISBN 3-540-64264-1 Springer-Verlag Berlin Heidelberg New York

© Springer-Verlag Berlin Heidelberg 1998
Printed in Germany

Typesetting: Camera-ready by author
SPIN 10631950   06/3142 – 5 4 3 2 1 0   Printed on acid-free paper

Lecture Notes in Computer Science 1377

Edited by G. Goos, J. Hartmanis and J. van Leeuwen

Lecture Notes in Computer Science 1517

Springer
Berlin
Heidelberg
New York
Barcelona
Budapest
Hong Kong
London
Milan
Paris
Santa Clara
Singapore
Tokyo

Foreword

The sixth international conference on Extending Data Base Technology, EDBT 98, took place in Valencia, Spain, between the 23rd and 27th of March 1998. Following a ten-year tradition of excellence, this sixth edition repeated the success of its predecessors: Venice in 1988, Venice again in 1990, Vienna in 1992, Cambridge in 1994, and Avignon in 1996. Firmly established as one of the leading forums in the database community, EDBT 98 has attracted 191 submissions worldwide. Of these, the Program Committee selected 32 papers which largely reflect the main trends in database research: data warehousing and the Internet, with a clear shift in focus from the database itself to the applications and uses of databases in complex environments. Databases seem, thus, to have reached a level of maturity which warrants their use as key building blocks of future information systems. Their functionality and characteristics are no longer the exclusive province of database researchers but a source of ideas, inspiration, and solutions to many in all areas of computer science. This edition of EDBT shows a thriving and fascinating world that, far from being in crisis, has become a crucial component of today's technological endeavors.

The program of the conference was organized around the scientific papers, with sessions ranging from similarity search and indexing to scientific databases, including, of course, the ubiquitous data warehousing, data mining, and Web databases. A keynote talk was given by Gerhard Weikum on issues of quality guarantees in information services. A panel, organized by Keith Jefferey with contributions by Stefano Ceri, Joachim Schmidt, Hans-Jörg Schek, and Andrea Servida, discussed the role of database technology in global information systems and its emphasis within the European Union's 5th Framework Programme for Research. The program was further augmented with six tutorials by F. Matthes (SAP R/3), S. Conrad and G. Saake (heterogeneous databases), F. Leymann (workflow management), C. Mohan (transaction processing), J. Chomicki and D. Toman (temporal databases), and S. Chaudhuri and U. Dayal (data warehousing and mining). In addition, for the first time in EDBT, the conference was complemented with two workshops: the Web and databases, and workflow management systems, organized by Paolo Atzeni and Omran Bukhres respectively.

A conference like EDBT requires the efforts of many people and it would take much more than the space available here to thank all of them. We appreciate the efforts of A. Olive in organizing the tutorials, O. Pastor for the workshops, K. Jefferey for the panel, A. de Miguel for the industrial sessions, and J.H. Canós for the demonstrations. We are also grateful to all the program committee members, and to all additional referees for their help and commitment. Special thanks also to the organization committee and the sponsors. Last but not least, we thank the publisher, Springer-Verlag, represented by Alfred Hofmann, for the smooth cooperation and for their efforts in making the contents of these proceedings available online.

Valencia/Zürich, March 1998

Hans-Jörg Schek, Felix Saltor,
Isidro Ramos, Gustavo Alonso

Sponsorship

Promoted by the EDBT Foundation in cooperation with the VLDB endowment

Sponsored by

> Universitat Politecnica de Valencia
> Generalitat Valenciana
> Ajuntament de Valencia
> The EDBT Foundation
> ETH Zurich
> Oracle
> Sybase
> Softlab
> Iberia

Conference Organization

Conference Chairperson: Felix Saltor (Universitat Politecnica de Catalunya)
Program Committee Chairperson: Hans-Jörg Schek (ETH Zurich)
Executive Committee Chair: Isidro Ramos (Universitat Politecnica de Valencia)
Tutorials Chair: Antoni Olive (Universitat Politecnica de Catalunya)
Panels Chair: Keith Jeffery (Rutherford Appleton Laboratory, CLRC)
Industrial Program Chair: Adoracion de Miguel (Universidad Carlos III)
Demonstrations Chair: Jose Hilario Canos (Universitat Politecnica de Valencia)
Program Committee Coordinator: Gustavo Alonso (ETH Zurich)
Social Events Chair: Matilde Celma (Universitat Politecnica de Valencia)
Demo Session Coordinator: Jose Angel Carsi (Universitat Politecnica de Valencia)

Local Organization Committee

M. Angeles Pastor   (Spain)
Laura Mota   (Spain)
Juan Carlos Casamayor (Spain)

Jose Hilario Canos   (Spain)
Oscar Pastor   (Spain)
M. Carmen Penades (Spain)

EDBT Foundation Executive Commitee

Paolo Atzeni (Italy)
Stefano Ceri (Italy)
Keith Jeffery (United Kingdom)

Michele Missikoff   (Italy)
Joachim W. Schmidt (Germany)

Program Committee

Additional Referees

Abiteboul, S.	Geppert, A.	Mueller, R.	Schuster, H.
Amann, B.	Gluche, D.	Märtens, H.	Schwarz, P.
Amato, G.	Goh, C.H.	Müller, R.	Schönhoff, M.
Anyanwu, K.	Gokkoca, E.	Nakano, M.	Sebastiani, F.
Araujo, R.	Gottlob	Nemoto, T.	Sehring, H.W.
Arpinar, S.	Grandi, F.	Nes, N.	Shafer, J.
Arpinar, B.	Grust, T.	Niederee, C.	Shah, K.
Baader, F.	Gunopulos, D.	Norrie, M.	Shibata, H.
Bechhofer, S.	Hagen, C.	Obermair, W.	Shintani, T.
Behm, A.	Han, Y.	Ohmori, T.	Shirai, H.
Berchtold, S.	Hara, T.	Papadopoulos, A.	Siebes, A.
Biskup, J.	Heuer	Paraboschi, S.	Simeon, J.
Boehlen, M.	Holliday, J.	Pastor, M.A.	Spaccapietra, S.
Bonatti, P.A.	Jonscher, D.	Pastor, O.	Spyratos, N.
Bouganim, L.	Kandzia, P.-T.	Patella, M.	Srikant, R.
Budiarto	Karagoz, P.	Paton, N.	Stanoi, I.
Cabibbo, L.	Kemme, B.	Pizzicannella, R.	Strässler, M.
Canós, J.H.	Kirby, G.	Posenato, R.	Tan, K.-L.
Casamayor, J.C.	Kradolfer, M.	Prabhakar, S.	Tatbul, N.
Chan, D.	Lalmas, M.	Preuner, G.	Teniente, E.
Ciaccia, P.	Larson, P.	Prueckler, T.	Theodoratos, D.
Cicekli, N.K.	Laurent, D.	Psaila, G.	Tombros, D.
Cichocki, A.	Lechtenboerger, J.	Quak, W.	Torlone, R.
Cingil, I.	Ligoudistianos, S.	Ramos, I.	Toroslu, I.H.
Comai, S.	Lopistéguy, P.	Riedel, H.	Torp, K.
Damiani, E.	Ludaescher, B.	Rudloff, A.	Ulusoy, O.
Dolin, R.	Luo, Z.	Rump, N.	Urpi, T.
Domenig, R.	Machado, M.L.	Saake, G.	Vassiliadis, P.
Ehmayer, G.	Mainetto, G.	Sampaio, P.	Virmani, A.
Erwig, M.	Manegold, S.	dos Santos, C.S.	Waas, F.
Fabret, F.	Manolopoulos, Y.	Sarawagi, S.	Weske, M.
Fauvet, M.-C.	Manthey, R.	Savino, P.	Wimmers, E.
Fayyad, U.	Meduna, A.	Schlegelmilch	Wu, D.
Formica, A.	Meghini, C.	Schneider, M.	
Fraternali, P.	Mogi, K.	Scholl, P.-C.	
Freitag, B.	Mohania, M.	Schoop, D.	
Geffner, S.	Monro, D.	Schroeder, G.	

Table of Contents

Algorithms for Data Mining

Modelling in OLAP

Query Processing and Storage Management

Aggregation and Summary Data

Object-Oriented and Active Databases

View Maintenance and Integrity

Databases and the Web

Workflow and Scientific Databases

Keynote Talk

On the Ubiquity of Information Services and the Absence of Guaranteed Service Quality

Gerhard Weikum

University of the Saarland, Saarbruecken, Germany
E-mail: weikum@cs.uni-sb.de, WWW: http://www-dbs.cs.uni-sb.de/

Extended Abstract

We are witnessing the proliferation of the global information society with a sheer explosion of information services on a world-spanning network. This opens up unprecedented opportunities for information discovery, virtual enterprises and cyberspace-based collaboration, and also more mundane things such as electronic commerce [1, 2]. Using such services is, however, often a frustrating experience. Many information services (including Web search engines) deliver poor results - inconsistent, arbitrarily inaccurate, or completely irrelevant data - to their clients, break easily and exhibit long outages, or perform so poorly that unacceptable response times ultimately render the offered service useless. The bottom line is that the quality of services is highly unpredictable, and service quality *guarantees* are usually absent in today's fast-moving IT world.

Contrast this situation with the evolution of database systems. Over the last three decades, database systems have developed an outstanding reputation for keeping mission-critical data consistent, virtually never losing data, providing high availability, excellent performance for a wide variety of workload patterns, and so on. The bottom line is that database systems have proven that they are among the most dependable, intensively stress-tested services within computer science and the IT business [3]. On the flip side of the coin, however, we have to admit that full-fledged database systems are typically heavy-weight platforms with a large "footprint", and many of their salient qualities can be achieved only in conjunction with a human support staff that takes care of system administration and performance tuning.

Database technology is widely viewed as the most promising candidate for a backbone of quality-conscious information services. But the database R&D community should not rest on achievements of the past. The rapidly evolving, highly diverse world of global information services calls for a new blend of database technology. Often only certain components of a database system are needed as building blocks that have to be integrated with other technologies such as workflow, multimedia, or security technologies; a prominent example for an application class with this characteristic is electronic commerce [4]. These building blocks should therefore be light-weight, easy-to-use, composable and adaptable, require "zero administration" and be self-tuning.

These aspects already constitute strategic research avenues that are database-oriented but also interact with other computer science and application fields [5].

An additional dimension that I wish to highlight and focus on in this talk is the need for *guaranteed service quality* of both building blocks and more comprehensive information services.

The objective of providing services with guaranteed quality poses a variety of research challenges. First and above all, we need a better understanding of what kinds of gurantees are useful and how to express them in a rigorous yet reasonably comprehensible manner. The overriding goal is to develop highly dependable systems. This includes provably correct behavior, high reliability and availability in the presence of component failures, and predictably good performance even under stress conditions. Thus service quality must comprise both qualitative and quantitative properties; examples can already be found in specific areas:

- On the qualitative side, guaranteed termination of workflows or other active application components is an example [6, 7]. In addition to the mere termination, one should ideally guarantee an outcome that is acceptable to the user in terms of her business or private goals (e.g., granting loans only to credit-worthy customers, or purchasing a gameboy within certain financial constraints). Thus, this kind of service quality requires formal reasoning on the specification of the workflow [8], but also failure-resilience and availability guarantees from an underlying recovery manager [9, 10].
- On the quantitative side, consider the notion of quality of service in the area of multimedia storage and communication [11, 12]. This involves quantifying the presentation quality of video and audio streams in terms of guaranteed bandwidth or guaranteed playback "smoothness". In addition, throughput and startup-latency metrics are of major interest, too, as storage servers and network switches serve many clients concurrently. Finally, the cost of such servers is a non-negligible issue, which demands good resource utilization. Then, the quality of service could be of stochastic nature for a better cost/performance ratio. For example, smooth playback could be guaranteed only with a specifiable probability close to one [13].

However, the world is not so simple to be categorized that easily. Many properties of information services for which we would like to establish service quality guarantees have both qualitative and quantitative facets. Sometimes, properties are perceived by the user as qualitative (or ordinal at best), but should ideally be quantified for comparison purposes. The quality of information retrieval services such as Web search engines falls into this grey area, and intelligent searching of multimedia documents or scientific data exhibits similar problems [14, 15].

In addition, one may often wish to trade off some quality of the delivered query results (e.g., completeness, accuracy, timeliness) for faster response time and/or lower resource consumption (including the money charged by a service). For example, one may prefer a few reasonably good matches within seconds over finding the best matches with a time-consuming or expensive service. Being able to cope with such tradeoffs in a predictable manner becomes even harder for "mixed" information services that combine information-retrieval-style searching

with SQL-style processing and optimization in a highly distributed and heterogeneous environment [16, 17].

Provided that the service quality guarantees of building blocks were well
defined, the next step would be to compose the building blocks into more comprehensive, value-added services that preserve these guarantees and transform
them into a higher level of service quality. Such compositions should ideally
be carried out with mathematical rigor to capture again the binding nature of
guarantees. To this end, higher-level services and also end-users may want to
establish a service quality "contract" with a used service. In the presence of
tradeoffs (e.g., service quality versus service charges), the contract may itself result from a negotiation process. Thus, information services also need to support
negotiability of their quality guarantees in a mostly automated manner (e.g.,
based on "agents" that act on behalf of the client's preferences).

Obviously, the problems sketched above call for intensive research efforts
to obtain a better fundamental understanding of service quality. Mathematical
modeling is a key asset in addressing these hard issues, but we also need research
on the system architecture and experimental side. This talk discusses directions
towards guaranteed service quality, using examples from workflow management
and multimedia information servers. The notion of service quality in these areas
is rather narrow, and such approaches must be generalized and broadened into
a science of service quality guarantees. Among the questions to be addressed
are: How should service quality properties be specified? How can we quantify
initially qualitative service properties? How can we cope with tradeoffs among
quantitative properties? How can we compose the service quality guarantees of
multiple building blocks into more comprehensive services that can again give
guarantees to their clients? The ultimate goal would be to provide even legally
binding guarantees for the ubiquitous information services of future generations.

References

1. Communications of the ACM Vol.40 No.2, February 1997, Special Anniversary Issue
   on "The Next 50 Years".
2. Lockemann, P.C., Kölsch, U., Koschel, A., Kramer, R., Nikolai, R., Wallrath, M.,
   Walter, H.-D.: The Network as a Global Database: Challenges of Interoperability,
   Proactivity, Interactiveness, Legacy, Proceedings of the 23rd International Conference on Very Large Data Bases (VLDB), Athens, Greece, 1997.
3. Silberschatz, A., Stonebraker, M., Ullman, J. (Editors): Database Research:
   Achievements and Opportunities Into the 21st Century, ACM SIGMOD Record
   Vol.25 No.1, March 1996.
4. Adam, N., Yesha, Y., et al.: Strategic Directions in Electronic Commerce and Digital
   Libraries, ACM Computing Surveys Vol.28 No.4, December 1996, pp. 818–835.
5. Silberschatz, A., Zdonik, S., et al.: Strategic Directions in Database Systems - Break-
   ing Out of the Box, ACM Computing Surveys Vol.28 No.4, December 1996, pp.
   764–778.
6. Reuter, A., Schneider, K., Schwenkreis, F.: ConTracts Revisited, in: Jajodia, S.,
   Kerschberg, L. (Editors), Advanced Transaction Models and Architectures, Kluwer
   Academic Publishers, 1997.

7. Alonso, G., Hagen, C., Schek, H.-J., Tresch, M.: Distributed Processing Over Stand-alone Systems and Applications, Proceedings of the 23rd International Conference on Very Large Data Bases (VLDB), Athens, Greece, 1997.
8. Muth, P., Wodtke, D., Weissenfels, J., Weikum, G., Kotz-Dittrich, A.: Enterprise-wide Workflow Management Based on State and Activity Charts, in: Dogac, A., Kalinichenko, L., Özsu, T., Sheth, A. (Editors), Advances in Workflow Management Systems and Interoperability, NATO Advanced Study Institute, Springer, 1998.
9. Kamath, M., Alonso, G., Günthör, R., Mohan, C.: Providing High Availability in Very Large Workflow Management Systems, Proceedings of the 5th International Conference on Extending Database Technology (EDBT), Avignon, France, 1996.
10. Lomet, D.: Persistent Applications Using Generalized Redo Recovery, Proceedings of the IEEE International Conference on Data Engineering (ICDE), Orlando, Florida, 1998.
11. Christodoulakis, S., Triantafillou, P.: Research and Development Issues for Large-Scale Multimedia Information Systems, ACM Computing Surveys Vol.27 No.4, December 1995, pp. 576-579.
12. Wolf, L.C., Griwodz, C., Steinmetz, R.: Multimedia Communication, Proceedings of the IEEE Vol.85 No.12, December 1997, pp. 1915-1933.
13. Nerjes, G., Muth, P., Weikum, G.: Stochastic Service Guarantees for Continuous Data on Multi-Zone Disks, Proceedings of the ACM International Symposium on Principles of Database Systems (PODS), Tucson, Arizona, 1997.
14. Faloutsos, C.: Searching Multimedia Databases By Content, Kluwer Academic Publishers, 1996.
15. Raghavan, P.: Information Retrieval Algorithms: A Survey, Proceedings of the ACM-SIAM Symposium on Discrete Algorithms, 1997.
16. Bulletin of the IEEE Technical Committee on Data Engineering Vol.19 No.1, March 1996, Special Issue on Integrating Text Retrieval and Databases.
17. Bulletin of the IEEE Technical Committee on Data Engineering Vol.19 No.4, December 1996, Special Issue on Query Processing for Non-Standard Data.

Similarity Search and Indexing

Processing Complex Similarity Queries
with Distance-Based Access Methods*

Paolo Ciaccia[1], Marco Patella[1], and Pavel Zezula[2]

[1] DEIS - CSITE-CNR, University of Bologna - Italy,
{pciaccia,mpatella}@deis.unibo.it
[2] IEI-CNR Pisa - Italy, zezula@iei.pi.cnr.it

Abstract. Efficient evaluation of similarity queries is one of the basic requirements for advanced multimedia applications. In this paper, we consider the relevant case where *complex* similarity queries are defined through a generic language $\mathcal{L}$ and whose predicates refer to a single feature F. Contrary to the language level which deals only with similarity scores, the proposed evaluation process is based on distances between feature values - known spatial or metric indexes use distances to evaluate predicates. The proposed solution suggests that the index should process complex queries *as a whole*, thus evaluating multiple similarity predicates at a time. The flexibility of our approach is demonstrated by considering three different similarity languages, and showing how the M-tree access method has been extended to this purpose. Experimental results clearly show that performance of the extended M-tree is consistently better than that of state-of-the-art search algorithms.

1 Introduction

Similarity queries are a primary concern in multimedia database systems, where users are interested in retrieving objects which best match query conditions. Efficient resolution of similarity queries is usually based on a process which includes the extraction of relevant features from the objects (e.g., color histograms from still images), and the indexing of such feature values, typically through either *spatial* access methods, such as the R-tree [Gut84], or *metric* trees, such as the M-tree [CPZ97]. In this context, low *distance* between feature values implies high similarity, and vice versa. In general, index support is experimentally shown to be valuable under many circumstances, even if the cost of evaluating a similarity query can sometimes be still very high – comparable to that of a sequential scan.

Efficient processing of *complex* similarity queries - queries with more than one similarity predicate - has some peculiarities with respect to traditional (Boolean) query processing which have been highlighted by recent works [CG96, Fag96, FW97]. The basic lesson is that, since the "similarity score" (*grade*) an object gets for the whole query depends on how the scores it gets for the single predicates are combined, predicates cannot be independently evaluated.

Example 1. Consider an image database where objects can be retrieved by means of predicates on shape and color features, and assume that the two sets of feature values are separately indexed. In order to retrieve the best match for the query (shape = 'circular') and (color = 'red') it is *not* correct to retrieve *only* the best match

---

* This work has been partially supported by the ESPRIT LTR project no. 9141, HERMES, and by Italian CNR project MIDA. The work of Pavel Zezula has also been supported by Grants GACR No. 102/96/0986 and KONTAKT No. PM96 S028.

for color (using an index on color) and the best match for shape (using an index on shape), since the best match for the *overall* query needs not to be the best match for the single conjuncts.   □

The state-of-the-art solution to the above kind of queries is Fagin's $\mathcal{A}_0$ algorithm [Fag96], which returns the k best matches (nearest neighbors) for a complex query, on the assumption that evaluation of the single predicates in the query is carried out by independent *subsystems*, and that access to one subsystem is "synchronized" with that to others (a special case of the $\mathcal{A}_0$ algorithm is described in Section 6).

In this paper we concentrate on a relevant class of complex similarity queries, which arises when all the similarity predicates refer to a single feature.

Example 2. Consider an image database whose objects can be retrieved using a *Query-by-Sketch* modality. When a user draws a shape on the screen, the system searches the DB, and returns those, say, 10 images which contain a shape best matching (according to given similarity criterion for shapes) the user's input. The user can then "refine" the search by selecting those objects which are similar to what he/she had in mind and which are actually not. Suppose two "positive" and one "negative" samples are specified. Now, the system has to search the DB for those 10 objects which are most similar to *both* positive samples, and, at the same time, *not* similar to the negative one. This interactive process can be iterated several times, until the user gets satisfied with system's output.   □

An interactive retrieval process, such as the one sketched above, typically occurs when querying multimedia repositories [Jai96], where the user has no clear idea on how to express what he/she is looking for, and relies on previous results to improve the effectiveness of subsequent requests.

Complex single-feature queries could be casted in the more general framework of multi-feature queries, however their nature suggests that a more efficient evaluation strategy could indeed be possible to devise. The one we propose starts from the idea to extend access methods in such a way that they can process complex queries *as a whole*, thus evaluating *multiple* predicates at a time. Since access methods typically evaluate the similarity of two objects by means of their distance in some feature space, we ground our proposed extension on a sound formal basis, which specifies how multiple distance measures (corresponding to multiple similarity predicates) should be combined to perform a both efficient and correct pruning of the search space. The three basic ingredients of the framework we introduce are: (a) a distance function, d, which compares feature values, (b) a functional mapping, h, from distances to similarity scores, and (c) a similarity language, $\mathcal{L}$, which, given scores for the single predicates, tells us how to combine them to yield a global score. Our solution is parametric on d, h, and $\mathcal{L}$, thus it provides a solution to the following general problem:
Given a similarity language $\mathcal{L}$, a distance function d, and a function h which converts distance values into similarity scores, **determine** how to efficiently evaluate a query Q expressed in the language $\mathcal{L}$, when Q consists of predicates on a single feature F, and values of F are indexed by a distance-based access method.

We show the feasibility of our approach by considering three different languages and by providing an extension of the M-tree access method [CPZ97]. Since the only assumption we need about the nature of the access method is that it uses distances to prune the search space, our results apply to *any* spatial (multi-dimensional) or metric access method. Experimental results show that our solution consistently outperforms state-of-the-art algorithms.

The rest of the paper is organized as follows. In Section 2 we provide the necessary definitions, review how access methods are used to solve simple similarity queries, and introduce three specific query languages for illustrative purpose. In Section 3 we establish the basis for evaluating similarity queries through distance measures, and Section 4 presents the basic result which allows a distance-based access method to process complex queries as a whole. In Section 5 we describe how the M-tree access method has been extended to this purpose. Section 6 shows some experimental results, and Section 7 considers related works and concludes.

2 Preliminaries

Consider a collection (class, relation, etc.) C of objects which are indexed on a feature F, whose values are drawn from a domain D, $D = dom(F)$. For simplicity, we assume that values of F univocally identify objects, thus no two objects have the same feature value.

A generic *similarity predicate* p on F has the form $F \sim v$, where $v \in D$ is a constant (*query value*) and $\sim$ is a similarity operator. Evaluating p on an object O returns a score (grade), $s(p, O.F) \in [0, 1]$, which says how similar is object O to the query value v. The evaluation of predicate p on all the objects in C then yields a "graded set" $\{(O, s(p, O.F))|O \in C\}$. For instance, evaluating the predicate color $\sim$ 'red' means to assign to each image in the collection a score assessing its "redness".

We consider two basic forms of similarity queries: *range* and *nearest neighbors* (best matches) queries. Given a predicate $p : F \sim v$, a *simple* range query returns all the objects whose similarity with respect to v is at least α (e.g. images which are "red enough"), whereas a *simple* nearest neighbors query would return the k ($k \geq 1$ being user-specified) objects having the highest similarity scores with respect to v (e.g. the 10 "most red" images), with ties arbitrarily broken.

Since our objective is to deal with *complex* (single-feature) similarity queries, we need a language $\mathcal{L}$ which allows multiple predicates to be combined into a *similarity formula*, f. The nature of the specific language is uninfluential to our arguments. We only require that, if $f = f(p_1, \ldots, p_n)$ is a formula of $\mathcal{L}$, then the similarity of an object O with respect to f, denoted $s(f, O.F)$, is computed through a corresponding *scoring function* [Fag96], s_f, which takes as input the scores of O with respect to the predicates of formula f, that is:

$$s(f(p_1, \ldots, p_n), O.F) = s_f(s(p_1, O.F), \ldots, s(p_n, O.F)) \tag{1}$$

Shortly, we will introduce three specific sample languages to construct similarity formulas. For the moment, we provide the following definitions which exactly specify the kinds of queries we are going to deal with:

Complex range query: Given a similarity formula $f \in \mathcal{L}$ and a minimum similarity threshold α, the query range(f, α, C) selects all the objects in C (with their scores) such that $s(f, O.F) \geq \alpha$.

Complex nearest neighbors (k-NN) query: Given a similarity formula f and an integer $k \geq 1$, the k-NN query NN(f, k, C) selects the k objects in C having the highest similarity scores with respect to f. In case of ties, they are arbitrarily broken.

2.1 Distance-based Access Methods

Evaluating the similarity of an object with respect to a query value can be done in several ways, depending on the specific feature. A common approach, which is the basis for efficiently processing similarity queries through indexing, is to have an *indirect* evaluation of similarity scores. In this case, what is actually measured is the *distance* between feature values, being understood that high scores correspond to low distances and low scores to high distances.

In general, distance evaluation is carried out by using a *distance function*, d, which, for any pair of feature values, yields a non-negative real value, $d : D^2 \to \Re_0^+$. Although arbitrary distance functions can in principle be used, it is both reasonable and useful to limit the analysis to "well-behaved" cases. In particular, we assume that d is a *metric*, that is, for each triple of values $v_x, v_y, v_z \in D$ the following axioms hold:

1. $d(v_x, v_y) = d(v_y, v_x)$ (*symmetry*)
2. $d(v_x, v_y) > 0$ ($v_x \neq v_y$) and $d(v_x, v_x) = 0$ (*non negativity*)

3. $d(v_x, v_y) \leq d(v_x, v_z) + d(v_z, v_y)$ (*triangle inequality*)

Relevant examples of metrics are, among others, the Minkowski (L_p) metrics over n-dimensional points, which are defined as $L_p(v_x, v_y) = (\sum_{j=1}^{n} \mid v_x[j] - v_y[j] \mid^p)^{1/p}$ ($p \geq 1$), and include the Euclidean (L_2) and the Manhattan, or "city-block", (L_1) metrics, and the Levenshtein (*edit*) distance over strings, which counts the minimal number of changes (insertions, deletions, substitutions) needed to transform a string into another one.

Most tree-like access methods able to index complex features share a substantial similar structure, which can be summarized as follows. Each *node* N (usually mapped to a disk page) in the tree corresponds to a *data region*, $Reg(N) \subseteq \mathcal{D}$. Node N stores a set of entries, each entry pointing to a child node N_c and including the specification of $Reg(N_c)$. All indexed keys (feature values, i.e. points of $\mathcal{D}$) are stored in the leaf nodes, and those keys in the sub-tree rooted at N are guaranteed to stay in $Reg(N)$.

Example 3. The R-tree [Gut84] organizes n-dimensional point objects by enclosing them into Minimum Bounding Rectangles (MBR). This principle is applied at all levels of the R-tree, so that the region of each node in the R-tree is a (hyper-)rectangle, defined as the MBR of its child regions. □

Example 4. The M-tree [CPZ97] can index objects over generic metric spaces (see also Section 5). Given a distance function d, the region of a node N is implicitly defined by the predicate $d(v_r, v) \leq r(v_r)$, where v_r is a so-called *routing object* (or routing key value), and $r(v_r)$ is the *covering radius* of v_r. The intuition is that all objects v reachable from node N are within distance $r(v_r)$ from v_r. Note that the actual "shape" of M-tree regions depends on the specific metric space $(\mathcal{D}, d)$. □

The usual strategy adopted by access methods to process *simple* range similarity queries consists of two basic steps:

1. Take as input a (single) query value, v_q, and a *maximum distance threshold*, $r(v_q)$. This defines a *query region*, centered at v_q. In general, $r(v_q)$ is inversely related to the minimum similarity one wants to accept in the result.
2. Search the index, and access all and only the nodes N such that $Reg(N)$ and the query region intersect. This is practically done by computing $d_{min}(v_q, Reg(N))$, that is, the minimum distance an object in $Reg(N)$ can have from the query value v_q. If $d_{min}(v_q, Reg(N)) \leq r(v_q)$ then N has to be accessed, otherwise it can be safely pruned from the search space.

In the case of k-NN queries, the basic difference with respect to above strategy is that the distance threshold $r(v_q)$ is a *dynamic* one, since it is given by the distance of the k-th *current* nearest neighbor from the query value v_q. Because of $r(v_q)$ dynamicity, algorithms for processing nearest neighbors queries also implement a policy to decide the order to visit nodes which have not been pruned yet. Details can be found in [RKV95] (for R-tree) and [CPZ97] (for M-tree).

If we try to naively generalize the above approach to complex queries, some difficulties arise, which are summarized by the following questions:

1. Can a "distance threshold" be defined for arbitrarily complex queries?
2. Can we always decide if a query region and a data region intersect?

It turns out that both questions have a *negative* answer, as we will show in Section 4, where we also describe how our approach can nonetheless overcome these limitations.

2.2 Similarity Languages

A similarity language $\mathcal{L}$ comes with a syntax, specifying which are valid (well-formed) formulas, and a semantics, telling us how to evaluate the similarity of an object with respect to a complex query. Although the results we present are language-independent, it also helps intuition to consider specific examples.

The first two languages we consider, $\mathcal{FS}$ (fuzzy standard) and $\mathcal{FA}$ (fuzzy algebraic), share the same syntax and stay in the framework of *fuzzy logic* [Zad65, KY95]. Their formulas are defined by the following grammar rule:

$$f ::= p \,|\, f \wedge f \,|\, f \vee f \,|\, \neg f \,|\, (f)$$

where p is a similarity predicate. The semantics of a formula f is given by the following set of recursive rules:

	$\mathcal{FS}$	$\mathcal{FA}$
$s(f_1 \wedge f_2, v)$	$\min\{s(f_1, v), s(f_2, v)\}$	$s(f_1, v) \cdot s(f_2, v)$
$s(f_1 \vee f_2, v)$	$\max\{s(f_1, v), s(f_2, v)\}$	$s(f_1, v) + s(f_2, v) - s(f_1, v) \cdot s(f_2, v)$
$s(\neg f, v)$	$1 - s(f, v)$	$1 - s(f, v)$

The last language we consider, $\mathcal{WS}$ (weighted sum), does not use logical connectives at all, but allows *weights* to be attached to the predicates, in order to reflect the importance the user wants to assign to each of them. A formula f has the form:

$$f ::= \{(p_1, \theta_1), (p_2, \theta_2), \dots, (p_n, \theta_n)\}$$

where each p_i is a similarity predicate, the θ_i's are positive weights, and $\sum_i \theta_i = 1$. The semantics of a $\mathcal{WS}$ formula f is simply $s(f, v) = \sum_{i=1}^{n} \theta_i \cdot s(p_i, v)$

Although the subject of deciding on which is the "best" language is not in the scope of the paper, it is important to realize that any specific language has some advantages and drawbacks, thus making the choice a difficult problem. We also remark that above languages are only a selected sample of the many one can conceive to formulate complex queries, and that our approach is not limited only to them. In particular, our results also apply to fuzzy languages, such as $\mathcal{FS}$ and $\mathcal{FA}$, when they are extended with weights, as shown in [FW97].

Example 5. Assume that we want to retrieve objects which are similar to both query values v_1 and v_2. With the $\mathcal{FS}$ and $\mathcal{FA}$ languages we can use the formula $f_1 = p_1 \wedge p_2$, where $p_i : F \sim v_i$. With $\mathcal{WS}$, assuming that both predicates have the same relevance to us, the formula $f_2 = \{(p_1, 0.5), (p_2, 0.5)\}$ is appropriate. Given objects' scores for the two predicates p_1 and p_2, Table 1 shows the final scores, together with the relative rank of each object. It is evident that objects' ranking highly depends on the specific language (see object O_1) – this can affect the result of nearest neighbors queries – and that the score of an object can be very different under different languages – this can influence the choice of an appropriate threshold for range queries. □

			$\mathcal{FS}$		$\mathcal{FA}$		$\mathcal{WS}$	
Object	$s(p_1, O_j.F)$	$s(p_2, O_j.F)$	$s(f_1, O_j.F)$	rank	$s(f_1, O_j.F)$	rank	$s(f_2, O_j.F)$	rank
O_1	0.9	0.4	0.4	4	0.36	3	0.65	1
O_2	0.6	0.65	0.6	1	0.39	2	0.625	3
O_3	0.7	0.5	0.5	3	0.35	4	0.6	4
O_4	0.72	0.55	0.55	2	0.396	1	0.635	2

Table 1. Similarity scores for complex queries.

Above example also clearly shows that determining the best match (the object with rank 1 in Table 1) for a complex query cannot be trivially solved by considering only the best matches for the single predicates. For instance, the best match for formula f_1 under $\mathcal{FA}$ semantics is object O_4, which is neither the best match for p_1 nor for p_2.

Similar considerations can be done for complex range queries too. Refer again to Table 1, and consider the query $\mathbf{range}(f_2, 0.63, \mathcal{C})$, to be evaluated under $\mathcal{WS}$ semantics. Given the threshold value 0.63, which leads to select objects O_1 and O_4, which are (if any) appropriate thresholds for the single predicates such that the correct answer could still be derived?

3 Evaluating Similarity Through Distance

The first step towards an efficient evaluation of complex queries concerns how to compute similarity scores when only distances between feature values can be measured, which is the usual case. For this we need the definition of a *correspondence function*.

Definition 1 : Correspondence function.
We say that $h : \Re_0^+ \to [0,1]$ is a (distance to similarity) correspondence function iff it has the two following properties:

$$h(0) = 1 \tag{2}$$

$$x_1 \leq x_2 \Rightarrow h(x_1) \geq h(x_2) \qquad \forall x_1, x_2 \in \Re_0^+ \tag{3}$$

In other terms, a correspondence function assigns maximum similarity in case of 0 distance (exact-match), and makes similarity inversely related to distance. Usually, correspondence functions are not considered "first-class" elements in the context of similarity processing. The reason is that either only simple queries are considered or no reference is done to the actual work performed by indexes [CG96]. In the enlarged context we consider, where both complex queries and access methods are present, correspondence functions have a primary role. Indeed, they represent the "missing link" of the chain leading from feature values to similarity scores. The essence of this chain is captured by the following definition.

Definition 2 : Distance-based similarity environment.
A distance-based similarity environment is a quadruple $\mathcal{DS} = (\mathcal{D}, d, h, \mathcal{L})$, where $\mathcal{D}$ is a domain of feature values, d is a metric distance over $\mathcal{D}$, h is a correspondence function, and $\mathcal{L}$ is a similarity language. □

Given any similarity environment $\mathcal{DS}$, we are now ready to perform sequential evaluation of arbitrarily complex similarity queries. The algorithm for range queries is described below; the one for nearest neighbors queries is based on the same principles, but it is not shown here for brevity.

Algorithm Range-Seq (sequential processing of range queries)

Input: similarity environment $\mathcal{DS} = (dom(F), d, h, \mathcal{L})$, collection $\mathcal{C}$,
formula $f = f(p_1, \ldots, p_n) \in \mathcal{L}$, minimum threshold α;
Output: $\{(O, s(f, O.F)) | O \in \mathcal{C}, s(f, O.F) \geq \alpha\}$;
1. For each $O \in \mathcal{C}$ do:
2.   For each predicate $p_i : F \sim v_i$ compute $d_i = d(v_i, O.F)$;
3.   Let $s_i = h(d_i)$, $i = 1, \ldots, n$;
4.   If $s(f, O.F) \stackrel{\Delta}{=} s_f(s_1, \ldots, s_n) \geq \alpha$ then add $(O, s(f, O.F))$ to the result;

Example 6. Consider the environment $\mathcal{DS} = (\Re^2, L_1, 1 - 0.1 \cdot x, \mathcal{FS})$, and the query $Q :$ $\text{range}(p_1 \wedge p_2, 0.8, \mathcal{C})$, with $p_i : F \sim v_i (i = 1, 2)$. Refer to Figure 1, where $v_1 = (3, 2)$ and $v_2 = (5, 3)$, and consider the point (feature vector) $v = (3.5, 1)$. To evaluate its score, we first compute $d_1 = L_1(v_1, v) = |3 - 3.5| + |2 - 1| = 1.5$ and $d_2 = L_1(v_2, v) = |5 - 3.5| + |3 - 1| = 3.5$ (line 2 of the Range-Seq algorithm). In step 3, we apply the correspondence function $h(x) = 1 - 0.1 \cdot x$ to the two distance values, thus obtaining $s_1 = h(d_1) = 0.85$ and $s_2 = h(d_2) = 0.65$. Finally, since we are using the $\mathcal{FS}$ semantics, we have to take the minimum of the two scores to compute the overall score, i.e. $s(p_1 \wedge p_2, v) = \min\{s_1, s_2\} = 0.65$. Since this is less than the threshold value 0.8, point v does not satisfy the range query Q. □

It is important to observe that the choice of a specific correspondence function can affect the result of similarity queries. This is easily shown by referring to the above example, and redefining h as $h(x) = 1 - 0.05 \cdot x$. After simple calculations, it is derived that $s(p_1 \wedge p_2, v) = 0.825$, thus point v will be part of the result.

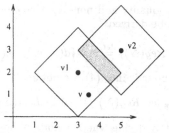

Fig. 1. The region of the query $\mathtt{range}((F \sim v_1) \wedge (F \sim v_2), 0.8, \mathcal{C})$ is shaded

4 Extending Distance-based Access Methods

The Range-Seq algorithm is correct but clearly inefficient for large objects' collections. Exploitation of an index built over a feature F is possible, in principle, with two different modalities. The "traditional" one independently.evaluates the predicates, and then combines the partial results *outside* of the index itself. This approach, besides being inefficient because it leads to access parts of the index more than once, cannot be applied at all for generic complex queries. The case of nearest neighbors queries has been analyzed in [Fag96]. Here the problem is that the best match for a complex query cannot be determined by looking only at the best matches of the single predicates (see also Example 5). In the case of complex range queries, independent evaluation is possible only under the strict assumption that a distance constraint for each single predicate in the query can be derived from the overall minimum similarity threshold, which is not always the case.

Example 7. Consider Example 6. In order to process the query $\mathtt{range}(p_1 \wedge p_2, 0.8, \mathcal{C})$, by independently evaluating predicates p_1 and p_2, we can proceed as follows. Since we are using the $\mathcal{FS}$ semantics and the correspondence function h, it has to be $\min\{1 - 0.1 \cdot d(v_1, v), 1 - 0.1 \cdot d(v_2, v)\} \geq 0.8$. This can also be expressed as $\max\{d(v_1, v), d(v_2, v)\} \leq 2$. It can be easily verified that if v satisfies above inequality, then v lies in the shaded query region of Figure 1. Since above constraint can be also written as $(d(v_1, v) \leq 2) \wedge (d(v_2, v) \leq 2)$, the complex query can be evaluated by independently performing two simple range queries, taking the intersection of objects' results, and then computing the final scores. □

Example 8. Assume now that the correspondence function has the form $h(x) = \exp(-x)$, and consider the query $\mathtt{range}(\{(p_1, 0.4), (p_2, 0.6)\}, 0.5, \mathcal{C})$ in the $\mathcal{WS}$ language. The similarity constraint is:
$$0.4 \cdot e^{-d(v_1, v)} + 0.6 \cdot e^{-d(v_2, v)} \geq 0.5$$
which cannot be decomposed into two *bounded* simple range queries. Indeed, if v is in the result, then v necessarily satisfies the two constraints (each using a single query value) $0.4 \cdot e^{-d(v_1, v)} + 0.6 \geq 0.5$ and $0.4 + 0.6 \cdot e^{-d(v_2, v)} \geq 0.5$, which are obtained by setting, respectively, $d(v_2, v) = 0$ and $d(v_1, v) = 0$. However, since the first constraint is satisfied by *any* $d(v_1, v)$ value, the corresponding simple range query is $d(v_1, v) \leq \infty$, which amounts to access the whole data collection. □

The second possibility of evaluating complex queries is the one we propose, and suggests that the index should process complex queries *as a whole*. We first show how queries in the two above examples would be managed by the new approach, then we generalize to generic similarity environments.

Example 9. Consider Example 7, and assume, without loss of generality, that feature values are indexed by an M-tree. We can prune a node N with routing object v_r and covering radius $r(v_r)$ if its region, $Reg(N)$, only contains points v such that

$$\min\{1 - 0.1 \cdot d(v_1, v), 1 - 0.1 \cdot d(v_2, v)\} < 0.8 \tag{4}$$

Because of the triangular inequality and non-negativity properties of d, the following lower bound on $d(v_i, v)$ can be derived:

$$d(v_i, v) \geq d_{min}(v_i, Reg(N)) \stackrel{\text{def}}{=} \max\{d(v_i, v_r) - r(v_r), 0\} \qquad i = 1, 2$$

If we substitute such lower bounds into (4), we obtain

$$\min\{1 - 0.1 \cdot d_{min}(v_1, Reg(N)), 1 - 0.1 \cdot d_{min}(v_2, Reg(N))\} < 0.8$$

From this, we can immediately decide whether node N has to be accessed or not. $\quad\square$

Example 10. Consider now Example 8. We can adopt the same approach as in Example 9. Node N can be pruned if each point v in its region satisfies $0.4 \cdot e^{-d(v_1, v)} + 0.6 \cdot e^{-d(v_2, v)} < 0.5$. By using the $d_{min}(v_i, Reg(N))$ lower bounds, it is obtained $0.4 \cdot e^{-d_{min}(v_1, Reg(N))} + 0.6 \cdot e^{-d_{min}(v_2, Reg(N))} < 0.5$. Once again, checking above constraint is all that is needed to decide if node N has to be accessed. $\quad\square$

In order to generalize our approach to generic similarity environments and arbitrarily complex queries, we need a preliminary definition.

Definition 3 : Monotonicity.
We say that a scoring function $s_f(s(p_1, v), \ldots, s(p_n, v))$ is monotonic increasing (respectively decreasing) in the variable $s(p_i, v)$ if, given any two n-tuples of scores' values $(s_1, \ldots, s_i, \ldots, s_n)$ and $(s_1, \ldots, s_i', \ldots, s_n)$ with $s_i \leq s_i'$, it is $s_f(s_1, \ldots, s_i, \ldots, s_n) \leq s_f(s_1, \ldots, s_i', \ldots, s_n)$ (resp. $s_f(s_1, \ldots, s_i, \ldots, s_n) \geq s_f(s_1, \ldots, s_i', \ldots, s_n)$). If a scoring function s_f is monotonic increasing (resp. decreasing) in all its variables, we simply say that s_f is monotonic increasing (resp. decreasing). $\quad\square$

Monotonicity is a property which allows us to somewhat predict the behavior of a scoring function in a certain data region, which is a basic requirement for deciding whether or not the corresponding node in the index should be accessed. Note that both queries in Examples 9 and 10 are monotonic increasing.

Before presenting our major result, it has to be observed that *a scoring function can be "monotonic in all its arguments" without being neither monotonic increasing nor monotonic decreasing* (on the other hand, the converse is true). For instance, $s(p_1, v) \cdot (1 - s(p_2, v))$, which is the scoring function of $p_1 \wedge \neg p_2$ in the $\mathcal{FA}$ language, is monotonic increasing in $s(p_1, v)$ and monotonic decreasing in $s(p_2, v)$.

In case a certain predicate occurs more than once in a formula, we need to distinguish its occurrences. For instance, the formula $f : p_1 \wedge \neg p_1$ with $p_1 : F \sim v_1$, has to be rewritten as, say, $p_1 \wedge \neg p_2$, with $p_2 : F \sim v_2$, and $v_1 \equiv v_2$. Under the $\mathcal{FA}$ semantics, say, the scoring function of f, that is $s(p_1, v) \cdot (1 - s(p_2, v))$, is now monotonic increasing in $s(p_1, v)$ and monotonic decreasing in $s(p_2, v)$. By distinguishing single occurrences of predicates, it can be seen that the $\mathcal{WS}$ language can only generate formulas having monotonic increasing scoring functions, whereas all scoring functions of formulas of languages $\mathcal{FS}$ and $\mathcal{FA}$ are guaranteed to be monotonic in all their arguments.

We are now ready to state our major result.

Theorem 4.
Let $\mathcal{DS} = (dom(F), d, h, \mathcal{L})$ be a similarity environment, $f = f(p_1, \ldots, p_n) \in \mathcal{L}$ ($p_i : F \sim v_i, i = 1 \ldots, n$) a similarity formula such that each predicate occurs exactly once, and $\mathcal{C}$ a collection of objects indexed by a distance-based tree $\mathcal{T}$ on the values of feature F. Let $s_f(s(p_1, v), \ldots, s(p_n, v))$ ($v \in \mathcal{D}$) be the scoring function of f. If s_f is monotonic in all its variables, then a node N of $\mathcal{T}$ can be pruned if

$$s_{max}(f, Reg(N)) \stackrel{\text{def}}{=} s_f(h(d_B(v_1, Reg(N))), \ldots, h(d_B(v_n, Reg(N)))) < \alpha \qquad (5)$$

where

$$d_B(v_i, Reg(N)) = \begin{cases} d_{min}(v_i, Reg(N)) & \text{if } s_f \text{ is monotonic increasing in } s(p_i, v) \\ d_{max}(v_i, Reg(N)) & \text{if } s_f \text{ is monotonic decreasing in } s(p_i, v) \end{cases} \quad (6)$$

with $d_{min}(v_i, Reg(N))$ ($d_{max}(v_i, Reg(N))$) being a lower (upper) bound on the minimum (maximum) distance from v_i of any value $v \in Reg(N)$, and where α is

- *the user-supplied minimum similarity threshold, if the query is* **range**(f, α, C);
- *the k-th highest similarity score encountered so far, if the query is* NN(f, k, C). *If less than k objects have been evaluated, then $\alpha = 0$.* □

Proof: Assume that $Reg(N)$ contains a point v^* such that $s_f(h(d(v_1, v^*)), \ldots, h(d(v_n, v^*))) \geq \alpha$. By construction, it is $d(v_i, v^*) \geq d_B(v_i, Reg(N))$, if s_f is monotonic increasing in $s(p_i, v)$, and $d(v_i, v^*) \leq d_B(v_i, Reg(N))$, if s_f is monotonic decreasing in $s(p_i, v)$. Since h is a monotonic decreasing function, it is also

$$h(d(v_i, v^*)) \leq (\geq) h(d_B(v_i, Reg(N))) \quad \text{if} \quad d(v_i, v^*) \geq (\leq) d_B(v_i, Reg(N))$$

Since s_f is monotonic in all its arguments, it is impossible to have

$$s_f(h(d(v_1, v^*)), \ldots, h(d(v_n, v^*))) > s_f(h(d_B(v_1, Reg(N))), \ldots, h(d_B(v_n, Reg(N))))$$

which proves the result. □

Theorem 4 generalizes to complex queries the basic technique used to process simple range and nearest neighbors queries. It does so by considering how a (single occurrence of a) predicate can affect the overall score, and by using appropriate bounds on the distances from the query values. These are then used to derive an upper bound, $s_{max}(f, Reg(N))$, on the maximum similarity score an object in the region of node N can get with respect to f, that is, $s_{max}(f, Reg(N)) \geq s(f, v)$, $\forall v \in Reg(N)$.

Example 11. A query which has been proved in [Fag96] to be a "difficult one" is NN$(p_1 \wedge \neg p_1, 1, C)$, with $p_1 : F \sim v_1$. This can be processed as follows. First, rewrite the formula as $p_1 \wedge \neg p_2$ ($p_2 : F \sim v_2, v_2 \equiv v_1$). Without loss of generality, assume the standard fuzzy semantics $\mathcal{FS}$, and the correspondence function $h(x) = 1 - 0.1 \cdot x$. The scoring function can therefore be written as $\min\{s(p_1, v), 1 - s(p_2, v)\}$. By substituting bounds on distances and applying the correspondence function we finally get:

$$s_{max}(p_1 \wedge \neg p_1, Reg(N)) = \min\{1 - 0.1 \cdot d_{min}(v_1, Reg(N)), 0.1 \cdot d_{max}(v_1, Reg(N))\}$$

where we have turned back to the original v_1 notation. □

Theorem 4 provides a general way to handle complex queries in generic similarity environments, using *any* distance-based index. The only part specific to the index at hand is the computation of the $d_{min}(v_i, Reg(N))$ and $d_{max}(v_i, Reg(N))$ bounds, since they depend on the kind of data regions managed by the index. For instance, in M-tree above bounds are computed as $\max\{d(v_i, v_r) - r(v_r), 0\}$ and $d(v_i, v_r) + r(v_r)$, respectively [CPZ97]. Simple calculations are similarly required for other metric trees [Chi94, Bri95, BO97], as well as for spatial access methods, such as R-tree (see [RKV95]).

4.1 False Drops at the Index Level

The absence of any specific assumption about the similarity environment and the access method in Theorem 4 makes it impossible to guarantee the absence of "false drops" at the level of index nodes. More precisely, if inequality (5) is satisfied, it is guaranteed that node N cannot lead to qualifying objects, and can therefore be safely pruned. This is also to say that $Reg(N)$ and the query region do not intersect. On the other hand, if (5) is *not* satisfied (i.e. $s_{max}(v, Reg(N)) \geq \alpha$) it can still be the case that $Reg(N)$ and the query region do not intersect.

Example 12. Consider the environment $\mathcal{DS} = (\Re^2, L_2, \exp(-x), \mathcal{FS})$, and the query range$(p_1 \wedge p_2, 0.5, \mathcal{C})$, with $p_i : F \sim v_i$, $v_1 = (1, 2)$ and $v_2 = (2, 2)$. Consider the M-tree data region: $Reg(N) = \{v | d(v_r = (1.5, 1), v) \leq r(v_r) = 0.43\}$. As Figure 2 shows, $Reg(N)$ does not intersect the query region, represented by the intersection of the two circles of radius $\ln(1/0.5)$ centered in v_1 and v_2. However, the maximum possible similarity for $Reg(N)$ is estimated as $\min\{e^{-(d(v_1, v_r) - r(v_r))}, e^{-(d(v_2, v_r) - r(v_r))}\}$ $\approx 0.502 > 0.5$. Therefore, node N cannot be pruned. □

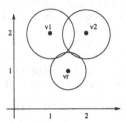

Fig. 2. The false drops phenomenon.

Although the phenomenon of false drops can lead to explore unrelevant parts of the tree, thus affecting the efficiency of the retrieval, it does not alter at all the correctness of the results, since, at the leaf level, we evaluate the actual similarities of the objects, for which no bounds are involved and actual distances are measured.

Resolving the false drop problem for generic similarity environments appears to be a difficult task. In order to derive a tighter $s_{max}(v, Reg(N))$ bound, the $n \cdot (n - 1)/2$ relative distances between the n query values could be taken into account. However, without specific assumptions on the similarity environment, additional hypotheses on the scoring functions (such as differentiability) seem to be needed to obtain major improvements. We leave this problem as a future research activity.

In the case of spatial access methods, which only manage similarity environments of type $\mathcal{DS}_{sam} = (\Re^n, L_p, h, \mathcal{L})$, that is, vector spaces with L_p (Euclidean, Manhattan, etc.) metrics,[3] the similarity bound established by (5) could be improved by trying to exploit the geometry of the Cartesian space. However, for arbitrarily complex queries this still remains a difficult task [SK97, HM95].

5   The Extended M-tree

In order to verify actual performance obtainable by processing complex queries with a distance-based access method, we have extended the M-tree. The M-tree stores the indexed objects into fixed-size nodes, which correspond to regions of the metric space. Each entry in a leaf node has the format $[v_j, \text{oid}(v_j)]$, where v_j are the feature values of the object whose identifier is $\text{oid}(v_j)$. The format of an entry in an internal node is $[v_r, r(v_r), \text{ptr}(N)]$, where v_r is a feature value (*routing object*), $r(v_r) > 0$ is its *covering radius*, and $\text{ptr}(N)$ is the pointer to a child node N. We remind that the semantics of the covering radius is that each object v in the sub-tree rooted at node N satisfies the constraint $d(v_r, v) \leq r(v_r)$.[4] Thus, the M-tree organizes the metric space into a set of (possibly overlapping) regions, to which the same principle is recursively applied.

Our M-tree implementation is based on the Generalized Search Tree (GiST) C++ package, a structure extendible both in the data types and in the queries it can support [HNP95]. In this framework, a specific access method is obtained by providing the code for a limited set of required methods. Among them, only the `Consistent` method is used

---

[3] Indeed, they can also manage quadratic distance functions, as shown in [SK97], but this does not make a substantial difference.

[4] For performance reasons, each entry also stores the distance between the feature value of that entry and the parent routing object. For more specific details see [CPZ97].

during the search phase, and had therefore to be modified to support complex queries. The Consistent method returns *false* iff all objects in the sub-tree of the considered node are guaranteed to be outside of the query region. The search algorithm uses this information to descend all paths in the tree whose entries are consistent with the query.

The new version of the Consistent method we have developed is based on the results obtained in the previous Section, and is fully parametric in the similarity environment $\mathcal{DS}$. The overall architecture of the method is shown in Figure 3.

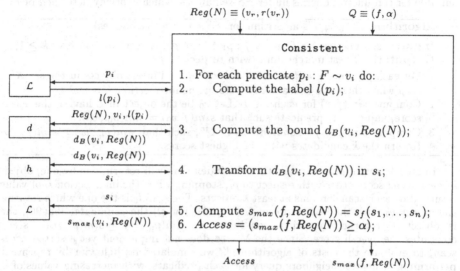

Fig. 3. The Consistent method.

The input of the Consistent method is an entry $Reg(N) \equiv (v_r, r(v_r))$, representing the region of node N, and a query $Q \equiv (f, \alpha)$, where $f = f(p_1, \ldots, p_n)$ is (a suitable encoding of) a formula of language $\mathcal{L}$, and α is a minimum similarity threshold. In order to optimize nearest neighbors queries, the new version of Consistent also returns an upper bound, $s_{max}(f, Reg(N))$, on the similarity between the objects in the region $Reg(N)$ and the formula f. At each step of the k-NN algorithm, the node with the highest bound is selected and fetched from disk.

The architecture of Consistent is independent of the similarity environment $\mathcal{DS}$, since all specific computations are performed by external modules implementing each component of the environment (these are shown on the left side in Figure 3). In particular, the two modules denoted with $\mathcal{L}$ are those which encode language-specific information. The execution flow closely follows the logic of Theorem 4 (refer to Figure 3): at step 2, we compute a Boolean *label* for each predicate p_i, to determine if the scoring function s_f is monotonic increasing or decreasing in the variable $s(p_i, v)$. Then, distance bounds are computed, depending on the value of $l(p_i)$, and transformed, by using the correspondence function h, into similarity bounds s_i. The overall upper bound $s_{max}(f, Reg(N))$ is then computed, by applying the scoring function s_f to the bounds obtained for all the predicates. Finally, if $s_{max}(f, Reg(N))$ is lower than α (*Access* = *false*) N can be pruned from the search.

6 Experimental Results

In this Section we compare the performance of the extended M-tree with that of other search techniques. For the sake of definiteness, we consider the specific similarity environment $\mathcal{DS} = ([0, 1]^5, L_\infty, 1 - x, \mathcal{FS})$, where $L_\infty(v_x, v_y) = \max_j\{|v_x[j] - v_y[j]|\}$. The results we present refer to 10-NN conjunctive queries $f : p_1 \wedge p_2 \wedge \ldots$, evaluated over a collection of 10^4 objects. These are obtained by using the procedure described in [JD88], which generates normally-distributed clusters. The intra-cluster variance is $\sigma^2 = 0.1$, and clusters' centers are uniformly distributed in the 5-dimensional unit hypercube. Unless otherwise stated, the number of clusters is 10. The M-tree implementation uses a node size of 4 KBytes.

The alternative search algorithms against which we compare M-tree are a simple linear scan of the objects – the worst technique for CPU costs, but not necessarily for I/O costs – and the $\mathcal{A}'_0$ algorithm [Fag96], a variant of the general $\mathcal{A}_0$ algorithm suitable for conjunctive queries under $\mathcal{FS}$ semantics, which is briefly described below.[5]

Algorithm $\mathcal{A}'_0$ (Fagin's algorithm for $\mathcal{FS}$ conjunctive queries)

Input: conjunctive $\mathcal{FS}$ formula $f : p_1 \wedge \ldots \wedge p_n$, collection $\mathcal{C}$, integer $k \geq 1$;
Output: the k best matches in $\mathcal{C}$ with respect to f;

1. For each p_i, open a *sorted access* index scan and insert objects in the set X^i; stop when there are at least k objects in the intersection $L = \cap_i X^i$.
2. Compute $sim(f, v)$ for each $v \in L$. Let v_0 be the object in L having the least score, and p_{i_0} the predicate such that $sim(f, v_0) = sim(p_{i_0}, v_0)$.
3. Compute $sim(f, v_c) \; \forall \; candidate \; v_c \in X^{i_0}$, such that $sim(p_{i_0}, v_c) \geq sim(p_{i_0}, v_0)$
4. Return the k candidates with the highest scores.

In step 1, *sorted access* means that the index scan will return, one by one, objects in decreasing score order with respect to p_i, stopping when the intersection L of values returned by each scan contains at least k objects. The scan i_0 is the one which returned the object v_0 with the least score in L (step 2). For all the *candidates* [Fag96], that is, objects v_c returned by such a scan *before* v_0 ($sim(p_{i_0}, v_c) \geq sim(p_{i_0}, v_0)$), step 3 computes the overall score. Since the M-tree does not implement yet a sorted access scan, to evaluate the costs of algorithm $\mathcal{A}'_0$ we simulated its behavior by repeatedly performing k_i nearest neighbors query for each predicate, with increasing values of k_i, until 10 common objects were found in the intersection. The sorted access costs are then evaluated as the costs for the last n queries (one for each predicate). Note that this is an optimistic cost estimate, since it is likely that a "real" sorted access scan would cost more than a single k_i nearest neighbors query which "magically" knows the right value of k_i. Step 3 is charged only with CPU costs, since we assume that all the *candidates* are kept in main memory.

Figures 4 and 5 compare CPU and I/O costs, respectively, for 10-NN queries consisting of the conjunction of two predicates, $f : p_1 \wedge p_2$, as a function of the distance between the two query objects. CPU costs are simply evaluated as the number of distance computations, and I/O costs are the number of page reads. As the graphs show, $\mathcal{A}'_0$ performs considerably better when the query objects are relatively "close", because in this case it is likely that the two query objects will have almost the same neighbors, thus leading to cheaper costs for the sorted access phase. On the other hand, the M-tree approach is substantially unaffected by the distance between the query objects. When query objects are "close" (i.e. the user asks for a conjunction of similar objects) the CPU costs for both approaches are very similar, while I/O costs for $\mathcal{A}'_0$ tend to be twice those of our approach. Comparison with linear scan shows that our approach is highly effective in reducing CPU costs, which can be very time-consuming for complex distance functions, and also lowers I/O costs. $\mathcal{A}'_0$, on the other hand, is much worse than linear scan for "distant" query objects.

Figures 6 and 7 show the effect of varying data distribution, by generating 10^3 clusters. Now the distribution of objects' relative distances has a lower variance with respect to the previous case, thus making more difficult the index task. Major benefits are still obtained from reduction of CPU costs, whereas I/O costs of M-tree are comparable to that of a linear scan only for not too far query objects.

---

[5] We have slightly changed notation and terminology to better fit our scenario. In particular, we access data through index scans, whereas Fagin considers generic independent *subsystems*.

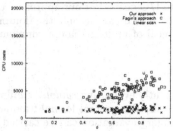

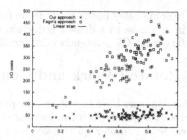

Fig. 4. CPU costs. $f : p_1 \wedge p_2$. 10 clusters   **Fig. 5.** I/O costs. $f : p_1 \wedge p_2$. 10 clusters

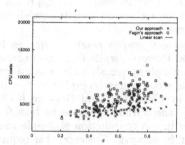

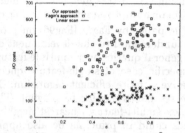

Fig. 6. CPU costs. $f : p_1 \wedge p_2$. 10^3 clusters   **Fig. 7.** I/O costs. $f : p_1 \wedge p_2$. 10^3 clusters

We now consider the case where one of the two predicates is negated i.e. $f : p_1 \wedge \neg p_2$. In this case, as Figures 8 and 9 show, the trend of index-based algorithms is somewhat inverted with respect to the previous cases, thus favoring, as to I/O costs, the linear scan when query objects are close. The performance degradation of M-tree in this case is because, due to negation, best matches are far away from both the query objects, thus leading to access a major part of the tree.

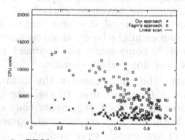

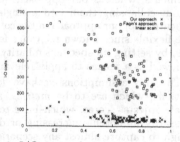

Fig. 8. CPU costs. $f : p_1 \wedge \neg p_2$. 10 clusters   **Fig. 9.** I/O costs. $f : p_1 \wedge \neg p_2$. 10 clusters

Finally, we compared our approach with $\mathcal{A}'_0$ in the case of n positive conjuncts, that is $f : p_1 \wedge \ldots \wedge p_n$, for n in the range $[2, 5]$. Results, not shown here, report that I/O savings are never less than 90%, while CPU savings have a decreasing trend, starting from 85% down to 45%. This is explained by observing that, at each call of the **Consistent** method, we evaluate distances with respect to all the predicates. On the other hand, $\mathcal{A}'_0$ algorithm does this only for the *candidate* objects, as above explained.

The overall conclusions we can draw from above results, as well as others not shown here for brevity, can be so summarized:

1. Processing complex queries as a whole is *always* better than performing multiple sorted access scans (as $\mathcal{A}'_0$ does), both as to I/O and CPU costs.
2. For a given formula, our approach is almost insensitive to the specific choice of the query objects, thus leading to stable performance. This is not the case for the $\mathcal{A}'_0$ algorithm.

3. In some cases linear scan can be preferable as to I/O costs, but our approach leads in any case to a drastic reduction of CPU costs, which can become the dominant factor for CPU-intensive distance functions typical of multimedia environments.

7 Related Work and Conclusions

In this paper we have considered the problem of efficiently evaluating *complex* similarity queries over generic feature domains. We have introduced a general formal framework to deal with complex queries and have shown how query evaluation can be carried out by using *any* access method which assesses similarity through distance measures, which is the usual case. Finally, we have demonstrated the effectiveness of our approach by extending the M-tree metric access method, and showing how it leads to considerable performance improvements over other query processing strategies.

The paper by Fagin [Fag96] on processing complex nearest neighbors queries has been fundamental to the development of our work. However, while Fagin is concerned with general queries over multiple features (and multiple systems), we have considered the specific case of single-feature queries and have consequently exploited this fact to derive a more efficient algorithm. The work by Chaudhuri and Gravano [CG96] addresses issues similar to [Fag96]. The strategy the authors propose to transform complex (multi-feature) nearest neighbors queries into a conjunction of simple range queries could in principle be also applied to our framework. However, this requires some knowledge of data and distance distributions, which might not be always available. Furthermore, and more important, it only applies if distance constraints can be derived for the single range queries, which is not always the case (see Example 8).

Our work shares some similarities with relevance feedback techniques used by text retrieval systems [Har92]. Such techniques derive a new query from a previous one and from user's relevance judgments on previous results. In our terminology, this amounts to a change of a (single) query value, trying to "move" it closer towards relevant documents, whereas our approach queries the database with *multiple* query values, without collapsing them into a single value. Although we have not worked out the implications of our approach in the context of document retrieval, it is clear that we are more flexible since known relevance feedback techniques might be obtained as special cases, by setting up specific similarity environments. In some sense, our approach can be viewed as a means to apply relevance feedback over *any* feature domain.

The only assumptions we have done throughout the paper concern the distance functions, which are to be *metrics*, and the *scoring functions* used to evaluate the overall objects' scores, which have to be monotonic in all their arguments (but not necessarily monotonic increasing or decreasing). Both these assumptions are general enough to capture almost any scenario of interest in multimedia environments.

We need the distance function to be a metric only for practical reasons, since no access method we are aware of is able to index over non-metric spaces. However, it is easy to see that relaxing this assumption would not affect our main formal result (Theorem 4). Thus, an hypothetical access method for non-metric spaces could exploit the results in this paper without modifications. A practical non-metric distance for which this would be helpful is described in [FS96].

We need scoring functions to be monotonic in all their arguments in order to derive similarity bounds within a data region, which is a basic requirement for Theorem 4 to apply. Although monotonicity is clearly a reasonable property to demand to a scoring function [Fag96], there are indeed cases for which it does not hold. For instance, assume one wants to retrieve all the objects v which are similar to v_1 as they are to v_2 (up to a certain tolerance ϵ), that is, $\mid s(F \sim v_1, v) - s(F \sim v_2, v) \mid \le \epsilon$. This "equi-similarity" (or "equi-distance") query does not fit our framework, however it appears that access methods *can* indeed be further extended to process it too. We plan to investigate this and similar problems in our future work.

Acknowledgements

We thank Fausto Rabitti, Pasquale Savino, and Roger Weber for helpful discussions about the subject of the paper. We also acknowledge the comfortable environment of the HERMES project within which this work has originated.

References

[BO97]   T. Bozkaya and M. Ozsoyoglu. Distance-based indexing for high-dimensional metric spaces. In *Proceedings of the 1997 ACM SIGMOD International Conference on Management of Data*, pages 357–368, Tucson, AZ, May 1997.

[Bri95]   S. Brin. Near neighbor search in large metric spaces. In *Proceedings of the 21st VLDB International Conference*, pages 574–584, Zurich, Switzerland, September 1995.

[CG96]   S. Chaudhuri and L. Gravano. Optimizing queries over multimedia repositories. In *Proceedings of the 1996 ACM SIGMOD International Conference on Management of Data*, pages 91–102, Quebec, Canada, June 1996.

[Chi94]   T. Chiueh. Content-based image indexing. In *Proceedings of the 20th VLDB International Conference*, pages 582–593, Santiago, Chile, September 1994.

[CPZ97]   P. Ciaccia, M. Patella, and P. Zezula. M-tree: An efficient access method for similarity search in metric spaces. In *Proceedings of the 23rd VLDB International Conference*, pages 426–435, Athens, Greece, August 1997.

[Fag96]   R. Fagin. Combining fuzzy information from multiple systems. In *Proceedings of the 15th ACM Symposium on Principles of Database Systems*, pages 216–226, Montreal, Canada, June 1996.

[FS96]   R. Fagin and L. Stockmeyer. Relaxing the triangle inequality in pattern matching. Research Report RJ 10031, IBM, June 1996.

[FW97]   R. Fagin and E.L. Wimmers. Incorporating user preferences in multimedia queries. In *Proceedings of the 6th ICDT International Conference*, pages 247–261, Delphi, Greece, January 1997.

[Gut84]   A. Guttman. R-trees: A dynamic index structure for spatial searching. In *Proceedings of the 1984 ACM SIGMOD International Conference on Management of Data*, pages 47–57, Boston, MA, June 1984.

[Har92]   D. Harman. Relevance feedback and other query modification techniques. In W.B. Frakes and R. Baeza-Yates, editors, *Information Retrieval: Data Structures and Algorithms*, chapter 11, pages 241–263. Prentice Hall PTR, 1992.

[HM95]   A. Henrich and J. Möller. Extending a spatial access structure to support additional standard attributes. In *Proceedings of the 4th International Symposium on Advances in Spatial Databases (SSD'95)*, volume 951 of *LNCS*, pages 132–151, Zurich, Switzerland, August 1995. Springer-Verlag.

[HNP95]   J.M. Hellerstein, J.F. Naughton, and A. Pfeffer. Generalized search trees for database systems. In *Proceedings of the 21st VLDB International Conference*, pages 562–573, Zurich, Switzerland, September 1995.

[Jai96]   R. Jain. Infoscopes: Multimedia information systems. In B. Furht, editor, *Multimedia Systems and Techniques*, chapter 7, pages 217–253. Kluwer Academic Publishers, 1996.

[JD88]   A.K. Jain and R.C. Dubes. *Algorithms for Clustering Data*. Prentice-Hall, 1988.

[KY95]   G.J. Klir and B. Yuan. *Fuzzy Sets and Fuzzy Logic*. Prentice Hall PTR, 1995.

[RKV95]   N. Roussopoulos, S. Kelley, and F. Vincent. Nearest neighbor queries. In *Proceedings of the 1995 ACM SIGMOD International Conference on Management of Data*, pages 71–79, San Jose, CA, May 1995.

[SK97]   T. Seidl and H.-P. Kriegel. Efficient user-adaptable similarity search in large multimedia databases. In *Proceedings of the 23rd VLDB International Conference*, pages 506–515, Athens, Greece, August 1997.

[Zad65]   L.A. Zadeh. Fuzzy sets. *Information and Control*, 8:338–353, 1965.

HySpirit – A Probabilistic Inference Engine for Hypermedia Retrieval in Large Databases

Norbert Fuhr, Thomas Rölleke*

University of Dortmund, Informatik 6, 44221 Dortmund, Germany
{fuhr,roelleke}@ls6.cs.uni-dortmund.de

Abstract. HySpirit is a retrieval engine for hypermedia retrieval integrating concepts from information retrieval (IR) and deductive databases. The logical view on IR models retrieval as uncertain inference, for which we use probabilistic reasoning. Since the expressiveness of classical IR models is not sufficient for hypermedia retrieval, HySpirit is based on a probabilistic version of Datalog. In hypermedia retrieval, different nodes may contain contradictory information; thus, we introduce probabilistic four-valued Datalog. In order to support fact queries as well as content-based retrieval, HySpirit is based on an open world assumption, but allows for predicate-specific closed world assumptions. For performing efficient retrieval on large databases, our system provides access to external data. We demonstrate the application of HySpirit by giving examples for retrieval on images, structured documents and large databases.

1 Introduction

Due to the advances in hardware, processing of multimedia data in digital form has become feasible. Currently, many research efforts for the development of multimedia information systems are undertaken. New multimedia applications like digital libraries, video-on-demand or electronic kiosks are reaching the end user. However, a crucial issue in most of these application is content-oriented access to multimedia objects. Whereas many technical problems can be solved in a satisfactory way, content-oriented multimedia retrieval is still in its infancy.

Classic information retrieval (IR) approaches originally developed for (unstructured) text documents can hardly be applied in multimedia environments, for three major reasons:

1. Since text retrieval typically only considers the presence/absence of terms, it is logically founded on propositional logic, where each term corresponds to a proposition, to which a document assigns truth values (see [23]). In multimedia IR, however, we have to deal with e.g. temporal or spatial relationships which cannot be expressed in this logic.
2. Classic IR models treat documents as atomic units. On the other hand, since multimedia documents comprise different media, they are always structured documents. Through the additional use of links, hypermedia documents have an even more complex structure. Therefore, document nodes linked together may form a single answer item.
3. Different document nodes may contain contradictory information, thus their combination cannot be handled properly by most models.

* This work was supported in part by the European Commission through the ESPRIT project FERMI (grant no. 8134)

What modern IR has to offer, however, is the principle of retrieval as uncertain inference ([22]): Let d denote a document and q a query, then retrieval can be viewed as estimation of the probability $P(d \rightarrow q)$ that the document implies the query. Thus, logic-based IR is similar to the logical view on databases, but uses uncertain inference instead of a deterministic one.

Most multimedia information systems are based on object-oriented database management systems (see e.g. the survey in [17]). For content-based retrieval, however, the query languages offered by these systems are not sufficient, due to their limited expressiveness and the inability to perform uncertain inference. For solving the first problem, different logical query languages have been discussed (see e.g. [1]). Recently, the issue of uncertain inference has gained more attention. Some approaches to multimedia IR based on textual annotations incorporate text retrieval methods like e.g. the vector space model which generate a ranking of documents (see e.g. [27]). Most approaches, however, are based on similarity of multimedia objects; for example, in image retrieval, typical methods compute similarity values for color, contour and texture (see e.g. [8]). However, the integration of these methods in a full-fledged database query language suffers from the fact that the latter typically is restricted to deterministic inference. So most approaches are of hybrid nature: the database query language is used for a pre-election of multimedia objects, for which then the similarity methods yield a ranking ([4]). However, the resulting query language has a limited expressiveness — e.g. when asking for the photographers of images similar to a given photo, it is not possible to project on the photographer's names. Furthermore, the hybrid query language lacks the closure property.

The latter problem is overcome by using a fuzzy or a probabilistic relational algebra ([21], [7], [10]). As a more expressive query language supporting uncertain inference, probabilistic Datalog (pD) is described in [15]. This approach yields probability intervals for derived facts; however, no implementation has been described so far. [16] presents a restricted pD system (no projection, no difference) yielding point probabilities by using a default independence assumption and explicit disjointness of events.

For probabilistic inference in IR, one must take into account that for large document collections, only minimum probabilistic information is available for the single events considered. Thus, successful probabilistic IR models are based on independence assumption, which results in point probabilities for the answers; for example, the IN-QUERY system ([3]) is based on Bayesian inference networks. However, as mentioned before, these approaches are restricted to propositional logic.

In [9], we have described a version of pD (see section 2.1) which is suited for IR applications, due to the simplifying assumptions about the dependence of events: basic events are independent by default, and disjointness of events can be specified explicitly. For the retrieval of hypermedia documents, we have proposed a model based on four-valued logic in [18] (see section 2.2).

In this paper, we present the hypermedia retrieval engine HySpirit (*H*ypermedia *S*ystem with *p*robabilistic *i*nference for the *r*etrieval of *i*nforma*t*ion). HySpirit combines pD with a four-valued logic, thus solving the three problems mentioned in the beginning: pD supports multimedia retrieval by using horn clause predicate logic instead of propositional logic. The four-valued logic solves the problem of retrieval of structured documents and of possible inconsistencies between the contents of document nodes. The resulting system offers several unique features:

– It is based on 4-valued Datalog.

- It yields probabilistic inference in 4-valued logic.
- It supports both open world and closed world assumptions.
- It performs efficient retrieval for large databases.

The remainder of this paper is structured as follows: first, we outline the major concepts of pD as well as our four-valued logic for retrieval of structured documents. Then we show how both approaches can be combined, by first presenting four-valued Datalog (4D), which is then extended to a probabilistic version, thus arriving at probabilistic four-valued Datalog (p4D). Based on this inference engine, we show how retrieval of hypermedia objects can be implemented. Finally, we demonstrate the application of HySpirit by giving examples for retrieval on images, structured documents and large databases.

2 Background

2.1 Probabilistic Datalog

Probabilistic Datalog is an extension of ordinary (two-valued) Datalog (2D). On the syntactical level, the only difference is that with facts, also a probabilistic weight may be given[1], e.g.

```
0.7 indterm(d1,ir). 0.8 indterm(d1,db). 0.5 link(d2,d1).
about(D,T) ← indterm(D,T).
about(D,T) ← link(D,D1) , about(D1,T).
q1(X) ← about(X,ir) , about(X,db).
```

Informally speaking, the probabilistic weight gives the probability that the following predicate is true. In our example, document d1 is with probability 0.7 about IR and with probability 0.8 about databases (DB). The rule for q1 searches for documents dealing with both of these topics. Assuming that index terms are stochastically independent, we can compute a probability of $0.7 \cdot 0.8 = 0.56$ for q1(d1). As a more complex example, consider the second rule for about(D,T) stating that in case we have hypertext links between documents a document is about a term if it is linked to another document indexed with this term: Then simple multiplication of the probabilistic weights involved in the inference process would give us results that are not consistent with probability theory, e.g. for document d2: $0.5 \cdot 0.7 \cdot 0.5 \cdot 0.8 = 0.14$. Here the probability 0.5 for the link between d2 and d1 is considered twice; the correct result would be 0.28.

Thus, we must keep track of the events that contribute to a derived fact. For this purpose, we assume that each fact for an extensional database (EDB) predicate corresponds to a basic (probabilistic) event, and assign it an unique event key. A fact derived for an intensional database (IDB) predicate relates to a Boolean combination of basic events of the EDB facts from which this fact was derived. Thus, we assign IDB facts additionally an event expression consisting of a Boolean combination of the event keys of the corresponding EDB facts. For each IDB fact, its probability is computed based on these event expressions (see [9] for the details).

Besides independent events, pD also supports disjoint events. As an example, assume that we have only uncertain information about the publication years of books (an imprecise attribute value), e.g.

```
0.2 py(d3,89). 0.7 py(d3,90). 0.1 py(d3,91).
```

---

[1] Currently, we are extending HySpirit in order to support probabilistic weights for rules, too.

Here the publication year of d3 is either 89, 90 or 91, with the probabilities 0.2, 0.7 and 0.1, respectively. Obviously, these facts represent disjoint events. In order to define certain tuples of a relation as disjoint events, a *disjointness key* can be declared for a predicate. For example, #py(dk,av) states that all tuples of predicate py which correspond in the first argument (dk = disjointness key value, av = attribute value) should be treated as disjoint events. (If no disjointness key is declared, then it is assumed that all attributes belong to the disjointness key, so this relation contains no disjoint events.) Now a query for books published after 89: q2(X) ← py(X,Y) , Y > 89 would yield q2(d3) with the correct probability $0.7 + 0.1 = 0.8$.

2.2 Retrieval of complex objects based on 4-valued logic

When going from classic text retrieval to hypertext retrieval, we have to solve the problems of retrieval of structured documents and of possible inconsistencies between the contents of document nodes.

From a logical point of view, a database is a collection (or more precisely, a conjunction) of formulas which are consistent. In contrast, in IR, documents may contain contradictory knowledge (e.g. assume a database with articles from different newspapers which may contain contradictory statements about the same events).

Concerning the retrieval of structured documents, from a database-oriented point of view, coping with document structure is not a difficult problem: Here the query formulation has to refer explicitly to the document structure (see e.g. [5]). However, for content-oriented retrieval, such a solution is not appropriate. When searching for content, a user will hardly ever bother about the structure of an item that answers his question. Thus, we need an approach that allows for a certain kind of abstraction from document structure.

The approach presented in [18] combines the two ideas of inconsistency handling and structural abstraction. For the latter, the concept of *contexts* is introduced: Theoretically, a context corresponds to a part of one or more aggregated documents which can be viewed by a user in a meaningful way. (Practically, the set of contexts considered as possible answers for a query is restricted in order to reduce the computational time for computing the answers). The exact definition of contexts depends on the specific data model.

The logical formula representing the content of a context is formed via a mapping called *augmentation*. In its most simple form, a context is represented as the conjunction of the logical formulas occurring in the corresponding part(s) of the document(s) (see also section 5).

The general retrieval strategy is to retrieve the minimum entities implying the query (e.g. in a digital library, the relevant paragraphs or sections instead of whole articles or books).

By forming contexts from several parts of a document or even from different documents (in case there is a hyperlink in between), we may get inconsistencies, i.e. the logical formulas of the context are inconsistent. In order to cope with this problem, we use a four-valued logic; thus, we are able to restrict the effects of inconsistency to those formulas that refer directly to the inconsistent statements.

For example, the following document d1 consists of three sections (s1, s2, s3), and we give the logical formulas describing the content (which are simple propositions in this case) in brackets.

```
d1[ s1[audio ∧ indexing    ]
    s2[image ∧ retrieval    ]
    s3[video ∧ ¬ retrieval] ]
```

Let us assume that any set of sections forms a context. In response to a query audio
∧ indexing, section s1 would be the most specific answer. For the query audio
∧ retrieval, {s1,s2} is an answer: since the corresponding context contains the
formula audio ∧ indexing ∧ image ∧ retrieval, it implies the query. However,
when we ask video ∧ retrieval, {s2,s3} is not an answer, since the context yields
image ∧ retrieval ∧ video ∧ ¬ retrieval, and thus we have an inconsistency
with respect to the proposition retrieval.

In two-valued logic, this inconsistency would lead to severe problems (e.g. {s2,s3}
would imply any query). Instead, we use a four-valued logic with the truth values unknown, true, false and inconsistent. Thus, in {s2,s3}, image and video are true, but
retrieval is inconsistent (all other propositions are unknown). Since inconsistency is
restricted to the proposition retrieval, we can e.g. infer that {s2,s3} is an answer to
image ∧ video, but not to image ∧ ¬video

In the following sections, we show how inference based on this logic can be implemented.

3 Four-valued Datalog

In this section, we describe the syntax of 4D, discuss its semantics and then show how
it can be implemented based on 2D.

The syntax of 4D is very similar to that of 2D. As basic elements, we have *variables* (starting with capital letters), *constants* (numbers or alphanumeric strings starting
with lower-case letters) and *predicates* (alphanumeric strings starting with lower-case
letters).

A *term* is either a constant or a variable. A *ground term* is a constant, and the *Herbrand Universe* of a Datalog program is the set of constants occurring in it.

An *atom* $q(t_1,\ldots,t_n)$ consists of an n-ary predicate symbol q and a list of arguments
$(t_1,\ldots,t_n)$ such that each t_i is a term. A *literal* is an atom $q(t_1,\ldots,t_n)$ (positive literal)
or a negated atom $\neg q(t_1,\ldots,t_n)$ (negative literal)

A 4D program is a set of clauses and declarations. Clauses have the form
$$h \leftarrow b_1,\ldots,b_n$$
where h and $b_1,\ldots,b_n$ are (positive or negative) literals. h is also called the clause head
and $b_1,\ldots,b_n$ its body. Both h and the list $b_1,\ldots,b_n$ can be missing. Thus, we have
three different types of clauses:

1. *Ground facts* consist of the head literal only, and all arguments must be constants.
   Note that 4D supports both positive and negative facts.
2. *Rules* consist of a head and a body. Rules also must be *safe*, i.e. all variables
   occurring in the head also must occur in the body of the rule.
3. A *goal clause* consisting of a body only represents a query to the Datalog program
   to be answered.

Declarations allow for specifying closed-world assumptions for predicates. Let q denote
a predicate, then q is closed via the declaration #close(q).

Now we briefly discuss the semantics of 4D. In the model-theoretic semantics of 2D,
an interpretation only contains the (unnegated) atoms of the Herbrand base. In contrast,

we now assume that for 4D, an interpretation may contain both positive and negated atoms. Thus, for a specific fact, a model may contain the positive atom, the negated atom, both the positive and the negated atom or none of both. This corresponds to the four truth values true (T), false (F), inconsistent(I) and unknown (U). For example, let the Herbrand base consist of the four atoms p(a), p(b), p(c) and p(d), and let $M =$ {p(b), ¬p(c), p(d),¬p(d)}. Then p(a) is unknown, p(b) is true, p(c) is false and p(d) is inconsistent. The actual definition of our logic is similar to the one described in [2] – see the truth tables below.

∧	T	F	U	I		∨	T	F	U	I		¬	
T	T	F	U	I		T	T	T	T	T		T	F
F	F	F	F	F		F	T	F	U	I		F	T
U	U	F	U	F		U	T	U	U	T		U	U
I	I	F	F	I		I	T	I	T	I		I	I

The crucial issue is the interpretation of rules. Since our goal is the development of a logic for retrieval, we want to restrict the inferential capabilities such that the system is not burdened with inferences which are not essential for retrieval, e.g. those yielding unknown as truth values. On the other hand, our system should be able to tolerate local inconsistencies. Thus, we follow the idea of [25] of viewing rules as conditional facts, not as implication formulas.

Let us consider a simple rule like $p \leftarrow q$. Concerning our model-theoretic semantics, we first have to decide when we consider this rule to be applicable: Whenever $q \in M$ or only if $q \in M \land (\neg q) \notin M$? Since we do not want to draw any more inferences from an inconsistent antecedent, we decide that the rule should only be applied in the latter case. Second, what should be the outcome of this rule: Only that $p \in M$ or that in addition $(\neg p) \notin M$? Here the latter choice corresponds to 2-valued logic, but raises two problems in 4-valued logic: First, we are not able to infer any inconsistent facts, and second, programs that would lead to inconsistent facts are incorrect. Since we want to allow for inconsistencies, we are left with the first choice here. Thus, we conclude that the positive atom is in the model, but we say nothing about the corresponding negative atom. This means that in our example p may be inconsistent in case there is evidence for the negative fact as well, and p is true when there is no such evidence[2].

More generally, for any instantiated rule of our 4D program
$$h \leftarrow b_1, \ldots, b_n$$
where h and $b_1, \ldots, b_n$ are (positive or negative) atoms now, M is a model for this rule if the following holds:

if $b_1 \in M \land (\neg b_1) \notin M \land \ldots \land b_n \in M \land (\neg b_n) \notin M$, then $h \in M$

As a simple example, assume a rule doc(X) ← book(X), from which we can conclude that doc(X) is true or inconsistent in case book(X) is true, but nothing else. If we also want to infer negative information, this has to be stated explicitly[3]. For example, if we assume that X is a student iff she is a person and enrolled, we can formulate this by the rules:

student(X) ← person(X), enrolled(X).
¬ student(X) ← ¬ person(X).
¬ student(X) ← ¬ enrolled(X).

---

[2] In [25], this combination of the two choices is called "conservative reasoning".
[3] Approaches for deriving negative information in two-valued Datalog have been described in [24] and [11].

In order to implement an inference engine for 4D, we map it onto 2D. The basic idea is that for each predicate q in 4D, we have two predicates p_q and n_q in 2D, where the first gives the positive information (true or inconsistent) and the latter the negative information (false or inconsistent) for q. Thus, the truth value of q for a specific fact depends in the following way on those of p_q and n_q for the same tuple:

p_q	n_q	q
T	T	I
T	F	T
F	T	F
F	F	U

For the description of this mapping, we use the following notations: Let q denote a predicate in 4D, which we map onto the two predicates p_q and n_q in 2D. Furthermore, h and b denote arbitrary literals, where p_h, n_h and p_b, n_b stand for the corresponding literals in 2D with the same number of arguments. Furthermore, let $X_1, \ldots, X_i, \ldots$ denote arbitrary variables with $X_i \not\equiv X_j$ for $i \neq j$. Then the elements of a 4D program are mapped in the following way:

1. Declaration of closed world assumptions for a predicate q (with k arguments) are mapped onto a rule yielding true for n_q if p_q is false:

$$\texttt{\#close}(q) \quad \longmapsto \quad n\_q(X_1, \ldots, X_k) \leftarrow \neg p\_q(X_1, \ldots, X_k).$$

2. In ground facts and rules, each positive literal in the body is replaced by the conjunction of the corresponding positive literal and the negation of the corresponding negative literal, and vice versa for negated literals. The head h is mapped onto the corresponding positive or negative literal in 2D, depending whether h is positive or negated:

$$h \leftarrow b_1, \ldots, b_n \quad \longmapsto \quad g \leftarrow r_1, \ldots, r_n \quad \text{with}$$

$$g \quad = \quad \begin{cases} p\_h, & \text{if } h \text{ is positive} \\ n\_h', & \text{if } h = \neg h' \end{cases}$$

$$r_i \quad = \quad \begin{cases} p\_b_i, \neg n\_b_i, & \text{if } b_i \text{ is a positive literal} \\ n\_b_i', \neg p\_b_i', & \text{if } b_i = \neg b_i' \end{cases}$$

3. A query has to be mapped onto three queries, one for each of the truth values T/F/I:

$$\leftarrow b_1, \ldots, b_n \quad \longmapsto \quad \begin{cases} \leftarrow r_1, \ldots, r_n. \\ \leftarrow s_1, \ldots, s_n. \\ \leftarrow t_1, \ldots, t_n. \end{cases} \quad \text{with (for } i = 1, \ldots, n)$$

$$r_i \quad = \quad \begin{cases} p\_b_i, \neg n\_b_i, & \text{if } b_i \text{ is a positive literal} \\ n\_b_i', \neg p\_b_i', & \text{if } b_i = \neg b_i' \end{cases}$$

$$s_i \quad = \quad \begin{cases} n\_b_i, \neg p\_b_i, & \text{if } b_i \text{ is a positive literal} \\ p\_b_i', \neg n\_b_i', & \text{if } b_i = \neg b_i' \end{cases}$$

$$t_i \quad = \quad p\_b_i, n\_b_i.$$

As an example for these mapping rules, consider the rules about students from above, to which we add the fact $\neg$ `person(fido)`. This program is mapped onto `n_person(fido)`.

p_student(X) ← p_person(X) , ¬ n_person(X), p_enrolled(X),
    ¬ n_enrolled(X).
n_student(X) ← n_person(X) , ¬ p_person(X).
n_student(X) ← n_enrolled(X), ¬ p_enrolled(X).

For the 4D query ?- student(X), we get the instances yielding a truth value of false
(i.e. fido) by means of the query ?- n_student(X) , ¬ p_student(X).

Since these mappings do not refer to pD, they can be used for implementing 4D
on top of an arbitrary Datalog engine. By using 4D instead of 2D, the complexity of
rule bodies is doubled, since any predicate q is replaced by two predicates p_q and n_q;
however, this has only a significant effect on computing time in case there are rules for
deriving negative information. Besides the possibility of handling inconsistent data, a
major advantage of 4D is the possibility of combining open world and closed world
assumptions in a Datalog engine which is able to perform rather efficient inferences.

In the following, we show how probabilities are added to 4D.

4 Probabilistic 4-valued Datalog

In probabilistic (two-valued) Datalog, we specify the probability of a fact being true.
For p4D, we not only must specify the probabilities of being true and false, but also for
being inconsistent; then the probability for unknown can be derived as the complement
to 1. Syntactically, we specify the probabilities of an event as a triple of values for
true/false/inconsistent. As shorthand, a pair of values stands for the probabilities of true
and false, a singular value is the probability of being true, and the other probabilities are
0. If no probability is given, a positive literal h stands for 1/0/0 h, and ¬ h is equivalent
to 0/1/0 h.

A model for p4D consists of a set of possible worlds $\mathcal{W}$, where each world is a
model for the corresponding deterministic 4-valued Datalog program; in addition, there
is a probability distribution on $\mathcal{W}$. For a Herbrand base $H = \{q(a), q(b), q(c), q(d)\}$, an
example model is shown here, where the last row gives the corresponding fact clause in
p4D:

0.3 W_1		q(b)	¬q(c)	q(d),¬ q(d)
0.5 W_2	q(a)	q(b)	q(c), ¬q(c)	q(d),¬ q(d)
0.2 W_3		¬q(b)	q(c)	q(d),¬ q(d)
	0.5/0/0 q(a)	0.8/0.2/0 q(b)	0.2/0.3/0.5 q(c)	0/0/1 q(d)

The syntax of p4D is an extension of that of 4D: disjointness keys must be declared
for all EDB predicates and probabilities are given for all truth values of facts:

- For each EDB predicate q with k arguments, a disjointness key has to be declared
  in the form $\#q(t_1, \ldots, t_k)$ where (for $i = 1, \ldots, k$) t_i=dk, if argument i is part of the
  disjointness key, and t_i=av otherwise.
- Let α_T, α_F and α_I denote probabilistic weights with $0 \leq \alpha_T, \alpha_F, \alpha_I \leq 1$. Then
  facts are denoted in the form $\alpha_T / \alpha_F / \alpha_I\ h$, where h is a positive literal containing
  constants as arguments only.

The mapping of p4D onto pD follows the same rules as those for 4D, with the
exception of facts. In the following, t, f and i denote specific constants standing for
the truth values true, false and inconsistent. For each fact in p4D, we generate three
facts in pD, namely one for each truth value T, F and I, with an additional argument
denoting the truth value. In order to ensure proper computation of probabilities, we

declare identical facts with different truth values as disjoint events. Thus, we also have to map the disjointness key declaration in the corresponding way:

- Disjointness key declarations have to be modified for considering the additional argument denoting the disjoint truth values. Furthermore, we have to generate rules that perform the mapping from the predicates with the prefixes $p\_$ and $q\_$ onto the corresponding EDB predicates:

$$\#q(t_1,\ldots,t_k) \quad \longmapsto \quad \#q(\mathtt{av},t_1,\ldots,t_k).$$
$$p\_q(X_1,\ldots,X_k) \leftarrow q(t,X_1,\ldots,X_k). \quad p\_q(X_1,\ldots,X_k) \leftarrow q(i,X_1,\ldots,X_k).$$
$$n\_q(X_1,\ldots,X_k) \leftarrow q(f,X_1,\ldots,X_k). \quad n\_q(X_1,\ldots,X_k) \leftarrow q(i,X_1,\ldots,X_k).$$

- Each p4D fact (with arguments $a_1,\ldots,a_k$) has to be mapped onto up to three pD facts for the truth values T, F and I (facts with zero weights may be omitted):

$$\alpha_T/\alpha_F/\alpha_I \, q(a_1,\ldots,a_k) \quad \longmapsto$$
$$\alpha_T \, q(t,a_1,\ldots,a_k). \quad \alpha_F \, q(f,a_1,\ldots,a_k). \quad \alpha_I \, q(i,a_1,\ldots,a_k).$$

Our implementation of p4D is based on the pD system presented in [19] which uses the magic sets strategy for modular stratified programs ([20]). The relational algebra expressions resulting from the magic set transformed Datalog rules are evaluated according to the probabilistic relational algebra described in [10]. Since the equivalences from relational algebra also hold for our probabilistic version, we can apply the corresponding strategies for query optimization. In [19], we show that the first step of the evaluation algorithm is almost identical to (and as efficient as) the evaluation of deterministic Datalog, we only have to add the construction of the event expressions. In a subsequent step, the computation of the corresponding probabilities is performed. Although probabilistic inference is NP-hard in the general case ([6]), the typical queries considered so far pose no complexity problems.

HySpirit is implemented in the object-oriented programming language BETA.[4] The current version of the BETA compiler does little optimization, thus the efficiency of HySpirit is rather limited at the moment. For implementing p4D, we use a preprocessor written in Perl that performs the mappings described before.

In order to cope with large databases, we need a facility for accessing external data. For this purpose, we have added the concept of external predicates to Hyspirit: External predicates are EDB predicates whose tuples are stored externally. Currently, external predicates are implemented via an SQL interface, where the evaluation of the predicate generates an SQL query which is sent to a relational DBMS, and the resulting relation is fed into HySpirit.

5 Retrieval of complex objects

Now we show how we can use p4D for the retrieval of complex objects. First, we discuss the case where content is represented in propositional logic.

---

[4] In principle, it also would have been possible to use an existing deductive database engine and extend it by facilities for handling probabilities and event expressions.

Let us consider the example from section 2.2, which can be stated in 4D as follows[5]:
`docterm(s1,audio). docterm(s1,indexing). docterm(s2,image).`
`docterm(s2,retrieval). docterm(s3,video).` ¬ `docterm(s3,retrieval).`
`part-of(s1,d1). part-of(s2,d1). part-of(s3,d1).`
`about(D,T)` ← `docterm(D,T).` ¬ `about(D,T)` ← ¬ `docterm(D,T).`
The rules for the predicate about allow for retrieval of single document nodes only. In order to use augmentation, we have to specify contexts and then add rules that perform the mapping of the propositions from the corresponding nodes into the context. For this purpose, let us assume that a context is defined via an accessibility relation, where `acc(C,N)` denotes that node `N` is accessible from context `C`. Then we can formulate the rules
`about(D,T)` ← `acc(D,D1), docterm(D1,T).`
¬ `about(D,T)` ← `acc(D,D1),` ¬ `docterm(D1,T).`
From these rules, we can also derive inconsistent knowledge in case we have access to two different nodes, one positively and one negatively indexed with the same term. On the other hand, if an accessible node has inconsistent knowledge with respect to docterm, then no further inferences are drawn from this fact.

For our example, let us assume that we only want to retrieve single sections or the whole document. For the latter, we define a probabilistic accessibility relation[6] with weights less than 1:
`0.6 acc(d1,s1). 0.6 acc(d1,s2). 0.6 acc(d1,s3).`
This probability assignment treats the elements of a context as stochastically independent and has two advantages:

1. If a query is fulfilled in a single element, then the element gets a higher weight than the surrounding context. For example, ← `about(D,audio),about(D,indexing)` would give the probabilities (for true/false/inconsistent) 1/0/0 for s1 and 0.6/0/0 for d1.

2. Contradictory information from different elements does not always lead to purely inconsistent statements, with a certain probability also each statement from the different elements is true, e.g. ← `about(D,retrieval)` yields 1/0/0 for s2 and for d1, we have 0.24/0.24/0.36, yielding true when `acc(d1,s2)` is true and `acc(d1,s3)` is not true, i.e. $0.6 \cdot (1 - 0.6) = 0.24$.

However, contradictions are obeyed, thus avoiding arbitrary combinations of statements from different elements. For example, consider the query
← `about(D,video), about(D,retrieval)`
for which d1 yields 0/0.24/0.36, since this query yields false when `acc(d1,s3)` is true and `acc(d1,s2)` is false, inconsistent if both are true and otherwise unknown. Here (as well as in the previous examples), the nonzero probability of unknown results from the fact that d1 itself contains no information w.r.t. the query, and the other elements of the context are accessible with a certain probability only.

Our general approach to hypermedia retrieval uses terminological logic (i.e. monadic (concepts) and dyadic predicates (roles) only) for describing multimedia objects

---

[5] For text documents, these facts can be generated automatically by an appropriate indexing procedure, where negative docterm facts may be produced for terms occurring in a part of a sentence preceded by a word indicating negation, like e.g. "no", "not", "except", . . .

[6] In principle, the accessibility relation also can be derived (by means of probabilistic rules) from information about the structure of the document.

(based on the multimedia terminological logic presented in [13]). We also can apply augmentation for terminological logic. For combining augmentation with terminological logic, we represent concepts by a single predicate `concept(C,D,I)`, where D refers to the document node, C to the concept name and I to the concept instance. In a similar way, we use the predicate `role(R,D,X,Y)` for a role R with arguments X and Y. Then we can formulate augmentation rules similar to those for propositional logic, e.g. for roles:

```
role(R,D,X,Y) ← acc(D,D1), role(R,D1,X,Y).
¬ role(R,D,X,Y) ← acc(D,D1), ¬ role(R,D1,X,Y).
```

Now assume that we have a document collection containing a proceedings volume p where article a1 states that M-JPEG is not a standard format for digital video and a2 claims that the contrary is true, i.e.

```
¬ role(stdformat,a1,video,m-jpeg). role(stdformat,a2,video,m-jpeg).
0.6 acc(p,a1). 0.6 acc(p,a2).
```

Searching for documents talking about standard formats for video

```
← role(stdformat,D,video,X)
```

would yield the probabilities 0.24/0.24/0.36 for p.

As an example for a closed world assumption, assume that we have an `author` predicate which we want to close:

```
author(d1,smith). #close(author).
```

Then the query ← `author(d1,miller)` would yield false.

For content-oriented facts, an open world assumption is more appropriate, e.g. ← `docterm(s1,retrieval)` gives unknown. Actually, classical models based on two-valued propositional logic use a closed world assumption (see e.g. [26]), thus always giving point probabilities for $P(d \rightarrow q)$. In contrast, an open world assumption (in combination with a probabilistic two-valued logic) would yield probability intervals for most documents (whereas our four-valued logic yields nonzero probabilities for unknown in these cases — see the examples from above). However, when using predicate logic for representing the content of documents, then the closed world assumption would lead to incorrect results. For example, in our document collection from above, any article not mentioning M-JEPG at all would be treated as evidence that this is not a standard for digital video. Thus, IR based on predicate logic requires an open world assumption.

6 Application

6.1 Image retrieval

As an example of multimedia retrieval, we are applying HySpirit for image retrieval. For this purpose, we use the output of the IRIS image indexing system ([12]). In contrast to many other approaches dealing with syntactic features of images only (i.e. contour, texture or color), IRIS performs semantic indexing by inferring semantic concepts from syntactic features. IRIS has been applied successfully to the domain of landscape photos, where it detects basic concepts like e.g. water, sand, stone, forest, grass, sky and clouds. By subdividing an image into tiles, IRIS identifies the concepts occurring in a tile. Then, for each concept, adjacent tiles with the same concept are joined and finally the corresponding minimum bounding rectangle (MBR) is computed. In addition to the position and the size of the MBR, IRIS also computes the certainty with which the concept is identified. The output of the indexing process for an image is a list of objects, where each consists of a concept and the corresponding parameters.

Fig. 1. Query result for images with water in front of stone

In HySpirit, each image object is represented as a fact of the form io(O, I, N, L, R, B, T), where O denotes the object id, I the id of the image, N the name of the concept (water, sand,...) and L, R, B, T are the coordinates of the MBR. The probabilistic weight of the fact gives the certainty with which the object was identified. Based on this representation, we can formulate queries for images with a certain content. As an example, the following query searches for images with water (lake, river, sea) in front of stone (rocks):

← io(OA,I,water,L1,R1,B1,T1), io(OB,I,stone,L2,R2,B2,T2), B1 <= B2

The top-ranking answers to this query (from a collection of 1200 photos, of which 300 contain landscapes) are shown in figure 1. Obviously, the IRIS system is doing well in finding stone, but has problems with identifying water.

6.2 Retrieval of complex documents

For demonstrating the retrieval of complex objects, we use a collection of manuals from the Perl documentation which have a two-level hierarchical document structure which is indicated in the original data by level-1 and level-2 headings. Each document is structured into a a description and additional texts (level-1 headings), and each of these may consist of several subtexts (level-2 headings). In the following examples, we use identifiers similar to path expressions for denoting the hierarchical level and the type of each document node (des for description, adt for additional text, and sub for subtext).

Information about the presence of a term T in a document node D of a document is represented by the predicate docterm(D,T). For example,

docterm(doc_46_des_1_sub_2,object)

denotes that the term "object" occurs in the document node "doc_46_des_1_sub_2". A query is a set of terms, where the predicate qt(T) denotes that term T ocurs in the current query. For performing probabilistic retrieval, we assume that terms form a disjoint concept space (see [26]), where the probability of a term is proportional to its idf weight.[7] The term probability is given by the predicate term(T).

---

[7] Let n_i denote the number of documents in which term t_i occurs, and N is the number of documents in the database. For the probability of term t_i, we assume that $P(t_i) \propto \log(N/n_i)$, with the additional constraint that the terms occuring in the database cover the complete event space: $\sum_{t_j} P(t_j) = 1$.

With the rules for the about predicate as described in section 5, we formulate the following retrieval rule:

`retrieve(D) ← about(D,T), qt(T), term(T).`

As an example, consider a query like "inheritance object oriented programming", where we derive from the term space the following conditional probabilities $P(t|q)$ for the term relation, where q is the set of query terms (all terms are stemmed):

`0.233 term(inherit). 0.148 term(object).`
`0.527 term(orient). 0.092 term(program).`

As an outline of the retrieval result, consider the ranking of the nodes of document "doc_46" which contains a top-ranked document node:

`1.000(doc_46_adt_4_sub_1). 0.165(doc_46_adt_2).`
`0.574(doc_46_adt_4).       0.119(doc_46_des_1).`
`0.369(doc_46).             0.091(doc_46_adt_3).`
`0.239(doc_46_des_1_sub_5). 0.091(doc_46_adt_2_sub_1).`
`0.239(doc_46_adt_2_sub_2).`

Note the non-monotonicity of the ranking: specific nodes (contexts) like subtexts are ranked higher than upper nodes like additional texts and the whole document, at the same time there are specific nodes which are ranked below upper nodes. We obtain this ranking using an accessibility value of 0.5, i.e. a document node accesses its subtrees with a probability of 0.5. (The greater the accessibility value is, the higher become the retrieval weights of upper nodes.)

Now, we take a closer look at the first and second ranked document nodes: The highest ranked node "doc_46_adt_4_sub_1" contains all query terms and is retrieved with a value of 1.0. This retrieved node corresponds to a text about guidelines for module creation in perl. The second ranked node "doc_46_adt_4" is retrieved because it comprises the top-ranked node and in addition it has an introductory part where the term "object" occurs. This context is about the creation, use, and abuse of modules in perl. It is retrieved with a probability value of $0.574 = 0.148 + 0.5 - 0.148 \cdot 0.5$, where the first addend stands for the query term occurring in the node and the second addend reflects the augmented weight from the subnode. In the analogous way, the other weights are computed, where the document nodes contain only some query terms and we achieve the interleaving of specific (small) and general (big) contexts.

The position of the retrieved nodes in the hierarchic document structure is illustrated in figure 2, where the numbers denote the ranks of the node in the result list. For supporting the browsing of the retrieved documents, we can exploit the ranking of document nodes. For example, we can present to the user some selected entry points into the complex object using the following strategy: we display only the top-ranked entry points into the document tree and

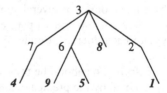

Fig. 2. Position of retrieved nodes in the document structure

we skip the nodes which are parents or childs of already presented entry points. This strategy would show only those nodes from figure 2 where the numbers are printed in bold italics.

6.3 Retrieval on a large database

For performing retrieval on large databases, we used a part of the TREC collection, namely 12 months of the AP newswire data comprising 259 MB of text (about 85000 documents). Indexing and retrieval was performed in the same way as with the Perl manuals, but no document structure was considered. The docterm relation generated for this data was stored in a relational database (Postgres), which consumed 1.5 GB of disc space (plus 500 MB for the index). The Hyspirit system and the database server were running on different workstations (170MHz Sun Ultrasparc with 64 MB main memory) connected by a 10 Mbs ethernet.

For our experiments, we used the first 150 TREC queries, but did not consider terms occurring in more than 1000 documents, thus leaving up to 55 terms per query, with an average of about 16 terms. This selection of query terms limits the number of retrieved documents. We retrieved up to 9000 documents for a single query (i.e. documents containing at least one term from the query). It turned out that the response time of HySpirit is proportional to the number of documents retrieved. On average, the system outputs 30 documents per second. Further investigations showed that one performance bottleneck is the database system. We can improve the performance of HySpirit by using a more efficient database management system and a parallel access strategy. In order to be able to consider all query terms, we could e.g. apply the strategy described in [14], where at most 1% of the documents in a collection (namely those containing the most significant query terms) are considered for ranking.

7 Conclusions and outlook

In this paper, we have presented the Hyspirit retrieval engine which is based on a probabilistic version of Datalog. We have shown that hypermedia retrieval requires the handling of inconsistent information and a combination of open and closed world assumptions. For this purpose, we have introduced probabilistic four-valued Datalog. Large databases can be handled in HySpirit by means of external predicates. Thus, HySpirit combines all essential concepts for retrieval on hypermedia databases.

The concept of external predicates allows for linking external data as well as external functions. This way, also multimedia similarity operators (e.g. for images) can be used in HySpirit (where the system itself handles references to the multimedia objects only). We are also aiming at increasing the expressiveness of pD by adding operators for deriving conditional probabilities, either as fraction of other probabilities (this would e.g. allow for normalizing the derived probabilities from section 6.2) or via a frequency operator estimating the relative frequency of certain facts.

The major idea underlying our work on Hyspirit is the development of a flexible tool for investigating retrieval strategies for hypermedia data. Once certain strategies have shown to be useful, a query language with appropriate high-level concepts can be developed along with an efficient retrieval engine.

Acknowledgements

We wish to thank Christian Altenschmidt, Achim Oberreuter and Claus-Peter Klas who implemented Hyspirit as part of their work for their diploma thesises and who also developed some of the applications. Umberto Straccia pointed us towards Wagner's work on reasoning with inconsistent knowledge.

References

1. Beeri C. and Kornatzky Y. A logical query language for hypermedia systems. *Information Sciences*, 77(1/2):1–37, 1994.
2. Belnap N. A useful four-valued logic. In Dunn J.M. and Epstein G.., editors, *Modern Uses of Multiple-Valued Logic*. Reidel, Dordrecht, 1977.
3. Callan J.P., Croft W.B., and Harding S.M. The INQUERY retrieval system. In *Proc. 3rd DEXA*, pages 78–83, 1992.
4. Chaudhuri S. and Gravano L. Optimizing queries over multimedia repositories. In *Proc. SIGMOD.*, pages 91–102, 1996.
5. Christophides V., Abiteboul S., and Cluet S. From structured documents to novel query facilities. In *Proc. SIGMOD*, pages 313–324, 1994.
6. Cooper G.F. The computational complexity of probabilistic inference using bayesian belief networks. *Artificial Intelligence*, 42:393–405, 1990.
7. Dey D. and Sarkar S. A probabilistic relational model and algebra. *ACM TOIS*, 21(3):339–369, 1996.
8. Flickner M., et al. Query by image and video content: The QBIC system. *Computer*, 28(9):23–32, 1995.
9. Fuhr N. Probabilistic datalog - a logic for powerful retrieval methods. In *Proc. SIGIR*, pages 282–290, 1995..
10. Fuhr N. and Rölleke T. A probabilistic relational algebra for the integration of information retrieval and database systems. *ACM TODS*, 14(1):32–66, 1997.
11. Gelfond M. and Lifschitz V. Logic programs with classical negation. *Logic Programming, Proc. 7th Conf.*, 1990.
12. Hermes Th., Klauck Ch., Kreyß J., and Zhang J. Image retrieval for information systems. In *Proc. IS&T/SPIE's Symposium on Electronic Imaging: Science & Technologie.*, 1995.
13. Meghini C. and Straccia U. A relevance terminological logic for information retrieval. In *Proc. SIGIR* , pages 197–205, 1996.
14. Moffat Alistair and Zobel Justin. Self-indexing inverted files for fast text retrieval. *ACM TOIS*, 14(4):349–379, October 1996.
15. Ng R. and Subrahmanian V. S. A semantical framework for supporting subjective and conditional probabilities in deductive databases. *J. Autom. Reas.*, 10:191–235, 1993.
16. Poole D. Probabilistic horn abduction and bayesian networks. *Artificial Intelligence*, 64:81–129, 1993.
17. Rakow T.C., Neuhold E.J., and Löhr M. Multimedia database systems - the notion and the issues. In *Proc. BTW*, pages 1–29, 1995. Springer.
18. Rölleke T. and Fuhr N. Retrieval of complex objects using a four-valued logic. In Frei H.-P., Harmann D., Schäuble P., and Wilkinson R., editors, *Proc. SIGIR* , pages 206–214, 1996.
19. Rölleke T. and Fuhr N. Probabilistic reasoning for large scale databases. In *Proc. BTW*, pages 118–132, 1997. Springer.
20. Ross K. Modular stratification and magic sets for datalog programs with negation. *J. ACM*, 41(6):1216–1266, November 1994.
21. Takahashi Y. Fuzzy database query languages and their relational completeness theorem. *IEEE TKDE*, 5(1):122, 1993.
22. van Rijsbergen C. J. A non-classical logic for information retrieval. *Computer Journal*, 29(6):481–485, 1986.
23. van Rijsbergen C. J. Towards an information logic. In *Proc. SIGIR*, pages 77–86, 1989.
24. Wagner G. A database needs two kinds of negation. In *Proc. MFDB*, pages 357–371, 1991.
25. Wagner G. Ex contradictione nihil sequitur. In *Proc. IJCAI*, pages 538–543, 1991.
26. Wong S.K.M. and Yao Y.Y. On modeling information retrieval with probabilistic inference. *ACM TOIS*, 13(1):38–68, 1995.
27. Zhang H.J., Smoliar S.W., and Tan Y.H. Towards automating content-based video indexing and retrieval. In *Proc. Multi-Media Modeling*, 1993.

Towards Optimal Indexing for Segment Databases

E. Bertino[1]   B. Catania[1]   B. Shidlovsky[2]

[1] Dipartimento di Scienze
dell'Informazione
Università degli Studi di Milano
Via Comelico 39/41
20135 Milano, Italy
e-mail: {bertino,catania}@dsi.unimi.it

[2] Rank Xerox Research Center
Grenoble Laboratory
6, chemin de Maupertuis
38240 Meylan, France
e-mail: chidlovskii@xrce.xerox.com

Abstract. Segment databases store N non-crossing but possibly touching segments in secondary storage. Efficient data structures have been proposed to determine all segments intersecting a vertical line (stabbing queries). In this paper, we consider a more general type of query for segment databases, determining intersections with respect to a generalized segment (a line, a ray, a segment) with a fixed angular coefficient. We propose two solutions to solve this problem. The first solution has optimal $O(\frac{N}{B})$ space complexity, where N is the database size and B is the page size, but the query time is far from optimal. The second solution requires $O(\frac{N}{B} \log_2 B)$ space, the query time is $O(\log_B \frac{N}{B}(\log_B \frac{N}{B} + \log_2 B + IL^*(B)) + \frac{T}{B})$, which is very close to the optimal, and insertion amortized time is $O(\log_B \frac{N}{B} + \log_2 B + \frac{1}{B}\log_B^2 \frac{N}{B})$, where T is the size of the query result, and $IL^*(B)$ is a small constant, representing the number of times we must repeatedly apply the $\log^*$ function to B before the result becomes ≤ 2.

1 Introduction

Background. Advanced database programming languages, such as constraint database languages, and new application domains, dealing with spatial, geographical, and temporal data, require managing data such as points, segments, and other geometrical entities. In this respect, an important issue is the development of new data structures supporting query and update operations with time and space complexity comparable to those of data structures for relational databases.

Complexity is expressed in terms of *input-output (I/O) operations*. An I/O operation is the operation of reading/writing one block of data from or to disk. Other parameters are respectively: N, the number of items in the database; B, the number of items per disk block; T, the number of items in the problem solution; $n = N/B$, the optimal number of blocks required to store the database; $t = T/B$, the optimal number of blocks to access for reporting the problem result. For 1-dimensional data, efficient data structures like B-trees and B$^+$-trees [8] process range queries in $O(\log_B n + t)$ I/O operations, require $O(n)$ blocks of secondary storage, and perform insertions/deletions in $O(\log_B n)$ I/O operations. All these complexities are worst-case.

A large amount of work has been carried out to obtain optimal I/O complexities for the so called "point databases". For such databases, which typically contain N points on the plane, several external-memory data structures have been developed. Those data structures are characterized by an I/O complexity for search and update operations comparable to the internal memory results [11, 14, 19, 21].

Compared to the "point database" case, much less work has been carried out for the so called "segment databases" which represent a more general case. A segment database stores in secondary storage N non-crossing but possibly touching plane segments (for brevity, called NCT segments). Segment databases are the basis for data representation in several large scale applications, including spatial databases and geographical information systems (GIS) [18], temporal databases [15] and constraint databases [13]. Among all possible applications, GIS certainly represent the main target of segment databases. Indeed, GIS databases often store data as layers of maps, where each map is typically stored as a collection of NCT segments.

Some relevant query types for segment databases can be reduced to a *stabbing query* on a set of 1-dimensional intervals. Given a set of input intervals and a point q, a stabbing query for q retrieves all intervals that contain q. As an example of query that can be reduced to a stabbing query, consider the query that, given a vertical line l, retrieves all (non necessarily NCT) segments intersected by l. This query can be reduced to a stabbing query against 1-dimensional segments which are x-projections of the database segments. An optimal solution to the stabbing query problem has been recently proposed in [3]. Other solutions have been discussed in [14, 20]. Optimal external memory algorithms for some other segment problems have been presented in [2]. Moreover, good average bounds for several segment problems can be obtained by using some typical spatial data structures, such as R-trees [10].

The problem. A more general and relevant problem in segment databases (especially for GIS) is to determine all segments intersecting a given query segment. In this paper we go one step towards the solution of this problem by investigating a weaker problem, consisting in determining all segments intersected by a given generalized query segment (a line, a ray, a segment), having a fixed angular coefficient. Without leading the generality of the discussion, we consider vertical query segments.[1] The corresponding query is called *VS query* (see Figure 1).

There exists a difference in the optimal time complexity between VS and stabbing queries even in internal memory. A space optimal solution for solving VS queries in internal memory has $O(\log^2 N + T)$ query complexity, uses $O(N)$ space and performs updates in $O(\log N)$ time [6] (with update we mean the insertion/deletion of a segment non-crossing, but possibly touching, the already stored ones). On the other hand, the optimal solution for solving stabbing queries in internal memory has $O(\log N + T)$ query complexity, uses $O(N)$ space and

---

[1] If the query segment is not vertical, coordinate axes can be appropriately rotated.

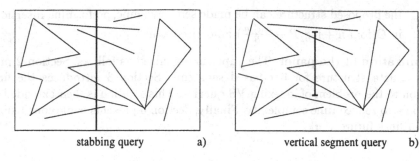

stabbing query   a)   vertical segment query   b)

Fig. 1. Vertical line queries vs vertical segment queries.

performs updates in $O(\log N)$ time [7]. VS queries are therefore inherently more expensive than stabbing queries. In this paper, we propose a $O(n \log_2 B)$ space solution having query I/O complexity very close to $O(\log_B^2 n + t)$. The solution is proposed for static and semi-dynamic (thus, allowing insertion) cases.

The proposed results. The data structures we propose to solve VS queries are organized according to two levels. At the top level, we use a primary data structure (called *first-level data structure*). One or more auxiliary data structures (called *second-level data structures*) are associated with each node of the first-level data structure. The second-level data structures are tailored to efficiently execute queries on a special type of segments, called *line-based segments*. A set of segments is line-based if all segments have an endpoint lying on a given line and all segments are positioned in the same half-plane with respect to such line. Thus, the main contributions of the paper can be summarized as follows (proofs of the proposed results are presented in [4]):

1. We propose a data structure to store and query line-based segments, based on *priority search trees* (PST for short) [7, 11], similar to the internal memory data structure proposed in [6]. The proposed data structure is then extended with the P-range technique presented in [21], to reduce time complexity.

2. We propose two approaches to the problem of VS queries:
   - In the first approach, the first-level structure is a binary tree, whereas the second-level structure, associated with each node of the first-level structure, is a pair of priority search trees, storing line-based segments in secondary storage. This solution uses $O(n)$ blocks of secondary storage and answers queries in $O(\log n(\log_B n + IL^*(B)) + t)$ I/O's. We also show how updates on the proposed structures can be performed in $O(\log n + \frac{\log_B^2 n}{B})$ amortized time.
   - In the second approach, to improve the query time complexity of the first solution, we replace the binary tree at the top level with a secondary storage interval tree [3]. The second-level structures are based on priority search trees for line-based segments and segment trees, enhanced with fractional cascading [5]. This solution uses $O(n \log_2 B)$ space and answers queries in $O(\log_B n(\log_B n + \log_2 B + IL^*(B)) + t)$ time. We also show how

the proposed structure can be made semi-dynamic, performing insertions in $O(\log_B n + \log_2 B + \frac{\log_B^2 n}{B})$ amortized time.

Organization of the paper. The paper is organized as follows. Section 2 proposes a data structure for line-based segments. Section 3 introduces the first solution to the problem of indexing VS queries. This solution is then extended in Section 4 to reduce time complexity. Finally, Section 5 presents some conclusions and outlines future work.

2 Data structures for line-based segments

Let S be a set of segments. S is *line-based* if there exists a line l (called *base line*) such that each segment in S has (at least) one endpoint on l and all the segments in S having only one end-point on l are located in the same half-plane with respect to l.

In the following, we construct a data structure for storing line-based segments in secondary storage and retrieving all segments intersected by a query segment q which is parallel to the base line. More precisely, the query object q may be a segment, a ray, or a line.[2] Since a segment query represents the most complex case, in the following we focus only on such a type of queries. Moreover, without loss of generality, through out Section 2, we restrict the presentation to horizontal base lines. This choice simplifies the description of our data structure making it consistent with the traditional way of drawing data structures. The query thus becomes a horizontal segment as well.

The solution we propose for storing a set of line-based segments is based on the fact that there exists an obvious relationship between a segment query against a set of line-based segments on the plane and a 3-sided query against a set of points (see Figure 2). Given a set of points in the plane and a rectangular region open in one of its sides, the corresponding 3-sided query returns all points contained in the (open) rectangle. A segment query defines in a unique way a 3-sided query on the point database corresponding to all segment endpoints not belonging to the base line. On the other hand, the bottom segment of a 3-sided query on such point database corresponds to a segment query on the segment database. However, these corresponding queries do not necessarily return the same answers. Indeed, although both queries often retrieve the same data (segment 1 in Figure 2), this is not always true. The intersection of a segment with the query segment q does not imply that the segment endpoint is contained in the 3-sided region (segment 2 in Figure 2). Also, the presence of a segment endpoint in the 3-sided region does not imply that the query segment q intersects the segment (segment 3 in Figure 2). Despite these differences, solutions developed for 3-sided queries can be successfully applied to line-based segments as well.

In internal memory, priority search trees [16] are used to answer 3-sided queries in optimal space, query, and update time. All proposals to extend pri-

---

[2] We assume that the query object belongs to the same half-plane where segment endpoints belong. Otherwise, no segment intersects the query.

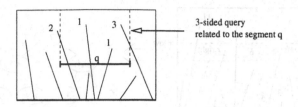

Fig. 2. A segment query on a set of line-based segments vs a 3-sided query on the endpoint set of the same segments.

ority search trees, for use in secondary storage, do not provide both query and space optimal complexities [11, 19, 21]. In [11], a solution with $O(n)$ storage and $O(\log n + t)$ query time was developed. Two techniques have been defined to improve these results. *Path-caching* [19] allows to perform 3-sided queries in $O(\log_B n)$, with $O(n \log_2 B \log_2 \log_2 B)$ space. A space optimal solution to implement secondary storage priority search trees is based on the *P-range tree* [21] and uses $O(n)$ blocks, performing 3-sided queries in $O(\log_B n + IL^*(B) + t)$ and updates in $O(\log_B n + \frac{\log_B^2 n}{B})$, where $IL^*(B)$ is a small constant, representing the number of times we must repeatedly apply the $\log^*$ function to B before the result becomes ≤ 2. [3]

As in the approach presented in [19, 21] for point databases, in order to define priority search trees for a set of line-based segments, a binary decomposition is first used and algorithms for retrieving all segments intersected by the query segment are developed. As a result, we obtain a binary tree structure in secondary storage of height $O(\log n)$, which meets all conditions required in [19, 21] for applying any advanced technique between path-caching and P-range tree.

Data structure. Let S be a set of N line-based segments. We first select a number B of segments from S with the topmost y-value endpoints and store them in the root r of the tree Tr under construction, ordered with respect to their intersections with the base line. [4] The set containing all other segments is partitioned into two subsets containing an equal number of elements. The top segment in each subset is then copied into the root. These segments are denoted respectively by *left* and *right*. A separator *low* is also inserted in the root, which is a horizontal line separating the selected segments from the others. Line *low* for a generic node v is denoted by $v.low$. A similar notation is used for *left* and *right* (see Figure 3). If $v.left.y$ ($v.right.y$) denotes the top y-value of segment $v.left$ ($v.right$) and $v.low.y$ denotes the y-value of line $v.low$, then $v.left.y \leq v.low.y$ and $v.right.y \leq v.low.y$.

The decomposition process is recursively repeated for each of the two subsets. Like external priority search trees in point databases, the resulting tree Tr is a balanced binary tree of height $O(\log n)$, occupying $O(n)$ blocks in external storage. The difference, however, is that no subtree in Tr defines a rectangular

---

[3] Unless otherwise stated all logarithms are given with respect to base 2.

[4] Note that the construction guarantees that each node is contained in exactly one block.

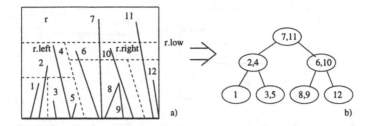

Fig. 3. a) An external PST for line-based segments; b) the corresponding binary tree, assuming $B = 2$. Non-horizontal dashed lines do not exist in the real data structure and are given only for convenience. Moreover segments $v.left$ and $v.right$, as well as line $v.low$, are shown only for the root r.

region in the plane. Indeed, in a point database, a vertical line is used as a separator between points stored in left and right subtrees. Instead, in a segment database, the line separating segments stored in left and right subtrees is often biased (see Figure 3).

Search algorithm. Let q be a horizontal query segment. We want to find all segments intersecting q. The search algorithm is based on the comparison of q with the stored segments.[5] The search is based on two functions $Find$ and $Report$. Function $Find$ is to locate the deepest-leftmost (deepest-rightmost) segment intersected by the query q, with respect to its storage position in Tr, and the node in Tr where the segment is located. Function $Report$ then uses the result of function $Find$ to retrieve all segments in Tr intersected by q, starting from the deepest-leftmost and deepest-rightmost segments intersecting the query. These functions are similar to the ones presented in [6] for the internal memory intersection problem, and satisfy the following properties:

- Function $Find$ maintains in a queue Q the nodes that should be analyzed to find the deepest-leftmost (the deepest-rightmost) segment intersecting the query segment. It can be shown that Q contains at most two nodes for each level of Tr, thereby assuring that the answer is found in $O(\log n)$ steps. Moreover, a constant space $O(1)$ is sufficient to store Q [6].
- Function $Report$ determines the deepest-leftmost and the deepest-rightmost segments intersecting the query, using function $Find$. Then, it visits the subtree rooted at the common ancestor of the nodes containing such segments and the path from such ancestor to the root of the tree. It can be proved that the number of nodes of such subtree, containing at least one segment non-intersecting q, is $O(\log n + t)$ [6].

Lemma 1. *[6] Let S be a set of line-based segments. Let q be a query segment. Let Tr be the priority search tree for S, constructed as above. Then:*

---

[5] Note that this is different from the approach usually used in PST for point databases. In that case, the comparison is performed against region boundaries. Such an approach is not possible for line-based segments, since no rectangular region is related to any subtree of Tr.

1. *Function Find returns the deepest-leftmost (the deepest-rightmost) segment bl_l (bl_r) in S intersected by q and the node it belongs to in $O(\log n)$ I/O's.*
2. *All T segments in S intersected by q can be found from Tr, bl_l and bl_r, in $O(\log n + \frac{T}{B})$ I/O's.* □

The following result summarizes the costs of the proposed data structure.

Lemma 2. *N line-based segments can be stored in a secondary storage priority search tree having the following costs: (i) storage cost is $O(n)$; (ii) horizontal segment query cost is $O(\log n + T/B)$, where T is the number of the detected intersections.* □

Despite the difference in the query results between a 3-sided query on a point database and a segment query on a segment database (see Figure 2), either the path-caching [19] or the P-range tree [21] methods can be applied for reducing the search time in a segment database, using an external PST. Since we will use some external PST on each level of the first-level data structures we are going to develop (see Section 3 and Section 4), we choose a linear memory solution based on P-range trees, obtaining an optimal space complexity in the data structure for storing line-based segments.

The application of the P-range tree technique to an external PST for line-based segments requires only one minor modification to the technique described in [21]. As for PST, the vertical line separator should be replaced by the queue Q and several procedures needed for the queue maintenance. Then, a comparison of a query point against a vertical line separator in a point database is replaced by the check of at most two nodes in queue Q, during the search in a segment database. Since the detection of the next-level node and the queue maintenance in a segment database takes $O(1)$ time, this substitution does not influence any properties of the P-range tree technique. This proves the following result.

Theorem 3. *N line-based segments can be stored in a secondary storage data structure having the following costs: (i) storage cost is $O(n)$; (ii) horizontal segment query cost is $O(\log_B n + IL^*(B) + t)$ I/O's; (iii) update amortized cost is $O(\log_B n + \frac{\log_B^2 n}{B})$.* □

3 External storage of NCT segments

In order to determine all NCT segments intersecting a vertical segment, we propose two secondary storage solutions, based on two-level data structures (denoted by 2LDS). Second-level data structures are based on the organization for line-based segments presented in Section 2. In the following, we introduce the first proposed data structure; the second one will be presented in Section 4.

First-level data structure. The basic idea is to consider a binary tree as first-level structure. With each node v of the tree, we associate a line $bl(v)$ (standing for *base line* of v) and the set of segments intersected by the line. More formally, let N be a set of NCT segments. We order the set of endpoints corresponding to such segments in ascending order according to their x-values. Then, we determine a vertical line partitioning such ordered set in two subsets of equal cardinality and we associate such vertical line with the base line $bl(r)$ of the root. All segments intersecting $bl(r)$ are associated with the root whereas all segments which are on the left (right) of $bl(r)$ and do not intersect it, are passed to the left (right) subtree of the root. The decomposition recursively continues until each leaf node contains B segments and fits as a whole in internal memory. The construction of base lines guarantees that the segments in a node v are intersected by $bl(v)$ but are not intersected by the base line of the parent of v. The tree height is $O(\log n)$.

Second-level data structures. Because of the above construction, each segment in an internal node v either lies on $bl(v)$ or intersects it. The segments which lie on the base line are stored in $C(v)$, an external interval tree [3] which requires a linear number of storage blocks and performs a VS query in $O(\log_B n + t)$ I/O's. Each segment which is intersected by $bl(v)$ has left and right parts. Left and right parts of all the segments are collected into two sets, called $L(v)$ and $R(v)$, respectively. Each of these sets contains line-based segments and can be efficiently maintained in secondary storage using the technique proposed in Section 2. Totally, each segment is represented at most twice inside the two-level data structure. Therefore, the tree stores N segments in $O(n)$ blocks in secondary storage. Figure 4 (b) illustrates the organization and content of the proposed 2LDS, for the set of segments presented in Figure 4 (a).

Search algorithm. Given a query segment of the form $x = x_0, a \le y \le b$, the search is performed on the first-level tree as follows. We scan the tree and visit exactly one node v for each level. In each node v, we first verify if x_0 equals the x-coordinate of the vertical line $bl(v)$. In such a case, all segments in $C(v)$, $L(v)$ and $R(v)$ intersected by q are retrieved and the search stops. Otherwise, if x_0 is lower than the x-coordinate of $bl(v)$, we visit only $L(v)$ and move to the left son of v. If x_0 is greater than the x-coordinate of $bl(v)$, we visit only $R(v)$ and move to the right son. The search for all segments T' inside one node intersected by the query requires $O(\log_B n + IL^*(B) + \frac{T'}{B})$ time. Since the height of the first-level data structure is $O(\log n)$ and each segment is reported at most twice,[6] the I/O complexity of the total search is $O(\log n(\log_B n + IL^*(B)) + t)$.

Updates. If updates are allowed, the binary tree should be replaced by a dynamic search-tree, for which efficient rebalancing methods are known. To maintain insertions and deletions of line-based segments in the data structure described above, we replace the binary tree with a $BB[\alpha]$-tree [6, 17], $0 < \alpha < 1 - 1/\sqrt{2}$. We store balance values in internal nodes of the $BB[\alpha]$-tree and maintain the optimal $O(\log n)$ height of the tree by performing $O(\log n)$ single or double rotations during an update. The update cost consists of $O(\log n)$ operations for the search and balance maintenance in the first-level tree and $O(\log_B n + \frac{\log_B^2 n}{B})$ operations for updating the second-level data structures. Therefore, the total update cost is $O(\log n + \frac{\log_B^2 n}{B})$. The cost is $O(\log n)$ for all real values of n (more exactly, for $n \in O(2^B)$).

---

[6] A segment is reported twice only if it intersects q and it is contained in a node v such that x_0 equals the x-coordinate of $bl(v)$.

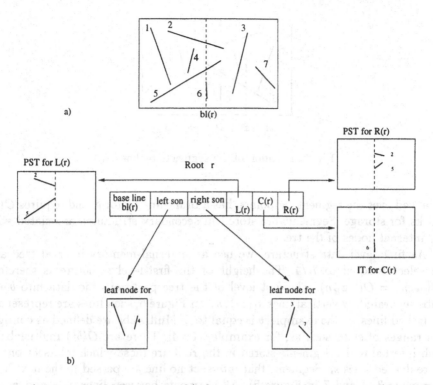

Fig. 4. a) A set of 7 NCT segments; b) the corresponding data structure ($B = 2$, PST stands for priority search tree, IT stands for interval tree).

Theorem 4. *N NCT segments can be stored in a secondary storage data structure having the following costs: (i) storage cost is $O(n)$; (ii) VS query time is $O(\log n(\log_B n + IL^*(B)) + t)$; (iii) update time is $O(\log n + \frac{\log_B^2 n}{B})$.* □

4 An improved solution to query NCT segments

In order to improve the complexity results obtained in the previous section, a secondary storage interval tree, designed for solving stabbing queries [3], is used as first-level data structure, instead of the binary tree. This modification, together with the use of the fractional cascading technique [5], improves the wasteful factor $\log n$ in the complexity results presented in Theorem 4, but uses $O(n \log_2 B)$ space.

4.1 First-level data structure

The *interval tree* is a standard dynamic data structure for storing a set of 1-dimensional segments [3, 9], tailored to support stabbing queries. The tree is

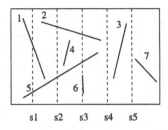

$s1 \quad s2 \quad s3 \quad s4 \quad s5$

Fig. 5. Partition of the segments by lines s_i.

balanced over the segment endpoints, has a branching factor b, and requires $O(n)$ blocks for storage. Segments are stored in secondary structures associated with the internal nodes of the tree.

As first level data structure, we use an external-memory interval tree and we select b equal to $B/4$. The height of the first-level structure is therefore $O(\log_b n) = O(\log_B n)$. The first level of the tree partitions the data into $b + 1$ slabs separated by vertical lines $s_1, \ldots, s_b$. In Figure 5, such lines are represented as dashed lines. In the example, b is equal to 5. Multislabs are defined as contiguous ranges of slabs such as, for example, $[1 : 4]$. There are $O(b^2)$ multislabs in each internal node. Segments stored in the root are those which intersect one or more dashed lines s_i. Segments that intersect no line are passed to the next level (segments 3, 4 and 7 in Figure 5). All segments between lines s_{i-1} and s_i are passed to the node corresponding to the i-th slab. The decomposition continues until each leaf represents B segments.

4.2 Second-level data structures

In each internal node of the first-level tree, we split all segments which do not lie on dashed lines s_i into *long* and *short* fragments. A long fragment spans one or more slabs and has both its endpoints on dashed lines. A short fragment spans no complete slab and has only one endpoint on the dashed line. Segments are split as follows (see Figure 6). If a segment completely spans one or more slabs, we split it into one long (central) fragment and at most two short fragments. The long fragment is obtained by splitting the segment on the boundaries of the largest multislab it spans. After this splitting, at most two additional short segments are generated. If a segment in the node intersects only one dashed line and spans no slab, it is simply split into two short fragments. In total, if k segments are associated with a node, the splitting process generates at most k long and $2k$ short fragments.

As before, segments lying on a dashed line s_i are stored in an external interval tree C_i. Short ad long fragments are stored as follows.

Short fragments. All short fragments are naturally clustered according to the dashed line they touch. Note that short fragments having one endpoint on line s_i are line-based segments and can be maintained in an external priority search tree as described in Section 2. Short line-based fragments which are located on

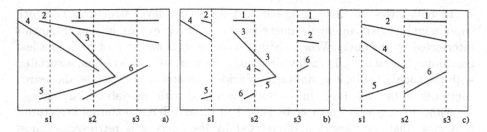

Fig. 6. The splitting of segments. a) Segments associated with a node; b) short fragments; c) long fragments.

the left of s_i are stored in an external PST L_i. Symmetrically, short fragments on the right side of s_i are stored in an external PST R_i. Totally, an internal node of the first-level structure contains $2b$ external PSTs for short fragments.

Long fragments. We store all long segments in an additional structure G which is essentially a segment tree [1, 7] based on dashed lines s_i, $i = 1, \ldots, b$. G is a balanced binary tree with $b - 2$ internal nodes and $b - 1$ leaves. Thus, in total it has $O(B)$ nodes.

Each leaf of the segment tree G corresponds to a single slab and each internal node v is associated with the multislab $I(v)$ formed by the union of the slabs associated with the leaves of the subtree of v. The root of G is associated with the multislab $[1 : b]$. Given a long fragment l which spans many slabs, the *allocation nodes* of l are the nodes v_i of G such that l spans $I(v_i)$ but not $I(par(v_i))$, where $par(v)$ is the parent of v in G. There are at most two allocation nodes of l at any level of G, so that, since the height of the segment tree is $\log_2 B$, l has $O(\log_2 B)$ allocation nodes [7].

Each internal node v of G is associated with a multislab $[i : j]$ and is associated with the ordered list (called *multislab list* $[i : j]$) of long fragments having v as allocation node, cut on the boundaries of $I(v)$. A B$^+$-tree is maintained on the list for fast retrieval and update.

Since the segment tree G contains $O(B)$ nodes, each containing a pointer to a B$^+$-tree in addition to standard node information, it can be stored in $O(1)$ blocks. In total, each segment may be stored in at most three external-memory structures. That is, if a segment spans the multislab $[i : j]$, the segment is stored in data structures L_i, R_j, and in $O(\log_2 B)$ allocation nodes of G. Since $b = B/4$, an internal node of the first-level structure has enough space to store all references to b structures C_i, b structures L_i, b structures R_i and one structure G. Thus, in total, the space utilization is $O(n \log_2 B)$.

Search algorithm. Given a query segment $x = x_0, a_1 \leq y \leq a_2$, a lookup is performed on the first-level tree from the root, searching for a leaf containing x_0. For each node, if x_0 equals the x-coordinate of any s_i, the interval tree C_i is searched together with the second-level structures R_i and L_i to retrieve the segments lying on s_i and short fragments intersected by the query segment. Otherwise, if x_0 hits the i-th slab, that is $s_i < x_0 < s_{i+1}$, then we check second-level structures R_i and L_{i+1}.

In both cases, we have to check also the second-level structures G which contain multislabs spanning the query value x_0 and retrieve all the long fragments intersected by the query. When visiting G, we scan from the root of G to a leaf containing the value x_0. In each visited node, we search the ordered list associated with the node. Finally, if x_0 does not coincide with any s_i in the node, the search continues on the next level, in the node associated with the slab containing x_0.

Although any segment may be stored in three different external structures, it is clear that each segment intersected by the query q is retrieved at most twice. Moreover, for each internal node, during the search we visit exactly two structures for short fragments and structure G for long ones. This proves the following lemma.

Lemma 5. *N NCT segments can be stored in a secondary storage data structure having the following costs: (i) storage cost is $O(n \log_2 B)$; (ii) VS query time is $O(\log_B n(\log_B n \log_2 B + IL^*(B)) + t)$.* □

To further reduce the search time, we extend this approach with fractional cascading [5] between lists stored on neighbor levels of structures G.

4.3 Fractional cascading

Fractional cascading [5] is a technique supporting the execution of a sequence of searches at a constant cost (in both internal memory and secondary storage) per search, except for the first one. The main idea is to construct a number of "bridges" among lists. Once an element is found in one list, the location of the element in other lists is quickly determined by traversing the bridges rather than applying the general search. Fractional cascading has been extensively used in internal-memory algorithms [5, 7, 12]. Recently, the technique has been also applied to off-line external-memory algorithms [2]. Our approach can be summarized as follows.

Data structure supporting fractional cascading. The idea is to create bridges between nodes on neighbor levels of the G structure, stored in one node of the first-level data structure. In particular, for an internal node of G associated with a multislab $[i : j]$, two sets of bridges are created between the node and its two sons associated with multislabs $[i : \frac{i+j}{2}]$ and $[\frac{i+j}{2} : j]$ (see Figure 7). Each fragment in the multislab list $[i : j]$ keeps two references to the nearest fragments in the list, which are bridges to left and right sons.

For multislabs $[i : j]$ and $[i : \frac{i+j}{2}]$ (and similarly for multislabs $[i : j]$ and $[\frac{i+j}{2} : j]$), the bridges are created in such a way that the following *d-property* is satisfied : *the number s of fragments in both multislab lists $[i : j]$ and $[i : \frac{i+j}{2}]$ between two sequential bridges is such that $d \leq s \leq 2d$, where d is a constant ≥ 2.*

The bridges between two multislab lists $[i : j]$ and $[i : \frac{i+j}{2}]$ are generated as follows. First we merge the two lists in one. All fragments in the joined list do not intersect each other and either touch or intersect line $s_{\frac{i+j}{2}}$. We scan the joined list given by the order of segment intersections with line $s_{\frac{i+j}{2}}$ and select each $d+1$-th

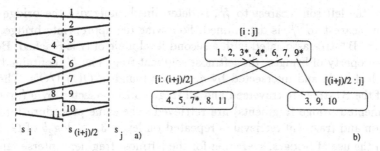

Fig. 7. "Bridges" in G. a) Long fragments stored in the node associated with multislab $[i : j]$ and in its two sons, associated with multislabs $[i : \frac{i+j}{2}]$ and $[\frac{i+j}{2} : j]$. b) Lists of fragments associated with nodes of the G structure. The lists are extended with bridge fragments ($d=2$). Bridges are shown by lines and augmented bridge fragments are marked with '*'.

fragment from the list as a bridge. If the fragment is from $[i : j]$ (like fragment 7 in Figure 7), we cut it on line $s_{\frac{i+j}{2}}$ and copy it in the multislab list $[i : \frac{i+j}{2}]$. Otherwise, if the fragment is from $[i : \frac{i+j}{2}]$ (like fragment 4 in Figure 7), we copy it in the multislab list $[i : j]$. Such a copy of the bridge is called *augmented bridge fragment*; in Figure 7 these fragments are marked with "*".[7] The position of the augmented bridge fragment in $[i : j]$ is determined by its intersection with line $s_{\frac{i+j}{2}}$. Analogously, the bridges are created between multislabs $[i : j]$ and $[\frac{i+j}{2} : j]$. Bridge fragments from a multislab list $[i : j]$ are copied (after the cutting) in the multislab list $[\frac{i+j}{2} : j]$ while bridge fragments from the multislab list $[\frac{i+j}{2} : j]$ are copied to $[i : j]$.

After bridges from the multislab list $[i : j]$ to both lists $[i : \frac{i+j}{2}]$ and $[\frac{i+j}{2} : j]$ are generated, the list $[i : j]$ contains original fragments (some of them are bridges to left or right son) and augmented bridge fragments copied from lists $[i : \frac{i+j}{2}]$ and $[\frac{i+j}{2} : j]$. In Figure 7, the list $[i : j]$ contains three augmented bridge fragments, respectively fragments 3, 4, and 9. All the fragments in $[i : j]$ are ordered by the points in which they intersect or touch line $s_{\frac{i+j}{2}}$.

Given an internal node v of G, associated with the multislab $[i : j]$, a B$^+$-tree is built from the multislab list $[i : j]$, after bridges to both sons are generated and copied in the list. After including augmented bridge fragments in all nodes of G, the space complexity is still $O(n \log_2 B)$.

Search algorithm. Let q be the vertical segment of the form $x = x_0, a_1 \leq y \leq a_2$. The VS query q is performed as described in Subsection 4.2, by modifying the search in G as follows. First we search in the B$^+$-tree associated with the root of G and detect the leftmost segment fragment f_l^1 intersected by q and associated with the root. This takes $O(\log_B n)$ steps. Then, the leaves of the B$^+$-tree are traversed and all fragments in the root of G intersected by q (except for the augmented bridge fragments) are retrieved. As a second step, if x_0 is lower than $s_{\frac{i+j}{2}}$, the

---

[7] Note that augmented bridge fragments are only used to speed up the search, they are never reported in the query reply.

bridge to the left son, nearest to f_l^1, is determined, otherwise the bridge to the right son, nearest to f_l^1, is determined. Following the appropriate bridge, a leaf node in the B$^+$-tree associated with a second level node of G is reached. Because of the d-property of bridges, the leftmost segment fragment f_l^2, contained in the reached leaf node and intersected by q, can be found in $O(1)$ I/O's. Then, the leaves of the B$^+$-tree are traversed and all fragments intersected by q (except for the augmented bridge fragments) are retrieved. The same procedure for bridge navigation and fragment retrieval is repeated on levels $3, \ldots, \log_2 b$ of G.

With the use of bridges, searching for the leftmost fragment intersecting q on all levels of G takes $O(\log_B n + \log_2 B)$ steps. Together with searching in second-level data structures for short fragments, the search time for one internal node a of the first-level structure is $O(\log_B n + \log_2 B + IL^*(B) + \frac{T'}{B})$, where T' is the number of segments in node a intersected by the query. Since any segment is stored in only one node of the first-level tree (whose height is $O(\log_B n)$) and each segment intersected by the query is reported at most twice, reporting all segments intersected by the query takes $O(\log_B n(\log_B n + \log_2 B + IL^*(B)) + t)$.

Insertions. The 2LDS proposed above has been designed for the static case. The extension of the proposed schema to the semi-dynamic case is based on: (i) the use of a weighted-balanced B-tree [3] as first-level data structure;[8] (ii) the use of a $BB[\alpha]$-tree [6, 17], $0 < \alpha < 1 - 1/\sqrt{2}$ as the second-level structure G for long fragments; (iii) the definition of some additional operations on multislab lists (similar to those presented in [12]), guaranteeing the $O(1)$ I/O amortized complexity of bridge navigation. Such extensions allow insertions to be executed in $O(\log_B n + \log_2 B + \frac{\log_B^2 n}{B})$ amortized time.

Theorem 6. *N NCT segments can be stored in a secondary storage data structure having the following costs: (i) storage cost is $O(n \log_2 B)$; (ii) VS query time is $O(\log_B n(\log_B n + \log_2 B + IL^*(B)) + t)$; (iii) insertion amortized time is $O(\log_B n + \log_2 B + \frac{\log_B^2 n}{B})$.* □

5   Concluding remarks

In this paper we have proposed two techniques to solve a vertical (or having any other fixed direction) segment query on segment databases. The most efficient technique has $O(n \log_2 B)$ space complexity and time complexity very close to $O(\log_B^2 n + t)$. Future work includes the extension of the proposed technique to deal with query segments having arbitrary angular coefficients and a comparison of the proposed technique with typical spatial data structures having good average bounds, such as R-trees [10].

---

[8] A weighted-balanced B-tree is a B-tree where the weight of a node (i.e., the number of elements stored in the subtree rooted at the node) is a function of the level to which the node belongs. It guarantees efficient rebalancing operations in external-memory.

References

1. L. Arge. The Buffer Tree: A New Technique for Optimal I/O Algorithms. In *LNCS 955: Proc. of the 4th Int. Workshop on Algorithms and Data Structures*, pages 334–345, 1995.
2. L. Arge, D.E. Vengroff, and J. S. Vitter. External-Memory Algorithms for Processing Line Segments in Geographic Information Systems. In *Proc. of the 3rd Annual European Symp. on Algorithms*, pages 295–310, 1995.
3. L. Arge and J. S. Vitter. Optimal Dynamic Interval Management in External Memory. In *Proc. of the Int. Symp. on Foundations of Computer Science*, pages 560–569, 1996.
4. E. Bertino, B. Catania, and B. Shidlovsky. Towards Optimal Indexing for Segment Databases. Extended version. Technical report, University of Milano, Italy, 1998.
5. B. Chazelle and L.J. Guibas. Fractional Cascading: I. A Data Structuring Technique. *Algorithmica*, 1(2):133–162, 1986.
6. S.W. Cheng and R. Janardan. Efficient Dynamic Algorithms for Some Geometric Intersection Problems. *Information Processing Letters*, 36(5):251–258, 1990.
7. Y.-J. Chiang and R. Tamassia. Dynamic Algorithms in Computational Geometry. *Proc. IEEE*, 80(9):1412–1434, 1992.
8. D. Comer. The ubiquitous B-tree. *Computing Surveys*, 11(2):121–138, 1979.
9. H. Edelsbrunner. A New Approach to Rectangular Intersection. Part I. *Int. J. Comp. Mathematics*, 13:209–219, 1983.
10. A. Guttman. R-trees: A Dynamic Index Structure for Spatial Searching. In *Proc. ACM SIGMOD Int. Conf. on Management of Data*, pages 47–57, 1984.
11. C. Icking, R. Klein, and T. Ottmann. Priority Search Trees in Secondary Memory. In *LNCS 314: Proc. of the Int. Workshop on Graph-Theoretic Concepts in Computer Science*, pages 84–93, 1988.
12. K. Mehlhorn and S. Naher. Dynamic Fractional Cascading. *Algorithmica*, 5(2):215–241, 1990.
13. P. Kanellakis, G. Kuper, and P. Revesz. Constraint Query Languages. *J. Comp. System Sciences*, 51(1):25–52, 1995.
14. P.C. Kanellakis, S. Ramaswamy, D.E. Vengroff, and J.S. Vitter. Indexing for Data Models with Constraints and Classes. *J. Comp. System Sciences*, 52(3):589–612, 1996.
15. M. Koubarakis. Database Models for Infinite and Indefinite Temporal Information. *Information Systems*, 19(2):141–173, 1994.
16. E.McCreight. Priority Search Trees. *SIAM Journal of Computing.* 14(2): 257–276, 1985.
17. J. Nievergelt and E. M. Reingold. Binary Search Tree of Bounded Balance. *SIAM J. Computing*, 2(1):33–43, 1973.
18. J. Paredaens. Spatial Databases, the Final Frontier. In *LNCS 893: Proc. of the 5th Int. Conf. on Database Theory*, pages 14–31, 1995.
19. S. Ramaswamy and S. Subramanian. Path-Caching: A Technique for Optimal External Searching. In *Proc. of the ACM Symp. on Principles of Database Systems*, pages 25–35, 1994.
20. S. Ramaswamy. Efficient Indexing for Constraints and Temporal Databases. In *LNCS 1186: Proc. of the 6th Int. Conf. on Database Theory*, pages 419–431, 1997.
21. S. Subramanian and S. Ramaswamy. The P-Range Tree: A New Data Structure for Range Searching in Secondary Memory. In *Proc. of the ACM-SIAM Symp. on Discrete Algorithms*, pages 378–387, 1995.

Query Optimisation in the Web

Fusion Queries over Internet Databases *

Ramana Yerneni[1], Yannis Papakonstantinou[2]
Serge Abiteboul[3], Hector Garcia-Molina[4]

[1] yerneni@cs.stanford.edu, Stanford University, USA
[2] yannis@cs.ucsd.edu, University of California, San Diego, USA
[3] serge.abiteboul@inria.fr, INRIA, France
[4] hector@cs.stanford.edu, Stanford University, USA

Abstract. Fusion queries search for information integrated from distributed, autonomous sources over the Internet. We investigate techniques for efficient processing of fusion queries. First, we focus on a very wide class of query plans that capture the spirit of many techniques usually considered in existing systems. We show how to efficiently find good query plans within this large class. We provide additional heuristics that, by considering plans outside our target class of plans, yield further performance improvements.

1 Introduction

In distributed information systems on the Internet, data sources often provide incomplete and overlapping information on a set of entities. A *fusion query* searches over these entities, looking for ones that satisfy given conditions.

To illustrate, consider databases operated by the Departments of Motor Vehicles (DMVs) of several states. Conceptually, each state database can be thought of as a relation R_i with the following attributes, among others: Driver's license number (L), Violation (V) and Date of violation (D). Figure 1 shows some sample relations for three DMVs. Now, consider a fusion query that searches for drivers who have both a "driving under the influence" (dui) and a "speeding" (sp) violation. For instance, the driver with license $J55$ satisfies this query because he has a dui infraction in the first state and a sp one in the second state. Notice that the information for a particular driver, say $J55$, may be dispersed among the sources, so the query conceptually (but not actually) "fuses" the information for each driver as it checks the constraints.

To express our sample query in SQL, we first let U be the union of all the $R_1, R_2, \ldots$ tables at the various DMVs, and then we write

```
SELECT   u1.L
FROM     U u1, U u2
WHERE    u1.L = u2.L AND   u1.V = sp AND u2.V = dui
```

* Research partially supported by the Wright Laboratory, Aeronautical Systems Center, Air Force Material Command, USAF, under Grant Number F33615-93-1-1339. This research was done when Papakonstantinou and Abiteboul were at Stanford.

R_1	L	V	D
	J55	dui	1993
	T21	sp	1994
	T80	dui	1993

R_2	L	V	D
	T21	dui	1996
	J55	sp	1996
	T11	sp	1993

R_3	L	V	D
	T21	sp	1993
	S07	sp	1996
	S07	sp	1993

Fig. 1. DMV Example.

This is the type of query we focus on in this paper.

We believe that such fusion queries are important now, and will become even more important in the future as integration systems cope with more and more information that has *not* been nicely structured and partitioned in advance. In a traditional distributed database environment, for instance, an administrator could determine in advance that all violations for licenses issued in a given state go to a particular database. This makes fusion query processing much simpler because we only have to perform the query locally at each database and union the results. However, in a world where sites and databases are autonomous, as in the Internet context, it is very difficult to agree on and enforce global partitions. For example, the California DMV may want to keep a record of all violations that occurred in its state regardless of the license's origin. At the same time, the California DMV may not have complete records for California drivers because the other DMVs may not notify the California DMV of infractions occurring in their states involving California drivers.

Fusion queries over Internet databases introduce tough performance challenges. Traditional query optimizers do not consider fusion queries in any special way. They treat them simply as queries involving join operations and union views. In addition, many optimizers rely on good fragmentation of data and assume that the number of sources is small. As we have argued earlier, such assumptions are not valid in the Internet context and this often leads conventional techniques to produce poor plans for fusion queries over Internet databases.

Our goal in this paper is to understand how fusion queries can be processed efficiently in the context of Internet databases. To gain this knowledge, we proceed in four steps:

1. To make our task more manageable, we only consider fusion queries that retrieve the merge attribute (e.g., driver's license) of the matching entities. If additional information on the matching entities (e.g., driver's address) is needed, a "second phase" query would be issued. The assumption eliminates some performance factors (e.g., when should additional attributes be fetched), but still lets us study the basic types of fusion query plans.

   Furthermore, the "two-phase" approach is sometimes used in practice so it is interesting in its own right. For instance, in a bibliographic search scenario, one first identifies the documents that satisfy the criteria, and then fetches the documents, usually a few at a time. The main reason why searches are split this way is that the full records of the matching entities may be very large and are often stored on separate systems altogether. Even when this is not the case, this two-phase processing may reduce cost because we do not pay the price of fetching full records until we know which ones are needed.

2. To understand the types of fusion query plans, we first narrow down the space of plans to those we call *simple plans* (Section 2). Simple plans are coordinated by a central site we call the *mediator*. The mediator can ask one or more data sources to evaluate a condition, obtaining a set of values for the merge attributes. The mediator can also perform one or more semijoins by sending a set of merge attribute values to a source and receiving that subset whose elements match a condition at the source.[5] Finally, the mediator can combine the sets of merge attribute values it obtains, via union or intersection operations. For our sample query, one simple plan, call it $\mathcal{P}_1$, could be as follows: First, the mediator asks each source to give it all L values for drivers with $V = dui$ (see Figure 1). Then the mediator unions all these sets of values, and sends the entire set to all sources, asking each to select the ones that have $V = sp$. The union of those answer sets would be the final answer. The class of simple plans includes all the strategies that most real world optimizers would currently develop for a fusion query, plus many other natural plans. Thus, even though we have narrowed down our search, we expect to still find some excellent plans in this space, at least as good as those found by current optimizers.

3. The class of simple plans is still too large to be searched in a brute force way for an optimal plan. Fortunately, using theorems we prove in [24], we can constrain our search to a much smaller class of plans, those we call *semijoin-adaptive*. Intuitively, these are simple plans that work on the conditions of the query in some order, one condition at a time. (Plan $\mathcal{P}_1$ above is also semijoin-adaptive, since it first considers one condition fully, and then moves on to the second one.) It turns out that semijoin-adaptive plans are very good under a general cost model that we use here. In particular, if there are only two query conditions, or if there are more conditions but they are independent, then the best semijoin-adaptive plan is also the best simple plan. In this case the optimizer can perform a significantly smaller search over the space of semijoin-adaptive plans, and still find the best simple plan. Even if the conditions of the query are not independent, the best semijoin-adaptive plan provides an excellent heuristic. Indeed, when dealing with autonomous sources over the Internet, we often have no information about the dependence of conditions, so using the best semijoin-adaptive plan is as good a guess as we can make. Section 3 presents an efficient optimization algorithm to find the best semijoin-adaptive plan for a given fusion query.

4. Once we find the best semijoin-adaptive plan, we consider some variations of this plan that make it non-simple but that may improve performance further. In other words, as a "postoptimization" step, we consider a class of plans that is larger than simple plans, but we only perform a local optimization

---

[5] Note that if the source does not directly support semijoins, the mediator can emulate them; see Section 2.3.

in the neighborhood of our best semijoin-adaptive plan. For example, one of the variations we consider is having the mediator use set difference. To illustrate, consider our sample plan $\mathcal{P}_1$. We leave the first part unchanged, obtaining the set $X_1 = \{J55, T80, T21\}$ of all L values that have $V = dui$. Now, instead of sending X_1 to all sources for a semijoin, we only send it to the first source. The first source (R_1) returns the subset of X_1 with $V = sp$, i.e., $Y_1 = \{T21\}$. Now the mediator knows that $T21$ is definitely an answer to the query, so when it goes to the other sources, it does not have to send the full X_1 set; instead it sends $X_1 - Y_1$, reducing the amount of data that must be sent to the source. Postoptimization techniques like this one are discussed in Section 4.

2 Framework

In this section, we provide the framework for fusion query processing. First, we define the operations and data exported by sources. Second, we formally define fusion queries. Then we describe the class of simple plans, and our cost model. Finally, we identify some important subsets of simple plans.

2.1 The Sources

In our framework, each source has a *wrapper* [19] that exports a relation[6]. All the source relations have the same attributes, which include the merge attribute M. Attribute M identifies the real-world entity that the tuple refers to. Internally, each source can use a different model, but the wrapper maps it to the common view we are using. Note that we use a relational framework here only for simplicity. The algorithms we propose in this paper can be extended in a straightforward way to other data models. Incidentally, our interest in the fusion problem emerged from the TSIMMIS project which uses a semistructured object model [18].

Wrappers support the following two types of operations:

- *Selection queries* denoted as $X := sq(c_i, R_j)$. This operation retrieves the set of items that satisfy c_i in source relation R_j (we use the term *item* to refer to a merge attribute value).
- *Semijoin queries* denoted as $X := sjq(c_i, R_j, Y)$. This operation computes the subset of Y items that satisfy c_i in R_j.

2.2 Fusion Queries

We use U to refer to the union of all the source relations R_j. The general form of fusion queries is:

---

[6] The wrapper can export other relations of course; here we focus on the one involved in the fusion query of interest.

```
SELECT  u₁.M
FROM    U u₁,...,U uₘ
WHERE   u₁.M = ... = uₘ.M AND  c₁  AND  ...  AND  cₘ
```

where each condition c_i, $i = 1, \ldots, m$ involves only one u_i variable and U attributes, and is supported by the wrappers.

2.3 Simple Plans

Under *simple plans*, mediators can issue selection and semijoin queries to the wrappers, and can themselves perform operations of the form $X := Y \ op \ Z$, where Y and Z are sets of items, and op is either a union ($\cup$) or an intersection ($\cap$). Notice that, in general, mediators perform other operations like joins. However, for fusion queries, union and intersection operations suffice. Figures 2(a), 2(b) and 2(c), later on in this section, give examples of simple plans for a fusion query with 3 conditions and 2 sources.

Simple plans are quite general and can represent many ways to efficiently process fusion queries. They allow the description of any plan obtained by standard algebraic optimization techniques such as pushing selection and projection operations to the sources. They also allow query rewriting using the distributivity of join and union, the commutativity and associativity of join and union, along with many techniques to reorder joins to efficiently process m-way joins, and the use of semijoin operations for efficient processing of joins in distributed environments. These are strategies that most optimizers typically use. Thus, if we are able to find the best simple plan, we believe we will have a plan that cannot be beaten by existing real-world optimizers.

Simple plans can be employed in many contexts with a wide range of source capabilities. All that is required is that the sources support selection and semijoin queries. Some sources may not be able to support semijoin queries. In this case, the mediator can emulate a semijoin query as a set of selection queries. The cost of the emulated operation may be higher than if the source supported the semijoin operation, and this will be taken into account in our cost model. If source R_j does not support $sjq(c_i, R_j, Y)$, the mediator can process this semijoin query by sending the source a set of individual selection queries, one for each value in Y. In order for this to work, the source should at least be able to handle selection conditions of the form c_i AND $M = m$, where m is a "passed binding" (from Y). If the source is incapable of supporting even such queries, we can assign an infinite cost to the semijoin query, indicating that it is an unsupported query and hence should not be used in any query plan.

2.4 Cost Model

In our domain of interest, the Internet databases, the most time consuming task is sending queries to the sources and receiving answers from them. Thus, we adopt a model that emphasizes these costs and neglects the cost of local processing at the mediator. In particular,

- Each $sq(c_i, R_j)$ and each $sjq(c_i, R_j, X)$ operation has a non-negative cost.
- If X, Y and Z are sets of items with $X = Y \cup Z$, the cost of $sjq(c_i, R_j, X)$ is at most as much as the sum of the costs of $sjq(c_i, R_j, Y)$ and $sjq(c_i, R_j, Z)$ for any c_i and R_j. In other words, there is no benefit in splitting a semijoin set X into semijoin sets Y and Z.
- The cost of local mediator operations, $\cup$ and $\cap$, is negligible.
- The cost of a query plan is the sum of the costs of the constituent $sq(c_i, R_j)$ and $sjq(c_i, R_j, X)$ operations. Thus, our focus is on total work involved in query execution, not on response time.

We do not make any assumptions as to how the costs of source queries are computed; they could take into account the cost of communicating with sources, and the cost of actually processing the queries at the sources. The costs can vary depending on the contents of R_j and X, and the selectivity of c_i.

We believe that our cost model is quite general. Many distributed database optimizers use cost models that are compatible with our cost model. In fact, our cost model allows for cost estimation that can deal with heterogeneous source characteristics while many other cost models do not.

2.5 Important Classes of Simple Plans

To conclude this section, we define some important classes of simple plans.

(a) A filter plan	(b) A semijoin plan	(c) A semijoin-adaptive plan
1) $X_{11} := sq(c_1, R_1)$	1) $X_{11} := sq(c_1, R_1)$	1) $X_{11} := sq(c_1, R_1)$
2) $X_{12} := sq(c_1, R_2)$	2) $X_{12} := sq(c_1, R_2)$	2) $X_{12} := sq(c_1, R_2)$
3) $X_1 := X_{11} \cup X_{12}$	3) $X_1 := X_{11} \cup X_{12}$	3) $X_1 := X_{11} \cup X_{12}$
4) $X_{21} := sq(c_2, R_1)$	4) $X_{21} := sjq(c_2, R_1, X_1)$	4) $X_{21} := sjq(c_2, R_1, X_1)$
5) $X_{22} := sq(c_2, R_2)$	5) $X_{22} := sjq(c_2, R_2, X_1)$	5) $X_{22} := sq(c_2, R_2)$
6) $X_2 := X_{21} \cup X_{22}$	6) $X_2 := X_{21} \cup X_{22}$	6) $X_2 := X_{21} \cup X_{22}$
7) $X_2 := X_2 \cap X_1$	7) $X_{31} := sq(c_3, R_1)$	7) $X_2 := X_2 \cap X_1$
8) $X_{31} := sq(c_3, R_1)$	8) $X_{32} := sq(c_3, R_2)$	8) $X_{31} := sq(c_3, R_1)$
9) $X_{32} := sq(c_3, R_2)$	9) $X_3 := X_{31} \cup X_{32}$	9) $X_{32} := sq(c_3, R_2)$
10) $X_3 := X_{31} \cup X_{32}$	10) $X_3 := X_2 \cap X_3$	10) $X_3 := X_{31} \cup X_{32}$
11) $X_3 := X_3 \cap X_2$		11) $X_3 := X_2 \cap X_3$

Fig. 2. Three simple plans

1. *Filter plans*: Filter plans are simple plans that use only selection queries and local operations at the mediator. Many traditional distributed query optimizers do not use semijoin operations. Such optimizers generate filter plans for fusion queries.

    Figure 2(a) shows an example filter plan for a fusion query with conditions c_1, c_2, and c_3 and sources R_1 and R_2. In this plan, the mediator pushes each condition to each source (six selection queries), and computes the final answer from the corresponding item sets.

2. *Semijoin plans*: These are simple plans that employ semijoin queries in a restricted fashion. A particular semijoin plan is determined first by an ordering, say, $c_1, ..., c_m$ of the query conditions. The set X_1 of items satisfying c_1 at some source is first retrieved by issuing selection queries, one for each of the n sources. Next, the second condition can be evaluated either in a similar fashion or by semijoin queries using X_1 as the semijoin set. In either case, the plan computes X_2, the set of items that satisfy c_1 at one source and c_2 at another (possibly the same) source. The process continues in a similar fashion for the rest of the conditions. In general, for a given ordering of the conditions, a particular semijoin plan is specified by deciding for each condition c_i (i in $[2..m]$), whether to evaluate c_i by selection queries or by semijoin queries using as semijoin set the set of items satisfying $c_1 \wedge ... \wedge c_{i-1}$. Figure 2(b) illustrates a semijoin plan for the same fusion query used in Figure 2(a). The second condition is evaluated by semijoin queries, and the others by selection queries. Observe that the first condition in a semijoin plan is always evaluated by selection queries.

Semijoin plans can be more efficient than filter plans. For instance, in Figure 2(b), the source with R_1 only returns a fraction of the items satisfying c_2, while the equivalent filter plan would have fetched all items in R_1 satisfying c_2. However, we can make semijoin plans even more effective by allowing them more flexibility. In particular, notice that for a given condition, semijoin plans either send selection queries to all sources or they send semijoin queries to all sources. This may be inefficient in an environment where the sources have widely different characteristics. For example, if the second source does not directly support semijoins (i.e., semijoins have to be emulated in an expensive manner) it may not be beneficial to process c_2 at the second source by a semijoin query. The class of plans described next has the ability to adapt to the characteristics of the sources.

3. *Semijoin-adaptive plans*: Like semijoin plans, these plans process one condition at a time, in some order $c_1, ..., c_m$. However, for each condition in $[2..m]$ and each source, the plan can choose independently between a selection query or a semijoin query. Figure 2(c) illustrates a semijoin-adaptive plan for the same sample query of the previous figures. As we can see, the plan processes c_2 at R_1 by issuing a semijoin query, and at R_2 by a selection query. Thus, the plan can use the best strategy at each source.

3 Finding Optimal Simple Plans

In this section we present three optimization algorithms — FILTER, SJ, and SJA — that compute the best filter, semijoin, and semijoin-adaptive plans respectively. These algorithms are very efficient, as they run in time linear in the number of sources participating in the fusion query.

INPUT: Conditions $c_1, \ldots, c_m$
Sources $R_1, \ldots, R_n$
Cost functions sq_cost and sjq_cost
OUTPUT: An optimal semijoin plan
METHOD:

$Optimal\_Plan\_Cost \leftarrow \infty$

for every ordering $[c_{o_1}, \ldots, c_{o_m}]$ of the conditions   *loop A*

$Plan \leftarrow [X_{11} := sq(c_{o_1}, R_1), \ldots, X_{1n} := sq(c_{o_1}, R_n), X_1 := \cup_{j=1,\ldots,n} X_{1j}]$

$Plan\_Cost \leftarrow \sum_{j=1,\ldots,n} sq\_cost(c_{o_1}, R_j)$

for $i = 2, \ldots, m$ *loop B*

$selection\_queries\_cost \leftarrow \sum_{j=1,\ldots,n} sq\_cost(c_{o_i}, R_j)$

$semijoin\_queries\_cost \leftarrow \sum_{j=1,\ldots,n} sjq\_cost(c_{o_i}, R_j, X_{i-1})$

if $selection\_queries\_cost < semijoin\_queries\_cost$

append to *Plan* the sequence of operations

$[X_{i1} := sq(c_{o_i}, R_1), \ldots, X_{in} := sq(c_{o_i}, R_n)]$

append to *Plan* the operation $X_i := X_{i-1} \cap (\cup_{j=1,\ldots,n} X_{ij})$

$Plan\_Cost \leftarrow Plan\_Cost + selection\_queries\_cost$

else

append to *Plan* the sequence of operations

$[X_{i1} := sjq(c_{o_i}, R_1, X_{i-1}), \ldots, X_{in} := sjq(c_{o_i}, R_n, X_{i-1})]$

append to *Plan* the operation $X_i := \cup_{j=1,\ldots,n} X_{ij}$

$Plan\_Cost \leftarrow Plan\_Cost + semijoin\_queries\_cost$

if $Plan\_Cost < Optimal\_Plan\_Cost$

$Optimal\_Plan \leftarrow Plan$

$Optimal\_Plan\_Cost \leftarrow Plan\_Cost$

Fig. 3. The SJ algorithm

We use cost functions $sq\_cost(c_i, R_j)$ and $sjq\_cost(c_i, R_j, X)$ to estimate the costs of the selection query $sq(c_i, R_j)$ and the semijoin query $sjq(c_i, R_j, X)$ respectively. In analyzing the complexity of the various algorithms presented in this section, we assume that sq_cost and sjq_cost take constant time per invocation. These functions can use whatever information is available at query optimization time, in order to estimate the costs. Techniques like those discussed in [5, 15, 25] can be employed in gathering the relevant statistical information that the cost functions need.

The FILTER algorithm: For a fusion query with m conditions and n sources, the most efficient filter plan is one that issues the mn source queries, pushing each condition to each source, and combining the results of these source queries to compute the answer to the fusion query. FILTER directly outputs such a plan without searching the plan space. Its running time is proportional to the size of the filter plan, which in turn is $O(mn)$, where m is the number of conditions and n is the number of sources.

INPUT: Conditions $c_1, \ldots, c_m$
        Sources $R_1, \ldots, R_n$
        Cost functions sq_cost and sjq_cost
OUTPUT: The optimal semijoin-adaptive plan
METHOD:

$\quad$ $Optimal\_Plan\_Cost \leftarrow \infty$
$\quad$ for every ordering $[c_{o_1}, \ldots, c_{o_m}]$ of the conditions $\hfill$ loop A
$\quad\quad$ $Plan \leftarrow [X_{11} := sq(c_{o_1}, R_1), \ldots, X_{1n} := sq(c_{o_1}, R_n), X_1 := \cup_{j=1,\ldots,n} X_{1j}]$
$\quad\quad$ $Plan\_Cost \leftarrow \sum_{j=1,\ldots,n} sq\_cost(c_{o_1}, R_j)$
$\quad\quad$ for $i = 2, \ldots, m$ $\hfill$ loop B
$\quad\quad\quad$ for $j = 1, \ldots, n$ $\hfill$ source loop
$\quad\quad\quad\quad$ if $sq\_cost(c_{o_i}, R_j) < sjq\_cost(c_{o_i}, R_j, X_{i-1})$
$\quad\quad\quad\quad\quad$ append to $Plan$ the operation $X_{ij} := sq(c_{o_i}, R_j)$
$\quad\quad\quad\quad\quad$ $Plan\_Cost \leftarrow Plan\_Cost + sq\_cost(c_{o_i}, R_j)$
$\quad\quad\quad\quad$ else
$\quad\quad\quad\quad\quad$ append to $Plan$ the operation $X_{ij} := sjq(c_{o_i}, R_j, X_{i-1})$
$\quad\quad\quad\quad\quad$ $Plan\_Cost \leftarrow Plan\_Cost + sjq\_cost(c_{o_i}, R_j, X_{i-1})$
$\quad\quad\quad$ append to $Plan$ the operation $X_i := X_{i-1} \cap (\cup_{j=1,\ldots,n} X_{ij})$
$\quad\quad$ if $Plan\_Cost < Optimal\_Plan\_Cost$
$\quad\quad\quad$ $Optimal\_Plan \leftarrow Plan$
$\quad\quad\quad$ $Optimal\_Plan\_Cost \leftarrow Plan\_Cost$

Fig. 4. The SJA algorithm

The SJ algorithm: SJ (see Figure 3) generates all possible $m!$ orderings of the conditions (see loop A). For each one of them, it generates the best *Plan* with respect to this ordering, estimates its cost, and eventually selects as *Optimal Plan* the one with the least cost among all orderings.

The best *Plan* with respect to a specific ordering $[c_{o_1}, \ldots, c_{o_m}]$ starts with a sequence of operations that evaluate c_{o_1} using selection queries. Then SJ goes over each one of the $m - 1$ conditions c_{o_i}, $i = 2, \ldots, m$ (see loop B) and decides whether c_{o_i} is evaluated by semijoin or selection queries. In particular, SJ sums up and compares the cost of the n selection queries against the cost of the n semijoin queries. The *Plan* and its cost are appropriately updated in each round. The complexity of SJ is $O((m!)mn)$ because loop A iterates $m!$ times, loop B iterates $m - 1$ times, and the operations inside loop B are of complexity $O(n)$.

The SJA algorithm: SJA (see Figure 4) differs from the SJ algorithm in that it makes a separate decision between selection and semijoin query for each condition at each source. In particular, SJA includes the "source loop" of Figure 4 where, for a given condition c_{o_i}, it decides, for each source R_j, whether the processing of c_{o_i} at R_j will be done with a semijoin query or a selection query.

It is easy to see that SJA's complexity is also $O((m!)mn)$ since the source loop iterates n times and the operations inside it cost $O(1)$. The complexity of

SJA is similar to that of SJ, despite the fact that the space of semijoin-adaptive plans is much larger than the space of semijoin plans (there are $O((m!)2^{m-2})$ semijoin plans assuming we do not consider semijoin plans that are equivalent with respect to our cost model, and there are $O((m!)2^{n(m-2)})$ semijoin-adaptive plans). Moreover, the optimal semijoin-adaptive plan is always at least as good as, and often much better than, the optimal semijoin plan, as shown in [24]. So, SJA is preferable to SJ.

The fact that the algorithms presented in this section run in time linear in the number of sources is very important when we deal with a large number of sources as is the case with integrating Internet sources.

The running times of SJ and SJA are exponential in the number of conditions. In most realistic scenarios, this is acceptable since the number of conditions (unlike the number of sources) is usually small. If the number of conditions is large, one may employ the efficient greedy versions of SJ and SJA that we present in [24]. Those algorithms run in $O(mn)$ time and still find optimal plans under many realistic cost models. However, they may end up with suboptimal, although still very good, plans under the general cost model that we consider here.

4 Postoptimization

In this section, we consider postoptimization techniques that can improve the plans generated by the SJA algorithm. First, we describe two such techniques. Then, we briefly discuss how we efficiently incorporated these techniques in an algorithm named SJA+. In [24], we describe a set of other postoptimization techniques that can further enhance the performance.

Loading entire sources. Instead of sending a set of queries to a source, the mediator may consider issuing a single query to load the entire source contents and using this result to evaluate all the queries of that source. This can be advantageous in fusion queries involving extremely small source databases or large number of conditions.

To illustrate, consider the two queries on R_3 in $\mathcal{P}_1$ (Steps 3 and 7 in Figure 5(a)). Let the cost of loading the entire contents of R_3 be lower than the cost of issuing the two queries on R_3. Plan $\mathcal{P}_{2a}$ in Figure 5(b) is the result of postoptimizing $\mathcal{P}_1$ by loading R_3 and replacing the two queries of $\mathcal{P}_1$ on R_3 by local computation at the mediator. Note that $lq(R_j)$ is a new operation type used to represent the loading of the entire relation R_j. Also, we use $sq(c_i, Y)$ to stand for the local application of the condition c_i on a set Y of items[7].

Using the difference operation. A significant portion of the cost of semijoin queries to sources is for the transmission of the semijoin sets of items. One way to reduce the size of the semijoin sets is to use the set *difference* operation in the local

---

[7] Strictly speaking, Y is not a set of items because it may also include values for non-merge attributes on which the condition has to be applied.

1) $X_{11} := sq(c_1, R_1)$
2) $X_{12} := sq(c_1, R_2)$
3) $X_{13} := sq(c_1, R_3)$
4) $X_1 := X_{11} \cup X_{12} \cup X_{13}$
5) $X_{21} := sq(c_2, R_1)$
6) $X_{22} := sjq(c_2, R_2, X_1)$
7) $X_{23} := sq(c_2, R_3)$
8) $X_2 := X_{21} \cup X_{22} \cup X_{23}$
9) $X_2 := X_2 \cap X_1$

(a) phase 1: $\mathcal{P}_1$

1) $X_{11} := sq(c_1, R_1)$
2) $X_{12} := sq(c_1, R_2)$
3) $Y := lq(R_3)$
4) $X_{13} := sq(c_1, Y)$
5) $X_1 := X_{11} \cup X_{12} \cup X_{13}$
6) $X_{21} := sq(c_2, R_1)$
7) $X_{22} := sjq(c_2, R_2, X_1)$
8) $X_{23} := sq(c_2, Y)$
9) $X_2 := X_{21} \cup X_{22} \cup X_{23}$
10) $X_2 := X_2 \cap X_1$

(b) loading sources: $\mathcal{P}_{2a}$

1) $X_{11} := sq(c_1, R_1)$
2) $X_{12} := sq(c_1, R_2)$
3) $X_{13} := sq(c_1, R_3)$
4) $X_1 := X_{11} \cup X_{12} \cup X13$
5) $X_{21} := sq(c_2, R_1)$
6) $Z_1 := X_1 - X_{21}$
7) $X_{22} := sjq(c_2, R_2, Z_1)$
8) $X_{23} := sq(c_2, R_3)$
9) $X_2 := X_{21} \cup X_{22} \cup X_{23}$
10) $X_2 := X_2 \cap X_1$

(c) using difference: $\mathcal{P}_{2b}$

1) $X_{11} := sq(c_1, R_1)$
2) $X_{12} := sq(c_1, R_2)$
3) $Y := lq(R_3)$
4) $X_{13} := sq(c_1, Y)$
5) $X_1 := X_{11} \cup X_{12} \cup X_{13}$
6) $X_{21} := sq(c_2, R_1)$
7) $Z_1 := X_1 - X_{21}$
8) $X_{22} := sjq(c_2, R_2, Z_1)$
9) $X_{23} := sq(c_2, Y)$
10) $X_2 := X_{21} \cup X_{22} \cup X_{23}$
11) $X_2 := X_2 \cap X_1$

(d) SJA+ choice: $\mathcal{P}_2$

Fig. 5. Postoptimization

computations at the mediator. This is particularly important if some sources do not support semijoins directly and the semijoin operation has to be emulated.

In Section 1, we gave a simple example of postoptimization using the difference operator. Here we give a second example, now couched in our notation. Consider again plan $\mathcal{P}_1$ of Figure 5(a). In Step 6, $\mathcal{P}_1$ issues a semijoin query. At the end of Step 4, X_1 contains all the items that satisfy c_1. In Step 5, X_{21} collects all the items of relation R_1 that satisfy condition c_2. From X_1 and X_{21}, we can find the set of items that have already satisfied c_1 and c_2. These items need not be sent to R_2 in Step 6, to ascertain the satisfaction of condition c_2. Thus, there is no need to send the entire set X_1 as the semijoin input in Step 6. Instead, we can just send $X_1 - X_{21}$. Figure 5(c) shows the resulting plan.

4.1 SJA+

The SJA+ algorithm incorporates the above two postoptimization techniques as follows. First, it mimics SJA to obtain the best semijoin-adaptive plan for the given query. Then, it uses the *difference* operation to prune the semijoin sets, in all the semijoin queries as described above. Finally, it considers the option of loading entire source contents to further improve the plan. Figure 5(d) shows a plan that may be obtained by SJA+, assuming that the plan of Figure 5(a) is obtained by SJA for the same fusion query.

The time complexity of SJA+ is $O((m!)mn + mn)$. The $(m!)mn$ term is the cost of SJA. The second term mn is for postoptimization, computed as follows. The postoptimization phase in SJA+ considers the semijoin queries of $(m-1)$ conditions to be improved upon, by using the difference operation. For each set of semijoin queries corresponding to a condition, SJA+ spends $O(n)$ time reducing the semijoin sets and modifying the semijoin queries appropriately. Thus, the postoptimization using the difference operation takes $O(mn)$ time. Then, for each of the n sources, SJA+ takes $O(m)$ time to decide on replacing all its queries by an lq operation and local computation at the mediator. The actual modification of the plan also takes $O(m)$ per source, because SJA+ will replace m steps by $1 + m$ steps (the first to load the entire source and the rest for local computation). Thus, the total postoptimization cost is $O(mn)$. Note that SJA+ has the same order of complexity as SJA. In particular, the postoptimization phase of SJA+ is very efficient.

We note that the postoptimization phase of SJA+ uses operations that are not allowed in simple plans as defined in Section 2. In this sense, SJA+ yields plans outside the space of simple plans. One could have considered this more general class of plans up front, and systematically searched for optimality within that space. We decided not to follow that approach because of the very large number of plans that must be then considered to find an optimal plan. For instance, a simple direct extension to the SJA algorithm to consider the set difference operations at the mediator would make its time complexity be exponential in n. Given that n is usually large in the application domains of interest to us, such algorithms are infeasible.

5 Fusion Queries in Existing Optimizers

The expansion of the Internet has led to mediator prototypes that combine information from multiple heterogeneous sources ([1, 10, 17, 23]). Similarly, prototypes for integrating databases have been developed, and recently integration products are being released or announced ([2, 9, 13]).

We note that there is a close connection between mediator-based systems and distributed database systems. Given this, many mediator systems have incorporated query processing and optimization techniques of distributed databases. There has been a great deal of published work on these techniques ([4, 16, 20, 22]). However, most of this work focuses on the efficient evaluation of Select-Project-Join (SPJ) queries. It does not adequately address the special needs of fusion queries.

In this section we study how existing optimizers would handle fusion queries, and we explore opportunities for improvement based on the ideas presented in this paper. The approaches taken by existing optimizers on fusion queries fall into three general categories, so we divide our discussion into three subsections.

Distribution of the join over the union. The first category contains optimizers that distribute the join operation in a fusion query over the underlying unions. This leads to a plan that is a union of SPJ subqueries, where each SPJ subquery can then be optimized using traditional methods. The plans for the constituent SPJ subqueries may involve semijoin operations.

Generating separate subplans for each of the SPJ subqueries can lead to inefficient query plans due to repeated evaluation of common subexpressions. Elimination of common subexpressions can be very cumbersome and expensive, when semijoin operations are used in the subplans. This task takes time that is exponential in the number of the constituent SPJ subqueries, which in turn is exponential in the size of the fusion query.

Examples of systems in our first category are Information Manifold [12], TSIMMIS [17], HERMES [23] and Infomaster [6]. Query processing in these systems is based on resolution ([3]), which leads to the distribution of the join over the union.

One obvious way in which systems taking this approach to fusion query processing can incorporate techniques discussed in our paper is to implement a module that checks if a query is a fusion query (by looking for the distinctive pattern of fusion queries) and invokes the algorithm (of Section 3) to generate the best semijoin-adaptive plan for the identified fusion query. This leads to a very efficient evaluation of fusion queries without incurring an extremely cumbersome optimization process involving common subexpression elimination.

Handling unions uniformly. The second approach to fusion query processing is to separately process the union views, and conceptually generate "temporary" relations. Selection conditions are applied as the temporary relations are computed. Then the temporary relations are joined.

Examples of systems using this approach are DB2 [7] and Tandem's NonStop SQL/MP [21]. These systems do not allow for the use of semijoin operations in the query plans. Thus, the plans they consider are characterized by the class of filter plans discussed in Section 2. A slight variation is to combine the steps of union view processing and the join processing. This variation allows for the use of semijoin operations. An example system that uses this variation is Tandem's NonStop SQL/MX [21]. With this variation, the set of query plans considered includes the class of filter plans and the class of semijoin plans, but not the class of semijoin-adaptive plans. This is because the various sources of a union view are treated homogeneously. That is, if two sources take part in a union view, they both get the same kind of source queries. Semijoin-adaptive plans can be obtained by allowing for heterogeneous treatment of the different elements of a union view. That is, one source in the union view may get a selection query while another source in the same union view may get a semijoin query.

Extensible optimizers Recent extensible optimizers ([8, 11, 14]) use flexible, rule-based approaches. The key to efficient fusion query processing in these systems lies in the set of rules defined. Rule-based optimization research has focused on the evaluation of Select-Project-Join queries. We believe that one can write rules, which embody our techniques, to achieve efficient fusion query processing in these optimizers. For example, it is easy to write rules in the Garlic system [10] that help generate efficient filter plans for fusion queries. Combining these with rules for semijoin operations, like the ones given in [10], we can generate semijoin plans for fusion queries. We believe that an extension of these rules (nontrivial, but perhaps not very difficult) may yield semijoin-adaptive plans for fusion queries. Another way to incorporate our techniques into optimizers following the rule-based approach is to have a rule that identifies a fusion query and generates the best semijoin-adaptive plan for it.

6 Conclusions

Fusion queries are important in environments where data is not well organized and partitioned across autonomous, distributed sites. In this paper we have developed a formal framework for optimizing fusion queries, and we have provided efficient algorithms to produce good query plans over broad scenarios. We have also described enhancements (postoptimizations) that can boost performance significantly, with relatively little additional optimization cost. As discussed in Section 5, our results can be useful for understanding the types of plans current optimizers generate for fusion queries, as well as for improving their performance.

In this paper, we focused on minimizing the total work in executing a query. One could also consider minimizing the *response time* of a query in a parallel execution model. This is a future direction of work we plan to undertake. Another important area of exploration involves moving away from the "two-phase" approach to fusion query processing (as discussed in Section 1). Then we need to consider query plans involving source queries that return other attributes in addition to the merge attributes and this takes us out of the space of simple plans. The techniques we have developed here may still be quite useful in finding very good plans in that more general space of fusion query plans.

References

1. Y. Arens, C. Chee, C. Hsu and C. Knoblock. Retrieving and Integrating Data from Multiple Information Sources. In *Journal of Intelligent and Cooperative Information Systems*, Vol. 2, June 1993.
2. J. Blakeley. Data Access for the Masses through OLE DB. In *Proc. ACM SIGMOD Conf.*, 161–172, 1996.
3. S. Ceri, G. Gottlobb, and L. Tanca. *Logic Programming and Databases, Surveys in Computer Science.* Springer-Verlag, 1990.
4. S. Ceri and G. Pelagatti. *Distributed Databases: Principles and Systems.* McGraw-Hill, 1984.

5. W. Du, R. Krishnamurthy and M. Shan. Query Optimization in Heterogeneous DBMS. In *Proc. VLDB Conference*, 277-291, 1992.

6. O. Duschka and M. Genesereth. Query Planning in Infomaster. In *Proc. ACM Symposium on Applied Computing*, 1997.

7. P. Gassner, G. Lohman, B. Schiefer and Y. Wang. Query Optimization in the IBM DB2 Family. In *IEEE Data Engineering Bulletin*, 16:4-18, 1993.

8. G. Graefe. The Cascades Framework for Query Optimization. In *Bulletin of the Technical Committee on Data Engineering*, 18:19–29, September 1995.

9. P. Gupta and E. Lin. DataJoiner: A Practical Approach to Multidatabase Access. In *Proc. PDIS Conference*, 264–264, 1994.

10. L. Haas, D. Kossman, E. Wimmers, and J. Yang. Optimizing Queries across Diverse Data Sources. In *Proc. VLDB Conference*, 1997.

11. L. Haas, J. Freytag, G. Lohman, and H. Pirahesh. Extensible Query Processing in Starburst. In *Proc. ACM SIGMOD Conference*, 377–388, 1989.

12. A. Levy, A. Rajaraman and J. Ordille. Query Processing in the Information Manifold. In *Proc. VLDB Conference*, 1996.

13. W. Litwin, L. Mark and N. Roussopoulos. Interoperability of Multiple Autonomous Databases. In *ACM Computing Surveys*, 22:267–293, 1990.

14. G. Lohman. Grammar-like Functional Rules for Representing Query Optimization Alternatives. In *Proc. ACM SIGMOD Conference*, 1988.

15. H. Lu, B. Ooi and C. Goh. Multidatabase Query Optimization: Issues and Solutions. In *Proc. RIDE-IMS '93*, 137–143, 1993.

16. T. Ozsu and P. Valduriez. *Principles of Distributed Database Systems*. Prentice Hall, 1991.

17. Y. Papakonstantinou. Query Processing in Heterogeneous Information Sources. Technical report, Stanford University Thesis, 1996.

18. Y. Papakonstantinou, H. Garcia-Molina, and J. Widom. Object Exchange across Heterogeneous Information Sources. In *Proc. ICDE Conference*, 251–260, 1995.

19. Y. Papakonstantinou, A. Gupta, H. Garcia-Molina, and J. Ullman. A Query Translation Scheme for the Rapid Implementation of Wrappers. In *Proc. DOOD Conference*, 161–186, 1995.

20. N. Roussopoulos and H. Kang. A Pipeline N-way Join Algorithm based on the 2-way Semijoin Program. In *IEEE Transactions on Knowledge and Data Engineering*, 3:486-495, December 1991.

21. S. Sharma and H. Zeller. Personal Communication with Sunil Sharma and Hans Zeller, Tandem Computers Inc. June, 1997.

22. A. Silberschatz, H. Korth and S. Sudarshan. *Database System Concepts*. McGraw-Hill, 1997.

23. V. Subrahmanian et al. HERMES: A Heterogeneous Reasoning and Mediator System. http://www.cs.umd.edu/projects/hermes/overview/paper.

24. R. Yerneni, Y. Papakonstantinou, S. Abiteboul and H. Garcia-Molina. Fusion Queries over Internet Databases (Extended Version). http://www-db.stanford.edu/pub/papers/fqo.ps

25. Q. Zhu and P. Larson. A Query Sampling Method for Estimating Local Cost Parameters in a Multidatabase System. In *Proc. ICDE*, 144–153, 1994.

Efficient Queries over Web Views

Giansalvatore Mecca,[1] Alberto O. Mendelzon,[2] Paolo Merialdo[3]

[1] DIFA, Università della Basilicata, Potenza, Italy
[2] Dept. of Computer Science, University of Toronto, Canada
[3] Dip. Informatica e Automazione, Università di Roma Tre, Roma, Italy

Abstract. Large web sites are becoming repositories of structured information that can benefit from being viewed and queried as relational databases. However, querying these views efficiently requires new techniques. Data usually resides at a remote site and is organized as a set of related HTML documents, with network access being a primary cost factor in query evaluation. This cost can be reduced by exploiting the redundancy often found in site design. We use a simple data model, a subset of the Araneus data model, to describe the structure of a web site. We augment the model with link and inclusion constraints that capture the redundancies in the site. We map relational views of a site to a navigational algebra and show how to use the constraints to rewrite algebraic expressions, reducing the number of network accesses.

1 Introduction

As the Web becomes a preferred medium for disseminating information of all kinds, the sets of pages at many Web sites have come to exhibit regular and complex structure not unlike the structures that are described by schemes in database systems. For example, Atzeni *et al.* [4] show how to describe the structure of the well-known Database and Logic Programming Bibliography at the University of Trier [9] using their own data model, the ARANEUS data model.

As these sites become large, manual navigation of these hypertext structures ("browsing") becomes clearly inadequate to retrieve information effectively. Typically, ad-hoc search interfaces are provided, usually built around full-text indexing of all the pages at the site. However, full-text queries are good for retrieving documents relevant to a set of terms, but not for answering precise questions, e.g. "find all authors who had papers in the last three VLDB conferences." If we can impose on such a site a database abstraction, say a relational schema, we can then use powerful database query languages such as SQL to pose queries, and leave it to the system to translate these declarative queries into navigation of the underlying hypertext.

In this paper we explore the issues involved in such a translation. In general, a declarative query will admit different translations, corresponding to different navigation paths to get to the data; for example, the query above could be answered by:

1. Starting from the home page, follow the link to the list of conferences, from here to the VLDB page, then to each of the last three VLDB conferences, extract a list of authors for each, and intersect the three lists.
2. As above, but go directly from the home page to the list of database conferences, a smaller page than the one that lists all conferences.

3. As above, but go directly from the home page to the VLDB page (there is a link).
4. Go through the list of authors, for each author to the list of their publications, and keep those who have papers in the last three VLDB's.

If we use number of pages accessed as a rough measure of query execution cost, we see there are large differences among these possible access paths, in particular between the last one and the other three. There are over 16,000 authors represented in this bibliography, so the last access path would retrieve several orders of magnitude more pages than the others. Given these large performance differentials, a query optimizer is needed to translate a declarative query to an efficient navigation plan, just as a relational optimizer maps an SQL query to an efficient access plan. In fact, there is an even closer similarity to the problem of mapping declarative queries to network and object-oriented data models, as we discuss in Section 2.

To summarize, our approach is to build relational abstractions of large and fairly well-structured web sites, and to use an optimizer to translate declarative queries on these relational abstractions to efficient navigation plans. We use a simple subset of the ARANEUS data model (ADM) to describe web sites, augmenting it with *link constraints* that capture the redundancy present in many web sites. For example, if we want to know who were the editors of VLDB '96, we can find this information in the page that lists all the VLDB conferences; we do not need to follow the link from this page to the specific page for VLDB '96, where the information is repeated. We also use *inclusion constraints*, that state that all the pages that can be accessed using a certain path can also be accessed using another path. We use a *navigational algebra* as the target language that describes navigation plans, and we show how to use rewrite rules in the spirit of relational optimizers, and taking link and inclusion constraints into account, to reduce the number of page accesses needed to answer a query.

When a query on the relational views is issued, it is repeatedly rewritten using the rules. This process generates a number of navigation plans to compute the query; the cost of these plans is then estimated based on a simple cost model that takes network accesses as the primary cost parameter. In this way, an efficient execution plan is selected for processing the query.

Query optimization is hardly a new topic; however, doing optimization on the Web is fundamentally different from optimizing relational or OO databases. In fact, the Web exhibits two peculiarities: the *cost model* and the *lack of control over Web sites*: (*i*) *the cost model*: since data reside at a remote site, our cost model is based on the number of network accesses, instead of I/O and CPU cost, and we allocate no cost to local processing such as joins; (*ii*) *the lack of control over the site*: unlike ordinary databases, sites are autonomous and beyond the control of the query system; first, it is not possible to influence the *organization of data* in the site; second, the site manager inserts, deletes and modifies pages without notifying remote users of the updates.

These points have fundamental implications on query processing. The main one is that we cannot rely on auxiliary access structures besides the ones already built right into the HTML pages. Access structures – like *indices* or *class extents* – are heavily used in optimizing queries over relational and object-oriented databases [14]. Most of the techniques proposed for query optimization rely on the availability of suitable access structures. One might think of extending such techniques to speed up the evaluation of queries by, for example, storing URLs in some local data structures, and then using them in query evaluation. However, this solution is in general unfeasible because, after the data structures have been constructed, they have to be maintained; and since our system is not notified of updates to pages, the only way of maintaining these structures is to actually navigate the site at query time checking for updates, which in general has a cost comparable to the cost of computing the query itself.

We therefore start our analysis under the assumption that the only access structures to pages are the ones built right into the hypertext. Due to space limitations, we concentrate on the issue of mapping queries on *virtual* relational views to navigation of the underlying hypertext, and develop an algorithm for selecting efficient execution plans, based on a suitable cost function. In [10], we study the problem of querying *materialized* views, and show how the same techniques developed for virtual views can be extended to the management of materialized views.

Outline of the Paper The outline of the paper is as follows. We discuss related work in Section 2. Sections 3 and 4 present our data model and our navigational algebra; the problem of querying virtual views is introduced in Section 5; the rewrite rules and the optimization algorithm are presented in Section 6; Section 7 discusses several interesting examples. Due to space limitations, the presentation is mainly informal. Details can be found in [10].

2   Related Work

Query optimization Our approach to query optimization based on algebraic rewriting rules is inspired on relational and object-oriented query optimization (e. g., [18], [5]). This is not surprising, since it has been noted in the context of object-oriented databases that relational query optimization can be well extended to complex structures ([14], [7]). However, the differences between the problem we treat here and conventional query optimization, which we listed in the Introduction, lead to rather different solutions.

Optimizing path expressions Evaluating queries on the Web has some points of contact with the problem of optimizing *path-expressions* [22] in object-oriented databases (see, for example, [6], [14]). Since path-expressions represent a powerful means to express navigation in object databases, a large body of research about query processing has been devoted to their optimization. In this research, the focus is on transforming *pointer chasing* operations – which are considered rather expensive – into *joins of pointer sets* stored in auxiliary access structures, such as class extents [7], access support relations [8] and join indices [19], [20].

Although it may seem that a similar approach may be extended to the Web, we show that the more involved nature of access paths in Web sites and the absence of *ad-hoc* auxiliary structures introduces a number of subtleties. We compare two main approaches to query optimization: (*i*) the first one, that we might call a *"pointer join"* approach, is inspired on object-oriented query optimization: it aims at reducing link traversal by manipulating (joining) pointer sets; (*ii*) the second is what we call a *"pointer chase"* approach, in which links between data are used to restrict network access to relevant items. An interesting result is that, in our cost model, sometimes navigation is less expensive than joins. This is different from object-oriented databases, where the choice between the two is generally in favor of the former [6].

Relational Views over Network Databases The idea of managing relational views over hypertextual sources is similar to some proposals (e.g., [21], [13], [16]) for accessing network databases through relational views: links between pages may recall set types that correlate records in the network model. However, in these works the focus is more on developing tools and methods for automatically deriving a relational view over a network database, than on query optimization. More specifically, one of the critical aspects of accessing data in the Web – i.e., selecting one among multiple paths to reach data – is not addressed.

Indices in Relational Databases It has already been noted in the previous section that our approach extends to the Web a number of query optimization techniques developed in the context of relational databases. Another related issue is the problem of selecting one among several indices available for a relation in a relational database (see, for example, [15] and [12]); this has some points in common with the problem of selecting one among different access paths for pages in a Web site; however, paths in the Web are usually more complex than simple indices, and our cost model is radically different from the ones adopted for relational databases.

Path Constraints The presence of *path constraints* on Web sites is the core of the approach developed in [1]. The authors recognize that important structural information about portions of the Web can be expressed by constraints; they consider the processing of queries in such a scenario, and discuss how to take advantage of constraints. The fundamental difference with our approach is that we work with an intensional description of Web data, based on a database-like data model, while the authors of [1] reason directly on the extension of data.

3 The Data Model

Our data model is essentially a subset of ADM [4], the ARANEUS data model; the notion of *page-scheme* is used to describe the (possibly nested) structure of a set of homogeneous Web pages; since we are interested in query optimization, in this paper we enrich the model with *constraints* that allow reasoning about redundancies in a site, e.g., multiple paths to reach the same data. From this perspective, a *scheme* gives a description of a portion of the Web in terms of page-schemes and constraints. It is important to note that this description of the Web portion is usually *a posteriori*, that is, both the page-schemes and the constraints are obtained, not from a forward engineering phase, but rather from a *reverse engineering* phase, which aims at describing the structure of an existing site. This analysis is conducted by a human designer, with the help of a number of tools which semi-automatically analyze the Web in order to find regular patterns.

3.1 Page-schemes

Each Web page is viewed as an object with a set of attributes. Structurally similar pages are grouped together into sets, described by *page-schemes*. Attributes may have simple or complex type. Simple type attributes are *mono-valued* and correspond essentially to text, images, or *links* to other pages. Complex type, *multi-valued* attributes are used to model collections of objects inside pages, and correspond to lists of tuples, possibly nested.

The set of pages described by a given page-scheme is an *instance* of the page-scheme. It is convenient to think of a page-scheme as a nested relation scheme, a page as a nested tuple on a certain page-scheme, and a set of similar pages as an instance of the page-scheme. There is one aspect of this framework with no counterpart in traditional data models. There are pages that have a special role: they act as "entry-points" to the hypertext. Typically, at least the home page of each site falls into this category. In ADM *entry points* are modeled as page-schemes whose instance contains only one tuple.

To formalize these ideas, we need two interrelated definitions for types and page-schemes, as follows. Given a set of *base types* containing the types *text* and *image*, a set of *attribute names* (or simply *attributes*), and a set of *page-scheme names*, the set of WEB *types* is defined as follows (each type is either mono-valued or multi-valued):

- each base type is a *mono-valued* WEB *type*;
- LINK TO P is a *mono-valued* WEB *type*, for each page-scheme name P;
- LIST OF$(A_1 : T_1, A_2 : T_2, \ldots, A_n : T_n)$ is a *multi-valued* WEB *type*, if $A_1, A_2, \ldots, A_n$ are attributes and $T_1, T_2, \ldots, T_n$ are WEB types;

A *page-scheme* has the form $P(URL, A_1 : T_1, A_2 : T_2, \ldots, A_n : T_n)$, where P is a page scheme name, each A_i is an attribute, each T_i is a WEB type, and URL is the Universal Resource Locator of P, and forms a key for P.

An *entry-point* is a pair (P, URL), where P is a page-scheme and URL is the URL for a page p which is the only tuple in the instance of P. As we suggested above, an *instance* of a page-scheme is a *page-relation*, i.e., a set of nested tuples, one for each of the corresponding pages, each with a URL and a value of the appropriate type for each page-scheme attribute. Entry points are page-relations containing a single nested tuple.

Note that we do not assume the availability of *page-scheme extents*: the only pages whose URL is known to the system are instances of entry points; any other page-relation can only be accessed by navigating the site starting from some entry point. It is also worth noting that, in order to see pages, i.e., HTML files, as instances of page-schemes, i.e., nested tuples, we assume that suitable *wrappers* [3, 2] are applied to pages in order to access attribute values.

We have experimented with our approach on several real-life Web sites. However, in this paper we choose to refer to a fictional site – a hypothetical university Web site – constructed in such a way as to allow us to discuss with a single and familiar example all relevant aspects of our work. Figure 1 shows some examples of page-schemes from such site.

3.2 Constraints

The hypertextual nature of the Web is usually associated with a high degree of redundancy. Redundancy appears in two ways. First, many pieces of information are replicated over several pages. Consider the Department example site: the name of a Department –say, *Computer Science*– can be found not only in the *Computer Science* Department page but also in many other pages: for instance, it is presumably used as an anchor in every page in which a link towards the department page occurs. Second, pages can be usually reached following different navigational paths in the site. To capture these redundancies so they can be

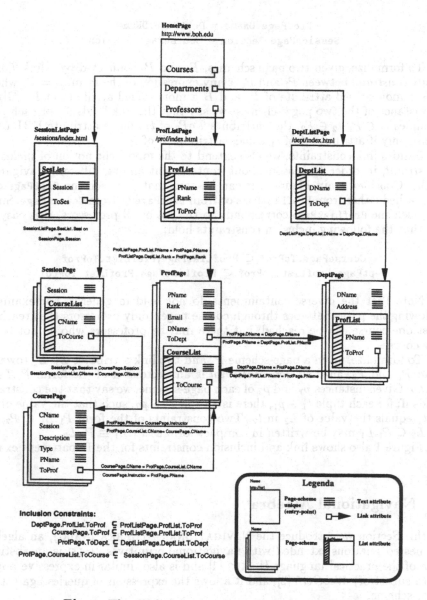

Fig. 1. The *Web-Scheme* of a University Web Site

exploited in query optimization, we enrich the model with two kinds of integrity constraints: *link constraints*, and *inclusion constraints*.

A *link constraint* is a predicate associated with a link. It is used to document the fact that the value of some attribute in the source page-relation equals the value of another attribute in a related tuple in the target page-relation. For example, with respect to Figure 1, this is the case for attribute DName in page-schemes DeptPage and ProfPage or for attribute Session in SessionPage and CoursePage. In our model, this can be documented by the following link constraints:

```
ProfPage.DName = DeptPage.DName
SessionPage.Session = CoursePage.Session
```

To formalize, given two page-schemes, P_1 and P_2 connected by a link ToP_2, a *link constraint* between P_1 and P_2 is any expression of the form: $A = B$, where A is a monovalued attribute of P_1 and B a monovalued attribute of P_2. Given an instance of the two page-schemes, we say that the link holds if: for each pair of tuples $t_1 \in P_1, t_2 \in P_2$, then attribute ToP_2 of t_1 equals attribute URL of t_2 if and only if attribute A of t_1 equals attribute B of t_2.

Besides link constraints, we also extend to the model the notion of *inclusion constraint*, in order to reason about containment among different navigation paths. Consider again Figure 1: it can be seen that page-scheme ProfPage can be reached either from ProfListPage or from DeptPage or from CoursePage. Since page-scheme ProfListPage corresponds to the list of all professors, it is easy to see that the following inclusion constraints hold:

```
CoursePage.ToProf ⊆ ProfListPage.ProfList.ToProf
DeptPage.ProfList.ToProf ⊆ ProfListPage.ProfList.ToProf
```

Note that the inverse containments do not hold in general. For example, following the path that goes through course pages, only professors that teach at least one course can be reached; but there may be professors who do not teach any courses.

To formalize, given a page-scheme P, and two link attributes L_1, L_2 towards P in P_1 and P_2, an *inclusion constraint* is an expression of the form: $P_1.L_1 \subseteq P_2.L_2$. Given instances p_1 and p_2 of each page-scheme, we say that the constraint holds if: for each tuple $t_1 \in p_1$, there is a tuple $t_2 \in p_2$, such that the value of L_1 in t_1 equals the value of L_2 in t_2. Two constraints of the form $P_1.L_1 \subseteq P_2.L_2$, $P_2.L_2 \subseteq P_1.L_1$ may be written in compact form as $P_1.L_1 \equiv P_2.L_2$.

Figure 1 also shows link and inclusion constraints for the Department example.

4 Navigational Algebra

In this Section we introduce the NAVIGATIONAL ALGEBRA (NALG), an algebra for nested relations extended with navigational primitives. NALG is an abstraction of the practical language ULIXES [4] and is also similar in expressive power to (a subset of) *WebOQL* [2], and it allows the expression of queries against an ADM scheme.

Besides the traditional selection, projection and join operators, in NALG two simple operators are introduced in order to describe navigation. The first operator, called *unnest page* is the traditional *unnest* [17] operator (μ), that allows to access data at different levels of nesting inside a page; instead of the traditional prefix notation: $\mu_A(R)$, in this paper we prefer to use a different symbol, $\diamond$, and an infix notation: $R \diamond A$. The second, called *follow link* and denoted by symbol $\longrightarrow$, is used to follow links. In some sense, we may say that $\diamond$ is used to navigate *inside* pages, i.e., inside the hierarchical structure of a page, whereas $\longrightarrow$ to navigate *outside*, i.e., between pages.

Note that the the selection-projection-join algebra is a sublanguage of our navigational algebra. In this way, we are able to manipulate both relational and navigational queries, as it is appropriate in the Web framework. To give an example, consider Figure 1. Suppose we are interested in the name and e-mail of all professors in the *Computer Science* department. To reach data of interest, we first need to navigate the site as follows:

$$\text{ProfListPage} \diamond \text{ProfList} \xrightarrow{ToProf} \text{ProfPage}$$

The semantics of this expression is as follows: entry point `ProfListPage` is accessed through its URL; the corresponding nested relation is *unnested* with respect to attribute `ProfList` in order to be able to access attribute `ToProf`; finally, each of these links is followed to reach the corresponding `ProfPage`. Operator $\xrightarrow{ToProf}$ essentially "expands" the source relation by joining it with the target one; the join is a particular one: since it physically corresponds to following links, it implicitly imposes the equality of the link attribute in the source relation with the URL attribute in the target one. We assume that attributes are suitably renamed whenever needed.

Since the result of the expression above is a (nested) relation containing a tuple for each tuple in page scheme `ProfPage`, the query *"Name and e-mail of all professors in the Computer Science Department"* can be expressed as follows:

$$\pi_{PName,e-mail}\left(\sigma_{DName='C.S.'}\left(\text{ProfListPage}\diamond\text{ProfList}\xrightarrow{ToProf}\text{ProfPage}\right)\right) \quad (1)$$

To formalize, the NAVIGATIONAL ALGEBRA is an algebra for the ADM model. The *operators* of the navigational algebra work on page-relations and return page-relations, as follows:

- *selection*, σ, *projection*, π and *join*, $\bowtie$, have the usual semantics;
- *unnest page*, $\diamond$, is a binary operator that takes as input a nested relation R and a nested attribute A of R; its semantics is defined as the result of unnesting R with respect to A: $R\diamond A = \mu_A(R)$.
- *follow link*, $\xrightarrow{L}$, is a binary operator that takes as input two page-relations, R_1, R_2, such that there is a link attribute, L from R_1 to R_2; the execution of expression $R_1 \xrightarrow{L} R_2$ corresponds to computing the join of R_1 and R_2 based on the link attribute, that is: $R_1 \xrightarrow{L} R_2 = R_1 \bowtie_{R_1.L=R_2.URL} R_2$. It thus "expands" the source relation following links corresponding to attribute L.

A NALG *expression* over a scheme S is any combination of operators over page-relations in S. With each expression it is possible to associate in the usual way a *query tree* (or *query plan*) in which leaf nodes correspond to page-relations and all other nodes to NALG operators (see Figures 2, 3).

Note that not all navigational algebra expressions are computable. In fact, the only page-relations in a Web scheme that are directly accessible are the ones corresponding to entry-points, whose URL is known and documented in the scheme; thus, in order to be computable, all navigational paths involved in a query must start from an entry point. We thus define the notion of *computable expression* as a navigational algebra expression such that all leaf nodes in the corresponding query plan are entry points.

5 Querying Virtual Views of the Web

Our approach to querying the Web consists in offering a relational view of data in a portion of the Web, and allowing users to pose queries against this view. In this paper we concentrate on *conjunctive queries*. When a query is issued to the system, the query engine transparently navigates the Web and returns the answer. We assume that the query engine has knowledge about the following elements: (*i*) the ADM scheme of the site; (*ii*) the set of relations offered as external view to the user; we call these relations *external relations*; (*iii*) for each external relation, one or more computable navigational algebra expression whose execution correspond to materializing the extent of that external relation. Note that the use of both ADM and the navigational algebra is completely transparent to the user, whose perception of the query process relies only on the relational view and the relational query language.

To give an example, suppose we consider the Department site whose scheme is reported in Figure 1. Suppose also we are interested in pieces of information about Departments, Professors, and Courses. We may decide to offer a view of the site based on the following external relations:

1. Dept(DName, Address);
2. Professor(PName, Rank, email);
3. ProfDept(PName, DName);
4. Course(CName, Session, Description, Type);
5. CourseInstructor(CName, PName);

In this case, in order to answer queries, the query engine must know the Web scheme in Figure 1 and the external scheme of items 1–5; moreover, it must also know how to navigate the scheme in order to build the extent of each external relation; this corresponds to associating with each external relation one or more computable NALG expressions, whose execution materializes the given relation. For example, with respect to external relations Dept, Professor and ProfDept above, we have the following navigations:

1. Dept(DName, Address)

   $= \pi_{DName, Address}(\text{DeptListPage} \diamond \text{DeptList} \overset{ToDept}{\longrightarrow} \text{DeptPage})$

2. Professor(PName, Rank, email)

   $= \pi_{PName, Rank, email}(\text{ProfListPage} \diamond \text{ProfList} \overset{ToProf}{\longrightarrow} \text{ProfPage})$

3. ProfDept(PName, DName)

   $= \pi_{PName, DName}(\text{ProfListPage} \diamond \text{ProfList} \overset{ToProf}{\longrightarrow} \text{ProfPage})$

   $= \pi_{PName, DName}(\text{DeptListPage} \diamond \text{DeptList} \overset{ToDept}{\longrightarrow} \text{DeptPage} \diamond \text{ProfList})$

We call these expressions the *default navigations* associated with external relations. There may be different alternative expressions associated with the same external relation (see 3). Note also that, for a given external relation, there may be other possible navigational expressions, "contained" in the default navigations. For example, professors may be reached also through their courses. However, it is not guaranteed that *all* professors may be reached using this path.

6 Query Optimization

When the system receives a query on the external view, it has to choose an efficient strategy to navigate the site and answer the query. The optimization proceeds as follows:

- the original query is translated into the corresponding projection-selection-join algebraic expression;
- this expression is converted into a computable NALG expression, which is repeatedly rewritten by applying NALG rewriting rules in order to derive a number of candidate execution plans, i.e., executable algebra expressions;
- finally, the cost of these alternatives is evaluated, and the best one is chosen, based on a specific cost model.

Since network accesses are considerably more expensive than memory accesses, we decide to adopt a simple *cost model* [10] based on the number of pages downloaded from the network. Thus, we aim at finding an execution plan for the query that minimizes the number of pages visited during the navigation. Note that the cost model can be made more accurate by taking into account also other parameters such as the size of pages, the deployment of Web servers over the network or the query *locality* [11]. Also, some expensive local operations should be considered. We omit these details here for the sake of simplicity. In the following section, we introduce a number of rewriting rules for the navigational algebra that can be used to this end. In [10] we develop an optimization algorithm based on these rules that, by successive rewritings, generates a number of candidate execution plans. Each of these is then evaluated based on the cost function, and the optimal one is chosen.

6.1 NALG Rewriting Rules

The first, fundamental rule simply says that, in order to evaluate a query that involves external relations, each external relation must be replaced by one of the corresponding NALG expressions. In fact, the extent of an external relation is not directly accessible, and must be built up by navigating the site.

Rule 1 [Default Navigation] *Each external relation can be replaced by any of its default navigations.*

Other rules are based on simple properties of the navigational algebra, and thus are rather straightforward, as follows.

Rule 2 *Given two relations R_1, R_2, such that R_1 has an attribute L of type* LINK TO R_2, *suppose that a link constraint $R_1.A = R_2.B$ is associated with L; then:* $R_1 \bowtie_{R_1.A=R_2.B} R_2 = R_1 \bowtie_{R_1.L=R_2.URL} R_2 = R_1 \xrightarrow{L} R_2$

Rule 3 *Given a relation R, suppose X is a set of non-nested attributes of R and A a nested attribute; then:* $\pi_X(R \diamond A) = \pi_X(R)$

Rule 4 *Given a relation R, suppose A is a nested attribute of R, and Y any set of non-nested attributes of R; then:* $(i) R \bowtie_Y R = R$; $(ii)(R \diamond A) \bowtie_Y R = R \diamond A$

Rule 5 *Given two relations R_1, R_2, suppose X is a set of attributes of R_1; suppose also that R_1 has an attribute L of type* LINK TO R_2; *then:*
$$\pi_X(R_1 \xrightarrow{L} R_2) = \pi_X(R_1)$$

The following two rules extend ordinary selection and projection pushing to navigations. They show how, based on link constraints, selections and projections can be moved down along a path, in order to reduce the size of intermediate results, and thus network accesses.

Rule 6 [Pushing Selections] *Given two relations R_1, R_2, such that R_1 has an attribute L of type* LINK TO R_2, *suppose that a link constraint $R_1.A = R_2.B$ is associated with L; then:* $\sigma_{B='v'}(R_1 \xrightarrow{L} R_2) = \sigma_{A='v'}(R_1) \xrightarrow{L} R_2$

Rule 7 [Pushing Projections] *Given two relations R_1, R_2, such that there is an attribute L in R_1 of type* LINK TO R_2, *suppose that a link constraint $R_1.A = R_2.B$ is associated with L; then:* $\pi_B(R_1 \xrightarrow{L} R_2) = \pi_A(\pi_{A,L}(R_1) \xrightarrow{L} R_2)$

We now concentrate on investigating the relationship between joins and navigations. The rules make use of link and inclusion constraints. The first rule (rule 8) states that, in all cases in which it is necessary to join the result of two different paths (denoted by R_1 and R_2) both pointing to R_3, it is possible to join the two sets of pointers in R_1 and R_2 *before* actually navigating to R_3, and *then* navigate the result.

Rule 8 [Pointer Join] *Given relations R_1, R_2 and R_3, such that both R_1 and R_2 have an attribute L of type* LINK TO R_3, *suppose that a link constraint $R_2.A = R_3.B$ is associated with L; then:*
$$(R_1 \xrightarrow{L} R_3) \bowtie_{R_3.B=R_2.A} R_2 = (R_1 \bowtie_{R_1.L=R_2.L} R_2) \xrightarrow{L} R_3$$

The second rule says that, in some cases, joins between page sets can be eliminated in favor of navigations; in essence, the join is implicitly computed by chasing links between pages.

Rule 9 [Pointer Chase] *Given relations R_1, R_2 and R_3, such that both R_1 and R_2 have an attribute L of type* LINK TO R_3; *suppose X is a set of attributes not belonging to R_1; suppose also that a link constraint $R_2.A = R_3.B$ is associated with L, and that there is an inclusion constraint $R_2.L \subseteq R_1.L$; then:* $\pi_X((R_1 \xrightarrow{L} R_3) \bowtie_{R_3.B=R_2.A} R_2) = \pi_X(R_2 \xrightarrow{L} R_3)$

7 Pointer-join vs Pointer-chase

Rules 8 and 9 essentially correspond to two alternative approaches to query optimization, which we have called the *"pointer join"* approach – aiming at reducing link traversal by pushing joins of link sets – versus a *"pointer chase"* approach – in which links between data are followed to restrict network access to relevant items. For a large number of queries, both strategies are possible. Our optimization algorithm is such that it generates and evaluates plans based on both strategies. In the following, we discuss this interaction between join and navigation in the Web and show that pointer chase is sometimes less expensive than joins.

Example 1. [**Pointer-Join**] Consider the scheme in Figure 1, and suppose we need to answer the following query: *"Name and Description of courses taught by full professors in the Fall session"*. The query can be expressed against the external view as follows:

$$\pi_{CName,Desc.}(\sigma_{Ses.='Fall',Rank='Full'}(\text{Professor}\bowtie\text{CourseInstructor}\bowtie\text{Course}))$$

Note that there are several ways to rewrite the query. For example, since external relation CourseInstructor has two different default navigations, by rule 1, the very first rewrite step originates two different plans. Then, the number of plans increases due to the use of alternative rules. We examine only two of these possible rewritings, based on a pointer-join and a pointer-chase strategy, respectively, and discuss the relationship between the two.

The first rewriting is essentially based on rule 8, and corresponds to adopting a traditional optimization strategy, in which link chasing is reduced by using joins. The rewriting goes as follows:

$$\pi_{CName,Descr}(\sigma_{Ses.='Fall',Rank='Full'}(\text{Professor}\bowtie_{PName}\text{CourseInstructor}$$
$$\bowtie_{CName}\text{Course}))$$

$$\overset{rule\ 1}{=}\ (1a)\ \pi_{CName,Descr}(\ \sigma_{Ses.='Fall',Rank='Full'}((\text{ProfListPage}\diamond\text{ProfList}\overset{ToProf}{\longrightarrow}$$
$$\text{ProfPage})$$
$$\bowtie_{PName}(\text{ProfListPage}\diamond\text{ProfList}\overset{ToProf}{\longrightarrow}\text{ProfPage}\diamond\text{CourseList})$$
$$\bowtie_{CName}(\text{SessionListPage}\diamond\text{SesList}\overset{ToSes}{\longrightarrow}\text{SessionPage}\diamond\text{CourseList}$$
$$\overset{ToCourse}{\longrightarrow}\text{CoursePage})))$$

$$\overset{rule\ 4}{=}\ (1b)\ \pi_{CName,Descr}(\sigma_{Ses.='Fall',Rank='Full'}((\text{ProfListPage}\diamond\text{ProfList}\overset{ToProf}{\longrightarrow}$$
$$\text{ProfPage}\diamond\text{CourseList})$$
$$\bowtie_{CName}(\text{SessionListPage}\diamond\text{SesList}\overset{ToSes}{\longrightarrow}$$
$$\text{SessionPage}\diamond\text{CourseList}\overset{ToCourse}{\longrightarrow}\text{CoursePage})))$$

$$\overset{rule\ 8}{=}\ (1c)\ \pi_{CName,Descr}(\sigma_{Ses.='Fall',Rank='Full'}(((\text{ProfListPage}\diamond\text{ProfList}\overset{ToProf}{\longrightarrow}$$
$$\text{ProfPage}\diamond\text{CourseList})$$
$$\bowtie_{ToCourse}(\text{SessionListPage}\diamond\text{SesList}\overset{ToSes}{\longrightarrow}\text{SessionPage}\diamond\text{CourseList}))$$
$$\overset{ToCourse}{\longrightarrow}\text{CoursePage}))$$

$$\overset{rule\ 6}{=}\ (1d)\ \pi_{CName,Descr}(((\sigma_{Rank='Full'}(\text{ProfListPage}\diamond\text{ProfList})\overset{ToProf}{\longrightarrow}$$
$$\text{ProfPage}\diamond\text{CourseList})$$
$$\bowtie_{ToCourse}(\sigma_{Ses.='Fall'}(\text{SessionListPage}\diamond\text{SesList})\overset{ToSes}{\longrightarrow}$$
$$\text{SessionPage}\diamond\text{CourseList}))$$
$$\overset{ToCourse}{\longrightarrow}\text{CoursePage})$$

First, by rule 1, each external relation is replaced by a corresponding default navigation (1a); then, rule 4 is applied to eliminate repeated navigations (1b); then, by rule 8, the join is pushed down the query plan: in order to reduce the number of courses to navigate, we join the two pointer sets in CourseList, and then navigate link ToCourse (1c); finally, based on link constraints, rule 6 is used to push selections down (1d). The plan can then be further rewritten to push down projections as well.

A radically different way of rewriting the query is based on rule 9; in this case, the first two rewritings are the same as above; then, by rule 9, the join is removed in favor of navigations in the site ; finally, projections are pushed down to generate plan (2d), as follows:

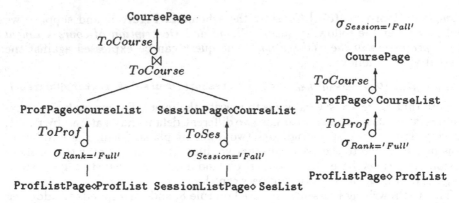

Fig. 2. Alternative Plans for the query in Example 1

$(2d)$ $\pi_{CName,Descr}(\sigma_{Ses.='Fall'}(\sigma_{Rank='Full'}(\text{ProfListPage}\diamond\text{ProfList})$
$\overset{ToProf}{\longrightarrow} \text{ProfPage}\diamond\text{CourseList}$
$\overset{ToCourse}{\longrightarrow} \text{CoursePage}))$

Plans corresponding to expressions $(1d)$ and $(2d)$ are represented in Figure 2. Plan $(1d)$ corresponds to: (i) finding all links to courses taught by full professors; (ii) finding all links to courses taught in the fall session; (iii) joining the two sets in order to obtain the intersection; (iv) navigate to the pages in the result. On the other hand, plan $(2d)$ corresponds to: (i) finding all full professors; (ii) navigating all courses taught by full professors; (iii) selecting courses in the fall section.

It is rather easy to see that plan $(1d)$ has a lower cost. In fact, plan $(2d)$ navigates *all* courses taught by full professors, and then selects the ones belonging to the result; on the contrary, in plan $(1d)$, pointers to courses are first selected, and then only pages belonging to the result are navigated.

The pointer-join strategy chosen by the optimizer in Example 1 is reminiscent of the ones that have been proposed for relational databases to optimize selections on a relation with multiple indices [12], and for object-oriented query processors to reduce pointer chasing in evaluating path-expressions – assuming a join index on professors and courses is available [8].

However, the following two examples show that, in the Web context, this is not always the optimal solution: in some cases, pointer-chasing is less expensive. This is shown in the following example.

Example 2. [**Pointer-chasing**] Consider the scheme in Figure 1, and suppose we need to answer the following query: *"Name and Email of Professors who are members of the Computer Science Department, and who are instructors of Graduate Courses"*. The query can be expressed on the external view as follows:

$\pi_{PName,Email}(\sigma_{DName='C.S.',Type='Graduate'}(\text{Course} \bowtie \text{CourseInstructor} \bowtie$
$\text{Professor} \bowtie \text{ProfDept}))$

We examine the two most interesting candidate execution plans. A pointer-join approach yields an expression (1), in which rule 8 is applied to join links ToProf

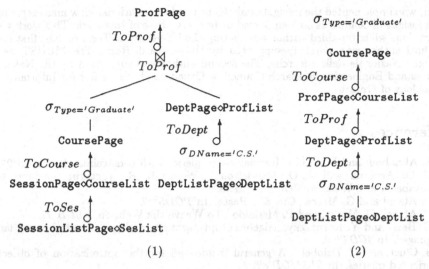

Fig. 3. Alternative Plans for the query in Example 2

in `CoursePage` and `ProfList` before navigating to `ProfPage`; then, rule 6 is used to push down selections. The alternative pointer-chasing strategy (2) corresponds to completely eliminate joins by replacing them with navigations. The query plans corresponding to these expressions are in Figure 3.

Let us compare the cost of the two plans. Plan (1) intersects two pointer sets, obtained as follows: the left-hand side path navigates the Computer Science Department page and retrieves all pointers to its members; the right-hand side path essentially downloads all session pages, and all course pages, and derives all pointers to instructors of graduate courses; then, the two pointer sets are joined, and URLs are navigated to build the result. On the contrary, plan (2) downloads all pages of professors in the Computer Science Department, and, from those, the pages of the corresponding courses. Now, a little reflection shows that plan (2) has a lower cost: navigating all instances of `CoursePage` in plan (1) makes it excessively expensive. In fact, due to the topology of the site, we know that there are several professors for each Department and several courses for each professor.

An intuitive explanation of this fact is the following: in this case, there is no efficient access structure to page-scheme `CoursePage`: in order to select graduate courses, it is necessary to navigate all courses; this makes the cost excessively high, and the pointer-join approach fails. On the contrary, following links from the Computer Science Department yields a reasonable degree of selectivity, that reduces the number of network accesses.

Based on the previous examples, we can conclude that ordinary pointer-join techniques do not transfer directly to the Web; a number of new issues have to be taken into account, namely, the different cost model and the absence of adequate access structures; in general, several alternative strategies, based on pointer-chasing, need to be evaluated.

Acknowledgments The authors would like to thank Paolo Atzeni and Giuseppe Sindoni, for useful discussions on early drafts of this paper. Special thanks go to Alessandro

Masci, who implemented the navigational algebra and the relational view manager, provided insightful comments and supported us in every phase of this work. This work was in part done while the third author was visiting the University of Toronto. The first and the third author were partially supported by Università di Roma Tre, MURST, and Consiglio Nazionale delle Ricerche. The second author was supported by the Natural Sciences and Engineering Research Council of Canada and the Center for Information Technology of Ontario.

References

1. S. Abiteboul and V. Vianu. Regular path queries with constraints. In *PODS'97*.
2. G. O. Arocena and A. O. Mendelzon. WebOQL: Restructuring documents, databases and Webs. In *ICDE'98*, 1998.
3. P. Atzeni and G. Mecca. Cut and Paste. In *PODS'97*.
4. P. Atzeni, G. Mecca, and P. Merialdo. To Weave the Web. In *VLDB'97*.
5. C. Beeri and Y. Kornatzky. Algebraic optimization of object-oriented query languages. In *ICDT'90*.
6. S. Cluet and C. Delobel. A general framework for the optimization of object-oriented queries. In *SIGMOD'82*.
7. B. P. Jenq, D. Woelk, W. Kim, and W. Lee. Query processing in distributed ORION. In *EDBT'90*.
8. A. Kemper and G. Moerkotte. Access support relations: An indexing method for object bases. *Information Systems*, 17(2):117–145, 1992.
9. M. Ley. Database systems and logic programming bibliography site. http://-www.informatik.uni-trier.de/~ley/db/index.html.
10. G. Mecca, A. Mendelzon, and P. Merialdo. Efficient queries over Web views. Technical Report n. RT-DIA-31-1998, Dipartimento di Informatica e Automazione, Università di Roma Tre, 1998. http://poincare.dia.uniroma3.it:8080/Araneus/.
11. A. Mendelzon, G. Mihaila, and T. Milo. Querying the World Wide Web. *Journal of Digital Libraries*, 1(1):54–67, April 1997.
12. C. Mohan, D. Haderle, Y. Wang, and J. Cheng. Single table access using multiple indexes: Optimization, execution, and concurrency control techniques. In *EDBT'90*.
13. S. Navathe. An intuitive view to normalize network structured data. In *VLDB'80*.
14. M. T. Özsu and J. A. Blakeley. Query processing in object-oriented database systems. In W. Kim, editor, *Modern Database Management – Object-Oriented and Multidatabase Technologies*, pages 146–174. Addison Wesley-ACM Press, 1994.
15. A. Rosenthal and D. S. Reiner. An architecture for query optimization. In *SIGMOD*, 1982.
16. A. Rosenthal and D. S. Reiner. Querying relational views of networks. In W. Kim, D. S. Reiner, and D. S. Batory, editors, *Query Processing in Database Systems*, pages 109–124. Springer-Verlag, 1985.
17. M.A. Roth, H.F. Korth, and A. Silberschatz. Extended algebra and calculus for ¬1NF relational databases. *ACM TODS*, 13(4):389–417, December 1988.
18. G. M. Shaw and S. B. Zdonik. An object-oriented query algebra. In *DBPL'89*.
19. P. Valduriez. Join indices. *ACM TODS*, 12(2):218–246, 1987.
20. Xie Z. and Han J. Join index hierarchies for supporting efficient navigations in object-oriented databases. In *VLDB'94*.
21. C. Zaniolo. Design of relational views over network schemas. In *SIGMOD* 1979.
22. C. Zaniolo. The database language GEM. In *SIGMOD* 1983.

Equal Time for Data on the Internet with WebSemantics*

George A. Mihaila[1], Louiqa Raschid[2] and Anthony Tomasic[3]

[1] Department of Computer Science, University of Toronto, Canada
[2] Maryland Business School and UMIACS, University of Maryland, USA
[3] INRIA Rocquencourt, 78153 Le Chesnay, France

Abstract. Many collections of scientific data in particular disciplines are available today around the world. Much of this data conforms to some agreed upon standard for data exchange, i.e., a standard schema and its semantics. However, sharing this data among a global community of users is still difficult because of a lack of standards for the following necessary functions: (i) data providers need a standard for describing or publishing available sources of data; (ii) data administrators need a standard for discovering the published data and (iii) users need a standard for accessing this discovered data. This paper describes a prototype implementation of a system, WEBSEMANTICS, that accomplishes the above tasks. We describe an architecture and protocols for the publication, discovery and access to scientific data. We define a language for discovering sources and querying the data in these sources, and we provide a formal semantics for this language.

1 Introduction

Recently, many standardized collections of scientific data, in specific disciplines, e.g., the environmental sciences, have become available. For example, governments have recognized that information about the environment has important consequences in the management of sustainable economic growth. As a result, many collections of environmental data, located around the world, are now available to scientists [Fra97]. Much of this data conforms to existing standards for the definition of data. These standards help scientists share information since each item of data is precisely defined. However, the sharing of information between scientists is still a very difficult process. Sharing is hindered by the lack of a standard system for *describing* the data that is available, the lack of a standard method for *discovering* the existence of data relevant to a problem, and the lack of a standard method for *accessing* discovered relevant data.

The World-Wide Web (WWW) provides a standard system for sharing documents. In this system there is a standard way to publish and access documents via the HTTP protocol and HTML document format standards. In addition,

* This research was partially sponsored by the National Science Foundation grant IRI9630102 and the Defense Advanced Research Projects Agency grant 01-5-28838

there is a standard way to discover relevant documents, through the use of search engines. Because of the inherent nature of documents, only a loose standard is required for the definition of the meaning of a document – the language in which the document is written.

Typed data cannot be shared using such a system, and in this paper we describe the implementation of a prototype system which permits publication, discovery and access to data. Our goal is to make the access to structured data as easy as access to documents, that is, to give "equal-time" to data on the Internet. Our approach extends the WWW with a protocol for publishing the existence of data sources in documents, via a *metadata description*. We then provide a language for discovering relevant published data sources via the metadata. The language combines features for searching over the metadata with features for searching relevant documents that contain this metadata. This approach smoothly integrates the functionality already existing on the WWW for searching documents with our extensions for searching over the metadata. Once relevant data sources have been found, a query language provides access to this data.

Consider a scientist who samples water in the Seine river at Notre Dame in Paris. She analyzes the sample for hydro-biological material. The schema describing the sample and the result of the analysis has been standardized in France by the *Secrétariat d'Administration National des Données Relatives à l'Eau (SANDRE)* (the national administration of water related data) [SAN95]. The schema includes a standard taxonomy of fauna, the list of fauna found in the sample, the method (from a standard set of methods) used to analyze the sample, the date, time, and duration of the sampling operation, etc. Suppose that this scientist has stored the results of the analysis in an `Oracle` database. This data source can be published via the WEBSEMANTICS system with an HTML file like the one shown in Fig. 1.

This document pairs machine-readable information for accessing the database with a description of the data in the database. More precisely, the new `WSSCI` tag contains WEBSEMANTICS *source connection information* such as the address of a *wrapper* module (needed to access the data), the Internet address of the database server, authentication information, etc. We say that this document is an WS-MXF (WEBSEMANTICS *Metadata Exchange Format*) document that *describes* the data source.

Suppose a second scientist knows that the server `www.env.org` has links to documents that publish data sources. Then, he can execute the following query:

Query 1.
select   *s*
from   Document *d* **such that** "http://www.env.org/" →* *d*,
         Source *s* **such that** *d* describes *s*
where   *d.text* **contains** "water pollution";

This query finds any WEBSEMANTICS document that is linked to the given server and that mentions water pollution. The query then extracts the information

```
<HTML>
<HEAD>
<TITLE>Environmental Data for Paris</TITLE>
<WSSCI WRAPPER = "http://www.cs.toronto.edu/ws/WS-Oracle.class"
      ADDR  = "server.env.org:8001"
      USER  = "guest" PASSWD = "1234" >
</HEAD>
<BODY>
This repository contains daily measurements of water pollution
quality parameters in Paris for the year 1996.  The data conforms
to the SANDRE standard.  The samples of water were obtained using
the following equipment:

etc.

</BODY>
</HTML>
```

Fig. 1. Publishing a data source in an HTML file

about data sources that are published in that document. The scientist can then *register* these data sources to his *catalog* of data sources. Registering a data source means that the set of types of the data source and other additional information are made available to the catalog. Once a catalog has been constructed, other scientists can query this catalog, identify data sources in the catalog and access the data from these sources. The details of data access are described in Sect.3.4.

To validate our research we have constructed WEBSEMANTICS with environmental information and a community of environmental scientists in mind. However, the underlying architecture and language are not specific to environmental data or scientific data in general. Given a standard semantic description for some data, WEBSEMANTICS can be utilized to share this data. For example, given a standardized semantic description of the want-ads of newspapers, (e.g., make, model, year, and price of a car for sale), users of the system can publish databases of want-ads and search for other databases of want-ads. WEBSEMANTICS provides the infrastructure for constructing this community of users.

The above example introduces several questions for which this paper gives preliminary answers. What metadata about data sources, in addition to the types, should be shared using the catalog? What metadata is obtained from the sources? What data model and language should be used to describe metadata of interest? How are text and type information combined in queries?

In summary, the contributions of this paper are as follows:

- A formal model and a physical architecture of a system which permits publication, discovery and access to data sources;
- A query language, WSQL, addressing the issue of resource discovery by context and allowing access to discovered relevant data;
- A formal calculus defining the semantics of the above query language.

The paper is organized as follows: Section 2 introduces a formal model of the objects manipulated by the system; Section 3 presents the WSQL language for the discovery, registration and access to data sources; Section 4 describes the semantics of the WSQL language; Section 5 describes the WEBSEMANTICS architecture; Section 6 describes related work; and Section 7 concludes the paper.

2 The WEBSEMANTICS Metadata Model

The WEBSEMANTICS system operates both at the data level (by providing uniform access to the tuples stored in repositories) and at the *metadata* level. In this section we introduce the metadata objects manipulated by the system: relational types, data sources, catalogs, active domains, WWW documents and links, which together form what we call the WEBSEMANTICS *universe*.

Definition 1. *The* WEBSEMANTICS *Universe is an 8-tuple* $WSU = (\mathcal{T}, \mathcal{S}, \mathcal{N}, \mathcal{C}, \mathcal{D}, \mathcal{L}, \rho_{\mathcal{L}}, \rho_{\mathcal{S}})$
where:

- $\mathcal{T}$ *is the set of all relational types exported by all sources;*
- $\mathcal{S}$ *is the set of all data sources;*
- $\mathcal{N}$ *is the set of all active domains for all sources.*
- $\mathcal{C}$ *is the set of all catalogs;*
- $\mathcal{D}$ *is the set of all the HTML documents in the WWW;*
- $\mathcal{L}$ *is the set of all links between documents;*
- $\rho_{\mathcal{L}} : \mathcal{D} \rightarrow 2^{\mathcal{L}}$ *is a mapping defining for each document the set of its outgoing links;*
- $\rho_{\mathcal{S}} : \mathcal{D} \rightarrow 2^{\mathcal{S}}$ *is a mapping defining for each document the set of sources it describes;*

The metadata model is represented by six *virtual relations*: Type, Source, Domain, Catalog, Document and Link. These relations are not materialized. Access to these virtual relations is distributed over various components in the WEBSEMANTICS architecture.

Definition 2. *A relational type is modeled by a tuple in the virtual relation* Type(name, attributes) *where:*

- name *is a string uniquely identifying the type;*
- attributes *is a set of pairs (*name, scalar_type*), where* scalar_type $\in$ {String, Int, Float, Boolean}.

Definition 3. *A data source is represented by a tuple in the virtual relation* Source(id, types, description, url, sci), *where:*

- id *is a string identifying the source;*
- types *is the set of all relational types available is this source (represented by* Type *tuples);*
- description *is a textual description of the data present in this source;*
- url *is the location of the HTML document publishing this source;*
- sci *is the source connection information tuple: a nested tuple with variable structure, containing at least a field named* wrapper, *containing the location of the wrapper, and possibly other fields (eg.* addr, username, passwd*).*

One component of the metadata maintained by WEBSEMANTICS is a compact representation of the current contents of data sources, also known as the *active domain*.

Definition 4. *The active domain of a source is modeled by a set of tuples in a virtual relation* Domain(source_id, type, attribute, values) *where:*

- source_id *is the source's identifier;*
- type *is the name of a relational type;*
- attribute *is the name of an attribute of the type* type;
- values *is a textual representation of a set of values for the specified attribute;*

A catalog C stores information about a collection of data sources and the types and domains exported by them:

Definition 5. *A catalog is represented by a tuple in the virtual relation* Catalog(addr, sources, types, domains) *where:*

- addr *is the RMI address of the catalog service;*
- sources *is a set of Source tuples;*
- types *is the set of all types exported by the sources registered in the catalog;*
- domains *is the set of all domains exported by the sources;*

We identify a catalog with its RMI address.

The WEBSEMANTICS system uses the World Wide Web for publishing data sources. The following definition refers to objects in the WWW: documents and links.

Definition 6. *A WWW document is modeled by a tuple in the virtual relation* Document(url, title, text, date), *where the attributes are the document's URL, title, text, and last modification date, respectively. We identify a document with its URL.*

A hypertext link is modeled by a tuple in the virtual relation Link(base, href, label), *where the* base *is the URL of the source document,* href *is the URL of the target document, and* label *is the link's labeling text.*

3 Locating, Registering and Querying Data Sources

In this section we introduce the WEBSEMANTICS Query Language (WSQL) which provides the following functions: 1) finding data sources published in WS-MXF documents on the WWW or registered in existing catalogs; 2) registering sources in a catalog; 3) selecting sources based on their contents; and 4) extracting data from sources. To accomplish these tasks, the WSQL language integrates constructs borrowed from WebSQL [MMM96] and OQL [C+96].

3.1 Finding Sources on the WWW

In Sect.1 we described the WEBSEMANTICS Metadata Exchange Format (WS-MXF) for publishing information about data sources in Web pages. In order to access this information, the WEBSEMANTICS system needs to locate these pages and extract the source connection information from them.

Consider the following scenario: researchers at an institute for environmental studies publish on the institute's Web server several HTML pages describing data sources containing measurements of various parameters. A scientist in a different location, interested in this data, knows only the home page of the institute, and would like to locate all data sources related to water pollution. Then, the following query would build the desired collection of sources:

Query 2.
select s
from Document d **such that** "http://www.env.org/" $\rightarrow^*$ d,
  Source s **such that** d describes s
where $d.text$ **contains** "water pollution";

The first construct in the **from** clause sets the range of the variable d to the set of all documents on the "www.env.org" server which are reachable from the root page. The path regular expression '$\rightarrow^*$' means "traverse any number of local links starting from the specified URL". The set of documents of interest is restricted by a predicate in the **where** clause which specifies a string containment condition on $d.text$. The second construct in the **from** clause sets the range of the variable s to the set of sources described in the documents which satisfy the predicate.

Path regular expressions, a construct borrowed from WebSQL, are regular expressions over the alphabet of link types: $\rightarrow$ — *local* link between documents on the same Web server, $\Rightarrow$ — *global* link to a different Web server, $\mapsto$ — *interior* link to a position in the same document, and $\overset{u}{\rightarrow}$ — a user defined link type[4].

---

[4] For more examples of WSQL queries, including user defined link types, one can see [MRT97]

3.2 Selecting Sources from Catalogs

We have seen in the previous section how we can extract sources from the WWW. Once specialized catalogs have been built, however, it is reasonable to pick certain sources directly from these catalogs, instead of exploring the WWW.

For instance, going back to our example with environmental data, assuming one knows the RMI addresses of several catalogs registering relevant data sources, one can extract sources of interest from these catalogs with the following query:

Query 3. Find all data sources containing mean values of the UV index for Paris, according to a specific list of catalogs.

select s
from Catalog c **in** { "rmi://an.env.org/WSCat", "rmi://rep.env.fr/WSCat" },
 Source s **in** $c.sources$,
 Domain d **in** $c.domains$,
where $d.type$ = "UVIndex" **and** $d.att$ = "city"
 and $d.values$ **contains** "Paris"
 and $d.source\_id$ = $s.id$;

3.3 Registering Sources

We have presented example queries to extract and build sets of data sources based on their metadata. In order to make such a set of sources available to the WEBSEMANTICS system they have to be registered in a catalog. This is accomplished by the **register** command, whose syntax is specified below:

register into catalog *catalog_address* (**sources** | **types**) *WSQL_query*

Thus, the **register** command can be used to register either a set of sources or a set of types, as computed by a WSQL query.

3.4 Selecting and Querying Data Sources

In the previous sections, we described the process of locating and registering data sources in a catalog. Once catalogs have been built, they can be queried to identify sources for data access. In this section, we describe the features of the WSQL language that can be used to select sources in a catalog and then extract tuples from these sources.

Although the WSQL language allows the user to combine the source discovery features with data extraction, we expect that most user queries will be executed against sources registered in the default catalog. To support the typical user, we expect that a WEBSEMANTICS database administrator will use the Web navigation and catalog interrogation features of WSQL to maintain the default catalog.

The WSQL features support the following operations:

- Selecting data sources from the catalog based on the meta-data describing them, for example, the types that are supported by each source, the textual descriptions of the data, the domains of some types, etc.
- Comparing the meta-data contents of two sources or the data contents of two sources.
- Combining source selection with data extraction.

Once the sources are selected from the catalog, then an appropriate subquery against the selected type(s) that are supported by that source will be submitted and answer tuples will be obtained as the result to this subquery. Answers from multiple sources will be combined by evaluating those operations in the WS query processor.

For example, if we are interested in all the measured values of the UV index in Canada in a specific day, we can write the following query:

Query 4.
select $x.uv\_index$
from   Source s,
          UVIndex x in s
where $s.types \supseteq \{$UVIndex$\}$ **and** $s.description$ **contains** "Canada"
         and $x.date = $ "30.06.1997" **and** $x.country = $ "Canada"

The set of sources that need to be contacted is restricted by explicitly including a content-dependent selection of the sources from the default catalog.

4   Formal Semantics

In this section we give a formal semantics for the WSQL language, by introducing a calculus and providing the translation rules from the language to this calculus.

We start by specifying the meaning of the various constructs in the **from** clause. Every variable in a query is defined by a *range*, i.e. a set of values. The query examples given so far illustrate several ways to specify a range. The following definition introduces domain calculus predicates for each of these syntactic constructs.

Definition 7. *Consider the* WebSemantics *universe* $WSU = (\mathcal{T}, \mathcal{S}, \mathcal{N}, \mathcal{C}, \mathcal{D}, \mathcal{L}, \rho_{\mathcal{L}}, \rho_{\mathcal{S}})$ *and a finite set* Λ *of link types. Consider also a multi-sorted collection of metadata variables* $V_{Meta} = \bigcup_{\mathcal{X} \in \{\mathcal{T}, \mathcal{S}, \mathcal{N}, \mathcal{C}, \mathcal{D}\}} V_{\mathcal{X}}$ *and a separate multi-sorted collection of data variables* $V_{Data} = \bigcup_{t \in \mathcal{T}} V_t$, *where the subscript specifies the sort of the variables. Also, denote by* $Dom_{Meta} = \bigcup_{\mathcal{X} \in \{\mathcal{T}, \mathcal{S}, \mathcal{N}, \mathcal{C}, \mathcal{D}\}} \mathcal{X}$, *the meta-data domain, and by* $Dom_{Data} = \bigcup_{t \in \mathcal{T}} Dom_t$, *the data domain, where for each type* $t \in \mathcal{T}$, Dom_t *is the set of all possible data tuples of type* t.

A range atom *is an expression of one of the following forms:*

- $Path(d, R, e)$, *where* $d \in \mathcal{D} \cup V_{\mathcal{D}}$, R *is a regular expression over* Λ, *and* $e \in V_{\mathcal{D}}$;

- $Describes(d, s)$, where $d \in \mathcal{D} \cup V_\mathcal{D}$ and $s \in V_\mathcal{S}$;
- $x \in extent(s, t)$, where $s \in V_\mathcal{S}$, $t \in \mathcal{T} \cup V_\mathcal{T}$, and $x \in V_\mathcal{T}$;
- $x \in \{c_1, ..., c_k\}$, where $x \in V_\mathcal{X}$ and $c_1, ..., c_k \in \mathcal{X}$ are constants $(\mathcal{X} \in \{\mathcal{T}, \mathcal{S}, \mathcal{N}, \mathcal{C}, \mathcal{D}\})$;
- $x \in u.attr$, where $u, x \in V_{Meta}$ and $attr$ is a set-valued attribute;

A range expression is an expression of the form $\{(x_1, ..., x_n) | A_1 \wedge ... \wedge A_m\}$, where $A_1, ..., A_m$ are range atoms and $x_1, ..., x_n$ are all the variables occurring in them.

Consider a valuation $\nu : V_{Meta} \cup V_{Data} \rightarrow Dom_{Meta} \cup Dom_{Data}$, such that for all variables $x \in V_\mathcal{X}$, $\nu(x) \in \mathcal{X}$. We extend ν to the identity function on $Dom_{Meta} \cup Dom_{Data}$. The following definition assigns semantics to range atoms.

Definition 8. *Let A be a range atom. We say that A is validated by the valuation ν if:*

- *for $A = Path(d, R, e)$, if there exists a simple path from $\nu(d)$ to $\nu(e)$ matching the regular expression R;*
- *for $A = Describes(d, s)$, if $\nu(s) \in \rho_\mathcal{S}(\nu(d))$ (the document $\nu(d)$ contains connection information for the source $\nu(s)$);*
- *for $A = x \in extent(s, t)$, if $\nu(x)$ is a data tuple of type $\nu(t)$ in source $\nu(s)$;*
- *for $A = x \in \{c_1, ..., c_k\}$, if $\nu(x) \in \{c_1, ..., c_k\}$;*
- *for $A = x \in u.attr$, if $\nu(x) \in \nu(u).attr$;*

Now we can give semantics to range expressions.

Definition 9. *Let $\mathcal{E} = \{(x_1, ..., x_n) | A_1 \wedge ... \wedge A_m\}$ be a range expression. Then, the set of tuples $\Psi(\mathcal{E}) = \{(\nu(x_1), ..., \nu(x_n)) | \nu \text{ is a valuation s.t. } A_1, ..., A_m \text{ are all validated by } \nu\}$ is called the range of $\mathcal{E}$.*

Range expressions model the syntactic constructs in the **from** clause. In order to model the **select** and **where** clauses, we need to include in our calculus the traditional relational operators *project* (π) and *select* (σ), with the standard semantics:

Definition 10. *Let $X = \{x_1, ..., x_n\} \subset V_{Meta} \cup V_{Data}$ be a set of variables. Let $T = \{(\nu_i(x_1), ..., \nu_i(x_n)) | \nu_i \text{ valuation}, i = 1, \cdots, m\}$ be a set of tuples. Let ϕ be a Boolean expression over the variables in X (involving any combination of equality, inequality, set containment and string containment tests). Then, the result of applying the select and project operators on T is:*

$$\sigma_\phi(T) = \{t \in T | \phi(t) = true\}$$

$$\pi_{x_{i_1}.a_{j_1}, ..., x_{i_k}.a_{i_k}}(T) = \{(x_{i_1}.a_{j_1}, ..., x_{i_k}.a_{i_k}) | (x_1, ..., x_n) \in T\}$$

We are now ready to specify the semantics of WSQL in terms of the introduced calculus. We first consider un-nested WSQL queries. Thus, a query of the form:

select L
from $C_1, C_2, ..., C_m$
where ϕ;

translates to the following calculus query:

$$\pi_L \sigma_\phi \{(x_1, ..., x_n) | A_1 \wedge ... \wedge A_m\}$$

where each range atom A_i is obtained from the corresponding condition in the **from** clause by applying the following transformation rules:

- if C_i = "Document e **such that** $d\ R\ e$", then $A_i = Path(d, R, e)$;
- if C_i = "Source s **such that** d **describes** s", then $A_i = Describes(d, s)$;
- if C_i = "$MetaType\ v$ **in** $\{c_1, ..., c_k\}$", then $A_i = v \in \{c_1, ..., c_k\}$ ($MetaType$ is any of the virtual relations introduced in Sect.2);
- if C_i = "$MetaType\ v = c$", then $A_i = v \in \{c\}$;
- if C_i = "$MetaType\ v$ **in** $u.attr$", then $A_i = v \in u.attr$;
- if C_i = "$t\ v$ **in** s", then $A_i = v \in extent(s, t)$;
- if C_i = "$t\ v$", then $A_i = v \in extent(s, t)$ and we introduce one extra atom $A_{m+1} = s \in C.sources$, where C is the default catalog and $s \in V_S$ is a new variable;

For example, Query 1 translates to the following calculus query:

$$\pi_s \sigma_{d.text \supset "water\ pollution"} \{(d, s) | Path(www.env.org, \rightarrow^*, d) \wedge Describes(d, s)\}$$

For queries that contain subqueries, the semantics is defined recursively starting from the inner-most subquery.

5 Architecture

In this section we introduce the WEBSEMANTICS architecture and components, and describe the functionality and interactions of these components.

We assume that a community of users in a specific discipline have agreed upon the data model, data exchange format, and semantics of the data to be shared, and have provided a set $\mathcal{T}$ of tuple types (in the relational data model). In other words, we assume *semantic homogeneity* within a well-defined application domain. Each type in $\mathcal{T}$ is defined by a set of named attributes having scalar types (*string, int, float*, etc.).

5.1 The WEBSEMANTICS Components

The WEBSEMANTICS system has a layered architecture of interdependent components (see Fig.2). We begin by introducing each layer, and leave the description of the way the components interact to the next section.

The *Data Source Layer* has two components, *data sources* and *wrappers*. Data providers create and manage a set S of autonomous *data sources*, that can be accessed over the Internet. These data sources can provide query capability ranging from full DBMS to simple scanning of files. WEBSEMANTICS provides uniform access to both kinds of sources, independent of the capability of the sources. This is accomplished using *wrapper* components. These components provide two kinds of functionality. First, they provide the metadata (types, domains, etc.) needed to register a data source in a *catalog* (the catalog component is described later). This functionality is defined by a *Metadata Protocol*. Second, wrappers accept a WEBSEMANTICS query and provide answers. This functionality is supported by the *Query and Answer Protocol*[5].

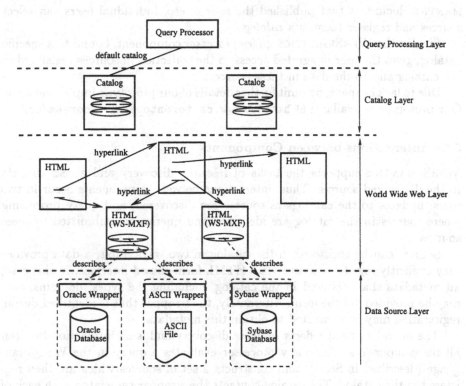

Fig. 2. The WEBSEMANTICS layers

The next layer is the *World Wide Web Layer*. This layer includes WEBSEMANTICS *documents* that publish data sources as well as other documents and data on the WWW. To publish a source, the provider needs to identify

---

[5] A more detailed description of WEBSEMANTICS wrappers and their supported protocols is given in [MRT97]

the location of the wrapper, and some wrapper-specific connection parameters, such as the address of the source, user name, password., etc. This information is made available by publishing it in a WWW-accessible HTML document using the WEBSEMANTICS metadata exchange format (WS-MXF), described in Sect.1. The collection of all HTML documents, including these WEBSEMANTICS documents, connected through hyperlinks, constitutes the *World Wide Web Layer*.

The next layer is the *Catalog Layer*. A *catalog* is a specialized repository storing collections of SCI tuples describing the source. In addition to this connection information, a catalog stores additional metadata characterizing the data source, such as the set of types exported by the source, the domain for a subset of attributes of some types, a textual description of the data source obtained from the WEBSEMANTICS document describing the source, the URL of the WEBSEMANTICS document that published the source, etc. Individual users can select sources and register them in a *catalog*.

Finally, the WEBSEMANTICS *query processor* component, bound to a specific catalog, gives the user integrated access to the collection of sources registered in the catalog and to the data in these sources.

Due to lack of space, we omit further details of our prototype implementation. Our prototype is available at `http://www.cs.toronto.edu/~georgem/ws/`.

5.2 Interactions between Components

WEBSEMANTICS supports the tasks of resource discovery and access to data in the discovered sources. Thus, interactions between components occur in two ways: updates to the catalogs as sources are discovered, and query processing where sources in the catalog are identified and queries are submitted to these sources.

Sources can be registered in the catalog in two ways. First, a data provider may explicitly register a source via a HTML forms based interface. In this case, all metadata that is stored in the catalog, including the types, domains, etc., may be provided via the form. Alternately, the wrapper that is identified during registration may be contacted to obtain this metadata.

The second method reflects resource discovery and is an interaction between all the components. The query processor evaluates a query in the WSQL language (described in Sect.3) and constructs a set of sources which are then registered in the catalog. The catalog contacts the wrapper associated with each of these sources via the Metadata Protocol to extract metadata about the sources, e.g., type and domain information.

Query processing proceeds as follows: a query, either generated by an application program, or entered through a parameterized user interface, is sent to the query processor. There are two phases to query processing. In the first phase, the set of data sources on which the query is to be evaluated must be bound. The query can declaratively specify the set of data sources to be used, in terms of selections on the default catalog, on other catalogs, or even by utilizing the resource discovery features of the language (that was used to discover sources).

If unspecified, the set of sources is bound to the set of all sources registered in the default catalog (bound to the query processor).

After the set of sources has been determined, the query processor issues sub-queries to each wrapper associated with some source. This time, the interaction with the wrapper is done via the Query and Answer protocol. The query processor combines the results, which are then returned to the user.

6 Related Work

Current research in mediation technology has proposed several techniques for describing, integrating or accessing structured data on the Internet. However, little research has been done for the problem of *locating* data sources on-the-fly and querying their contents. This is the main contribution of WEBSEMANTICS. However, WEBSEMANTICS is not a stand-alone technology, and it depends on the existence of other technologies. In this section, we review this research.

There are currently numerous wrapper mediator architectures, as proposed in [ACPS96, HKWY97, G+96, KLSS95, R+89, P+96, TRV96, Wie92]. These systems differ widely in the capabilities of mediators and in the capabilities of wrappers. However, we believe that interoperation between WEBSEMANTICS and these systems is possible. WEBSEMANTICS differs in two distinct ways from these systems. Wrappers developed for Garlic [HKWY97] and the Information Manifold [KLSS95] assume the location of the data sources, types, and wrapper capability, are embedded within the wrappers. Wrappers for DISCO [TRV96] and TSIMMIS [GM+95, VP97] use declarative languages to export types and query capabilities. The location of components is embedded within the mediators. Our main contribution is an architecture that uses WWW documents to publish the location of components (wrappers and data sources) and a uniform query language to locate data sources (based on metadata) and to access data from the sources.

Distributed information retrieval systems, for example the Harvest/Essence information retrieval based system [B+95] are indirectly related to our work. Essence is a customizable information extraction system that is used to extract and structure mostly textual information from documents in Harvest. It exploits the formats of common file types and extracts contents of files. The result is a summary object (a SOIF record). Collections of SOIF records are indexed and organized into *brokers*. Brokers provide information retrieval search on their associated SOIF records. The information stored in SOIF records is similar to the metadata about sources maintained by WEBSEMANTICS catalogs. However, these systems focus on passive documents and information retrieval search, whereas we focus on querying strictly typed data in both active and passive data repositories.

The importance of the World Wide Web as a repository of information has generated an increasing interest in the research community for the design of high-level, declarative languages for querying it. WebSQL [MMM96] integrates textual retrieval with structure and topology-based queries. There, a minimalist relational approach is taken: each Web document is associated with a tuple in a virtual **Document** relation and each hypertext link with a tuple in a virtual **Anchor** relation. In order to query these virtual tables, one must first define computable sub-domains, either using keyword matching or through controlled navigation starting from known URLs. Another Web query language, W3QS [KS95] includes the specification of syntax and semantics of a SQL-like query language (W3QL) that provides simple access to external Unix programs, advanced display facilities for gathered information, and view maintenance facilities.

Recently there is an increasing interest within the World Wide Web Consortium (W3C) for providing standard formats for machine-readable resource content descriptions, to allow for the automation of Web information retrieval and processing. Among the currently evolving standards we can mention the Resource Description Framework [RDF] and the Meta Content Framework [MCF]. Both standards use the Extensible Markup Language [XML] as a common data encoding format and provide a framework for defining and publishing a shared vocabulary of entities and properties of these entities. Clearly, a system like WEBSEMANTICS would benefit from such standardization efforts.

7 Conclusion

We have presented a system, WEBSEMANTICS, that provides a multi-layered infrastructure for publishing, discovering and accessing structured data on the Internet. Thus, the *Data Source Layer* contains *sources*, which contain data stored in either an active repository (such as a DBMS) or a passive collection of files and *wrappers*, which are software components that isolate the differences in query capabilities and data exchange formats between data sources and also provide metadata information about the contents of sources. To allow for dynamic location of data sources we proposed a special type of HTML document pairing data source connection information with a textual description of the data source content. This provides an easy way to publish sources and allows the use of information retrieval techniques for the location of relevant data sources. Thus, the second layer is the *World Wide Web Layer* containing all the HTML documents together with the hyperlinks between them. The third layer, the *Catalog Layer*, consists of *catalogs*, which are specialized repositories storing connection information and metadata about data sources (such as types, active domain, and natural language description). Finally, the *Query Processing Layer* provides content-dependent selection of sources and integrated data access.

We introduced a formal model, meant to capture the concepts manipulated by the system and the relationships between them. Furthermore, we introduced a declarative query language, WSQL whose purpose is to facilitate discovery and registration of data sources, content-dependent selection of sources and data access. We specified the semantics of this language by defining a domain calculus over the previously introduced model.

References

[ACPS96]   S. Adali, K. S. Candan, Y. Papakonstantinou, and V. S. Subrahmaniam. Query caching and optimization in distributed mediator systems. In *Proceedings of the ACM SIGMOD'96*, pages 137–148, 1996.

[B+95]   C. Bowman et al. The Harvest information discovery and access system. *Computer Networks and ISDN Systems*, 28:119–125, 1995.

[C+96]   R.G.G. Cattell et al. *The Object Database Standard - ODMG 93, Release 1.2*. Morgan Kaufmann, 1996.

[Fra97]   Michael J. Franklin, editor. *SIGMOD Record*, volume 26, March 1997. Special Section on Environmental Information Systems.

[G+96]   G. Gardarin et al. IRO-DB: A distributed system federating object and relational databases. In O.A. Bukhres and A.K. Elmagarmid, editors, *Object-Oriented Multidatabase Systems : A solution for Advanced Applications*. Prentice Hall, 1996.

[GM+95]   H. Garcia-Molina et al. Integrating and accessing heterogeneous information sources in TSIMMIS. In *Proceedings of the AAAI Symposium on Information Gathering*, pages 61–64, Stanford, California, March 1995.

[HKWY97]   L. M. Haas, D. Kossmann, E. L. Wimmers, and J. Yang. Optimizing queries across diverse data sources. In *Proceedings of VLDB'97*, pages 276–285, 1997.

[KLSS95]   T. Kirk, A. Y. Levy, Y. Sagiv, and D. Srivastava. The Information Manifold. In *Proc. of the AAAI Spring Symposium on Information Gathering in Distributed Heterogeneous Environments*, Stanford, CA, March 1995.

[KS95]   D. Konopnicki and O. Shmueli. W3QS: A query system for the World Wide Web. In *Proceedings of VLDB'95*, pages 54–65, 1995.

[MCF]   Meta Content Framework using XML. http://www.w3.org/TR/NOTE-MCF-XML.

[MMM96]   A. O. Mendelzon, G. A. Mihaila, and T. Milo. Querying the World Wide Web. In *Proceedings of PDIS'96*, pages 80–91, 1996.

[MRT97]   G. A. Mihaila, L. Raschid, and A. Tomasic. Equal Time for Data on the Internet with WebSemantics. Technical report, University of Toronto, 1997. http://www.cs.toronto.edu/~georgem/ws/ws.ps.

[P+96]   Y. Papakonstantinou et al. Capabilities-based query rewriting in mediator systems. In *Proceedings of PDIS'96*, 1996.

[R+89]   M. Rusinkiewicz et al. Query processing in a heterogeneous multidatabase environment. In *Proceedings of the IEEE Symposium on Parallel and Distributed Processing*, 1989.

[RDF]   Resource Description Framework (RDF). http://www.w3.org/RDF/.

[SAN95]   *Secrétariat d'Administration National des Données Relatives à l'Eau*. Sandre, Rue Edouard Chamberland, 87065 Limoges, France, 1995.

[TRV96]   A. Tomasic, L. Raschid, and P. Valduriez. Scaling heterogeneous databases and the design of DISCO. In *Proceeding of ICDCS'96*, 1996.

[VP97]   V. Vassalos and Y. Papakonstantinou. Describing and using query capabilities of heterogeneous sources. In *Proc. of VLDB'97*, pages 256–265, 1997.

[Wie92]   G. Wiederhold. Mediators in the architecture of future information systems. *Computer*, 25(3):38–49, March 1992.

[XML]   Extensible Markup Language (XML). http://www.w3.org/XML.

Algorithms for Data Mining

Pincer-Search: A New Algorithm for Discovering the Maximum Frequent Set

Dao-I Lin and Zvi M. Kedem

Department of Computer Science
Courant Institute of Mathematical Sciences
New York University
{lindaoi, kedem}@cs.nyu.edu

Abstract. Discovering frequent itemsets is a key problem in important data mining applications, such as the discovery of association rules, strong rules, episodes, and minimal keys. Typical algorithms for solving this problem operate in a bottom-up breadth-first search direction. The computation starts from frequent 1-itemsets (minimal length frequent itemsets) and continues until all maximal (length) frequent itemsets are found. During the execution, every frequent itemset is explicitly considered. Such algorithms perform reasonably well when all maximal frequent itemsets are short. However, performance drastically decreases when some of the maximal frequent itemsets are relatively long. We present a new algorithm which combines both the bottom-up and top-down searches. The primary search direction is still bottom-up, but a restricted search is also conducted in the top-down direction. This search is used only for maintaining and updating a new data structure we designed, the maximum frequent candidate set. It is used to prune candidates in the bottom-up search. A very important characteristic of the algorithm is that it does not require explicit examination of every frequent itemset. Therefore the algorithm performs well even when some maximal frequent itemsets are long. As its output, the algorithm produces the maximum frequent set, i.e., the set containing all maximal frequent itemsets, which therefore specifies immediately all frequent itemsets. We evaluate the performance of the algorithm using a well-known benchmark database. The improvements can be up to several orders of magnitude, compared to the best current algorithms.

1 Introduction

A key component of many data mining problems is formulated as follows. Given a large database of sets of items (representing market basket data, episodes, etc.), discover all the frequent *itemsets* (sets of items), where a frequent itemset is one that occurs more than a user-defined number of times (minimum *support*) in the database. Depending on the semantics attached to the input database, the frequent itemsets, and the term "occurs," we get the key components of different data mining problems such as association rules (e.g., [2] [7] [11]), strong rules (e.g., [15]), episodes (e.g., [9]) and minimal keys (e.g., [6]).

Typical algorithms for finding the *frequent set*, i.e., the set of all frequent itemsets [1], operate in a *bottom-up* breadth-first fashion (e.g. [2] [3] [4] [7] [10] [11] [13] [14] [16]). The computation starts from frequent 1-itemsets (minimal length frequent itemsets at the bottom) and then extends one level up in every pass until all maximal (length) frequent itemsets are discovered. *All* frequent itemsets are *explicitly examined* and discovered by these algorithms. When all maximal frequent itemsets are short, these algorithms perform reasonably well. However, performance drastically decreases when any of the maximal frequent itemsets becomes longer, because a maximal frequent itemset of size l implies the presence of $2^l - 2$ non-trivial frequent itemsets (its nontrivial subsets) as well, each of which is explicitly examined by such algorithms. In data mining applications in which items are correlated, maximum frequent itemsets could be long [4].

Therefore, instead of examining and "assembling" all the frequent itemsets, an alternative approach might be to "shortcut" the process and attempt to search for maximal frequent itemsets "more directly," as they immediately specify all frequent itemsets. In many data mining applications, it suffices to know only the support of maximal frequent itemsets and a few of their subsets.

Finding the *maximum frequent set* (or MFS), the set of all maximal frequent itemsets, is essentially a search problem in a hypothesis search space (a binomial graph). The search for the maximum frequent set can proceed from the 1-itemsets to n-itemsets (bottom-up) or from the n-itemsets to 1-itemsets (top-down).

We present a novel *Pincer-Search* algorithm which searches for MFS from *both bottom-up and top-down directions*. It performs well even when the maximal frequent itemsets are long.

The bottom-up search is similar to the *Apriori* [2] and the *OCD* [11] algorithms. However, the top-down search is unique. It is implemented efficiently by introducing an auxiliary data structure, the *maximum-frequent-candidate-set* or MFCS, as explained later. By incorporating the computation of MFCS in our algorithm, we are able to efficiently approach MFS from both top-down and bottom-up directions. Unlike the bottom-up search that goes up one level in each pass, MFCS set can help the computation "move down" many levels in one pass.

In this paper, we apply the MFCS concept to association rules mining. Popular benchmark databases designed by Agrawal and Srikant [2] have been used in [3], [13], [14], [16], and [19]: we use these same benchmarks to evaluate the performance of our algorithm. In most cases, our algorithm not only reduces the number of passes of reading the database but also can reduce the number of candidates (for whom support is counted). In such cases, both I/O time and CPU time are reduced by eliminating the candidates that are subsets of maximal frequent itemsets found in MFCS.

The organization of the rest of the paper is as follows. The procedures for mining association rules, the cost of the processes, and the properties that can be used to reduce the cost will be discussed in Section 2. Section 3 will describe our algorithm and the ideas behind it. Two technical issues and the techniques to address them will also be discussed in this section. Section 4 presents the results of our experiments. Section 5 briefly discusses the related research. A somewhat more detailed description of the algorithm can be found in [8].

2 Association Rule Mining

This section we briefly introduce the association rule mining problem, following to the extent feasible the terminology of [1].

2.1 The Setting of the Problem

Let $I = \{i_1, i_2, \ldots, i_m\}$ be a set of m distinct items. A *transaction* T is defined as any subset of items in I. A database D is a set of transactions. A set of items is called an *itemset*. The number of items in an itemset is called the *length* of an itemset. Itemsets of some length k are referred to as k-itemsets.

A transaction T is said to *support* an itemset $X \subseteq I$ if it contains all items of X, i.e., $X \subseteq T$. The fraction of the transactions in D that support X is called the *support* of X, denoted as support(X). An itemset is *frequent* if its support is above some user-defined minimum support threshold. Otherwise, it is *infrequent*.

An *association rule* has the form $R : X \rightarrow Y$, where X and Y are two non-empty and non-intersecting itemsets. The *support for rule* R is defined as support($X \cup Y$). A *confidence* factor defined as support($X \cup Y$)/support(X), is used to evaluate the strength of such association rules. The semantics of the confidence of a rule indicates how often it can be expected to apply, while its support indicates how trustworthy this rule is.

The problem of association rule mining is to discover all rules that have support and confidence greater than some user-defined minimum support and minimum confidence thresholds, respectively. Association rules that satisfy these requirements are *interesting*.

The normally followed scheme for mining association rules consists of two stages [2]:

1. the discovery of frequent itemsets, followed by
2. the generation of association rules.

The *maximum frequent set* (MFS) is the set of all the *maximal frequent itemsets*. (An itemset is a maximal frequent itemset if it is frequent and no proper superset of it is frequent.) Obviously, an itemset is frequent if and only if it is a subset of a maximal frequent itemset. Thus, it is necessary to discover only the maximum frequent set during the first stage. Of course, an algorithm for that stage may explicitly discover and store some other frequent itemsets as a necessary part of its execution—but minimizing such effort may increase efficiency.

It is also important to note that interesting association rules can be generated by examining the maximum frequent set first, and then proceeding to their subsets if the generated rules have the required confidence. Usually, only a few rules will be interesting. Therefore, while generating rules, all one needs to know is the support of the maximal frequent itemsets and of the itemsets "a little" shorter. If the maximum frequent set is known, one can easily generate the required subsets and count their supports by reading the database once.

The discovery of the maximum frequent set dominates the performance of the whole process. Therefore, we explicitly focus the paper on the discovery of this set.

2.2 A Common Approach to the Discovery of Frequent Itemsets

A typical frequent itemsets discovery process follows a standard scheme. Throughout the execution, the set of all itemsets is partitioned, perhaps implicitly, into 3 sets:

1. *frequent:* This is the set of those itemsets that have been discovered as frequent
2. *infrequent:* This is the set of those itemsets that have been discovered as infrequent
3. *unclassified:* This is the set of all the other itemsets.

Initially, the frequent and the infrequent sets are empty. The process terminates when every itemset is either in the frequent set or in the infrequent set.

We now briefly sketch a realization of this process as in, e.g., [2]. This is a *bottom-up* approach. It consists of repeatedly applying a *pass*, itself consisting of two steps. At the end of pass k all frequent itemsets of size k or less have been discovered. As the first step of pass $k + 1$, itemsets of size $k + 1$ each having two frequent subsets of size k are generated. Some of these itemsets are *pruned*, as they do not need to be processed further. Specifically, itemsets that are supersets of infrequent itemsets are pruned (and discarded), as of course they are infrequent. The remaining itemsets form the set of *candidates* for this pass. As the second step the support for these itemsets is computed, and they are classified as either frequent or infrequent. Note that *every* frequent itemset is a candidate at some pass, and is *explicitly* considered..

The support of the candidate is computed by reading the database. The cost of the frequent itemsets discovery process comes from the reading of the database (I/O time) and the generation of new candidates (CPU time). The number of candidates dominates the entire processing time. Reducing the number of candidates not only can reduce the I/O time but also can reduce the CPU time, since fewer candidates need to be counted and generated. Thus reducing the number of candidates is of critical importance for the efficiency of the process.

2.3 Our Approach to Reducing the Number of Candidates

Consider *any process* for classifying itemsets and some point in the execution where some itemsets have been classified as frequent, some as infrequent, and some are still unclassified. Two observations can be used to immediately classify some of the unclassified itemsets:

Observation 1: If an itemset is infrequent, all it supersets must be infrequent, and they do not need to be examined further

Observation 2: If an itemset is frequent, all its subsets must be frequent, and they do not need to be examined further

Note that the bottom-up process described above uses only the first observation to reduce the number of candidates. Conceivably, a process that relies on both observation to prune candidates could be much more efficient than a process that relies on *only* the first or the second.

3 A New Algorithm for Discovering the Maximum Frequent Set

3.1 Combining Top-down and Bottom-up Searches

It is possible to search for maximal frequent itemsets either *bottom-up* or *top-down*. If all maximal frequent itemsets are expected to be small (close to 1 in size), it seems efficient to search for them bottom-up. If all maximal frequent itemsets are expected to be long (close to n in size) it seems efficient to search for them top-down.

In a "pure" bottom-up approach, only Observation 1 above is used to prune candidates. This is the technique that existing algorithms ([2] [3] [4] [7] [10] [11] [13] [14] [16]) use to decrease the number of candidates. In a "pure" top-down approach, only Observation 2 is used to prune candidates. We will show that by relying on *both* observations we are able to make use of the information gathered in one direction to prune more candidates during the search in the other direction.

If some maximal frequent itemset is found in the top-down direction, then this itemset can be used to eliminate (possibly many) candidates in the bottom-up direction. The subsets of this frequent itemset can be pruned because they are frequent (Observation 2). Of course, if an infrequent itemset is found in the bottom-up direction, then it can be used to eliminate some candidates found so far in the top-down direction (Observation 1). This "two-way approaching" method can fully make use of both observations and thus speed up the search for the maximum frequent set.

We have designed a combined search algorithm for discovering the maximum frequent set. It relies on a new data structure during its execution, the *maximum-frequent-candidate-set,* or MFCS for short, which we define next.

Definition 1. Consider some point during the execution of an algorithm for finding MFS. Some itemsets are frequent, some infrequent, and some unclassified. The maximum-frequent-candidate-set (MFCS) is a minimum cardinality set of itemsets such that the union of all the subsets of its elements contains all the frequent itemsets but does not contain any infrequent itemsets, that is, it is a minimum cardinality set satisfying the conditions

$$\text{FREQUENT} \subseteq \cup \{2^X \mid X \in \text{MFCS}\}$$

$$\text{INFREQUENT} \cap \{2^X \mid X \in \text{MFCS}\} = \emptyset$$

where FREQUENT and INFREQUENT, stand respectively for sets of all frequent and infrequent itemsets (classified as such so far).

Thus obviously at any point of the algorithm MFCS is a superset of MFS. When the algorithm terminates, MFCS and MFS are equal.

The computation of our algorithm follows the bottom-up (breadth-first) search approach. We base our presentation on the *Apriori* algorithm [2], and for greatest ease of exposition we present our algorithm as a modification to that algorithm.

Briefly speaking, in each pass, in addition to counting supports of the candidates in the bottom-up direction, the algorithm also counts supports of the itemsets in MFCS: this set is adapted for the top-down search. This will help in pruning candidates, but will also require changes in candidate generation, as explained later.

Consider a pass k, during which itemsets of size k are to be classified. If some itemset that is an element of MFCS, say X, of cardinality greater than k is found to be frequent in this pass, then all its subsets must be frequent. Therefore, all of its subsets of cardinality k can be pruned from the set of candidates considered in the bottom-up direction in this pass. They, and their supersets will never be candidates throughout the rest of the execution, potentially improving performance. But of course, as the maximum frequent set is finally computed, they "will not be forgotten."

Similarly, when a new infrequent itemset is found in the bottom-up direction, the algorithm will use it to update MFCS. The subsets of MFCS must not contain this infrequent itemset.

Figure 1 conceptually shows the combined two-way search. MFCS is initialized to contain a single element, the itemset of cardinality n containing all the elements of the database. As an example of its utility, consider the first pass of the bottom-up search. If some m 1-itemsets are infrequent after the first pass (after reading the database once), MFCS will have one element of cardinality $n - m$. This itemset is generated by removing the m infrequent items from the initial element of MFCS. In this case, the top-down search goes down m levels in one pass. In general, unlike the search in the bottom-up direction which goes up one level in one pass, *the top-down search can go down many levels in one pass.*

By using the MFCS, we will be able to discover some maximal frequent itemsets in early passes. This early discovery of the maximal frequent itemsets can reduce the number of candidates and the passes of reading the database which in turn can reduce the CPU time and I/O time. This is especially significant when the maximal frequent itemsets discovered in the early passes are long.

For our approach to work efficiently, we need to address two issues. First, how to update MFCS efficiently? Second, once the subsets of the maximal frequent itemsets found in the MFCS are removed, how do we generate the correct candidate set for the subsequent passes in the bottom-up direction?

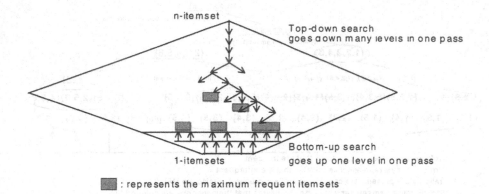

n-itemset

Top-down search
goes down many levels in one pass

Bottom-up search
goes up one level in one pass

1-itemsets

☐ : represents the maximum frequent itemsets

Fig. 1. The search space

3.2 Updating MFCS Efficiently

Consider some itemset Y that has been "just" classified as infrequent and assume that it is a subset of some itemset that is an element of MFCS. To update MFCS, we replace X by $|Y|$ itemsets, each obtained by removing from X a single item (element) of Y. We do this for each newly discovered infrequent itemset and each of its supersets that is an element of MFCS. Formally, we have the following *MFCS-gen* algorithm (shown here for pass k).

Algorithm: *MFCS-gen*
1. **for all itemsets** $s \in S_k$
2.   **for all itemsets** $m \in$ MFCS
3.   **if** s **is a subset of** m
4.   MFCS := MFCS $\setminus \{m\}$
5.   **for all items** $e \in$ **itemset** s
6.   **if** $m \setminus \{e\}$ **is not a subset of any itemset in the MFCS**
7.   MFCS := MFCS $\cup \{m \setminus \{e\}\}$
8. **return MFCS**

Example Suppose $\{\{1,2,3,4,5,6\}\}$ is the current ("old") value of MFCS and two new infrequent itemsets $\{1,6\}$ and $\{3,6\}$ are discovered. Consider first the infrequent itemset $\{1,6\}$. Since the itemset $\{1,2,3,4,5,6\}$ (element of MFCS) contains items 1 and 6, one of its subsets will be $\{1,6\}$. By removing item 1 from itemset $\{1,2,3,4,5,6\}$, we get $\{2,3,4,5,6\}$, and by removing item 6 from itemset $\{1,2,3,4,5,6\}$ we get $\{1,2,3,4,5\}$. After considering itemset $\{1,6\}$, MFCS becomes $\{\{1,2,3,4,5\}, \{2,3,4,5,6\}\}$. Itemset $\{3,6\}$ is then used to update this MFCS. Since $\{3,6\}$ is a subset of $\{2,3,4,5,6\}$, two itemsets $\{2,3,4,5\}$ and $\{2,4,5,6\}$ are generated to replace $\{2,3,4,5,6\}$. The itemset $\{2,3,4,5\}$ is a subset of the itemset $\{1,2,3,4,5\}$ in the new MFCS, and it will be removed from MFCS. Therefore, MFCS becomes $\{\{1,2,3,4,5\}, \{2,4,5,6\}\}$. The top-down arrows in Fig. 2 show the updates of MFCS.

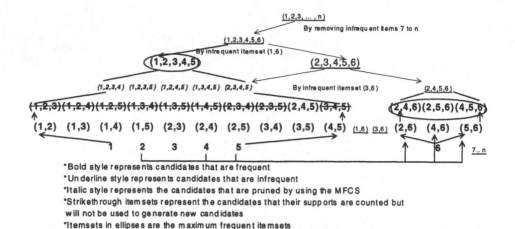

*Bold style represents candidates that are frequent
*Underline style represents candidates that are infrequent
*Italic style represents the candidates that are pruned by using the MFCS
*Strikethrough itemsets represent the candidates that their supports are counted but
  will not be used to generate new candidates
*Itemsets in ellipses are the maximum frequent itemsets

Fig. 2. Two-way search

Lemma 2. *The algorithm MFCS-gen correctly updates* MFCS.

3.3 A New Candidate Generation Method

The Apriori-gen algorithm [2] consists of *join* and *prune* procedures. The *join* procedure combines two frequent k-itemsets that have the same $(k-1)$-prefix, generating a new candidate $(k+1)$-itemset. Thus, a preliminary candidate set is generated. Following the *join* procedure, the *prune* procedure is used to remove from the preliminary candidate set all itemsets c such that some k-subset of c is not in the frequent set L_k. In other words, the supersets of an infrequent itemset are pruned.

In our algorithm, after a maximal frequent itemset is added to MFS, all of its subsets in the frequent set (as computed so far) will be removed. We show by example that if the original *join* procedure is applied some of the needed itemsets could be missing from the candidate set. Consider Fig. 2. Suppose the original frequent itemset L_3 is $\{\{1,2,3\}, \{1,2,4\}, \{1,2,5\}, \{1,3,4\}, \{1,3,5\}, \{1,4,5\}, \{2,3,4\}, \{2,3,5\}, \{2,4,5\}, \{2,4,6\}, \{2,5,6\}, \{3,4,5\}, \{4,5,6\}\}$. Assume itemset $\{1,2,3,4,5\}$ in MFCS is determined to be frequent. Then all 3-itemsets of the original frequent set L_3 will be removed from it by our algorithm, except for $\{2,4,6\}$, $\{2,5,6\}$, and $\{4,5,6\}$. Since the Apriori-gen algorithm uses a $(k-1)$-prefix test on the frequent set to generate new candidates and no two itemsets in the current frequent set $\{\{2,4,6\}, \{2,5,6\}, \{4,5,6\}\}$ share a 2-prefix, no candidate will be generated by applying the *join* procedure on this frequent set. However, the correct candidate set should be $\{\{2,4,5,6\}\}$.

It is easy to recover missing candidates. We sketch two ways.

The first way is by recovering the missing candidates using the current frequent set and the MFS. All required candidates can be obtained by restoring some itemsets to the current frequent set. They will be extracted from MFS, which implicitly maintains all frequent itemsets discovered so far. The first group of itemsets that needs to be restored contains those k-itemsets that have the same $(k-1)$-prefix as an itemset in the current frequent set.

Consider then in pass k, an itemset X in MFS and an itemset Y in the current frequent set such that $|X| > k$. Suppose that the first $k-1$ items of Y are in X and the $(k-1)$st item of Y is equal to the jth item of X. We obtain the k-subsets of X that have the same $(k-1)$-prefix as Y by taking one item of X that has an index greater than j and combining it with the first $k-1$ items of Y, thus getting one of these k-subsets. After these k-itemsets are found, we recover candidates by combining them with the itemset Y as follows:

Algorithm: The *recovery* procedure

```
1.  for all itemsets l in L_k
2.    for all itemsets m in MFS
3.      if the first k − 1 items in l are also in m
4.      /* suppose m.item_j = l.item_{k−1} */
5.        for i from j + 1 to |m|
6.          C_{k+1} := C_{k+1} ∪ {{l.item_1, l.item_2, ..., l.item_k, m.item_i}}
```

Example See Fig. 2. MFS is $\{\{1,2,3,4,5\}\}$ and the current frequent set is $\{\{2,4,6\},$ $\{2,5,6\}, \{4,5,6\}\}$. The only 3-subset of $\{\{1,2,3,4,5\}\}$ that needs to be restored for the itemset $\{2,4,6\}$ to generate a new candidate is $\{2,4,5\}$. This is because it is the only subset of $\{\{1,2,3,4,5\}\}$ that has the same length and the same 2-prefix as the itemset $\{2,4,6\}$. By combining $\{2,4,5\}$ and $\{2,4,6\}$, we recover the missing candidate $\{2,4,5,6\}$. No itemset needs to be restored for itemsets $\{2,5,6\}$ and $\{4,5,6\}$.

The second group of itemsets that need to be restored consists of those k-subsets of MFS having the same $(k-1)$-prefix but have no common superset in the MFS. A similar procedure can be applied to them.

The second way, which we do not describe here further, is based on replacing the $(k-1)$-prefix test in the *join* procedure of the Apriori-gen algorithm by a $(k-1)$-overlap test.

After the recovery stage, we proceed to the prune stage. Instead of checking to see if all k-subsets of an itemset X are in C_{k+1}, we can simply check to see if X is a subset of an itemset in the current MFCS.

Algorithm: The new *prune* procedure

```
1.  for all itemsets c in C_{k+1}
2.    if c is not a subset of any itemset in the current MFCS
3.      delete c from C_{k+1}
```

3.4   The Pincer-Search Algorithm

We now present our complete algorithm, *The Pincer-Search Algorithm*, which relies on the combined approach for determining the maximum frequent set. Lines 9 to 12 constitute our *new* candidate generation procedure.

Algorithm: The Pincer-Search algorithm
1. $L_0 := \emptyset$; $k := 1$; $C_1 := \{\{i\} \mid i \in I\}$
2. MFCS := $\{\{1, 2, \ldots, n\}\}$; MFS := $\emptyset$
3. while $C_k \neq \emptyset$
4.   read database and count supports for C_k and MFCS
5.   MFS := MFS $\cup$ {frequent itemsets in MFCS}
6. L_k := {frequent itemsets in C_k} \ {subsets of MFS}
7. S_k := {infrequent itemsets in C_k}
8.   call the *MFCS-gen* algorithm if $S_k \neq \emptyset$
9.   call the *join* procedure to generate C_{k+1}
10. if any frequent itemset in C_k is removed in line 8
11.   call the *recovery* procedure to recover candidates to C_{k+1}
12. call new *prune* procedure to prune candidates in C_{k+1}
13. $k := k + 1$
14. return MFS

Lemma 3. *The new candidate generation algorithm generates the complete candidate set.*

Theorem 4. *Pincer-Search algorithm generates all maximal frequent itemsets.*

In general, one may not want to use the "pure" version of the Pincer-Search algorithm. For instance, in some case there may be many 2-itemsets, but only a few of them are frequent. In this case it may not be worthwhile to maintain the MFCS, since there will not be many frequent itemsets to discover. In that case, we may simply count candidates of different sizes in one pass, as in [2] and [11]. The algorithm we have implemented is in fact an adaptive version of the algorithm described above. This adaptive version does not maintain the MFCS, when doing so would be counterproductive. This is also the algorithm whose performance is being evaluated in Section 4. Thus the very small overhead of deciding when to use the MFCS is accounted in the performance evaluation of our Pincer-Search algorithm.

4 Performance Evaluation

A key question can be informally stated: "Can the search in the top-down direction proceed fast enough to reach a maximal frequent itemset faster than the search in the bottom-up direction?". There can be no categorical answer, as this really depends on the distribution of the frequent and infrequent itemsets. However, according to both [2] and our experiments, a large fraction the 2-itemsets will usually be infrequent. These infrequent itemsets will cause MFCS to go down the levels very fast, allowing it to reach some maximal frequent itemsets after only a few passes. Indeed, in our experiments, we have found that, in most cases, many of the maximal frequent itemsets are found in MFCS in very early passes. For instance, in the experiment on database T20.I15.D100K (Fig. 4), all maximal frequent itemsets containing up to 17 items are found in 3 passes only!

The performance evaluation presented compares our adaptive Pincer-Search algorithm to the Apriori algorithm [2]. We restrict this comparison both for space limitation and because it is sufficiently instructive to understand the characteristics of the new algorithm's performance.

4.1 Preliminary Discussion

Auxiliary Data Structures Used Since we are interested in studying the effect of using MFCS to reduce the number of candidates and the number of passes, we didn't use more efficient data structures, such as hash tables (e.g., [2] [14]), to store the itemsets. We simply used a link-list data structure to store the frequent set and the candidate set.. The databases used in performance evaluation, are the synthetic databases used in [2].

Also, as done in [13] and [17], we used a one-dimensional array and a two-dimensional array to speed up the process of the first and the second pass correspondingly. The support counting phase runs very fast by using an array, since no searching is needed. No candidate generation process for 2-itemsets is needed because we use a two-dimensional array to store the support of all combinations. We start using a link-list data structure after the third pass. For a fair comparison, the number of candidates shown in the figures does not include the candidates in the first two passes. The number of the candidates in the Pincer-Search algorithm includes the candidates in MFCS.

Scattered and Concentrated Distributions For the same number of frequent itemsets, their distribution can be *concentrated* or *scattered*. In concentrated distribution, on each level the frequent itemsets have many common items: the frequent items tend to cluster. If the frequent itemsets do not have many common elements, the distribution is scattered. We will present experiments to examine the impact of the distribution type on the performance of the two algorithms.

The number of the maximal frequent itemsets $|L|$ is set to 2000, as in [2], in the first set of experiments. The frequent itemsets found in this set of experiments are rather scattered. To produce databases having a concentrated distribution of the frequent itemsets, we adjust the parameter $|L|$ to a smaller value. The value of $|L|$ is set to 50 in the second set of experiments. The minimum supports are set to higher values so that the execution time will not be too long.

Non-Monotone Property of the Maximum Frequent Set For a given database, both the number of candidates and the number of frequent itemsets increase as the minimum support decreases. However, this is *not* the case for the number of the maximal frequent itemsets. For example, when minimum support is 9%, the maximum frequent set may be {{1,2}, {1,3}, {2,3}}. When the minimum support decreases to 6%, the maximum frequent set can become {{1,2,3}}. The number of the maximal frequent itemsets decreased from 3 to 1.

This "nonmonotonicity" does not help bottom-up breadth-first search algorithms. They will have to discover the entire frequent itemsets before the maximum frequent set is discovered. Therefore, in those algorithms, the time, the number of candidates, and the number of passes will monotonically increase when the minimum support decreases.

However, when the minimum support decreases, the length of some maximal frequent itemsets may increase and our MFCS may reach them faster. Therefore, our algorithm *does have* the potential to benefit from this nonmonotonicity.

4.2 Experiments

The test databases are generated synthetically by an algorithm designed by the **IBM Quest** project. The synthetic data generation procedure is described in detail in [2], whose parameter settings we follow. The number of items N is set to 1000. $|D|$ is the number of transactions. $|T|$ is the average size of transactions. $|I|$ is the average size of maximal frequent itemsets.

Scattered Distributions The results of the first set of experiments are shown in Fig. 3. The best improvement occurs for database T10.I4.D100K and minimum support of 0.5%. Pincer-Search runs 1.7 times faster than the Apriori. The improvement came from reducing the number passes of reading the database and the number of candidates.

In the experiment on database T5.I2.D100K, Pincer-Search used more candidates than Apriori. That is because of the number of additional candidates used in MFCS is more than the number of extra candidates pruned relying on MFCS. The maximal frequent itemsets, found in the MFCS, are so short that not too many subsets can be pruned. However, the I/O time saved more than compensated for the extra cost. Therefore, we still get an improvement.

Depending on the distribution of the frequent itemsets, it is also possible that our algorithm might spend time counting the support of the candidates in MFCS while still not finding any maximal frequent itemsets from MFCS. For instance, our algorithm took more time than the Apriori algorithm on the case when the minimum support is set to 0.75% and the database is T10.I4.D100K. However, since there were only a few candidates in MFCS, the difference is quite small.

Concentrated Distributions In the second set of experiments we study the relative performance of the two algorithms on databases with such distributions. The results are shown in Fig. 4. In the first experiment, we use the same T20.I6.D100K database as in the first set of experiments, but the parameter $|L|$ is set to 50. The improvements of Pincer-Search begin to increase. When the minimum support is 18%, our algorithm runs about 2.3 times faster than the *Apriori* algorithm.

The non-monotone property of the maximum frequent set, considered in Section 4.1, reflects on this experiment. When the minimum support is 12%, both

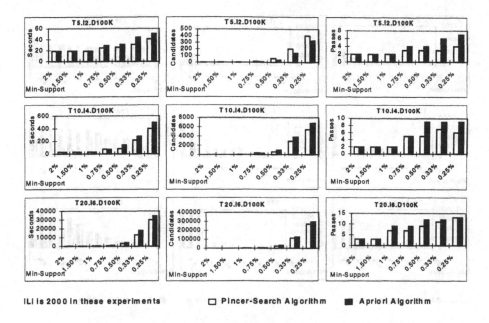

ILI is 2000 in these experiments   □ Pincer-Search Algorithm   ■ Apriori Algorithm

Fig. 3. Relative time, candidates, and passes (scattered distribution)

the Apriori and the Pincer-Search algorithms took 8 passes to discover the maximum frequent set. But, when the minimum support decreases to 11%, the maximal frequent itemsets become longer. This forced the Apriori algorithm to take more passes (9 passes) and consider more candidates to discover the maximum frequent set. In contrast, MFCS allowed our algorithm to reach the maximal frequent itemsets faster. Pincer-Search took only 4 passes and considered fewer candidates to discover all maximal frequent itemsets.

We further increased the average size of the frequent itemsets in the next two experiments. The average size of the maximal frequent itemsets was increased to 10 in the second experiment and database T20.I10.D100K was used. The best case, in this experiment, is when the minimum support is 6%. Pincer-Search ran approximately 23 times faster than the Apriori algorithm. This improvement mainly came from the early discovery of maximal frequent itemsets which contain up to 16 items. Their subsets were not generated and counted in our algorithm. As shown in this experiment, the reduction of the number of candidates can significantly decrease both I/O time and CPU time.

The last experiment ran on database T20.I15.D100K. As shown in the last row of Fig. 4, Pincer-Search took as few as 3 passes to discover all maximal frequent itemsets which contain as many as 17 items. This experiment shows improvements of more than 2 orders of magnitude when the minimum supports are 6% and 7%. One can expect even greater improvements when the average size of the maximal frequent itemsets is further increased.

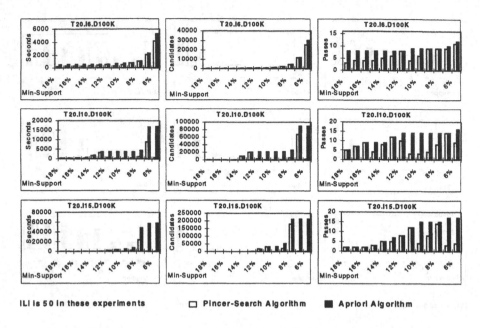

Fig. 4. Relative time, candidates, and passes (concentrated distribution)

5 Related Work

Reading the database repeatedly can be very time consuming. *Partition* [16] and *Sampling* [18] proposed effective ways to reduce the I/O time. However, they are still inefficient when the maximal frequent itemsets are long. The Pincer-Search algorithm presents a new approach that can reduce both I/O and CPU time.

DIC is an interesting algorithm relying on combining variable length candidates in a single pass [4].

A randomized algorithm for discovering the maximum frequent set was presented by Gunopulos *et al.* [6]. We present a deterministic algorithm for solving this problem.

Our work was inspired by the notion of *version space* in Mitchell's machine learning paper [12]. We found that if we treat a newly discovered frequent itemset as a new *positive training instance*, a newly discovered infrequent itemset as a new *negative training instance*, the candidate set as the *maximally specific generalization* (S), and the MFCS as the *maximally general generalization* (G), then we will be able to use a two-way approaching strategy to discover the maximum frequent set (*generalization* in his terminology) efficiently.

6 Acknowledgments

This research was partially supported by the National Science Foundation under grant number CCR-94-11590 and by the Intel Corporation. We thank Rakesh

Agrawal and Ramakrishnan Srikant for kindly providing us the synthetic data generation program. We thank Sridhar Ramaswamy for his very valuable comments and suggestions.

References

1. R. Agrawal, T. Imielinski, and A. Swami. Mining association rules between sets of items in large databases. In *Proc. SIGMOD*, May 1993.
2. R. Agrawal and R. Srikant. Fast algorithms for mining association rules in large databases. In *Proc. 20th VLDB*, Sept. 1994.
3. R. Agrawal and J. Shafer. Parallel mining of association rules. *IEEE Trans. on Knowledge and Data Engineering*, Jan. 1996.
4. S. Brin, R. Motwani, J. Ullman, and S. Tsur. Dynamic itemset counting and implication rules for market basket data. In *Proc. SIGMOD*, May 1997.
5. U. Fayyad, G. Piatetsky-Shapiro, P. Smyth, and R. Uthrusamy (Eds.). *Advances in Knowledge Discovery and Data Mining*. AAAI Press, Menlo Park, CA, 1996.
6. D. Gunopulos, H. Mannila, and S. Saluja. Discovering all most specific sentences by randomized algorithm. In *Proc. Intl. Conf. of Database Theory*, Jan. 1997.
7. J. Han and Y. Fu. Discovery of multiple-level association rules from large databases. In *Proc. 21st VLDB*, Sept. 1995.
8. D. Lin and Z. Kedem. Pincer-Search: A new algorithm for discovering the maximum frequent set. *Technical Report TR1997-742*, Dept. of Computer Science, New York University, Sept. 1997.
9. H. Mannila and H. Toivonen. Discovering frequent episodes in sequences. In *Proc. KDD'95*, Aug. 1995.
10. H. Mannila and H. Toivonen. Levelwise search and borders of theories in knowledge discovery. *Technical Report TR C-1997-8*, Dept. of Computer Science, U. of Helsinki, Jan. 1997.
11. H. Mannila, H. Toivonen, and A. Verkamo. Improved methods for finding association rules. In *Proc. AAAI Workshop on Knowledge Discovery*, July 1994.
12. T. Mitchell. Generalization as search. *Artificial Intelligence*, Vol. 18, 1982.
13. B. Özden, S. Ramaswamy. and A. Silberschatz. Cyclic Association Rules. In *Proc. 14th Intl. Conf. on Data Engineering*, 1998, to appear.
14. J. Park, M. Chen, and P. Yu. An effective hash-based algorithm for mining association rules. In *Proc. ACM-SIGMOD*, May 1995.
15. G. Piatetsky-Shapiro. Discovery, analysis, and presentation of strong rules. *Knowledge Discovery in Databases*, AAAI Press, 1991.
16. A. Sarasere, E. Omiecinsky, and S. Navathe. An efficient algorithm for mining association rules in large databases. In *Proc. 21st VLDB*, Sept. 1995.
17. R. Srikant and R. Agrawal. Mining generalized association rules. IBM Research Report RJ 9963, June 1995.
18. H. Toivonen. Sampling large databases for association rules. In *Proc. 22nd VLDB*, Sept. 1996.
19. M. J. Zaki, S. Parthasarathy, M. Ogihara, and W. Li. New algorithms for fast discovery of association rules. In *Proc. KDD'97*, Aug. 1997.

Multivariate and Multidimensional OLAP[*]

Shin-Chung Shao

Department of Information Management
NanHwa Management College, Fo-Kuan University
Da-Lin, Chia-Yih, Taiwan, ROC
scshao@acm.org

Abstract. The author presents a new relational approach to multivariate and multidimensional OLAP. In this approach, a multivariate aggregate view (MAV) is defined. MAV contains categorized univariate and multivariate aggregated data, which can be used to support many more advanced statistical methods not currently supported by any OLAP models. The author shows that MAV can be created, materialized, and manipulated using SQL commands. Thus, it can be implemented using commercial relational DBMS. A query rewrite algorithm is also presented to convert aggregate queries to base tables into those to MAV. Therefore, users need not to know the existence and definition of MAV in order to share materialized data. Incremental update of MAV created from single base table is also considered. The application of MAV to data mining is presented to illustrate the use of multivariate and multidimensional OLAP.

1. Introduction

The goal of on-line analytical processing (OLAP) and data warehousing is to enable enterprises to gain competitive advantages by providing fast and better support of data analyses on data stored in corporate databases [4]. One of the main approaches to OLAP is the data cube model [6]. A data cube, also referred to as a *summary table*, is defined by a set of dimension attributes, a set of measure attributes, and one or more aggregation types. Conceptually, it can be viewed as an aggregate query defined by SELECT D, *Aggr*(X) ... FROM <*table names*> GROUP BY D, where *Aggr*( ) denotes an aggregate function, X is a measure attribute, and D is the set of dimension attributes. Usually, data cubes are materialized to speed up aggregate query processing or to provide inputs to more advanced data analysis.

[6] proposes the cube operator to SQL which is a convenient way of creating 2^d cubes in a single command, where d is the number of dimensions. [1] and [20] propose efficient algorithms to implement the cube operator. [8] develops optimal policy on choosing cells to materialize when it is too expensive to materialize all cells. [7] introduces the generalized projections which capture aggregations, groupbys and

---

[*] This work was supported by the National Science Council, Republic of China, under Contract NSC 87-2416-H-145-001.

many others in a unified framework. Query rewrite rules are also developed to convert aggregate queries on base tables into queries on data cubes. [19] presents algorithms to answer to aggregate queries using materialized views. Issues on maintaining consistency between base tables and materialized data cubes have been addressed in [2], [12], [15].

When users want to perform data analyses, e.g., analysis of variance, linear regression, partial correlation analysis, that are more advanced than simple tabulation of summary data, they can retrieve summary data from data cubes, and input them into statistical packages, the so-called *macro data analyses*. In contrast, data analyses performed on source data are referred to as *micro data analyses*. In Section 2, we will show that the differences between results of a micro data analysis and that of a macro data analysis may be significant, which implies that directly performing data analysis on data cubes may lead to incorrect results.

In this paper, the author presents a new relational approach to OLAP so that a wide range of commonly used statistical methods can be supported in accurate as well as efficient fashion. In this approach, a new data construct, called multivariate aggregate view (MAV), is proposed. The major distinction between MAV and conventional data cubes is that we include the cross-product matrix $X'X$ in data cubes, where X denotes a matrix containing values of measure attributes, and X' denotes transpose of X. Since $X'X$ is a symmetric matrix, we use $((p^2 + p)/2)$ attributes to represent its triangular part, where p is the number of measure attributes. Thus the costs of maintaining $X'X$ is not significant. On the other hand, by providing $X'X$, most statistical methods can be supported as accurate as performing micro data analyses, and as efficient as performing macro data analyses.

This paper is organized as follows. In Section 2 the author will present a motivating example to illustrate the differences between micro data analysis and macro data analysis. The author will also show that by including $X'X$ in data cubes many more advanced statistical methods can be supported. Section 3 will introduce MAV, including its definition, creation, materialization, manipulation and maintenance in a relational database. In Section 4 the author will illustrate an application of MAV to support data mining, namely, *mining regression rules and regression trees*. Section 5 concludes this paper.

2. Motivating Example and Implications

Traditionally, performing analyses on large data sets follows an indirect manner. Summaries or indices, i.e., macro data, such as Dow-Jones, Standard & Poor 500 and national census statistics, are first derived from source data and published or stored in public media such as newspapers, journals, CD-ROMs, or more recently, data cubes. Analysts then collect macro data from these media and perform further analyses, e.g., correlation analysis, linear regression, and time series analysis.

In Section 2.1, the author will show that performing linear regression following the macro data analysis approach may lead to inaccurate results. The author also show in Section 2.2 that by including $X'X$ in data cubes many more advanced statistical methods can be supported in the fashion like performing macro data analysis while their results can be as accurate as performing micro data analyses. Section 2.3 will show the distributive property of $X'X$ so that $X'X$ in different cells can be added up, and incremental update of $X'X$ can be supported.

2.1 Motivating Example

Suppose the national census database maintains a table containing state residence, personal incomes and savings as shown in Table 1. Table 2 is a summary table containing average incomes and average savings categorized by states, which are derived from data in Table 1. Performing linear regression analysis of savings on incomes using the micro data and macro data in Table 1 and Table 2, yield, respectively:

$$L_1 : S_{1i} = -504.5 + 0.13 I_{1i} \text{ (Equation of fitted line using micro data in Table 1)}$$

$$L_2 : S_{2j} = 992.7 + 0.09 I_{2j} \text{ (Equation of fitted line using macro data in Table 2)}$$

where S_{1i} and I_{1i} , $i = 1, 2, ..., 10$, denote individual savings and incomes listed in Table 1, and S_{2j} and I_{2j} , $j = 1, 2, 3$, denote average savings and incomes listed in Table 2, respectively. The plots of data points and fitted lines are shown in Figure 1.

It is obvious that the difference between L_1 and L_2 is significant. Therefore, performing linear regression on macro data stored in summary tables (data cubes) may lead to inaccurate results. That is, in performing macro data analyses, we are implicitly trading accuracy for efficiency.

To perform a multiple linear regression, the unbiased least squares estimator of the regression coefficients β in regression equation: $Y = X\beta + \varepsilon$ can be derived using the following formulae:

$$\hat{\beta} = (X'X)^{-1}(X'Y)$$

where X is an $(n \times p)$ matrix containing p explanatory variables and Y is an $(n \times 1)$ column vector denoting response variable. Notice that the order of $X'X$ and $X'Y$ are given by $(p \times p)$ and $(p \times 1)$, respectively, regardless how large n is. Therefore, if we maintain $X'X$ and $X'Y$ in data cubes, we may derive estimate of β without referring to X and Y. Therefore, we may support linear regression in a manner as accurate as performing micro data analysis and as efficient as performing macro data analysis[1].

---

[1] Other statistics relevant to linear regression, e.g., R-squared, adjusted R-squared, variance of error terms, can also be derived from $X'X$ and $X'Y$, without referring to the very large X and Y. For computing formulas of these statistics, see [10], [13].

State	Income	Saving	State	Income	Saving
CA	21,000	1,400	TN	14,000	1,500
CA	28,000	3,000	TN	19,000	1,800
CA	32,500	3,150	TN	31,000	3,100
CA	41,000	4,200	WY	21,000	2,400
CA	54,000	6,500	WY	32,000	6,500

Table 1. Source Census Data

State	Avg(Income)	Avg(Saving)
CA	35,300	3,650
TN	21,333	2,133
WY	26,500	4,450

Table 2. Summary Table of Census Data

Plots of Data Points and Fitted Lines

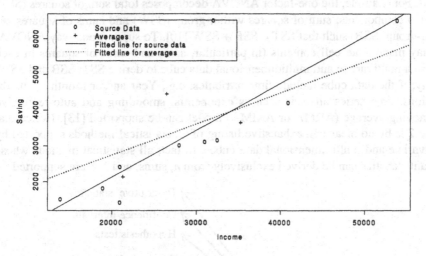

Fig. 1: Plots of Data Points and Fitted Lines

2.2 Supporting More Statistical Methods

The advantages of maintaining the cross-product matrix in data cubes can be further achieved by exploiting the derivation relationships among statistical methods, as illustrated in Figure 2. A data object O_1 is said to *be derivable from* another data object O_2, if $O_1 = f(O_2)$, where $f(\ )$ denotes a function. In Figure 2, we use arcs to represent derivation relationships. It is obvious that n (count), sums of each variable in X, and $X'X$ are derivable from X. Since $X'X$ contains sum of squares in its diagonal elements, statistics relevant to descriptive statistics (average, variance, standard deviation and standard error), estimation of confidence intervals, and hypothesis tests (z tests, t tests, and F tests) can be derived. Moreover, relevant statistics in correlation analysis (correlation matrix), partial correlation analysis, canonical correlation analysis, principal component analysis, and factor analysis can be derived from $X'X$ [3], [10]. Therefore, many univariate and multivariate statistical methods are supported.

Now we consider the multidimensionality of micro data. Let D and X denote the set of categorical (dimension) attributes and the set of numeric-valued (measure) attributes defined in a source table, respectively, and let $Aggr()$ denote a set of aggregate functions used to derive count, sums and cross-product matrix from X. The query SELECT D, $Aggr$(X) GROUP BY D results in a d-dimensional multivariate data cube. Each row contains a set of univariate and multivariate aggregated data, which can be used to support univariate and multivariate statistical methods illustrated in Figure 2. Furthermore, since the data cube is multidimensional, categorical data analyses such as cross-tabulation analysis, analysis of variance (ANOVA), multivariate analysis of variance (MANOVA), χ^2 test of independence, can also be supported. For example, the one-factor ANOVA decomposes total sum of squares (SST) into two components: sum of squares within-group (SSW) and sums of squares between-group (SSB) such that SST = SSB + SSW [10]. To support one-way ANOVA, we may manipulate cell contents (in particular, sums and sums of squares in each row) in a multivariate and multidimensional data cube to derive SST, SSB and SSW. Finally, if the data cube include time attributes, e.g., Year and/or Month, as its dimensions, time series analysis such as exponential smoothing and auto-regressive and moving-average (ARMA or ARIMA) model can be supported [13]. Notice that Figure 2 is by no means an exhaustive listing of all statistical methods supported by multivariate and multidimensional data cubes. In fact, all statistical methods whose relevant statistics can be derived exclusively from n, sums, and $X'X$ are supported.

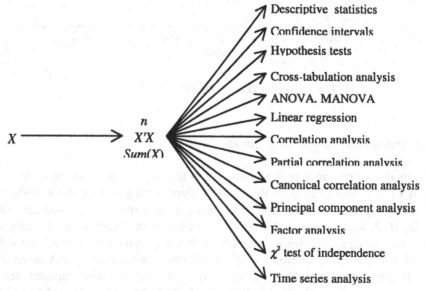

Fig.2: Derivation Relationships.

2.3 Distributive Property of Cross-product Matrix

We consider a nice property, the *distributive property*, of aggregate functions. An aggregate function $f(\ )$ is said to be distributive if $f(X) = f(X_1) + f(X_2) + ... + f(X_m)$, where $X = [X_1' \mid X_2' \mid ... \mid X_m']$, i.e., X_1, X_2, ... X_m vertically partition X. [7] shows that aggregate functions such as count and sum are distributive so that aggregated data in different cells can be added up, and incremental update of data cubes can be supported.

Recall that $X'X$ contains sums of squares as its diagonal elements and sums of cross-products as its off-diagonal elements, it is easy to see that:

$$\sum x_i^2 = \sum x_{1i}^2 + \sum x_{2i}^2 + \cdots + \sum x_{mi}^2$$

$$\sum x_i.y_i = \sum x_{1i}y_{1i} + \sum x_{2i}y_{2i} + \cdots + \sum x_{mi}y_{mi}$$

where x_i and y_i denote the i-th row of different columns in X, and x_{ji} and y_{ji}, $j = 1$, 2, ..., m, denote the i-th row of different columns in the submatrix X_j. From the above formulas, it follows that the cross-product matrix $X'X$ is also distributive, and thus combining $X'X$ in different rows and incremental update of $X'X$ are also supported. For example, if we have maintained $X'X$ for incomes and savings categorized by states, i.e., each row contains an $X'X$ for a given state. Then to derive the $X'X$ for *all* states, we can add up (matrix addition) the $X'X$ in all rows. The distributive property of $X'X$ has important implications to manipulation and maintenance of multivariate and multidimensional data cubes, as will be seen in Section 3.

3. Multivariate Aggregate Views

The purpose of this section is to show how to represent, create, manipulate, and maintain multivariate and multidimensional data cubes in a relational database. We will represent a multivariate and multidimensional data cube as a materialized multivariate aggregate view (MAV), and show how to create, retrieve, and update MAV using SQL commands and triggers.

3.1 Definition and Representation of MAV

An MAV is defined by a quadruple: MAV = <T, D, X, A>. T denotes a base table or a derived table (a view) containing micro data, D is a set of dimension attributes, X is a set of p numeric-valued measure attributes, and A is a composite data object containing aggregated data. Let X denote the micro data matrix contained in T, i.e., $X = \pi_x(t)$, where π denotes the generalized (duplicates allowed) project operator, and t is an instance of T. D partitions X in such a way that $G_D(\pi_x(t))$, where G denotes the group-by operator with D as operand. Thus, X is partitioned into $(m_1 \times m_2 \cdots \times m_d)$ submatrices, where d is the number of dimension attributes and m_k, $k = 1, ..., d$, is the number of distinct values in $D_t \in D$. For each submatrix X_t, a set of aggregated data, denoted by A_t, is derived by:

$$A_t = \{\text{Count}(x_i), \text{Sum}(x_i), \text{SS}(x_i), \text{SCP}(x_i, x_j) \mid x_i \in X_t, x_j \in X_t, x_i \neq x_j\}$$

where x_i and x_j are two distinct columns in X_t, $\text{SS}(x_i)$ and $\text{SCP}(x_i, x_j)$ denote sum of squares of x_i and sum of cross-products of x_i and x_j, respectively. The collection of all A_t makes up A. That is, A contains $(m_1 \times m_2 \dots \times m_d)$ component objects, each containing a count, p summations, and a cross-product matrix derived from a partitioned submatrix. The collection of $\text{SS}(\ )$ forms the diagonal elements of $X'X$ and the collection of $\text{SCP}(\ )$ forms the off-diagonal elements of $X'X$.

MAV can be represented, created and materialized in a relational database by an SQL command:

```
SELECT D, Count(*), Sum(X₁), …, Sum(X₁ * X₁), …, Sum(X₁ * X₂), …
INTO <MAV Name>
FROM T
GROUP BY D
```

The number of attributes in an MAV table is given by $d + 1 + p + (p^2 + p) / 2$, where the first d attributes are for dimension attributes, the next one is for Count(*), the next p attributes following Count(*) are for $\text{Sum}(X_i)$, and the rest are for sums of squares and sums of cross-products. To support query rewriting (see Section 3.2), we set restrictions on naming convention. We use MAV_T as the name of the MAV created from T. For dimension attributes, we use the same names as they are defined in T. For aggregated attributes, we use _Count, Sum_X$_i$, SS_X$_i$, and SCP_X$_i$_X$_j$ to denote Count(*), $\text{Sum}(X_i)$, $\text{SS}(X_i)$ and $\text{SCP}(X_i\_X_j)$, respectively. We assume that X_i and X_j are sorted by alphabetic order in SCP.

Example 1: Suppose the national census database defines a table Census = <Year, State, Sex, Income, Saving>. Let D = {Year, State, Sex} and X = {Income, Saving}, then MAV_Census can be created as:

```
SELECT Year, State, Sex, Count(*) as _Count, Sum(Income) as
       Sum_Income, Sum(Saving) as Sum_Saving, Sum(Income ^
       2) as SS_Income, Sum(Saving ^ 2) as SS_Saving,
       Sum(Income * Saving) as SCP_Income_Saving
INTO MAV_Census
FROM Census
GROUP BY Year, State, Sex
```

Assuming that Census contains data spanning fifty years in fifty states, then MAV_Census contains 9 attributes and $(50 \times 50 \times 2)$ records. Since insertions and deletions to MAV tables rarely happen, to speed up query processing we may create index on each of these dimensional attributes.

3.2 Manipulation of MAV

Since MAVs are represented as tables in a relational database, we may issue SQL queries to manipulate their contents. In particular, we consider queries having the following syntax:

```
SELECT [D ,] Sum(A_i), ...
FROM MAV_T
[WHERE <Predicates on D>]
[GROUP BY D]
[HAVING <Predicates on Sum(A_i)>]
```

where $D' \subset D$ and A_i denotes an aggregated attribute in MAV_T. Notice that we use, by distributive property, Sum( ) to aggregate values of aggregated attributes.

Example 2: The yearly average incomes and savings of all Californians from 1960 to 1990 (a bivariate time series), and the $X'X$ of incomes and savings of all states in 1990 can be derived from MAV_Census, respectively, by the following two queries:

```
SELECT Year, Sum(Sum_Income) / Sum(_Count),
    Sum(Sum_Saving) / Sum(_Count)
FROM MAV_Census
WHERE State = "CA" and Year Between 1960 and 1990
GROUP BY Year

SELECT Sum(SS_Income), Sum(SS_Saving), Sum(SCP_Income_Saving)
FROM MAV_Census
WHERE Year = 1990
```

In a multi-user and very large database environment, users may not know the existences and definitions of all data cubes. Therefore, casual (valid) users may directly issue time consuming aggregate queries to base tables. To avoid this problem, an efficient query rewrite algorithm is presented below, which converts aggregate queries to T into those to MAV_T.

Let T denote a base table, MAV_T be an MAV defined over T with dimension attribute set D and measure attribute set X. Consider an aggregate query to T, denoted by Q(T), having the syntax:

```
SELECT [D'], Aggr(Y), ...
FROM T
[WHERE <Predicate on D>]
[GROUP BY D']
[Having <Predicate on Aggr(Y)>
```

where $D' \subset D$, $Y \subset X$, Aggr $\in$ {Count, Sum, Avg, SS, SCP}. Notice that we introduce two additional aggregate operators SS (a unary operator) and SCP (a binary operator) to SQL to represent sum of squares and sum of cross-products, respectively. It can be shown that there exists an aggregate query to MAV_T, denoted by Q(MAV_T), such that Q(T) is equivalent to Q(MAV_T) in the sense that they produce the same results when evaluating against any instance of T. In particular, Q(MAV_T) can be constructed using the following query rewrite algorithm.

```
Query rewrite algorithm:
Input: Q(T) such that D'⊂D, Y⊂X, and Aggr∈{Count,Sum,Avg,SS,SCP}
{
    For each Aggr(Y) in the SELECT and in the HAVING clause {
        if Aggr ∈ {Count, Sum, SS}
            replace Aggr(Y) by Sum(Aggr_Y)
        else if Aggr = Avg
            replace Avg(Y) by (Sum(Sum_Y) / Sum(_Count))
        else replace SCP(Y1, Y2) by Sum(SCP_Y1_Y2)
    }
    replace T by MAV_T in the FROM clause
} /* the WHERE clause and the GROUP BY clause remain unchanged */
```

Example 3: The first query below can be converted into the second query below.

```
SELECT Year, Avg(Income), Avg(Saving), SS(Income)
FROM Census
WHERE State = "CA" and Year Between 1960 and 1990
GROUP BY Year
HAVING Avg(Income) >= 10000

SELECT Year, (Sum(Sum_Income) / Sum(_Count)),
    (Sum(Sum_Saving) / Sum(_Count)), Sum(SS_Income)
FROM MAV_Census
WHERE State = "CA" and Year Between 1960 and 1990
GROUP BY Year
HAVING (Sum(Sum_Income) / Sum(_Count)) >= 10000
```

3.3 Maintenance of MAV

When source data contained in T have been modified, MAV_T must be updated to maintain consistency between source data and aggregated data. In the context of very large databases, aggregated data are often updated using incremental update mechanisms. Incremental update refers to updating derived data using only modifications made to its source data. This subsection shows how to incrementally update MAV_T using triggers and stored procedures.

Let X_{old} and X_{new} denote instances of a dynamic data set X evaluated at times t_1 and t_2, $t_2 > t_1$, respectively, $X_{inserted}$ and $X_{deleted}$ denote rows inserted into, and deleted from X during (t_1, t_2). By distributive property of aggregate functions, $Aggr(X_{new}) = Aggr(X_{old}) + Aggr(X_{inserted}) - Aggr(X_{deleted})$, where $Aggr \in \{Count, Sum, SS, SCP\}$.

Incremental update of MAV_T can be implemented as a two-phase process. In the first phase, records inserted into and deleted from T are maintained in temporary tables in the course of database operations. When MAV_T is to be updated the second phase updating MAV is invoked. Let T_inserted and T_deleted be two temporary tables holding records inserted into, and deleted from T during two consecutive updates. Then the first phase can be implemented as the following trigger:

(1) ```
create trigger insert_T
on T
for insert
as
insert into T_inserted select * from inserted
```

(2)  ```
create trigger delete_T
on T
for delete
as
insert into T_deleted select * from deleted
```

(3) ```
create trigger update_T
on T
for update
as
insert into T_inserted select * from inserted
insert into T_deleted select * from deleted
```

where inserted and deleted denote records inserted into, and deleted from T in an insertion/deletion/update transaction. When the second phase, i.e., updating MAV_T, is invoked, MAV_T can be updated using the following batch of commands:

```
/* Block 1 */
  select * into tempMAV from MAV_Census
  union all
  (select year, state, sex, count(*) _count,
    sum(income) sum_income, sum(saving) sum_saving,
    sum(income * income) SS_income,
    sum(saving*saving) SS_saving,
    sum(income*saving) SCP_income_saving
  from insert_census
  group by year, state, sex)
  union all
  (select year, state, sex, -count(*) _count,
    - sum(income) sum_income,
    -sum(saving) sum_saving,
    -sum(income*income) SS_income,
    -sum(saving*saving) SS_saving,
    -sum(income*saving) SCP_income_saving
  from delete_census
  group by year, state, sex)

/* Block 2 */
  select year, state, sex, sum(_count) _count,
    sum(sum_income) sum_income,
    sum(sum_saving) sum_saving,
    sum(SS_income) SS_income,
    sum(SS_saving) SS_saving,
    sum(SCP_income_saving) SCP_income_saving
```
```

```
  into temp2
  from tempMAV
  group by year, state, sex

/* Block 3 */
  delete MAV_census
  insert MAV_census select * from temp2
  drop table temp2
  drop table tempMAV
  delete delete_census
  delete insert_censusinsert into temp
```

In Block 1, three MAV instances, the non-updated MAV_T, MAV created from T_inserted, and MAV created from T_deleted, are unioned (duplicates allowed). Notice that all aggregated attributes in MAV created from deleted_T are prefixed by a minus sign. In Block 2 we take summation of values of aggregated attributes in the unioned MAV table. In Block 3 all temporary tables generated in the update process is removed.

4. Application of MAV to Support Data Mining

The application of MAV to support data mining, also referred to as knowledge discovery in databases (KDD) [5], is presented in this section. In particular, we consider the support of *mining regression rules and regression trees* [18]. A regression rule can be represented as: $Pred(D) \rightarrow Y = X\beta$, where D denotes a set of categorical variables, i.e., dimension attributes, $Pred(D)$ denotes a conjunctive predicate over D, and $Y = X\beta$ is a regression equation. The regression equation is conditioned on a conjunctive predicate defined over D. Regression rules are useful to represent relationships hidden in mixtures of categorical data and numeric data, while other kinds of rules, e.g., classification rules, and association rules [5], deal mainly with categorical data. In the national census database example, regression rules can be regression equations of saving on income, conditioning on year, state, and sex. That is, we want to mine rules like If (year between 1950 and 1955) and (state = "CA") and (sex = "Male") Then (Saving = $a + b$ * Income).

In general, there may exist a set of such regression rules. They can be presented as a tree graph, called the regression tree, to assist understanding, interpreting, and applying these rules. In a regression tree, each non-leaf node represents a dimension attribute and each edge represents a distinct value in the domain of that attribute. Each leaf node links to a regression equation. A path from the root node to a leaf node specifies a regression rule. Figure 3 is an example of the regression tree mined from our national census database example. In Figure 3, the left-most path specifies the rule: If (Sex = "Female") and (State = "AK") and (Year = 1950) Then (Saving = -3122 + 0.42 * Income). Notice that we also include "ALL" as an edge of each node to represent all values (including missing values) of that attribute. Therefore, the right-most path denotes the rule given by: (unconditioned) Saving = -1950 + 0.40 *

Income, which is equivalent to the results of applying linear regression on all income and saving data in the census table.

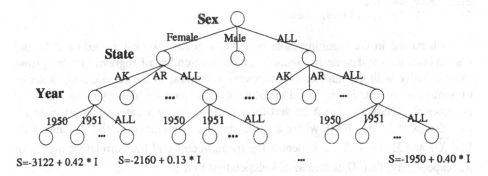

Fig. 3: An Example of Regression Tree

The command syntax for mining regression rules from data stored in a relational database is:

```
SELECT D, Y, X
FROM table name
[WHERE conditions on D]
MINE REGRESSION RULE Y ~ X
WITH CONFIDENCE c
GROUP BY D
```

where c denotes a threshold used to filter out those insignificant rules. A regression equation with measure of goodness-of-fit r, e.g., adjusted R-squared, is said to be significant if $r \geq c$, otherwise, it is said to be insignificant. Notice that the SELECT clause, the FROM clause, the WHERE clause, and the GROUP BY clause are similar to those in SQL syntax. In fact, we will use these clauses to construct queries to MAV. As an example, the following command mines the regression rules/tree illustrated in Figure 3:

```
SELECT Year, State, Sex, Income, Saving
FROM Census
MINE REGRESSION RULE Saving ~ Income
WITH CONFIDENCE 0.7
GROUP BY Year, State, Sex
```

The process of mining regression rules/trees can be divided into three stages: aggregated data derivation, search space reduction, and estimation. MAV provides necessary and sufficient data for the last two steps. In the first stage the command is converted into an aggregate query to MAV_Census. This can be done by an obvious generalization of the query rewrite algorithm presented in Section 3.2. Due to space limitation, we do not show the modified query rewrite algorithm. The above command can be converted into:

```
SELECT Year, State, Sex, Sum(_Count),
    Sum(Sum_Income), Sum(Sum_Saving),
    Sum(SS_Income), Sum(SS_Saving), Sum(SCP_Income_Saving)
FROM MAV_Census
GROUP BY Year, State, Sex
```

Each record in the resulting table contains a count, two sums, and an $X'X$, and corresponds to a leaf node in Figure 3. Since the number of regression rules grows exponentially with the number of dimension attributes, in the second stage a series of homogeneity tests is conducted to reduce search space by identifying *independent* categorical variable(s). Let X be vertically partitioned by a categorical attribute D_i, i.e., $X = [X_1' \mid X_2 ' \mid ... \mid X_k']$, where k is the number of elements in the domain of D_i. Let $\overline{X}_j$ and Σ_j, $j = 1, 2, ..., k$, denote the mean vector and the correlation matrix of X_j, respectively, then D_i is said to be independent to X if:

$$\overline{X}_1 = \overline{X}_2 = \cdots = \overline{X}_k \text{, and}$$

$$\Sigma_1 = \Sigma_2 = \cdots = \Sigma_k$$

Under the normality assumption, if D_i is independent to X, then we may remove all nodes of D_i from the regression tree, thus the regression tree is shrunken and the number of regression rules to be estimated in the third stage may be significantly reduced. The test of independent categorical attribute can be done by homogeneity tests, which require count, sums, and $X'X$ as inputs. Therefore, the resulting table of the above aggregate query to MAV_Census can provide sufficient information to conduct homogeneity tests. In the third stage regression equations are estimated by applying the formulae illustrated in Section 2.1 to each record in the resulting table.

5. Conclusion

In this paper the author proposed a new approach to multivariate and multidimensional OLAP to support more advanced data analyses. An MAV contains not only many univariate summary tables of counts, sums (and averages), but also an $X'X$ in each row. In this fashion, all statistical methods using sums of squares and sums of cross-products can be supported in a manner which is as accurate as performing a micro data analysis, and as efficient as performing a macro data analysis. Moreover, by exploiting the query rewrite algorithm, users can directly issue aggregate queries to base tables. These queries can be converted into those to corresponding MAV. Therefore, users don't need to comprehend the definitions of all existing summary tables in order to use them. Incremental update of MAV is also sketched to maintain consistency between base data and derived data. Thus, MAV provides an ideal bridge linking very large database and advanced data analyses.

A series of related research projects is being conducted. This includes (1) the assessment of differences (in terms of error rates) between micro and macro data analyses, (2) the application of MAV to real world data and its performance evaluation, (3) the support of scientific computing, e.g., singular value decomposition, eigenvalues and eigenvectors, using MAV [11].

References

1. Agarwal, S., R. Agrawal, P. M. Deshpande, A. Gupta, J. F. Naughton, R. Ramakrishnan and S. Sarawagi: *On the Computation of Multidimensional Aggregates*, in Proc. Of the 22nd VLDB Conference, Mumbai, India, 1996, 506-521.
2. Agrawal, D., A. El Abbadi, A. Singh and T. Yurek: *Efficient View Maintenance Warehouses*, In Proc. Of the 1997 ACM SIGMOD International Conference on Management of Data, Tucson, Arizona, USA, May 1997, 117-127.
3. Anderson, T.W. : *An Introduction to Multivariate Statistical Analysis*, Second Edition, New York, Wiley, 1984.
4. Surajit Chaudhuri and Umeshwar Dayal. *Data Warehousing and OLAP for Decision Support*. In Proc. Of the 1997 ACM SIGMOD International Conference on Management of Data, Tucson, Arizona, USA, May 1997, 507-508.
5. U. Fayyad, G.P. Shapiro, P. Smyth and R. Uthurusamy (editors): *Advances in Knowledge Discovery and Data Mining*, AAAI Press/The MIT Press, 1996.
6. J. Gray, A. Bosworth, A. Layman, and H. Pirahesh. Data Cube: *A relational aggregation operator generalizing group-by, cross-tab, and sub-total*, In Proc. Of the twelve IEEE International Conference on Data Engineering, New Orleans, LA, Feb. 1996, 152-159.
7. A. Gupta, V. Harinarayan and D. Quass: *Aggregate-Query Processing in Data Warehousing*, in Proc. Of the 21st VLDB Conference, Zurich, Switzerland, 1995, 358-369.
8. V. Harinarayan, A. Rajaraman and J. Ullman: *Implementing Data Cubes Efficiently*, In Proc. Of the 1996 ACM SIGMOD International Conference on Management of Data, Montreal, Canada, June 1996, 205-216.
9. C. T. Ho, R. Agrawal, N. Megiddo and R. Srikant: *Range Queries in OLAP Data Cubes*, In Proc. Of the 1997 ACM SIGMOD International Conference on Management of Data, Tucson, Arizona, USA, May 1997, 73-88.
10. J. D. Jobson: *Applied Multivariate Data Analysis, Vol II: Categorical and Multivariate Methods*, Springer-Verlag, 1992.
11. F. Korn, H.V. Jagadish, and C. Faloutsos: *Efficiently Supporting Ad Hoc Queries in Large Datasets of Time Sequences*, In Proc. Of the 1997 ACM SIGMOD International Conference on Management of Data, Tucson, Arizona, USA, May 1997, 289-300.
12. I. S. Mumick, D. Quass and B. S. Mumick: *Maintenance of Data Cubes and Summary Tables in a Warehouse*, In Proc. Of the 1997 ACM SIGMOD International Conference on Management of Data, Tucson, Arizona, USA, May 1997, 100-111.
13. R. S. Pindyck and D. L. Rubinfeld: *Econometric Models and Economic Forecasts*, Third Edition, McGraw-Hill Inc., 1991.
14. D. Quass and J. Widom: *On-Line Warehouse View Maintenance*, in In Proc. Of the 1997 ACM SIGMOD International Conference on Management of Data, Tucson, Arizona, USA, May 1997, 393-404.
15. N. Roussopoulos, Y. Kotidis and Mema Roussopoulos: *Cubtree: Organization of and Bulk Incremental Updates on the Data Cube*, In Proc. Of the 1997 ACM SIGMOD International Conference on Management of Data, Tucson, Arizona, USA, May 1997, 89-99.

16. A. Segev and S. C. Shao: *Statistical Computing in A Database Environment*, Technical Report 35436, Lawrence Berkeley Lab., Berkeley, CA 94720, January 1994.

17. S. C. Shao: *Statistical Computing in the Database Environment: A New Paradigm*, Ph.D Dissertation, Haas School of Business, Univ. of California at Berkeley, 1994.

18. B.Y Sher, S.C. Shao and W.S. Hsieh: *Mining Regression Rules and Regression Tree*, to appear in Proc. of PAKDD-98, Lecture Notes in Artificial Intelligence, Springer-Verlag, April 1998.

19. D. Srivastava, S. Dar, H. V. Jagadish and A. Y. Levy: *Answering Queries with Aggregation Using Views*, in Proc. Of the 22nd VLDB Conference, Mumbai, India, 1996, 318-329.

20. Y. Zhao, P. Deshpande and J. F. Naughton: *An Array-Based Algorithm for Simultaneous Multidimensional Aggregates*, in Proc. Of the 1997 ACM SIGMOD International Conference on Management of Data, Tucson, Arizona, USA, May 1997, 159-170.

Incremental Generalization for Mining in a Data Warehousing Environment

Martin Ester, Rüdiger Wittmann

Institute for Computer Science, University of Munich
Oettingenstr. 67, D-80538 Muenchen, Germany
{ester | wittman}@informatik.uni-muenchen.de
http://www.dbs.informatik.uni-muenchen.de

Abstract. On a data warehouse, either manual analyses supported by appropriate visualization tools or (semi-) automatic data mining may be performed, e.g. clustering, classification and summarization. Attribute-oriented generalization is a common method for the task of summarization. Typically, in a data warehouse update operations are collected and applied to the data warehouse periodically. Then, all derived information has to be updated as well. Due to the very large size of the base relations, it is highly desirable to perform these updates incrementally. In this paper, we present algorithms for incremental attribute-oriented generalization with the conflicting goals of good efficiency and minimal overly generalization. The algorithms for incremental insertions and deletions are based on the materialization of a relation at an intermediate generalization level, i.e. the anchor relation. Our experiments demonstrate that incremental generalization can be performed efficiently at a low degree of overly generalization. Furthermore, an optimal cardinality for the sets of updates can be determined experimentally yielding the best efficiency.

Keywords: Data Mining, Data Warehouses, Generalization, Database Updates.

1 Introduction

Many companies have recognized the strategic importance of the knowledge hidden in their large databases and have built data warehouses. A *data warehouse* contains information collected from multiple data sources, integrated into a common repository and extended by summary information (such as aggregate views) for the purpose of analysis [MQM 97]. Often, a data warehouse - used for online analytical processing - is implemented as a collection of materialized views, i.e. a (possibly extended) copy of the operational data bases - used for online transaction processing [Huy 97].

On a data warehouse, either manual analyses supported by appropriate visualization tools or (semi) automatic data mining may be performed. *Data mining* has been defined as the application of data analysis and discovery algorithms that - under acceptable computational efficiency limitations - produce a particular enumeration of patterns over the data [FSS 96]. Several data mining tasks have been identified [FSS 96], e.g. clustering ([EKX 95], [EKSX 96]), classification [HF 96] and summarization ([AS 94], [HCC 93]). Typical results of data mining are as follows:

- clusters of items which are typically bought together by some class of customers (clustering in a sales transactions data warehouse)
- rules discriminating disease A from disease B (classification in a medical data warehouse)
- description of the typical WWW access patterns (summarization in the data warehouse of an internet provider).

In this paper, we assume the data warehouse to be implemented as a relational database which is a common approach.

Generalization is an important method for the task of summarization. *Attribute-oriented generalization* [HCC 93] of a relation is the process of replacing the attribute values by a more general value, one attribute at a time, until the relation fulfills some termination condition, e.g. the number of its tuples becomes less than a threshold. The reduction of the number of tuples enables effective and efficient manual analyses as well as automatic data mining on the generalized relations [HF 96].

Typically, a data warehouse is not updated immediately when insertions and deletions on the operational databases occur. Update operations are collected and applied to the data warehouse periodically, e.g. each night [MQM 97]. Then, all patterns derived from the warehouse by some data mining algorithm have to be updated as well. This update has to be efficient enough to be finished before the operation of the warehouse starts again, e.g. in the next morning. Due to the very large size of the base relations, it is highly desirable to perform these updates incrementally [Huy 97], e.g. to consider only the old generalized relations and the tuples to be inserted or deleted, instead of applying the generalization algorithm to the (very large) updated base relation.

The problem of incrementally updating mined patterns on changes of the database has just started to receive some attention. [CHNW 96] describes an efficient method for incrementally modifying a set of association rules [AS 94] mined from a database. In [HCC 93], the incremental update of generalized relations is discussed but no algorithms are presented. The goal of this paper is to propose algorithms for incremental attribute-oriented generalization and to evaluate their performance both, in terms of efficiency and effectivity.

The rest of the paper is organized as follows. Section 2 introduces the concepts of attribute-oriented generalization and presents a new algorithm. In section 3, we discuss the requirements for incremental generalization. Section 4 presents incremental algorithms for insertion and deletion to a relation with derived generalizations. In section 5, we report the results of our performance evaluation. Section 6 summarizes the contributions of this paper and discusses several issues for further research.

2. Attribute-Oriented Generalization

Attribute-oriented generalization [HCC 93] of a relation is the process of replacing the attribute values by a more general value, one attribute at a time, until the number of tuples of the relation becomes less than a specified threshold. The more general value is taken from a concept hierarchy which is typically available for most attributes in a data warehouse. In the following, we introduce some notions needed for a more formal specification.

Definition 1: card(R), d_i

Let R be a relation with attributes A_i, $1 \leq i \leq k$, $card(R)$ be the number of tuples of R and d_i be the number of different values of A_i in R.

Definition 2: $[A_{i1}, , , A_{im}], A_{ij}^{\ l}$

We denote the sequence of attributes selected for generalization (*attribute sequence* for short) by $[A_{i1}, , , A_{im}], A_{ij} \varepsilon \{A_1, \ldots, A_k\}$ and l *consecutive selections* of attribute A_{ij} by $A_{ij}^{\ l}$.

Definition 3: concept hierarchy, ANY, height

The *concept hierarchy* of A_i, which is not mandatory, is a balanced tree and is denoted by C_i. Its nodes represent the possible values (concepts) of A_i and its edges represent the is-a (superterm) relation between the concepts of the connected nodes.

The root of each concept hierarchy contains the special concept *ANY* which is a superterm of all other values (concepts).

Let the *height* of the leaves of a concept hierarchy be 0. The *height* of an interior node of a concept hierarchy is the height of its direct children plus 1.

Definition 4: base relation, generalized relation, fully generalized relation

Let R be a relation. We call R a *base relation* if all attribute values are from leaves of their respective concept hierarchy, i.e. if no generalization has been performed.

R is called a *generalized relation* if it has been derived from some base relation by performing one or more generalizations. Each generalized relation has an additional attribute *support* counting the number of tuples of the base relation subsumed by the generalized tuple.

We call R a *fully generalized relation w.r.t. T*, denoted by R_T, if $card(R) \leq T$.

Definition 5: generalization level

Let R be a relation and A_i, $1 \leq i \leq k$, be one of its attributes. The *generalization level of* A_i, denoted as g_i, is defined as the height of the values of A_i in their respective concept hierarchy. The *generalization level of R*, denoted as G_R, is defined as:.

$$G_R = \sum_{i=1}^{K} g_i$$

The basic algorithm presented in [HCC 93] is presented in figure 1. This algorithm has some drawbacks. Typically, after the first phase $card(R)$ is much larger than T and, in the worst case, even $card(R) = T^k$, i.e. the second phase is of primary importance. Furthermore, in [HCC 93] the strategy for attribute selection in the second phase is not specified. In practical applications, not only one but several threshold values T may be of interest. E.g., a value of 10 may be required for manual analysis by a manager, a value of 200 may be useful for analysis by some technical staff, and $T = 10.000$ may be appropriate to efficiently run a classification algorithm. Each of the T values requires an independent run of the generalization algorithm, since the selection of the next attribute depends on the value of T in the first phase, i.e. if $d_i < T$ then A_{i+1} is selected. E.g., the attribute sequences for $T = 10$ and $T = 20$ may be $[A_1^{\ l}]$ and $[A_1^{\ l-1}, A_2]$ resp. implying that the fully generalized relation for $T = 20$ cannot be used as input to create the fully generalized relation for $T = 10$.

These drawbacks are caused by the following features of the basic generalization algorithm: first, by the two phases of generalization and, second, by the depth first approach to attribute selection in the first phase. Therefore, we propose a modified generalization algorithm using a single phase and following a breadth first approach. In each

```
FOR each attribute Aᵢ DO
   calculate dᵢ;
   WHILE dᵢ > T DO
      IF Cᵢ available THEN
         FOR each tuple of R DO
            replace the value of Aᵢ by its predecessor in Cᵢ;
         END FOR;
         Sort R, eliminate redundant tuples, update support;
         calculate dᵢ;
      ELSE
         eliminate Aᵢ from R;
         Sort R, eliminate redundant tuples and update
         support;
      END IF;
   END WHILE;
END FOR first phase;
/* All attributes Aᵢ have at most T different values in R */
WHILE card(R) > T DO
   Select next Aᵢ according to some strategy;
   IF Cᵢ available THEN
      FOR each tuple of R DO
         replace the value of Aᵢ by its predecessor in Cᵢ;
      END FOR;
   ELSE
      eliminate Aᵢ from R;
   END IF;
   Sort R, eliminate redundant tuples and update support;
END WHILE second phase;
```

figure 1: Basic_Generalize(Relation R, Threshold T)

iteration, the attribute A_i with the maximum d_i value is selected for generalization. If this criterion yields several attributes then from these the A_i with minimum g_i is chosen. This strategy of selection yields a fully generalized relation with similar numbers of attribute values at similar conceptual levels for all remaining attributes.

Our algorithm called *Homogeneous_Generalize* takes a list of T values sorted in descending order as argument and is presented in figure 2. *Homogeneous_Generalize* obtains the fully generalized relations for multiple values of T in one run which is the contents of lemma 1. Consequently, the generalization for multiple T values can be performed as efficient as for a single T value.

Lemma 1

Algorithm Homogeneous_Generalize is *correct* for multiple values of T, i.e. the fully generalized relations for each element t of T_List are identical with the relation obtained when performing Homogeneous_Generalize with a single value of $T = t$.

Proof Idea: The attribute selection of Homogeneous_Generalize is independent of the T values.

```
WHILE card(R) > LAST(T_List) DO
    Select Aᵢ with maximum dᵢ;
    IF Aᵢ not unique THEN
        Select from those Aᵢ the one with minimum gᵢ;
        IF Aᵢ not unique THEN
            Select first of those Aᵢ in lexicographic order;
        END IF;
    END IF;
    IF Cᵢ available THEN
        FOR each tuple of R DO
            replace the value of Aᵢ by its father in Cᵢ;
        END FOR;
        calculate dᵢ;
        increment gᵢ;
    ELSE
        eliminate Aᵢ from R;
    END IF;
    Sort R, eliminate redundant tuples and update support;
    IF card(R) < NEXT(T_List) THEN
        store R as the result for T = NEXT(T_List)
    END IF;
END WHILE;
```

figure 2: Homogeneous_Generalize(Relation R, Thresholds T_List)

3. Requirements for Incremental Generalization

Updates of the base relation require updates of all derived relations. We call these updates of the generalized relations *incremental* if they do not require a new run of the generalization algorithm on the updated base relation but only on a generalized relation different from the base relation. In this section, we discuss the general requirements for an incremental generalization algorithm, i.e. efficiency, correctness and avoidance of overly generalization.

Clearly, the goal of incremental generalization is a significant gain in *effciency* vs. non-incremental generalization so that the derived relations can be updated during the time when the data warehouse is not used, e.g. during night.

We call an incremental generalization algorithm *correct* if the resulting fully generalized relation is identical to the result of applying the non-incremental generalization algorithm to the updated base relation.

The problem of overly generalization was informally introduced in [HCC 93] without presenting exact definitions and solutions. To define overly generalization, we introduce some notions.

Definition 6: overly generalized

A fully generalized relation R is called *overly generalized* w.r.t. some generalization algorithm, if its generalization level G_R is larger than the generalization level obtained when applying this generalization algorithm to the base relation of R.

Definition 7: unnecessary generalizations, overly generalization factor

Let G_{Rnew} be the generalization level of a fully generalized relation R obtained when applying a generalization algorithm to the updated base relation. Let G_{Rinc} be the generalization level of the fully generalized relation R obtained when applying the same generalization algorithm to an updated generalized relation different from the base relation. We define the *number of unnecessary generalizations* of R, denoted as NUG_R, as follows:

$$NUG_R = G_{Rinc} - G_{Rnew}$$

If $G_{Rnew} \neq 0$, then we define the *overly generalization factor* of R (denoted as OGF_R):

$$OGF_R = \frac{NUG_R}{G_{Rnew}} + 1$$

The overly generalization factor measures the relative number of unnecessary generalizations. If $NUG_R = 0$, then $OGF_R = 1$. The following very small example shows that, in general, after deletions from the base relation overly generalization cannot be avoided unless the generalization algorithm is applied to the whole updated base relation.

Example

We assume a base relation with attributes "sex" and "age" and the following tuples:

Sex	Age	Support
male	45	1
female	48	1
male	62	1

Let $T = 2$, $d_{Sex} = 2$, $d_{Age} = 3$. "Age" is the first attribute selected for generalization resulting in the following relation:

Sex	Age	Support
male	medium	1
female	medium	1
male	old	1

Now $d_{Sex} = d_{Age} = 2$ and $g_{Sex} < g_{Age} = 1$. "Sex" is the next attribute selected for generalization resulting in the fully generalized relation with $card(R) \leq T = 2$:

Sex	Age	Support
ANY	medium	2
ANY	old	1

Now, let the tuple (male,45,1) be deleted from the base relation.

A naive incremental algorithm proceeds as follows. First, the deleted tuple is generalized to the level of the fully generalized relation in order to determine which generalized tuple is afflicted by the deletion. In this example, it is the tuple (ANY, medium, 2). Second, the support of this tuple is decreased. Finally, the resulting relation is returned as the result of the incremental generalization:

Sex	Age	Support
ANY	medium	1
ANY	old	1

However, $NUG_R = 2$ for this relation since the updated base relation, depicted below, immediately fulfills the termination condition $card(R) \leq T = 2$:

Sex	Age	Support
female	48	1
male	62	1

Whereas in many data warehouses no deletions are performed, there are important cases where deletions are desirable:

- a data warehouse of an internet provider may contain a relation with the following schema keeping track of the accesses to the WWW pages of the provider:

Source URL	Destination URL	User	Day	Time
. . .	. . .	. . .	. . .	. . .

  Often, URL's are changed or deleted and analyses of the data warehouse should not consider these old URL's so that deletions will be performed for the tuples related to these URL's.

- imagine a protein database with a relation describing protein surface points with the following schema:

Protein Name	X	Y	Z	Electrostatic Potential	Hydrophobicity
. . .	.	. .	. .	. . .	. . .

  The protein data are obtained by complex analyses. The results of these analyses may be improved for a protein, e.g. using better equipment. Then, the tuples related to that protein have to be updated, i.e. they are first deleted and then reinserted with new attribute values.

Therefore, we have to deal with the problem of overly generalization. Clearly, if overly generalization occurs, the condition of correctness is violated as well. Thus, we have the following trade-off between correctness and overly generalization vs. efficiency:

- if we require strict correctness and no overly generalization then the generalization algorithm has to be applied to the updated base relation - which is very large - and is inefficient.

- if we do not care about overly generalization then we may run the generalization algorithm on the updated fully generalized relation - which is relatively small - and is very efficient.

In the following section, we present an approach to find a reasonable compromise between these conflicting requirements.

4. Incremental Generalization Algorithms

While the goal of efficiency requires to perform updates on the fully generalized relations, the goal of avoiding overly generalization requires to perform updates on the base relation. To find a reasonable compromise, we introduce the concept of anchor relations with a generalization level in between the base and the fully generalized relation (subsection 4.1). In subsections 4.2 and 4.3, incremental algorithms for insertions and deletions based on these anchor relations are presented.

4.1 Construction of the Anchor Relation

Our incremental approach to generalization is as follows:
  1.) insertions and deletions are performed on the anchor relation
  2.) the generalization algorithm is applied to the updated anchor relation.

Thus, the anchor relation is the relation used as input for incremental generalization. On one hand, the cardinality of the anchor relation should be significantly smaller than the cardinality of the base relation R. On the other hand, the cardinality of the anchor relation should be significantly larger than the cardinality of all fully generalized relations derived from R. Typically, the relevant thresholds T and, consequently, the cardinality of the fully generalized relations depend on the cardinality of the base relation, i.e. they are proportional to $card(R)$. Therefore, we specify the cardinality of the anchor relation as a certain fraction of the cardinality of the base relation. This fraction is a parameter (called anchor reduction factor) which can be set by the database administrator using his knowledge of the relevant generalization thresholds. In the following, we define the related notions.

Definition 8: anchor reduction factor, anchor threshold

Let ARF denote the *anchor reduction factor*. We define the *anchor threshold* for the base relation R, denoted by T_{Anc}, as

$$T_{Anc} = \frac{card(R)}{ARF}$$

The *anchor relation* of R, denoted as R_{Anc}, is the first generalization of R with $card(R_{Anc}) \leq T_{Anc}$.

4.2 Incremental Insertions

After insertions of tuples to the base relation R, a generalized relation derived from R may violate its threshold T, i.e. further generalization(s) are required. We assume that insertions are not performed tuple by tuple but that sets of tuples of considerable size are inserted at the same time. This approach is used in a data warehouse context: A data warehouse is not updated continously, but insertions and deletions of the base relations are collected and are applied to the data warehouse periodically, e.g. during the night. Then, all derived information, e.g. generalized relations derived from the warehouse, have to be updated as well before the operation of the warehouse starts again, e.g. in the next morning.

On insertion of a set of tuples to the base relation, these tuples are generalized to the generalization level of the anchor relation R_{Anc}. For all of these generalized tuples already present in R_{Anc}, the support of the existing tuple is incremented. If one of these generalized tuples is new in the anchor relation it is inserted with a support of 1. The generalization algorithm has to be applied to the updated anchor relation only if at least one new tuple was inserted to the anchor relation. In figure 3, the incremental insertion algorithm is presented.

```
FOR each t IN T_Set DO
    generalize t to the generalization level of R_Anc
        and store the resulting tuple in R';
end FOR;
Sort R', eliminate redundant tuples and update support;
new-start := FALSE;
FOR each t' IN R' DO
    IF NOT(t' IN R_Anc) THEN
        new-start := TRUE;
    END IF;
    insert t' into R_Anc;
END FOR;
Sort R_Anc, eliminate redundant tuples and update support;
IF new_start THEN
    Homogeneous_Generalize(R_Anc, Threshold_List);
ELSE
    FOR each t' IN R' DO
        FOR each threshold IN Threshold_List DO
            generalize t' to the generalization level of the fully
            generalized relation for threshold (R_thr) and increment
            support of the respective tuple in R_thr;
        END FOR each threshold;
    END FOR each t';
END IF new_start;
```

figure 3: Incremental_Insert(Relation R, Set_Of_Tuples T_Set)

4.3 Incremental Deletions

In section 3, we demonstrated that deletions of tuples from the base relation R may result in an overly generalization of a generalized relation derived from R which should be avoided as far as possible. As in the case of insertions, we assume that deletions are not performed tuple by tuple but that sets of tuples of considerable size are deleted at the same time.

On deletion of a set of tuples from the base relation, these tuples are generalized to the generalization level of the anchor relation R_{Anc}. For all of these generalized tuples, the support of the related tuple in R_{Anc} is decremented and if the support becomes 0 this tuple is deleted. The generalization algorithm has to be applied to the updated anchor relation only if at least one tuple was deleted from R_{Anc}. This application is due to the fact that a generalized relation derived from R_{Anc} may now have become overly generalized. Otherwise, if no tuple was deleted from R_{Anc} then no tuple will be deleted in a generalized relation derived from it since the support of tuples increases monotonically during generalization. Then, only the support of the related tuples in the fully generalized relations derived from R_{Anc} is decremented. In figure 4, the incremental deletion algorithm is presented:

```
FOR each t IN T_Set DO
   generalize t to the generalization level of R_Anc
      and store the resulting tuple in R';
end FOR;
Sort R', eliminate redundant tuples and update support;
new-start := FALSE;
FOR each t IN R_Anc DO
   decrement support of t by support of t IN R';
   IF remaining support of t = 0 THEN
      delete t from R_Anc;
      new-start := TRUE;
   END IF;
END FOR;
Sort R_Anc, eliminate redundant tuples and update support;
IF new_start THEN
   Homogeneous_Generalize(R_Anc, Threshold_List);
ELSE
   FOR each t' IN R' DO
      FOR each threshold IN Threshold_List DO
         generalize t' to the generalization level of the fully
         generalized relation for threshold (R_thr) and decrement
         support of the respective tuple in R_thr;
      END FOR each threshold;
   END FOR each t';
END IF new_start;
```

figure 4: Incremental_Delete(Relation R, Set_Of_Tuples T_Set)

5. Performance Evaluation

The proposed algorithms were implemented in C/Embedded SQL using ORACLE 7 on an HP 9000/735 workstation with HP-UX 9.01. In this section, we explain the design of the experiments (subsection 5.1) and present their results for incremental insertions (subsection 5.2) and deletions (subsection 5.3).

5.1 Design of the Experiments

We used real data from the protein database BIOWEPRO as test data. The goal of the BIOWEPRO project is to support protein-protein docking. A necessary condition for protein-protein docking is the complementarity of the interaction sites with respect to surface shape, electrostatic potential, hydrophobicity etc. The protein-protein docking database manages the 3D coordinates of the protein surface points as well as several geometric and physicochemical features for each point of the protein surface. The database is modeled as a relation with 9 attributes with a concept hierarchy each.

We chose a relation containing 112300 tuples, called the *source relation*, from which we derived several smaller relations by selecting a given percentage of all tuples. The tuples for the base relation were taken from the begin of the source relation and the tuples to be inserted were taken from the end. This was due to the fact that neighboring tuples in the relation are likely to represent neighboring points on the protein surface which have similar attribute values. Thus, the inserted tuples tend to have attribute values different from the existing tuples of the base relation implying a significant number of new tuples in the anchor relation.

Clearly, the performance results depend on a lot of parameters. We chose the following as *fixed parameters*:
- concept hierarchies
  The height of the concept hierarchies was 3 or 4.
- generalization threshold
  We set the generalization threshold to 50.

We chose the following as *variable parameters*: cardinality of the base relation, number of inserted tuples, number of deleted tuples and anchor reduction factor (*ARF*).

5.2 Results for Insertions

The efficiency of the incremental algorithms has to be compared with the efficiency of the non-incremental algorithm which is, therefore, evaluated first. Figure 5 presents the runtime of algorithm *Homogeneous_Generalize* depending on the cardinality of the base relation, i.e. *card(R)*. This figure confirms the expectation that the runtime is $O(n \log n)$ with $n = card(R)$ due to the dominating influence of the sorting step of the generalization algorithm [HCC 93]. Furthermore, figure 5 shows that the runtime is quite large even for relatively small relations.

The runtime of both, incremental insertions and deletions consists of two components:
- T_1 : runtime for generalizing the inserted / deleted tuples to the level of the anchor relation
- T_2 : runtime for updating (and possibly generalizing) the anchor relation

T_2 depends on the number of updates and on the cardinality of the anchor relation. Figure 6 shows the runtime for sets of incremental insertions on a base relation of 20.000 tuples depending on the number of new tuples for several *ARF's*. This runtime decreases significantly with increasing *ARF* (and decreasing cardinality of the anchor relation) and increases superlinearly with increasing number of inserted tuples.

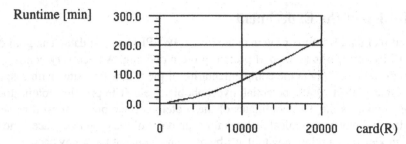

figure 5: Runtime of (non-incremental) algorithm Homogeneous_Generalize

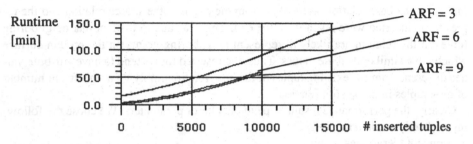

figure 6: Runtime of sets of incremental insertions for card(R) = 20000

In the following, we analyze the runtime for a single incremental insertion by calculating the average over all insertions. Figure 7 depicts the average runtime for one incremental insertion to a base relation of 20000 tuples depending on the total number of insertions with different anchor reduction factors.

Runtime of a single insertion [sec]

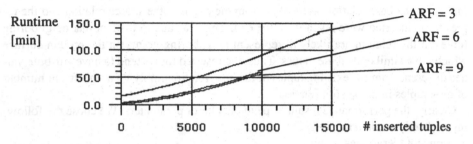

figure 7: Runtime of single incremental insertions for card(R) = 20000

We observe that the average runtime first decreases and then increases again. This is due to the following facts. The insertion of a single tuple (into the base relation) which creates a new tuple in the anchor relation causes the application of the generalization algorithm to the anchor relation. Therefore, the incremental insertion algorithm has a considerable minimum runtime which increases only slightly if several new tuples are created in the anchor relation. This minimum runtime can be regarded as an additive constant and its influence decreases with increasing size of the set of insertions because the ratio of the runtime (of the incremental insertion algorithm) and the number of inserted tuples decreases. On the other hand, the runtime of attribute-oriented generalization is $O(n \log n)$ for a relation of n tuples, i.e. superlinear, implying that the above ratio, i.e. the runtime of a single insertion, increases with increasing number of inserted tuples.

Due to these two conflicting trends, there is an *optimal cardinality* of the sets of insertions, i.e. a cardinality minimizing the ratio of of the runtime of the incremental insertion algorithm and the number of inserted tuples. Our experimental evaluation indicates that the minimum runtime and, consequently, the optimal cardinality increases with increasing cardinality of the anchor relation.

Thus, the set of all insertions should be split into subsets of the optimal cardinality to speed up the overall runtime. Figure 8 compares the runtime for insertions to a base relation R with $card(R)=5000$ and $ARF=3$ for the three different approaches:
- apply the generalization algorithm to the updated base relation (*non-incremental*)
- apply the incremental insertion algorithm to the whole set of insertions (*incremental-standard*)
- split the whole set of insertions into subsets with optimal cardinality and apply the incremental insertion algorithm to all of these subsets (*incremental-optimal*).

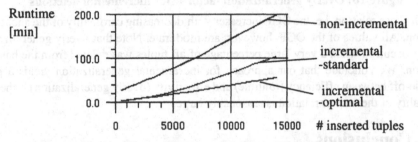

figure 8: Comparison of efficiency for the different strategies

Figure 8 demonstrates that the incremental approach is always significantly more efficient than the non-incremental one. Furthermore, inserting optimal sets of tuples reduces the runtime even more. And, finally, this gain in efficiency increases with increasing cardinality of the base relation and with increasing number of tuples to be inserted.

5.3 Results for Deletions

The runtimes for sets of incremental deletions are similar to those for insertions. Figure 9 depicts the runtime for sets of incremental deletions on a base relation of 20.000 tuples depending on the number of deleted tuples for several $ARF's$. This runtime decreases with increasing ARF and increases superlinearly with increasing number of deleted tuples.

In the following, we analyze the overly generalization factor (OGF) of the incremental deletions. We incrementally deleted 90 % of the tuples of the resp. base relations and calculated the resulting OGF. Figure 10 depicts the OGF after these incremental deletions depending on the ARF for different cardinalities of the base relation R.

We observe that the OGF increases with increasing ARF and decreasing cardinality

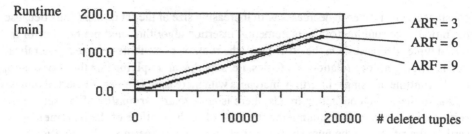

figure 9: Runtime of sets of incremental deletions for card(R) = 20000

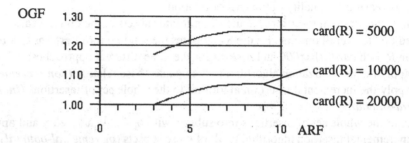

figure 10: Overly generalization factor after incremental deletions

of the base relation, i.e. the OGF increases with decreasing cardinality of the anchor relation. All values of the OGF, however, are moderate. Note that overly generalization only occurred when a very large percentage of all tuples was deleted from the base relation. We conclude that our approach for incremental generalization yields a good trade-off between efficiency (runtime) and effectivity (overly generalization) if the cardinality of the anchor relation is reasonably large.

6. Conclusions

Attribute-oriented generalization is a common method for the data mining task of summarization [HCC 93]. In this paper, we presented the algorithm Homogeneous_Generalize for attribute-oriented generalization with two important changes compared to the algorithm proposed in [HCC 93]: First, it has a single phase and strategy instead of two phases with different selection strategies. Second, it uses a breadth first approach instead of a depth first approach. The advantages of Homogeneous_Generalize are as follows: It obtains the fully generalized relations for multiple values of the generalization threshold in one run. Algorithm Homogeneous_Generalize is better suited for incremental updates since it obtains similar generalization levels for each attribute.

Typically, updates of an operational database are collected and applied to the data warehouse periodically. Then, all derived information, e.g. a generalized relation, has to be updated as well. We call updates of a generalized relation incremental if they do not require a new run of the generalization algorithm on the updated base relation. We discussed the requirements for incremental generalization, i.e. efficiency, correctness and avoidance of overly generalization. In particular, we showed that overly generalization may occur if deletions are performed on the base relation and introduced the overly generalization factor (OGF) as its measure. We presented algorithms for incremental insertions and deletions based on the materialization of a relation at an intermediate generalization level, i.e. the anchor relation. Our experiments demonstrate that incremental generalization can be performed efficiently with a low OGF.

Our experiments revealed the existence of an optimal cardinality for the sets of updates yielding a nearly linear runtime. A method for the automatic calculation of these optimal cardinalities and an algorithm to split the actual set of updates into subsets of (nearly) optimal cardinality should be developed. Furthermore, the performance of incremental generalization in other applications should be investigated.

References

[AS 94]   Agrawal R., Srikant R.: *"Fast Algorithms for Mining Association Rules"*, Proc. 20th Int. Conf. on Very Large Data Bases, Santiago, Chile, 1994, pp. 487-499.

[CHNW 96] Cheung D.W., Han J., Ng V.T., Wong Y.: *"Maintenance of Discovered Association Rules in Large Databases: An Incremental Technique"*, Proc. 12th Int. Conf. on Data Engineering, New Orleans, USA, 1996, pp. 106-114.

[EKX 95]   Ester M., Kriegel H.-P., Xu X.: *"A Database Interface for Clustering in Large Spatial Databases"*, Proc. 1st Int. Conf. on Knowledge Discovery and Data Mining, Montreal, Canada, 1995, AAAI Press, 1995, pp. 94-99.

[EKSX 96] Ester M., Kriegel H-P, Sander J. and Xu X.: *"A Density-Based Algorithm for Discovering Clusters in Large Spatial Databases with Noise"*, Proc. 2nd Int. Conf. on Knowledge Discovery and Data Mining, Portland, Oregon, 1996, pp. 226-231.

[FSS 96]   Fayyad U., Piatetsky-Shapiro G., and Smyth P.: *"Knowledge Discovery and Data Mining: Towards a Unifying Framework"*, Proc. 2nd Int. Conf. on Knowledge Discovery and Data Mining, Portland, Oregon, 1996, pp.82-88.

[HCC 93]   Han J., Cai Y., Cercone N.: *"Data-driven Discovery of Quantitative Rules in Relational Databases"*, IEEE Transactions on Knowledge and Data Engineering, Vol.5, No.1, 1993, pp. 29-40.

[HF 96]   Han J., Fu Y.: *"Exploration of the Power of Attribute-Oriented Induction in Data Mining"*, in *Advances in Knowledge Discovery and Data Mining*, AAAI/MIT Press, 1996, pp. 399-421.

[Huy 97]   Huyn N.: *"Multiple-View Self-Maintenance in Data Warehousing Environments"*, Proc. 23rd Int. Conf. on Very Large Data Bases, Athens, Greece, 1997, pp. 26-35.

[MQM 97]   Mumick I.S., Quass D., Mumick B.S.: *"Maintenance of Data Cubes and Summary Tables in a Warehouse"*, Proc. ACM SIGMOD Int. Conf. on Management of Data, 1997, pp. 100-111.

Modelling in OLAP

Modeling Large Scale OLAP Scenarios

Wolfgang Lehner

University of Erlangen-Nuremberg, Dept. of Database Systems, Martensstr. 3
D-91058 Erlangen, Germany

Abstract. In the recent past, different multidimensional data models were introduced to model OLAP ('Online Analytical Processing') scenarios. Design problems arise, when the modeled OLAP scenarios become very large and the dimensionality increases, which greatly decreases the support for an efficient ad-hoc data analysis process. Therefore, we extend the classical multidimensional model by grouping functionally dependent attributes within single dimensions, yielding in real orthogonal dimensions, which are easy to create and to maintain on schema design level. During the multidimensional data analysis phase, this technique yields in nested data cubes reflecting an intuitive two-step navigation process: classification-oriented 'drill-down'/ 'roll-up' and description-oriented 'split'/ 'merge' operators on data cubes. Thus, the proposed NESTED MULTIDIMENSIONAL DATA MODEL provides great modeling flexibility during the schema design phase and application-oriented restrictiveness during the data analysis phase.

1 Introduction

In the last few years, "Online Analytical Processing" (OLAP, [5]) and the corresponding multidimensional data model has become a major research area in the database community ([1], [10], [7], [9]). The promising turnover estimates for OLAP applications results in the appearance of different commercial products as well ([2], [8], [13], [14], etc.). One consequence of the OLAP-fever is the rejuvenation of the multidimensional data model. Moreover, the multidimensional view of data seems natural and appropriate for a wide range of scientific applications ([20]) such as market analysis, population analysis, geographic information analysis or cost accounting but needs a conceptual extension to model complex application scenarios appropriately.

To motivate our modeling approach and to show that the proposed approach ("THE NESTED MULTIDIMENSIONAL DATA MODEL") is 'not yet another data model' but provides necessary extensions in different directions, we refer to an example which stems from a cooperation with an industrial partner, a large european market retail research company. In their business, facts like sales or stock values of single articles in single shops at a specific period of time are monitored and collected to form the raw database ("micro data"). In a second phase, the raw database is analyzed in two ways: On the one hand, the data is aggregated along a predefined classification hierarchy. As pointed out later in more detail, one may imagine a classification hierarchy as a tree of 'high-level' business terms, identifying classes of single basic items ("Video" identifies all video equipment articles). On the other hand, the data is split into characteristic features of the single articles or shops. For example, each shop holds descriptive information about its purchase class or its shop type ('Cash&Carry', 'Retail', 'Hypermarket'). In the product dimension, each article of the 250.000 monitored products belongs to one of the 400 product families. Furthermore, each article is characterized by five attributes valid for all products (brand, package type, ...) and about 15 attributes which are valid only in the product family or product group to which the article belongs to (video system only for the product group "Video", water usage only for the product family "Washers"). Thus, a typical query may look like:

"Give me the total sales values for all product families subsumed by the product group 'Video' sold in shops in 'Germany' divided into different regions and split these values in such a way that the market shares of different brands are compared to the shop type where the corresponding articles have been sold",

which could be specified in SQL like:

select sum(SALES)
from ...
where Product_Group = 'Video',
*   Shop_Country = 'Germany'*
group by Product_Family, Product_Brand,
*   Shop_Region, Shop_Type*

SALES			Product_Group = 'Video'			
			CAMC		VCR	
			Sony	JVC	JVC	Grundig
Shop_Country = 'Germany'	North	C&C	12	11	37	58
		Retail	31	35	32	66
	South	HyperM	22	18	32	67
		Retail	51	46	54	57

According to the number of group-by attributes, this sample query would intuitively produce a 4-dimensional data cube. As we will show in this paper, this query corresponds only to a two-dimensional, but nested data cube (look at the prefixes of the attribute identifiers), where the additional characterizations like 'Brand' and 'ShopType' are nested into a classification based low-dimensional data cube stretched by product families and different geographic regions[1].

Structure of the paper

The paper is structured as follows: In the next section we will show that either the classical as well as all proposed extensions to the multidimensional model will fail in modeling the application scenario. Section 3 details the notion of a complex dimensional structure, whereas section 4 introduces the notion of 'Multidimensional Objects' which arises, when dimensional structures are brought into a multidimensional analysis context. Section 5 defines formally as well as guided by the ongoing market research example, the different operators on multidimensional objects. The paper concludes with a summary and a conclusion.

2   Related Work

As illustrated in figure 1, the general idea of the multidimensional data model is that each dimension of a multidimensional data cube, e.g. Products, Shops, or Time, can be seen as part of the primary key, spanning the cartesian product with the elements of the dimensions. Consequently, any combination of the composite primary key identifies exactly a single cell within the cube. In the classical multidimensional model as implemented in different OLAP products ([2], [8], [13], [14], etc.), classification hierarchies can be

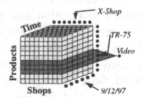

Fig. 1. General Idea of the multidim. Model

---

1. As pointed out in [6], a statistical table might be used to visualize a multi-dimensional data cube. Due to problems in drawing such cubes, we will follow this advice throughout the paper.

defined on the dimensional elements to identify business terms like 'Video' in figure 2. According to the classes within the hierarchies, operators are defined to slice/dice the data cube, i.e. selecting a subcube addressed by high-level terms.

To reflect dimensional attributes, i.e. features or properties describing single dimensional elements in the pure multidimensional model, each dimensional attribute must be modeled as an own dimension of the data cube. Referring again to the market research example, with 250.000 products classified in 400 product families and each family with about 15 features, the obviously three

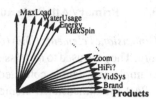

Fig. 2. Naive modeling approach

dimensional problem (Products, Shops, Time) explodes to a problem with 400*15=6000 dimensions to represent only the description of the articles (figure 2).

The consequence of this approach is that from a conceptual point of view, (n-1) dimensions functionally depend on the true dimension, holding the dimensional elements. This means that more than one "dimension" (Brand, VidSys, ...) refers to a single basic object, i.e. a single article in the ongoing example. From an implementation point of view, this approach leads to a high dimensionality and an extremely sparse data cube.

Neither an extended multidimensional model in the modern OLAP community nor the stream of statistical and scientific databases ([12], [19]) has addressed the problem of representing dimensional attributes (or features, properties, etc.) appropriately. Proposals on *multidimensional models* were made to transform cells to dimensions and vice versa ([1]), add complex statistical functions ([10]), or define a sophisticated mapping to the relational model ([7]). Also the historic stream of the *graphically oriented data models* like SUBJECT ([4]), GRASS ([16]), STORM ([17]), STORM+ ([3]) basically only knows classification and cross-product nodes to represent the corresponding data schema. Although these approaches enable the same grouping techniques, the basic problem of a single and therefore high dimensional data cube still remains.

The following consequences can be extracted from the discussion of related work: Firstly, current multidimensional data models are not capable to model dimensions of complex structure, which in reality reflect the user's world. Secondly, beyond classification-oriented analysis ("vertical analysis", drill-down operations), the characteristics or feature descriptions offer a new way of feature-oriented analysis ("horizontal analysis", feature splits). Thirdly, a carefully performed schema design process helps to define a reasonable space for the execution of queries as a basis for efficient query optimization techniques.

3 Dimensional Structures

In the context of multidimensional data models, the notion of a 'dimension' has a large number of different interpretations. Sometimes, a dimension reflects an edge of a multidimensional data cube without further structuring. In most cases, a dimension consists of multiple hierarchically structured classifications based on a set (or list) of basic values. In our approach, a dimension is a very complex entity enabling the proper structuring of the world of interest. Furthermore, we propose that dimensions are orthogonal to each other, meaning that no dimension depends on the existence of other dimensions leading to a clean schema design.

3.1 Primary Attribute and Dimensional Elements

Dimensional elements (DE) (or basic objects) are the basic units of a dimensional structure. They are used to address the micro data, i.e. measures or facts. Since in the ongoing example raw data is collected on a single article basis, these single article identifiers reflect the dimensional elements within the product dimension. Furthermore, dimensional elements are instances of the primary attribute (PA) of a dimension. As illustrated in figure 3, for example 'TR-75' is a dimensional element for the primary attribute 'ArticleID'.

3.2 Classification Attributes

Based on the dimensional elements, a balanced tree-structured *classification hierarchy* ([21]) can be defined to identify business terms like product families, groups, and areas in the product dimension (figure 3a) or cities, regions, and countries in a geographical dimension (figure 4). Each *classification node* (C), e.g. 'Video', is an instance of a corresponding *classification attribute* (CA). Thus, on the attribute level, the hierarchy of classification nodes corresponds to a list of classification attributes (CA_i, i=1,...,δ) denoted as *categorization* of that dimension. The root node of the classification hierarchy is a specific 'ALL'-node, covering all dimensional elements. For consistency reasons, this root node is the single instance of the highest classification attribute TOP (CA_δ), which is always member of each categorization.

3.3 Dimensional Attributes

As pointed out earlier, *dimensional attributes* (DA) reflect features or properties of dimensional elements. The important characteristic is that the existence of properties depends on the nodes of the classification hierarchy. For example, only video equipment has a property describing the video system, implying that the property 'VidSys' depends on the classification node 'Video' (figure 3b). Naturally, properties may also be valid for all dimensional elements thus depending on root node 'ALL' of that dimension. During the schema design phase, it may often not be clear which attributes may be used as *classification attributes* and which attributes may be used for further character-

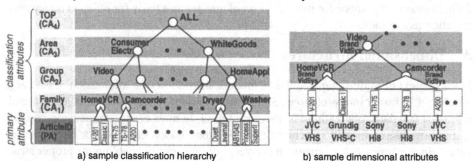

a) sample classification hierarchy   b) sample dimensional attributes

Fig. 3. Classification hierarchy and dimensional attributes of the product dimension

izing, i.e. as *dimensional attributes* ([18]). A candidate classification attribute must at least be valid for all dimensional elements and must functionally determine other classification attributes. For example, each article belongs to a product family and the family attribute determines the product group and the product area attributes. If more than one attributes are classification candidates, either the underlying implementation supports multiple classifications or the *most natural* one ([11]) must be selected as the classification attribute.

3.4 Node Domains

For a specific classification node, the distinction of classification attributes and dimensional attributes allows to define node domains with regard to the different direction.

Definition: A *classification-oriented node domain* $DOM(C_{|CA})$ holds all classification or basic objects subsumed by the current node C according to a given classification attribute (CA). If the classification attribute (CA) is equal to the classification attribute of the node C, then $DOM(C_{|CA}) := \left(C \right)$.

Definition: A *feature-oriented node domain* $DOM(C_{|DA})$ holds all instances of the subsumed dimensional elements for a specific dimensional attribute (DA).

Definition: A node domain without an attribute specification is called the *Null-domain* of that node ($DOM(C_{|})= \left(\ \right)$).

Following the example of figure 3b, the node domain of "Video" according to the product family classification attribute results in
$$DOM(Video_{|Family}) = \begin{pmatrix} Camcorder \\ HomeVCR \end{pmatrix}.$$
Otherwise, the node domain according to the feature 'Brand' results in
$$DOM(Video_{|Brand}) = \begin{pmatrix} Sony \\ JVC \\ Grundig \end{pmatrix}.$$
As final examples, the brand domains of camcorders and HomeVCRs are:
$$DOM(Camcorder_{|Brand}) = \begin{pmatrix} Sony \\ JVC \end{pmatrix} \quad DOM(HomeVCR_{|Brand}) = \begin{pmatrix} JVC \\ Grundig \end{pmatrix}$$

To exemplify the following definitions in the multidimensional context, we extend our ongoing market research example by a second *Shops* dimension. Therefore, we assume the categorization *(Country, Region, City, ShopID)*. At the instance level, we pick the country Germany, which is divided into northern and southern regions. From a possible large list of dimensional attributes (ShopType, PurchaseClass, BranchStore, ...), we pick the feature 'ShopType' with the node domains shown in figure 4).

4 Nested Multidimensional Data Cubes

While the dimensional structures model the business terms of the users' world in a very complex and powerful way, the multidimensional context uses these information for gaining analyses access to the measures or facts. This section starts with the formal definition of "Primary and Secondary Multidimensional Objects" reflecting the multidimensional view of classification and dimensional attributes. Using these mechanisms, this section focuses on the introduction of "Multidimensional Objects" (MOs), representing a consistent and intuitive view to nested multidimensional data cubes.

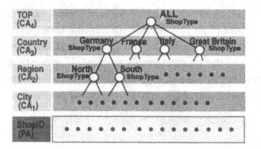
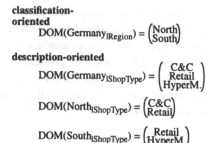

classification-
oriented
$$DOM(Germany_{|Region}) = \binom{North}{South}$$

description-oriented
$$DOM(Germany_{|ShopType}) = \begin{pmatrix} C\&C \\ Retail \\ HyperM. \end{pmatrix}$$

$$DOM(North_{|ShopType}) = \binom{C\&C}{Retail}$$

$$DOM(South_{|ShopType}) = \binom{Retail}{HyperM.}$$

Fig. 4. Sample node domains of the shop dimension

4.1 Granularity and Range Specification

Definition: A *context descriptor schema* (DS) is an n-tuple $(A_1, ..., A_n)$ where each element A_i is either a primary attribute (PA) or a categorization attribute (CA)[2].

Definition: A *context descriptor* (D) is an n-tuple $(c_1, ..., c_n)$ where each c_i is a node of the classification level described by A_i of the corresponding context descriptor schema.

In the two-dimensional context stretched by the product and shops dimension, (*'Video'*, *'Germany'*) is a valid context descriptor for the context descriptor schema *(Product.Group, Shops.Country)*. With an explicit schema descriptor, the context descriptor is also written as *(Product.Group='Video', Shops.Country='Germany')*.

4.2 Primary Multidimensional Objects

Definition: A *primary multidimensional object* (PMO) is a quintuple (M, DS, D, t_A, t_D) consisting of an unique cell identifier M, a context descriptor schema DS denoting the granularity of the cell, a context descriptor D specifying the selection criteria, an aggregation type $t_A \in \{\Sigma, \phi, c\}$, and a data type $t_D \in \{N, Z, R\}$.

As introduced in [15], the aggregation type describes the aggregation operators which are applicable to the modeled data (Σ: data can be summarized, ϕ: data may be used for average calculations, c: constant data implies no application of aggregation operators). The cardinality of the context descriptor D reflects the dimensionality of the corresponding data cube. Furthermore, the context descriptor D may be compared to the 'where-clause' of a SQL select-statement, thus specifying the partition (or sub-cube) size. The context descriptor schema DS of a PMO may be seen as the list of 'group by' attributes, resulting in a specification of the data granularity.

Examples

If all attributes of the context descriptor schema DS of a PMO are primary attributes from different dimensions, the PMO reflects *micro data*. If at least one attribute of DS is a categorization attribute, the PMO describes *macro data*. For the ongoing example, the PMO

$P_1 = (SALES, (P.ArticleID, S.ShopID), (P.Group = 'Video', S.Country = 'Germany'), \Sigma, N)$

---

2. In the multidimensional context, each primary or classification attribute is prefixed with the dimension identifier, e.g. "Product.Family" or "Shops.Region".

describes a summarizable two-dimensional micro data object for accessing video sales figures of single articles in single shops for all of Germany. Substituting the context descriptor schema of PMO P_1 by the context descriptor schema *(P.Family, S.Region)* leads to the PMO

$P_2 = (SALES, (P.Family, S.Region), (P.Group = 'Video', S.Country = 'Germany'), \Sigma, \mathbf{N})$

for the description of macro data holding aggregation values of P_1. As a final example, the following PMO P_3 holds one-dimensional price figures for video equipment:

$P_3 = (PRICE, (P.ArticleID), (P.Group = 'Video'), \phi, \mathbf{R})$

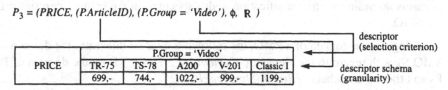

PRICE	P.Group = 'Video'				
	TR-75	TS-78	A200	V-201	Classic I
	699,-	744,-	1022,-	999,-	1199,-

descriptor (selection criterion)

descriptor schema (granularity)

Domain of a PMO

Definition: The *domain of a PMO* is defined by the cartesian product of the classification-oriented node domains of each context descriptor element:
$DOM(P) = \bigotimes_{i=1}^{n} DOM(c_i|_{CA_i})$, where c_i is the i-th component of the context descriptor D and CA_i is the i-th component of the context descriptor schema DS of the PMO.

The following figure 5 details the definition of the domain for the PMO P_2. The classification node 'Video' has 'Camcorder' and 'HomeVCR' as children at the family level. On the geographical dimension, 'Germany' is divided into the regions 'North' and 'South'.

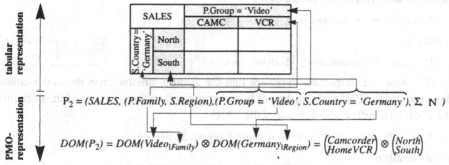

Fig. 5. Domain of the sample PMO P_2

Definition: A *constant primary multidimensional object* is a PMO where the context descriptor schema DS as well as the context descriptor are empty, the aggregation type is 'c', and the data type is $t_D \in \{\mathbf{N}, \mathbf{Z}, \mathbf{R}\}$.

For example, the PMO $(TAX, (), (), c, \mathbf{R})$ may hold the constant factor for the applicable tax which is invariant according to all dimensions.

4.3 Secondary Multidimensional Objects

Definition: A *secondary multidimensional object* (SMO) is a tuple (D, DA), where D is a context descriptor, and DA is a set of dimensional attributes applicable to the context descriptor $D = (c_1, ..., c_n)$. The set of dimensional attributes results in $DA \subseteq \bigcup_{i=1}^{n} DA_i$, where DA_i is the set of dimensional attributes of the classification node c_i.

Definition: The *domain of an SMO* is the cartesian product of the feature-oriented domains according to the classification nodes specified in the context descriptor D of the SMO.

In analogy to the domain of a PMO, the following figure 6 illustrates the domain of an SMO S_1 with regard to the element *('Camcorder', 'North')* from the domain of PMO P_2 and the feature schema *{Brand, ShopType}*.

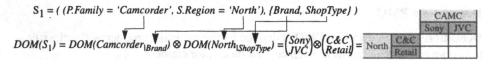

$$DOM(S_1) = DOM(Camcorder_{\mid Brand}) \otimes DOM(North_{\mid ShopType}) = \binom{Sony}{JVC} \otimes \binom{C\&C}{Retail} = North \begin{array}{|c|c|} \hline C\&C & \\ \hline Retail & \\ \hline \end{array}$$

Fig. 6. Domain of the sample SMO S_1

At this point, it is worth to note that in a pure classification-oriented multidimensional environment, the component DA of an SMO would simply result in an empty set of dimensional attributes, resulting in a seamless extension to the classical multidimensional model. Thus, the domain of the SMO

$$S_2 = (\ (P.Family = 'Camcorder', S.Region = 'North'), \{ \ \} \ )$$

results in

$$DOM(S_2) = DOM(Camcorder_{\mid}) \otimes DOM(North_{\mid}) = (\ ).$$

Furthermore, it is important to realize that the feature schema depends on the context descriptor of the PMO. The instances however depend on the elements of the domain of the PMO! Therefore, the domain of the SMO

$$S_1' = (\ (P.Family = 'VCR', S.Region = 'North'), \{Brand, ShopType\})$$

would result in

$$DOM(S_1') = DOM(VCR_{\mid Brand}) \otimes DOM(North_{\mid ShopType}) = \binom{JVC}{Grundig} \otimes \binom{C\&C}{Retail},$$

which is different from $DOM(S_1)$.

4.4 Multidimensional Objects

Definition: A *multidimensional object* (MO) is a tuple (P, DA), where P is a valid PMO and DA is a set of dimensional attributes for defining the corresponding nested SMOs.

The following figure 7 illustrates two multidimensional objects MO_1 and MO_2. Both MOs have the same primary multidimensional object (P_2) but different feature split schema (left: none; right: by Brand and ShopType). Each element of the PMO points to an SMO (left: 0-dimensional, right: 2-dimensional). Each element of an SMO points to

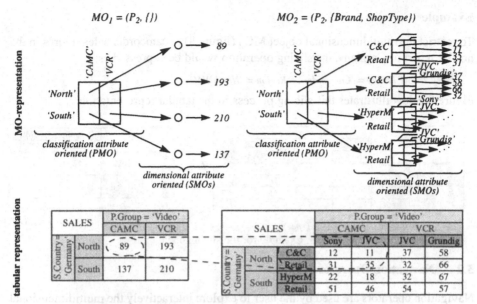

Fig. 7. Sample MOs representing context-sensitive nested data cubes

the real sales figure for the current context. The lower half of figure 7 shows the tabular representation of both MOs (MO_1 and MO_2). As depicted in this representation, each cell of MO_1 (0-dimensional SMO) is expanded by an inner 2-dimensional SMO in MO_2 (dark shaded).

Explicit modeling of dimensional attributes in dimensional structure, as discussed in section 3 results in nested multidimensional data cubes during the data analysis phase. The next section will explain the different operators to work with such data cubes, specified formally in multidimensional objects.

5 Operators on Multidimensional Objects

In this section, the 'traditional' operators like slicing, aggregation operations and cell-oriented joins of two data cubes are defined on the basis of PMOs. The extension of nested SMOs implies two new operators ("split" and "merge") which dramatically improve the power and flexibility of the whole analysis process.

5.1 Sub-Cube Selection according to Classification Attributes (Slicing)

The result of a *slicing operation* is a MO which inherits all components of the source MO except the context descriptor. The new context descriptor D, given as parameter to the operator is "smaller", i.e. more restrictive than the one from the source MO.

MO' := σ(D)MO

The slice operator has no effect on the source MO when the schema of the new context descriptor is finer than the context descriptor schema (data granularity) of the source MO.

Example

To restrict the multidimensional object MO_2 (figure 8) to camcorder sales figures in the northern part of Germany, the slicing operation would be expressed as:

$MO_2' := \sigma(P.Family = 'Camcorder', S.Region = 'North')MO_2$

Figure 8 below illustrates this slicing process in the tabular representation.

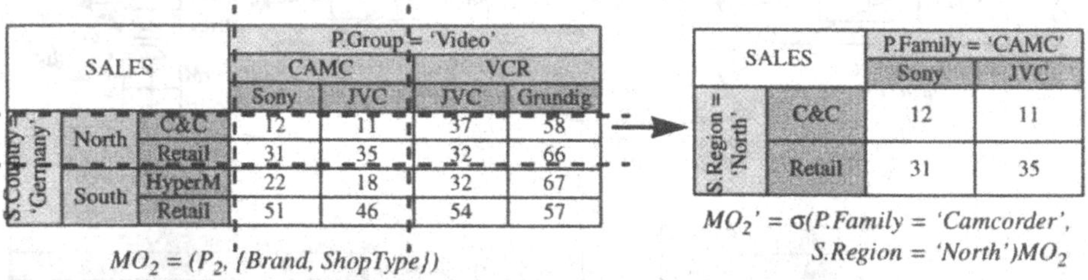

SALES			P.Group = 'Video'			
			CAMC		VCR	
			Sony	JVC	JVC	Grundig
S.Country 'Germany'	North	C&C	12	11	37	58
		Retail	31	35	32	66
	South	HyperM	22	18	32	67
		Retail	51	46	54	57

$MO_2 = (P_2, \{Brand, ShopType\})$

SALES		P.Family = 'CAMC'	
		Sony	JVC
S.Region 'North'	C&C	12	11
	Retail	31	35

$MO_2' = \sigma(P.Family = 'Camcorder',$
$S.Region = 'North')MO_2$

Fig. 8. Example for the slicing operator

5.2 Navigation Operators

Navigation operators are used by the user to explore interactively the multidimensional analysis context. As pointed out in section 2, the classical multidimensional model only supports *classification-oriented navigation* ('vertical analysis') proposing 'drill-down' and 'roll-up' operations. In our data and user interactivity model, these operations are used in a first analysis phase to find an interesting context. These operations are based on the PMO-part of multidimensional objects. The explicit modeling of dimensional attributes yields in an additional analysis phase. Based on the SMO-part of multidimensional objects the selected analysis context can be further and detailed investigated by a dimensional attribute-oriented navigation process ('horizontal analysis'), which is enabled by the new operators 'split' and 'merge'.

PMO-oriented Navigation along the Classification Hierarchy

- The *drill-down* operator ("give details") corresponds to an implicit de-aggregation process according to the aggregation type t_A of the source MO,

  $MO' := \downarrow(DS)MO$

  where at least one attribute of the new descriptor schema DS (data granularity) is 'finer' than the attributes of the descriptor schema of the source MO. The 'drill-down' operator has no effect, if all attributes of the descriptor schema of the source MO correspond to primary attributes in their dimensions.

- The *roll-up* operator ("hide details") corresponds to an implicit aggregation process according to t_A of MO,

  $MO' := \uparrow(DS)MO$

  where at least one attribute of the new descriptor schema (data granularity) is 'coarser' than the attributes of the descriptor schema of the source MO. Furthermore, the roll-up operator may result in an implicit 'un-slice' operator, because the selection of a parent node within the classification hierarchy may release an earlier performed selection criterion during in the analysis process. If all attributes of the descriptor schema of the source MO correspond to the TOP-attribute, the 'roll-up'-operator has no effect.

Examples

The tabular representation in figure 9 below show a sequence of two drill-down operations (from left to the right) or, from left to the right, the inverse roll-up operations.

- $MO_1 = \downarrow(P.Family, S.Region)MO'_1$
  $MO'_1 = \downarrow(P.ArticleID, S.Region)MO_1$

- $MO_1 = \uparrow(P.Family, S.Region)MO''_1$
  $MO'_1 = \uparrow(P.Group, S.Region)MO_1$

MO'_1 MO_1 MO''_1

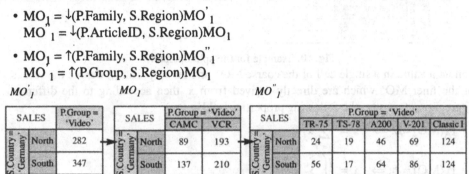

SALES	P.Group = 'Video'
North	282
South	347

S.Country = 'Germany'

↓(P.Family, S.Region)

SALES	P.Group = 'Video'	
	CAMC	VCR
North	89	193
South	137	210

S.Country = 'Germany'

↓(P.Article, S.Region)

SALES	P.Group = 'Video'				
	TR-75	TS-78	A200	V-201	Classic I
North	24	19	46	69	124
South	56	17	64	86	124

S.Country = 'Germany'

Fig. 9. Example of the drill-down operator

SMO-oriented Navigation along dimensional attributes

- The *split operator* adds a valid feature (DA_i) to the set of dimensional attributes, thus incrementing the dimensionality of the nested SMOs.
  $MO' := \rightarrow(DA_i)MO$ where $DA(MO') = DA(MO) \cup \{DA_i\}$.

- The *merge operator* removes a specific dimensional attribute (DA_i) from the MO's dimensional attribute set, thus decrementing the dimensionality of the nested SMO.
  $MO' := \leftarrow(DA_i)MO$ where $DA(MO') = DA(MO) \setminus \{DA_i\}$.

Examples

Once MO_1 is selected by use of PMO-oriented operations, it serves as the basis for SMO-oriented analysis. As shown in the figure 10 below, the first split operation is made according to the dimensional attribute 'ShopType' of the geographical dimension. Further split operations to increase or merge operations to undo former split operations are also seen in figure 10. The necessary transformations from MO_1 to MO_2 (figure 7) and vice versa are specified as follows:

- $MO_2 = \rightarrow(Brand)(\rightarrow(ShopType)MO_1)$ // expand the nested SMOs

- $MO_1 = \leftarrow(ShopType)(\leftarrow(Brand)MO_2)$ // collapse the nested SMOs

5.3   Implicit Aggregation

The use of navigation operations also implicitly performs an aggregation process corresponding to the default aggregation type (t_A) of the source MO. Consider two MOs (MO' and MO'') with the same descriptor $D = (c_1,...,c_n)$ where MO' is coarser (either classification-oriented or dimensional attribute-oriented) than MO''. Furthermore, let x

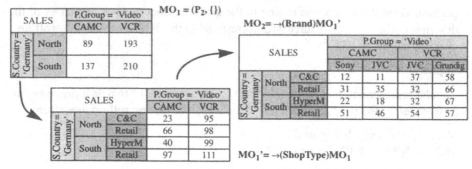

Fig. 10. Example for the split operator

denote a value in a single cell of the coarse MO" and let x_j ($j=1,...,\kappa$) denote the values of the finer MO' which are directly derived from x, then according to the different aggregation types t_A, the following properties hold:

- $t_A(MO) = \Sigma: \Rightarrow \quad x = \sum_{j=1}^{\kappa} x_j$

- $t_A(MO) = \phi: \Rightarrow \quad x = \frac{1}{\kappa}\left(\sum_{j=1}^{\kappa} x_j\right)$

- $t_A(MO) = c: \Rightarrow \quad x = x_1 = ... = x_\kappa$

In the case of a classification-based relationship, κ corresponds to the size of the domain, which is computed by the cartesian product of the node domains according to the finer descriptor schema $DS(MO) = (A_1,...,A_n)$.

$$\kappa = \prod_{i=1}^{n} \left|DOM(c_i\big|_{A_i})\right|$$

In the case of a dimensional attribute-based relationship, the cartesian product of the node domains according to the set of dimensional attributes $DA(MO) = \{DA_1, ..., DA_m\}$ determines the number of the new cells, i.e. the size of the SMO of the finer MO.

$$\kappa = \prod_{k=1}^{m} \left|DOM(c_i\big|_{DA_k})\right| (\forall c_i \in D)$$

Example

Referring to the definition of MO_1 and MO_2, the following figure 11 shows that summing up all partial sums generated by two successive split operations, is equal to the total sales figure of MO_1.

	CAMC	$MO_1 = (P, \{\})$	$MO_2 = (P, DA)$		CAMC	
					Sony	JVC
North	89	$x = 89$	$x = \sum_{j=1}^{4} x_j$	North C&C	12	11
				Retail	31	35

Fig. 11. Implicit aggregation when performing navigation operators

This implicit aggregation process holds for classification-oriented navigation operators as well.

5.4 Explicit Aggregation Operator

The result of an *aggregation operation* reflects the original MO with a new context descriptor schema DS, which is "coarser" than the original one (like 'roll-up'). The single numeric values are aggregated according to the explicitly specified operator.

$$MO' := \theta(DS)MO$$

where $\theta \in \{$ SUM, AVG, MIN, MAX, COUNT $\}$, if $t_A(MO) = \Sigma$.
where $\theta \in \{$ AVG, MIN, MAX $\}$, if $t_A(MO) = \phi$.
where $\theta = ID$, if $t_A(MO) = c$.

Example

To sum up all video equipment sales to the family level in the product dimension and upto different regions specified in the geographic dimension, i.e. generate MO_1 of the ongoing example, the following expression must be stated:

$$MO_1 := SUM(P.Family, S.Region) (P_1, \{\})$$

5.5 Cell-Oriented Operators

The objectives of a *cell-oriented operator* are the cells themselves, thus resulting in a MO with the same context descriptor D and the same context descriptor schema DS.

- unary operators: $MO' := \theta(MO)$ where $\theta \in \{$ -, abs, sign $\}$
- binary operators: $MO' := \theta(MO_1, MO_2)$ where $\theta \in \{$ *, / , +, -, min, max$\}$
  before performing any binary cell-oriented operator, the dimensionality as well as the context descriptor schema of each MO are aligned. Furthermore, if the MOs obtain different aggregation types, the resulting MO gets the strongest type according to the ordering $(c < \phi < \Sigma)$.

Example

To calculate the purchase of each article, the MOs M'=(P1,{}) and M''=(P3,{}) are joined by the multiplication operator. Since M'' is one-dimensional, it is expanded to the second geographical dimension of M'. Furthermore, the resulting MO M has aggregation type Σ because $t_A(M')=\Sigma$ is stronger than $t_A(M'')=\phi$. Thus, $M := *(M', M'')$, where

$$M = ((PURCHASE, (P.ArticleID, S.ShopID), (P.Group = 'Video', S.Country = 'Germany'), \Sigma, N), \{\}).$$

As seen in this section, on the one hand the defined set of operators on multidimensional objects enables a simple navigation process through the multidimensional analysis context performing implicit aggregation operations. Furthermore, this navigation process is extended through split/merge operators hiding the nested cube model of the conceptual layer for the user, which, of course, is only faced with the tabular representation at the external layer. On the other hand, explicit aggregation and cell-oriented operators allow the specification of sophisticated statistical analysis queries against the multidimensional cube.

6 Summary and Conclusion

This paper motivates and formally describes an extended multidimensional data model. The extension is based on the fundamental distinction between classification attributes and dimensional attributes within a single dimension. This approach leads to functionally independent dimensions at the schema design level and to low-dimensional but nested data cubes during the analysis process. The described model is currently being implemented within the CubeStar-project at our department (http://www6.informatik.uni-erlangen.de/Research/cubestar/index.html) on top of a relational model. In opposite to the well-known Star-/Snowflake schema, the nested multidimensional model requires an alternative cube-to-relation mapping approach.

Although the proposed nested multidimensional data model allows the flexible modeling of statistical and scientific application scenarios, there still remain some open issues which must be solved: From a modeling point of view, versioning of dimensional structures must be supported by the data model. Since all multidimensional models handle the time dimension equally to other dimensions, the special characteristics of time must be considered and mechanisms like 'transaction/valid time' must be transferred from different temporal models. From an implementation point of view, redundancy-based query optimization, i.e. supporting of pre-aggregates reflects a major requirement for an efficient ad-hoc analysis process. Therefore, already existing work must be extended to the model of context-sensitive and nested data cubes. Nevertheless, we believe that our modeling approach is an adequate basis for solving all these problems.

Acknowledgements

I would like to thank Prof. Shoshani for the valuable discussions. Moreover, I acknowledge Prof. Wedekind, J. Albrecht, and H. Günzel for helpful comments on a draft of the paper.

References

1. Agrawal, R.; Gupta, A.; Sarawagi, S.: Modeling Multidimensional Databases, in: *13th International Conference on Data Engineering*, (ICDE'97, Birmingham, U.K., April 7-11), 1997, pp. 232-243

2. *Essbase Analysis Server - Bringing Dynamic Data Access and Analysis to Workgroups Across the Enterprise*, Product Information, Arbor Software Corporation, 1995

3. Bezenchek, A.; Massari, F.; Rafanelli, M.: "STORM+: statistical data storage and manipulation system", in: *11th Symposium on Computational Statistics*, (Compstat '94, Vienna, Austria, Aug. 22-26), 1994

4. Chan, P.; Shoshani, A.: SUBJECT: A Directory Driven System for Organizing and Accessing Large Statistical Data Bases, in: *7th International Conference on Very Large Data Bases* (VLDB'81, Cannes, France, Sept. 9-11), 1981, pp. 553-563

5. Codd, E.F.: Codd, S.B.; Salley, C.T.: *Providing OLAP (On-line Analytical Processing) to User Analysts: An IT Mandate*, White Paper, Arbor Software Corporation, 1993

6. Gray, J.; Bosworth A.; Layman A.; Pirahesh, H.: Data Cube: A Relational Aggregation Operator Generalizing Group-By, Cross-Tab, and Sub-Total, in: *12th IEEE International Conference on Data Engineering* (ICDE´96, New Orleans, Louisiana, Feb. 26 -Mar. 1), 1996, pp. 152-159

7. Gyssens, M.; Lakshmanan, L.V.S.: A Foundation for Multi-Dimensional Databases, in: *23th International Conference on Very Large Data Bases* (VLDB'97, Athen, Greece, Aug. 25-29), 1997, pp. 106-115

8. *The INFORMIX-MetaCube Approach*, Product Information, Informix Software, Inc., 1996

9. Lehner, W.; Ruf, T.; Teschke, M.: CROSS-DB: A Feature-extended Multi-dimensional Data Model for Statistical and Scientific Databases, in: *5th International Conference on Information and Knowledge Management*, (CIKM'96, Rockville, Maryland, Nov. 12-16), 1996, pp. 253-260

10. Li, C; Wang, X.S.: A Data Model for Supporting On-Line Analytical Processing, in: *5th International Conference on Information and Knowledge Management*, (CIKM'96, Rockville, Maryland, Nov. 12-16), 1996, pp. 81-88

11. Lorenzen, P.; *Constructive Philosophy*, Amherst, Univ. of Massachusetts Press, 1987

12. Michalewicz, Z. (Ed.): *Statistical and Scientific Databases*, New York, Ellis Horwood, 1991

13. *The Case for Relational OLAP*, White Paper, MicroStrategy, Inc., 1995

14. *Personal Express Language Reference Manual, Volumes I / II*, Oracle Cooperation, 1996

15. Rafanelli, M.; Ricci, F.: Proposal of a Logical Model for Statistical Databases, in: *2nd International Workshop on Statistical Database Management*, Los Altos, CA, 1983

16. Rafanelli, M.; Ricci, F.: A Graphical Approach for Statistical Summaries: The GRASS Model, in: *ISMM International Symposium on Microcomputers and their Applications*, 1987

17. Rafanelli, M.; Shoshani, A.: STORM: A Statistical Object Representation Model, in: *5th International Conference on Statistical and Scientific Database Management* (5SSDBM, Charlotte, NC, April 3-5), 1990, pp. 14-29

18. Shoshani, A.; Lehner, W: *Are classifications and attributes orthogonal to each other?*, personal communication, 1997

19. Shoshani, A.: Statistical Databases: Characteristics, Problems, and Some Solutions, in: *8th International Conference on Very Large Data Bases* (VLDB'82, Mexico City, Mexico, Sept. 8-10), 1982, pp. 208-222

20. Shoshani, A.: OLAP and Statistical Databases: Similarities and Differences, in: *16th ACM SIGACT-SIGMOD-SIGART Symposium on Principles of Database Systems*, (PODS'97, Tucson, Arizona, 13-15 May), 1997, pp. 185-196

21. Smith, J.M.; Smith, D.C.P.: Database Abstractions: Aggregation and Generalization, *ACM Transactions on Database Systems 2(1977)2*, pp. 105-133

Discovery-Driven Exploration of OLAP Data Cubes[*]

Sunita Sarawagi   Rakesh Agrawal   Nimrod Megiddo

IBM Almaden Research Center, 650 Harry Road, San Jose, CA 95120, USA

Abstract. Analysts predominantly use OLAP data cubes to identify regions of anomalies that may represent problem areas or new opportunities. The current OLAP systems support hypothesis-driven exploration of data cubes through operations such as drill-down, roll-up, and selection. Using these operations, an analyst navigates unaided through a huge search space looking at large number of values to spot exceptions. We propose a new discovery-driven exploration paradigm that mines the data for such exceptions and summarizes the exceptions at appropriate levels in advance. It then uses these exceptions to lead the analyst to interesting regions of the cube during navigation. We present the statistical foundation underlying our approach. We then discuss the computational issue of finding exceptions in data and making the process efficient on large multidimensional data bases.

1 Introduction

On-Line Analytical Processing (OLAP) characterizes the operations of summarizing, consolidating, viewing, applying formulae to, and synthesizing data along multiple dimensions. OLAP software helps analysts and managers gain insight into the performance of an enterprise through a wide variety of views of data organized to reflect the multidimensional nature of enterprise data [Col95]. An increasingly popular data model for OLAP applications is the multidimensional database [OLA96][AGS97], also known as the data cube [GBLP96]. A data cube consists of two kinds of attributes: *measures* and *dimensions*. The set of dimensions consists of attributes like product names and store names that together form a key. The measures are typically numeric attributes like sales volumes and profit. Dimensions usually have associated with them *hierarchies* that specify aggregation levels. For instance, *store name* → *city* → *state* is a hierarchy on the *store* dimension and *UPC code* → *type* → *category* is a hierarchy on the *product* dimension.

Hypothesis-driven Exploration A business analyst while interactively exploring the OLAP data cube is often looking for regions of anomalies. These anomalies may lead to identification of problem areas or new opportunities. The exploration typically starts at the highest level of hierarchies of the cube dimension. Further, navigation of the cube is done using a sequence of "drill-down"

---

[*] This is an abridged version of the full paper that appears in [SAM98].

(zooming in to more detailed levels of hierarchies), "roll-up" (zooming out to less detailed levels) and "selection" (choosing a subset of dimension members) operations. From the highest level of the hierarchy, the analyst drills-down to the lower levels of hierarchies by looking at the aggregated values and visually identifying interesting values to follow. Thus, drilling-down the product dimension from product category to product type may lead to product types whose sale exhibited some anomalous behavior. A further drill down may lead to individual product UPC codes causing this anomaly. If an exploration along a path does not lead to interesting results, the analyst rolls-up the path and starts pursuing another branch. A roll-up may lead to the top-level of hierarchy and then further drill-down may continue along another dimension.

This "hypothesis-driven" exploration for anomalies has several shortcomings. The search space is very large — typically, a cube has 5–8 dimensions, each dimension has a hierarchy that is 2–8 levels deep and each level of the hierarchy has ten to hundreds of members [Col95]. Simply looking at data aggregated at various levels of details to hunt down an anomaly that could be one of several million values hidden in detailed data is a daunting task. Furthermore, the higher level aggregations from where an analyst starts may not even be affected by an anomaly occuring underneath either because of cancellation of multiple exceptions or because of the large amount of data aggregated. Even if one is viewing data at the same level of detail as where the anomaly occurs, it might be hard to notice the exception because of large number of values.

Discovery-driven Exploration We propose a new "discovery-driven" method of data exploration where an analyst's search for anomalies is guided by precomputed indicators of exceptions at various levels of detail in the cube. This increases the chances of user noticing abnormal patterns in the data at any level of aggregation.

We present a formal notion of exceptions. Intuitively, we consider a value in a cell of a data cube to be an exception if it is significantly different from the value anticipated based on a statistical model. This model computes the anticipated value of a cell in context of its position in the data cube and combines trends along different dimensions that the cell belongs to. Thus, for instance, a large increase in sales in december might appear exceptional when looking at the time dimension but when looking at the other dimensions like product this increase will not appear exceptional if other products also had similar increase. The model allows exceptions to be found at all levels of aggregation.

We present computation techniques that make the process of finding exceptions efficient for large OLAP datasets. Our techniques use the same kind of data scan operations as required for cube aggregate computation [AAD+96] and thus enables overlap of exception finding with routine aggregate precomputation. These techniques recognize that the data may be too large to fit in main memory and intermediate results may have to be written to disk requiring careful optimization.

Paper layout The paper is organized as follows. In Section 2 we demonstrate a scenario of the use of our proposed method. Section 3 gives the statistical model we use to compute the anticipated value of a cell and the rationale for choosing this model. Computation techniques are discussed in Section 4. Refer to [SAM98] for some performance results and experience with real-life datasets that illustrates the effectiveness of the proposed approach. We conclude with a summary and directions for future work in Section 5.

2 An Illustrative Example

We illustrate our proposed method using an example session with our prototype implementation. This prototype uses the Microsoft Excel spreadsheet, extended with appropriate macros, as the front-end for user-interaction. The backend is the well-known OLAP product, Arbor Essbase [Arb] that computes and stores the exceptions using the techniques we present in Sections 3 and 4.

To keep the example brief, we will consider a three-dimensional data cube with dimensions Product, Market, and Time. There is a hierarchy Market $\rightarrow$ Region $\rightarrow$ ALL on the Market dimension. The data for this cube is taken from a sample OLAP database distributed with Essbase [Arb].

We annotate every cell in all possible aggregations of a data cube with a value that indicates the degree of "surprise" that the quantity in the cell holds. The surprise value captures how anomalous a quantity in a cell is with respect to other cells. The surprise value of a cell is a composite of the following three values (we give definitions and discuss how these values are determined in Section 3):

1. SelfExp: represents the surprise value of the cell relative to other cells at the same level of aggregation.
2. InExp: represents the degree of surprise somewhere beneath this cell if we drill down from the cell.
3. PathExp: represents the degree of surprise for each drill-down path from the cell.

Product	(All)
Region	(All)

Sum of Sales	Month											
	Jan	Feb	Mar	Apr	May	Jun	Jul	Aug	Sep	Oct	Nov	Dec
Total		2%	0%	2%	2%	4%	3%	0%	-8%	0%	-3%	4%

Figure1. Change in sales over time

Consider a user looking at the monthly sales as a percentage difference from the previous month. Suppose the user starts by viewing the data aggregated over all products and markets for different months of the year as shown in Figure 1.

To find out what parts of the cube may be worthy of exploring further in terms of exceptions, the user invokes a "highlight exceptions" button that colors the background of each cell based on its SelfExp value. In addition, each cell is surrounded with a different colored box based on the InExp value. In

Region	(All)											
Avg.Sales	Month											
Product	Jan	Feb	Mar	Apr	May	Jun	Jul	Aug	Sep	Oct	Nov	Dec
Birch-B		10%	-7%	3%	-4%	15%	-12%	-3%	1%	■	-14%	-10%
Chery-S		1%	1%	4%	3%	5%	5%	-9%	-12%	1%	-5%	5%
Cola		-1%	2%	3%	4%	9%	4%	1%	-11%	-8%	-2%	7%
Cream-S		3%	1%	6%	3%	3%	8%	-3%	-12%	-2%	1%	10%
Diet-B		1%	1%	-1%	2%	1%	2%	0%	-6%	-1%	-4%	2%
Diet-C		3%	2%	5%	2%	4%	7%	-7%	-12%	-2%	-2%	8%
Diet-S		2%	-1%	0%	0%	4%	2%	4%	-9%	5%	-3%	0%
Grape-S		1%	1%	0%	4%	5%	1%	3%	-9%	-1%	-8%	4%
Jolt-C		-1%	-4%	2%	2%	0%	-4%	2%	6%	-2%	0%	0%
Kiwi-S		2%	1%	4%	1%	-1%	3%	-1%	-4%	4%	0%	1%
Old-B		4%	-1%	0%	1%	5%	2%	7%	-10%	3%	-3%	1%
Orang-S		1%	1%	3%	4%	2%	1%	-1%	-1%	-6%	-4%	9%
Sasprla		-1%	2%	1%	3%	-3%	5%	-10%	-2%	-1%	1%	5%

Figure2. Change in sales over time for each product

both cases, the intensity of the color is varied with the degree of exception. In Figure 1, the months with a thick box around them have a high $InExp$ value and thus need to be drilled down further for exceptions underneath them. Darker boxes (e.g., around "Aug", "Sep" and "Oct") indicate higher values of $InExp$ than the lighter boxes (e.g., around "Feb" and "Nov").

There are two paths the user may drill down along from here: Product and Region. To evaluate which of these paths has more exceptions, the user selects a cell of interest and invokes a "path exception" module that colors each aggregated dimension based on the surprise value along that path. These are based on the $PathExp$ values of the cell. In Figure 1 (top-left part) the path along dimension Product has more surprise than along Region indicated by darker color. Drilling-down along Product yields 143 different sales values corresponding to different Product-Time combinations as shown in Figure 2. Instead of trying to find the exceptions by manual inspection, the user can click on the "highlight exception" button to quickly identify the exceptional values. In this figure, there are a few cells with high $SelfExp$ values and these appear as cells with a different background shade than the normal ones (darker shades indicate higher surprise). For instance, sales of "Birch-B(eer)" shows an exceptional difference of 42% in the month of "Oct". In addition, three other cells are also indicated to have large $SelfExp$ values although the sales values themselves (6% for <Jolt-C, Sep>, -12% for <Birch-B, Jul>and -10% for <Birch-B, Dec>) are not exceptionally large when compared with all the other cells. The reason why these cells are marked as exceptions will be explained in Section 3.

Figure 2 also shows some cells with large $InExp$ values as indicated by the thick boxes around them. The highest $InExp$ values are for Product "Diet-S(oda)" in the months of "Aug" and "Oct". The user may therefore choose to explore further details for "Diet-Soda" by drilling down along Region. Figure 3 shows the sales figures for "Diet-Soda" in different Regions. By highlighting

Product	Diet-S											
Avg.Sales	Month											
Region	Jan	Feb	Mar	Apr	May	Jun	Jul	Aug	Sep	Oct	Nov	Dec
C		0%	-2%	0%	1%	4%	1%	5%	-6%	2%	-2%	-2%
E		0%	2%	-8%	7%	0%	5%	40%	10%	33%	2%	8%
S		0%	-1%	3%	-2%	2%	-2%	19%	-1%	12%	-1%	0%
W		5%	1%	0%	-2%	6%	6%	2%	-17%	9%	-7%	2%

Figure3. Change in sales of Product "Diet-Soda" over time in each Region

exceptions in this plane, the user notices that in Region "E" (for Eastern), the sales of "Diet-Soda" has decreased by an exceptionally high value of 40% and 33% in the months of "Aug" and "Oct" respectively. Notice that the sales of "Diet-Soda" in the Product-Time plane aggregated over different Regions (Figure 2) gives little indication of these high exceptions in the Region-Product-Time space. This shows how the $\mathcal{I}$nExp value at higher level cells may be valuable in reaching at exceptions in lower level cells.

Market	(All)											
Product	Cola											
Avg.Sales	Month											
Region	Jan	Feb	Mar	Apr	May	Jun	Jul	Aug	Sep	Oct	Nov	Dec
C		3%	1%	4%	1%	4%	10%	-11%	-14%	-3%	5%	11%
E		-3%	3%	4%	4%	13%	2%	0%	-10%	-13%	-3%	8%
S		2%	-1%	1%	9%	6%	3%	21%	-15%	1%	-5%	4%
W		-2%	2%	2%	4%	12%	1%	1%	-9%	-11%	-4%	6%

Figure4. Change in sales over Time for Product "Cola" in different Region

There are no other cells with high $\mathcal{I}$nExp in Figure 3. Therefore, the user may stop drilling down and go back to the Product-Time plane of Figure 2 to explore other cells with high $\mathcal{I}$nExp. Suppose, he chooses to drill-down along Product "Cola" in "Aug". Figure 4 shows the exceptions for "Cola" after drilling down along Region. The "Central" Region has a large $\mathcal{I}$nExp and may be drilled down further, revealing the $\mathcal{S}$elfExp values in the Market-time plane for "Cola".

3 Defining exceptions

Intuitively, a value in a cell of a data cube is an exception if it is surprising. There could be several interpretations of this notion. We present the approach we use. In [SAM98] we discuss the alternatives we considered before deciding on our approach.

Product	Birch-B
Region	E

Sum of Sales	Month											
State	Jan	Feb	Mar	Apr	May	Jun	Jul	Aug	Sep	Oct	Nov	Dec
Massachusetts		0%	-4%	0%	-8%	0%	-2%	0%	7%	35%	-14%	-16%
New-Hampshire		5%	10%	-13%	17%	3%	14%	-27%	-17%	57%	-11%	-41%
New-York		18%	-10%	8%	-4%	24%	-19%	-1%	1%	44%	-15%	-3%

Figure5. Change in sales over Time for Product "Birch-B"

Our choice of exception model was motivated by the following desiderata:

1. We need to consider variation and patterns in the measure value across all dimensions that a cell belongs to. This helps us find values that are exceptional within the context of a particular aggregation. It is not enough to simply treat the values in a cube as a flat set and call extreme values in the set as exceptions. For instance, consider the example data cube from Figure 2. If we ignored cell positions, possibly only <Birch-B, Oct> would be marked as an exception. However, we identify several other exceptions. Interestingly, the entry <Birch-B, Dec> with value -10% is marked as an exception whereas entry <Birch-B, Nov> with a higher value -14% is not because for the "Dec" column almost all other product have a large positive value whereas in the "Nov" column most other products also have a negative value. In the "Sep" column, "Jolt-C" has a relatively large positive value since most other products have a negative value and is therefore marked as an exception.
2. We need to find exceptions at all aggregated group-bys of the cube, and not only at the detailed level because it simplifies end-user comprehensibility through concise representation. For instance, ⟨Birch-B,Oct⟩ is an exception at the ⟨Product,Month⟩ group-by (Figure 2) and that means we do not need to mark as exceptions all the high values for ⟨Birch-B,Oct, *⟩ at the ⟨Product,Month,State⟩ group-by (Figure 5).
3. The user should be able to interpret the reason why certain values are marked as exceptions. A typical OLAP user is a business executive, not necessarily a sophisticated statistician. Our method therefore should not require the user to make choices between complex statistical models and the process of finding exceptions should be fairly automated.
4. The procedure for finding exceptions should be computationally efficient and scale for large datasets commonly found in OLAP databases. Also, it should be generalizable and efficient for the range of dimensions that are common in OLAP (typically 3 to 8) and handle hierarchies on dimensions.

3.1 The Model

Consider first the problem of finding exceptions in the most detailed values of the data cube. We call a value an exception if it differs significantly from the anticipated value calculated using a model that takes into account all aggregates (group-bys) in which the value participates. This model was inspired by the table analysis methods [HMJ88] used in the statistical literature.

For a value $y_{i_1 i_2 \ldots i_n}$ in a cube C at position i_r of the rth dimension d_r ($1 \leq r \leq n$), we define the anticipated value $\hat{y}_{i_1 i_2 \ldots i_n}$ as a function f of contributions from various higher level group-bys as:

$$\hat{y}_{i_1 i_2 \ldots i_n} = f(\gamma^G_{(i_r | d_r \in G)} | G \subset \{d_1, d_2, \ldots d_n\}) \tag{1}$$

We will refer to the γ terms as the *coefficients* of the model equation. The way these coefficients are derived is explained in Section 3.4. The different functional forms function f can take is discussed in Section 3.3.

We clarify Eq. 1 by illustrating for the case of a cube with three dimensions A, B, C. The anticipated value $\hat{y}_{ijk}$ for the ith member of dimension A, jth member of dimension B and kth member of dimension C, is expressed as a function of seven terms obtained from each of the seven group-bys of the cube as:

$$\hat{y}_{ijk} = f(\gamma, \gamma_i^A, \gamma_j^B, \gamma_k^C, \gamma_{ij}^{AB}, \gamma_{jk}^{BC}, \gamma_{ik}^{AC})$$

The absolute difference between the actual value, $y_{i_1 i_2 \ldots i_n}$ and the anticipated value $\hat{y}_{i_1 i_2 \ldots i_n}$ is termed as the residual $r_{i_1 i_2 \ldots i_n}$ of the model. Thus,

$$r_{i_1 i_2 \ldots i_n} = |y_{i_1 i_2 \ldots i_n} - \hat{y}_{i_1 i_2 \ldots i_n}| \ .$$

Intuitively, any value with a *relatively* large value of the residual is an exception. A statistically valid definition of "relatively large" requires us to scale the values based also on the anticipated standard deviation $\sigma_{i_1 i_2 \ldots i_n}$ associated with the residuals. Thus, we call a value an exception if the standardized residual, $s_{i_1 i_2 \ldots i_n}$, defined as

$$s_{i_1 i_2 \ldots i_n} = \frac{|y_{i_1 i_2 \ldots i_n} - \hat{y}_{i_1 i_2 \ldots i_n}|}{\sigma_{i_1 i_2 \ldots i_n}} \tag{2}$$

is higher than some threshold τ. We use $\tau = 2.5$ corresponding to a probability of 99% in the normal distribution. In Section 3.5 we discuss how we estimate the standard deviations.

3.2 Exceptions at Higher Levels of Group-bys

Exceptions at higher level group-bys of the cube can be found by separately fitting the model Eq. 1 on aggregated values at each group-by of the data cube using different values of n. For instance, for a cube with three dimensions A, B, C we will need one equation at the most detailed level ABC where $n = 3$, three equations for group-bys AB, BC and CA where $n = 2$, and three equations for group-bys A, B and C where $n = 1$. The OLAP user specifies the aggregate function to be used for summarizing values at higher levels of the cube. For instance, a user might specify "sum" or "average" of sales as the aggregate function. Accordingly, exceptions in "total" or "average" sales will be reported at various group-bys of the cube.

3.3 Functional forms of f

The function f in Eq. 1 can take a form which is:

- Additive: the function f returns the sum of its arguments.
- Multiplicative: the function f returns the product of its arguments.

Other (more complex) functional forms for f are also possible — most of them involving different mixtures of additive and multiplicative terms [HMJ88]. A significantly different approach in this category is the one suggested in [Man71] where factor analytic models like the singular value decomposition [CL86] are used to fit a model based on a mixture of additive and multiplicative terms. The main demerit of these models is the high overhead of computing them and the lack of generalizations of the models to more than 2-3 dimensions and hierarchies.

In our experience with OLAP datasets, the multiplicative form provided better fit than the additive form. (See [SAM98] for an intuitive reason for this.) For ease of calculation, we transform the multiplicative form to a linear additive form by taking a log of original data values. We thus have

$$\hat{l}_{i_1 i_2 \ldots i_n} = \log \hat{y}_{i_1 i_2 \ldots i_n} = \sum_{G \subset \{d_1, d_2, \ldots d_n\}} \gamma^G_{(i_r | d_r \in G)} \qquad (3)$$

For a three-dimensional cube, this equation takes the form:

$$\hat{l}_{ijk} = \log \hat{y}_{ijk} = \gamma + \gamma^A_i + \gamma^B_j + \gamma^C_k + \gamma^{AB}_{ij} + \gamma^{BC}_{jk} + \gamma^{AC}_{ik}.$$

3.4 Estimating model coefficients

We now discuss how we estimate the coefficients of the model equation. Two possible approaches are:

1. Mean-based estimates: For deriving these estimates we assume the logarithms of the values are distributed normally with the same variance. The following approach yields the least-squares estimates in that case [HMT83]:
   - $\gamma = \ell_{+\ldots+}$ which is the grand mean or average. Note that a "+" in the ith index denotes an aggregation along the ith dimension.
   - $\gamma^{A_r}_{i_r} = \ell_{+..+i_r+..+} - \gamma$ where $\ell_{+..+i_r+..+}$ is the mean over all values along i_rth member of dimension A_r. Thus, $\gamma^{A_r}_{i_r}$ denotes how much the average of the values along i_rth member of dimension A_r differs from the overall average.
   - $(\gamma)^{A_r A_s}_{i_r i_s} = \ell_{+..+i_r+..+i_s+..+} - \gamma^{A_r}_{i_r} - \gamma^{A_s}_{i_s} - \gamma.$

   In general, the coefficients corresponding to any group-by G are obtained by subtracting from the average ℓ value at group-by G all the coefficients from higher level group-bys. Intuitively, the coefficients reflect an adjustments to the mean of the corresponding group-by after all higher-level adjustments are taken into account. If a user is navigating the data cube top-down, then the coefficients reflect how different the values at more detailed levels are, based on the general impressions formed by looking at higher level aggregates. This helps provide easy grasp of why certain numbers are marked exceptions.

2. Other robust estimates: The main shortcoming of the mean-based approach is that it is not robust in the presence of extremely large outliers. Therefore, a number of methods including the median polish method [HMJ88] and the square combining method [HMJ88] have been proposed. These are all based on using robust estimates of central tendency like "median" or "trimmed-mean" instead of "mean" for calculating the coefficients. Trimmed-mean of a set of values is defined as the mean of the values left after a certain fraction of the extreme values (largest and smallest) have been trimmed off.

We used the 75% trimmed-mean where 25% of the extreme values are trimmed off and the mean is taken of the middle 75% numbers. By dropping 25% of the extreme numbers, we make the method robust to outliers.

3.5 Estimating standard deviation

In classical Analysis of Variance (ANOVA) methods [Mon91], the standard deviation for all the cells is assumed to be identical. The variance (square of standard deviation) is estimated as the sum of squares of the residuals divided by the number of entries. We found that this method provides poor fits on OLAP data. In the analysis of contingency tables [BFH75], where cell entries represent counts, the Poisson distribution is assumed. This assumption implies that the variance is equal to the mean. When the entries are not counts (e.g., large dollar values), this typically leads to an underestimate of the variance.

The method we use for estimating variance is based on a slight modification of the previous models. We model the variance as a power ρ of the mean value $\hat{y}_{i_1...i_n}$ as:

$$\sigma^2_{i_1 i_2...i_n} = (\hat{y}_{i_1 i_2...i_n})^\rho .$$

To calculate ρ we use the maximum likelihood principle [CL86] on data assumed to be distributed normally with the mean value $\hat{y}_{i_1 i_2...i_n}$. According to the latter, one can derive that the estimated value of ρ must satisfy:

$$\sum \frac{(y_{i_1 i_2...i_n} - \hat{y}_{i_1 i_2...i_n})^2}{(\hat{y}_{i_1 i_2...i_n})^\rho} \cdot \log \hat{y}_{i_1 i_2...i_n} - \sum \log \hat{y}_{i_1 i_2...i_n} = 0 . \tag{4}$$

The method we used for solving the equation to find ρ is discussed in [SAM98].

3.6 Summarizing exceptions

As discussed in Section 2, we need to summarize exceptions in lower levels of the cube as single values at higher levels of cube. We present concise definitions of the $\mathcal{S}$elfExp,$\mathcal{I}$nExp and $\mathcal{P}$athExp quantities we associate with each cell for this purpose. In [SAM98] more formal definitions appear.

$\mathcal{S}$elfExp: denotes the exception value of the cell. This quantity is defined as the scaled absolute value of the residual defined in Eq. 2 with a cut-off threshold of τ.

InExp: denotes the total degree of surprise over *all* elements reachable by drill-downs from this cell. We define it formally as the maximum SelfExp value over all cells underneath this cell.

PathExp: denotes the degree of surprise to be anticipated if drilled down along a particular path for each possible drill down path from the cell. We define PathExp as the maximum of the SelfExp over all cells reachable by drilling down along that path.

4 Computation Techniques

At first glance, our approach may appear unrealizable in practice because of the apparent high cost of computing exceptions at every cell of every group-by of the cube. In this section, we present fast computation techniques that make our approach feasible for large OLAP databases. There are three logical phases in the computation of exceptions in the entire cube:

1. The first phase involves the computation of the aggregate values (as specified by the user-provided aggregate function) over which exceptions will be found at each group-by of the cube. This is essentially the problem of cube computation and efficient computation techniques for this problem have been developed in [AAD+96].
2. The next phase is *model fitting*, *i.e.*, finding the coefficients of the model equation and using them to find the residuals as discussed in Section 3.1.
3. The final phase involves summarizing exceptions found in the second phase as discussed in Section 3.6. Computationally, this phase is similar to phase 1 with a few differences as discussed in [SAM98].

4.1 Model fitting

In general, we need to fit separate equations for different group-bys of the cube as discussed in Section 3.2. We will first consider the scenario where a single equation is fit on the base level data. Later in Section 4.2, we will discuss how to simultaneously fit multiple equations, one for each of the group-bys of the cube.

We first present a method called **UpDown** that is directly based on Eq. 3 and later present improvements.

The UpDown Method Recall from Section 3.4 that the coefficients at each group-by G of the cube is equal to the average value at G minus the sum of the coefficients of all group-bys that are subsets of G. Thus, an efficient way to compute the coefficients is the following two pass approach: First in the **up-phase**, compute the average ℓ value (call it **avg-1**) at each group-by starting from the most detailed group-by. This is computationally similar to the cube computation of phase 1 where we compute the user specified aggregate function (call it **user-agg**). Thus, phase-1 and the **up-phase** of phase 2 can be combined to save on the disk scan and sorting costs. Then in the **down-phase**, subtract from each group-by G the coefficients of all its subsets starting from the least detailed group-by (ALL).

Find-coefficients
Up-phase:
    For each group-by G starting from the most detailed group-by
        Compute the **user-agg** and **avg-1** values from one of its parents
Down-phase:
    For each group-by G starting from the least detailed
        Compute coefficient at G by subtracting from **avg-1** values, coefficients
            from **all** group-bys H where $H \subset G$.

Example: Consider cube ABC. We first compute the average value for each of the $2^3 - 1 = 7$ group-bys of the cube by starting from the ABC group-by and computing the average at AB, AC and BC from ABC, computing the average at A from one of AB or AC and so on, using the cube computation methods of [AAD+96]. We then compute the coefficient starting from ALL. The coefficient of each member of group-by A is the average value at the member minus the coefficient of its parent ALL, the coefficients at AB is the average at AB minus the coefficients at A, B and ALL and so on. Finally, we subtract from the average ℓ value at ABC coefficients at AB, AC, BC, A, B, C and ALL.

Analysis The **down-phase** is computationally rather intensive because, in general, for computing the coefficients of a n attribute group-by we need to subtract coefficients from $2^n - 1$ other group-bys. This is equivalent to joining the n-attribute group-by with $2^n - 1$ other group-bys. When the size of these group-bys is large, computing so many multi-attribute joins per group-by can incur large sorting and comparison costs. This straightforward computation can be improved further as discussed in [SAM98].

Rewriting We now discuss further ways of speeding up computation by rewriting Eq. 3. Instead of the $2^n - 1$ terms in Eq. 3, we express the expected value as a sum of n terms as follows:

$$\hat{\ell}_{i_1 \ldots i_n} = g^1 + \ldots + g^n, \ where \ g^r = \mathrm{avg}_{i_r}(\ell_{i_1 \ldots i_n} - g^1 - \ldots - g^{r-1}) \qquad (5)$$

As an example, consider a cube with three dimensions A, B, C.

$$\hat{\ell}_{ijk} = g^1_{ij} + g^2_{ik} + g^3_{jk}, \ where,$$
$$g^1_{ij} = \mathrm{avg}_k(\ell_{ijk})$$
$$g^2_{ik} = \mathrm{avg}_j(\ell_{ijk} - g^1_{ij})$$
$$g^3_{jk} = \mathrm{avg}_i(\ell_{ijk} - g^1_{ij} - g^2_{ik}).$$

The coefficients from the original Eq. 3 can be rewritten in terms of the new coefficients as:

$$r_{ijk} = \ell_{ijk} - (g^1_{ij} + g^2_{ik} + g^3_{jk})$$

$$\gamma_{ij} = g_{ij}^1 - g_i^1 - g_j^1, \text{ where } g_i^1 = \text{avg}_j(g_{ij}^1), \ g_j^1 = \text{avg}_i(g_{ij}^1 - g_i^1),$$
$$\gamma_{ik} = g_{ik}^2 - g_k^2, \text{ where } g_k^2 = \text{avg}_i(g_{ik}^2),$$
$$\gamma_{kj} = g_{jk}^3$$
$$\gamma_i = g_i^1 - g^1, \text{ where } g^1 = \text{avg}_i(g_i^1)$$
$$\gamma_j = g_j^1$$
$$\gamma_k = g_k^2$$
$$\gamma = g^1$$

Lemma 1. *Equations 3 and 5 yield the same set of residuals when the cube contains no missing data. [Proof appears in [SAM98].]*

When a cube does contain missing data, the residuals could differ depending on the number of missing values. One should evaluate the coefficients iteratively ([HMJ88], chapter 4) for producing accurate least squares fit in such cases. However, these methods are not practical for our goal of pre-mining an entire large database since they require multiple passes (often 10 or more) of data. Our implementation ignores the missing values in the calculation of the coefficients in both equations by calculating the average only over the values actually present.

Computing with Eq. 5 The rewritten formula can be computed as follows. First compute g^1 by averaging the starting $\ell_{i_1 \ldots i_n}$ values along dimension i_n, subtract values g^1 from the original ℓ values, average the subtracted value along dimension i_{n-1} to compute g^2, subtract the values at g^2 from the modified ℓ values and so on until all dimensions are aggregated. The final ℓ value directly gives us the residual. Next, compute the other coefficients of the equation by recursively repeating the process for higher level aggregates on the average g values just calculated. These operations can be overlapped with the computation of the **user-agg** function of phase-1 as follows:

Compute(G)
    Mark G as computed.
    For each immediate child H of G not marked computed
        Compute and store the **user-agg** and **avg-g** values at H from G
        Subtract the **avg-g** value at H from G
    For each H above
        Compute(H) /* on the **avg-g** values. */
    Initial call: Compute(Base level cube)

Example In Figure 6 we show the example of a three attribute group-by and the sequence of computations needed for getting its coefficients and residuals. An upward arrow denotes the averaging phase and a downward arrow denotes the subtraction phase. The numbers beside each edge denotes the order in which these operations are performed. We first average ABC along C to obtain AB, subtract the values at AB from ABC, average ABC along B to obtain AC, and so on until BC is subtracted from ABC. Next, we compute the coefficient at AB

by averaging its g values along dimension B to obtain A, subtract out the results from AB and so on. When computing coefficient at AC we do not average and subtract along A because A has already been computed by averaging AB.

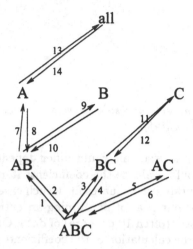

Figure6. Fitting single equation for a three-attribute cube

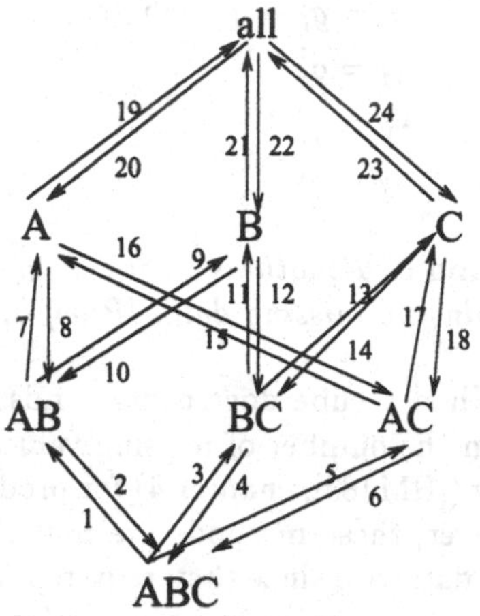

Figure7. Fitting multiple equations for a three-attribute cube

Benefits of rewriting The advantage of rewriting Eq. 3 into Eq. 5 as above is three fold. First we can compute the residuals of a k-dimensional cube by joining it with at most k other group-bys instead of $2^k - 1$ group-bys as in Eq. 3, an exponential difference in the number of join (subtraction) operations. Second, we can compute the residuals the same time as we compute the aggregate values in phase 1 and thus save on the sorting and comparison costs. Finally, there is no additional sorting cost beyond cube computation since, unlike in the UpDown method, the subtraction operation is followed immediately after the aggregation operation. Thus, not only are the number of join operations exponentially smaller but also the cost of each join is significantly reduced since the joins require the same sorting order as the aggregation that precedes it.

Alternative Rewritings There are other ways in which we could have rewritten Eq.3. For instance, for $n = 3$ another way of rewriting the equation is:

$$\hat{\ell}_{ijk} = g_{ij}^{AB} + \gamma_k^C + \gamma_k^{AC} + \gamma_k^{BC}, \text{where}$$
$$g_{ij}^{AB} = \text{avg}_k(\ell_{ijk})$$

The above equation uses four terms whereas Eq. 5 requires only three.

The goal in rewriting the equation in terms of as few coefficients as possible is to reduce the computation cost. Eq. 5 involves the fewest number of terms in each equation. It is because any equation equivalent to Eq. 3 must contain at least n terms since we must have at least one term from each of the $n - 1$ dimensional group-bys.

4.2 Simultaneous computation of multiple equations

We can adapt our method for fitting single equations to the case where we fit simultaneously multiple equations — one for each group-by of the cube. We proceed bottom up and first compute the residuals for the bottom-most group-by using the aggregation and subtraction operations with respect to its immediate children group-bys as in the single equation case. At the end of this, the residuals for the bottom-most group-by are already computed. Thus, we can drop the g terms calculated so far and start to fit the equations of the $n-1$ attribute group-bys on the aggregated function **user-agg**. Each of these $n-1$ dimensional group-bys can now be treated independently and we can recursively fit equations for each group-by of the cube as shown in the pseudo-code below.

ComputeMulti(G)
    For each immediate child H of G
        Compute the **avg-g** values at H by aggregating G
        If G is the smallest parent of H
            also, compute and store **user-agg** function along with above step
        Subtract the **avg-g** value at H from G
    For each H whose **user-agg** function computed above
        ComputeMulti(H) /* on the **user-agg** function values. */
Initial call: ComputeMulti(Base level cube)

Note the two key differences between the routine Compute() for the single equation case and ComputeMulti() for the multi equation case. First, for each group-by *all* of its immediate children are used instead of just the un-computed ones as in the single equation case. Second, for each group-by we start from the aggregate function value for that group-by rather than the g values computed from the previous group-by.

Example Figure 7 shows the sequence of aggregation and subtraction operations that happen when fitting multiple equations using the rewrite procedure.

5 Conclusion

We developed a novel method of effectively navigating large OLAP data cubes. Our method guides the user to interesting regions exhibiting anomalous behavior using pre-computed exceptions. This method enhances a user's capability of discovering interesting areas in the data compared with the current manual discovery.

We presented the statistical foundation of our methodology for identifying exceptions, which was chosen after considering a number of other competing techniques and suitably adapted so as to best match the requirements of OLAP datasets. The coefficients at different levels of the cube have the property that they reflect adjustments to the combined average value obtained from higher level aggregations of the cube. As the user typically navigates the data cube top-down, this enables the user to very naturally capture the context in which the value was declared an exception. In [SAM98] we present how our model handles hierarchies and ordered dimensions like time.

We devised methods of efficiently computing exceptions. Novel rewriting techniques are used to reduce the cost of model fitting and modifying the computation flow so as to mesh exception finding with cube computation. Our experiments (detailed in [SAM98]) show that these techniques yield almost a factor of three to four performance improvement. We have applied our technique on several real-life OLAP datasets with interesting results. In [SAM98] we report some of these findings.

Future work in the area should incorporate methods for model selection and user customization of the definition of exceptions.

References

[AAD+96] S. Agarwal, R. Agrawal, P.M. Deshpande, A. Gupta, J.F. Naughton, R. Ramakrishnan, and S. Sarawagi. On the computation of multidimensional aggregates. In *Proc. of the 22nd Int'l Conference on Very Large Databases*, pages 506–521, Mumbai (Bombay), India, September 1996.

[AGS97] Rakesh Agrawal, Ashish Gupta, and Sunita Sarawagi. Modeling multidimensional databases. In *Proc. of the 13th Int'l Conference on Data Engineering*, Birmingham, U.K., April 1997.

[Arb] Arbor Software Corporation. *Application Manager User's Guide, Essbase version 4.0.* http://www.arborsoft.com.

[BFH75] Y. Bishop, S. Fienberg, and P. Holland. *Discrete Multivariate Analysis theory and practice.* The MIT Press, 1975.

[CL86] William W. Cooley and Paul R Lohnes. *Multivariate data analysis.* Robert E. Krieger publishers, 1986.

[Col95] George Colliat. OLAP, relational, and multidimensional database systems. Technical report, Arbor Software Corporation, Sunnyvale, CA, 1995.

[GBLP96] J. Gray, A. Bosworth, A. Layman, and H. Pirahesh. Data cube: A relational aggregation operator generalizing group-by, cross-tabs and sub-totals. In *Proc. of the 12th Int'l Conference on Data Engineering*, pages 152–159, 1996.

[HMJ88] D. Hoaglin, F. Mosteller, and Tukey. J. *Exploring data tables, trends and shapes.* Wiley series in probability, 1988.

[HMT83] D.C. Hoaglin, F. Mosteller, and J.W. Tukey. *Understanding Robust and Exploratory Data Analysis.* John Wiley, New York, 1983.

[Man71] J. Mandel. A new analysis of variance model for non-additive data. *Technometrics*, 13:1–18, 1971.

[Mon91] D.G. Montgomery. *Design and Analysis of Experiments*, chapter 13. John Wiley & sons, third edition, 1991.

[OLA96] The OLAP Council. *MD-API the OLAP Application Program Interface Version 0.5 Specification*, September 1996.

[SAM98] Sunita Sarawagi, Rakesh Agrawal, and Nimrod Megiddo. Discovery-driven exploration of OLAP data cubes. Research Report RJ 10102 (91918), IBM Almaden Research Center, San Jose, CA 95120, January 1998. Available from http://www.almaden.ibm.com/cs/quest.

A Logical Approach to Multidimensional Databases*

Luca Cabibbo and Riccardo Torlone

Dipartimento di Informatica e Automazione, Università di Roma Tre
Via della Vasca Navale, 79 — I-00146 Roma, Italy
E-mail: {cabibbo,torlone}@dia.uniroma3.it

Abstract. In this paper we present $\mathcal{MD}$, a logical model for OLAP systems, and show how it can be used in the design of multidimensional databases. Unlike other models for multidimensional databases, $\mathcal{MD}$ is independent of any specific implementation (relational or proprietary multidimensional) and as such it provides a clear separation between practical and conceptual aspects. In this framework, we present a design methodology, to obtain an $\mathcal{MD}$ scheme from an operational database. We then show how an $\mathcal{MD}$ database can be implemented, describing translations into relational tables and into multidimensional arrays.

1 Introduction

An enterprise can achieve a great competitive advantage from the analysis of its historical data. For instance, the identification of unusual trends in sales can suggest opportunities for new business, whereas the analysis of past consumer demand can be useful for forecasting production needs. A *data warehouse* is an integrated collection of enterprise-wide data, oriented to decision making, that is built to support this activity [8, 9]. Actually, data analysis is not performed directly on the data warehouse, but rather on special data stores derived from it, often called *hypercubes* or *multidimensional* "fact" tables. These terms originate from the fact that the effectiveness of the analysis is related to the ability of describing and manipulating factual data according to different and often independent perspectives or "dimensions," and that this picture can be naturally represented by means of n-dimensional arrays (or cubes). As an example, in a commercial enterprise, single sales of items (the factual data) provide much more information to business analysts when organized according to dimensions like category of product, geographical location, and time. The collection of fact tables of interest for an enterprise forms a *multidimensional database*.

Traditional database systems are inadequate for multidimensional analysis since they are optimized for on-line transaction processing (OLTP), which corresponds to large numbers of concurrent transactions, often involving very few records. Conversely, multidimensional database systems should be designed for

---

* This work was partially supported by *CNR* and by *MURST*.

the so-called *on-line analytical processing* [5] (OLAP), which involves few complex queries over very large numbers of records. Current technology provides both OLAP data servers and client analysis tools. OLAP servers can be either relational systems (ROLAP) or proprietary multidimensional systems (MOLAP). A ROLAP system is an extended relational system that maps operations on multidimensional data to standard relational operations (SQL). A MOLAP system is instead a special server that directly represents and manipulates data in the form of multidimensional arrays. The clients offer querying and reporting tools, usually based on interactive graphical user interfaces, similar to spreadsheets.

In the various systems [11], multidimensional databases are modeled in a way that strictly depends on the corresponding implementation (relational or proprietary multidimensional). This has a number of negative consequences. First, it is difficult to define a design methodology that includes a general, conceptual step, independent of any specific system but suitable for each. Second, in specifying analytical queries, the analysts often need to take care of tedious details, referring to the "physical" organization of data, rather than just to the essential, "logical" aspects. Finally, the integration with database technology and the optimization strategies are often based on ad-hoc techniques, rather than any systematic approach. As others [1, 7], we believe that, similarly to what happens with relational databases, a better understanding of the main problems related to the management of multidimensional databases can be achieved only by providing a logical description of business data, independent of the way in which data is stored.

In this paper we study conceptual and practical issues related to the design of multidimensional databases. The framework for our investigation is $\mathcal{MD}$, a logical model for OLAP systems that extends an earlier proposal [3]. This model includes a number of concepts that generalize the notions of dimensional hierarchies, fact tables, and measures, commonly used in commercial systems. In $\mathcal{MD}$, dimensions are linguistic categories that describe different ways of looking at the information. Each dimension is organized into a hierarchy of levels, corresponding to different granularity of data. Within a dimension, levels are related through "roll-up" functions and can have descriptions associated with them. Factual data is represented by f-tables, the logical counterpart to multi-dimensional arrays, which are functions associating measures with symbolic coordinates.

In this context, we present a general design methodology, aimed at building an $\mathcal{MD}$ scheme starting from an operational database described by an Entity-Relationship scheme. It turns out that, once facts and dimensions have been identified, an $\mathcal{MD}$ database can be derived in a natural way. We then describe two practical implementations of $\mathcal{MD}$ databases: using relational tables in the form of a "star" scheme (as in ROLAP systems), and using multidimensional arrays (as in MOLAP systems). This confirms the generality of the approach.

The paper is organized as follows. In the rest of this section, we briefly compare our work with relevant literature. In Section 2 we present the $\mathcal{MD}$ model. Section 3 describes the design methodology referring to a practical example. The implementation of an $\mathcal{MD}$ database into both relational tables and multidimensional arrays is illustrated in Section 4. Finally, in Section 5, we draw some final conclusions and sketch further research issues.

Related work. The term OLAP has been recently introduced by Codd et al. [5] to characterize the category of analytical processing over large, historical databases (data warehouses) oriented to decision making. Further discussion on OLAP, multidimensional analysis, and data warehousing can be found in [4, 8, 9, 12]. Recently, Mendelzon has published a comprehensive on-line bibliography on this subject [10].

The $\mathcal{MD}$ model illustrated in this paper extends the multidimensional model proposed in [3]. While the previous paper is mainly oriented to the introduction of a declarative query language and the investigation of its expressiveness, the present paper is focused on the design of multidimensional databases.

The traditional model used in the context of OLAP systems is based on the notion of star scheme or variants thereof (snowflake, star constellation, and so on) [8, 9]. A star scheme consists of a number of relational tables: (1) the fact tables, each of which contains a composed key together with one or more measures being tracked, and (2) the dimension tables, each of which contains a single key, corresponding to a component of the key in a fact table, and data describing a dimension at different levels of granularity. Our model is at an higher level of abstraction than this representation, since in $\mathcal{MD}$ facts and dimensions are abstract entities, described by mathematical functions. It follows that, in querying an $\mathcal{MD}$ database, there is no need to specify complex joins between fact and dimension tables, as it happens in a star scheme.

To our knowledge, the work by Golfarelli et al. [6] is the only paper that investigates the issue of the conceptual design of multidimensional databases. They propose a methodology that has some similarities with ours, even though it covers only conceptual aspects (no implementation issue is considered). Conversely, our approach relies on a formal logical model that provides a solid basis for the study of both conceptual and practical issues.

Other models for multidimensional databases have been proposed (as illustrated next) but mainly with the goal of studying OLAP query languages. A common characteristic of these models is that they are generally oriented towards a specific implementation, and so less suitable to multidimensional design than ours.

Agrawal et al. [1] have proposed a framework for studying multidimensional databases, consisting of a data model based on the notion of multidimensional cube, and an algebraic query language. This framework shares a number of characteristics and goals with ours. However, $\mathcal{MD}$ is richer than the model they propose, as it has been defined mainly for the development a general design methodology. For instance, dimensional hierarchies are part of the $\mathcal{MD}$ model, whereas, in Agrawal's approach, they are implemented using a special query language operator. Moreover, their work is mainly oriented to an SQL implementation into a relational database. Conversely, we do not make any assumption on the practical realization of the model.

Gyssens and Lakshmanan [7] have proposed a logical model for multidimensional databases, called MDD, in which the contents are clearly separated from structural aspects. This model has some characteristic in common with the star scheme even though it does not necessarily rely on a relational implementation. Differently from our approach, there are some multidimensional features that are not explicitly represented in the MDD model, like the notion of aggregation levels in a dimension. Moreover, the focus of their paper is still on the development of querying and restructuring languages rather than data modeling.

2 Modeling Multidimensional Databases

The MultiDimensional data model ($\mathcal{MD}$ for short) is based on two main constructs: dimension and f-table. *Dimensions* are syntactical categories that allow us to specify multiple "ways" to look at the information, according to natural business perspectives under which its analysis can be performed. Each dimension is organized in a hierarchy of *levels*, corresponding to data domains at different granularity. A level can have *descriptions* associated with it. Within a dimension, values of different levels are related through a family of *roll-up functions*. *F-tables* are functions from *symbolic coordinates* (defined with respect to particular combinations of levels) to *measures*: they are used to represent factual data.

Formally, we fix two disjoint countable sets of *names* and *values*, and denote by $\mathcal{L}$ a set of names called *levels*. Each level $l \in \mathcal{L}$ is associated with a countable set of values, called the *domain of l* and denoted by DOM(l). The various domains are pairwise disjoint.

Definition 1 (Dimension). *An $\mathcal{MD}$ dimension consists of:*

- *a finite set of levels $L \subseteq \mathcal{L}$;*
- *a partial order $\preceq$ on the levels in L — whenever $l_1 \preceq l_2$ we say that l_1 rolls up to l_2;*
- *a family of roll-up functions, including a function R-UP$_{l_1}^{l_2}$ from DOM(l_1) to DOM(l_2) for each pair of levels $l_1 \preceq l_2$ — whenever R-UP$_{l_1}^{l_2}(o_1) = o_2$ we say that o_1 rolls up to o_2.*

A dimension with just one level is called *atomic*. For the sake of simplicity, we will not make any distinction between an atomic dimension and its unique level.

Definition 2 (Scheme). *An $\mathcal{MD}$ scheme consists of:*

- *a finite set D of dimensions;*
- *a finite set F of f-table schemes of the form $f[A_1 : l_1\langle d_1 \rangle, \ldots, A_n : l_n\langle d_n \rangle] : l_0\langle d_0 \rangle$, where f is a name, each A_i $1(\leq i \leq n)$ is a distinct name called attribute of f, and each l_i $(0 \leq i \leq n)$ is a level of the dimension d_i;*
- *a finite set Δ of level descriptions of the form $\delta(l) : l'$, where l and l' are levels and δ is a name called description of l.*

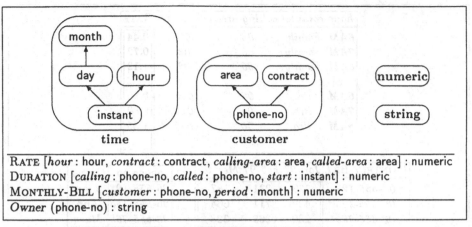

RATE [*hour*: hour, *contract*: contract, *calling-area*: area, *called-area*: area] : numeric	
DURATION [*calling*: phone-no, *called*: phone-no, *start*: instant] : numeric	
MONTHLY-BILL [*customer*: phone-no, *period*: month] : numeric	
Owner (phone-no) : string	

Fig. 1. The sample TelCo scheme

Note that in an f-table we annotate the dimension corresponding to each level: this is because a level may belong to different dimensions. However, we will omit the dimensions in an f-table scheme when they are clear from the context.

Consider for instance a telecommunication company interested in the analysis of its operational information. Data about phone calls can be organized along dimensions **time** and **customer**. The corresponding hierarchies are depicted on top of Figure 1. Two further atomic dimensions are used to represent **numeric** values and **strings**. Level phone-no (telephone numbers) rolls up to both area (the geographical area in which the telephone is located, identified by an area code) and contract (characterized by rates at different hours). The domain associated with the level instant contains timestamps like *Jan 5, 97, 10AM:45:21*. This value rolls up to *10AM* in the level hour and to *Jan 5, 97* in the level day. Several f-tables can be defined in this framework, as described in the same figure. RATE represents the cost for a minute of conversation between a customer in a *calling-area* (having a contract of type *contract*) and a customer in a *called-area*, and starting at a specific *hour*. The second f-table associates with each call (issued by a *calling* to a *called* party at some time) the DURATION in seconds. MONTHLY-BILL is a derived f-table that aggregates the revenues by phone number and month. Finally, *Owner* is a level description associating the name of a customer with a phone number.

Instances can be defined over f-tables as follows.

Definition 3 (Coordinate and Instance). *Let* $S = (D, F, \Delta)$ *be an* $\mathcal{MD}$ *scheme. A (symbolic) coordinate over an f-table scheme* $f[A_1 : l_1\langle d_1\rangle, \ldots, A_n : l_n\langle d_n\rangle] : l_0\langle d_0\rangle$ *in F is a function mapping each attribute name* A_i ($1 \leq i \leq n$) *to an element in* DOM(l_i). *An instance over f is a partial function that maps coordinates over f to elements of* DOM(l_0). *An instance over a level description* $\delta(l) : l'$ *in* Δ *is a partial function from* DOM(l) *to* DOM(l').

An *entry* of an f-table instance f is a coordinate over which f is defined. The actual value that f associates with an entry is called a *measure*.

hour	contract	calling-area	called-area	RATE
6AM	Family	06	02	0.44
7AM	Family	06	02	0.72
8AM	Family	06	02	1.12
		...		...
6AM	Pro	06	055	0.80
7AM	Pro	06	055	0.80
8AM	Pro	06	055	1.35
		...		...

MONTHLY-BILL	Jan-97	Feb-97	Mar-97
06-555-123	129	231	187
06-555-456	429	711	664
02-555-765	280	365	328

phone-no	Owner
06-555-123	John
06-555-456	Ann
02-555-765	Mary

Fig. 2. A sample instance over the TelCo scheme

A possible instance over the TelCo scheme is shown in Figure 2. A symbolic coordinate over the f-table RATE is [hour : 7AM, contract : Family, calling-area : 06, called-area : 02]. The actual instance associates the measure 0.72 with this entry. The description Owner associates the string John with the value 06-555-123 of level phone-no. Note that two different graphical representations for f-tables are used in Figure 2: a table for RATE and an array MONTHLY-BILL. This suggests that several implementations of a same f-table are possible.

It is apparent that our notion of "symbolic coordinate" is related with that of "tuple" in the relational model. It can also be noted that the notation we use for symbolic coordinates resembles subscripting into a multi-dimensional array (although in a non-positional way). There is however an important difference between f-tables and multi-dimensional arrays. Specifically, in arrays, "physical" coordinates vary over intervals within linearly-ordered domains, whereas we do not pose any restrictive hypothesis on the domains over which coordinates range. In this sense, our notion of coordinate is "symbolic."

Roll-up functions are a distinctive feature of our model: they describe *intensionally* how values of different levels are related. Such a description is indeed independent of any effective implementation, which can be based on stored relations, built-in functions, or external procedures. Moreover, roll-up functions provide a powerful tool for querying multidimensional data, since they allow us to specify how data must be aggregated, and how f-tables involving data at different levels of granularity can be joined [3].

3 Design of MultiDimensional Databases

In this section we show how $\mathcal{MD}$ schemes can be obtained from conceptual schemes. We assume to have an E-R scheme [2] at our disposal describing an (integrated) view of operational databases. We assume that this scheme describes a "primitive" data warehouse containing all the operational information that can support our business processing, but not yet tailored to this activity. The construction of this scheme can require a number of foregoing activities, including the reverse-engineering of several data sources and their integration into a global conceptual scheme; we will not discuss these activities here, since they are beyond the scope of the paper. We make however a number of assumptions on the initial E-R scheme. First, we assume that the scheme does not contain generalization hierarchies and that all its attributes are simple (no multivalued or composed attributes). Then, we assume that the scheme is complete, in the sense that it contains all the information that can be extracted from our operational databases and that can be used in the analytical processing. Finally, we assume that the scheme is fully normalized and minimal, that is, all the concepts appear only once (no derived concepts).

The methodology we propose for building an $\mathcal{MD}$ database starting from a pre-existing E-R scheme consists of four steps.

1. Identification of facts and dimensions.
2. Restructuring of the E-R scheme.
3. Derivation of a dimensional graph.
4. Translation into the $\mathcal{MD}$ model.

Actually, the first two steps are not strictly sequential, but in many cases proceed in parallel: during the restructuring of the E-R scheme, selected facts and dimensions can be refined and modified. Then, the process proceeds sequentially, since each phase requires the completion of the previous one.

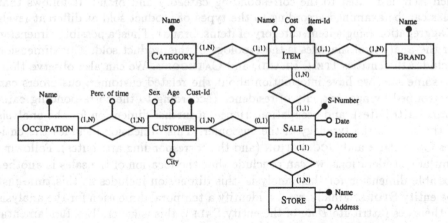

Fig. 3. An E-R scheme describing the Retail operational database

The methodology will be illustrated in the remaining of the section referring to the Retail database, whose E-R scheme is reported in Figure 3 (we adopt the notation used in the book [2]). This scheme describes a number of information about a company holding a chain of stores in which several products are sold. Some information about frequent customers of the company are available.

3.1 Identification of Facts and Dimensions

The first activity consists in a careful analysis of the given E-R scheme whose aim is the selection of the facts, the measures, and the dimensions of interest for our business processing. We call *facts* the concepts in the E-R scheme (entities, relationship, or attributes) on which the decision-making process is focused. A *measure* is instead an atomic property of a fact that we intend to analyze (generally a numeric attribute of a fact or a count of its instances). Finally, a *dimension* is a subscheme of the given E-R scheme that describes a perspective under which the analysis of a fact can be performed.

Let us consider the Retail database. We could be interested, on one hand, in the identification of trends in the volume of sales and in the corresponding incomes and, on the other hand, in the analysis of the variation of production costs of the items on sale. Thus, in this case the facts are the entity SALE and the attribute *Cost* of the entity ITEM. The measures for the former fact are the number of sales (count of instances of the entity) and the incomes of the sales (attribute *Income*). The only measure for the latter is the value of the cost itself. Note that, in some cases, a fact has several aspects that need to be evaluated, in others the measure of a fact coincides with the fact itself.

Along a dimension, the analysis of a fact is performed by consolidating (i.e., aggregating) data [5]. Therefore, we can identify a dimension by navigating the scheme, starting from each fact and including concepts that suggest a way to group data (for example, entities related by one-to-many relationships, or categorical attributes like age or sex). Let us consider for instance the fact entity SALE. We can see that each sale is related to the corresponding item sold and each item is related to the corresponding category and brand. It follows that sales can be examined according to the types of product sold at different levels of aggregation (single item, category of items, brand). Thus, a possible dimension for the analysis of the sales is the typology of the product sold. This dimension includes the entities ITEM, BRAND, and CATEGORY. We can also observe that, for some sale, we have information about the related customer; customers can be grouped by age, sex, city of residence (according to the corresponding categorical attributes), and occupation. Hence, a further dimension for the analysis of the sales is the typology of the customer. This dimension includes the entities CUSTOMER and OCCUPATION (and the corresponding attributes). Following similar considerations, we can conclude that the location of the sales is another possible dimension for their analysis: this dimension includes at this time just the entity STORE. Finally, we can identify a temporal dimension for the analysis of the sales (attribute *Date* of the entity SALE): this is generally a fundamental dimension in multidimensional processing.

3.2 Restructuring of the E-R Scheme

This activity consists in a reorganization of the original E-R scheme in order to describe facts and dimensions in a better, more explicit way. The goal of this step is the production of a new E-R scheme that can be directly mapped to the $\mathcal{MD}$ model. We believe that it is useful to perform this activity within the E-R model since, in this way, the mapping between the operational and the multidimensional database can be easily derived.

The restructuring can be divided into a number of activities as described in the following paragraphs.

Representing facts as entities. Generally, facts correspond to entities of the initial E-R scheme, but they can also be described by attributes or relationships. In these cases, they need to be translated into entities (according to the usual information-preserving transformations [2]) since facts become of central interest in the analytical processing. Also, this transformation simplifies the steps that follows the restructuring phase.

For instance, in our example, the production cost of the items is represented by means of an attribute. This attribute can be easily transformed into an entity COST OF ITEM by adding a one-to-one relationship between the new entity and the entity ITEM, as shown in Figure 4. Each instance of this new entity is identified (externally) by the corresponding item.

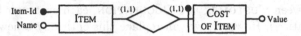

Fig. 4. A restructuring of the entity ITEM in the E-R scheme in Figure 3

Adding dimensions. It may happen that, for some fact in the E-R model, there are dimensions of interest for its analysis that are missing in the scheme (and therefore, according to our hypotheses, are not represented extensionally in the operational databases) but can be derived either from external databases or from meta-information associated with our data sources. For instance, we could be interested in the temporal validity of a fact or in the geographical origin of certain information. Such dimensions need to be represented explicitly in the E-R scheme.

Let us consider the cost of the items in our `Retail` database. It is reasonable that in the ordinary transaction processing we are only interested in the current cost of an item and therefore no historical information is available about it. Assume however that we know the exact time of the update operations, and that the costs change once for month on the average. Since an effective analysis of costs can be performed only if we compare them in different periods of time, we need to add temporal information about costs. According to the meta-information available, this can be done by restructuring the entity COST OF ITEM as described in Figure 5. From a practical point of view, this historical data can be obtained from the operational database by means of incremental updates that add, each month, a new instance to the entity COST OF ITEM, according to the current value of the attribute *Cost* in the original database.

Refining the levels of each dimension. Within each dimension, we need to select and represent in an explicit way the various levels of aggregation that

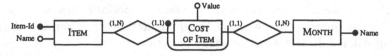

Fig. 5. A restructuring of the entity COST OF ITEM in Figure 4

are of interest in the analysis of facts (e.g., category and brand of an item) and distinguish them from the concepts that are only descriptive but cannot be used in the analysis since do not allow to perform aggregations (e.g., address and telephone number of a store). In practice, this step requires to perform one of the following transformations: replacing many-to-many relationships, adding new concepts (entities or attributes) to represent new levels of interest, selecting a simple identifier for each level entity, and removing irrelevant concepts.

Let us consider the dimension customer in our example. Within this dimension we can aggregate customers according to their age, sex, and city of residence (through the corresponding attributes of the entity CUSTOMER). If we need to aggregate customers also with respect to their occupation, we cannot use directly the corresponding entity since, according to the many-to-many relationship between CUSTOMER and OCCUPATION, each customer has in general several occupations. However, we can replace this entity by a new entity MAIN OCCUPATION describing the occupation of a customer in most of the time, so that the relationship is transformed from many-to-many into one-to-many (see Figure 6). Let us now turn our attention to the dimension location that contains just the entity STORE. We could be interested in aggregating the stores according to the city and to the geographical area (note that this information can be derived from the attribute *Address* and from "built-in" knowledge). This can be made explicit by adding new entities CITY and AREA as shown in Figure 6. For the new entities, it is important to choose a simple identifier (possibly natural if one exists). Finally, let us consider the dimension time, assuming that the dimension product does not require restructuring. We would like to aggregate sales according, for instance, to days, months, special periods (e.g., Easter, school opening, Christmas), quarters, and years. This can be done, again according to built-in knowledge, by adding new entities and one-to-many relationships as shown in Figure 6. When all the dimensions have been examined in this way, the final step consists in removing all the concepts contained in the scheme (entities, attributes, and relationships) that are useless in the analysis processing (among them, uninteresting levels of aggregation).

The E-R scheme we obtain in our example after the restructuring phase is reported in Figure 6. Note that the scheme has been annotated with facts and dimensions. Note also that a dimension does not include descriptive attributes (e.g., attribute *Address* of entity STORE).

3.3 Derivation of a Dimensional Graph

Starting from the restructured E-R scheme, we can now derive a special graph that we call *dimensional*. A dimensional graph represents, in a succinct way,

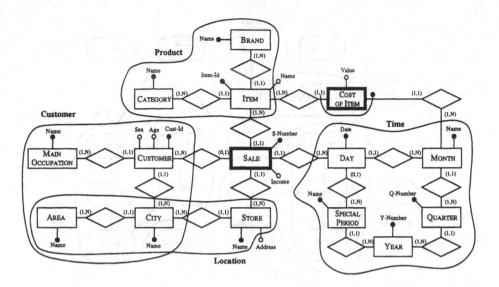

Fig. 6. A restructuring of the E-R scheme reported in Figure 3

facts and dimensions of the restructured E-R scheme. In particular, each node of the graph corresponds to a specific concept (entity or attribute) and represents a domain as follows: if the node corresponds to an entity, it represents the domain of the key of the entity; if the node corresponds to an attribute, it represents the domain of the attribute. The arc between two nodes represents a function between the corresponding domains (the arc is dashed if the function is partial). Figure 7 reports the dimensional graph obtained from the E-R scheme in Figure 6. In this graph, the node ITEM represents the domain of the attribute *Item-Id*; similarly, the node MONTH represents the domain of the attribute *Name* of the corresponding entity; instead, the node INCOME represents the domain of the attribute *Income* of the entity SALE. It is easy to see that this graph can be derived automatically and has the same information content as the original scheme. Note also that the dimensions become sub-graphs of the dimensional graph. In the dimensional graph we can distinguish four kinds of nodes: *fact nodes* are denoted by bold margins (they originate from fact entities); *level nodes* are those occurring in a dimension; *descriptive nodes* are the nodes outside the dimensions that have an incoming arc outgoing from a level node (they originate from descriptive attributes); and *measure nodes* are the nodes outside the dimensions that have an incoming arc outgoing from a fact node (they originate from measures).

3.4 Translation into the $\mathcal{MD}$ Model

The $\mathcal{MD}$ dimensions can be directly derived from the dimensional graph. Specifically, we have an $\mathcal{MD}$ dimension for each dimension of the dimensional graph and, for each dimension, we have an $\mathcal{MD}$ level for each node and a roll-up function for each arc of the corresponding sub-graph. The sub-graphs of the di-

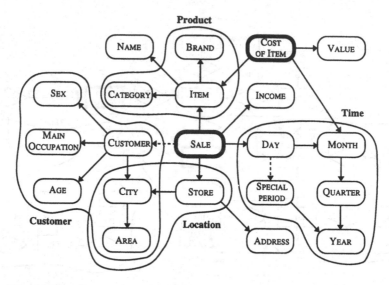

Fig. 7. The dimensional graph obtained from the scheme in Figure 6

mensional graph associated with the various dimensions denote the partial order on the $\mathcal{MD}$ levels. We need also to define a number of atomic dimensions to represent measure nodes and descriptive nodes. In our example, we can define a **numeric** dimension for sale incomes and item costs, and a dimension **string** for item names and store addresses. We can then define a $\mathcal{MD}$ level description for each descriptive node. In our example, we have a description *Name* of the level item and a description *Address* of the level store.

F-tables can be defined as follows. For each fact node in the dimensional graph, we first select a combination of levels from the "associated" dimensions, that is, the dimensions for which there is an arc from the fact node to them. More than one level can be selected for each dimension and not all the dimensions associated with a fact node must be chosen. Then, we need to define a mapping θ, possibly involving aggregations, describing the result of the f-table. This mapping can be: (1) a count of a collection of facts, or (2) an expression over a measure. The f-table instance can be built as follows: for each possible tuple t of values over the chosen levels, we have a collection Φ_t of instances of the fact (for instance, in our example, given a specific item and a day, we have a set of sales associated with them). Then, the tuple t becomes an entry of the f-table, and the measure associated with this entry is obtained by applying the mapping θ to Φ_t.

In the **Retail** database, we have already identified three measures: (1) the number of items sold, (2) the revenues, and (3) the cost of items. The first two measures are described daily for each item and store, whereas the third is given on a monthly basis. These measures can be represented by the following f-tables.

1. SALE[*period* : day, *product* : item, *location* : store] : numeric, defined over the fact SALE by the mapping **count**(SALE);
2. REVENUE[*period* : day, *product* : item, *location* : store] : numeric, defined over the fact SALE by the mapping **sum**(INCOME(SALE));

3. COSTOFITEM[*period* : month, *product* : item] : numeric, defined over the fact
   COST OF ITEM by the mapping VALUE(COST OF ITEM).

We can also be interested in some partially aggregated data. For instance, the analysis of the customers' purchases, by age, category of items, and year, can be performed with the following f-table:

PURCHASEBYAGE[*age* : age, *products* : category, *period* : year] : numeric,

which is defined over the fact SALE by the mapping sum(INCOME(SALE)).

4 Implementation of MultiDimensional Databases

In this section we show how an $\mathcal{MD}$ database can be practically implemented, using a relational database (as in ROLAP systems) or a set of multidimensional arrays (as in MOLAP systems).

4.1 Relational Databases

The natural representation of a multidimensional database in the relational model consists of a collection of "fact" and "dimension" tables. The former are normalized, whereas the latter can be denormalized. Since there exist several different definitions of star schemes, we refer in the following to a basic formulation [8, 9]. We develop the mapping for a star scheme; however, the approach can be easily adapted to variants of this model (e.g., the snowflake scheme).

A *star scheme* representing an $\mathcal{MD}$ database can be built as follows. We have: (1) a relation scheme R_d for each non-atomic dimension d, and (2) a relation scheme R_f for each f-table f. The atomic dimensions do not need to be represented since they generally correspond to basic domains.

- R_d contains an attribute A_l for each level l occurring in d, an attribute A_δ for each description δ of a level in d, and an attribute A_d denoting a (generated) key for R_d.
- R_f contains an attribute A_f for the measure of f and, for each attribute A_i of f over a level $l\langle d \rangle$, an attribute A_i whose domain coincides with the domain of the key A_d of the relation R_d.

The corresponding instances are defined as follows.

- The relation R_d contains a tuple t_v for each value v of each level l occurring in d. The tuple t_v is defined as follows: $t_v.A_d$ is a unique identifier k_v for the value v; $t_v.A_l = v$; for each description δ of l, $t_v.A_\delta = \delta(v)$; for each level l' to which l rolls up, $t_v.A_{l'} = \text{R-UP}_l^{l'}(v)$ and, for each description δ' of l', $t_v.A_{\delta'} = \delta'(\text{R-UP}_l^{l'}(v))$. The other attributes carry nulls.
- The relation R_f contains a tuple t_e for each entry e of f. If e equals $[A_1 : v_1, \ldots, A_n : v_n]$ and v_0 is the corresponding measure, then $t_e.A_f = v_0$ and, for each attribute A_i, $t_e.A_i = k_{v_i}$ $(1 \leq i \leq n)$. Note that a value v in the entry is represented by k_v (which is a key for the dimension relation identifying v), rather than by v itself.

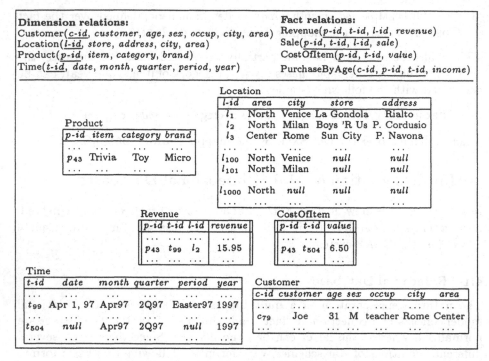

Dimension relations:
Customer(*c-id, customer, age, sex, occup, city, area*)
Location(*l-id, store, address, city, area*)
Product(*p-id, item, category, brand*)
Time(*t-id, date, month, quarter, period, year*)

Fact relations:
Revenue(*p-id, t-id, l-id, revenue*)
Sale(*p-id, t-id, l-id, sale*)
CostOfItem(*p-id, t-id, value*)
PurchaseByAge(*c-id, p-id, t-id, income*)

Location

l-id	area	city	store	address
l_1	North	Venice	La Gondola	Rialto
l_2	North	Milan	Boys 'R Us	P. Cordusio
l_3	Center	Rome	Sun City	P. Navona
...	...	...	...	...
l_{100}	North	Venice	null	null
l_{101}	North	Milan	null	null
...	...	...	...	...
l_{1000}	North	null	null	null
...	...	...	...	...

Product

p-id	item	category	brand
...	...	...	...
p_{43}	Trivia	Toy	Micro
...	...	...	...

Revenue

p-id	t-id	l-id	revenue
...	...	...	...
p_{43}	t_{99}	l_2	15.95
...	...	...	...

CostOfItem

p-id	t-id	value
...	...	...
p_{43}	t_{504}	6.50
...	...	...

Time

t-id	date	month	quarter	period	year
...	...	...	...	...	...
t_{99}	Apr 1, 97	Apr97	2Q97	Easter97	1997
...	...	...	...	...	...
t_{504}	null	Apr97	2Q97	null	1997
...	...	...	...	...	...

Customer

c-id	customer	age	sex	occup	city	area
...	...	...	...	...	...	...
c_{79}	Joe	31	M	teacher	Rome	Center
...	...	...	...	...	...	...

Fig. 8. Star scheme of the Retail database

As an example, the star scheme representation of the the Retail database is shown in Figure 8. Note that the instance is just outlined. The relation Location is more detailed to show the structure of a dimension table.

The scheme so obtained can be optimized in several ways. For instance, relation schemes corresponding to different f-tables over the same levels can be merged, suitable indexes can be defined, and some views involving aggregation can be materialized [4]. The issue of optimization is however beyond the scope of this paper.

4.2 Multidimensional Arrays

We now briefly outline how an $\mathcal{MD}$ database can be represented by means of multidimensional arrays. Since there is no agreed model for MOLAP systems, we assume that factual data are represented by means of matrices whose indexes range over contiguous, initial segments of the natural numbers.

First of all, for each dimension d of our $\mathcal{MD}$ scheme we define a bijection β_d assigning a unique integer to each value of each level in d. More specifically, if m is the number of those values, β_d associates with each of them an integer varying from 1 to m (and vice versa). In this way, we obtain a one-to-one correspondence between symbolic and numeric coordinates. Then, an f-table $f[A_1 : l_1\langle d_1\rangle, \ldots, A_n : l_n\langle d_n\rangle] : l_0\langle d_0\rangle$ is represented by a n-dimensional matrix, storing each measure v_0, corresponding to the symbolic entry $[A_1 : v_1, \ldots, A_n : v_n]$, in the cell having physical coordinate $[\beta_{d_1}(v_1), \ldots, \beta_{d_n}(v_n)]$.

An $\mathcal{MD}$ dimension can be represented by means of a special data structure, with a hierarchical organization according to the partial order between the levels. This data structure is used to store both the roll-up functions and the assignment between values of levels and integers. We can then use this structure as an index to access the multidimensional arrays. The resulting scheme can be tuned by using the tools provided by the specific storage system chosen.

5 Conclusions

In this paper we have proposed a framework, based on a logical data model, for the design of multidimensional databases. Another fundamental aspect of OLAP systems is querying, a task that can be pursued using different paradigms. On one hand, the final user should be enabled to perform point-and-click operations by means of graphical metaphors. On the other hand, the sophisticated user that needs to express more complex queries should be allowed to use a declarative, high-level language. Finally, query optimization can be effectively performed by using a procedural, algebraic language, possibly referring to the underlying representation of data. We have started the study of declarative query languages for OLAP systems in [3]. We are currently investigating the other paradigms, arguing that $\mathcal{MD}$ is well-suited for the manipulation of multidimensional databases, since it allows the user to disregard implementation aspects.

References

1. R. Agrawal, A. Gupta, and S. Sarawagi. Modeling multidimensional databases. In *13th Int. Conf. on Data Engineering*, pages 232–243, 1997.
2. C. Batini, S. Ceri, and S. Navathe. *Conceptual Database Design*. Benjamin/Cummings, 1992.
3. L. Cabibbo and R. Torlone. Querying multidimensional databases. In *6th Int. Workshop on Database Programming Languages (DBPL'97)*, 1997.
4. S. Chaudhuri and U. Dayal. An overview of Data Warehousing and OLAP technology. *ACM SIGMOD Record*, 26(1):65–74, March 1997.
5. E.F. Codd, S.B. Codd, and C.T. Salley. Providing OLAP (On Line Analytical Processing) to user-analysts: an IT mandate. Arbor Software White Paper, *http://www.arborsoft.com*.
6. M. Golfarelli, D. Maio, and S. Rizzi. Conceptual design of data warehouses from E/R schemes. In *31st Hawaii Intl. Conf. on System Sciences*, 1998.
7. M. Gyssens and L.V.S. Lakshmanan. A foundation for multi-dimensional databases. In *33rd Int. Conf. on Very Large Data Bases*, pages 106–115, 1997.
8. W.H. Inmon. *Building the Data Warehouse*. John Wiley & Sons, 2nd ed., 1996.
9. R. Kimball. *The Data Warehouse Toolkit*. John Wiley & Sons, 1996.
10. A. O. Mendelzon. Data warehousing and OLAP: a research-oriented bibliography. *http://www.cs.toronto.edu/~mendel/dwbib.html*.
11. N. Pendse and R. Creeth. The OLAP Report. *http://www.olapreport.com*.
12. A. Shoshani. OLAP and statistical databases: 6imilarities and differences. In *16th ACM SIGACT SIGMOD SIGART Symp. on Principles of Database Systems*, pages 185–196, 1997.

Query Processing and Storage Management

Efficient Dynamic Programming Algorithms for Ordering Expensive Joins and Selections

Wolfgang Scheufele*   Guido Moerkotte

Universität Mannheim
Lehrstuhl für Praktische Informatik III
68131 Mannheim, Germany
e-mail: {ws|moer}@pi3.informatik.uni-mannheim.de

Abstract. The generally accepted optimization heuristics of pushing selections down does not yield optimal plans in the presence of expensive predicates. Therefore, several researchers have proposed algorithms to compute optimal processing trees for queries with expensive predicates. All these approaches are incorrect—with one exception [3]. Our contribution is as follows. We present a formally derived and correct dynamic programming algorithm to compute optimal bushy processing trees for queries with expensive predicates. This algorithm is then enhanced to be able to (1) handle several join algorithms including sort merge with a correct handling of interesting sort orders, to (2) perform predicate splitting, to (3) exploit structural information about the query graph to cut down the search space. Further, we present efficient implementations of the algorithms. More specifically we introduce unique solutions for efficiently computing the cost of the intermediate plans and for saving memory space by utilizing bitvector contraction. Our implementations impose no restrictions on the type of query graphs, the shape of processing trees or the class of cost functions. We establish the correctness of our algorithms and derive tight asymptotic bounds on the worst case time and space complexities. We also report on a series of benchmarks showing that queries of sizes which are likely to occur in practice can be optimized over the unconstrained search space in less than a second.

1 Introduction

Traditional work on algebraic query optimization has mainly focused on the problem of ordering joins in a query. Restrictions like selections and projections are generally treated by "push-down rules". According to these, selections and projections should be pushed down the query plan as far as possible. These heuristic rules worked quite well for traditional relational database systems where the evaluation of selection predicates is of neglectable cost and every selection reduces the cost of subsequent joins. As pointed out by Hellerstein, Stonebraker [5], this is no longer true for modern database systems like object-oriented DBMSs

---

* Research supported by the German Research Association (DFG) under contract Mo 507/6-1.

that allow users to implement arbitrary complex functions in a general-purpose programming language. In this paper we present a dynamic programming algorithm for computing optimal bushy processing trees with cross products for conjunctive queries with expensive join and selection predicates. The algorithm is then enhanced to (1) handle several join algorithms including sort merge with a correct handling of interesting sort orders, to (2) perform predicate splitting, to (3) exploit structural information about the query graph to cut down the search space. There are no restrictions on the shape of the processing trees, the structure of the query graph or the type of cost functions. We then focus on *efficient algorithms* with respect to both the asymptotic time complexity and the hidden constants in the implementation. Our dynamic programming algorithm and its enhancements were formally derived by means of recurrences and time and space complexities are analyzed carefully. We present details of an efficient implementation and sketch possible generalizations. More specifically we introduce unique solutions for efficiently computing the cost of the intermediate plans and for saving memory space by utilizing bitvector contraction. A more detailed description of our algorithm can be found in our technical report [10].

The rest of the paper is organized as follows. Section 2 summarizes related work and clarifies the contribution of our approach over existing approaches. Section 3 covers the background for the rest of the paper. In section 4 we present the dynamic programming algorithm for ordering expensive selections and joins. Section 5 discusses the problems to be solved in an efficient implementation of these solutions. One of its main contributions is to offer a possibility for a fast computation of cost functions. This is a major point, since most of the optimization time in a dynamic programming approach is often spent on computing costs. A second major point introduces techniques for space saving measures. In section 6 we discuss several possible generalizations of our algorithm accounting for interesting sort orders, the option to split conjunctive predicates, and the exploitation of structural information from the join graph. Section 7 shows the results of timing measurements and section 8 concludes the paper.

2 Related Work and Contribution

Only few approaches exist to the problem of ordering joins and selections with expensive predicates. In the LDL system [4] and later on in the Papyrus project [1] expensive selections are modelled as artificial relations which are then ordered by a traditional join ordering algorithm producing left-deep trees. This approach suffers from two disadvantages. First, the time complexity of the algorithm cannot compete with the complexity of approaches which do not model selections and joins alike and, second, left-deep trees do not admit plans where more than one cheap selection is "pushed down". Another approach is based upon the "predicate migration algorithm" [5, 6] which solves the simpler problem of interleaving expensive selections in an existing join tree. The authors of [5, 6] suggest to solve the general problem by enumerating all join orders while placing the expensive selections with the predicate migration algorithm—in combination with a system R style dynamic programming algorithm endowed with pruning. The predicate migration approach has several severe shortcomings. It may degenerate to exhaustive enumeration, it assumes a linear cost model and it does not always yield optimal results [2]. Recently, Chaudhuri and Shim presented a dynamic programming algorithm for ordering joins and expensive selections [2]. Although they claim that their algorithm computes optimal plans for all cost functions, all query graphs, and even when the algorithm is generalized to bushy processing trees and expensive join predicates, the alleged correctness has not been proved at all. In fact, it is not difficult to find counterexamples disproving the correctness for even the simplest cost functions and processing trees. This bug was later discovered and the algorithm restricted to work on regular cost functions only [3]. Further, it does not generate plans that contain cross products. The algorithm is not able to consider different join implementations. Especially the sort merge join is out of the scope of the algorithm due to its restriction to regular cost functions. A further disadvantage is that the algorithm does not perform predicate splitting. The contribution of our algorithm and its enhancements are: (1) It works on arbitrary cost functions. (2) It generates plans with cross products. (3) It can handle different join algorithms. (4) It is capable of exploiting interesting sort orders. (5) It employs predicate splitting. (6) It uses structural information to restrict the search space. Our final contribution are tight time and space bounds.

3 Preliminaries

We consider simple *conjunctive queries* [12] involving only single table selections and binary joins (selection-join-queries). A query is represented by a set of relations $R_1, \ldots, R_n$ and a set of query predicates $p_1, \ldots, p_n$, where p_k is either a join predicate connecting two relations R_i and R_j or a selection predicate which refers to a single relation R_k (henceforth denoted by σ_k). All predicates are assumed to be either *basic predicates* or conjunctions of basic predicates (*conjunctive predicates*). Basic predicates are simple built-in predicates or predicates defined via user-defined functions which may be expensive to compute.

Let $R_1, \ldots, R_n$ be the relations involved in the query. Associated with each relation is its *cardinality* $n_i = |R_i|$. The predicates in the query induce a *join graph* $G = (\{R_1, \ldots, R_n\}, E)$, where E contains all pairs $\{R_i, R_j\}$ for which exists a predicate p_k relating R_i and R_j. For every join or selection predicate $p_k \in P$, we assume the existence of a *selectivity* f_k [12] and a cost factor c_k denoting the costs for a single evaluation of the predicate.

A *processing tree* for a select-join-query is a rooted binary tree with its internal nodes having either one or two sons. In the first case the node represents a selection operation and in the latter case it represents a binary join operation. The tree has exactly n leaves, which are the relations $R_1, \ldots, R_n$. Processing trees are classified according to their shape. The main distinction is between *left-deep trees* and *bushy trees*. In a left-deep tree the right subtree of an internal node does not contain joins. Otherwise it is called a *bushy tree*.

There are different implementations of the join operator each leading to different cost functions for the join and hence to different cost functions for the whole processing tree. We do not want to commit ourselves to a particular cost function, instead the reader may select his favorite cost function from a large class of *admissible cost functions* which are subject to the following two requirements. First, the cost function is *decomposable* and thus can be computed by means of recurrences. Second, the costs of a processing tree are *(strictly) monotonously increasing with respect to the costs of its subtrees*. This seems to be no major restriction for "reasonable" cost functions. It can be shown [9] that such cost functions guarantee that every optimal solution satisfies the "principle of optimality" which we state in the next section. In order to discuss some details of an efficient implementation we assume that the cost function can be written as a recurrence involving several auxiliary functions, an example is the *size function* (the number of tuples in the result of a subquery).

4 The Dynamic Programming Algorithm

Let us denote the set of relations occurring in a bushy plan P by $Rel(P)$ and the set of relations to which selections in P refer by $Sel(P)$. Let R denote a set of relations. We denote by $Sel(R)$ the set of all selections referring to some relation in R. Each subset $V \subseteq R$ defines an *induced subquery* which contains all the joins and selections that refer to relations in V only. A *subplan P'* of a plan P corresponds to a subtree of the expression tree associated with P. A *partition* of a set S is a pair of nonempty disjoint subsets of S whose union is exactly S. For a partition S_1, S_2 of S we write $S = S_1 \uplus S_2$. By a *k-set* we simply mean a set with exactly k elements.

Consider an optimal plan P for an induced subquery involving the nonempty set of relations $Rel(P)$ and the set of selections $Sel(P)$. Obviously, P has either the form $P \equiv (P_1 \bowtie P_2)$ for subplans P_1 and P_2 of P, or the form $P \equiv \sigma_i(P')$ for a subplan P' of P and a selection $\sigma_i \in Sel(P)$. The important fact is now that the subplans P_1, P_2 are necessarily *optimal plans* for the relations $Rel(P_1), Rel(P_2)$ and the selections $Sel(P_1), Sel(P_2)$, where $Rel(P_1) \uplus Rel(P_2) = Rel(P)$, $Sel(P_1) = Sel(P) \cap Sel(R_1)$, $Sel(P_2) = Sel(P) \cap Sel(R_2)$. Similarly, P' is an optimal bushy plan for the relations $Rel(P')$ and the selections $Sel(P)$, where $Rel(P') = Rel(P)$, $Sel(P') = Sel(P) - \{\sigma_i\}$. Otherwise we could obtain a cheaper plan by replacing the suboptimal part by an optimal one which would be a contradiction to the assumed optimality of P (note that our cost function is decomposable and monotone). The property that optimal solutions of a problem can be decomposed into a number of "smaller", likewise optimal solutions of the same problem, is known as *Bellman's optimality principle*. This leads immediately to the following recurrence for computing an optimal bushy plan[1] for a set of relations R and a set of selections S.

---

[1] min() is the operation which yields a plan with minimal costs among the addressed set of plans. Convention: $\min_\emptyset(\ldots) := \lambda$ where λ denotes some artificial plan with cost ∞.

$$
\mathrm{opt}(R,S) = \begin{cases} \min(\min_{\emptyset \subset R' \subset R}(\mathrm{opt}(R', S \cap \mathrm{Sel}(R'))) \bowtie & \text{if } \emptyset \subseteq S \subseteq R, \\ \quad \mathrm{opt}(R \setminus R', S \cap \mathrm{Sel}(R \setminus R'))) & \\ \quad \min_{\sigma_i \in S}(\sigma_i(\mathrm{opt}(R, S \setminus \{\sigma_i\})))) & \\ R_i & \text{if } R = \{R_i\}, \\ & \quad S = \emptyset \end{cases} \tag{1}
$$

The join symbol $\bowtie$ denotes a join *with the conjunction of all join predicates* that relate relations in R' to relations in $R \setminus R'$. Considering the join graph, the conjuncts of the join predicate correspond to the predicates associated with the edges in the cut $(R', R \setminus R')$. If the cut is empty the join is actually a *cross product*.

In our first algorithm we will treat such joins and selections with conjunctive predicates as single operations with according accumulated costs. The option to split such predicates will be discussed in section 6.2 where we present a second algorithm.

Based on recurrence (1), there is an obvious recursive algorithm to solve our problem but this solution would be very inefficient since many subproblems are solved more than once. A much more efficient way to solve this recurrence is by means of a table and is known under the name of *dynamic programming* [8, 11]. Instead of solving subproblems recursively, we solve them one after the other in some appropriate order and store their solutions in a table. The overall time complexity then becomes (typically) a function of the number of distinct subproblems rather than of the larger number of recursive calls. Obviously, the subproblems have to be solved in the right order so that whenever the solution to a subproblem is needed it is already available in the table. A straightforward solution is the following. We enumerate all subsets of relations by increasing size, and for each subset R we then enumerate all subsets S of the set of selections occurring in R by increasing size. For each such pair (R, S) we evaluate the recurrence (1) and store the solution associated with (R, S).

For the following algorithm we assume a given select-join-query involving n relations $\mathcal{R} = \{R_1, \ldots, R_n\}$ and $m \leq n$ selections $S = \{\sigma_1, \ldots, \sigma_m\}$. In the following, we identify selections and relations to which they refer. Let P be the set of all join predicates $p_{i,j}$ relating two relations R_i and R_j. By R_S we denote the set $\{R_i \in \mathcal{R} \mid \exists \sigma_j \in S : \sigma_j \text{ relates to } R_i\}$ which consists of all relations in $\mathcal{R}$ to which some selection in S relates. For all $U \subseteq \mathcal{R}$ and $V \subseteq U \cap R_S$, at the end of the algorithm $T[U, V]$ stores an optimal bushy plan for the subquery (U, V).

proc Optimal-Bushy-Tree(R, P)
1   **for** $k = 1$ **to** n **do**
2   **for all** k-subsets M_k of R **do**
3   **for** $l = 0$ **to** $\min(k, m)$ **do**
4   **for all** l-subsets P_l of $M_k \cap R_S$ **do**
5                   $best\_cost\_so\_far = \infty$;
6   **for all** subsets L of M_k with $0 < |L| < k$ **do**
7                       $L' = M_k \setminus L, \; V = P_l \cap L, \; V' = P_l \cap L'$;
8                       $p = \bigwedge\{p_{i,j} \mid p_{i,j} \in P, \; R_i \in V, \; R_j \in V'\}$; $//$ $p=true$ might hold
9                       $T = (T[L, V] \bowtie_p T[L', V'])$;
10   **if** $Cost(T) < best\_cost\_so\_far$ **then**
11                          $best\_cost\_so\_far = Cost(T)$;
12                          $T[M_k, P_l] = T$;
13   **fi**;
14   **od**;
15   **for all** $R \in P_l$ **do**
16                      $T = \sigma_R(T[M_k, P_l \setminus \{R\}])$;
17   **if** $Cost(T) < best\_cost\_so\_far$ **then**
18                          $best\_cost\_so\_far = Cost(T)$;
19                          $T[M_k, P_l] = T$;
20   **fi**;
21   **od**;
22   **od**;
23   **od**;
24   **od**;
25 **od**;
26 **return** $T[R, S]$;

Complexity of the algorithm: In [10] we show that the number of considered partial plans is $3^n(5/3)^m + (2m/3 - 2) \cdot 2^n(3/2)^m + 1$ which we can rewrite as $[3(5/3)^c]^n + (2cn/3 - 2)[2(3/2)^c]^n + 1$ if we replace m by the fraction of selections $c = m/n$. Assuming an asymptotic optimal implementation of the enumeration part of the algorithm (see section 5), the amount of work per considered plan is constant and the asymptotic time complexity of our algorithm is $O([3\,(5/3)^c]^n + n[2\,(3/2)^c]^n)$. Assuming that the relations are re-numbered such that all selections refer to relations in $\{R_1, \ldots, R_m\}$, the space complexity of the algorithm is $O(2^{n+m})$. Note that not every table entry $T[i, j], 0 \leq i < n, 0 \leq j < m$ represents a valid subproblem. In fact, the number of table entries used by the algorithm to store the solutions of subproblems is $2^n(3/2)^m - 1$. In section 5.3 we discuss techniques to save space.

5   An Efficient Implementation

5.1   Fast Enumeration of Subproblems

The frame of our dynamic programming algorithm is the systematic enumeration of subproblems consisting of three nested loops iterating over subsets of relations and predicates, respectively.

The first loop enumerates all nonempty subsets of the set of all relations in the query. It turns out that enumerating all subsets strictly by increasing size seems not to be the most efficient way. The whole point is that the order of enumeration only has to guarantee that for every enumerated set S, all subsets of S have already been enumerated. One of such orderings, which is probably the most suitable, is the following. We use the standard representation of n-sets, namely bitvectors of length n. A subset of a set S is then characterized by a bitvector which is component-wise smaller than the bitvector of S. This leads to the obvious ordering in which the bitvectors are arranged according to their value as binary numbers. This simple and very effective enumeration scheme (*binary counting method*) is successfully used in [13]. The major advantage is that we can pass over to the next subset by merely incrementing an integer, which is an extremely fast hardwired operation.

The next problem is to enumerate subsets S of a fixed subset M of a set Q. If Q has n elements then we can represent M by a bitvector m of length n. Since M is a subset of Q some bit positions of m may be zero. Vance and Maier propose in [13] a very efficient and elegant way to solve this problem. In fact, they show that the following loop enumerates all bitvectors S being a subset of M, where $M \subseteq Q$.

$S = 0;$
repeat

$\quad \cdots$
$\quad S = M \mathbin{\&} (S - M);$
until $S = 0$

We assume two's-complement arithmetic. Bit-operations are denoted as in the language C. As an important special case, we mention that $M \mathbin{\&} -M$ yields the bit with the *smallest* index in M. Similarily, one can count downward using the operation $S = M \mathbin{\&} (S - 1)$. Combining these operations, one can show that the operation $S = M \mathbin{\&} ((S \mid (M \mathbin{\&} (S - 1))) - M)$ (with initial value $S = M \mathbin{\&} -M$) iterates through each single bit in the bitvector M in order of increasing indices.

5.2 Efficient Computation of the Cost Function

Now, we discuss the efficient evaluation of the cost function within the nested loops. Obviously, for a given plan we can compute the costs and the size in (typically) linear time but there is a even more efficient way using the recurrences for these functions. If R', R'' and S', S'' are the partitions of R and S, respectively, for which the recurrence (1) assumes a minimum, we have

$$Size(R, S) = Size(R', S') * Size(R'', S'') * Sel(R', R''),$$

where

$$Sel(R', R'') := \prod_{R_i \in R', R_j \in R''} f_{i,j}$$

is the product of all selectivities between relations in R' and R''. Note that the last equation holds for *every* partition R', R'' of R independent of the root operator in an optimal plan. Hence we may choose a certain partition in order to simplify the computations. Now if $R' = U_1 \uplus U_2$ and $R'' = V_1 \uplus V_2$, we have the following recurrence for $Sel(R', R'')$

$$Sel(U_1 \uplus U_2, V_1 \uplus V_2) = Sel(U_1, V_1) * Sel(U_1, V_2) * Sel(U_2, V_1) * Sel(U_2, V_2)$$

Choosing $U_1 = \alpha(R)$, $U_2 := \emptyset$, $V_1 = \alpha(R \setminus U_1)$, and $V_2 := R \setminus U_1 \setminus V_2$, where the function α is given by $\alpha(A) := \{R_k\}$, $k = \min\{i \mid R_i \in A\}$
leads to

$$Sel(\alpha(R), R \setminus \alpha(R)) =$$
$$Sel(\alpha(R), \alpha(R \setminus \alpha(R))) * Sel(\alpha(R), (R \setminus \alpha(R)) \setminus \alpha(R \setminus \alpha(R))) =$$
$$Sel(\alpha(R), \alpha(R \setminus \alpha(R))) * Sel(\alpha(R), (R \setminus \alpha(R \setminus \alpha(R))) \setminus \alpha(R))$$

Defining the *fan-selectivity* $Fan\_Sel(R)$ as $Sel(\alpha(R), R \setminus \alpha(R))$, gives the simpler recurrence

$$Fan\_Sel(R) = Sel(\alpha(R), \alpha(R \setminus \alpha(R))) * Fan\_Sel(R \setminus \alpha(R))$$
$$= f_{i,j} * Fan\_Sel(R \setminus \alpha(R \setminus \alpha(R))) \qquad (2)$$

where we assumed $\alpha(R) = \{R_i\}$ and $\alpha(R \setminus \alpha(R)) = \{R_j\}$.

As a consequence, we can compute $Size(R, S)$ with the following recurrence

$$Size(R, S) = Size(\alpha(R), S \cap \alpha(R)) * Size(R \setminus \alpha(R), (R \setminus \alpha(R)) \cap S) \qquad (3)$$
$$* Fan\_Sel(R)$$

We remind that the single relation in $\alpha(R)$ can be computed very efficiently via the operation $a \& - a$ on the bitvector of R. Recurrences (2) and (3) are illustrated in the following figure. The encircled sets of relations denote the nested partitions along which the sizes and selectivities are computed.

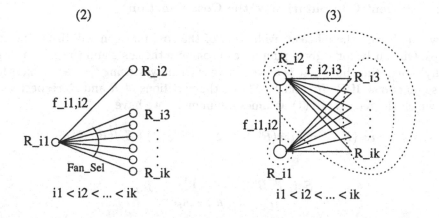

(2)   (3)

i1 < i2 < ... < ik   i1 < i2 < ... < ik

5.3 Space Saving Measures

Another problem is how to store the tables without wasting space. For example, suppose $n = 10$, $m = 10$ and let r and s denote the bitvectors corresponding to the sets R and S, respectively. If we use r and s directly as indices of a two-dimensional array $cost[][]$, about 90% of the entries in the table will not be accessed by the algorithm. To avoid this immense waste of space we have to use a *contracted version* of the second bitvector s.

Definition 1. *(bitvector contraction)*
Let r and s be two bitvectors consisting of the bits $r_0 r_1 \ldots r_n$ and $s_0 s_1 \ldots s_n$, respectively. We define the contraction of s with respect to r as follows:

$$
contr_r(s) = \begin{cases}
\epsilon & \text{if } s = \epsilon \\
contr_{r_1 \ldots r_n}(s_1 \ldots s_n) & \text{if } s \neq \epsilon \text{ and } r_0 = 0 \\
s_0\, contr_{r_1 \ldots r_n}(s_1 \ldots s_n) & \text{if } s \neq \epsilon \text{ and } r_0 = 1
\end{cases}
$$

Example Let us contract the bitvector $s = 0101001111$ with respect to the bitvector $r = 1110110100$. For each bit s_i of s, we examine the corresponding bit r_i in r. If r_i is zero we "delete" s_i in s, otherwise we retain it. The result is the contracted bitvector 010001.

The following figure shows the structure of the two-dimensional ragged arrays. The first dimension is of fixed size 2^n, whereas the second dimension is of size 2^k where k is the number of common nonzero bits in the value of the first index i and the bitvector of all selections $sels$. The number of entries in such a ragged array is $\sum_{k=0}^{m} \binom{m}{k} 2^k 2^{n-m} = [2(\frac{3}{2})^c]^n$. Note that this number equals 2^n for $m = 0$ and 3^n for $m = n$. A simple array would require 4^n entries. The figure below shows the worst case where the number of selections equals the number of relations.

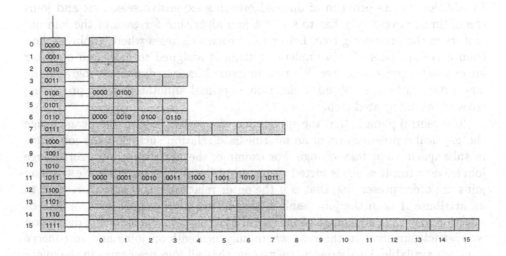

The simplest way would be to contract the second index on the fly for each access of the array. This would slow down the algorithm by a factor of n. It would be much better if we could contract all relevant values in the course of the other computations—therefore not changing the asymptotic time complexity. Note that within our algorithm the first and second indices are enumerated by increasing values which makes a contraction easy. We simply use pairs of indices i, ic, one uncontracted index i and its contracted version ic and count up their values independently.

As mentioned before, in the two outermost loops bitvector contraction is easy due to the order of enumeration of the bitvectors. Unfortunately, this does not work in the innermost loop where we have to contract the result of a conjunction of two contracted bitvectors again. Such a "double contraction" cannot be achieved by simple counting or other combinations of arithmetic and bit operations. One possible solution is to contract the index in the innermost loop on the fly, another is to tabulate the contraction function. Since tabulation seems slightly more efficient, we apply the second method. Before entering the innermost loop we compute and store the results of all contraction operations which will occur in the innermost loop. The computation of contraction values can now be done more efficiently since we do not depend on the specific order of enumeration in the innermost loop. The values in the table can be computed bottom-up using the recurrence given in Definition 1. Due to contraction the new time complexity of the algorithm is $O((n + 1)[3(5/3)^c]^n + n[2(3/2)^c]^n + (cn)^2 2^n)$ whereas the new space complexity is $O([2(3/2)^c]^n + 2^n)$.

6 Some Generalizations

6.1 Different Join Algorithms

In addition to the problem of optimal ordering expensive selections and joins the optimizer eventually has to select a join algorithm for each of the join operators in the processing tree. Let us call processing trees where a join method from a certain pool of join implementations is assigned to each join operator an *annotated processing tree*. We now describe how our dynamic programming algorithm can be generalized to determine optimal annotated bushy processing trees in one integrated step.

The central point is that the application of a certain join method can change the physical representation of an intermediate relation such that the join costs in subsequent steps may change. For example, the application of a sort-merge join leaves a result which is sorted with respect to the join attribute. Nested loop joins are order preserving, that is if the outer relation is sorted with respect to an attribute A then the join result is also sorted with respect to A. A join or selection may take advantage of the sorted attribute. In the following discussion we restrict ourselves to the case where only nested-loop joins and sort-merge joins are available. Furthermore, we assume that all join predicates in the query are equi-joins so that both join methods can be applied for every join that occurs.

This is not a restriction of the algorithm but makes the following discussion less complex.

Consider an optimal bushy plan P for the relations in $Rel(P)$ and the selections in $Sel(P)$. Again we can distinguish between a join operator representing the root of the plan tree and a selection operator representing the root. In case of a join operator we further distinguish between the join algorithms nested-loop (nl) and sort-merge (sm). Let $C_a(R, S)$ be the costs of an optimal subplan for the relations in R and selections in S, where the result is sorted with respect to the attribute a (of some relation $r \in R$). $C(R, S)$ is similar defined, but the result is not necessarily sorted with respect to any attribute. Now, the optimality principle holds both for $C(R, S)$ and $C_x(R, S)$ for all attributes x in the result of the query (R, S) and one can easily specify two recurrences which compute $C(R, S)$ and $C_{a|b}(R, S)$ in terms of $C(R', S'), C_a(R', S')$ and $C_b(R', S')$ for "smaller" subproblems (R', S'), respectively. Here $a|b$ denotes the join attribute in the result of an equi-join with respect to the attributes a and b.

Time Complexity: The number of considered partial plans is $O(n^2[3(5/3)^c]^n + cn^3[2(3/2)^c]^n)$. Similarly, the asymptotic number of table entries in our new algorithm is $O(n^2[2(3/2)^c]^n)$.

6.2 Splitting Conjunctive Predicates

So far our algorithm does consider joins and selections over *conjunctive predicates* which may occur in the course of the algorithm as indivisible operators of the plan. For example, consider a query on three relations with three join predicates relating all the relations. Then, every join operator in the root of a processing tree has a join predicate which is the conjunction of two basic join predicates. In the presence of expensive predicates this may lead to suboptimal[2] plans since there may be a cheaper plan which splits a conjunctive join predicate into a join with high selectivity and low costs and a number of (secondary) selections with lower selectivities and higher costs. Consequently, we do henceforth consider the larger search space of all queries formed by joins and selections with *basic predicates* which are equivalent to our original query.

The approach is similar to our first approach but this time we have to take into account the basic predicates involved in a partial solution. First, we replace all conjunctive selection and join predicates in the original query by all its conjuncts. Note that this makes our query graph a multigraph. Let $p_1, \ldots, p_m$ be the resulting set of basic predicates. We shall henceforth use bitvectors of length m to represent sets of basic predicates. Let us now consider an optimal plan P which involves the relations in R and the predicates in P. We denote the costs of such an optimal plan by $C(R, P)$. Obviously, the root operator in P is either a cross product, a join with a basic predicate h_1 or a selection with a basic predicate h_2. Hence, exactly one of the following four cases holds:

---

[2] with respect to the larger search space defined next

$P \equiv P_1 \times P_2$ (**cross product**): $Rel(P) = Rel(P_1) \uplus Rel(P_2)$, $Pred(P) = Pred(P_1) \uplus Pred(P_2)$. The induced join graphs of P_1 and P_2 are not connected in the induced join graph of P. Besides, the subplans P_i $(i = 1, 2)$ are optimal with respect to the corresponding sets $Rel(P_i)$, $Pred(P_i)$.

$P \equiv P_1 \bowtie_{h_1} P_2$ (**join**): $Rel(P) = Rel(P_1) \uplus Rel(P_2)$ and $Pred(P) = Pred(P_1) \uplus Pred(P_2) \uplus \{h_1\}$. The induced join graphs of P_1 and P_2 are connected by a bridge h_1 in the induced join graph of P. Furthermore, the subplans P_1, P_2 are optimal with respect to the corresponding sets $Rel(P_i)$, $Pred(P_i)$.

$P \equiv \sigma_{h_1}(P_1)$ (**secondary selection**): $Rel(P) = Rel(P_1)$ and $Pred(P) = Pred(P_1) \uplus \{h_1\}$. The subplan P_1 is optimal with respect to the corresponding sets $Rel(P_1)$ and $Pred(P_1)$.

$P \equiv \sigma_{h_2}(P_1)$ (**single table selection**): $Rel(P) = Rel(P_1)$ and $Pred(P) = Pred(P_1) \uplus \{h_2\}$. The subplan P_1 is optimal with respect to the corresponding sets $Rel(P_1)$ and $Pred(P_1)$.

Again, it is not difficult to see that the optimality principle holds and one can give a recurrence which determines an optimal plan $opt(R, P)$ for the problem (R, P) by iterating over all partitions of R applying the corresponding cost function according to one of the above cases. More details can be found in the technical report [10].

Complexity Issues: Let $m > 0$ be the number of different basic predicates (joins and selections) and n the number of base relations. We derived the following upper bound on the number of considered partial plans $m2^m3^n - 3m2^{m+n-1} + m2^{m-1} = O(m2^m3^n)$.
As to the space complexity, one can easily give an upper bound of 2^{n+m} on the number of table entries used by the algorithm.

6.3   Using Structural Information from the Join Graph

So far we concentrated on *fast enumeration* without analyzing structural information about the problem instance at hand. To give an example, suppose our query graph to be 2-connected. Then every cut contains at least two edges; therefore the topmost operator in a processing tree can neither be a join nor a cross product. Hence, our second algorithm iterates in vain over all 2^n partitions of the set of all n relations.

We will now describe the approach in our third algorithm which uses *structural information* from the join graph to avoid the enumeration of unnecessary subproblems. Suppose that a given query relates the relations in R and the predicates in P. We denote the number of relations in R by n, the number of predicates in P by m and the number of selections by s. Consider any optimal processing tree T for a subquery induced by the subset of relations $R' \subseteq R$ and the subset of predicates $P' \subseteq P$. The join graph induced by the relations R and the predicates P is denoted by $G(R, P)$. Obviously, the root operator in T is either *a cross product, a join, a secondary selection* or *a single table selection*. Depending on the operation in the root of the processing tree, we can classify the graph $G(R', P')$ as follows. If the root operation is a cross product, then $G(R', P')$ decomposes into *two components*. Otherwise, if it is a join with (basic) predicate h then $G(R', P')$ contains a *bridge* h. If it is a secondary selection with (basic) predicate h then $G(R', P')$ contains an *edge* h. And, if it is a single table selection with predicate h then $G(R', P')$ contains a *loop* h.

Consequently, we can enumerate all possible cross products by building all partitions of the set of components of $G(R', P')$. All joins can be enumerated by considering all bridges of $G(R', P')$ as follows. Suppose that the bridge is the basic predicate h and denote the set of components resulting from removing the bridge by C. Now, every possible join can be obtained by building all partitions of the components in C and joining them with the predicate h. All secondary selections can be enumerated by just considering every edge (no loops) as selection predicate. And, if we step through all loops in $G(R', P')$ we enumerate all single table selections. In a sense we are tackling subproblems in the reverse direction than we did before. Instead of enumerating all partitions and analyzing the type of operation it admits we consider types of operations and enumerate the respective subproblems.

Complexity: One can show that the number of considered partial plans is at most $2^{m-1}(3^n - 1) + 2m(3/2)^{m-1}(3^n - 1) + m2^{m-1}(2^n - 1)$ and the asymptotic worst-case time complexity is $O(2^m 3^n + m(3/2)^m 3^n + (m + n)2^{m+n} - m2^m)$. Furthermore, the number of table entries used by the algorithm is 2^{n+m}.

The above time and space complexities are generous upper bounds which do not account for the structure of a query graph. For an acyclic join graph G with n nodes, $m = n - 1$ edges (no loops and multiple edges) and s loops (possibly some multiple loops) the number of considered partial plans is bound by $2^s[4^n(n/2 - 1/4) + 3^n(2n/9 - 2/9 + s/6)]$ and the asymptotic time complexity is $O(2^s(n^2 4^n + (n^2 + s)3^n))$.

7 Performance Measurements

In this section we investigate how our dynamic programming algorithms perform in practice. Note that we give no results of the quality of the generated plans, since they are optimal. The only remaining question is whether the algorithm can be applied in practice since the time bounds seem quite high. We begin with algorithm Optimal-Bushy-Tree(R,P) without enhancements. The table below shows the timings for random queries with $n = 10$ relations and query graphs with 50% of all possible edges having selectivity factors less than 1. Join predicates are cheap (i.e. $c_p = 1$) whereas selection predicates are expensive (i.e. $c_p > 1$). All timings in this section were measured on a lightly loaded Sun SPARCstation 20 with 128 MB of main memory. They represent averages over a few hundred runs with randomly generated queries.

10 relations *sel* :	0	1	2	3	4	5	6	7	8	9	10
time [s]:	< 0.1	< 0.1	< 0.1	0.1	0.2	0.5	0.9	2.1	4.3	8.1	13.5

Let us now consider algorithm Optimal-Bushy-Tree(R,P) enhanced by splitting join predicates.

The next table shows running times for random queries on $n = 5$ relations. We varied the number of predicates from 0 to 16, the fraction of selections was held constant at 50%. For this example we used a modified "near-uniform" random generation of queries in order to produce connected join graphs whenever possible, i.e. we did only produce queries where the number of components equals $\max(n - p + s, 1)$.

$n = 5$ p:	0	1	2	3	4	5	6	7	8
time [s]:	< 0.001	< 0.001	< 0.001	0.001	0.001	0.002	0.003	0.006	0.011
p:	9	10	11	12	13	14	15	16	
time [s]:	0.022	0.043	0.084	0.177	0.364	0.801	1.763	3.899	

Finally, we considered queries with 10 predicates, out of which 5 are selections. By varying the number of relations from 1 to 10, we obtained the following timings.

$p = 10, s = 5$ n:	1	2	3	4	5	6	7	8	9	10
time [s]:	-	0.004	0.008	0.018	0.043	0.122	0.374	1.204	4.151	13.927

More performance measurements can be found in the technical report [10].

8 Conclusion

We presented a novel dynamic programming algorithm for the problem to determine optimal bushy processing trees with cross products for conjunctive queries with expensive selection and join predicates. Several enhancements were discussed giving our algorithm a leading edge over the only correct algorithm existing so far [3]. Our main focus was on developing *asymptotically efficient algorithms* that also admit extremely *efficient implementations* which make the algorithms competitive in operation.

Our algorithm and its enhancements compare to the algorithm of Chaudhuri and Shim [3] as follows. It works on arbitrary cost functions whereas the algorithm of Chaudhuri and Shim is confined to regular cost functions—excluding e.g. sort-merge joins. Our algorithm incorporates cross products, different join and selection algorithms and predicate splitting, none of them is supported by the algorithm of Chaudhuri and Shim. Furthermore we describe how to use structural information from the join graph to cut down the size of the search space. This is orthogonal to the cost-driven pruning techniques described in [3]. We also derived tight bounds on the asymptotic worst-case time complexity.

Acknowledgement We thank S. Helmer and B. Rossi for careful reading of a first draft of the paper.

References

1. S. Chaudhuri and K. Shim. Query optimization in the presence of foreign functions. In *Proc. Int. Conf. on Very Large Data Bases (VLDB)*, pages 529–542, Dublin, Ireland, 1993.
2. S. Chaudhuri and K. Shim. Optimization of queries with user-defined predicates. In *Proc. Int. Conf. on Very Large Data Bases (VLDB)*, pages 87–98, Bombay, India, 1996.
3. S. Chaudhuri and K. Shim. Optimization of queries with user-defined predicates. Technical report, Microsoft Research, Advanced Technology Division, One Microsoft Way, Redmond, WA 98052, USA, 1997.
4. R. Gamboa D. Chimenti and R. Krishnamurthy. Towards an open architecture for $\mathcal{LDL}$. In *Proc. Int. Conf. on Very Large Data Bases (VLDB)*, pages 195–203, Amsterdam, Netherlands, August 1989.
5. J. Hellerstein and M. Stonebraker. Predicate migration: Optimizing queries with expensive predicates. In *Proc. of the ACM SIGMOD Conf. on Management of Data*, pages 267–277, Washington, DC, 1993.
6. J. M. Hellerstein. Practical predicate placement. In *Proc. of the ACM SIGMOD Conf. on Management of Data*, pages 325–335, Minneapolis, Minnesota, USA, May 1994.
7. A. Kemper, G. Moerkotte, and M. Steinbrunn. Optimization of boolean expressions in object bases. In *Proc. Int. Conf. on Very Large Data Bases (VLDB)*, pages 79–90, 1992.
8. M. Minoux. *Mathematical Programming. Theory and Algorithms.* Wiley, 1986.
9. T. L. Morin. Monotonicity and the principle of optimality. *J. Math. Anal. and Appl.*, 1977.
10. W. Scheufele and G. Moerkotte. Efficient dynamic programming algorithms for ordering expensive joins and selections. Forthcoming Technical Report, Lehrstuhl für Praktische Informatik III, Universität Mannheim, 68131 Mannheim, Germany, 1998.
11. C. E. Leiserson T. H. Cormen and R. L. Rivest. *Introduction to Algorithms.* MIT Press, Cambridge, Massachusetts, USA, 1990.
12. J. D. Ullman. *Principles of Database and Knowledge-Base Systems*, volume II: The New Technologies. Computer Science Press, 1989.
13. B. Vance and D. Maier. Rapid bushy join-order optimization with cartesian products. In *Proc. of the ACM SIGMOD Conf. on Management of Data*, pages 35–46, Toronto, Canada, 1996.

Improving the Query Performance of High-Dimensional Index Structures by Bulk Load Operations

Stefan Berchtold[1], Christian Böhm[2], and Hans-Peter Kriegel[2]

1 AT&T Labs Research, 180 Park Avenue, Florham Park, NJ 07932
2 University of Munich, Oettingenstr. 67, D-80638 München

Abstract. In this paper, we propose a new bulk-loading technique for high-dimensional indexes which represent an important component of multimedia database systems. Since it is very inefficient to construct an index for a large amount of data by dynamic insertion of single objects, there is an increasing interest in bulk-loading techniques. In contrast to previous approaches, our technique exploits a priori knowledge of the complete data set to improve both construction time and query performance. Our algorithm operates in a mannar similar to the Quicksort algorithm and has an average runtime complexity of $O(n \log n)$. We additionally improve the query performance by optimizing the shape of the bounding boxes, by completely avoiding overlap, and by clustering the pages on disk. As we analytically show, the split strategy typically used in dynamic index structures, splitting the data space at the 50%-quantile, results in a bad query performance in high-dimensional spaces. Therefore, we use a sophisticated unbalanced split strategy, which leads to a much better space partitioning. An exhaustive experimental evaluation shows that our technique clearly outperforms both classic index construction and competitive bulk loading techniques. In comparison with dynamic index construction we achieve a speed-up factor of up to 588 for the construction time. The constructed index causes up to 16.88 times fewer page accesses and is up to 198 times faster (real time) in query processing.

1. Introduction

Multimedia database systems gain more and more importance in both database research and industry. In contrast to standard database systems, multimedia applications require similarity search as a basic functionality. A widely applied technique for searching a multimedia database for similar objects is the so-called feature transformation where important properties of the database object are transformed into a high-dimensional point, the so-called feature vector [10, 15, 18]. Usually, multidimensional index structures are used to manage the set of feature vectors. Most of the research regarding multidimensional index structures [1, 5, 4, 19, 14] focuses on a good search performance. Therefore, the performance of the proposed index structures for insert operations is sufficient only when inserting a relatively small amount of data, e.g. a single data item [4, 14]. A typical database application, however, starts with an empty database which will continuously grow due to multiple insert operations. It is not appropriate to use an index structure in the beginning of this process because having only a relatively small amount of high-dimensional feature vectors, a sequential scan of the data will be much faster than an index based search [7, 2]. However, if the size of the database reaches a certain threshold, the use of an index structure is required. In another scenario, we might want to replace a legacy system managing a large amount of data by a multimedia database system. In both cases, we face the problem to build an index file from a large amount of data i.e. to bulk-load the index.

On the other hand, we may draw some advantage from the fact that we do not only know a single data item - as in case of a normal insertion operation - but a large amount of data items. It is common knowledge that we can achieve a higher fanout and storage utilization using bulk load operations resulting in a slightly better search performance. But, do we exhaust all the potential of this information by increasing the storage utilization? As we show in this paper, we do not.

In this paper, we propose a new bulk-loading technique[1] for R-tree-like index structures. In contrast to other bulk-loading techniques, our algorithm exploits a priori knowledge of the complete data set to achieve a better data space partitioning. An arbitrary storage utilization can be chosen, including a near-100%[2] utilization. Furthermore, if we choose a storage utilization lower than 100%, we use the gained freedom for an acceleration of the construction. During the bulk-load operation, the complete data is held on secondary storage. Therefore, only a small cache in main memory is required and cost intensive disk operations such as random seeks are minimized. The basic idea of our technique is to split the data space recursively in a top-down fashion using hyperplanes as separators between the partitions. The hyperplanes are defined by a split dimension (the normal vector of the hyperplane) and a split value (defining the actual location of the hyperplane). Space partitioning is done by an algorithm that is similar to the well-known Quicksort algorithm although operating on secondary storage. Our technique is invariant against a specific split strategy i.e., gives us the freedom to partition the space according to arbitrary split dimensions and split values. We use this freedom to create a optimized space partitioning that is unbalanced and therefore cannot be achieved by a dynamic index structure. Note that, although partitioning is unbalanced, our algorithm guarantees that the resulting index structure is balanced. The paper is concluded by a variety of experimental results that demonstrate the advantage of our technique in comparison with dynamic indexing and other bulk loading techniques. We analytically show in Appendix A that our bulk-load operation can be done in average $O(n \log n)$ time.

2. Bulk-loading Multidimensional Index Structures

In this section, we will give an overview of the related research: A variety of high-dimensional index structures has been proposed in the past. The most well-known index structures are the TV-tree [14], the SS-tree [19], the SR-tree [13] and the X-tree [4]. However, none of these index structures supports an efficient bulk-load operation by itself.

On the other hand, some bulk-load techniques have been proposed. For example, the Hilbert R-tree [12] is created by externally sorting all the data vectors according to their Hilbert value and assigning equally sized, subsequential portions of the sorted data to data pages. Finally, the bounding boxes of the data pages are stored in directory pages clustering these directory pages recursively until we reach a single root node. The costs for bulk loading a Hilbert R-tree are obviously in $O(n \log n)$ due to external sorting. However, a

---

1. Frequently, bulk-loading an index is also called bottom-up construction of the index because we first construct the data pages which are at the "bottom" of the index structure and then construct the directory pages. As this term is misleading because we actually partition the data space in a top-down fashion, we omit this term and use bulk-loading or simply index construction instead.
2. "near 100%" means 100% up to round-up effects.

major drawback of the Hilbert R-tree is that Hilbert ordering degenerates in higher dimensions leading to a bad query performance.

As an alternative, we can divide the data space into partitions that correspond to data pages. This partitioning of the data space can be done in a top-down fashion which means that we hierarchically divide the d-dimensional space using $(d$-1)-dimensional hyperplanes as borderlines between the partitions. In addition, however, we have to assure that a directory can be built on top of this space partitioning. In [11], Jain and White introduced the VAM-Split R-tree and the VAM-Split KD-tree. VAM-Split trees are rather similar to KD-trees [16], however in contrast to KD-trees, split dimensions are not chosen in a round robin fashion but depending on the maximum variance. VAM Split trees are built in main memory and then stored to secondary storage. Therefore, the size of a VAM-Split tree is limited by the available main memory.

In [6], van den Bercken, Seeger and Widmayer proposed buffer trees which potentially work on all multidimensional index structures. The buffer tree is a derivative of the data structure to be constructed with two major modifications: First, an additional buffer is assigned to every directory page, and second, the capacity of a directory page may differ from the capacity of the target index structure. The buffer of every directory page is partially held in main memory and partially laid out on secondary storage. During the bulk load, each tuple is inserted into the buffer of the root node. If the buffer of the root node overflows, all objects in the buffer are dispatched to the next deeper index level. This process continues until the data level is reached. The general advantage of the buffer tree approach is that algorithms designed for tuning the query performance of the target index structure can be applied without modification. Obviously, the resulting index has the same properties as a dynamically constructed index.

None of these algorithms, however, uses the available knowledge of a large amount of data to improve the performance of the resulting index structure.

3. Our New Technique

In this section, we present our new bulk-loading technique. The index construction algorithm is a recursive algorithm comprising the following subtasks:

- determining the tree topology (height, fanout of the directory nodes, etc.)
- the split strategy
- external bisection of the data set on secondary storage
- constructing the index directory.

Although all these subtasks run in a nested fashion, we will present them separately to maintain clarity. However, we cannot regard the split strategy and the bisection independently from the tree topology. For example, we can only determine the exact topology of a subtree if we know the exact number of data objects stored in this subtree. This exact number, however, depends on the results of previous splits and bisections. Thus, although we separately describe the parts of the algorithms, we have to keep in mind the special requirements and prerequisites of the other parts.

An example will clarify the idea of our algorithm: Let us assume that we have given 10,000 two-dimensional data items and we can take from several properties our index structures that 10,000 items will fill a tree of height 3 having 6 entries in the root node (determination of tree topology). Thus, we first call the recursive partitioning algorithm

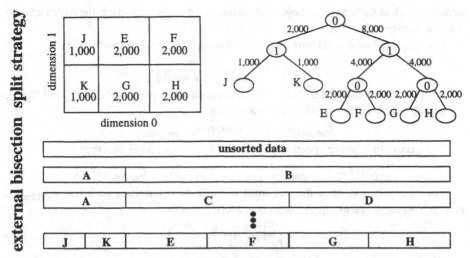

Fig. 1: Basic Idea of Our Technique

which applies the split strategy to our 10,000 data items and gets the following back: *"The 10,000 items should be first split according to dimension 0 such that partition A contains 2,000 items and partition B contains 8,000 items. Then we should split partition B according dimension 1 such that partition C and D each contain 4,000 items. Again, we should split C and D according to dimension 0 that each of the partitions E, F, G, and H each contain 2,000. Finally, we should split partition A according to dimension 1 into partitions J and K such that J and K contain each 1,000 data items."* Note that, this information could also be seen as a binary tree (split tree) having split dimensions as nodes and amounts of data as denotations of edges. The upper part of Figure 1 depicts the result of the split strategy and the according split tree. As a next step, the top-down partitioning algorithm calls the external[1] bisection algorithm which divides the previously unsorted data into the six desired portions (E, F, ... J, K). This is depicted in the lower part of Figure 1. At this point, we partitioned into the six subtrees of our root node. Note that, the data inside the partitions (J, K, ..., G, H) remains unsorted during the bisection i.e., there exists no ordering inside of J, for example. As a last step, we recursively apply our algorithm to the six partitions until we reach the data pages and write the corresponding directory to the secondary storage.

3.1 Determination of the Tree Topology

The first prerequisite of our algorithm is to determine the topology of the tree resulting from our bulk-load operation. The topology of a tree includes the height of the tree, the fanout of the directory nodes on the various tree levels, the capacity of data pages, and the number of objects stored in each subtree. However, we do not regard the exact number of objects stored in a tree, but a range between a maximum and a minimum number. The topology of the tree only depends on static information which is invariant during the con-

---

1. "External" means that the data to be bisected is located on secondary storage and the algorithm also operates on disk.

struction such as the number of objects, the dimension of the data space, the page capacity and the storage utilization.

Let $C_{max,data}$ be the maximum number of data objects in a data page where

$$C_{max,\,data} = \left\lfloor \frac{pagesize}{sizeof(dataobject)} \right\rfloor,$$

$C_{max,dir}$ analogously the maximum fanout of a directory page, and $C_{eff,data}$ and $C_{eff,dir}$ the average capacity of a data/directory page with

$$C_{eff,data} = storageutilization \cdot C_{max,\,data}.$$

The maximum number of data objects stored in a tree with height h then is:

$$C_{max,tree}(h) = C_{max,data} \cdot C_{max,dir}^{h-1} \qquad C_{eff,tree}(h) = C_{eff,data} \cdot C_{eff,dir}^{h-1}.$$

Therefore, the height of the tree must initially be determined such that $C_{eff,tree}$ is greater than the actual number of objects n. More formally:

$$h = \left\lceil \log_{C_{eff,dir}}(\frac{n}{C_{eff,data}}) \right\rceil + 1$$

Note that we have to evaluate this formula only once in order to determine the level of the root node of the index. As the X-tree and other R-tree related index structures are always height-balanced, we can easily determine the level of subtrees by decrementing the level of the parent node of the subtree. Now, we have to determine the fanout of the root node of a tree T with height h when filled with n data objects. Let us assume that every subtree of height $(h-1)$ is filled according to its average capacity $C_{eff,tree}(h-1)$. Thus, the fanout is the quotient of n and the average capacity of the subtrees:

$$fanout(h, n) = min(\left\lceil \frac{n}{C_{eff,tree}(h-1)} \right\rceil, C_{max,dir}) = min(\left\lceil \frac{n}{C_{eff,data} \cdot C_{eff,dir}^{h-2}} \right\rceil, C_{max,dir}).^1$$

Obviously, a 100% storage utilization in every node can be achieved only for certain values of n. Usually, the number of nodes in each level must be rounded-up. Thus, the data nodes and their parents are utilized best according to the desired storage utilization while the worst utilization typically occurs in the top levels of the tree. In general, our algorithm creates the highest possible average storage utilization below the chosen one.

3.2 The Split Strategy

Once we laid down the fanout f of a specific directory page P, the split strategy has to be applied to determine f subsets of the current data. As we regard the split strategy as an replaceable part of our algorithm, we only describe the requirements of a split strategy in this section. A detailed description of our optimized split strategy we be given in section 4.

Assuming that the dataset is bisected repeatedly, the split strategy determines the binary *split tree* for a directory page, which has f leaf nodes and may be arbitrarily unbalanced. Each non-leaf node in the split tree represents a hyperplane (the split plane) splitting the data set into two subsets. The split plane can be described by the split dimension and the numbers of data objects (NDO) on each side of the split plane. Thus, a split strategy has to determine the split dimension and the ratio between the two NDOs. Furthermore, we allow the split strategy to produce not only constant ratio but a interval of acceptable ratios. We will use this freedom later, to accelerate the bisection algorithm.

---

1. The minimum is required due to round-off effects

Note that the split strategy does not provide the position of the split plane in terms of attribute values. We determine this position using the bisection algorithm.

3.3 External Bisection of the Data Set

Our bisection algorithm is comparable to the well-known Quicksort algorithm [9, 17]. Note that, the actual goal of the bisection algorithm is to divide the array such that a specific proportion in the number of objects results which has fuzzily defined as an interval.

The basic idea of our algorithm is to adapt Quicksort as follows: Quicksort makes a bisection of the data according to a heuristically chosen pivot value and then recursively calls Quicksort for both subsets. Our first modification is to make only one recursive call for the subset which contains the split interval. We are able to do that because the objects in the other subsets are on the correct side of the split interval anyway and need no further sorting[1]. The second modification is to stop the recursion if the position of the pivot value is inside the split interval. The third modification is to choose the pivot values according to the proportion rather than trying to reach the middle of the array.

Additionally, our bisection algorithm operates on secondary storage. In our implementation, we use a sophisticated scheme reducing disk i/o and especially random seek operations much more than a normal caching algorithm would be able to. The algorithm runs in two modes: an internal mode, if the data set to be partitioned fits in the main memory cache, and an external mode, if it does not. In general, the internal mode is a modified Quicksort algorithm as explained above. The external mode is more sophisticated: First, the pivot value is determined a sample which fits into main memory and can be loaded without causing too many random seek operations. We use a simple heuristic to sample the data, which loads subsequent blocks from three different places in the data set. A complete internal bisection is run on the sample data set to determine the pivot value as well as possible. In the following external bisection, transfers from and to cache are always processed with a blocksize half the cache size, however, the cache does not exactly represent two blocks on disk. Each time, the data pointers of internal bisection meet at the bisection point, one of the sides of the cache contains more objects than fit in one block. Thus, one block, starting from the bisection point, is written back to the file and the next block is read and internally bisected again. All remaining data is written back in the very last step in the middle of the file where additionally a fraction of a block has to be processed. Now we test if the bisection point of the external bisection is in the split interval. In case the point is outside, another recursion is required.

3.4 Constructing the Index Directory

As the data partitioning is done by a recursive algorithm, the structure of the index is represented by the recursion tree. Therefore, we are able to created a directory node after the completion of the recursive calls for the child-nodes. These recursive calls return the bounding boxes and the according secondary storage addresses to the caller, where the informations are collected. There, the directory node is written, the bounding boxes are combined to a single bounding box comprising all child-boxes, and the result is again propagated to the next-higher level.

---

1. Note that our goal is not to sort the data but to divide the data into two partitions. Therefore, if we know that some part of the data belongs to a certain partition, we are not supposed to further sort it.

Thus, a depth-first post-order sequentialization of the index is written to disk. The sequentialization starts with a sequence of datapages, followed by the directory-page which is the common parent of these data pages. A sequence of such blocks is followed by a second-level directory page, and so on. The root page of the directory is the last page in the index file. As geometrically neighboring data pages are also likely to be in the same hierarchical branch, they are well clustered.

4. Improving the Query Performance

In dynamic index construction, the most important decision in split processing is the choice of the split axis whereas the split value is rather limited. Heavily unbalanced splits, such as a 10:1 proportion are commonly regarded as undesired because storage utilization guarantees would become impossible, if pages with deliberately low filling degree are generated in an uncontrolled manner. Moreover, for low-dimensional spaces, it is beneficial to minimize the perimeter of the bounding boxes i.e., to shape the bounding boxes such that all sides have approximately the same length [5]. But, there are some effects in high-dimensional data spaces leading to performance deterioration when minimizing the perimeter.

The first observation in a high-dimensional index is that, at least when applying balanced partitioning on a uniformly distributed dataset, the data space cannot be split in each dimension. Assuming for example a 20-dimensional data space which has been split exactly once in each dimension, would require $2^{20} = 1,000,000$ data pages or 30,000,000 objects if the effective page capacity is 30 objects. Therefore, the data space is usually split once in a number d' of dimensions. In the remaining $(d - d')$ dimensions it has not been split and the bounding boxes include almost the whole data space in these dimensions. As we assume the d-dimensional unit hypercube as data space, the bounding boxes have approximately side length 1/2 in d' dimensions and approximately side length 1 in $(d - d')$ dimensions. The maximum split dimension d' can be determined from the number N of objects stored in the database:

$$d' = \log_2(\frac{N}{C_{eff}}) \cdot {}^1$$

The second observation is that a similar property holds for typical range queries. If we assume that the range query is a hypercube and should have a selectivity s, then the side length q is the dth root of s: $q = \sqrt[d]{s}$. For a 20-dimensional range query with selectivity 0.01% we get a side length $q = 0.63$ which is larger than half of the extension of the data space in this direction.

It becomes intuitively clear that a query with side length larger than 1/2 must intersect with every bounding box having at least side length 0.5 in each dimension. However, we are also able to model this effect more accurate: The performance of a multi-dimensional range query is usually modeled by the means of the so-called Minkowski sum which transforms the range query into an equivalent point query by enlarging the bounding boxes of the pages accordingly [2]. In low-dimensional spaces, usually so-called boundary effects are neglected i.e., the data space is assumed to be infinite and everywhere filled with objects at the same density.

---

1. For a more detailed description of these effects, we refer the reader to [2].

To determine the probability that a bounding box intersects the query region, we consider the portion of the data space in which the center point of the query must be located, such that query and bounding box intersect. Therefore, we move the center point of the query (the query anchor) to each point of the data space marking the positions where the query rectangle intersects the bounding box. (c.f. Figure 3). The resulting set of marked positions is called the Minkowski sum which is the original bounding box having all sides enlarged by the query side length q and directly corresponds to the intersection probability[1].

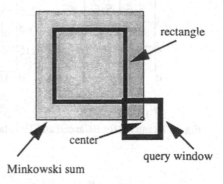

Fig. 2: The Minkowski Sum

Let $LLC_{i,j}$ and $URC_{i,j}$ denote the coordinates of the "lower left" and "upper right" corner of bounding box i ($0 \leq j < d$). The expected value $P(q)$ for page accesses upon processing a range query with side length q then is:

$$P_{no\_bound\_eff}(q) = \sum_i \prod_{j=0}^{d-1} (URC_{i,j} - LLC_{i,j} + q)$$

We have to adapt this formula to boundary effects, especially to consider that the query hypercube is always positioned completely in the d

$$P_{bound\_eff}(q) = \sum_i \prod_{j=0}^{d-1} \frac{min(URC_{i,j}, 1-q) - max(LLC_{i,j} - q, 0)}{1-q}.$$

The minimum and maximum is required to cut the parts of the Minkowski sum exceeding the data space. The denominator $(1 - q)$ is required due to the same reason as the stochastic "event space" of the query anchor is not $[0 ... 1]$ but rather $[0 ... 1-q]$. As an example, the results of three different partitionings for 6 pages in 2-d space and their expected page accesses for a range query with side length 0.6 are illustrated in Figure 3. All bounding boxes have an area of 1/6. The individual access probability is depicted inside the boxes. The first partitioning corresponds to a balanced split strategy optimized for square-like bounding boxes. The second corresponds to a strategy, cutting a slice with area 1/6 from the lower part of the remaining space. The dimensions are in this case changed periodically. The third strategy is similar to the second, with the only exception that slices are cut from the lower and the higher end, before the dimensions are changed. We can take from this simple 2-dimensional example that, for large queries, the performance is slightly (30%) improved if the pages are split unbalanced. This is due to the fact that close to the border of the data space, there arise long pages with a low access probability. We will see in the following refinement of the model that this effect is amplified in high-dimensional space. The model for balanced splits can be simplified if the number of data pages is a power of two. Then, all pages have extension 0.5 in d' dimensions, lying on the lower or the upper half of the data space, and full extension in the remaining dimensions:

---

1. Note hereby that the volume of the data space is 1.

224

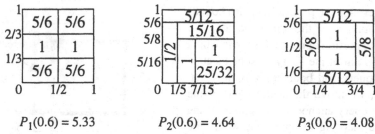

$$P_1(0.6) = 5.33 \qquad P_2(0.6) = 4.64 \qquad P_3(0.6) = 4.08$$

Fig. 3: Examples for Balanced and Unbalanced Split Strategies in 2-Dimensional Space

$$P_{balanced}(q) = \frac{N}{C_{eff}} \cdot \min(1, \left(\frac{0.5}{1-q}\right)^{\log_2(\frac{N}{C_{eff}})}).$$

In contrast, the performance of unbalanced partitioning is difficult to model. To get a coarse approximation of the improvement potential, we assume that the data pages are positioned on concentric cubic shells as in the third partitioning in Figure 3. Note that, this partitioning cannot be reached in the presence of an overlap-free R-tree directory. For simplicity, we further assume an infinite number of pages. Then, the volume met by the query can be individually determined for each set of pages connected to a side of the data space, depending on the position $[p_0, ..., p_{d-1}]$ of the query anchor:

$$V_i(p_i) = \frac{(1-2p_i)^d}{2d}.$$

As we have $2d$ such volumes, all met by a query with side length larger than 0.5, we have to build the average over all possible positions of p_i:

$$P_{unbalanced}(q) = \frac{2dN}{C_{eff} \cdot (1-q)} \cdot \int_0^{1-q} V_i(p_i)dp_i = \frac{N \cdot (1-(2q-1)^{d+1})}{2C_{eff} \cdot (1-q) \cdot (d+1)}.$$

While for queries larger than 0.5, all pages have to be read according to our model for balanced splits, efficient query processing is still possible in the model for unbalanced split. (c.f. Figure 4)

Thus, we implemented the following unbalanced split strategy: If the current data set fits into main memory, then we determine the dimension d_s where the space partition to be split has maximal extension. Otherwise, we apply the same criterion to a sample of the current data set which is taken as mentioned in section 3.3.

Once d_s has been determined, we split the space according to the given ratio. Then, we split the larger partition on the opposite side using the same ratio and split dimension. Thus, we have symmetrically split the space into three portions, a large partition in the middle of the space and two equally sized small partitions at the border of the space. If the remaining large partition contains more elements than the capacity of a subtree, we again choose an appropriate split dimension for the remaining partition and split it according to the given ratio. This process continues until the size of the remaining partition is below the capacity of a subtree. Note that we do not have the full freedom of splitting anywhere in the last step of this process, unless we produce underfilled pages.

5. Experimental Evaluation

To show the practical relevance of our bottom-up construction algorithm and of our techniques for unbalanced splitting, we performed an extensive experimental evaluation, comparing the following index construction techniques:

- Dynamic index construction by repeatedly inserting objects
- Hilbert R-tree construction by sorting the objects according to their Hilbert values
- our bottom-up construction method using
  - balanced (1:1) splitting
  - moderately balanced (3:1)
  - heavily (9:1) unbalanced splits

All experiments have been computed on HP9000/780 workstations with several GBytes of secondary storage. Although our technique is applicable to most R-tree-like index structures, we decided to use the X-tree as an underlying index structure because according to [4], the X-tree outperforms other high-dimensional index structures. All programs have been implemented object-oriented in C++. Our experimental evaluation comprises real and synthetic data. Our real data set consists of text data, describing substrings from a large text database. We converted the text descriptors to 300,000 points in a 16-dimensional data space (19 MBytes of raw data). The synthetic data set consists of two million uniformly distributed points normalized in the 16-dimensional unit hypercube. The total amount of disk space occupied by the created indexes is about 2.8 GBytes. The index construction time for all our experiments sums up to several weeks. Please note that we decided not to compare our technique to the technique of van Bercken and Seeger, proposed in [6], because they proof for their technique that the resulting index structure is identical to a dynamically created index structure. Therefore, an experiment would lead to exactly the same result as the experiment with the dynamic index structure.

In our first experiment, we compared the construction times for various indexes. The external sorting procedure of our construction method was allowed to use only a relatively small cache (32 kBytes). In our experiments we used a storage utilization of 80%. In contrast, the Hilbert construction method was implemented using internal sorting due to simplicity. Therefore, the construction time of the Hilbert method is under-estimated in the experiments. Due to the restricted implementation, all Hilbert-constructed indexes have a storage utilization near 100%.

Figure 5 shows the construction time of dynamic index construction and the bottom-up methods. In the left diagram, we fixed the dimension to 16 and varied the database size

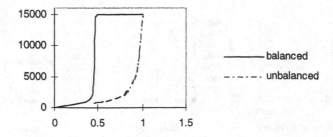

Fig. 4: Estimated Page Accesses for Balanced and Unbalanced Split Strategies

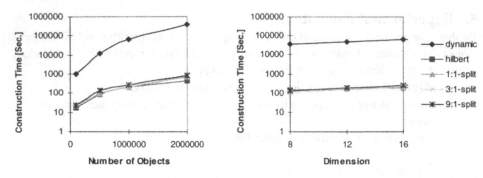

Fig. 5: Performance of Index Construction Against Database Size and Dimension

from 100,000 to 2,000,000 objects of synthetic data. The resulting speedup of the bulk-loading techniques over dynamic construction was so enormous that we decided to use a logarithmic scale, whereas the bottom-up methods differ only slightly in performance. The Hilbert technique was the best method having a construction time between 17 and 429 seconds. In contrast, the dynamic construction time ranged from 965 to 393,310 seconds (4 days, 13 hours). The right diagram in Figure 5 shows the construction time with varying index dimension. Here, the database size was fixed to 1,000,000 objects. It can be seen that the speed-up factors of the construction methods (between 240 and 320) are rather independent from the dimension of the data space.

In the next series of experiments on uniform data, depicted in Figure 6, we determined the query performance of the differently constructed indexes. As a query type, we used region queries because region queries serve as a basis for more complex queries such as nearest neighbor queries and, therefore, are fundamental in multimedia databases. In the left diagram, 16-dimensional indexes with between 100,000 and two million objects were queried with a constant selectivity of about 0.3‰. The diagram in the middle shows dimensions varying from 8 to 16 with a constant number of objects (1,000,000) and again a constant query. Note that, the highest speedup (16.8) of our technique over the dynamic index could be measured in the highest dimension and the largest database. The right part of Figure 6 shows the performance of a 16-dimensional index filled with 1,000,000 objects. We varied the selectivity of the query from $6.55 \cdot 10^{-13}$ % to 18.5%, corresponding to an edge length of the query hypercube varying from 0.2 to 0.9 and determined the number of page accesses. The result of this experiment is that the Hilbert constructed index

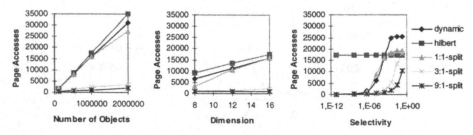

Fig. 6: Performance of Range Queries

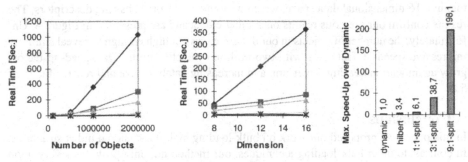

Fig. 7: Real Time for Executing Range Queries

has a unsatisfactory performance and therefore is unsuitable to index high-dimensional data spaces. Even very small query windows revealed a full scan of the complete index. However, dynamically and bottom-up constructed indexes with balanced splits had a very similar performance. Due to the sophisticated split strategy of the X-tree, the over-lap-free directory of the bottom-up constructed index does not lead to significant performance improvements. However, the benefits of unbalanced splitting can be ob-served at configuration. Especially the heavily unbalanced split leads to an index showing a very good performance also on very large queries. The speed-up factor over the bal-anced split reaches 15.6 at a query edge length of 0.6 and it is more than 15.7 times faster than the dynamically constructed index.

Nevertheless, range query evaluation is clearly disk i/o bound, as can be seen in Figure 7. Here we measured the real time for query execution, comprising cpu time and the times for disk i/o which are predominant. It is remarkable that, in contrast to the experiments counting page accesses, the balanced splitting bottom-up method outperforms the dynam-ic construction, too, and that the speedup-factors are one order of magnitude higher than the speed-up factors for page accesses. This is due to the much better disc clustering of our construction method. Data pages in a common subtree of the index are laid out contigu-ously on disk. These pages have often to be loaded commonly, such that disk head movements are often avoided. In contrast, if a dynamic index structure splits a page, one of the resulting new pages occupies the place of the old page whereas the second page is ap-pended at the end of the file. Thus, neighboring pages are rather declustered than clustered.

In a last series of experiments we determined the behavior of our technique on real data, stemming from an information retrieval application. We used 300,000 feature vec-

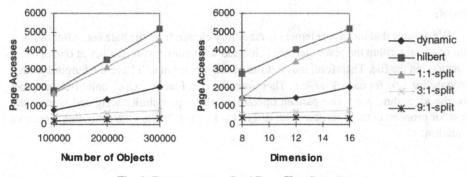

Fig. 8: Experiments on Real Data (Text Descriptors)

tors in a 16-dimensional data space, which we converted from substring descriptors. The results confirm our previous results on synthetic data and are presented in Figure 8. Unfortunately, the number of objects in our database was not high enough to reveal similarly impressive speed-up factors as with two million synthetic points. The speed-up factors grow again with increasing dimension and increasing database size and reach a factor of 5.8.

6. Conclusions

In this paper, we proposed our work on bulk-loading high-dimensional index structures. In contrast to other bulk-loading techniques, our method not only provides a very good performance when creating the index but also when querying the index. This is caused by the fact that we use a sophisticated split strategy, which leads to a much better space partitioning. In contrast with normal multidimensional index structures, we used an unbalanced split instead of a 50%-quantile split. We showed both analytically and experimentally that our technique outperforms other techniques by up to two orders of magnitudes. The average time complexity of our technique is $O(n \log n)$.

In the future, we will focus on the development of a multithreaded or parallel version of our algorithm which could reveal further performance enhancements because a higher degree of parallelity between cpu and disk i/o processor could be achieved.

Another important research issue is handling massive insert operations in an existing dynamic index and the reorganization of an existing index in order to improve the query performance.

Appendix A: Analytical Evaluation of the Bulk-Loading Algorithm

In this section, we will show that our bottom-up construction algorithm has an average complexity $O(n \log n)$. Unless no further caching is provided (which is true for our application, but cannot be guaranteed for the operating system) and provided that seeks are randomly distributed over a large file, the i/o processing time can be determined as $t_{i/o} = t_{seek} \cdot seek\_ops + t_{contiguous} \cdot amount$, where typical values for current devices could be $t_{seek} = 10 \ ms$ per seek operation and $t_{contiguous} = 220 \ ns$ per byte.

Lemma 1:

The bisection algorithm has complexity $O(n)$.

Proof:

We assume that the pivot element is randomly chosen from the data set. After the first run of the algorithm the pivot element is located with uniform probability at one of the n positions in the file. Therefore, the next run of the algorithm will have the length k with a probability $1/n$ for each $1 < k < n$. Therefore, the cost function $C(n)$ comprises the cost for the algorithm, $n + 1$ comparison operations plus a probability weighted sum of the cost for processing the algorithm with length $k - 1$, $C(k)$. We get the following recursive equation:

$$C(n) = n + 1 + \sum_{k=1}^{n} \frac{C(k-1)}{n},$$

which can be solved by multiplying with n and subtracting the same equation for $n-1$

$$n \cdot C(n) - (n-1) \cdot C(n-1) = n \cdot (n+1) - n \cdot (n-1) + \sum_{k=1}^{n} C(k-1) - \sum_{k=1}^{n-1} C(k-1).$$

This can be simplified to $C(n) = 2 + C(n-1)$ and, as $C(1) = 1$, $C(n) = 2 \cdot n = O(n)$.
q.e.d.

Lemma 2:

(1) The amount of data read or written during one recursion of our technique does not exceed four times the filesize.

(2) The number of seek operations required is bounded by

$$\text{seek\_ops}(n) \le \frac{8 \cdot n \cdot \text{sizeof(object)}}{\text{cachesize}} + 2 \cdot \log_2(n)$$

Proof:

(1) follows directly from Lemma 1 because every compared element has to be transferred from and to disk at most once.

(2) In each run of the external bisection algorithm, file i/o is processed with a block-size of cachesize/2. The number of blocks read in each run is therefore

$$\text{blocks\_read}_{\text{bisection}}(n) = \frac{n \cdot \text{sizeof(object)}}{\text{cache\_size}/2} + 1$$

because one extra read is required in the final step. The number of write operations is the same such that

$$\text{seek\_ops}(n) = 2 \cdot \sum_{i=0}^{r_{\text{interval}}} \text{blocks\_read}_{\text{run}}(i) \le \frac{8 \cdot n \cdot \text{sizeof(object)}}{\text{cachesize}} + 2 \cdot \log_2(n) \qquad \text{q.e.d.}$$

Lemma 3:

Our technique has an average case complexity $O(n \log n)$, unless the split strategy has a complexity worse than $O(n)$.

Proof:

For each level of the tree, the complete dataset has to be bisectioned as often as the height of the split tree. As the height of the split tree is limited by the directory page capacity, there are at most $h(n) \cdot C_{\text{max,dir}} = O(\log n)$ bisection runs necessary. Our technique has therefore complexity $O(n \log n)$. \qquad q.e.d.

References

1. Berchtold S., Böhm C., Braunmueller B., Keim D. A., Kriegel H.-P.: *'Fast Similarity Search in Multimedia Databases'*, Proc. ACM SIGMOD Int. Conf. on Management of Data, 1997, Tucson, Arizona.

2. Berchtold S., Böhm C., Keim D., Kriegel H.-P.: *'A Cost Model For Nearest Neighbor Search in High-Dimensional Data Space'*, ACM PODS Symposium on Pricinples of Database Systems, Tucson, Arizona, 1997, SIGMOD BEST PAPER AWARD.
3. Berchtold S., Kriegel H.-P.: *'S3: Similarity Search in CAD Database Systems'*, Proc. ACM SIGMOD Int. Conf. on Management of Data, 1997, Tucson, Arizona.
4. Berchtold S., Keim D., Kriegel H.-P.: *'The X-tree: An Index Structure for High-Dimensional Data'*, 22nd Conf. on Very Large Databases, 1996, Bombay, India, pp. 28-39.
5. Beckmann N., Kriegel H.-P., Schneider R., Seeger B.: *'The R*-tree: An Efficient and Robust Access Method for Points and Rectangles'*, Proc. ACM SIGMOD Int. Conf. on Management of Data, Atlantic City, NJ, 1990, pp. 322-331.
6. van den Bercken J., Seeger B., Widmayer P.:, *'A General Approach to Bulk Loading Multidimensional Index Structures'*, 23rd Conf. on Very Large Databases, 1997, Athens, Greece.
7. Faloutsos C., Barber R., Flickner M., Hafner J., et al.: *'Efficient and Effective Querying by Image Content'*, Journal of Intelligent Information Systems, 1994, Vol. 3, pp. 231-262.
8. Friedman J. H., Bentley J. L., Finkel R. A.: *'An Algorithm for Finding Best Matches in Logarithmic Expected Time'*, ACM Transactions on Mathematical Software, Vol. 3, No. 3, September 1977, pp. 209-226.
9. C.A.R. Hoare, *'Quicksort'*, Computer Journal, Vol. 5, No. 1, 1962.
10. Jagadish H. V.: *'A Retrieval Technique for Similar Shapes'*, Proc. ACM SIGMOD Int. Conf. on Management of Data, 1991, pp. 208-217.
11. Jain R, White D.A.: *'Similarity Indexing: Algorithms and Performance'*, Proc. SPIE Storage and Retrieval for Image and Video Databases IV, Vol. 2670, San Jose, CA, 1996, pp. 62-75.
12. Kamel I., Faloutsos C.: *'Hilbert R-tree: An Improved R-tree using Fractals'*. Proc. 20th Int. Conf. on Very Large Databases (VLDB'94), pp. 500-509
13. Katayama N., Satoh S.: *'The SR-tree: An Index Structure for High-Dimensional Nearest Neighbor Queries'*, Proc. ACM SIGMOD Int. Conf. on Management of Data, 1997.
14. Lin K., Jagadish H. V., Faloutsos C.: *'The TV-tree: An Index Structure for High-Dimensional Data'*, VLDB Journal, Vol. 3, pp. 517-542, 1995.
15. Mehrotra R., Gary J.: *'Feature-Based Retrieval of Similar Shapes'*, Proc. 9th Int. Conf. on Data Engeneering, April 1993
16. Robinson J. T.: *'The K-D-B-tree: A Search Structure for Large Multidimensional Dynamic Indexes'*, Proc. ACM SIGMOD Int. Conf. on Management of Data, 1981, pp. 10-18.
17. R. Sedgewick: *'Quicksort'*, Garland, New York, 1978.
18. Seidl T., Kriegel H.-P.: *'Efficient User-Adaptable Similarity Search in Large Multimedia Databases'*, Proc. 23rd Int. Conf. on Very Large Databases (VLDB'97), Athens, Greece, 1997.
19. White D.A., Jain R.: *'Similarity indexing with the SS-tree'*, Proc. 12th Int. Conf on Data Engineering, New Orleans, LA, 1996.

display. With VBR, this variation is not bounded. The VBR schemes have the advantage that, for the same average bandwidth as CBR, they can maintain a more constant quality in the delivered images by utilizing more megabits per second when needed, e.g., when there is more action in a scene. The focus of this study is on VBR encoded continuous media and techniques that ensure their hiccup-free display.

To support a hiccup-free display of VBR encoded continuous media, one must analyze both the network and the disk subsystem. A number of studies have analyzed each component in isolation. For the network, the previous studies [4, 5, 13, 11, 10, 6] have striven to reduce the rate variability of the VBR clips. For the disk storage subsystem, the previous studies [3, 2, 12] have focused on data placement, admission control, and scheduling techniques. In this study, we provide a framework that affiliates disk subsystem with network through the investigation of the role of bandwidth smoothing algorithms to schedule the disk bandwidth for continuous display of VBR video clips. The contribution of this study is a taxonomy that includes all possible techniques. In this taxonomy, $Universal - CR^2$ and $Atomic - VR^2\ FIT$ techniques have been applied to the disk subsystem. However, the applications of $Universal - CR^2\ FIT$, $Universal - CR^2\ VITAL$, $Atomic - CR^2$, and $Atomic - VR^2\ VITAL$ techniques to the disk subsystem are novel. We evaluate these techniques based on three criteria:

1. Throughput: Number of simultaneous displays supported by a technique assuming a fixed system configuration.
2. Startup latency: The amount of delay incurred from when a request references a video clip to the onset of its display.
3. Cost per stream: The amount of resources required by a technique (computed as cost) to support a fixed number of simultaneous displays.

The results demonstrate that $Atomic - VR^2\ VITAL$ is superior to others.

The rest of this paper is organized as follows. After a brief description of the related studies in Section 2, Section 3 presents a taxonomy of disk retrieval techniques and eight specific algorithms in support of VBR video. This section describes how the different algorithms map into a single taxonomy and which algorithm is used to represent a technique in the taxonomy. In Section 4, a case study is presented where each algorithm is applied to movie clips obtained from the Universal Studios. Analytical models are desinged to compute the cost per stream and the average startup latency for the different approaches. These analytical models are applied to the case study. Brief conclusions and future research directions are offered in Section 5.

2 Related Work

Two studies [3, 2] have proposed alternative approaches for placement of data with VBR objects: constant time length and constant data length. In the first approach, the blocks of the video data are variable in length with constant real-time display. The blocks in the other approach are fixed in length with

An Evaluation of Alternative Disk Scheduling Techniques in Support of Variable Bit Rate Continuous Media

Jaber A. Al-Marri and Shahram Ghandeharizadeh

Computer Science Department
University of Southern California
Los Angeles, California 90089
{ almarri, shahram} @pollux.usc.edu

Abstract. A number of recent studies have investigated scheduling techniques in support of variable bit rate (VBR) video. When compared with constant bit rate (CBR) video, VBR has a lower storage and bandwidth requirement while providing the same quality of images. However, a VBR video clip might exhibit a significant variance in the bit rate required to support its continuous display. The previous studies have proposed techniques to support the display of a VBR clip from two different perspectives: disk storage subsystem and the network. In this study, we propose a taxonomy of VBR disk scheduling techniques that includes those proposed for the network. The results demonstrate that a new class of disk scheduling techniques, termed $Atomic - VR^2\ VITAL$, is superior. Algorithms used to represent this class were adopted from the networking literature.

1 Introduction

Due to several advances in computer processing, storage performance, and high speed communications, a number of data intensive applications have become viable. Examples include digital libraries, distance learning, video-on-demand, shopping and entertainment services, etc. Continuous media, digital audio and video, play a major role in these applications. The principle characteristics of continuous media is their sustained bit rate requirement. For example, digital component video based on the CCIR 601 standard requires 270 Megabits per second (Mbps) for its continuous display. If a system delivers a clip at a rate lower than its prespecified rate without special precautions (e.g., prefetching), the user might observe frequent disruptions and delays with video and random noises with audio. These artifacts are collectively termed *hiccups*. The bandwidth requirement of a clip (along with its size) can be reduced using compression techniques due to redundancy in data. With continuous media, compression techniques can be classified as either CBR or VBR. With both approaches, the data must still be delivered at a prespecified rate. Typically CBR schemes allow some bounded variation of this rate based on some amount of memory at the

variable real-time display. We refer to the first approach in this study as *Atomic*–VR^2 *FIT*. The constant data length approach is referred to as $Universal - CR^2$ in this study. A statistical admissions control based on a number of service classes corresponding to various probabilities of loss is described in [3]. Three techniques are provided for computing loss probabilities: histogram convolution, Central Limit Theorem, and Cramer's rule. Scalability is achieved by allowing appropriate frames of MPEG to be dropped without fully suspending service to an active display. A number of deterministic and statistical admissions control policies for each of the data placement approaches is outlined in [2]. Based on one disk experiments, the two approaches are compared using a statistical admission control policy.

A stochastic model that guarantees an upper bound of the number of hiccup observed by the streams is described in [12]. All the data fragments stored on the disks have the same display time. We refer to this approach as *Atomic* – VR^2 *FIT* in this study. The Laplace-Stieltjes transform of the service time distribution is derived for the model based on batched disk service under a multi-user load of the concurrently served continuous data streams. Chernoff bounds are applied to the tail of the service time distribution and the resulting distribution of the glitch rate per stream.

Several other studies [9, 8] have investigated the traffic generated by VBR streams. Two network service models are proposed by these studies: deterministic guaranteed service [9] and renegotiated CBR service [8]. These studies focus on network scheduling while we focus on disk scheduling. In the network scheduling, the researchers aim to minimize the peak bandwidth, minimize the number of bandwidth increases, and maximize the number of bandwidth decreases. However, in disk scheduling, we strive to maximize the number of concurrent users, minimize the client buffer, and minimize the startup latency time.

Our work incorporates and extends these schemes. We propose a taxonomy that reveals all possible strategies that can be used to support a deterministic disk retrieval of VBR objects. We evaluate each strategy individually. Then, we compare and contrast the different strategies with one another.

3 A Taxonomy of Disk Retrieval of VBR Objects

A taxonomy of disk retrieval techniques that can guarantee a hiccup-free display of VBR objects is shown in Figure 1. There are two main techniques that produce a retrieval plan to transmit an object from a server to a client. The first technique employs a constant transmission rate (say 4 Mbps). We term this technique *Constant Retrieval Rate* (CR^2). The second technique, termed *Variable Retrieval Rate* (VR^2), utilizes more than one transmission rate. With VR^2, the retrieval plan of an object is divided into a number of time intervals. The server may use a different transmission rate for each of these intervals. If the intervals length is constant, the technique is termed *Fixed tIme inTerval* (FIT). For example, with a 3-hour presentation, the server might transmit the object at 8 Mbps for the first hour, 4 Mbps for the second hour, and 2 Mbps for the third

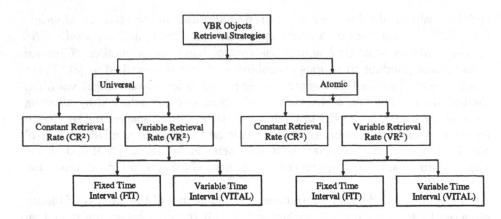

Fig. 1. A taxonomy of disk retrieval of VBR objects

hour. If the intervals have variable length, the technique is termed *VarIable Time intervAL (VITAL)*. A disk retrieval strategy determines the manner in which these techniques are employed. While a *Universal* strategy enforces a single retrieval plan on all objects in the repository, an *Atomic* strategy produces a different retrieval plan for each of these objects.

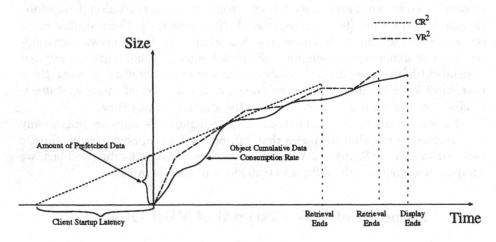

Fig. 2. CR^2 vs. VR^2

Figure 2 shows CR^2 and VR^2. In this figure, the solid line represents the number of bytes (y-axis) consumed by the client as a function of time (x-axis). To ensure a hiccup-free display, the amount of data delivered by a technique must suffice that consumed by the client. This fact is depicted in the figure by drawing the lines (dotted lines) corresponding to CR^2 and VR^2 above the solid line. CR^2 is represented as a straight line because it retrieves data at a constant rate (constant slope). However, VR^2 is represented as a piecewise line due to the variation of rates (slopes). The intersection of CR^2 line with the y-axis specifies the amount of data that a client must prefetch before its display is started. The intersection of CR^2 line with x-axis determines the time (client startup latency) required to materialize the prefetched amount of data. Obviously, one may draw different CR^2 lines with different slopes. (The slope of a line specifies the constant bandwidth required to support a hiccup-free display.) Different lines would resemble a tradeoff between the bandwidth required by the schedule and the amount of data that a client must be prefetched (i.e., client startup latency). It is possible to devise algorithms with different objectives, e.g., minimize the bandwidth requirement while the prefetched amount of data is less than 32 Megabytes (MB). Figure 3 shows both $VITAL$ and FIT. While FIT divides a retrieval plan into intervals of equal length, $VITAL$ attempts to adjust to the need of an object.

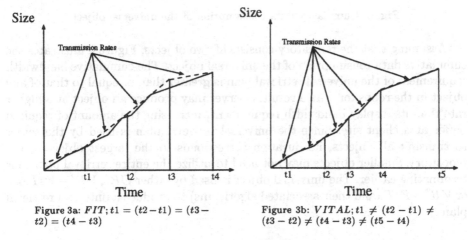

Figure 3a: FIT; $t1 = (t2 - t1) = (t3 - t2) = (t4 - t3)$

Figure 3b: $VITAL$; $t1 \neq (t2 - t1) \neq (t3 - t2) \neq (t4 - t3) \neq (t5 - t4)$

Fig. 3. VR^2

Term	Definition
O	Total number of objects in the repository
T	Display time length of the longest object
$C(j,i)$	Amount of data consumed at time i by object j
$S(i)$	Amount of data consumed at time i by universal object
$Mbps$	Megabits per second
GB	Gigabytes
MB	Megabytes

Table 1. List of terms used repeatedly in this research and their definitions

With *Atomic*, each object in the repository has an individual retrieval plan. However, with *Universal*, a single retrieval plan is employed for all objects. This plan is computed as follows. *Universal* constructs a "universal object" whose consumption rate is computed as defined by the maximum consumption rate required by an object per unit of time (refer to Table 1 for the definition of the parameters in this equation):

$$S(i)_{1 \leq i \leq T} = \max \ C(j,i)_{1 \leq j \leq O} \tag{1}$$

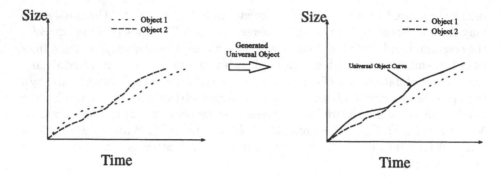

Fig. 4. Cumulative data consumption of the universal object

Assuming that the repository consists of two objects, Figure 4 illustrates the cumulative data consumption of the universal object. The cumulative bandwidth requirement of the universal retrieval plan is greater than or equal to that of any object in the repository. As a result, a server may produce an object at a higher rate than its display bandwidth requirement, increasing the amount of required buffer at a client site. Since the universal retrieval plan is used by the server to transmit all objects, its duration corresponds to the largest object in the repository. Smaller objects may not need to utilize the entire retrieval plan thus terminating earlier. The universal object is used by either CR^2, $VR^2 - VITAL$, or $VR^2 - FIT$ (and their associated algorithms) to produce a universal retrieval plan.

3.1 Eight Bandwidth Smoothing Algorithms

Bandwidth smoothing algorithms are created to compute a retrieval plan for the delivery of an object which simplifies the allocation of resources in the server and the network. They strive to remove the burstiness in VBR objects without causing startup latency. By eliminating burstiness, they improve the utilization of server and network resources. A bandwidth smoothing algorithm produces a retrieval plan, which reduces the variance of the transmission rates, for a compressed object based on the a priori knowledge of the frame sizes in the compressed object while avoiding both underflow and overflow of the client buffer. The smoothing is done by prefetching frames in advance of each burst. Consequently, a larger client buffer results in a less bursty retrieval plan for an object.

Bandwidth algorithms [4, 7, 5, 13, 11, 10, 6] generate retrieval plans that consist of a number of time intervals based on the frame lengths and the client buffer. During each interval, a portion of an object is transmitted using a constant rate. The time duration of an interval depends on the client buffer and the degree of burstiness in the object. Different smoothing algorithms produce different retrieval plans for an object. These plans may differ in the number of intervals, length of the intervals, and the consumption rate requirement in each interval. This is due to the different metrics that they aim to optimize. Table 2 depicts the classification of the algorithms into three possible categories: CR^2,

$VR^2 - FIT$, and $VR^2 - VITAL$. We now describe each of these algorithms in turn.

Smoothing Algorithm	CR^2	$VR^2 - FIT$	$VR^2 - VITAL$
ABA	√	√	√
SWS	√	√	√
CRTT	√	-	-
PCRTT	√	√	√
RCBS	-	√	-
CBA	-	-	√
MCBA	-	-	√
MVBA	-	-	√

Table 2. Classification of bandwidth smoothing algorithms

Algorithm 1: Average Bandwidth Allocation (ABA)

ABA [6] is a simple algorithm that groups an arbitrary number of frames together into a "chunk" and computes its average bandwidth requirement. The average bandwidth of a chunk is used to transmit its frames. Basically, a chunk is a collection of disk blocks that are retrieved at the average bandwidth requirement of a chunk. To guarantee a hiccup-free display, the first chunk must be buffered in its entirety at the client prior to display. The buffer requirement becomes impractical when ABA assumes large chunk size. Smoothing of the bandwidth across chunks is not considered by ABA.

ABA algorithm may produce a plan for CR^2 by grouping the entire frames of an object together into one chunk. This implies that a client must cache an object in its entirety prior to initiate its display, incurring a high startup latency. ABA algorithm generates a plan for VR^2 when an object's frames are grouped into more than one chunk. If each chunk contains the same number of frames, the generated plan is $VR^2 - FIT$. Otherwise, it is $VR^2 - VITAL$.

Algorithm 2: Sliding Window Smoothing (SWS)

SWS [6] is similar to ABA except that it attempts to smooth the bandwidth within chunks using a sliding window. It groups an arbitrary number of chunks into a window and smoothes them. The smoothing process is based on prefetching of frames with large sizes. Frames must be prefetched in order to guarantee a hiccup-free display. The smoothing process starts from the last chunk working itself back to the first chunk. When the bandwidth of a chunk is above the average bandwidth of the window as a whole, the difference between the chunk bandwidth and the average bandwidth is transfered to an earlier chunks whose bandwidth is below the average bandwidth. This results in prefetching of those frames that have large sizes. SWS smoothes the bandwidth of an object better than ABA when the window size is sufficiently large. Even though it may require buffers at the client to accommodate its prefetching of frames, its total memory requirement at the client is far less than ABA. Plans for CR^2, $VR^2 - FIT$, and $VR^2 - VITAL$ can be produced by SWS in a similar manner to ABA.

Algorithm 3: Constant-Rate Transmission and Transport (CRTT)

CRTT [11] is an algorithm that produces a constant transmission rate for an object. As input, this algorithm consumes the client buffer size and the startup latency time in terms of number of frames. As output, it produces two curves. The first represents the minimum bit rate requirement that guarantees a hiccup-free display. The second designates the maximum bit rate requirement which guarantees no overflow at the client buffer. The intersection of these two curves identifies the feasible region of constant bandwidth that can be used to represent the object. This algorithm might require a large client buffer. It supports CR^2.

Algorithm 4: Piecewise-Constant-Rate Transmission and Transport (PCRTT)

PCRTT [10] algorithm divides an object stream into fixed time intervals. The bandwidth rate of each interval is represented by the slope of the line connecting interval points. To guarantee a hiccup-free display, PCRTT algorithm vertically offsets the lines of the intervals until they are above the object consumption curve, see Figure 5. This algorithm results in a startup latency. The piecewise-linear curve that is generated by PCRTT is used to determine the minimum client buffer which might be large.

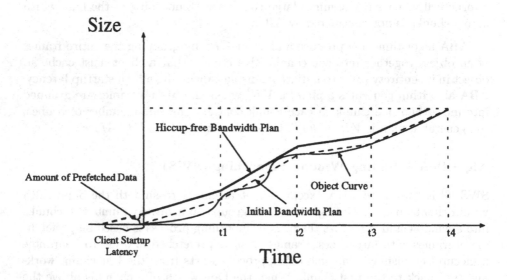

Fig. 5. Creation of PCRTT intervals

PCRTT algorithm can generate a plan for CR^2 by considering an object stream as one interval. In addition, PCRTT algorithm can produce a plan for VR^2 by dividing an object stream into more than one interval. If all intervals have the same time length, the resulting plan is $VR^2 - FIT$. Otherwise, it is $VR^2 - VITAL$.

Algorithm 5: Rate-Constrained Bandwidth Smoothing (RCBS)

Given a maximum bandwidth rate constraint, RCBS [4] examines each frame in an object and ensures its bandwidth does not exceed this maximum by prefetching data. RCBS examines the frames starting from the end of the object and maintains the excess data that should be prefetched. If the bandwidth of a frame is greater than the bandwidth constraint, the excess bandwidth is distributed among the preceding frames as long as it does not cause the bandwidth of the preceding frames to violate the constraint. An example of the effect of RCBS on an object bandwidth is shown in Figure 6. Conceptually, RCBS runs a knife across the frames' bandwidth. RCBS minimizes the amount of prefetched data. However, it maximizes the variability of the bandwidth allocation and the number of bandwidth changes. It also increases the variability of the time between bandwidth changes. RCBS produces a retrieval plan for an object by smoothing its frames. Since frames are considered fixed time interval of the same time length, the plan produced by RCBS is $VR^2 - FIT$.

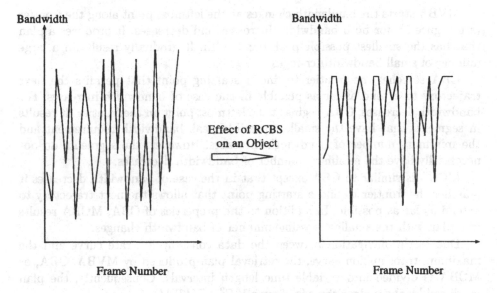

Fig. 6. RCBS example

Algorithms 6,7, and 8: MVBA, CBA, and MCBA

Minimum Variability Bandwidth Allocation (MVBA) [13], Minimum Changes Bandwidth Allocation (MCBA) [5], and Critical Bandwidth Allocation (CBA) [7, 6] algorithms are similar in nature. They consumes as input the accumulative data consumption rate curve of an object and the client buffer size in order to produce a maximum transmission curve that denotes the upper limits beyond which the client buffer overflows. They navigate between these two curves to generate a piecewise-linear curve. They differ in how they choose the starting point for the next interval when bandwidth either increases or decreases, see Figure 7.

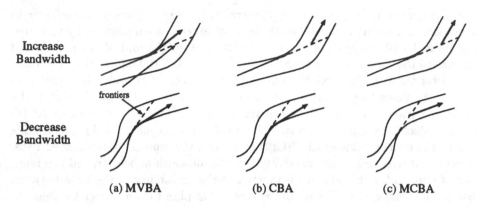

Increase
Bandwidth

frontiers

Decrease
Bandwidth

(a) MVBA   (b) CBA   (c) MCBA

Fig. 7. MVBA, CBA, and MCBA differences

MVBA starts the bandwidth changes at the leftmost point along the frontier (see Figure 7), for both bandwidth increases and decreases. It produces a plan that has the smallest possible peak bandwidth. It gradually results in a large number of small bandwidth changes.

CBA searches the frontier to find a starting point that permits the next trajectory to extend as far as possible in the case of bandwidth increases. For bandwidth decreases, CBA begins at the leftmost point on the frontier. It results in segments that have the smallest possible peak bandwidth requirement and the minimum number of bandwidth increases. However, the segments do not necessarily have the minimum number of bandwidth decreases.

MCBA is similar to CBA except that in the case of bandwidth decreases it searches the frontier to find a starting point that allows the next trajectory to extend as far as possible. In addition to the properties of CBA, MCBA results in a plan with the smallest possible number of bandwidth changes.

Due to the navigation between the data consumption rate curve and the maximum transmission curve, the retrieval plan produced by MVBA, CBA, or MCBA is divided into variable time length intervals. Consequently, the plan produced by these algorithms is of type $VR^2 - VITAL$.

3.2 Eight Algorithms and One Taxonomy

CR^2, $VR^2 - VITAL$, and $VR^2 - FIT$ may produce retrieval plans using one of the bandwidth smoothing algorithms. These algorithms strive to minimize the burstiness in the transmission of the objects by using the a priori knowledge of the objects frame sizes. Next, we identify the algorithm used to represent CR^2, $VR^2 - VITAL$, and $VR^2 - FIT$.

The CR^2 strategy can be implemented using either ABA, SWS, CRTT or PCRTT. Both ABA and SWS are inappropriate because they require a client to cache an object in its entirety prior to initiating the display in order to guarantee hiccup-free display. This increases the cost per stream and results in a long client startup latency. Even though CRTT provides a larger number of alternative plans than PCRTT, it is more complex and has a longer execution time. In addition, a plan produced by PCRTT matches well with the best plan produced by CRTT. We chose PCRTT to represent CR^2 class of algorithms.

The VR^2-FIT strategy can be implemented using either PCRTT or RCBS[1]. We chose PCRTT because RCBS requires the designer to input a maximum threshold for the data production. An optimal maximum bandwidth rate constraint is not easy to identify and such a choice might differ from one object to another.

The $VR^2-VITAL$ strategy can be realized using either ABA, SWS, PCRTT, MVBA, CBA, or MCBA. We selected MVBA, CBA, and MCBA to produce plans for $VR^2 - VITAL$. We eliminated ABA, SWS, and PCRTT because they require the intervals to be identified manually ahead of time prior to their execution (which might be impractical for certain class of applications). Moreover, MVBA, CBA, and MCBA minimize the amount of buffer required at the client site and require no client startup latency when compared with ABA, SWS, and PCRTT.

4   A Case Study with Movie Clips from Universal Studios

	Resources			Frame Sizes			
	Size (GB)	Time (min)	Rate (Mbps)	Avg (bytes)	Max (bytes)	Min (bytes)	Std (bytes)
Movie1	3.01	85.30	4.82	25277	154853	383	15601
Movie2	2.97	97.83	4.15	21735	117980	921	14866
Movie3	2.53	110.89	3.12	16347	143916	396	13196
Movie4	2.59	103.12	3.44	18010	164885	380	14429
Movie5	2.65	65.95	5.48	28707	158886	1348	22540

Table 3. Movies statistics

In order to provide an effective comparison of the different strategies, we require a large collection of video trace data to represent the diverse multimedia bandwidth requirements. We obtained MPEG-2 trace data for five real movies from Universal Studios that are stored in Digital Versatile Discs (DVDs). The frame rate of each movie is 25 frames/second. Each movie is segmented into chapters. The number of chapters in a movie typically range between 9 to 14. Each chapter is saved as a file. Table 3 shows some statistics about these movies. Using these

---

[1] ABA and SWS require to prefetch the first interval to guarantee a hiccup-free display. When the interval length is long, they incur a long startup latency by requiring the client to prefetch a significant amount of data. They behave similar to PCRTT when the interval length is short. Hence, we ignore ABA and SWS.

five movies, we constructed a repository of 100 movies. The first five movies are the original traces. The remaining 95 movies consist of 12 chapters. The chapter of each movie was selected randomly from those of the five original movies.

				Client Buffer Size (MB)			Client Startup Latency (sec)		
				Max	Min	Avg	Max	Min	Avg
CR^2	PCRTT			3368.60	1843.77	2571.12	512.32	512.32	512.32
VR^2 FIT	PCRTT	Interval Length	1 min	3155.26	1587.44	2341.32	2.60	2.60	2.60
			2 min	3155.78	1587.96	2341.93	4.28	4.28	4.28
			5 min	3158.57	1591.66	2344.66	11.00	11.00	11.00
			10 min	3165.82	1598.01	2350.91	25.20	25.20	25.20
			15 min	3172.41	1598.87	2353.04	32.00	32.00	32.00
VR^2 $VITAL$	CBA	Buffer Size	4 MB	3154.80	1587.31	2340.84	0	0	0.00
			8 MB	3154.94	1587.91	2340.98	0	0	0.00
			16 MB	3155.30	1588.94	2341.11	0	0	0.00
			32 MB	3158.80	1591.84	2344.08	0	0	0.00
			64 MB	3167.58	1597.74	2351.06	0	0	0.00
	MCBA	Buffer Size	4 MB	3154.80	1587.31	2340.84	0	0	0.00
			8 MB	3154.94	1587.91	2341.16	0	0	0.00
			16 MB	3155.30	1588.94	2341.17	0	0	0.00
			32 MB	3158.80	1591.84	2344.08	0	0	0.00
			64 MB	3167.58	1597.74	2351.06	0	0	0.00
	MVBA	Buffer Size	4 MB	3154.80	1587.31	2340.84	0	0	0.00
			8 MB	3154.94	1587.91	2340.99	0	0	0.00
			16 MB	3155.30	1588.94	2341.11	0	0	0.00
			32 MB	3158.80	1591.84	2344.08	0	0	0.00
			64 MB	3167.58	1597.74	2351.06	0	0	0.00

Table 4. Smoothing bandwidth algorithms statistics for $Universal$

Using PCRTT, CBA, MCBA, and MVBA algorithms, we generated retrieval plans for each object in the repository. These retrieval plans correspond to $Atomic$ and $Universal$. In the case of $VR^2 - FIT$, we tried different interval lengths in order to evaluate the approach appropriately. We produced interval plans for five different interval lengths: 1-minute, 2-minute, 5-minute, 10-minute, and 15-minute. With $VR^2 - VITAL$, we attempted different client buffer sizes that are commonly used in the current personal computers: 4 MB, 8 MB, 16 MB, 32 MB, and 64 MB. We selected the interval lengths with $VR^2 - FIT$ in terms of minutes rather than seconds because we wanted the number of intervals to be relatively similar to the ones generated by $VR^2 - VITAL$. The maximum number of intervals produced for an object by $VR^2 - VITAL$ was 250 using MVBA with 4 MB client buffer size. Consequently, we generated 42 retrieval plans for each object in the repository. Half of these retrieval plans belong to $Atomic$ and the other half belong to $Universal$. One out of the 21 retrieval plans in a strategy represents CR^2. Five retrieval plans correspond to $VR^2 - FIT$. The other fifteen retrieval plans represent $VR^2 - VITAL$. The total number of retrieval plans of the repository is 4200.

A retrieval plan might consist of one or more intervals. An interval is represented by a length and a constant consumption rate. The length of the interval is expressed in terms of frames. A frame is displayed in 0.04 second since the frame rate of each movie is 25 frames/second ($\frac{1}{25} = 0.04$). The constant consumption rate is expressed in terms of bits per frame (bits per 0.04 second).

				Client Buffer Size (MB)			Client Startup Latency (sec)		
				Max	Min	Avg	Max	Min	Avg
CR^2	PCRTT			372.23	45.27	189.41	500.20	0.12	184.29
VR^2		Interval	1 min	11.21	6.02	8.49	17.72	4.16	8.85
	PCRTT		2 min	24.05	8.73	14.80	31.52	5.56	15.74
FIT		Length	5 min	53.48	16.01	34.77	78.72	12.92	35.45
			10 min	99.61	21.29	59.86	130.64	17.48	59.91
			15 min	133.36	30.66	81.91	166.84	25.28	79.79
		Buffer	4 MB	3.99	3.99	3.99	0	0	0.00
			8 MB	7.99	7.98	7.99	0	0	0.00
	CBA		16 MB	15.99	15.98	15.99	0	0	0.00
		Size	32 MB	31.99	31.98	31.99	0	0	0.00
			64 MB	64.00	63.96	63.99	0	0	0.00
VR^2		Buffer	4 MB	3.99	3.99	3.99	0	0	0.00
			8 MB	7.99	7.98	7.99	0	0	0.00
	MCBA		16 MB	15.99	15.98	15.99	0	0	0.00
$VITAL$		Size	32 MB	31.99	31.98	31.99	0	0	0.00
			64 MB	64.00	63.96	63.99	0	0	0.00
		Buffer	4 MB	3.99	3.98	3.99	0	0	0.00
			8 MB	7.99	7.98	7.99	0	0	0.00
	MVBA		16 MB	15.99	15.98	15.99	0	0	0.00
		Size	32 MB	31.99	31.98	31.99	0	0	0.00
			64 MB	63.99	34.99	62.50	0	0	0.00

Table 5. Smoothing bandwidth algorithms statistics for *Atomic*

Tables 4 and 5 summarize the retrieval plans for *Universal* and *Atomic*, respectively. The first column designates the approach. The second column indicates the name of the smoothing algorithm used. The fourth one describes either the constant interval length for $VR^2 - FIT$ or the buffer size that is used in the smoothing algorithms for $VR^2 - VITAL$. The client buffer refers to the actual client buffer size that is required in order to avoid a memory overflow. For instance, even though we used a 4 MB buffer with MVBA algorithm to smooth the universal object curve in the case of *Universal*, the actual average client size is 2340.84 MB. The reason of this difference is because the server transmits data based on the bandwidth plan for the universal object curve while the consumption rate is based on the individual objects. Columns 8 to 10 contain the client startup latency information. For example, in the case of $Universal - CR^2$, when the system transmits an object to a client, the client must wait 512.32 seconds from the transmission time before it initiates the display of the object. This allows the system to accumulate enough data in the client that guarantees hiccup-free display.

In order to compare the different approaches, we designed analytical models to compute the cost per stream. These models quantify the amount of memory required by each approach as a function of a prespecified amount of disk bandwidth to support a fixed number of simultaneous displays. In addition, we have developed models to estimate the average startup latency incurred by each approach as a function of a theoretical upper bound. These models as well as a discussion about data placement, admission control, and multi-zone disks, are eliminated from this presentation due to space limitations (for a complete description see [1]). These models are applied to the case study presented in this section. The following provides a summary of our obtained results. The reported number of simultaneous displays is a theoretical upper bound, hence, the presented cost per stream is a theoretical minimum.

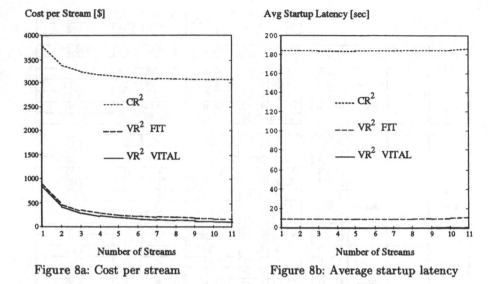

Figure 8a: Cost per stream   Figure 8b: Average startup latency

Fig. 8. Comparison of the techniques of *Atomic*

Universal is considered to be an infeasible strategy due to its large cost per stream. The cheapest approach with *Universal* costs approximately 8 times that of the most expensive approach with *Atomic*. Figure 8 shows a comparison of $Atomic-CR^2$, $Atomic-VR^2$ FIT, and $Atomic-VR^2$ $VITAL$. In these figures, the x-axis is the number of simultaneous displays supported by the system. In Figure 8a, the y-axis is the cost per stream while, in Figure 8b, the y-axis is the average startup latency. The minimum cost per stream of $Atomic - CR^2$ is $3059.72 when the system is configured to support 11 simultaneous streams per disk. This configuration incurs a startup latency of 186.19 seconds on the average. The minimum cost per stream of $Atomic-VR^2$ FIT is $168.81 when the interval length is 1-minute. This configuration also supports 11 simultaneous streams per disk and incurs a 10.21 seconds average startup latency. The minimum cost per stream of $Atomic - VR^2$ $VITAL$ is $108.52 using MVBA and a 4 MB cache at each client. With this technique, the system supports 11 simultaneous streams per disk and incurs a 0.86 second average startup latency.

When $Atomic-VR^2$ $VITAL$ is compared with $Atomic-CR^2$, it reduces the cost per stream by a factor of 27 and the average startup latency by a factor of 215. When compared with $Atomic - VR^2$ FIT, $Atomic - VR^2$ $VITAL$ reduces the cost per stream by 55% and the average startup latency by a factor of 10. It is clearly a superior approach.

5   Conclusion and Future Research Directions

In this study, we classified and evaluated disk scheduling techniques in support of hiccup-free display of VBR encoded clips. These techniques are categorized in two groups: *Universal* and *Atomic*. Evaluation of the different approaches was based on analytical models that compute the cost per stream and the average startup latency. Our cost analysis demonstrated the superiority of *Atomic* over *Universal*. From the list of alternative *Atomic* approaches, $VR^2 - VITAL$ is the most cost effective technique. While the cost of both memory and disk is decreasing (Moore's Law), our final observations remain unchanged as long as the cost reduction for both types of storage is almost identical. In the future, we intend to evaluate our taxonomy based on simulation models and include designs to support VCR functions.

6 Acknowledgments

We wish to thank the anonymous referees for their valuable comments.

References

1. J. A. Al-Marri and S. Ghandeharizadeh. An evaluation of alternative disk scheduling techniques in support of variable bit rate continuous media. Technical Report USC-CS-TR98-666, USC, 1997.
2. E. Chang and A. Zakhor. Admissions control and data placement for vbr video servers. In *Proceedings of the IEEE International Conference on Images Processing (ICIP)*, volume 1, pages 278–282, Austin, Texas, November 1994.
3. E. Chang and A. Zakhor. Variable bit rate mpeg video storage on parallel disk arrays. In *First International Workshop on Community Networking Integrated Multimedia Services to the Home*, pages 127–137, San Francisco, July 1994.
4. W. Feng. Rate-constrained bandwidth smoothing for the delivery of stored video. *To appear in IS&T/SPIE Multimedia Networking and Computing*, February 1997.
5. W. Feng, F. Jahanian, and S. Sechrest. Optimal buffering for the delivery of compressed prerecorded video. In *Proceedings of the IASTED/ISMM International Conference on Networks*, January 1995.
6. W. Feng and S. Sechrest. Critical bandwidth allocation for delivery of compressed video. *Computer Communications*, 18:709–717, October 1995.
7. W. Feng and S. Sechrest. Smoothing and buffering for delivery of prerecorded compressed video. In *Proceedings of the IS&T/SPIE Symposium on Multimedia Computing and Networking*, pages 234–242, February 1995.
8. M. Grossglauser, S. Keshav, and D. Tse. Rcbr: A simple and efficient service for multiple time-scale traffic. In *Proceedings of the ACM SIGCOMM*, pages 219–230, August 1995.
9. E. W. Knightly, D. E. Wrege, J. Liebeherr, and H. Zhang. Fundamental limits and tradeoffs of providing deterministic guarantees to vbr video traffic. In *Proceedings of the ACM SIGMETRICS*, pages 98–107, May 1995.
10. J. M. McManus and K. W. Ross. Prerecorded vbr sources in atm networks: Piecewise-constant-rate transmission and transport. *Submitted for publication*, September 1995.
11. J. M. McManus and K. W. Ross. Video on demand over atm: Constant-rate transmission and transport. In *Proceedings of IEEE INFOCOM*, pages 1357–1362, March 1996.
12. G. Nerjes, P. Muth, and G. Weikum. Stochastic service guarantees for continuous data on multi-zone disks. In *Proceedings of the 16th Symposium on Principles of Database Systems*, Tucson, Arizona, May 1997.
13. J. D. Salehi, Z. L. Zhang, J. F. Kurose, and D. Towsley. Supporting stored video: Reducing rate variability and end-to-end resource requirements through optimal smoothing. In *Proceedings of ACM SIGMETRICS*, pages 222–231, May 1996.

Buffer Management in Distributed Database Systems: A Data Mining-Based Approach *

L. Feng[1]   H. Lu[2]   Y.C. Tay[2]   K.H. Tung[2]

[1] The Hong Kong Polytechnic University, Kowloon, Hong Kong
[2] National University of Singapore, Kent Ridge Road, Singapore 119260

Abstract. In this paper, we propose a data mining-based approach to public buffer management in distributed database systems where database buffers are organized into two areas: public and private. While the private buffer areas contain pages to be updated by particular users, the public buffer area contains pages shared among users from different sites. Different from traditional buffer management strategies where limited knowledge of user access patterns is used, the proposed approach discovers knowledge from page access sequences of user transactions and uses it to guide public buffer placement and replacement. The knowledge to be discovered and the discovery algorithms are discussed. The effectiveness of the proposed approach was investigated through a simulation study. The results indicate that with the help of the discovered knowledge, the public buffer hit ratio can be improved significantly.

1 Introduction

Due to the higher cost of fetching data from disk than from RAM, most database management systems (DBMSs) use a main-memory area as a buffer to reduce disk accesses. In a distributed database system, database is spread among several sites over a computer network. In order to support concurrency control as well as reduce the disk I/O time, an approach of using two levels of buffer in distributed systems has been proposed [20, 8, 6]. The basic idea is to have two levels of buffers: a public buffer area to accommodate data pages shared among a number of users and a set of private buffers for individual users from different sites. With two levels of buffers, the private buffer is searched first when a user submits a request for a page. If no such page exists, the public buffer is then searched and if hit, the required page is copied from the public buffer into the corresponding private buffer for use, otherwise, the page is read from disk directly. A user transaction only updates data pages in the private buffers. When the transaction commits, all updated pages in his/her private buffer are written back to the disk. To maintain buffer coherency, copies of these updated pages in the public buffer and other private buffers should be updated accordingly as well.

There are three basic buffer management issues in such a system:

---
* The first two authors' work is partially supported by NUS academic research fund RP 3950660 and Hughes Research Laboratory Grant 3044GP.95-120

- **public buffer placement problem**: When a page which is not in the public buffer is read from disk into a private buffer, should the page be placed in the public buffer as well? Intuitively, pages that will not or seldom be referenced by other users afterwards should not enter the public buffer.
- **public buffer replacement problem**: When a public buffer frame is needed to bring in a page from disk, and all current buffer frames are in use, which page from the public buffer should be replaced?
- **private buffer replacement problem**: When a private buffer frame is needed to bring in a page from the public buffer or disk, and all current buffer frames are in use, which page from this private buffer should be replaced?

Among the above three issues, buffer replacement problem has been extensively studied. An early survey can be found in [9]. The most popular and simple buffer replacement strategy is LRU, the Least Recently Used [15, 3]: When a new buffer frame is needed, the page in the buffer that has not been accessed for the longest time is replaced. LFU (Least Frequently Used) policy is another simple but effective buffer replacement policy based on the frequency a page is referenced [16]. It relates a reference count to each page, and replaces the one with the smallest reference count when a buffer frame is needed.

In database buffer management, in addition to buffer replacement, *buffer allocation* is also an important and closely related issue and is often studied together. It addresses the problem of how many buffer frames should be allocated to a particular query. Sacco and Schkolnick, after studying the page reference behavior of queries, proposed the well-known hot set model to determine the optimal buffer space allocation for a query [17, 18]. Chou and Dewitt [7] extended this model with the DBMIN algorithm that separates the modeling of the reference behavior from any particular buffer management algorithm.

The above mentioned buffer management strategies for both allocation and replacement do not distinguish the importance of queries. Carey, Jauhari and Livny proposed two priority buffer management algorithms, Priority-LRU and Priority-DBMIN, to deal with the situation where database transactions are of different priority levels [4]. The major difference between the new schemas and the non-priority equivalents is that the priority strategies allow higher priority transactions to steal buffer pages from lower priority transactions. Their approaches were further developed that led to a strategy called Priority-Hints, which utilizes priority hints provided by the database access methods to instruct the buffer management [10]. With the similar idea, Chan, Ooi and Lu suggested to allow an access method to pass replacement hints to the buffer manager by assigning priority values to the buffer pages, and always select the page with the lowest priority value for replacement [5].

More recently, O'Neil and Weikum pointed out that it is difficult to design a query plan-based buffering algorithm that works well in a multitasking systems [15, 19]. They presented a self-reliant full buffer variant algorithm of LRU called LRU-K. The basic idea is to keep track of the times of the last K references to popular database pages and use this information to statistically estimate the inter-arrival times of references on a page by page basis. With K = 2, LRU-2 replaces the page whose penultimate access is the least recent among all penultimate accesses. Their experiments show LRU-K has significant cost/performance advantages over conventional algorithms like LRU, sometimes as high as 40%. To reduce the overhead cost of LRU-K, Johnson and Shasha presented a 2Q algorithm that behaves as well as LRU-2 but has constant time overhead [11]. 2Q follows the same principle as LRU-K, i.e., basing buffer priority on sustained popularity rather than on a single access.

Inspired by the recent development in data mining research and observing that LRU-K and 2Q algorithms outperform other strategies because they use more information about page references than the other strategies, we initiated a study on data mining-based buffer management. The basic idea of such an approach is rather simple: database access histories are collected and knowledge that can guide the buffer management is extracted. At run-time, the buffer manager uses the discovered knowledge to make decisions related to buffer allocation, placement, or replacement. The key issues to the success of the approach include:

1. what type of knowledge should be discovered;
2. how the knowledge discovered can be used effectively in run-time; and
3. whether the knowledge discovered from the access reference history can be generalized.

In this paper, we report some preliminary results on applying the approach to the problems of *public buffer placement and public buffer replacement* described earlier. One of the major reasons to choose them as the subject of our preliminary study is that little related work has been reported and the buffer replacement strategy used in most of the previous work is the simplest one, LRU [6].

In this paper, we propose the form of knowledge to be discovered from user access patterns and demonstrate through simulation that the approach does improve the hit ratio of public buffer significantly. Limited by resources, we did not address the third issue in this paper. However, based on an earlier study by Kearns and DeFazio, who have demonstrated that the database reference patterns exhibited by a transaction change very little over time [12], we assume that users in a database system have relative stable access preferences from a long period of view. Furthermore, data collection and knowledge discovery can be performed periodically so that the knowledge used can best reflect the current user access patterns.

Developing a new and effective approach to solve traditional database buffer management problems is only one of the tangible contributions of our study. The more important contribution of the paper is that, it is a first try to apply data mining technologies to database management itself. It is our fond hope that the work reported here will stimulate the interests to make database management a new application area of data mining technologies.

The remainder of the paper is organized as follows. Section 2 presents a data mining-based approach towards public buffer management in distributed DBMSs. Section 3 describes a simulation model used in our study with the results presented in Section 4. Section 5 concludes the paper with a brief discussion of future work.

2 Data Mining-Based Buffer Management

In this section, we describe our data mining-based approach to database buffer management in distributed DBMSs. In particular, we are interested in the problem of public buffer management in a distributed database system with two levels of buffers. After introducing the framework of such approach, we propose to use two types of knowledge about user access behavior, and describe how such knowledge can be mined. The public buffer placement policy and replacement policy based on mined knowledge are presented at the end of the section.

2.1 The framework

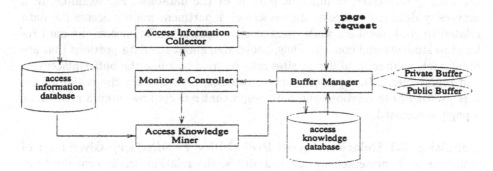

Fig. 1. Data mining-based buffer management

Figure 1 shows the framework of a data mining-based buffer management approach. In addition to the traditional buffer manager in a distributed DBMS, three new components *Access Information Collector* , *Access Knowledge Miner* and *Monitor and Controller* are introduced in the buffer management process. These components cooperate as follows:

- The Buffer Manager is responsible for all the operations on the buffer, including buffer search, buffer placement and buffer replacement, etc. Different from traditional buffer managers where most decision making rules are hardcoded, it uses the access knowledge database in its decision making process.
- The Monitor and Controller monitors the pre-specified performance metrics of buffer management, e.g., hit ratio. When the hit ratio is below certain level, it signifies that the stored access knowledge may be outdated. New access information should be collected and the access knowledge database should be updated by mining from the new data sets.
- When access information is to be collected, the Access Information Collector records the page requests of each transaction. The collected data are preprocessed according to the requirement of data mining process. The results are stored in an access information database.

– After enough data are collected, the Access Knowledge Miner will apply the mining algorithms to the collected data. The access knowledge discovered is used to update the access knowledge database. This process runs off-line.

2.2 Mining knowledge about user access behavior

As in every data mining application, we need identify what to be mined. In the public buffer management problem, we identify two types of knowledge, *access probability* and *associated access,* motivated by our understanding of the characteristics of database accesses.

Access probability In distributed database systems, users from different sites are usually interested in different portion of the database. For example, in a university database, users at the personnel department mainly access the data related to staff members while users at the registrar's office access the data related to students and courses. Thus, knowledge about the data portions that are of interests to users at different sites may be used to guide the buffer placement and replacement. To represent such knowledge, we introduce the notion of *access probability* to relations and data pages that reflects how often a relation or a page is accessed.

Definition 2.1 Relation Access Probability $ProbRel(s,r)$. Given a set of transactions T presented by users at site s, the relation access probability of site s to relation r is the fraction of transactions that access relation r to the total transactions of site s, i.e., $ProbRel(s,r) = \frac{|T_r|}{|T|}$, where $T_r = \{t_r \mid t_r \in T \wedge t_r \mapsto r\}$, and $t_r \mapsto r$ represents that transaction t_r accesses relation r.

Definition 2.2 Page Access Probability $ProbPage(s,p_r)$. Given a set of transactions T presented by users at site s, the page access probability of site s to relation r's page p is the fraction of transactions that access relation r's page p to the transactions that access relation r, i.e., $ProbPage(s,p_r) = \frac{|T_{p_r}|}{|T_r|}$, where $T_r = \{t_r \mid t_r \in T \wedge t_r \mapsto r\}$, $T_{p_r} = \{t_{p_r} \mid t_{p_r} \in T_r \wedge t_{p_r} \mapsto p\}$.

Associated access Another observation from the user access pattern is that, there usually exists some coherent relationship among successive accesses within a database transaction. In other words, some *associations* among pages referenced may exist in page reference sequences of user transactions. That is, *if certain pages have been accessed, then there are some other pages will be most likely accessed as well,* Such association results from several factors. One is due to semantic relationship among the data. For example, after a student record is accessed, the related pages containing his/her course information are more likely to be accessed also. Other reasons resulting in association among pages include physical data organization, query processing methods, etc. For example, a nested loops join will repeatedly scan a set of pages a number of times. The same set of index pages are always accessed before a data page is accessed. Apparently, if we can discover such associations among page references, we may be able to predict future page requests from the pages that have already been accessed by a transaction.

Mining association rules from transactional data is a classic data mining problem [1]. The main applications reported are related to the market ananlysis of sales data. We here apply the similar concept and define associated page access rules as follows.

Definition 2.3 Associated Access $AssoAccess(s, prepages \Rightarrow aftpages)$. Given a set of transactions T presented by users at site s, the associated access $prepages \Rightarrow aftpages$ of site s is that, access to page set $prepages$ imply the accesses to page set $aftpages$, with support s and confidence c defined as: $s = \frac{|T_{p+a}|}{|T|}$, $c = \frac{|T_{p+a}|}{|T_p|}$, where

$$T_{p+a} = \{t_{p+a} \mid t_{p+a} \in T \wedge \forall p_i \in prepages \ (t_{p+a} \mapsto p_i) \wedge$$
$$\forall p_j \in aftpages \ (t_{p+a} \mapsto p_j)\},$$
$$T_p = \{t_p \mid t_p \in T \wedge \forall p_i \in prepages \ (t_p \mapsto p_i)\}$$

Mining access probability and associated access rules To mine the above defined knowledge about user access behavior, the Access Information Collector collects and preprocesses the page access information (e.g., removing locality from page references, etc.), and stores the access information into the access information database, which contains records with the following form: *(transaction_id, site_id, list_of_relations, list_of_pages for each accessed relation)*.

Mining access probabilities is a simple counting process: both $ProbRel(s,r)$ and and $ProbPage(s,p_r)$ can be computed by scanning the access information data. The mining of associated access rules consists of two steps:

- Finding all sets of pages that have support greater than the minimum support. Such page sets are called frequent sets, or largesets. Here, we adopted the Apriori algorithm [2]. It first finds the largesets of one page. Using the largesets of $k - 1$ pages, the algorithm finds largesets of k pages recursively.
- Using the found largesets to generate the desired rules. That is, for every largeset l, find all non-empty subsets of l. For every such subset a, output a rule of the form $a \Rightarrow (l - a)$ if the ratio of support(l) to support(a) achieves the desired confidence level.

The output of the Access Knowledge Miner is stored in an access knowledge database. The access probabilities are stored in two tables, *ProbRel* and *ProbPage*, with the following schema:

ProbRel(**relation_id, site**, probability)
ProbPage(**page_id, site**, probability)

For a large database system with a number of sites, the size of table *ProbPage* could be reasonably large. To be able to retrieve the probability of certain page efficiently, index could be built on page_id. The associated access rules can also be stored in tables. However, as the number of pages in the left and right hand side of the rules varies, such rules can be simply stored in text files and a run-time data structure is used to hold the rules in memory. By controlling the thresholds of support and confidence levels, the number of such rules can be adjusted so that the space and computational overhead are tolerable.

2.3 Applying access knowledge in public buffer management

After obtaining the data mining results, we can use them to guide public buffer placement and replacement. To do so, we use $interest(p_r)$ to measure how likely page p_r tends to be accessed by users from all sites.

Definition 2.4 Page Interest $interest(p_r)$. The access interest that users from N sites show on page p_r is defined as:

$$interest(p_r) = \sum_{s=1}^{N} SiteAccessProb_s(p_r)$$

where values of both $interest(p_r)$ and $SiteAccessProb_s(p_r)$ are changing at run-time as follows:

Case 1 From the definition, the probability that users from site s access page p_r is equal to $ProbRel(s,r) * ProbPage(s, p_r)$.

Case 2 Once relation r is accessed, $ProbRel(s,r)$ becomes 1, and $SiteAccessProb_s(p_r) = ProbPage(s, p_r)$.

Case 3 When users from site s accessed all *prepages* of certain association rule(s), and page p_r belongs to *aftpages* of the rule(s), then $SiteAccessProb_s(p_r)$ becomes c, where c is the maximum confidence value of all these rules.

Case 4 After page p_r has been referenced and retrieved into the private buffer of site s, these users will no longer search p_r from the public buffer. That is, $SiteAccessProb_s(p_r)$ becomes 0.

As a summary, we have

$$SiteAccessProb_s(p_r) = \begin{cases} ProbRel(s,r) * ProbPage(s, p_r) & \text{(Case 1)} \\ ProbPage(s, p_r) & \text{(Case 2)} \\ c & \text{(Case 3)} \\ 0 & \text{(Case 4)} \end{cases}$$

With the *interest* of each page, the public buffer placement and replacement policies can be simply described as follows:

- placing those pages whose *interests* are greater than a pre-determined value into the public buffer; and
- replacing the page with the least *interest* in the public buffer when a buffer frame is needed.

Astute readers may argue that the updating of the interest measure of pages will incur high overhead, especially when the database is large, as the number of pages in the database are very large, and the number of associated access rules are also large. To make a compromise, access probability thresholds are introduced to discretize the relation or page access probability: for a relation(page) whose access probability is below the threshold value, its access probability will be set to 0, otherwise to 1. With such simplification, we maintain two bit arrays $RelBit_r[N]$ and $PageBit_{p_r}[N]$ for each relation r and each page p_r of r, where N is the number of total sites in the whole system. $RelBit_r[s] = 1$ means that users from site s have high possibility to access relation r, and 0 otherwise. So is $PageBit_{p_r}[s]$. As the Page Access Probability is calculated on the premise that its corresponding relation has been accessed, users at site s are supposed to access page p_r afterwards if and only if $(RelBit_r[s] = 1) \land (PageBit_{p_r}[s] = 1)$. The page *interest* that users from all sites show on certain page can thus be redefined as follows:

Definition 2.5. Refined Page Interest $interest'(p_r)$. The access interest that users from N sites show on page p_r is defined as:

$$interest'(p_r) = \sum_{s=1}^{N} SiteAccessProb'_s(p_r)$$

where

$$SiteAccessProb'_s(p_r) = \begin{cases} 1 \text{ if } (RelBit_r[s] = 1) \land (PageBit_{p_r}[s] = 1), \\ 0 \text{ otherwise.} \end{cases}$$

With the refined page interest measure, we can have the following public buffer placement policy *PIG0 (Page Interest Greater than 0)*, and public buffer replacement policy *LPI (Least Page Interest)*.

PIG0 Public Buffer Placement Policy

When a private buffer requests a page p_r that does not exist in the public buffer, page p_r should be placed into the public buffer if and only if there exists at least one site s user, such that both $RelBit_r[s]$ and $PageBit_{p_r}[s]$ are 1, in other words, the refined page *interest* of p_r is greater than 0, i.e.,

$$\exists s\ (RelBit_r[s] = 1 \land PageBit_{p_r}[s] = 1) \Leftrightarrow (interest'(p_r) > 0)$$

LPI Public Buffer Replacement Policy

When a new public buffer frame is needed for a page about to be read in from disk, and all current buffer frames are in use: the page p'_r to be replaced is the one whose refined page *interest* is less than any page p_r in the public buffer, i.e.,

$$interest'(p'_r) = Min(interest'(p_r))$$

3 A Simulation Model

In this section, we describe our simulation model of a distributed DBMS concentrating on the buffer management functions and the synthetic data generated for studying the performance.

The model consists of three major components: the distributed database itself; a *Source* which generates the workload of the system; and a *buffer manager* which implements the public buffer management algorithm. The major parameters and their values are summarized in Table 1

The distributed database is modeled as a collection of *relations*, and each relation is modeled as a collection of pages, including index pages and data pages. The buffer manager component encapsulates the details of database buffer management schema. It consists of two parts, the private buffer manager and the public buffer manager. In this study we are only concerned with the public buffer management. *pub_buf_size* is the public buffer size, measured in the percent of total number of database pages *num_pages*, and *private_buf_size_s* is the site s's private buffer size ($1 \le s \le num\_site$). *threshold* is the access probability threshold defined to filter and refine the original relation and page access probabilities.

The source module is the component responsible for modeling the workload in the distributed DBMS. Users access the distributed database through transactions. A transaction is a sequence of read and write requests. The system at each site can execute multiple requests coming from all sites concurrently on the premise that data consistency is not violated. There are totally *num_sites* number of sites in the system. The number of transactions presented by users from site s ($1 \le s \le num\_sites$) is *num_trans_s*. *max_rels_per_trans* is the maximum number of relations that can be accessed by one transaction. Each request can reference at most *max_pages_per_request* number of pages.

Each transaction is supposed (but not unrealistic [13]) to access database pages with a Zipfian distribution, that is, the probability for referencing a page with page number less than or equal to i is $(i/num\_pages)^{loga/logb}$ with a and b between 0 and 1. The meaning of a and b is that a fraction a of the references accesses a fraction b of the *num_pages* pages (and the same relationship holds recursively by within the fraction b of hotter pages and the fraction $1-b$ of colder pages) [11, 15, 19]. In addition, observing that users from different sites tend to be interested in different relations and pages, i.e., have different hot relations and pages, we use *hot_rel_overlap* and *hot_page_overlap* to simulate the overlapped hot relations and pages for users from two successive sites. To model the coherent associated accesses in one transaction, we determine a potentially largeset number *num_largesets*. In each largeset, the maximum number of relations is *max_rels_per_largeset*. The maximum and minimum number of pages per relation in a largeset is *max_pages_per_largeset_rel* and *min_pages_per_largeset_rel* respectively. *support* and *confidence* are support and confidence levels regarding the association rules.

The values given in Table 1 are used in our simulation. The system consists of 8 sites. There are totally 20 relations and 30000 pages in a database. Each re-

The Distributed Database		
num_sites	no. of sites in the system	8
num_rels	no. of relations in database	20
num_pages	no. of pages in database	30,000
rel_size_r	no. of pages in relation r	1,500
The Buffer Management		
pub_buf_size	public buffer size relative to the DB size	2.5-12.5%
private_buf_size_s	site s's private buffer size	
threshold	relation/page access probability threshold	0-70%
The Workload		
Transaction Parameters		
num_trans_s	no. of transactions posed by site s user	100
max_rels_per_trans	max. no. of relations per transaction	5
hot_rel_overlap	overlap of hot relation among sites	0-100%
hot_page_overlap	overlap of hot page per relation among sites	0-100%
Request Parameters		
max_pages_per_request	max. no. of pages per request	20
num_requests	no. of requests executed by one site	100,000
Associated Access Parameters		
num_largesets	no. of potentially largesets	5
max_rels_per_largeset	max. no. of relations in a largeset	3
max_pages_per_largeset_rel	max. no. of pages per relation in a largeset	10
min_pages_per_largeset_rel	min. no. of pages per relation in a largeset	30
support	support level of associated access rules	40-100%
confidence	confidence level of associated access rules	98 %

Table 1. The parameters and values

lation has 1500 pages. At least 100 transactions are presented by users from each site. The maximum number of relations referenced by a transaction is 5. Each request of a transaction accesses at most 20 pages. There are totally 100,000 requests coming from 8 sites. For each user, the page reference frequency distribution is skewed, in that *a* percent of transactions accesses *b* percent of database relations and pages. Here, we assign 80% to *a* and 20% to *b*. To simulate different hot spots for users at different sites, we use the term *overlap*, ranging from 0% to 100%, to express the overlapped hot portions between two successive sites. For associated accesses, we allocate 5 potential largesets, with each containing 1-3 relations. Each relation in a largeset refers to 3-10 pages. The confidence level for association rules is set to 98%, and the support level is selected from 40% to 100% according to different data sets being generated. Public buffer size is varied from 2.5% to 12.5% of the total pages. As we do not consider private buffer management issues in the paper, we do not limit the size of private, and simply assume that private buffer frames will be available when it is requested.

The relation/page access probability threshold is set from 0 to 70%.

To conduct the performance study using the model, two types of workload were generated. One is to simulate the historical data (training data) and the others are used as testing data to evaluate algorithms. Different random seeds are used in generating different data sets. Each data set, a steam of page accesses, was generated in three steps. The first step is to mark hot relations and hot pages of each relation for users from different sites. The 80-20 rule is used here: 20% of pages were marked as hot pages. The second step is to generate a sequence of page accesses for users at each individual site. Again, using the 80-20 rule, 80% of accesses will be hot pages. The associated access within a transaction were obtained in the similar manner as generating synthetic data sets for general association rules. To form a single stream, each user's access stream was broke into *requests*. The number of pages of each request was determined randomly. Requests from different sites were randomly picked to form a single access stream, that are used either as training data or test data.

4 Experiments and Results

In this section, we present the performance results using the simulation model defined in the previous section. Since the purpose of introducing public buffer is to reduce the number of disk I/Os, the major performance measure used in the simulation is the public buffer hit ratio, i.e., the ratio between the number of pages found in the public buffer and the total number of pages requested. The three buffer management strategies studied are:

PGI0-LPI Using PIG0 and LPI described in Section 2 as the placement and replacement policies, respectively.

PGI0-LRU Similar to PIG0-LPI except that LRU is used as the replacement policy.

ANY-LRU No data mining results are used. While LRU is used as its replacement policy, every page requested from the database is placed into the public buffer.

4.1 Experiment 1: the effect of public buffer size

This experiment investigated the impact of buffer size when it was varied from 2.5% to 12.5% of the total number of database pages. The results obtained with *threshold* equal to 15 and 30% are shown in Figure 2. *hot_rel_overlap* and *hot_page_overlap* are both set to 75%. For each setting, five testing data sets with different random seeds were used and the average is used in the curve. It is evident that the buffer hit ratio increases with the size of public buffer under all three policies, as more pages can be kept inside the buffer pool. Two algorithms PIG0-LPI and PIG0-LRU, which utilize data-mining results more or less, are superior over algorithm ANY-LRU which does not take historical access knowledge into consideration. For instance, at buffer size 2.5% and *threshold* 30%, the

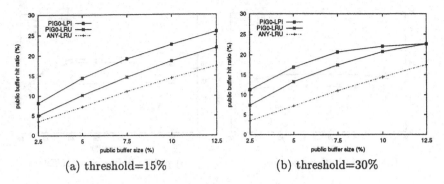

(a) threshold=15%   (b) threshold=30%

Fig. 2. Public buffer hit ratio versus public buffer size

hit ratio of ANY-LRU is 3.49%, while those of PIG0-LRU and PIG0-LPI reach 7.45% and 11.34% respectively, about 53% and 69% more. Comparing PIG0-LRU and PIG0-LPI, we may find that, with suitable access probability threshold, PIG0-LPI can achieve higher hit ratio than PIG0-LRU. This is because the former algorithm replaces pages according to the estimation of their future usage from historical transactions, while the latter simply uses LRU replacement policy, where too little information is considered in making replacement decision.

From this basic experiment, we can see that both PIG0-LRU and PIG0-LPI outperform traditional ANY-LRU. PIG0-LPI, which applys data mining results as much as possible to solve both public buffer placement and replacement problems, comes out the best of the three.

4.2 Experiment 2: the effect of access probability threshold

Experiment 2 studied the impact of access probability threshold by varying the threshold for different buffer sizes. Two sets of the results are presented in Figure 3 where the buffer sizes are 5 and 10% of the database size, respectively. Since ANY-LRU algorithm does not use information related to the threshold, its curves are flat as expected. For PIG0-LRU and PIG0-LPI, there exists a range of thresholds during which the hit ratio is higher. This is also expected: when the threshold is set too lower, pages with less access probabilities are mistakenly assumed as frequently accessed pages, and thus they are treated equally the same as those actually popular ones. On the other hand, when choosing a higher threshold, more pages with relatively reasonable access probabilities are exempted from consideration and given lower priorities in using the buffer.

One interesting observation is that, with high threshold, the performance of two data mining based strategies performs similarly. When buffer size is large and threshold is high, they even perform worse than LRU policy. The reason could be that, when the threshold is high enough, more site's access probabilities to certain pages have simply been abstracted into 0. For each page resident in

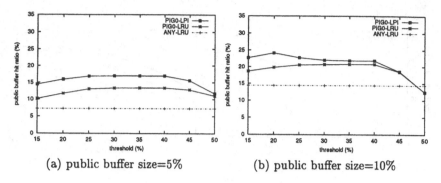

(a) public buffer size=5%   (b) public buffer size=10%

Fig. 3. Public buffer hit ratio versus threshold

the buffer, its total page *interest* can be quickly reduced to 0 along with the access evolution (LPG0-LPI algorithm also sets the corresponding page access probability for a site as 0 once the site accesses this page). On this situation, the LRU replacement policy of PIG0-LPI and ANY-LRU plays a major role. Therefore, the behavior of PIG0-LRU and PIG0-LPI are quite similar at higher thresholds. When buffer size enlarges, since pages passing the threshold can stay longer inside the buffer, they have the chance to endure more references coming from all the sites before being kicked out. So even lower thresholds are adopted at this time, *interests* of the pages in the buffer may still be decreased into 0 by setting the access probabilities to 0 when database accesses evolve, which thus makes LRU dominate LPG0-LPI's replacement decision as well, just like that in LPG0-LRU.

4.3 Experiment 3: the effect of hot overlap

Experiment 3 examines the impact of access locality by varying *hot_rel_overlap* and *hot_page_overlap* from 0% to 100%. Here, hot overlap=100% means that all users have exactly the same hot relations and pages, and 0% indicates that access from two consecutive sites have totally different hot relations and pages. Sample results for buffer size 5 and 10% are shown in Figure 4.

From the results, we can see that, while the hot overlap between two successive sites is below 50%, the public buffer hit ratios under the three policies hardly change, but from above 50%, all three policies improve their hit ratios greatly. This invariance and hereafter improvement can be explained as follows: With higher locality, accesses from all sites start to concentrate on a smaller number of relations and pages. The reference frequencies to these hot spots are much higher than when the locality is low. For ANY-LRU which places any page into the public buffer as long as private buffers request, the page referenced by users at one site at larger overlaps are more likely to belong to the hot portions of other sites, and it may be accessed by those sites later as well. Therefore, the

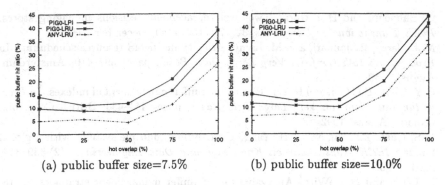

(a) public buffer size=7.5% (b) public buffer size=10.0%

Fig. 4. Public buffer hit ratio versus hot relation/page overlap

placement decision made by ANY-LRU tends to be reasonable at larger overlaps. Meanwhile, the LRU replacement policy that ANY-LRU adopts also seems to behave correctly as well, since LRU always chooses the least referenced page to replace and keeps those frequently referenced pages (hot portions) resident in the buffer. This is also the reason why the performance gains of LPG0-LPI and LPG0-LRU over ANY-LRU decrease from 69%, 56% (under hot overlap 50%) to 41%, 34% (under hot overlap 100%) when the buffer size is 5.0%.

5 Conclusion

The work reported here is a preliminary step towards data mining based database buffer management. While the initial results seem promising, there remain a number of interesting problems and opportunities for future work. As we are only concerned with public buffer management issue here, one important future work is to investigate how data mining results can be applied to private buffer management. Another aspect we plan to study is to utilize discovered knowledge to solve both public and private buffer allocation problems. Incremental maintenance of the discovered knowledge is also a critical point worth studying in the future. Finally, as the cross-site buffer invalidation effect is ignored in this paper, it should be interesting to see how it will affect the performance of the system.

References

1. R. Agrawal, T. Imielinski, and A. Swami. Mining association rules between sets of items in large databases. In *Proc. of the 1993 ACM SIGMOD Int'l Conf. on management of data*, pages 207–216, Washington D.C., USA, May 1993.
2. R. Agrawal and R. Srikant. Fast algorithms for mining association rules. In *Proc. of the 20th Conf. on Very Large Data Bases*, pages 478–499, Santiago, Chile, September 1994.

3. Ö. Babaoğlu and D. Ferrari. Two-level replacement decisions in paging stores. *IEEE Transactions on Computers*, 32(12):1151–1159, December 1983.

4. M.J. Carey, R. Jauhari, and M. Livny. Priority in DBMS resource scheduling. In *Proc. of the 15th Conf. on Very Large Data Bases*, pages 397–410, Amsterdam, August 1989.

5. C.Y. Chan, B.C Ooi, and H. Lu. Extensible buffer management of indexes. In *Proc. of the 18th Conf. on Very Large Data Bases*, pages 444–454, British Columbia, Canada, August 1992.

6. M.S. Chen, P.S. Yu, and T.H. Yang. On coupling multiple systems with a global buffer. *IEEE Transactions on Knowledge and Data Engineering*, 8(2):339–344, April 1996.

7. H. Chou and D. DeWitt. An evaluation of buffer management strategies for relational database systems. In *Proc. of the 11th Conf. on Very Large Data Bases*, pages 127–141, Stickhilm, Sweden, August 1985.

8. A. Dan, D.M. Dias, and P.S. Yu. Analytical modelling of a hierarchical buffer for a data sharing environment. In *Proc. of the ACM SIGMETRICS*, pages 156–167, San Diego, CA, May 1991.

9. W. Effelsberg and T. Haerder. Principles of database buffer management. *ACM Transaction on Database Systems*, 9(4):560–595, December 1984.

10. R. Jauhari, M.J. Carey, and M. Livny. Priority-hints: an algorithm for priority-based buffer management. In *Proc. of the 16th Conf. on Very Large Data Bases*, pages 708–721, Brisbane, Australia, August 1990.

11. T. Johnson and D. Shasha. 2Q: A low overhead high performance buffer management replacement algorithm. In *Proc. of the 20th Conf. on Very Large Data Bases*, pages 439–450, Santiago, Chile, September 1994.

12. J.P. Kearns and S. DeFazio. Diversity in database reference behavior. *Performance Evaluation Review*, 17(1):11–19, May 1989.

13. D.E. Knuth. *The Art of Computer Programming, Vol.3: Sorting and Searching*. Addison-Wesley, 1973.

14. V.F. Nicola, A. Dan, and D.M. Dias. Analysis of the generalized clock buffer replacement scheme for database transaction processing. *ACM SIGMETRICS and PERFORMANCE*, 20(1):35–46, June 1992.

15. E.J. O'Neil, P.E. O'Neil, and G. Weikum. The LRU-K page replacement algorithm for database disk buffering. In *Proc. of the 1993 ACM SIGMOD Int'l Conf. on management of data*, pages 297–306, Washington D.C., USA, August 1993.

16. J.T. Robinson and M.V. Devarakonda. Data cache management using frequency-based replacement. In *Proc. of the 1990 ACM SIGMOD Int'l Conf. on management of data*, pages 134–142, Brisbane, August, August 1990.

17. G.M. Sacco and M. Schkolnick. A mechanism for managing the buffer pool in a relational database system using the hot set model. In *Proc. of the 8th Conf. on Very Large Data Bases*, pages 257–262, Mexcio City, September 1982.

18. G.M. Sacco and M. Schkolnick. Buffer management in relational database systems. *ACM Transactions on Database Systems*, 11(4):473–498, December 1986.

19. G. Weikum, C. Hasse, A. Mönkeberg, and P. Zabback. The comfort automatic tuning project. *Information Systems*, 19(5):381–432, May 1994.

20. P.S. Yu, D.M. Dias, J.T. Robinson, B.R. Iyer, and D.W. Cornell. On coupling multi-systems through data sharing. *Proc. of the IEEE*, 75(5):573–587, May 1987.

Aggregation and Summary Data

Complex Aggregation at Multiple Granularities

Kenneth A. Ross[1], Divesh Srivastava[2], Damianos Chatziantoniou[3]

[1] Columbia University, New York, NY 10027, USA
[2] AT&T Labs–Research, Florham Park, NJ 07932, USA
[3] Stevens Institute of Technology, Hoboken, NJ 07030, USA

Abstract. Datacube queries compute simple aggregates at multiple granularities. In this paper we examine the more general and useful problem of computing a complex subquery involving multiple dependent aggregates at multiple granularities. We call such queries "multi-feature cubes." An example is "Broken down by all combinations of month and customer, find the fraction of the total sales in 1996 of a particular item due to suppliers supplying within 10% of the minimum price (within the group), showing all subtotals across each dimension." We classify multi-feature cubes based on the extent to which fine granularity results can be used to compute coarse granularity results; this classification includes distributive, algebraic and holistic multi-feature cubes. We provide syntactic sufficient conditions to determine when a multi-feature cube is either distributive or algebraic. This distinction is important because, as we show, existing datacube evaluation algorithms can be used to compute multi-feature cubes that are distributive or algebraic, without any increase in I/O complexity. We evaluate the CPU performance of computing multi-feature cubes using the datacube evaluation algorithm of Ross and Srivastava. Using a variety of synthetic, benchmark and real-world data sets, we demonstrate that the CPU cost of evaluating distributive multi-feature cubes is comparable to that of evaluating simple datacubes. We also show that a variety of holistic multi-feature cubes can be evaluated with a manageable overhead compared to the distributive case.

1   Introduction

Decision support systems aim to provide answers to complex queries posed over very large databases. The databases may represent business information (such as transaction data), medical information (such as patient treatments and outcomes), or scientific data (such as large sets of experimental measurements). The vast quantities of data contain enough information to answer questions of importance to the application user. Useful queries in the domains above include:

- Broken down by supplier, month and item, find the total sales in 1996, including all subtotals across each dimension.
- Broken down by hospital, diagnosis and treatment, find the average life expectancy, including all subtotals across each dimension.

The electronic mail addresses of the authors are kar@cs.columbia.edu, divesh@research.att.com and damianos@cs.stevens-tech.edu.

Each of these queries is an example of a datacube query [GBLP96]. Datacube queries allow one to compute aggregates of the data at a variety of granularities. The first query above would generate aggregate data at eight different granularities including total sales by (a) supplier, (b) month, (c) item, (d) supplier and month, (e) supplier and item, (f) month and item, (g) supplier, month and item, and (h) the empty set (i.e., the total overall sales). A datacube could be computed by separately computing the aggregate at each granularity. However, it is also possible to compute aggregates at several coarser levels of granularity at the same time as computing aggregates at finer levels of granularity. Such algorithms are presented in [GBLP96, AAD+96, ZDN97, RS97].

A different kind of decision support query has been considered in [CR96], involving aggregation queries in which multiple dependent aggregates are computed within each group. An example of such a query is the following:

Q0: For each item, find its minimum price in 1996, and the total sales among all minimum price tuples.

[CR96] presented an extended SQL syntax that allows a succinct representation of such queries. An experimental study demonstrated that such queries can be efficiently evaluated. In contrast, standard SQL representations of the same queries are verbose and redundant, leading to queries that are hard to understand, to maintain, and to optimize.

In this paper, we consider complex decision support queries in which multiple dependent aggregates are computed at a variety of granularities. In particular, we would like to be able to ask queries like that of Query Q0 above, but replacing the phrase "For each item" by "Grouping by all subsets of {supplier, month, item}." We call such queries *multi-feature cubes*, and illustrate the practical utility of such queries using a number of examples. The main contributions of this paper are the following.

Classification (Section 4) We classify multi-feature cubes based on their *degree of incrementality*. We extend the notions of *distributive*, *algebraic*, and *holistic* aggregates from [GBLP96] to our more general context.

Identification (Section 5) We provide syntactic sufficient conditions on multi-feature cube queries to determine when they are distributive or algebraic. The evaluation of such queries can be performed particularly efficiently, so it is important to be able to identify them syntactically. These conditions admit a large class of multi-feature cube queries beyond those expressible as simple datacubes.

Evaluation (Section 6) We present an algorithm that incrementally computes the coarser granularity output of a distributive multi-feature cube using the finer granularity output of the multi-feature cube. We show that this algorithm can be used in conjunction with previously proposed techniques for efficiently evaluating datacubes to evaluate multi-feature cubes that are distributive or algebraic, with the same I/O complexity. We also discuss the suitability of previously proposed datacube evaluation techniques for efficiently evaluating holistic multi-feature cubes.

Performance (Section 7) We evaluate the CPU performance of computing multi-feature cubes using the datacube evaluation algorithm of Ross and Srivastava [RS97]. Using a variety of synthetic, benchmark and real-world data sets, we demonstrate that the CPU cost of evaluating distributive multi-feature cubes is comparable to that of evaluating simple datacubes. We also show that a variety of holistic multi-feature cubes can be evaluated with a manageable overhead compared to the distributive case.

We can hence ask considerably more sophisticated queries than datacube queries without incurring a significant cost increase! All the examples in this paper will use the relation SUPPLIES(Supplier, Customer, Item, Year, Month, Day, Price, Sales, Delay) from a business application database. Suppliers supply items to customers. The unit price and sales (in dollars) of items ordered by the customer from the supplier on the given date are stored in Price and Sales. Orders placed on that date are delivered after Delay days.

2 Background

2.1 The Datacube: Aggregation at Multiple Granularities

In [GBLP96], Gray et al. present the datacube, which allows the computation of aggregates of the data at multiple granularities. We refer the reader to [GBLP96] for the syntax and semantics of such queries in general, and present an example below to aid intuition.

Example 2.1: Suppose that we want to ask the following datacube query: grouping by all subsets of {Supplier, Customer, Item, Month}, find the total sales among all tuples from 1996. One could write this query as:

```
SELECT    Supplier, Customer, Item, Month, SUM(Sales)
FROM      SUPPLIES
WHERE     Year = 1996
CUBE BY   Supplier, Customer, Item, Month
```

The meaning of this datacube is the union of the results of 16 SQL queries, obtained as follows: for each subset $\tilde{B}$ of the CUBE BY attributes, the CUBE BY clause is replaced by GROUP BY $\tilde{B}$, and any attribute in the SELECT clause not in $\tilde{B}$ is replaced by the special constant value ALL.[4]   □

2.2 Querying Multiple Features of Groups

In [CR96], Chatziantoniou and Ross present an extension of SQL that allows one to query multiple features of groups in relational databases. We refer the reader to [CR96] for the syntax and semantics of such queries, and present an example below to aid intuition.

---

[4] Recall that in standard SQL only attributes in the GROUP BY clause, aggregates and constant values can appear in the SELECT clause.

Example 2.2: Suppose that we want to ask the following query: for each customer, for each item, and for each month in 1996, find the total sales among all minimum price suppliers of that item for that month. In the SQL extension of [CR96], one could write this query as:

```
SELECT    Customer, Item, Month, SUM(R.Sales)
FROM      SUPPLIES
WHERE     Year = 1996
GROUP BY  Customer, Item, Month : R
SUCH THAT R.Price = MIN(Price)
```

The meaning of this query can be understood as follows. First, all tuples in the SUPPLIES relation that satisfy the condition "Year = 1996" are selected, and these tuples are grouped based on their values of the grouping attributes Customer, Item and Month into multiple groups, say $g_1, \ldots, g_r$. For each group of tuples g_i, the minimum price m_{g_i} among the tuples of g_i is computed, and grouping variable R ranges over all tuples in group g_i whose price is equal to m_{g_i}. The sum of sales of the tuples in g_i that R ranges over is then computed, and associated with the values of the grouping attributes of g_i in the query result. □

3 Multi-Feature Cubes

The work of Chatziantoniou and Ross from Section 2.2 motivates us to try to ask more general queries at multiple granularities. Consider Example 2.2 once more, and suppose that we wish to ask the same query at different time granularities. For example, finding minimum price suppliers over the whole year, and summing their sales, is commonly called a "roll-up" query. If we wish to find the minimum price suppliers on each day, and sum their sales, then we would be "drilling down" to a finer granularity. If we wish to answer this query at all possible granularities within a given set of grouping variables, then we are performing an operation analogous to the datacube, which we call a *multi-feature cube*.

Example 3.1: We shall use the following queries throughout this paper:

Q1: Grouping by all subsets of {Supplier, Customer, Item, Month} find the minimum price among all tuples from 1996, and the total sales among all such minimum price tuples.

Q2: Grouping by all subsets of {Supplier, Customer, Item, Month} find the minimum price among all tuples from 1996, and the fraction of the total sales due to tuples whose delay is less than 10 days and whose price is within 25%, within 50% and within 75% of the minimum price.

Q3: Grouping by all subsets of {Supplier, Customer, Item, Month} find the minimum price among all tuples from 1996, the maximum and minimum delays within the set of all minimum price tuples, and the fraction of the total sales due to tuples that have maximum delay within the set of all minimum price tuples, and the fraction of the total sales due to tuples that have minimum delay within the set of all minimum price tuples. □

```
Q:   SELECT      B₁, ..., Bₖ, f₁(A₁), ..., fₙ(Aₙ)
     FROM        T₁, ..., Tₚ
     WHERE       Cond
     CUBE BY     B₁, ..., Bₖ : R₁, ..., Rₘ
     SUCH THAT   S₁ AND ... AND Sₘ
```

Fig. 1. Syntax for Multi-Feature Cube Queries

Just as the multi-feature queries of [CR96] can be expressed using standard features of SQL such as views and/or subqueries, multi-feature cubes can also be expressed using the datacube and views/subqueries. However, as argued in [CR96], the resulting expressions are both complex and repetitious, leading to queries that are difficult to understand, maintain, and optimize, Thus, we prefer to extend the succinct syntax of [CR96] with the CUBE BY clause of [GBLP96].

3.1   A Combined Syntax for Multi-Feature Cubes

A *multi-feature cube* query Q has the syntax described in Figure 1. The FROM and the WHERE clauses in the multi-feature cube are identical to the corresponding clauses in the syntactic extensions of [CR96] and [GBLP96], which are unchanged from standard SQL. The CUBE BY clause in the multi-feature cube combines the CUBE BY clause from [GBLP96] with the specification of grouping variables $R_1, \ldots, R_m$ of the GROUP BY clause from [CR96]. The SELECT and the SUCH THAT clauses in the multi-feature cube are identical to the corresponding clauses in the syntactic extension of [CR96]. The meaning of the multi-feature cube is the union of the results of all 2^k queries of the form:

```
SELECT      B₁, ..., Bₖ, f₁(A₁), ..., fₙ(Aₙ)
FROM        T₁, ..., Tₚ
WHERE       Cond
GROUP BY    B̃ : R₁, ..., Rₘ
SUCH THAT   S₁ AND ... AND Sₘ
```

where $\tilde{B}$ is an arbitrary subset of $\{B_1, \ldots, B_k\}$, and any B_i not in $\tilde{B}$ that appears in the SELECT clause is evaluated as the special constant value ALL.

When we require that grouping variable R_j ranges over a *subset* of the tuples that grouping variable R_i (where $i < j$) ranges over, we simply write "R_j in R_i" in the condition S_j of the SUCH THAT clause. This notation is a convenient shorthand for a query in which the conditions in the SUCH THAT clause for S_i are repeated in S_j (for R_j rather than R_i).

Example 3.2: We now express the queries of Example 3.1 using our syntax.

```
Q1:  SELECT      Supplier, Customer, Item, Month, MIN(Price), SUM(R.Sales)
     FROM        SUPPLIES
     WHERE       Year = 1996
     CUBE BY     Supplier, Customer, Item, Month : R
     SUCH THAT R.Price = MIN(Price)
```

```
Q2:  SELECT     Supplier, Customer, Item, Month, MIN(Price),
                SUM(R1.Sales), SUM(R2.Sales), SUM(R3.Sales), SUM(Sales)
     FROM       SUPPLIES
     WHERE      Year = 1996
     CUBE BY    Supplier, Customer, Item, Month : R1, R2, R3
     SUCH THAT  R1.Price <= 1.25*MIN(Price) AND R1.Delay < 10
                AND R2.Price <= 1.50*MIN(Price) AND R2.Delay < 10
                AND R3.Price <= 1.75*MIN(Price) AND R3.Delay < 10

Q3:  SELECT     Supplier, Customer, Item, Month, MIN(Price), MIN(R1.Delay),
                MAX(R1.Delay), SUM(R1.Sales), SUM(R2.Sales), SUM(R3.Sales)
     FROM       SUPPLIES
     WHERE      Year = 1996
     CUBE BY    Supplier, Customer, Item, Month : R1, R2, R3
     SUCH THAT  R1.Price = MIN(Price) AND R2 in R1 AND R2.Delay =
                MIN(R1.Delay) AND R3 in R1 AND R3.Delay = MAX(R1.Delay)
```

4   Classifying Multi-Feature Cubes

To better understand issues arising in the evaluation of multi-feature cubes, we propose a classification based on the notion of incremental evaluability.

Definition 4.1: (Group, Granularity) Let Q be a multi-feature cube query on a database D, and let $B_1, \ldots, B_k$ be the attributes mentioned in the CUBE BY clause of Q. Each instance v of attributes $B_1, \ldots, B_k$ (including instances involving the special ALL value) is called a *group*.

Groups v and v' are said to be *at the same level* if they take the value ALL on exactly the same attributes. The set of all groups at the same level is called a *granularity*, and is denoted by its set of non-ALL attributes. Group v' is *coarser than* v (or, v is *finer than* v') if $v' \neq v$ and every non-ALL value of a (grouping) attribute in v' is also the value of that attribute in v. Also, the granularity of such a group v' is said to be *coarser than* the granularity of group v. □

Datacubes and multi-feature cubes can be evaluated using multiple passes over the base data. While such an evaluation technique may be required in general, a large number of datacubes (those using distributive aggregate functions, in the terminology of [GBLP96]) can be evaluated much more efficiently, by *incrementally* computing the output of the datacube at a coarser granularity using only the output of the datacube at a finer granularity. We capture this property in our definition of *distributive* multi-feature cubes.

Definition 4.2: (Distributive Multi-Feature Cube) Consider the multi-feature cube Q given by the syntax of Figure 1. Let $\tilde{B}_1$ and $\tilde{B}_2$ denote arbitrary subsets of the CUBE BY attributes $\{B_1, \ldots, B_k\}$, such that $\tilde{B}_1$ is a subset of $\tilde{B}_2$. Let Q_i, $i \in \{1, 2\}$ denote the query:

```
SELECT   B_1, ..., B_k, f_1(A_1), ..., f_n(A_n)
FROM     T_1, ..., T_p
```

```
WHERE     Cond
GROUP BY  B̃ᵢ : R₁, ..., Rₘ
SUCH THAT S₁ AND ... AND Sₘ
```

where any B_j not in $\tilde{B}_i$ appearing in the SELECT clause is evaluated as the constant value ALL.

Query Q is said to be a *distributive* multi-feature cube if there is a computable function F such that for all databases D and all Q_1 and Q_2 as above, $output(Q_1, D)$ can be computed via F as $F(output(Q_2, D))$. □

Proposition 4.1: Datacubes that use only distributive aggregate functions are distributive multi-feature cubes. □

Example 4.1: We show that Query Q1 is a distributive multi-feature cube. Suppose that we have computed the aggregates for the granularity Supplier, Customer, Item, Month and have kept both MIN(Price) and SUM(R.Sales) for each group. We now wish to compute the aggregates for the granularity Supplier, Customer, Item. We can combine the twelve pairs of values (one per month) into an annual pair of values, as follows: (a) Compute the minimum of the monthly MIN(Price) values. This is the annual MIN(Price) value. (b) Add up the SUM(R.Sales) for those months whose monthly MIN(Price) value is equal to the annual MIN(Price) value. This is the annual SUM(R.Sales) value. □

However, multi-feature cubes may be non-distributive even when *each* aggregate function in the SELECT and SUCH THAT clauses is distributive. Query Q2 from Example 3.2 is such a non-distributive cube, as the following example illustrates.

Example 4.2: Consider Query Q2, which determines the fraction of the total sales due to tuples whose delay is less than 10 days and whose price is within 25%, within 50% and within 75% of the minimum price.

Suppose that we've computed these aggregates for the granularity Supplier, Customer, Item, Month and have kept all of MIN(Price), SUM(R1.Sales), SUM(R2.Sales), SUM(R3.Sales) and SUM(Sales) for each group. We now wish to compute the aggregates for the granularity Supplier, Customer, Item. Unfortunately, we cannot simply combine the twelve tuples of values (one per month) into a global tuple of values. Suppose that (for some group) the minimum price over the whole year is $110, but that the minimum price for January is $120. Then we do not know how to combine January's SUM(R2.Sales) of $1000 into the yearly SUM(R2.Sales) since we do not know what fraction of the $1000 came from tuples with price at most $165; the figure of $1000 includes contributions from tuples with price up to $180. □

While not all multi-feature cubes are distributive, it is sometimes possible to "extend" multi-feature cubes by adding aggregates to the SELECT clause, such that the modified multi-feature cube *is* distributive. For example, a datacube that has AVG(Sales), but neither COUNT(Sales) nor SUM(Sales), in its SELECT clause, can be extended to a distributive multi-feature cube by adding SUM(Sales) to the SELECT clause. The average sales at coarser granularities can now be computed from the average sales and the total sales at finer granularities.

Definition 4.3: (Algebraic and Holistic Multi-Feature Cubes) Consider a multi-feature cube Q. Q is said to be an *algebraic* multi-feature cube if there exists a Q' obtained by adding aggregates to the SELECT clause, such that Q' is distributive. Otherwise, Q is said to be a *holistic* multi-feature cube. □

Query Q2 from Examples 3.2 and 4.2 above, is an example of a holistic multi-feature cube since no extension of Query Q2 would be distributive.

5 Identifying Distributive Multi-Feature Cubes

In this section, we identify natural syntactic conditions on multi-feature cubes for them to be distributive. Our first step is to define a binary relation "$\prec$" on the grouping variables $R_1, \ldots, R_m$, based on the pattern of attribute references in the SUCH THAT clause.

Definition 5.1: ($R_i \prec R_j$) Grouping variable R_i is said to be $<$ grouping variable R_j if the condition S_j (defining R_j) in the SUCH THAT clause refers to an attribute of R_i. Define $\prec$ to be the reflexive, transitive closure of $<$. □

Note that the syntactic restrictions on the conditions in the SUCH THAT clause of multi-feature cubes, from Section 3.1, guarantee that "$\prec$" is a partial order.

Our next step is to identify the pattern of accesses of different grouping variables, i.e., the relationships between the tuples within a group over which the grouping variables range. The following definition identifies an important access pattern of grouping variables.

Definition 5.2: ($R_i \sqsubset R_j$) Grouping variable R_i is $\sqsubset$ grouping variable R_j, if R_j always ranges over a subset of the tuples that R_i ranges over. □

It is important to understand that $R_i \prec R_j$ does not necessarily imply that $R_i \sqsubset R_j$. However, as we show later, such a condition on grouping variables that are related by the partial order "$\prec$" is essential for a multi-feature cube to be distributive. In general, $R_i \sqsubset R_j$ if and only if condition S_j (parameterized by the attributes of R_j) implies condition S_i (parameterized by the attributes of R_i). In many cases we can identify that $R_i \sqsubset R_j$ simply by checking that S_j contains the shorthand "R_j in R_i."

The multi-feature cube graph, defined below, captures most of the important relationships between grouping variables, and the nature of the defining conditions in the SUCH THAT clause for the grouping variables.

Definition 5.3: (Multi-Feature Cube Graph) Given a multi-feature cube query Q, the *multi-feature cube graph* of Q, denoted by $MFCG(Q)$ is a labeled, directed, acyclic graph defined as follows.

The nodes of $MFCG(Q)$ are the grouping variables $R_1, \ldots, R_m$ in the CUBE BY clause of Q, along with an additional node R_0.

There is a directed edge $(R_i, R_j), i < j$, in $MFCG(Q)$ if $R_i \sqsubset R_j$ and there does not exist R_k different from R_i and R_j, such that $R_i \sqsubset R_k \sqsubset R_j$. For every node R_j, $j \neq 0$, such that there is no edge of the form (R_i, R_j) in $MFCG(Q)$, add an edge (R_0, R_j).

If there is an edge (R_i, R_j) in $MFCG(Q)$, node R_i is referred to as a *parent* of node R_j. If there is a path from R_i to R_j, in $MFCG(Q)$, node R_i is referred to as an *ancestor* of node R_j.

Node R_0 is associated with the empty label. Each node R_i, $i \neq 0$, in $MFCG(Q)$ is labeled with those aggregate conditions that appear in S_i, the defining condition for R_i in the SUCH THAT clause of Q, but are not part of the label of an ancestor of R_i in $MFCG(Q)$. □

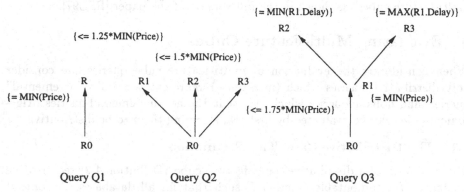

Fig. 2. Example Multi-Feature Cube Graphs

Figure 2 presents the multi-feature cube graphs for Queries Q1, Q2 and Q3. As a final step before identifying conditions for distributivity of multi-feature cubes, we define what it means for a *set* of aggregate functions of attributes to be distributive. This generalizes the characterization, from [GBLP96], of a *single* distributive aggregate function.

Definition 5.4: A set $\tilde{\mathcal{F}}$ of aggregate functions of attributes $f_1(A_1)$, ..., $f_n(A_n)$ is said to be *distributive*, if (1) each aggregate function f_i is either distributive or algebraic, and (2) for algebraic aggregate functions f_i, such that $f_i(A_i) \in \tilde{\mathcal{F}}$, other aggregate functions of attributes in $\tilde{\mathcal{F}}$ provide the necessary additional information needed for the incremental computation of $f_i(A_i)$. □

For example, the set {MIN(Price), AVG(R.Sales)} is not distributive, but the set {MIN(Price), AVG(R.Sales), SUM(R.Sales)} is distributive.

Theorem 5.1: Consider a multi-feature cube query Q. Let $\tilde{R}$ denote the set $\{R_1, \ldots, R_m\}$ of grouping variables in Q. Query Q is *distributive* if each of the following conditions is satisfied:

C1. The set of $f_i(A_i)$'s in the SELECT clause of Q is distributive.
C2. For any $R_i, R_j \in \tilde{R}$, $R_i \prec R_j$ implies $R_i \sqsubseteq R_j$.
C3. The multi-feature cube graph $MFCG(Q)$ is a tree with at most one aggregate condition on each node. Further, the aggregate condition (if any) associated with node R_j is of one of the forms[5] $R_j.A_k = \text{MAX}([R_i.]A_k)$, or

---
[5] $R_0.A_k$ is written simply as A_k.

$R_j.A_k = \text{MIN}(\text{[}R_i.\text{]}A_k)$, where R_i is the parent of R_j in $MFCG(Q)$.

C4. For each aggregate of the form $\text{MAX}(\text{[}R_j.\text{]}A_i)$ (or $\text{MIN}(\text{[}R_j.\text{]}A_i)$) in the SUCH THAT clause of query Q, $\text{MAX}(\text{[}R_j.\text{]}A_i)$ (resp. $\text{MIN}(\text{[}R_j.\text{]}A_i)$) appears in the SELECT clause of Q. □

Example 5.1: Consider Queries Q1, Q2 and Q3 from Example 3.2. The first and third queries satisfy the conditions of Theorem 5.1, but the conditions in the SUCH THAT clause of the second query violate Condition C3. □

The conditions of Theorem 5.1 can be easily modified to identify algebraic multi-feature cubes, as shown in the full version of the paper [RSC97].

6 Evaluating Multi-Feature Cubes

When considering the evaluation of multi-feature cube queries, we consider only distributive queries which (in a sense) represent the "fully incremental" queries, and holistic queries which represent the non-incremental queries. Algebraic queries can be evaluated by first transforming them to be distributive.

6.1 The Distributive Case: The F Function

The definition of a distributive multi-feature cube (Definition 4.2) requires the existence of a computable function F such that for all databases, the output of the multi-feature cube for a coarser granularity can be computed from the output of the multi-feature cube for finer granularities via F.[6]

When the multi-feature cube is just a simple datacube, the computation of the output for a coarser granularity from the output for a finer granularity is simple for the standard SQL aggregate functions. For example, the value of MAX(A) for a coarser group can be computed by taking the maximum of all the MAX(A) values in its finer groups, and the value of COUNT(A) for a coarser group can be computed as the sum of all the COUNT(A) values in its finer groups. The following example presents the F function for a simple multi-feature cube.

Example 6.1: Consider again Query Q1, which computes the minimum price among all tuples from 1996, and the total sales among all such minimum price tuples, for all subsets of {Supplier, Customer, Item, Month}. The specification of Example 3.2 satisfies the conditions of Theorem 5.1.

We now give the function F to compute coarser granularity results from finer granularity results on this query. Suppose that $\{v_1, \ldots, v_t\}$ are all of the groups at a fine granularity, and v is a coarser group for which we want to generate the output. The aggregates for each group v_j will be a pair of the form (p_j, t_j), where p_j is the minimum price, and t_j is the total sales. We process groups v_j one by one as follows, adjusting the aggregates (p, t) for the coarser group v as we go. F has a local flag f that is initially set to false, indicating that no groups have been processed.

---

[6] Note that the output of the multi-feature cube at the finest granularity cannot be computed using the function F. This computation can be performed using the techniques suggested in [CR96].

- If f is false then f is set to true, and $(p, t) = (p_j, t_j)$
- else if $(p_j < p)$ then $(p, t) = (p_j, t_j)$
- else if $(p_j = p)$ then $t = t + t_j$
- else do nothing.

At the end of the scan, we return (p, t). □

The multi-feature cube graph of Query Q1 is a simple chain with a single grouping variable, as can be seen from Figure 2. A general algorithm that is applicable whenever the conditions of Theorem 5.1 are satisfied has to deal with many grouping variables and tree-structured multi-feature cube graphs, and is given as **Incremental-Eval** in the full version of the paper [RSC97].

6.2 Algorithms for Distributive Multi-Feature Cubes

Several algorithms have been proposed for computing the datacube [GBLP96, AAD+96, ZDN97, RS97]. The details of these algorithms are not important here. All of these algorithms attempt to compute the datacube by utilizing the lattice structure of the various granularities. Finer granularity results are combined to give results at the next coarser granularity. Some of these algorithms perform optimizations based on the estimated size of answers of groups within the datacube. There are two crucial features of distributive multi-feature cubes that allow the algorithms mentioned above to apply:

1. Coarser granularity aggregates can be computed from finer granularity aggregates by distributivity. In particular, the function F to compute the coarser aggregates can be automatically derived. This F function plays the role that addition would play in evaluating a datacube with aggregate SUM.
2. The size of the output for each group is constant (one tuple of fixed size per group) and is easily derived from the query syntax. Thus one can use the same estimation techniques as used in the algorithms above to estimate the size of intermediate results, and employ the same optimization strategies.

As a result of these observations, it becomes clear that each of these algorithms can also be applied to distributive multi-feature cubes *without any increase in I/O complexity* compared with a simple datacube. Since F may be harder to compute than a simple aggregate like SUM, there might be an increase in the CPU cost. We address this concern in detail in Section 7.

6.3 The Holistic Case

The algorithms that have been proposed for computing the datacube [GBLP96, AAD+96, ZDN97, RS97] can be divided into two approaches:

- Algorithms that use main memory essentially for storing the input relation, typically in a partitioned and/or sorted fashion [AAD+96, RS97]. Datacube tuples are computed, and immediately flushed to output buffers.
- Algorithms that use main memory essentially for storing the (partially computed) output, typically as a k-dimensional array [GBLP96, ZDN97].

Of these, the algorithms in the first approach are better suited to computing holistic multi-feature cubes. The reason is that the first approach lends itself to the possibility of maintaining all tuples from a group of the input relation simultaneously in memory, allowing for the computation of the holistic multi-feature aggregate over this group. The second approach, on the other hand, maintains partially computed aggregates, obtained by scanning the input relation; such incremental computation cannot be performed for holistic multi-feature cubes.

7 Experimental Evaluation

We used the techniques proposed by Ross and Srivastava [RS97] to implement a variety of multi-feature cube queries. The software used is extensible with respect to the aggregate functions used; arbitrary distributive or non-distributive aggregate functions can be written and linked to the cube-computation code.

For distributive aggregates, the software works as follows: First, combine all tuples that share all CUBE BY attributes into a single tuple using the combination function F (which exists for distributive aggregates). After doing so, multiple sorting and scanning steps compute the cube result, as described in [RS97].

For holistic aggregates, there is no initial combining step. Multiple sorting and scanning steps compute the cube result. Unlike the case for distributive cubes, fine granularity results are not used to compute coarse granularity results; the aggregates are computed separately at each granularity.

The CPU performance measurements given below were generated on an UltraSparc 2 (200MHZ) running Solaris. The machine used had 128MB of RAM, and in all cases, the input relations used were able to fit in RAM. We would expect analogous results for larger tables using the divide and conquer approach of [RS97]. The reported time is the CPU time reported by the operating system, which was always very close to the elapsed time. CPU time measurement commenced after the input was read, and the writing of the output result was suppressed in order to avoid introducing I/O cost.

We ran four multi-feature cube queries, numbered B1 through B4. For comparison purposes, we also ran two datacube queries, numbered C1 and C2, with distributive aggregate functions. B1 and B2 are distributive, while B3 and B4 are holistic. All queries were run over an input with seven attributes, including four CUBE BY attributes (G1–G4) and three aggregated attributes (A1–A3). We used three different data sources for the input: (a) a uniform, randomly generated data set, (b) data generated according to the TPC-D benchmark [Tra95], and (c) data from real-world measurements of cloud coverage over the globe for a period of one month [HWL94]. The meaning of each attribute is given below.

Table	G1	G2	G3	G4	A1	A2	A3
TPC-D	Part	Supplier	Date	Return code	Discount	Quantity	Price
Cloud	Latitude	Longitude	Day	Hour	Weather code	low-cloud amount	total cloud amount
Random	Uniformly generated						

Query B1 outputs the maximum A1 value, as well as the maximum A3 value among all tuples having maximum A1 value in the group. Query B2 outputs the maximum A1 value, and then among tuples having maximum A1 value in the group it selects two subgroups: those with minimum A2 value, and those with maximum A2 value. (The minimum and maximum A2 values are also output.) For each of the three groups the maximum A3 value within the group is output. Query B3 finds (and outputs) the maximum A1 value within the group, and then computes (and outputs) the maximum A3 value in three subgroups: those tuples that have an A1 value more than 25% of maximum, those tuples that have an A1 value more than 50% of maximum, and those tuples that have an A1 value more than 75% of maximum. Query B4 finds the maximum A1 value and the maximum A2 value within a group. It then computes the maximum A3 value for all tuples in the group that have both an A1 value greater than 50% of maximum, and an A2 value greater than 50% of maximum. The maximum A1 and A2 values, together with the computed maximum A3 value are output; if no input tuples satisfy the conditions, then no output tuple is generated. Query C1 outputs the maximum A1 and A3 values, and Query C2 outputs the maximum A1, A2, and A3 values, along with the minimum A1, A2 and A3 values.

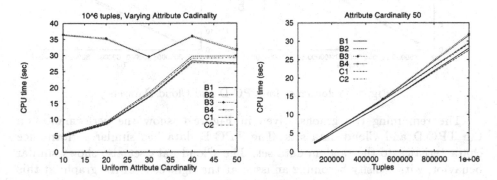

Fig. 3. Performance for Random Datasets

We present four performance graphs. The first two, given in Figure 3 show the performance on the random datasets.

In the left graph, we fix the input size at 10^6 tuples, and vary the (uniform) attribute cardinality. For low cardinality, the cube is *dense*, since the number of combinations of input **CUBE BY** attributes is 10^4, much smaller than the number of tuples. For high cardinality, the cube is sparse ($50^4 > 10^6$). The graph shows that for sparse data, at the right edge of the graph, the aggregate functions perform comparably, within a fairly narrow range. However, for dense data, the distributive functions perform substantially better than the holistic functions. The reason for this behavior is the initial combining step that is performed for distributive aggregates but not for holistic aggregates. In the distributive case, the initial data set will collapse to 10^4 tuples after combining when the cardinality is 10, meaning that all of the subsequent work is performed on 10^4 tuples rather than 10^6 tuples.

In the right graph, we show how the performance scales with the number of tuples when the attribute cardinality is 50. As the number of tuples increases, the density gradually increases, and so the holistic cubes begin to be more expensive at the right edge of the graph. If one looks closely, the other curves are divided into two groups with the curves in each group being very close to one another. One group consists of B1 and C1, and the other consists of B2 and C2. Both B1 and C1 have two output aggregates, while both B2 and C2 have six output aggregates. Thus, the complexity seems to be determined more by the *number* of output columns than by whether the distributive aggregate function is simple or complex. In other words, *there is negligible apparent overhead for evaluating a complex distributive multi-feature cube when compared with a simple datacube having the same number of output columns.*

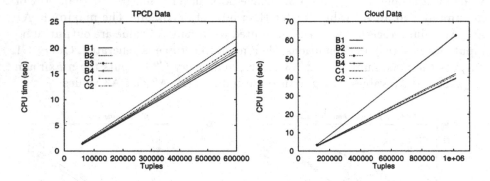

Fig. 4. Performance for TPC-D and Cloud Datasets

The remaining two graphs, given in Figure 4, show the performance on the TPC-D and Cloud data sets. The TPC-D data has similar performance characteristics to the random data set. The Cloud data set also shows similar behavior, with density becoming an issue at the right edge of the graph; at this point only 70% of the tuples remain after the initial combining step.

While holistic multi-feature cubes are sometimes significantly more expensive than distributive cubes, we can see that computing them involves a CPU cost that is relatively manageable.

8 Conclusions

We have considered multi-feature cube queries, a natural class of complex queries involving multiple dependent aggregates computed at multiple granularities, that are practically very useful. We have classified multi-feature cube queries according to the degree of incrementality by which coarser granularity results can be computed from finer granularity results. We have identified syntactic sufficient conditions that allow us to recognize multi-feature cubes that are distributive or algebraic. We have shown that a number of existing algorithms can be used for the evaluation and optimization of distributive (or algebraic) multi-feature cubes without any increase in I/O cost, and with a negligible increase in CPU cost. This is an important subclass of multi-feature cube queries that is no more difficult to compute than datacube queries, and which includes many sophisticated queries not easily expressed as datacube queries.

Other authors have introduced new algebraic operators and/or syntaxes for multidimensional data analysis [AGS97, LW96]. However, none of these proposals considers the issue of multiple dependent aggregates within a group. As a result, the specification of most of the examples presented in this paper using their approaches would require multiple views or subqueries, leading to the problems outlined in [CR96].

Acknowledgements

We would like to thank Ted Johnson for his comments on this paper. The research of Kenneth A. Ross and Damianos Chatziantoniou was supported by a grant from the AT&T Foundation, by a David and Lucile Packard Foundation Fellowship in Science and Engineering, by a Sloan Foundation Fellowship, by an NSF Young Investigator Award, and by NSF CISE award CDA-9625374.

References

[AAD+96] S. Agarwal, R. Agrawal, P. M. Deshpande, A. Gupta, J. F. Naughton, R. Ramakrishnan, and S. Sarawagi. On the computation of multidimensional aggregates. In *Proceedings of VLDB*, pages 506–521, 1996.

[AGS97] R. Agrawal, A. Gupta, and S. Sarawagi. Modeling multidimensional databases. In *Proceedings of IEEE ICDE*, 1997.

[CR96] D. Chatziantoniou and K. A. Ross. Querying multiple features of groups in relational databases. In *Proceedings of VLDB*, pages 295–306, 1996.

[GBLP96] J. Gray, A. Bosworth, A. Layman, and H. Pirahesh. Datacube : A relational aggregation operator generalizing group-by, cross-tab, and sub-totals. In *Proceedings of IEEE ICDE*, pages 152–159, 1996. Also available as Microsoft Technical Report MSR-TR-95-22.

[HWL94] C. J. Hahn, S. G. Warren, and J. London. Edited synoptic cloud reports from ships and land stations over the globe, 1982-1991. Available from http://cdiac.esd.ornl.gov/cdiac/ndps/ndp026b.html, 1994.

[LW96] C. Li and X. S. Wang. A data model for supporting on-line analytical processing. In *Proceedings of CIKM*, pages 81–88, 1996.

[RS97] K. A. Ross and D. Srivastava. Fast computation of sparse datacubes. In *Proceedings of VLDB*, pages 116–125, 1997.

[RSC97] K. A. Ross, D. Srivastava and D. Chatziantoniou. Complex aggregation at multiple granularities. AT&T Technical Report, 1997.

[Tra95] Transaction Processing Performance Council (TPC), 777 N. First Street, Suite 600, San Jose, CA 95112, USA. *TPC Benchmark D (Decision Support)*, May 1995.

[ZDN97] Y. Zhao, P. M. Deshpande, and J. F. Naughton. An array-based algorithm for simultaneous multidimensional aggregates. In *Proceedings of ACM SIGMOD*, pages 159–170, 1997.

Parallel Processing of Multiple Aggregate Queries on Shared-Nothing Multiprocessors

Fukuda Takeshi and Hirofumi Matsuzawa

{fukudat, matuzawa}@trl.ibm.co.jp
IBM Tokyo Research Laboratory
1623-14, Shimotsuruma, Yamato City, Kanagawa Pref. 242, Japan

Abstract. Decision support systems that include on-line analytical processing and data mining have recently attracted research attention. Such applications treat data in very large databases as multidimensional data cubes. Each cell of a data cube typically is some aggregation, such as total sales volume, that is of interest to analysts. Since it may be necessary to compute many cells, and the performance is critical, we propose parallel algorithms that compute multiple aggregate queries in data cubes on a shared-nothing multiprocessor with high-bandwidth communication facilities. We evaluate the algorithms on the basis of analytical modeling and an implementation on an IBM SP2 system.

1 Introduction

Aggregation is one of the most important operations in decision support systems (DSSs). *On-line analytical processing* (OLAP) [4] applications often require data to be summarized in very large databases (so-called *data warehouses*) across various combinations of attributes. [10] proposed a *data cube* operator that generalizes the SQL **group-by** construct to support multidimensional data analysis. Data cubes provide a typical view of the data in DSS applications. They can be used to visualize the data in a graphical way, and allow data-mining algorithms to find important patterns automatically [7, 6, 21]. Techniques for effective computation of data cubes have attracted considerable research interest [11, 14, 15, 12, 18, 2].

Since "on-line" means interactive, the response time is crucial in OLAP environments. To reduce the response times, most OLAP systems pre-compute frequently used aggregates. These materialized aggregate views are commonly referred to as *summary tables*. Summary tables can be used to help answer other aggregate queries. [11] discussed how materialized aggregate views can be used to help answer aggregate queries.

The pre-computation cost should also be small, since it determines how frequently the aggregates are brought up to date. It is difficult to pre-compute a complete data cube, because such a cube can be very large. [14] presented a greedy algorithm for deciding what subset of data cubes should be pre-computed. The algorithm selects a near-optimal collection of aggregate queries in a data cube. Recently [2] discussed various optimization techniques for computing related *multiple* aggregates, which may be chosen by the algorithm in [14].

Query-optimizing methods for aggregate queries have been thoroughly investigated, and are summarized in [9]. A few parallel algorithms for aggregate queries have been reported in the literature. To process data cubes, we need to handle *multiple* aggregate queries. Applying conventional parallel algorithms to aggregate queries in a data cube operator would appear to be straightforward. But, as we explain later, there may be so many queries that conventional methods will not work well.

Motivating Example

Example 1.1 Consider a relation of tens of millions of bank customers. It has 30 numeric attributes such as `Age`, `CheckAccountBalance`, and `FixedDeposit-Balance`, and 100 categorical attributes such as `Sex`, `Occupation`, `CardLoan-Delay`, and `CreditCardClass`. An analyst wants to discover any unknown patterns and rules in the database.

Both the number of records and the number of attributes in this example were taken from a real-life data set. As we will explain, the total size of aggregates to be pre-computed will be very large, even though the algorithm proposed in [14] can select the best subset of the data cube to reduce the response time for probable queries, since the number of dimensions is so large.

Numeric attributes are normally used as *measures* to aggregate values, but they can be used as *dimensions* to make groups. Since the domain size of a numeric attribute such as `CheckAccountBalance` tends to be very large, grouping over such attributes will hardly summarize the data at all. Analysts are not interested in how many customers have exactly the same amount of money, but would like to know the customer distribution along the numeric dimension. Thus the domain of such numeric attributes should be divided into a certain number of buckets, say 100, and grouping over the bucket number will provide an answer to the question.

As we have 130 dimensions, the size of the whole data cube is huge (2^{130} vertices). For simplicity, let us assume that each attribute A_i (either numeric or categorical; $i = 1, 2, \ldots, 130$) has 100 distinct, uniformly distributed values. We adopt the cost model used in [14], in which the aggregate query processing cost is proportional to the size of the source relation of the query. Figure 1 shows the size of the data cube. There is no point in materializing an aggregate with four or more dimensions, because the size of the result will not be any smaller than that of the raw data (100^4 is larger than the size of the raw data, 10^7) and hence the results of four-or-more-dimensional aggregates provide no help in answering other aggregate queries. Therefore, materializing a three-dimensional aggregate will yield the largest benefit. Similarly, the second-best to the forty-fourth-best choices are three-dimensional aggregates. For all one-dimensional aggregates to be computable not from the raw data but from a materialized view, it is necessary to pre-compute $\lceil 130/3 \rceil = 44$ three-dimensional aggregates. If we want to make all two-dimensional aggregates computable from a materialized view, we need to pre-compute at least $\lceil \binom{130}{2}/3 \rceil = 2,795$ three-dimensional aggregate queries. Since we assumed that each attribute is distributed uniformly, every three-dimensional query produces $100^3 = 1,000,000$ tuples. Even though the

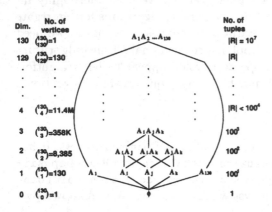

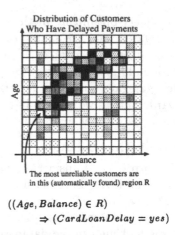

Fig. 1. Example of a data-cube lattice   **Fig. 2.** Example rule

actual database has skewed data distributions and the tuple size of each query result is very small, the total size of the summary tables will be too large to fit into main memory.   □

Example 1.2 Let us consider another scenario, using the same bank customer database. Aggregate queries can also be used for data mining. Data mining algorithms presented in [7, 6, 21] can discover interesting association rules with one or two numeric attributes, such as "*a customer whose age and balance falls in some two-dimensional region tends to delay his/her card loan payment with high probability.*" The rule characterizes a target property ("unreliable" customers) by using two numeric attributes (age and balance). The algorithms can derive the rule from the distribution (**count()**), in terms of age and balance, of all customers and that of customers who have delayed their payments at some time. Figure 2 illustrates the customer distribution and the region of the rule, where the brightness and saturation of each pixel, respectively, represent the number of all customers and the ratio of unreliable customers. Such association rules can be used to construct accurate decision trees and regression trees [5, 17].

In general, we do not know beforehand which combinations of numeric attributes adequately characterize the target property. Therefore, we usually compute all the potential rules, sort them in order of interestingness, and then select good ones.

This mining process requires computation of the distributions of all customers and unreliable customers along any two-dimensional combinations of numeric attributes. Since we have 30 numeric attributes, the number of queries for obtaining the necessary two-dimensional data distributions is $\binom{30}{2} = 435$.

We have focused on the target property represented by the expression "Card-LoanDelay = yes". However, any conditional expression can be a target, and we may have any number of targets. The simplest form of a target condition is "attribute = value". It is natural for *data mining* to use all pairs of categorical attributes and their values as target properties, because every attribute in the database represents some property of interest. We have 100 categorical attributes, each with between two and several dozens of possible values. Therefore the potential number of target properties will range from 100 to several thousand.

Let us assume that we have 500 target properties. Since we can share the computation necessary to create common groupings, the number of queries is still $\binom{30}{2} = 435$, which is the same as when we have only one target. But the tuple size of each query result is to be multiplied so that it contains 503 fields (2 for bucket numbers, 1 for counting all customers, and 500 for counting target properties). The typical number of buckets for each numeric attribute is between 20 and 400. Thus the number of groups in a query will be $20^2 = 400$ to $400^2 = 160,000$. Remember that the original data has 130 attributes and 10^7 records. Consequently, the total result is much larger than the original database. □

As we have seen in the examples, some decision support applications require computation of a large number of aggregate queries on a relation. The results of the queries can be used as materialized views and for data mining. Since serial algorithms would take a very long time, we investigate parallel algorithms on shared-nothing parallel architectures.

In this paper, we focus on computing a given set of aggregate queries on a single relation in parallel. The source relation may be a base relation (raw data) or another previously computed aggregate table. We evaluate three parallel algorithms on the basis of both analytical and empirical studies, and present a way of choosing the best one. Unexpectedly, a broadcasting algorithm outperforms other algorithms for problems of certain sizes.

We assume that the part of the data cube to be computed and the relation from which the aggregates are to be computed have already been decided through the use of other query optimization techniques such as [14, 2]. We also assume that the aggregating functions are *distributive*[10]. Distributive functions, such as count(), min(), max(), and sum(), can be partially computed and later combined.

The rest of this paper is organized as follows. In Section 2, we introduce three conventional parallel algorithms for processing single aggregate queries. In Section 3, we extend those algorithms so that they can handle multiple aggregate queries efficiently, and describe simple analytical cost models of the algorithms. In Section 4, we compare the algorithms by using these cost models. In Section 5, we describe implementations of the algorithms and give their performance results. In Section 6, we present our conclusions and discuss future work.

2 Algorithms for Single Queries

The literature contains only a few studies of parallel aggregate processing. Two conventional parallel algorithms, *Two-Phase* and *Repartitioning*, are mainly used for computing *single* aggregate queries. These algorithms will be explained later. [3] analyzed two algorithms for aggregate processing on tightly coupled multiprocessors with a shared disk cache. One is similar to the Two-Phase algorithm,

while the other broadcasts all tuples so that each node can use the entire relation. The latter approach has been considered impractical on shared-nothing
multiprocessors [19]. Recently, however, high-bandwidth multiprocessor interconnects, such as the High-Performance Switch (HPS) [20] for the IBM SP2 [1],
and low-cost gigabit LAN adaptors for PCs, have become available, and will
soon be common. Thus we should evaluate the feasibility of the broadcasting
approach with high-performance networks using such equipment.

In this section, we describe the Two-Phase, Repartitioning, and Broadcasting
algorithms for processing single aggregate queries.

We assume that the source relation is partitioned in round-robin fashion, and
that aggregation on a node is performed by hashing. The underlying uniprocessor-
hash-based aggregation works as follows:

1. All tuples of the source relation are read, and a hash table is constructed by hashing
   on the **group-by** attributes of the tuple. Note that the memory requirement for
   the hash table is proportional to the number of groups seen.
2. When the group values do not all fit into the memory allocated for the hash table,
   the tuples that do not belong to groups in the memory are hash-partitioned into
   multiple (as many as necessary to ensure no future memory overflow) bucket files
   on disk.
3. The overflow bucket files are processed one by one in the same way as in Step 1.

Two-Phase Algorithm (2P): The Two-Phase (2P) algorithm [9] simply partitions input data. In its first phase, each node (processor) in the system computes
aggregates on its local partition of the relation. In the second phase, these partial results are collected to one of the nodes, which merges them to produce the
final results. The second phase can be parallelized by hash-partitioning on the
group-by attributes.

As explained in [3, 19], 2P has two problems when the grouping selectivity
is high. First, since a group value may be accumulated on all the nodes, the
memory requirement for each node can be as large as the overall result, which
may not fit into main memory. Second, duplication of aggregation work in the
first phase and the second phase becomes significant [19]. As we have seen in the
examples, the total size of the aggregates may be very large in DSS applications.
Thus the effectiveness of this algorithm is not clear.

Repartitioning Algorithm (Rep): The Repartitioning algorithm [19] partitions groups, and can thus work well for large numbers of groups. It redistributes
the data on the **group-by** attributes, and then performs aggregation on each partition in parallel.

This algorithm is efficient when the grouping selectivity is high, because it
eliminates duplication of work by processing each value for aggregation just once.
It also reduces the memory requirement, since each group value is stored in only
one place. However, when the grouping selectivity is so low that the number of
groups is smaller than the number of processors, this algorithm cannot use all
the processors, which severely affects the performance.

Broadcasting Algorithm (BC): The *Broadcasting* (BC) algorithm [3] broadcasts all local disk pages to all nodes. Receiving the entire source relation, each

node computes aggregations for groups assigned to it. Since each group value is stored in only one place, the memory requirement of this algorithm is the same as that of the Rep algorithm. The BC algorithm computes both groups and aggregations on receiving nodes. In contrast, the Rep algorithm computes groups of tuples on nodes where the source data are read.

When the system does not support broadcast efficiently, this algorithm is inferior to the Rep algorithm, since the amount of data passed through the network is larger than when the Rep algorithm is used.

When the number of groups is smaller than the number of nodes, the BC algorithm cannot use all the processors, for the same reason as in Rep.

3 Algorithms for Multiple Queries

Let Q be the number of queries. Obviously, by applying the algorithms for single aggregate queries sequentially Q times, we can process all of the queries. However, such trivial algorithms can be improved by using the fact that all the queries have the same source relation.

In this section, we describe three algorithms for multiple queries, m2P, mRep, and mBC, which are based on the 2P, Rep, and BC algorithms, respectively. The main idea is that by processing multiple queries simultaneously we can share common processes.

We also present simple analytical cost models, which were developed to predict the relative performance of algorithms for various execution environments and problem sizes. Similar models have been presented previously [19]. We compare the algorithms in Section 4.

For simplicity, the models include no overlaps between CPU, I/O, and message-passing operations, and all processors work completely in parallel. These assumptions allow us to compute the performance by summing up the partial I/O and CPU performance on a single node.

The parameters of the models are listed in Table 1. We assume that there are Q aggregate queries on a single relation, and that each query contains A aggregate functions. We also assume that these queries are being performed directly on a base relation stored on disks. $|R|$ is the number of tuples in the source relation, and S is the grouping selectivity, which is the ratio of the number of groups to the number of tuples of the source relation. Therefore, the number of groups $|G|$ is equal to $|R|S$. p represents the projectivity, which is the ratio of the output tuple size to the input tuple size. To model the data-mining example, we make A and p high (100 and 50%, respectively). Most parameters were measured by using Database SONAR [8], a prototype data-mining system running on a 16-node IBM SP2 [1] with a High-Performance Switch (HPS) [20]. The SP2 also has an ordinary 10 Mb/s Ethernet. Including the MPI [16] protocol overhead, the point-to-point transfer rate of the HPS is about 40 MB/s, and that of the Ethernet is about 0.8 MB/s. Note that the HPS transfer rate is much faster than the ordinary disk I/O speed (about 5 MB/s).

Symbol	Description	Value
N	Number of nodes	Variable
R	Size of relation in bytes	5 GB
$|R|$	No. of tuples in R	10 million
R_i	No. of tuples on node i	$|R|/N$
$|R_p|$	No. of repartitioned tuples	$\max(|R_i|, 1/S/Q)$
Q	No. of aggregate queries	Variable
T	No. of scans of the source data	Variable
A	No. of aggregate functions / query	100
S	Grouping selectivity of a query	Variable
S_l	Phase 1 selectivity (for 2P)	$\min(SN, 1)$
S_g	Phase 2 selectivity (for 2P)	$\min(1/N, S)$
p	Projectivity	0.5
$|G|$	No. of result tuples	$|R|S$
$|G_i|$	No. of result tuples on node i	$R_i S_l$
P	Page size	4 KB
M	Size of hash table	50 MB
mips	CPU speed	120 MIPS
IO	Time to read a page	0.8 ms
t_r	Time to read a tuple	200 / mips
t_w	Time to write a tuple	200 / mips
t_h	Time to compute hash	200 / mips
t_a	Time to compute an aggregate	40 / mips
t_m	Time to send a page	0.1 ms
t_b	Time to broadcast a page	$(N-1)t_m$

Table 1. Parameters for the cost model

3.1 Two-Phase Algorithm (m2P)

The m2P algorithm processes Q queries simultaneously. In its first phase, each node reads its local source relation, and computes aggregations of Q queries. The second phase merges the partial results in parallel. Since only a single scan of source data is necessary, the scan cost is minimum. However, the memory requirement is multiplied by Q, and 2P requires as much main memory for each node as the overall result size. Therefore memory overflow is liable to happen, necessitating extra IOs for bucket files.

If we divide Q queries into $1 \leq T \leq Q$ parts (each part consists of Q/T queries), and process each part simultaneously, the cost of scans will increase on the one hand, and the cost of extra IOs will be reduced on the other. Therefore, to achieve the best performance, we may have to control the number of scans (T) and trade off the cost of extra IOs against the cost of scans.

The cost model of this algorithm is as follows:

1. Scanning cost: $(R_i/P) * IO * T$
2. Selection cost: $|R_i| * t_r * T$
3. Local aggregation cost: $|R_i| * (t_h + t_a * A) * Q$
4. Cost of extra write/read required for the tuples not processed in the first pass: $(R_i * p * Q - M/S_l * T)/P * 2 * IO$
5. Cost of generating result tuples: $|G_i| * t_w * Q$
6. Cost of sending/receiving: $G_i/P * t_m * Q$
7. Cost of computing the final aggregates: $|G_i| * (t_r + t_a * A) * Q$

8. Cost of generating result tuples: $|G_i| * S_g * t_w * Q$
9. Cost of extra write/read required for the tuples not processed in the first pass: $(G_i * Q - M/S_g * T)/P * 2 * IO$
10. Cost of storing to local disk: $G_i * S_g/P * IO * Q$

The cost model of 2P for single queries is its special case when $Q = T = 1$.

3.2 Repartitioning Algorithm (mRep)

The mRep processes multiple queries simultaneously, using Rep for each query. It seems to be suitable for multiple queries, since multiple queries require a lot of main memory and the base algorithm (Rep) uses main memory efficiently. However, we need to make partitioning independent for each query, because each query may have a different **group-by** clause. Therefore, to process Q queries simultaneously, each node reads a tuple, computes the groups that the tuple belongs to for all Q queries, and then sends the tuple to Q (possibly different) nodes. The communication cost of the mRep algorithm for Q queries is Q times larger than that of the Rep algorithm for a single query.

The cost model of this algorithm is as follows:

1. Scanning cost: $(R_i/P) * IO * T$
2. Selection cost: $|R_i| * t_r * T$
3. Cost of hashing to find the destination and writing to communication buffer: $|R_i| * (t_h + t_w) * Q$
4. Repartitioning send/receive: $R_p/P * p * t_m * Q$
5. Aggregation cost: $|R_p| * (t_r + t_a * A) * Q$
6. The tuples not processed in the first pass need an extra write/read: $(R_p * p * Q - M/S * T)/P * 2 * IO$
7. Cost of generating result tuples: $|R_p| * S * t_w * Q$
8. Cost of storing to local disk: $R_p * S/P * p * IO * Q$

3.3 Broadcasting Algorithm (mBC)

The mBC algorithm simply processes Q queries simultaneously, using BC for each query. As we will see in the next section, for a single query the BC algorithm is slower than the others, since its network cost is very high. However, the communication cost of the mBC algorithm is the same for multiple queries as for a single query, while the other algorithms have communication costs proportional to Q. Therefore, the mBC algorithm may outperform the other algorithms when there are multiple queries.

Broadcasting is usually more expensive than simple point-to-point message passing. When the network does not efficiently support broadcasting and allows only one point-to-point communication at a time, as in the case of ordinary Ethernets, it is necessary to use serialized $N * (N - 1)$ point-to-point communications for an all-to-all broadcast. Therefore, letting t_m be a point-to-point communication cost, we assume that the broadcasting cost t_b is $N * (N - 1) * t_m$.

Some multiprocessor interconnects such as ATM switches and HPS for IBM SP2 allow multiple pairs of processors to communicate simultaneously. When this kind of network is available, an all-to-all broadcast can be performed in only $N-1$ stages of point-to-point communication. Thus, the all-to-all broadcast cost t_b is $(N-1)*t_m$. Since our test bench, an IBM SP2, has the above kind of network, we use this model of the broadcasting cost.

The following is the cost model of the broadcasting algorithm:

1. Scanning cost: $(R_i/P)*IO*T$
2. Broadcasting cost: $(R_i/P)*t_b*T$
3. Cost of getting tuples from the communication buffer: $|R|*t_r*T$
4. Hashing cost: $|R|*t_h*Q$
5. Aggregation cost: $|R_p|*t_a*A*Q$
6. Cost of extra write/read required for the tuples not processed in the first pass: $(R_p*p*Q-M/S*T)/P*2*IO$
7. Cost of generating result tuples: $|R_p|*S*t_w*Q$
8. Cost of storing to local disk: $R_p*S/P*p*IO*Q$

3.4 Number of Scans

All the algorithms have trade-offs between the scan cost and the cost of extra IOs. As we can see from the cost models, we need to know the grouping selectivities (S) of queries in order to optimize the number of scans. The grouping selectivities are also necessary for deciding a good subset of a data cube to be pre-computed (using the algorithm presented in [14]). Statistical procedures such as [13] can be used to estimate the grouping selectivities. Thus we assume in the following sections that we have an estimate of the grouping selectivity for each query.

4 Analytical Evaluation

In this section, we evaluate the performance of the algorithms from various perspectives.

Grouping Selectivity: As explained in [19], m2P and mRep are expected to be sensitive to grouping selectivity. Figure 3 shows the relationship between the number of groups per query, $|G|$ (proportional to the grouping selectivity) and the response times of these algorithms for a configuration of 16 processors with high-speed interconnects. The number of queries (Q) is 100, in this case. Surprisingly, mBC outperforms both m2P and mRep when the number of groups falls within the range $[5 \cdot 10^3, 1.5 \cdot 10^5]$. mRep wins when the selectivity is within the range $[1.5 \cdot 10^5, 3 \cdot 10^6]$. In this range of selectivity, mRep iteratively scans the source relation to avoid extra IOs, because iterative scans are cheaper than extra IOs. When the grouping selectivity is higher than $3 \cdot 10^6$, however, mBC wins again. The reason for this is as follows. The high grouping selectivity requires so many scans to avoid extra IOs that the cost of iterative scans becomes more than the cost of extra IOs. Therefore, both mRep and mBC scan the source relation only once and use necessary extra IOs. The costs of extra IOs of mRep and mBC are the same, but the communication cost of mRep for a single scan is $p*Q/(N-1)$ times larger than that of mBC, which affects the performance of mRep.

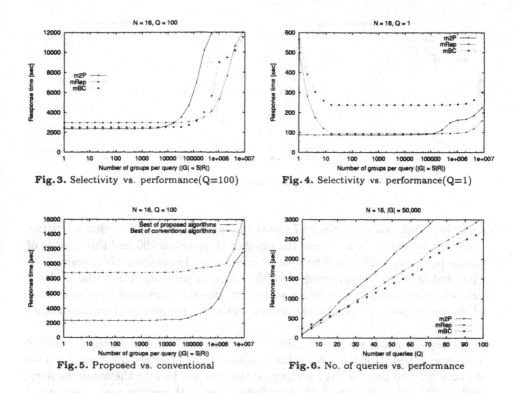

Fig. 3. Selectivity vs. performance(Q=100)

Fig. 4. Selectivity vs. performance(Q=1)

Fig. 5. Proposed vs. conventional

Fig. 6. No. of queries vs. performance

When the number of groups is small ($[1, 5 \cdot 10^3]$), m2P is a little faster than mBC. m2P has a shoulder (a point at which the response time starts to increase), indicating that the local result overflows the main memory of a single node ($|G| = |M|/Q \approx 2,000$). mBC also has a shoulder, which shows that the overall result becomes larger than the total main memory of the multiprocessor ($|G| = N|M|/Q \approx 32,000$).

The switching point of m2P and mBC is within the range of typical numbers of groups ($[400, 160,000]$) for the data mining applications explained in Example 1.2.

Figure 4 shows a case in which there is only one query. As expected, m2P works well when the selectivity is low, while mRep beats the other algorithms when the selectivity is high. mBC does not win for any selectivities.

Figure 5 compares the best performance of the proposed algorithms (m2P, mRep, and mBC) with that of the conventional algorithms (2P, Rep, and BC) when there are 100 queries. We can see that the best of the proposed algorithms is about 4 times faster than the best of the conventional algorithms for a wide range of grouping selectivities.

Number of Queries: To determine how many queries are necessary for mBC to outperform other algorithms, we examined their performance, fixing the number of groups. Figure 6 shows the relationship between the number of queries and the response times when the number of groups per query ($|G|$) is 50,000. We can see that mBC outperforms other algorithms when there are 25 or more queries.

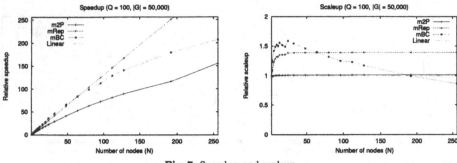

Fig. 7. Speedup and scaleup

Speedup and Scaleup: Figure 7 shows the speedup and scaleup characteristics of the algorithms in a case where the number of queries is 100 and the number of groups per query is 50, 000. The relative speedup is the response time normalized with that of a hash-based serial algorithm on a single node, where the problem size is kept constant. The relative scaleup is also the normalized response time when the number of tuples in the source relation is proportional to the number of nodes.

The speedup and scaleup of mBC are better than linear when the number of processors is less than 150. This is because the serial algorithm must employ a lot of extra I/Os to process data for groups that cannot fit into the main memory, while mBC can reduce the I/Os by effective use of the entire main memory of the system. The scaleup of mBC has a peak when the number of nodes is 24. At this point, the main memory size of the entire system is almost the same as the total size of the results, so the whole memory is fully utilized. As the number of processor increases beyond 24, the amount of memory that is not used increases and the broadcasting cost, which is proportional to the number of processors, overshadows the benefit gained.

The speedup and scaleup of mRep are superlinear and stable, because mRep uses main memory efficiently, and its communication cost is independent of the number of processors. m2P has a linear scaleup. The speedup of m2P decreases as the number of processors increases, because the partial result size ($|G_i|$) remains constant, and hence the computation cost of the second phase affects the speedup performance.

Note that the speedup and scaleup performance are very sensitive to the problem size (Q and G). When the problem is small, m2P scales well, while mRep and mBC do not.

Switching Points: Figure 8 shows how the best algorithm for a 16-node system depends on the problem size — the number of queries (Q) and the number of groups per query ($|G|$). The switching points of m2P and mBC lie on a line parallel to the dotted line labeled "$|M| = Q|G|$", on which the entire result size is equal to the main memory size of a single node.

From this analytical evaluation, we can conclude that none of the algorithms

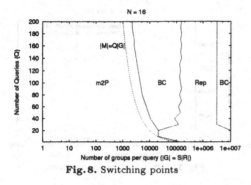

Fig. 8. Switching points

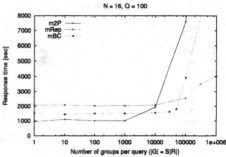

Fig. 9. Selectivity vs. performance(Q=100)

gives a satisfactory performance for the entire range of problem sizes, and that it is necessary to choose whichever of them is best according to the overall result size and the available memory size. The mBC algorithm for multiple queries may be practical when high-speed networks are available, and if the result size is larger than the main memory size of a single node.

5 Empirical Evaluation

The cost models that we used in Section 4 are very simple; they do not include several factors, such as network contentions and overlaps of I/O and CPU, which may strongly affect the performance. It was therefore necessary to validate our analytical conclusions by conducting experiments on a real system.

We implemented m2P, mRep, and mBC in Database SONAR [8] using standard MPI communication primitives [16]. Conformity with the standard makes the implementations portable to any parallel architectures, including workstation clusters.

All experiments were performed on a 16-node IBM SP2 Model 9076-304. Each node in the system has a 66-MHz POWER2 processor, 256 MB of real memory, a 2-MB L2 cache, and a SCSI-2W 4-GB HDD. The processors all run under the AIX 4.1 operating system and communicate with each other through the High-Performance Switch [20] with HPS adaptors. We assigned 50 MB of main memory for hash tables on each node. We randomly generated 10 million 500-byte tuples of test data with 130 attributes, and divided the data evenly among all the nodes of the system. Thus each node had about 298 MB of a relation. Since the prototype system is not a real database system and has no concurrency control, the implementations are more CPU-efficient than complete database systems. The response times shown below are the averages for several runs.

Grouping Selectivity Figure 9 shows the relationship between the number of groups and the response times of the implementations for 100 aggregate queries. We can see almost the same characteristics as in Figure 3. The mBC algorithm actually outperforms m2P and mRep when the number of groups per query falls

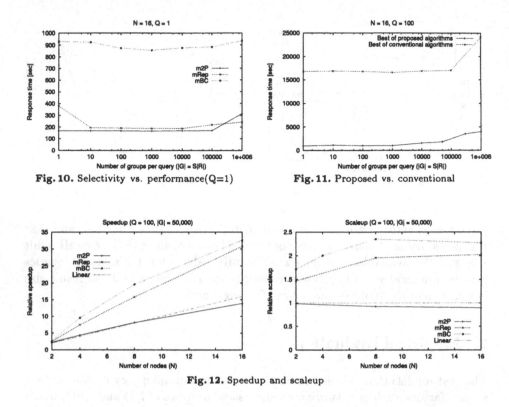

Fig. 10. Selectivity vs. performance(Q=1)

Fig. 11. Proposed vs. conventional

Fig. 12. Speedup and scaleup

within the range $[2 \cdot 10^3, 10^5]$. The measured response times are comparable with the response times predicted by the analytical models.

Figure 10 shows that mBC does not win for any number of groups per query when there is only one query. m2P and mRep work well when the grouping selectivity is low and high, respectively. mBC does not work well for single aggregate queries.

Figure 11 compares the best performance of the proposed algorithms (m2P, mRep, and mBC) with that of the conventional algorithms (2P, Rep and BC), when there are 100 queries. We can see that the best of the proposed algorithms is about 16 times faster than the best of the conventional algorithms for a wide range of grouping selectivities.

Speedup and Scaleup Since we have only a 16-node system, we could not measure the performance of a configuration with more than 16 nodes. Figure 12 shows the speedup and scaleup performance when there are 100 queries and the number of groups per query is 50, 000. Observe that the speedup and scaleup of mRep and mBC are better than linear, and that those of m2P are almost linear, as explained in Section 4. The measured speedup and scaleup performance of mBC decline a little earlier than the analytical cost model predicts. The reason for this is as follows. We used an MPI broadcast primitive in the implementation, which uses $\lceil \log N \rceil$ stages of communications. Each node of the system broadcasts, and only one broadcast can be performed at a time. Thus the necessary number of communication stages is $N\lceil \log N \rceil$, which is more than estimated by the cost model. As mentioned in Section 4, the cost can be reduced to $N - 1$ stages by using point-to-point communication primitives. It is therefore possible to have an implementation that gives a better performance.

6 Conclusion

We have presented three parallel algorithms — Two-Phase (m2P), Repartitioning (mRep), and Broadcasting (mBC) — for multiple aggregate queries, and compared them by using analytical cost models and conducting experiments on a real system.

Although the Broadcasting algorithm has been considered impractical for today's shared-nothing parallel architectures, we proved that it works well for multiple aggregate queries when high-speed networks are available and if the total result is larger than the main memory of a single node. Recently, high-performance networks have become a kind of commodity. It is thus now practical to use the Broadcasting algorithm for processing multiple aggregate queries on shared-nothing multiprocessors.

Since none of the existing algorithms gives a satisfactory performance for the entire range of problem sizes, it is necessary to choose whichever of them is best according to the overall result size and the available memory size. Switching points for the algorithms can be decided by using analytical cost models.

Future Work In this paper, we have ignored the relations among multiple queries and treated them as independent. But actual queries in DSS applications are often interrelated, and thus several optimization techniques can be applied, as explained in [2] for serial processors. We are investigating possible optimizations for parallel processors.

References

1. Tilak Agerwala, Joanne L. Martin, Jamshed H. Mirza, David C. Sadler, Daniel M. Dias, and Marc Snir. SP2 system architecture. *IBM Systems Journal*, 34(2):152–184, 95.
2. Sameet Agrawal, Rakesh Agrawal, Prasad M. Deshpande, Ashish Gupta, Jeffrey F. Naughton, Raghu Ramakrishnan, and Sunita Sarawagi. On the computation of multidimensional aggregates. In *Proceedings of the 22nd VLDB Conference*, September 1996.
3. Dina Bitton, Haran Boral, David J. DeWitt, and W. Kevin Wilkinson. Parallel algorithms for the excecution of relational database operations. *ACM Trans. on Database Systems*, 8(3):324–353, September 1983.
4. E. F. Codd, S. B. Codd, and C. T. Salley. Beyond decision support. *Computerworld*, 27(30), July 1993.
5. Takeshi Fukuda, Yasuhiko Morimoto, Shinichi Morishita, and Takeshi Tokuyama. Constructing efficient decision trees by using optimized association rules. In *Proceedings of the 22nd VLDB Conference*, pages 146–155, 1996.

6. Takeshi Fukuda, Yasuhiko Morimoto, Shinichi Morishita, and Takeshi Tokuyama. Data mining using two-dimensional optimized association rules: Scheme, algorithms, and visualization. In *Proceedings of the ACM SIGMOD Conference on Management of Data*, pages 13–23, June 1996.

7. Takeshi Fukuda, Yasuhiko Morimoto, Shinichi Morishita, and Takeshi Tokuyama. Mining optimized association rules for numeric attributes. In *Proceedings of the Fifteenth ACM SIGACT-SIGMOD-SIGART Symposium on Principles of Database Systems*, pages 182–191, June 1996.

8. Takeshi Fukuda, Yasuhiko Morimoto, Shinichi Morishita, and Takeshi Tokuyama. Sonar: System for optimized numeric association rules. In *Proceedings of the ACM SIGMOD Conference on Management of Data*, page 553, June 1996.

9. Goetz Graefe. Query evaluation techniques for large databases. *ACM Computing Surveys*, 25(2):73–170, June 1993.

10. Jim Gray, Adam Bosworth, Andrew Layman, and Hamid Pirahesh. Data cube: A relational aggregation operator generalizing group-by, cross-tab, and sub-totals. Technical report, Microsoft, November 1995.

11. Ashish Gupta, Venky Harinarayan, and Dallan Quass. Aggregate-query processing in data warehousing environments. In *Proceedings of the 21st VLDB Conference*, pages 358–369, 1995.

12. Himanshu Gupta, Venky Harinarayan, Anand Rajaraman, and Jeffrey D. Ullman. Index selection for OLAP. Working Paper, 1996.

13. Peter J. Haas, Jeffrey F. Naughton, S. Seshadri, and Lynne Stokes. Sampling-based estimation of the number of distinct values of an attribute. In *Proceedings of the 21st VLDB Conference*, pages 311–322, 1995.

14. Venky Harinarayan, Anand Rajaraman, and Jeffrey D. Ullman. Implementing data cubes efficiently. In *Proceedings of the ACM SIGMOD Conference on Management of Data*, pages 205–216, June 1996.

15. Theodore Johnson and Dennis Shasha. Hierarchically split cube forests for decision support: description and tuned design. Working Paper, 1996.

16. Message Passing Interface Forum. *MPI: A Message-Passing Interface Standard*, May 1994.

17. Yasuhiko Morimoto, Hiromu Ishii, and Shinichi Morishita. Efficient construction of regression trees with range and region splitting. In *Proceedings of the 23rd VLDB Conference*, pages 166–175, August 1997.

18. Sunita Sarawagi, Rakesh Agrawal, and Ashish Gupta. On computing the data cube. Technical Report RJ10026, IBM Almaden Research Center, 1996.

19. Ambuj Shatdal and Jeffrey F. Naughton. Adaptive parallel aggregation algorithms. In *Proceedings of the ACM SIGMOD Conference on Management of Data*, pages 104–114, May 1995.

20. Cralg B. Stunkel, Dennis G. Shea, Bülent Abali, Mark G. Atkins, Carl A. Bender, Don G. Grice, Peter Hochschild, Doug J. Joseph, Ben J. Nathanson, Richard A. Swetz, Robert F. Stucke, Mickey Tsao, and Philip R. Varker. The SP2 high-performance switch. *IBM Systems Journal*, 34(2):185–204, 95.

21. Kunikazu Yoda, Takeshi Fukuda, Yasuhiko Morimoto, Shinichi Morishita, and Takeshi Tokuyama. Computing optimized rectilinear regions for association rules. In *Proceedings, Third International Conference on Knowledge Discovery and Data Mining*, pages 96–103, August 1997.

Minimizing Detail Data in Data Warehouses

M. O. Akinde, O. G. Jensen, and M. H. Böhlen *

Department of Computer Science, Aalborg University,
Frederik Bajers Vej 7E, DK–9220 Aalborg Øst, Denmark,
e-mail: <strategy | guttorm | boehlen>@cs.auc.dk

Abstract. Data warehouses collect and maintain large amounts of data from several distributed and heterogeneous data sources. Because of security reasons, operational requirements, and technical feasibility it is often impossible for data warehouses to access the data sources directly. Instead data warehouses have to replicate legacy information as detail data in order to be able to maintain their summary data.

In this paper we investigate how to minimize the amount of detail data stored in a data warehouse. More specifically, we identify the minimal amount of data that has to be replicated in order to maintain, either incrementally or by recomputation, summary data defined in terms of *generalized project-select-join* (GPSJ) views. We show how to minimize the number of tuples and attributes in the current detail tables and even aggregate them where possible. The amount of data to be stored in current detail tables is minimized by exploiting smart duplicate compression in addition to local and join reductions. We identify situations where it becomes possible to omit the typically huge fact table and prove that these techniques in concert ensure that the current detail data is minimal in the sense that no subset of it permits to accurately maintain the same summary data. Finally, we sketch how existing maintenance methods can be adapted to use the minimal detail tables we propose.

1 Introduction

A data warehouse materializes summarized data in order to provide fast access to data integrated from several distributed and heterogeneous data sources [10]. At an abstract level, summarized data can be considered as materialized views over base tables in the data sources. Particularly important are materialized views that involve aggregation because data warehouse clients often, if not always, require summarized data [12, 15].

When source data is modified, summarized data must be updated eventually to reflect the changes. This is accomplished either by recomputing summary data or by incrementally maintaining it. While incrementally maintaining summary data is substantially cheaper than recomputing it this is not always possible [6, 13]. In addition to the performance penalty recomputation imposes, data

---

* This research was supported in part by the Danish Technical Research Council through grant 9700780 and Nykredit, Inc.

warehouses have to face a potentially worse problem. It is hardly ever possible to directly access the data sources and thus the base tables needed to recompute summary data. In other words, recomputation might not even be feasible because of the lack of base data. The typical solution is to maintain detail data in data warehouses, which accounts for or at least aggravates the storage problems of data warehouses [11, 12].

Figure 1 illustrates the structure of a data warehouse and its interaction with the operational data store [10]. We assume that the current detail data mirrors the (current) data of the data sources. Summarized data aggregates current (and old) detail data in terms of GPSJ views. GPSJ views are project-select-join views extended with aggregation and grouping. They represent the single most important class of SQL statements used in data warehousing [12, p.14].

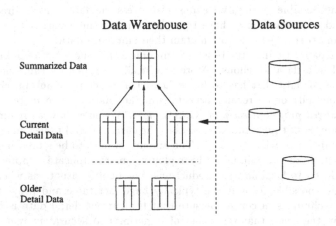

Fig. 1. The Basic Data Warehouse Framework

This paper addresses the problem of minimizing the amount of current detail data such that the summarized data (materialized GPSJ views) is still accurately maintainable. The set of current detail tables is minimal in the sense that only tables needed for maintaining the summarized data are included and no extraneous tuples or attributes are included in these tables; i.e. the summarized data and the set of minimal detail data is self-maintainable.

Given a GPSJ view, we apply local and join reductions to derive the minimal set of detail data that is sufficient to maintain the view. We show how smart duplicate compression has to be exploited to minimize the amount of detail data. More precisely, we compress duplicates by aggregating the current detail data, while making sure they keep being sufficient to maintain the summary table. For star schemas this technique results in enormous storage space savings as illustrated below.

Each base table referenced in a materialized GPSJ view is associated with an auxiliary view. However, sometimes an auxiliary view is not needed to maintain the materialized view, and thus does not need to be stored in the data warehouse.

We give the conditions for eliminating an auxiliary view, and as a side-effect show how key constraints and group-by attributes can be utilized to reduce the cost of incremental maintenance of the summary data.

1.1 Motivating Example

As a running example, we consider a data warehouse of retail sales for a grocery chain. The sales data is stored in the `sale` fact table with the schema

```
sale(ID, timeID, productID, storeID, price).
```

The warehouse also stores the following three dimension tables, which contain information about dates, products, and stores, respectively.

```
time(ID, day, month, year)
product(ID, brand, category)
store(ID, street_address, city, country, manager)
```

We assume referential integrity constraints from (1) `sale.productID` to `product.ID`, (2) from `sale.timeID` to `time.ID`, and (3) from `sale.storeID` to `store.ID`. As an example of a GPSJ view consider the following query, which, for each month, retrieves the total number of products sold by the grocery chain along with the total price of these sales and the number of different brands sold.

```
CREATE VIEW product_sales AS
SELECT time.month, SUM(price) AS TotalPrice, COUNT(*) AS TotalCount,
       COUNT(DISTINCT brand) AS DifferentBrands
FROM sale, time, product
WHERE time.year = 1997 AND
      sale.timeID = time.ID AND
      sale.productID = product.ID
GROUP BY time.month
```

The current detail data necessary to maintain the `product_sales` view consists of three auxiliary views.

```
CREATE VIEW timeDTL AS          CREATE VIEW productDTL AS
SELECT ID, month                SELECT ID, brand
FROM time                       FROM product
WHERE year = 1997
```

```
CREATE VIEW saleDTL AS
SELECT timeID, productID, SUM(price) AS SalePrice,
       COUNT(*) AS SaleCount
FROM sale
WHERE timeID IN (SELECT ID FROM timeDTL) AND
      productID IN (SELECT ID FROM productDTL)
GROUP BY timeID, productID
```

The product_sales view can now be reconstructed from these three auxiliary views without ever accessing the original fact and dimension tables.

```
CREATE VIEW product_sales AS
SELECT timeDTL.month, SUM(saleDTL.SalePrice) AS TotalPrice,
       SUM(SaleCount) AS TotalCount,
       COUNT(DISTINCT productDTL.brand) AS DifferentBrands
FROM saleDTL, timeDTL, productDTL
WHERE saleDTL.timeID = timeDTL.ID AND
      saleDTL.productID = productDTL.ID
GROUP BY timeDTL.month
```

In order to illustrate the savings in terms of storage space we compare the size of auxiliary views to the size of the original fact and dimension tables. Consider the following numbers based on real-life case studies of data warehouses [12, p.46-47,62]. We only give the numbers for the fact table because the size of dimension tables is insignificant in comparison to the fact table.

```
Time dimension: 2 years × 365 days = 730 days.
Store dimension: 300 stores, reporting sales each day.
Product dimension: 30,000 products in each store, 3,000 sell each
       day in a given store.
Transactions per product: 20

Number of tuples in fact table: 730 × 300 × 3000 × 20
       = 13,140,000,000
Fact table size: 13,140,000,000 × 5 fields × 4 bytes = 245 GBytes
```

The product_sales view only retrieves products from 1997, so the time dimension is halved assuming an even distribution of product sales over the two years. Further, the store dimension can be ignored, as it is not referenced in the view. If all 30,000 different products in the grocery chain are sold each day, which is the worst case for smart duplicate compression, then the auxiliary view saleDTL has the following size.

```
Number of tuples in the auxiliary view: 365 × 30000 = 10,950,000
Auxiliary view size: 10,950,000 × 4 fields × 4 bytes = 167 MBytes
```

In other words, in order to maintain the product_sales summary table we can reduce the size of the fact table a data warehouse has to maintain from 245 GBytes to 167 MBytes.

1.2   Related Work

Many incremental view maintenance algorithms have been developed, but most of them have been developed for traditional, centralized database environments where the view maintenance system is assumed to have full control and access to the database [3, 6–8, 15]. Segev et al. [16–18] study materialized views in distributed systems. However, they only consider views over a single base table.

Maintenance algorithms for views with aggregation have received little attention only [6, 7, 15]. A recent paper [13] proposes a method for efficiently maintaining materialized views with aggregation and how to maintain a large set of summary tables defined over the same base tables. Common to all these approaches is the fact that, in the general case, they have to resort to recomputations and queries involving base tables. These may not always be accessible, as with the case of legacy systems or highly secure data. In addition, [13] requires the presence of referential integrity constraints between base tables.

It is possible to avoid recomputation by making views self-maintainable [2, 5]. Determining the minimum amount of extra information required to make a given view self-maintainable is an open research problem [19]. Hull and Zhou [9] make views self-maintainable by pushing down projections and selections to the base tables and storing these at the data warehouse. Quass et al. [14] present an algorithm for making views self-maintainable using key and referential integrity constraints. However, their algorithm is limited to handling *project-select-join* (PSJ) views; that is, views consisting of a projection followed by a selection followed by a cross-product over a set of base tables.

In this paper, we extend the framework in [14] to handle *generalized project-select-join* (GPSJ) views, that is, views consisting of a generalized projection, i.e., a projection enhanced with aggregation and grouping, followed by a selection followed by a cross-product over a set of base tables. We consider all the SQL aggregates, as well as the use of the DISTINCT keyword. In addition to the use of key and referential integrity constraints, we show how the duplicate-eliminating property of generalized projection and group-by attributes can be exploited to minimize the amount of data stored in the data warehouse.

1.3 Paper Outline

The paper proceeds as follows. Section 2 presents notation and assumptions along with a brief explanation of the basic framework for deriving auxiliary views. Section 3 presents an algorithm for deriving a set of auxiliary views that is sufficient to maintain GPSJ views. Conclusions are given in Section 4.

2 Preliminaries

In Section 2.1 we present the notation used in this paper along with some basic assumptions. Section 2.2 introduces the framework for deriving auxiliary views.

2.1 Notation and Assumptions

We denote the *materialized GPSJ view* by V, its set of *auxiliary views* by $\mathcal{X}$, and the set of *base tables* referenced in V by $\mathcal{R} = \{R_1, R_2, \ldots, R_n\}$. We assume that no base table contains null values. For simplicity, we also assume that each base table R_i contains a single attribute key.

We use the *generalized projection* operator, Π_A, to represent aggregation [4]. Generalized projection is an extension of duplicate-eliminating projection, where the schema A can include both aggregates and regular attributes. For simplicity, all aggregates are assumed to be on single attributes. An *aggregate* $f(a_i)$ denotes the application of f to the attribute a_i, where $f \in \{\text{MIN}, \text{MAX}, \text{COUNT}, \text{SUM}, \text{AVG}\}$. An expression list is a list of attributes and/or aggregates. Regular attributes in A become *group-by attributes* for the aggregates and are denoted $GB(A)$. We say that that an attribute is *preserved* in V if it appears in A, either as a regular attribute or in an aggregate.

GPSJ views are relational algebra expressions of the form $V = \Pi_A \sigma_S (R_1 \bowtie_{C_1} R_2 \bowtie_{C_2} \ldots \bowtie_{C_{n-1}} R_n)$ where A is the schema of V, S is the set of conjunctive selection conditions on $\mathcal{R}$, and C_1 to C_{n-1} are join conditions. C_i is the join condition $R_i.b = R_j.a$, where a is a key of R_j. While we limit ourselves to views joining on keys in this paper, our techniques can be extented to a broader class of GPSJ views.

We assume insertions, deletions and updates of base tables. We say that a base table R_i has *exposed updates* if updates can change values of attributes involved in selection or join conditions. Exposed updates are propagated as deletions followed by insertions. We assume that no superfluous aggregates [1] are used in the view.

2.2 Framework for Deriving Auxiliary Views

Given a view V defined over a set of base tables $\mathcal{R}$ we want to derive a set of auxiliary views $\mathcal{X}$ such that $\{V\} \cup \mathcal{X}$ is self-maintainable (i.e., can be maintained upon changes to $\mathcal{R}$ without requiring access to the base tables). The set of base tables $\mathcal{R}$ constitutes one such set of auxiliary views. It is possible to reduce the size of this set of auxiliary views using *local* and *join reductions* on $\mathcal{R}$.

Local Reductions. Local reductions result from pushing down projections and local conditions (i.e., selection conditions involving attributes from a single table as opposed to those involving attributes from different tables, which are called join conditions) to each base table $R_i \in \mathcal{R}$ [9, 14].

Projections for GPSJ views store only those attributes of R_i which are preserved in V or are involved in join conditions. Note that, unlike for PSJ views, we do not explicitly require the storage of keys in order to maintain the auxiliary views.

We refer to the use of projections and local conditions to reduce the number of attributes and tuples in an auxiliary view as local reductions.

Join Reductions. Join reductions result from exploiting key and referential integrity constraints [14]. Consider a join $R_i \bowtie_{R_i.b = R_j.a} R_j$, where $R_j.a$ is the

---

[1] An aggregate function $f(a_i)$ is superfluous, if it can be replaced by a_i without changing the semantics of the statement.

key of R_j and there is a referential integrity constraint from $R_i.b$ to $R_j.a$. This means that each tuple in R_i joins with exactly one tuple in R_j, and that there is no tuple in R_i not joinable with a tuple in R_j. As a result insertions to R_j can never join with already existing tuples in R_i.

We say that R_i *depends* on R_j if V contains a join condition $R_i.b = R_j.a$, where a is a key of R_j, referential integrity exists between R_i and R_j, and R_j does not have exposed updates [14]. Join reductions limit the number of tuples in the auxiliary view X_{R_i} to those that can join with tuples in other auxiliary views of $\mathcal{X}$. More precisely, if R_i depends on R_j we perform a semijoin, i.e., a join reduction, of X_{R_j} on R_i.

Recollect that exposed updates change the values of attributes involved in local or join conditions. If we attempted the join reduction $X_{R_i} = R_i \ltimes X_{R_j}$ in the presence of exposed updates on R_j, then it would be possible for an updated tuple in R_j to join with an existing tuple in R_i, where the old value did not pass local selection conditions and hence was not in X_{R_j}.

3 Deriving Auxiliary Views

In this section we present an algorithm that, given a GPSJ view V, derives a set of self-maintainable auxiliary views sufficient to maintain V. In Section 3.1 we examine how different types of aggregates in a GPSJ view can influence the amount of auxiliary data needed to maintain the view, and we define the concept of a completely self-maintainable aggregate set. Section 3.2 describes how auxiliary views are minimized, and explains how duplicate compression can be used to further reduce auxiliary views. In Section 3.3 we present the conditions for omitting an auxiliary view. The algorithm for deriving auxiliary views is found in Section 3.4.

3.1 Classification of Aggregates

Aggregates can be divided into two classes depending on whether or not they are *self-maintainable*. An aggregate $f(a_i)$, where a_i is an attribute of the base table R_i, is self-maintainable, if $f(a_i)$ can be incrementally maintained upon changes to R_i. If $f(a_i)$ is not incrementally maintainable, then it must be recomputed from the base table upon changes to R_i, and, consequently, an auxiliary view for R_i is required. Thus, $f(a_i)$ is said to be a *self-maintainable aggregate* (SMA), if the new value of $f(a_i)$ can be computed solely from the old value of the aggregate and from the change to the base table R_i. Furthermore, a *self-maintainable aggregate set* (SMAS) is a set of aggregates, where the new values of the aggregates can be computed solely from the old values of the aggregates and from the changes to the base tables. The five SQL aggregates are categorized in Table 3.1 [13].

Aggregates, which are SMASs with respect to both insertions and deletions do not require auxiliary data to be maintained upon any change to their respective base tables. Therefore we define a *completely self-maintainable aggregate set* (CSMAS) as:

Table 1. Classification of SQL aggregates. An aggregate can be a SMA (or SMAS) with respect to insertion($\triangle$) and deletion(∇) respectively

Aggregate	SMA	SMAS
COUNT	$\triangle/\nabla$	$\triangle/\nabla$
SUM	$\triangle$	$\triangle/\nabla$, if COUNT is included
AVG	Not a SMA	$\triangle/\nabla$, if COUNT and SUM are included
MAX/MIN	$\triangle$	$\triangle$

Definition 1 (Completely self-maintainable aggregate set). *A set of aggregates is completely self-maintainable if the new values of the aggregates can be computed solely from the old values of the aggregates and from the changes to the base tables in response to both insertions and deletions.*

Table 2 categorizes each of the five SQL aggregates as either CSMASs or non-CSMASs. Note that if the DISTINCT keyword is used, then the aggregate is always a non-CSMAS and is not replaced. This is so because an aggregate must be distributive[2] or be replaceable by distributive aggregates in order to be self-maintainable, and the DISTINCT keyword makes an aggregate non-distributive.

Table 2. Classification of SQL aggregates

Aggregate	Replaced By	Class
COUNT	COUNT(*)	CSMAS
SUM	SUM, COUNT(*)	CSMAS
AVG	SUM, COUNT(*)	CSMAS
MAX/MIN	Not replaced	non-CSMAS

Henceforth we assume that aggregates appearing in view definitions are replaced according to Table 2. Note that because null-values are not considered any COUNT can be replaced by a COUNT(*).

3.2 Minimizing Auxiliary Views

The algorithm presented in Section 3.4 derives a set of auxiliary views $\mathcal{X}$, where each auxiliary view $X_{R_i} \in \mathcal{X}$ is an expression on the following form:

---

[2] Distributive aggregates can be computed by partitioning their input into disjoint sets, aggregating each set individually, and then further aggregating the result from each set into the final result. The SQL aggregates, COUNT, SUM, MIN, and MAX, are distributive.

$$X_{R_i} = (\Pi_{A_{R_i}} \sigma_S R_i) \ltimes_{C_1} X_{R_{j1}} \ltimes_{C_2} X_{R_{j2}} \ltimes \ldots \ltimes_{C_n} X_{R_{jn}}, \text{where}$$

> A_{R_i} is the expression list defined over the set of attributes in R_i preserved in V or involved in join conditions after applying smart duplicate compression.
>
> S is the local condition on R_i.
>
> $R_{j1}, R_{j2}, \ldots, R_{jn}$ is the set of tables R_i depends on.
>
> C_{j_k} is the join condition $R_i.b = R_{j_k}.a$, where a is the key of R_{j_k} referenced by $R_i.b$.

Each auxiliary view X_{R_i} is a selection and a generalized projection on a base table R_i followed by zero or more semi-joins with other auxiliary views. Local and join reductions are applied as discussed in Section 2.2.

Smart Duplicate Compression. Smart duplicate compression exploits the duplicate-eliminating property of the generalized projection to minimize auxiliary views while ensuring that they are still self-maintainable.

Consider an auxiliary view `sale'` for the `sale` fact table that is required by the `product_sales` view defined in Section 1.1. Assume the `sale'` auxiliary view is a result of local reductions and generalized projection. As duplicate elimination occurs, we are unable to determine the number of tuples in each group, which means that the `product_sales` view can not be maintained. Therefore we include a `COUNT(*)` in the auxiliary view. This results in the `sale'` auxiliary view becoming self-maintainable, as `COUNT(*)` is a CSMAS. Table 3 shows an example instance of the `sale'` auxiliary view.

Table 3. An example instance of the `sale'` auxiliary view after adding `COUNT(*)`

timeID	productID	price	COUNT(*)
1	1	20	15
1	2	40	9
1	2	50	2
2	1	15	5
2	1	25	8

The `product_sales` view retrieves the total sales price, `SUM(sale.price)`. SUM is a CSMAS, and all CSMASs can be replaced by a set of distributive aggregates. Distributive aggregates can be computed by partitioning their input into disjoint sets, aggregating each set individually, and then further aggregating the result from each set into the final result. This means that we can aggregate the `sale'` auxiliary view and still maintain the `product_sales` view. Table 4 shows an instance of the **sale′** auxiliary view after local reductions and smart duplicate compression.

Table 4. The **sale′** auxiliary view after smart duplicate compression

timeID	productID	SUM(price)	COUNT(*)
1	1	300	15
1	2	460	11
2	1	275	13

We formalize smart duplicate compression on an auxiliary view X_{R_i} with the schema $A_{X_{R_i}}$ after local reductions in the following steps.

Algorithm 3.1 Smart duplicate compression for auxiliary views.

1. Include a COUNT(*) in X_{R_i} unless this is superfluous.
2. For each attribute $a_i \in A_{X_{R_i}}$
   If a_i is not used in non-CSMASs, join conditions, or group-by clauses,
   Then replace all CSMASs over a_i by the appropriate set of aggregates in Table 2.

Note that if an aggregate is superfluous, there is no need to replace the attribute with it. An example of this occurs when an auxiliary view includes the key of its base table, and results in the auxiliary view degenerating into a PSJ view.

Maintainance Issues under Duplicate Compression. The theory of deriving maintenance expressions for GPSJ views in general is beyond the scope of this paper and the interested reader is referred to [15] instead. However, the presence of compressed duplicates requires changes to the maintenance of the views which we discuss below. If aggregates are not limited to the root table[3] or if non-CSMASs are present in the view, it may become necessary to compute the values of an aggregate from tuples in the auxiliary views.

Recall that CSMASs can be computed by partitioning their inputs into disjoint sets. This means that the value of a CSMASs can be computed from aggregated values in the auxiliary view. Thus we compute a COUNT(*) in V by summing up the counts in the auxiliary view of the root table. Similarly, a SUM can be recomputed by adding the appropriate aggregates in the auxiliary view.

However, when computing a CSMAS from an attribute in the auxiliary view (as may happen if an attribute of a base table is involved in both a CSMAS and

---

[3] The root table is the base table at the root of the extended join graph (see Section 3.3). In a star schema, this would be the fact table.

a non-CSMAS or the attribute is involved in a CSMAS not on the root table), it becomes necessary to use the COUNT(*) on the root table (referred to as cnt_0) to account for duplicates. Thus, for any aggregate $f(a)$ in A, where a is an attribute in R_i which is not maintained by an aggregate in $\mathcal{X}$, we compute the value of f as $f(a * cnt_0)$.

Assume that we define a view product_sales_max as follows:

```
CREATE VIEW product_sales_max AS
SELECT sale.productID, MAX(sale.price) AS MaxPrice, SUM(sale.price)
       AS TotalPrice, COUNT(*) AS TotalCount,
FROM sale
GROUP BY sale.productID
```

The auxiliary view for product_sales_max would then be:

```
CREATE VIEW saleDTL AS
SELECT productID, price, COUNT(*) AS SaleCount
FROM sale
GROUP BY productID
```

To recompute the value of SUM(sales.price) from saleDTL, one could then create the following view:

```
CREATE VIEW product_sales_max AS
SELECT productID, MAX(price) AS MaxPrice, SUM(price*SaleCount) AS
       TotalPrice, SUM(SaleCount) AS TotalCount,
FROM saleDTL
GROUP BY productID
```

Note that this approach only holds true for CSMASs. MAX and MIN and aggregates using the DISTINCT keyword already ignore duplicates and can be recomputed directly from the auxiliary views.

3.3 Eliminating an Auxiliary View

Under certain circumstances an auxiliary view X_{R_i} for a base table R_i is not required for propagating insertions, deletions, and updates to the materialized GPSJ view V or the other auxiliary views. When this happens, it becomes unnecessary to materialize the auxiliary view for that base table.

For PSJ views it is sufficient that R_i transitively depends on all other base tables in $\mathcal{R}$, and that it is not in the *Need* set of any other base table $R_j \in \mathcal{R}$ for X_{R_i} to be eliminated [14]. Informally, the *Need* set of a base table R_i is the minimal set of base tables with which R_i must join, so that the unique set of tuples in V associated with any given tuple in R_i can be identified. In general, if R_j is in the *Need* set of R_i, then X_{R_j} is required to propagate the effect of deletions and protected updates to R_i on V.

Due to the presence of aggregates in GPSJ views, we must also require that attributes in R_i are not involved in non-CSMASs. By definition non-CSMASs cannot be incrementally maintained for both insertions and deletions. As a result, it may sometimes be necessary to recompute the values of the aggregates from the auxiliary views, thereby preventing the elimination.

Join graphs are used to define the *Need* functions associated with PSJ views [14]. Due to the complexities added by generalized projection, we extend this concept and define the *extended join graph G(V)*.

Definition 2 (Extended Join Graph). *Given a GPSJ view V, the extended join graph G(V) is a directed graph $\langle \mathcal{R}, \varepsilon \rangle$ where $\mathcal{R}$ is the set of base tables referenced in V and forms the vertices of the graph. There exists a directed edge $e(R_i, R_j) \in \varepsilon$ from R_i to R_j if V contains a join condition $R_i.b = R_j.a$ and a is a key of R_j. A vertex $R_i \in \mathcal{R}$ is annotated with g, if R_i contains attributes involved in group-by clauses in V. If one of the attributes is a key of R_i, it is annotated with k instead.*

For the purpose of this paper, we assume that the graph is a tree (i.e., there is at most one edge leading into any vertex and no cycles), and that it has no self-joins. As both star schemas and snowflake structures have tree graphs, this assumption still allows us to handle a broad class of views occurring in practice. The base table at the root of the tree is referred to as the *root table*, R_0. Figure 2 shows the extended join graph for the product_sales view.

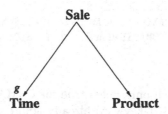

Fig. 2. The extended join graph for the product_sales view

The following definition is used to determine the *Need* set of a base table R_i. Unlike for PSJ views [14], we are not required to join with all other base tables, if the key of R_i is not preserved in V. Instead we use the $Need_0$ function to find a set of group-by attributes that forms a combined key to V.

Definition 3.

$$Need(R_i, G(V)) = \begin{cases} \emptyset & \text{if } R_i \text{ is a vertex annotated with } k, \\ \{R_j\} \cup Need(R_j, G(V)) & \text{if } R_i \text{ is not a vertex annotated with } k \\ & \text{and there exists an } R_j \text{ such that} \\ & e(R_j, R_i) \in G(V) \text{ and } i \neq 0, \\ Need_0(R_0, G(V)) & \text{otherwise.} \end{cases}$$

$Need_0(R_0, G(V))$ performs a depth-first traversal of the extended join graph, in order to find the minimal set of base tables, whose group-by attributes form a combined key to V. If none of the keys of the base tables are preserved in V, then $Need_0(R_0, G(V))$ includes all base tables, but R_0, containing attributes involved in group-by clauses in V, annotated R_g, and the base tables between the root table and R_g in the extended join graph. As we require all group-by attributes to be projected in the view, these always form a combined key to the view. However, if a key of a base table R_i is preserved in V, then it is not necessary to include the base tables appearing in the subtree of R_i in $Need_0(R_0, G(V))$. The reason is that each tuple in R_i joins with exactly one tuple in each of the base tables in the subtree of R_i. This means that when we group on the key of R_i, any group-bys on attributes of base tables in the subtree of R_i can not increase the total number of groups in V, and therefore are not needed in the combined key to the view. $Need_0(R_i, G(V))$ is defined as follows:

Definition 4.

$$
Need_0(R_i, G(V)) = \begin{cases} \bigcup_{R_j \in G(V)} \{R_j\} \cup Need_0(R_j, G(V)) \\ \quad \text{if there exists an edge } e(R_i, R_j) \text{ and } R_i \text{ is not} \\ \quad \text{vertex annotated with } k \text{ and there exists an } R_k \\ \quad \text{annotated with } k \text{ or } g \text{ in the subtree of } R_j, \\ \emptyset \quad \text{otherwise.} \end{cases}
$$

Note that $Need$ functions define the minimal set of tables with which R_i must join to maintain the view. This can be exploited in view maintenance [1].

3.4 Algorithm for Deriving Auxiliary Views

Our algorithm employs the concept of completely self-maintainable aggregates along with local/join reduction and smart duplicate compression to derive the minimum set of auxiliary views necessary to maintain a specified generalized project-select-join view.

Algorithm 3.2 Creation of minimum auxiliary views for generalized project-select-join views.

---

1. Construct the extended join graph $G(V)$.
2. For each base table $R_i \in \mathcal{R}$ calculate $Need(R_i, G(V))$ and check whether R_i transitively depends on all other base tables in $\mathcal{R}$.

   If this is the case, and R_i is not in the $Need$ set of any other base table in $\mathcal{R}$, and none of the attributes of R_i are involved in non-CSMASs, then X_{R_i} can be omitted.

   Else $X_{R_i} = (\Pi_{A_{R_i}} \sigma_S R_i) \ltimes_{C_1} X_{R_{j1}} \ltimes_{C_2} X_{R_{j2}} \ltimes \ldots \ltimes_{C_n} X_{R_{jn}}$, where A_{R_i} is an expression list over the attributes of R_i after local reduction and smart duplicate compression. C_j is the join condition $R_i.b = R_j.a$, where a is a key of R_i and R_i is dependent on $R_{j1}, R_{j2}, \ldots, R_{jn}$.

We state a theorem regarding the correctness and minimality of the auxiliary views derived by the above algorithm.

Theorem 1. *Let V be a view defined by a generalized project-select-join view with a tree-structured join graph. The set of auxiliary views $\mathcal{X}$ derived by Algorithm 3.2 is the unique minimal set of views $\mathcal{X}$ that can be added to V such that $\mathcal{X} \cup \{V\}$ is self-maintainable under insertions, deletions, and updates to the base tables $\mathcal{R}$ referenced in V.*

We say that the auxiliary views $\mathcal{X}$ derived by the algorithm are minimal in the sense that no subset of it permits us to accurately maintain V. By this we mean that neither an auxiliary view nor any attributes or tuples in an auxiliary view can be removed without sacrificing the maintainability of $\mathcal{X} \cup V$. The proof involves three steps. First, we show that each auxiliary view $X_{R_i} \in \mathcal{X}$ is minimal. Secondly, we show that each auxiliary view X_{R_i} is necessary to maintain V. Finally, we prove that $\mathcal{X}$ is self-maintable. The complete proof had to be omitted due to space limitations. It can be found in [1].

4 Conclusions

This paper presents an algorithm for making GPSJ views, the single most important class of views in data warehouses, self-maintainable by materializing a set of auxiliary views such that the original view and the auxiliary views taken together are self-maintainable.

We complete local and join reductions [14] with smart duplicate compression, which is inherent to GPSJ views with aggregation, and show that this allows to significantly reduce the amount of detail data that has to be stored in a data warehouse.

The work suggests several lines of future research.

Our approach could be extended to old detail data. Old detail data is often append-only data. This makes it possible to relax the definition of CSMA because only insertions have to be considered. This implies that old detail data can be reduced even further and it should also be possible to simplify (and speed up) the incremental maintenance.

Another future research direction is the generalization of GPSJ views. While GPSJ views are appropriate for data warehouses (they fit the template structure of data warehouse query tools such as Star Tracker [12, p.321]) it can still be useful to generalize them to include restrictions on groups (the HAVING clause in SQL), nested subqueries, and general expressions in the select clause.

An automation of the proposed techniques should start out with the definition of an abstract notation for classes of summary data. Our algorithm should then be extended to determine the minimal set of detail data for classes of summary data.

Finally, it could also be attractive to trade accuracy for space. It is one of our assumptions that summary data shall be maintained accurately. It is interesting to investigate frameworks where summary data is not accurate but a (good) approximation. Such an approach might allow further reductions of the size of the detail data.

References

1. M. O. Akinde, O. G. Jensen, and M. H. Böhlen. Minimizing Detail Data in Data Warehouses. R-98-5002, Aalborg University, 1998.
2. J. A. Blakely, N. Coburn, and P. A. Larson. Updating Derived Relations: Detecting Irrevelant and Autonomously Computable Updates. In *ACM Transactions on Database Systems*, pages 14(3):369–400. Los Alamitos, USA, September 1989.
3. S. Ceri and J. Widom. Deriving Production Rules for Incremental View Maintenance. In *Proceedings of the Seventeenth International Conference on Very Large Databases*, pages 577–589. Barcelona, Spain, September 1991.
4. A. Gupta, V. Harinarayan, and D. Quass. Aggregate-Query Processing in Data Warehousing Environments. In Umeshwar Dayal, Peter M. D. Gray, and Shojiro Nishio, editors, *Proceedings of the Twenty-first International Conference on Very large Databases*. Zurich, Switzerland, September 1995.
5. A. Gupta, H. V. Jagadish, and I. S. Mumick. Data Integration using Self Maintainable Views. Technical report, AT&T Bell Laboratories, November 1994.
6. T. Griffin and L. Libkin. Incremental Maintenance of Views with Duplicates. In M. Carey and D. Schneider, editors, *Proceedings of the ACM SIGMOD Conference on Management of Data*, pages 328–339. San Jose, CA, USA, May 1995.
7. A. Gupta, I. S. Mumick, and V. S. Subrahmanian. Maintaining Views Incrementally. In *Proceedings of the ACM SIGMOD Conference on Management of Data*, pages 157–166. Washington D.C., USA, May 1993.
8. J. V. Harrison and S. W. Diettrich. Maintenance of Materialized Views in a Deductive Database: An Update Propagation Approach. In *Proceedings of the Sixth International Conference of Data Enginerring*, pages 56–65, 1992.
9. R. Hull and G. Zhou. A Framework for Supporting Data Integration using the Materialized and Virtual Approaches. In *Proceedings of the ACM SIGMOD Conference on Management of Data*. Montreal, Quebec, Canada, June 1996.
10. W. H. Inmon, C. Imhoff, and G. Battas. *Building the Operational Data Store*. John Wiley & Sons, Inc., 1996.
11. W. H. Inmon. *Building the Data Warehouse*. John Wiley & Sons, Inc., 1992.
12. R. Kimball. *The Data Warehouse Toolkit*. John Wiley & Sons, Inc., 1996.
13. I. S. Mumick, D. Quass, and B. S. Mumick. Maintenance of Data Cubes and Summary Tables in a Warehouse. In *Proceedings of the ACM SIGMOD Conference on Management of Data*. Tuscon, Arizona, USA, May 1997.
14. D. Quass, A. Gupta, I. S. Mumick, and J. Widom. Making Views Self-Maintainable for Data Warehousing. In *Proceedings of the Conference on Parallel and Distributed Information Systems*. Miami Beach, Florida, USA, December 1996.
15. D. Quass. Maintenance Expressions for Views with Aggregation. In *ACM Workshop on Materialized Views: Techniques and Applications*. Montreal, Canada, June 1996.
16. A. Segev and W. Fang. Currency-based Updates to Distributed Materialized Views. In *Proceedings of the Sixth International Conference of Data Enginerring*, pages 512–520. Los Alamitos, USA, 1990.
17. A. Segev and W. Fang. Optimal Update Policies for Distributed Materialized Views. In *Management Science*, pages 37(7):851–870, July 1991.
18. A. Segev and J. Park. Updating Distributed Materialized Views. In *IEEE Transactions on Knowledge and Data Engineering*, pages 1(2):173–184, 1989.
19. J. Widom. Research Problems in Data Warehousing. In *Proceedings of the Fourth International Conference on Information and Knowledge Management*, November 1995.

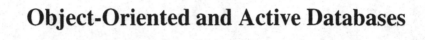

Object-Oriented and Active Databases

Static Management of Integrity in Object-Oriented Databases: Design and Implementation

Véronique Benzaken* and Xavier Schaefer*

Abstract. In this paper, we propose an efficient technique to statically manage integrity constraints in object-oriented database programming languages. We place ourselves in the context of a simplified database programming language, close to O_2, in which we assume that updates are undertaken by means of methods. An important issue when dealing with constraints is that of efficiency. A naïve management of such constraints can cause a severe floundering of the overall system. Our basic assumption is that the run-time checking of constraints is too costly to be undertaken systematically. Therefore, methods that are always safe with respect to integrity constraints should be proven so *at compile time*. The run-time checks should only concern the remaining methods. To that purpose, we propose a new approach, based on the use of predicate transformers combined with automatic theorem proving techniques, to prove the *invariance* of *integrity constraints* under complex *methods*. We then describe the current implementation of our prototype, and report some experiments that have been performed with it on non trivial examples. The counterpart of the problem of program verification is that of program correction. Static analysis techniques can also be applied to solve that problem. We present a systematic approach to undertake the automatic correction of potentially unsafe methods. However, the advantages of the latter technique are not as clear as those of program verification. We will therefore discuss some arguments for and against the use of method correction.

1 Introduction

Efforts on object-oriented database programming languages have mainly been devoted to the integration of elaborated type systems and persistence mechanisms in a uniform way. However, many specific database functionalities have not been taken into account by those works. In particular, functionalities such as view management, role definition and integrity constraints are either absent from, or only roughly supported by most (object-oriented) database programming languages. For the last five years, efforts in the database programming language community have been devoted to the definition of languages integrating such functionalities [1, 33, 2, 3]. Nevertheless, most object-oriented database programming languages are not able to take into account integrity constraints in a global and declarative way.

Integrity constraints reflect the user's concern that the information stored should represent the real world faithfully. The data should respect at any moment a set of conditions, called *semantic integrity constraints*. For example, assume that our database stores some persons who have a spouse. A reasonable integrity constraint imposed on this data could be:

No person can be married to itself

Integrity constraint management has always been presented as one of the great promises of database systems. To date, that *basic* facility should be provided by any object-oriented database system. However, no real database system has kept that promise in a satisfactory way.

One of the assumptions that has discouraged people from using integrity constraints is that constraints should be checked *systematically* at run-time, after each update. Despite the several optimisation techniques that have been proposed ([28, 26, 22] [9, 24, 20, 35, 8, 4, 25]) in order to improve dynamic checking, system performances are still greatly affected. Considering the efficiency problems that most database systems already have without having to deal with integrity constraints, one understands why integrity has more or less been left aside.

The situation can be significantly improved by detecting, at *compile time*, which updates preserve integrity. As in our framework such updates are undertaken by means of methods, a method that will never violate an integrity constraint should be proven safe at compile time.

---

* C.R.I., Université de Paris I - Panthéon - Sorbonne, 90, Rue de Tolbiac, 75013 Paris, France. e-mail {benzaken,schaefer}@univ-paris1.fr.

Indeed, the run-time checking (systematically generated by the compiler) of this constraint can be entirely avoided after the execution of this method. To illustrate our motivation let us consider the simple example suggested previously. We consider a database that stores some information about people: their name and their spouse. A database schema of such a database could be as shown in Figure 1. Consider the following constraint:

```
class Person type tuple (
            name: string,
            spouse: Person
            )
method marry(q: Person)
end;
```

Fig. 1. A simple schema

"No person can be married to itself."

Such a constraint will be written at the schema level in a first-order like language:

forall x in Persons: x.spouse≠x;

where the notation x.spouse denotes the extraction of attribute spouse of object x and where Persons is defined as the following persistent root:

name Persons: set (Person);

This command declares an entry point in the database, which is a container for objects that are instances of class Person. Let us now consider the following implementation of method marry

```
method marry(q:Person) in class Person{
    self.spouse:=q;            <set the spouse attribute of the receiver to q>
    q.spouse:=self; }          <set the spouse attribute of parameter to self>
```

That update can clearly violate the integrity constraint given previously, in particular when self is equal to q. The integrity constraint manager will therefore have to check the constraint after each execution of method marry. That can be done in several ways. It can either check the constraint as it is, i.e. check that (x.spouse≠x) for any Person x in the set Persons. It can also undertake an optimised run-time check. This test can be obtained with the techniques mentioned previously [28, 26, 22, 9, 24] [20, 35, 8, 4, 25]. In our case, such techniques can reduce the test to just testing that (q.spouse≠q) and (self.spouse≠self).

An important point is that such an optimisation is possible only for very simple constraints. Most of the time, the run-time checking overhead remains. Moreover, such optimisations are unable to produce the "minimal" run-time test. In our case, the minimal test is just to check that (self≠q) before performing the assignment.

As far as the programmer is concerned, the best solution, in terms of efficiency, is not to let the system generate the run-time test. The programmer that wants to tune his database should introduce some "minimal" run-time test directly into the implementation of methods. Method marry becomes as shown in Figure 2.

Note that taking such precautions can be dangerous because, as constraints can evolve, the programmer might also have to change the appropriate tests he has included in his programs. However, in real systems, this style of programming called *defensive programming* is often used, and therefore has to be taken into account.

If the programmer has already taken appropriate precautions with respect to integrity inside the programs, the overhead of run-time integrity checking can be avoided, as it is redundant with those precautions. Also, the user does not have to suffer from mysterious program failures (due to constraint violations) anymore.

```
method marry(q:Person)
in class Person {
    if (self≠q){
       self.spouse:=q;
       q.spouse:=self;}}
```

Fig. 2. Method marry

However, we first have to make sure that those precautions are indeed sufficient, i.e., that this method will *never* violate the integrity constraint. That must be proven formally, automatically and at compile-time. The first contribution of this paper is to provide a technique for doing so as well as a prototype implementing it.

We insist that our aim is *not* to encourage defensive programming, but as this style of programming is widely used in real systems, it should be detected at compile-time to improve the efficiency of integrity management.

Our approach undertakes a very detailed analysis of methods and provides some precise information on the impact they have upon constraints. Partial but reliable information concerning methods is obtained by means of *predicate transformers* [16, 17]. A predicate transformer is a function that takes for input a formula and a program (in our case, a method), and yields another formula. There are two kinds of predicate transformers:

- A *forward* predicate transformer is a function that, given a method m and a constraint C satisfied by the input data of m (which is the usual assumption as methods are run on a consistent state[1]), returns a formula $\overrightarrow{m}(C)$ that is necessarily satisfied by the output data of m.
- A *backward* predicate transformer is a function that, given a method m and a constraint C, returns a sufficient condition on the input data of m for C to be satisfied by the output data. This condition is denoted $\overleftarrow{m}(C)$.

Both predicate transformers can be used to detect at compile-time that a method m will never violate a constraint C. Using the forward predicate transformer, as done in [6], we have to prove that $\overrightarrow{m}(C) \Rightarrow C$. If we use the backward predicate transformer, we have to prove that $C \Rightarrow \overleftarrow{m}(C)$. To prove both implications, we use classical theorem proving techniques (the tableau method and resolution).

Our approach has been implemented and provides some positive results on some real, non-trivial examples. We insist that it is *fully automatic*, in the sense that this technique is embedded in the compiler technology and no human intervention is required at any stage. We will of course compare the results obtained by the two predicate transformers.

Another important question is whether there is a systematic way of automatically correcting the faulty version of marry, to yield a safe version of marry. The answer to this question is positive, and the *backward* predicate transformer can be used to this purpose. However, the advantages of the latter technique are not as clear as for the former one. Its assessment is still the subject of ongoing research, so we will give some arguments for and against its use in a real system.

The paper is organised as follows. In Section 2 we informally present our framework: an object-oriented database programming language allowing the definition of integrity constraints in a global and declarative way. In Section 3 we describe an intermediate language in which complex instructions will be translated and give the reasons for such a translation. In Section 4, we define our two predicate transformers. We shall purposely focus on the *forward* predicate transformer. Most remarks about the forward predicate transformer can be applied to the backward predicate transformer. We describe in Section 5 the implementation of our current prototype and give results of experiments. In particular, we will compare the results provided by the two predicate transformers. In section 6, we present a technique to undertake the automatic correction of unsafe methods. In Section 7 we compare ourselves to different approaches that have been proposed in the database field. We finally conclude in Section 8.

2 An object-oriented database programming language with constraints

Our framework consists in a very simple database model with object-oriented features very close to O_2 [15]. The programmer can define, together with the usual classes and methods, some *semantic integrity constraints* which are well formed formulae on a specific language. However, we point out that the specificities of the data model are not essential to our approach. We present, through examples, the ingredients of our language:

---

[1] This corresponds to the classical notion of *coherence* in databases.

classes and persistent roots, integrity constraints and methods. To focus on important issues, we will reduce the use of concepts that are not essential to our approach.

2.1 Classes and persistent roots

In order to illustrate the main concepts of our framework, let us start with the simple schema given in Figure 3. We define three classes (Person, Parent and Employee).

```
class Person type tuple(          class Parent inherit Person type tuple(
    name: string,                     children: set (Person))
    spouse: Person,               method marry(q: Person);
    bestfriend: Person,               separate();
    money: integer )                  spend(amount:integer);
method marry(q: Person);          end;
    separate();                   class Employee inherit Person type tuple(
    spend(amount: integer);           boss: Person)
    setbestfriend(p: Person);     method separate();
end;                              end;

name Persons: set (Person);
name Parents: set (Parent);
name Employees: set (Employee);
```

Fig. 3. A schema

Both of them have tuple-structured types. A Person has a name, a spouse, a bestfriend and some money. The classes Parent and Employee inherit from Person, their respective types are subtypes of the one of class Person. Thus attributes name, spouse, bestfriend and money are inherited in classes Parent and Employee. Methods marry and separate have been redefined in class Parent and Employee. Such a redefinition obeys the covariant rule (see [7] for an enlightening discussion on the consequences in O_2 and [11] for a more general framework). The semantics of inheritance is the usual inclusion semantics. We also define three persistent names Persons, Parents and Employees, as a set of Persons (respectively Parents, Employees). Persistence is achieved by reachability from those persistent names. This means that every object reachable from those names is automatically stored on disk at the end of programs. Unreachable objects are garbage-collected.

2.2 Integrity constraints

That schema is quite simple but many constraints can already be stated; some examples are given on Figure 4. Constraints are closed first-order formulae built on the following language:

- The symbols includes constants (0, 1,..., nil, etc.), and variables (x, y, etc.).
- Terms are built as follows: if t is a term, and a an attribute, then $t.a$ is a term. It denotes the extraction of field a of object t.
- Formulae are built in the usual way by using connectives ($\land$, $\lor$, $\neg$, etc.) and quantifiers (forall, exists).

The semantics, i.e., the truth or falsity of those constraints with respect to a specific database should be clear. As usual, a database can be seen as a structure, that is a domain together with a set of relationships between elements of that domain. A database B is coherent with respect to an integrity constraint C if it is a model of C, written $B \models C$.

2.3 Methods

Methods are building blocks which allow to update the data stored in the database. If no precautions are taken by the application programmer, such updates could lead to inconsistent database states. We give in Figure 5 the implementation of the methods in class Person. Those methods are safe with respect to at least one of the constraints previously declared. Appart from method separate defined in class Person, which is "naturally" safe, all those methods use defensive programming. The methods of Figure 6 are de-

C1: **exists** x **in Persons:** x**.spouse=nil;**
There must be at least one **Person** who is not married.
C2: **forall** x **in Persons:** x**.spouse**$\neq x$**;**
A **Person** cannot be married to itself.
C3: **forall** x **in Parents:** x**.spouse** $\notin x$**.children;**
No **Parent** can be married to one of its children.
C4: **forall** x **in Employees:** x**.spouse=nil** $\Rightarrow x$**.boss**$\neq$**nil;**
An **Employee** who is not married must have a boss.
C5: **forall** x **in Persons:** x**.money** > 0**;**
A **Person** must have some money.
C6: **forall** x **in Parents:** x**.spouse=nil** $\Rightarrow \neg$ (**exists** $y \in x$**.children**)**;**
A **Parent** who is not married cannot have any children.
C7: **exists** x **in Persons:** x**.bestfriend=nil**
There must be at least one **Person** who has no best friend.

Fig. 4. Integrity constraints

`method separate()`
`in class Person {`
`    self.spouse:=nil;}`
	`method spend(amount:integer)`
	`in class Person {`
	`    if (self.money-amount>0)`
	`        self.money:=self.money-amount;}`

`method marry(q:Person)`
`in class Person{`
`    if (self`$\neq$`q){`
`        self.spouse:=q;`
`        q.spouse:=self;}}`
	`method setbestfriend(q:Person)`
	`in class Person{`
	`    if (exists u in Persons: u`$\neq$`self`
	`∧ u.bestfriend=nil)`
	`        self.bestfriend:=q;}`

Fig.5. Implementation of methods of class `Person`

`method separate()`
`in class Employee{`
`    if (self.boss`$\neq$`nil)`
`        self.spouse:=nil;}`
	`method separate`
	`in class Parent{`
	`    if (`$\neg$`(exist u ∈ self.children))`
	`        self.spouse:=nil;}`

`method marry(q:Person)`
`in class Parent{`
`    if (self `$\neq$` q`
`       ∧ `$\neg$`(q ∈`
`self.children)`
`       ∧ `$\neg$`(self ∈`
`q.children)){`
`        self.spouse:=q;`
`        q.spouse:=self;}}`
	`method spend (amount:integer)`
	`in class Parent{`
	`    if (self.money-amount>0)`
	`        self.money=self.money-amount;`
	`    forall u where (u in self.children) do {`
	`        if (u.money-amount>0)`
	`            u.money=u.money-amount;}}`

Fig. 6. Implementation of methods for class `Parent` and `Employee`

fined or overridden for the subclasses `Parent` and `Employee`. They are still safe with respect to at least one of the constraints given previously.

When methods are overridden (as it is the case for methods `marry` and `separate`) we shall adopt the following notation in the sequel. We note for any overridden method m, $m = \{m_1, ..., m_n\}$ where $m_1, ..., m_n$ are all the different implementations of method m in the system. For example, `separate` has three different implementations, respectively in the classes `Person`, `Employee` and `Parent`.

3 Translation of methods into an intermediate form

The task of analysing computer languages can be difficult, particularly when dealing with object-oriented programming languages in which objects that are involved in an update are reached in a *navigational* way. Defining predicate transformers directly on the source language can be a painstaking task and proving that they are correctly defined (which must always be done) can be very difficult. In order to compensate for that extra complexity, our technique is to:

- First, translate the source language into an intermediate form.
- Then, undertake the static analysis on that intermediate form.

We give in this section a short illustration of the complexity problem that occurs in object-oriented languages. This illustration will help justify the intermediate language we consider in the next section. The complexity of instructions in object-oriented languages is due to the way the objects are referenced. Let us see a simple assignment instruction:

`p.spouse.spouse:=q.spouse`

That update is not about p or q but about objects that can be *reached* from p and q. That instruction groups in fact two radically different operations:

- First, it determines the objects that are used for the update. To that purpose, it *navigates* along the paths defined by the attributes. In our case, the objects that are used in the update are denoted by p.spouse and q.spouse. Let us call them o_1 and o_2.
- Then, it undertakes the update. The update has become: o_1.spouse:=o_2,

That decomposition has to be done formally and systematically. To that purpose we will use a simple new instruction:

`forone` *object* `where` *condition* `do` *instruction*.

That instruction executes *instruction*, where *object* denotes the only object that satisfies *condition*. With that new construct, the original instruction p.spouse.spouse:=q.spouse will be translated into:

```
forone o₁ where p.spouse=o₁
do forone o₂ where q.spouse=o₂
do o₁.spouse:=o₂
```

That translation simplifies considerably the matter of defining a static analysis for object-oriented programming languages. Indeed, with such a translation we can avoid defining a complex analysis for the assignment. We just have to define how to deal with the `forone` and we can consider assignments of the form:

"variable.attribute := variable"

instead of the more general form[2]:

"expression.attribute := expression".

The translation of database programming languages into that intermediate language is straightforward. We give in the following definition the syntax of the whole intermediate language we shall use.

---

[2] Handling more complex statements is the subject of ongoing research.

Definition 1. *A method is a program* $m(p_1, ..., p_n)$ =instruction *where* m *is the* name *of the method,* $p_1,...,p_n$ *are its parameters, and* instruction *is the* body *of* m *that is syntactically defined as follows:*

instruction *::=* *variable . attribute :=* *variable*
        | instruction ; instruction
        | { instruction }
        | if condition then instruction
        | forone variable where condition do instruction
        | forall variable where condition do instruction

We only consider instructions there and not methods returning expressions as we are only interested in updates (side effects) which can alter the integrity of data. Following [11], self can be considered as the first parameter of methods. To avoid heavy notation, we have not mentioned the class for which a method is defined. An abuse of notation we will make quite freely is to identify a method with its body, i.e., the list of instructions it executes. This has no consequences when methods are not overloaded. We will deal with overloaded methods in a specific section.

4 Safe database schemas via predicate transformers

We describe in this section our technique to prove automatically whether methods are consistent with respect to integrity constraints. The program analysis framework we develop has been greatly inspired by the works of Dijkstra on predicate transformers [16, 17] and of course the seminal work on Hoare logic [21]. It can also be seen as an instance of abstract interpretation [13, 14, 23].

The central concept of our approach is that of predicate transformers. We define in the following two predicate transformers and show how to use them to undertake automatic program verification. The forward predicate transformer has for input a precondition ϕ and a method m and generates a post-condition $\overrightarrow{m}(\phi)$. The backward predicate transformer has for input a post-condition ϕ and a method m and generates a precondition $\overleftarrow{m}(\phi)$. The correctness of the two predicate transformers can be formulated as follows:

– Provided ϕ is true before the execution of m, $\overrightarrow{m}(\phi)$ is true after.
– Provided $\overleftarrow{m}(\phi)$ is true before the execution of m, ϕ is true after.

The application of predicate transformers to our problem is natural. A method m cannot violate C if $\overrightarrow{m}(C) \Rightarrow C$ or $C \Rightarrow \overleftarrow{m}(C)$.

While correctness is achieved, for some complex languages with some sophisticated features such as aliasing, Clarke [12] has shown that completeness cannot be obtained. Our predicate transformers, cannot claim to produce the most-precise information about program behaviour (i.e., strongest post-conditions or weakest pre-condition). Still, they manage to produce some partial, but very useful information.

We will purposely present the *forward* predicate transformer with more details that the backward predicate transformer. Most remarks that we make about the former can be easily applied to the latter.

4.1 A forward predicate transformer.
In this section, we define a forward predicate transformer, by induction, both on the structure of the methods and the structure of the initial formulae. For the sake of clarity, we shall first describe how to deal with simple instructions. We shall show how it is used to prove method safety. Then, we shall describe the predicate transformer for loops and recursive methods. Finally, we present the treatment of overridden methods.

Simple methods
As our work involves first-order logic with equality, we will use the "=" symbol to denote equality in the formulae we manipulate. We will use the "≡" symbol to denote equality in the meta-language.

Definition 2. *Let m be a method (see Definition 1). We define the predicate transformer $\vec{m}$ of m, by induction, as follows ($\vec{m}$ denotes a formula). Let ϕ and ψ be formulae. Let u, v, x and y be terms and a be an attribute:*

- *Formula parse:*

  1. $\vec{m}\,((\phi)) \equiv (\vec{m}\,(\phi))$

  2. $\vec{m}\,(\phi \wedge \psi) \equiv \vec{m}\,(\phi) \wedge \vec{m}\,(\psi)$

  3. $\vec{m}\,(\phi \vee \psi) \equiv \vec{m}\,(\phi) \vee \vec{m}\,(\psi)$

  4. $\vec{m}\,(\texttt{forall } x:\ \phi(x)) \equiv \texttt{forall } x: \vec{m}\,(\phi(x))$

  5. $\vec{m}\,(\texttt{exists } x:\ \phi(x)) \equiv \texttt{exists } x: \vec{m}\,(\phi(x))$

- *Method parse:*

  6. If: $m \equiv u.a := v$ and ϕ is a literal[3] , then:

    - *If $\phi \equiv (x.a = y)$ then $\vec{m}\,(\phi) \equiv (u = x \wedge u.a = v) \vee (u \neq x \wedge u.a = v \wedge x.a = y)$*

    - *If $\phi \equiv (x.a \neq y)$ then $\vec{m}\,(\phi) \equiv (u = x \wedge u.a = v) \vee (u \neq x \wedge u.a = v \wedge x.a \neq y)$*

    - *Else: $\vec{m}\,(\phi) \equiv \phi \wedge u.a = v$*

    With (1-5), we can assume without loss of generality that ϕ is a literal.

  7. If: $m \equiv i_1;i_2$ then: $\vec{m}\,(\phi) \equiv \vec{i_2}\,(\vec{i_1}\,(\phi))$

  8. If: $m \equiv \{i\}$ then: $\vec{m}\,(\phi) \equiv \vec{i}\,(\phi)$

  9. If: $m \equiv \texttt{if } \psi \texttt{ then } i$ then: $\vec{m}\,(\phi) \equiv \vec{i}\,(\psi \wedge \phi) \vee (\neg\psi \wedge \phi)$

  10. If: $m \equiv \texttt{forone } v \texttt{ where } \psi(v) \texttt{ do } i$ then: $\vec{m}\,(\phi) \equiv \texttt{exists } v: \vec{i}\,(\psi(v) \wedge \phi)$

This definition allows to capture (partially) the semantics of updates. For example, point (6) first item above only states that if the instruction to be executed is an assignement of the form $u.a := v$ and if the pre-condition satisfied before the assignement is of the form $x.a = y$ then you are faced with two distinct cases: either x equals u and therefore the effect of executing the assignement will be captured by $u = x \wedge u.a = v$, or x is different from u and in this case the effect of the assigment will be $x \neq u \wedge u.a = v \wedge x.a = y$. We assume that there is no ambiguity between symbols. If necessary, we can always rename all the variables and parameters that are used in constraints and methods. In the following, we will have to interpret formulae with free variables. To that purpose, we will write $\mathcal{B}_\sigma$ the database $\mathcal{B}$ provided with the assignment of free variables σ.

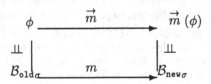

Fig. 7. Predicate transformer diagram

Theorem 1. *Let $\mathcal{B}_{\text{old}}$ a database, m a method, and $\mathcal{B}_{\text{new}}$ the result of the execution of m on $\mathcal{B}_{\text{old}}$. Let ϕ a formula, and σ an assignment for the free variables of ϕ. We have:*

$$\mathcal{B}_{\text{old}\sigma} \models \phi \implies \mathcal{B}_{\text{new}\sigma} \models \vec{m}\,(\phi)$$

that is, the predicate transformer $\vec{m}$ of m is correct.

---

[3] A *literal* is either an atom or the negation of an atom. An *atom* is an expression $a(t_1, ..., t_n)$, where a is a relation and $t_1,...,t_n$ are terms.

The proof of this theorem is given in [5]. This relationship is illustrated by the diagram in Figure 7. We can now use that predicate transformer to tell if a method can never violate an integrity constraint. The following corollary is a consequence of Theorem 1.

Corollary 1. *Let C be a constraint and m be a method. If $\vec{m}\,(C) \Rightarrow C$ then m is safe with respect to C.*

To establish that method m is safe with respect to C, we have to prove that $\vec{m}\,(C) \Rightarrow C$. We point out that powerful methods have been developed in the field of automated theorem proving in first-order logic: resolution, paramodulation, tableaux method...A property of all those proof techniques is that they are *complete*: if a formula is true, then those proof techniques find a proof for the formula in a finite time. The real problem occurs when the formula is *not* true. In that case, the theorem prover keeps on looking for a proof whereas none exists! Practically, theorem provers always look for a proof in a limited search space. So, our technique will:

- detect as being safe some safe methods (depending on the search space devoted to the computation).
- detect as being unsafe some safe methods and all unsafe methods.

Methods with loops

Database programming languages allow the use of a specific loop. In our kernel language, it is defined as:

forall variable where condition do instruction

The "forall" instruction executes "*instruction*" for every element, denoted by "*variable*", that satisfies "*condition*". The way we define a predicate transformer is very similar to the way Hoare logic deals with "while" loops. It amounts to computing an "invariant" for the loop instruction, that is, a formula which is preserved by the loop. Intuitively, the idea is that if "*instruction*" is safe with respect to a constraint, then the overall "forall" instruction will also be safe (i.e., the constraint is a logical consequence of the current value of the predicate transformer). Suppose we are proving the safety of a method m with respect to a constraint C, and that m contains a loop l defined as $l \equiv$"forall x where F do i". We define the predicate transformer of that loop as follows:

$$\vec{l}\,(\phi) = \begin{cases} C & \text{if } \phi \Rightarrow C \text{ and } \vec{i}\,(C) \Rightarrow C \\ \text{true} & \text{otherwise.} \end{cases}$$

Theorem 2. *Let $\mathcal{B}_{old}$ be a database, m be a method with loops statements, and $\mathcal{B}_{new}$ the database obtained after an execution of m. Let ϕ a formula, and σ an assignment for the free variables of ϕ. We have:*

$$\mathcal{B}_{old_\sigma} \models \phi \implies \mathcal{B}_{new_\sigma} \models \vec{m}\,(\phi)$$

that is, the predicate transformer $\vec{m}$ of m is correct.

The proof of this theorem relies on the fact that the composition of correct predicate transformers is still correct and can also be found in [5]. Note that the effect of a loop may depend on the order in which the elements $a_1, ..., a_n$ are chosen. However, the predicate transformer provides some reliable information which is independent from any order. Again we have:

Corollary 2. *Let C be a constraint and m be a method with loops statements. m is safe with respect to C if $\vec{m}\,(C) \Rightarrow C$.*

Recursion and overridden methods

As far as recursion is concerned, we adapt the usual techniques that have been defined in the field of static analysis. To oversimplify, we consider that any recursive method m can be written as shown in Figure 8. Where *"base case"* denotes the test to stop recursion and *"recursive call"* denotes a call to m with an object that can be reached from "self" or any parameter of m. We define the predicate transformer of m as follows:

method m (*parameters*) in class κ
{if *base case*
then i
else *recursive call*}

Fig. 8. Recursive method

$$\overrightarrow{m}(\phi) = \left\{ \begin{array}{l} C \quad \text{if } \phi \Rightarrow C \text{ and } \overrightarrow{i}(C) \Rightarrow C \\ \text{true otherwise.} \end{array} \right.$$

The predicate transformer is still correct. Therefore the following holds:

Theorem 3. *Let $\mathcal{B}_{old}$ be a database, m be a recursive method, and $\mathcal{B}_{new}$ the database obtained after an execution of m. Let ϕ a formula, and σ an assignment for the free variables of ϕ. We have:*

$$\mathcal{B}_{old_\sigma} \models \phi \implies \mathcal{B}_{new_\sigma} \models \overrightarrow{m}(\phi)$$

The proof can be found in [5]. Again we have:

Corollary 3. *Let C be a constraint and m be a recursive method.*

m *is safe with respect to C if $\overrightarrow{m}(C) \Rightarrow C$.*

The application of our approach to overridden methods is straightforward. Intuitively, an overridden method is safe if every branch defined for it is safe.

Theorem 4. *Let $m = \{m_1, \ldots, m_n\}$ be an overloaded method. Let C be an integrity constraint, m is safe with respect to C if the following holds*

$$\forall i \in \{1, \ldots, n\}, \overrightarrow{m_i}(C) \Rightarrow C.$$

We would like the reader to notice that our static analysis ensures modularity. Indeed, if one add a new branch for a method m, provided that this new branch is in turn safe, this update will not alter the safety of those programs which were calling m. No further verifications are required.

We have described in this section a *program analysis framework* for the language defined in the previous section. Our machinery can fail in proving the safety of some safe methods, but it will never manage to prove the safety of a method which is not safe. It errs on the side of caution (our technique is sound but not complete).

4.2 A backward predicate transformer

In this section, we define a backward predicate transformer. As opposed to the forward predicate transformer, a backward predicate transformer is a function that, given a program m and a formula ϕ, yields a sufficient condition on the input data of m in order for the output data to satisfy ϕ. We will give less details about the backward predicate transformer than we have done for the forward one. In particular, we will not show how to deal with loops and recursion. The approach used for the forward predicate transformer can be extended quite simply to the backward predicate transformer.

Definition 3. *Let m be a method (see Definition 1). We define the backward predicate transformer $\overleftarrow{m}$ of m, by induction, as follows. Let ϕ and ψ formulae. u, v, x and y are terms and a is an attribute:*

– *Formula parse:*

    1. $\overleftarrow{m}((\phi)) \equiv (\overleftarrow{m}(\phi))$

2. $\overleftarrow{m}(\phi \wedge \psi) \equiv \overleftarrow{m}(\phi) \wedge \overleftarrow{m}(\psi)$

3. $\overleftarrow{m}(\phi \vee \psi) \equiv \overleftarrow{m}(\phi) \vee \overleftarrow{m}(\psi)$

4. $\overleftarrow{m}(\texttt{forall } x: \phi(x)) \equiv \texttt{forall } x: \overleftarrow{m}(\phi(x))$

5. $\overleftarrow{m}(\texttt{exists } x: \phi(x)) \equiv \texttt{exists } x: \overleftarrow{m}(\phi(x))$

– *Method parse:*

6. *If:* $m \equiv \texttt{u.a} := \texttt{v}$ *and* ϕ *is a literal, then:*

   - *If* $\phi \equiv (x.a = y)$ *then* $\overleftarrow{m}(\phi) \equiv (u = x \wedge v = y) \vee (u \neq x \wedge x.a = y)$
   - *If* $\phi \equiv (x.a \neq y)$ *then* $\overleftarrow{m}(\phi) \equiv (u = x \wedge v \neq y) \vee (u \neq x \wedge x.a \neq y)$
   - *Else:* $\overleftarrow{m}(\phi) \equiv \phi$

   With (1-5), we can assume without loss of generality that ϕ *is a literal.*

7. *If:* $m \equiv i_1; i_2$ *then:* $\overleftarrow{m}(\phi) \equiv \overleftarrow{i_1}(\overleftarrow{i_2}(\phi))$

8. *If:* $m \equiv \{i\}$ *then:* $\overleftarrow{m}(\phi) \equiv \overleftarrow{i}(\phi)$

9. *If:* $m \equiv \texttt{if } \psi \texttt{ then } i$ *then:* $\overleftarrow{m}(\phi) \equiv (\psi \wedge \overleftarrow{i}(\phi)) \vee (\neg\psi \wedge \phi)$

10. *If:* $m \equiv \texttt{for one v where } \psi(v) \texttt{ do } i$ *then:* $\overleftarrow{m}(\phi) \equiv \texttt{exists } v: \psi(v) \; \overleftarrow{i} \wedge (\phi)$

The correctness property holds for the backward predicate transformer. It consists in establishing the opposite relationship from the one we showed for the forward predicate transformer.

Theorem 5. *Let* $\mathcal{B}_{old}$ *a database,* m *a method, and* $\mathcal{B}_{new}$ *the same database after an execution of* m. *Let* ϕ *a formula, and* σ *an assignment for the free variables of* ϕ. *We have:*

$$\mathcal{B}_{old\sigma} \models \overleftarrow{m}(\phi) \implies \mathcal{B}_{new\sigma} \models \phi$$

that is, the predicate transformer $\overleftarrow{m}$ *of* m *is correct.*

The proof is also given in [5]. We can now state a new safety criterion, which is symmetrical to the one already stated. This criterion gives us potentially a new way of proving that a method is safe with respect to a constraint.

Corollary 4. *Let* C *be a constraint and* m *be a method.* m *is safe with respect to* C *if* $C \Rightarrow \overleftarrow{m}(C)$.

In the next section, we will compare both approaches (forward and backward) to prove that a method preserves a constraint.

5 Implementation

We present in this section the prototype that has been implemented. In fact, there are two prototypes. The first (resp. second) one uses the forward (resp. backward) predicate transformer. We will give the results that we have obtained on the examples given earlier. This will provide us with a practical comparison of the forward and backward predicate transformers. The prototypes are in fact pre-processors for O_2. We will briefly sketch in the following several important points about the whole process. The first shows how the predicate transformers are put into practice in the prototypes.

5.1 Implementing the predicate transformers: from theory to practice

The predicate transformers as described in Section 4 are not directly suited to automation. Our experiment has shown that the formulae generated can be quite big, but that also the situation can be greatly improved by the use of appropriate heuristics. We use a very simple and pragmatic method to reduce the size of the output formulae. The first obvious way to do that is to simplify the input formula. The input formula can be simplified when it includes redundancies or contradictions. Another improvement, which is less trivial, is to include explicitly in the formula some facts that are implicit in that formula. This increases the size of the input formula but has the consequence of decreasing the size of the output formula. We insist that all those manipulations preserve the semantics of formulae.

Normalisation

First, we systematically put the input formula into prenex disjunctive normal form. Therefore, each formula is of the form:

$$Q_1 x_1, ... Q_n x_n, E_1 \lor ... \lor E_m$$

where the Q_i's are quantifiers and the E_i's, are a conjunction of literals ($L_1 \land ... \land L_k$).

Dealing with contradictions and redundancies

Once the formula has been normalised, we make a simple analysis of each E_i to get rid of contradictions and redundancies. The search for those is very limited (we would otherwise need a theorem prover). The redundancies we deal with are very simple: when a literal occurs twice in an environment, one occurrence can obviously be removed. Moreover, when a contradiction is detected in an environment E, E can be removed from the disjunction of environments. We point out that such a removal should be done *before* applying the predicate transformer. The reader interested could find details in [5] The rules that are used to detect contradictions are the axioms of equality (reflexivity, symmetry, transitivity) and functions ($x = y \Rightarrow f(x) = f(y)$).

Making the input formula more explicit

Another improvement can be obtained by including in the input formula some information that is implicit in that formula. Again, the reader interested will find all details in [5] Our experiment has shown that in some cases, it has allowed to reduce and simplify the output formula in a drastic way (from a formula with hundreds of literals to a formula with just one literal). For the sake of brevity, we will not describe these extra improvements, as they follow the spirit of those that have been presented previously. The reader interested could find details in [31].

5.2 Automatic theorem proving techniques

While attempting to prove that a method m is safe w.r.t. a constraint C, we either have to prove that $\overrightarrow{m}(C) \Rightarrow C$, or that $C \Rightarrow \overleftarrow{m}(C)$. In both cases, we use some automated theorem proving techniques. An important result of our experiment is that the theorem prover suited to the backward analysis is not the same as the one suited to the forward one.

The result provided by both predicate transformers ($\overrightarrow{m}(C)$ and $\overleftarrow{m}(C)$) is (nearly) in disjunctive normal form. Proving that $\overrightarrow{m}(C) \Rightarrow C$ or $C \Rightarrow \overleftarrow{m}(C)$ is respectively proving that $\overrightarrow{m}(C) \land \neg C$ or $C \land \neg \overleftarrow{m}(C)$ is unsatisfiable. The first formula is nearly in disjunctive normal form, whereas the second one is nearly in conjunctive normal form. Resolution accepts clausal form (conjunctive normal form). The tableaux method undertakes a kind of run time normalisation into disjunctive normal form. We therefore have used two different theorem provers: a resolution based theorem prover for the backward analysis, and a tableaux method theorem prover for the forward analysis. The resolution theorem prover is Otter [27], and the tableaux theorem prover is taken from [18].

5.3 Practical experiments

Our experiment has been done on a Sun sparc (sun4m) server running Solaris 2.3 OS. The integrity constraint manager has been run on all the examples given above. The results of that experiment are given Figure 9.

method	class	constraint	forward	backward
separate	Person	C1	0.21s.	0.12s.
separate	Employee	C1	0.27s.	0.23s.
separate	Parent	C1	0.29s.	0.57s.
separate	Parent	C6	1.21s.	2.48s.
separate	Employee	C4	1.06s.	0.22s.
marry	Person	C2	0.41s.	0.33s.
marry	Parent	C2	1.30s.	9.04s
marry	Parent	C3	3.60s.	1h.06min.35s.
spend	Person	C5	3.68s.	76.42s.
spend	Parent	C5	1.71s.	153.04s
setbestfriend	Person	C7	3.26s.	0.31s.

Fig. 9. Results.

The times given are only a rough guide of the efficiency of the method. They show that, in many cases, a proof can be obtained quite fast (see method separate with constraint C1). In some other cases, although quite simple, the proof might need some extra time (for instance, method spend with constraint C5).The reasons for such differences between proofs are not clear. A further study should focus on the assessment of the cost of the analysis. However, we insist that our method is run at *compile-time* and once and for all. Note that for simple examples, the prototype that uses the backward predicate transformer is slightly more efficient than the prototype that uses the forward predicate transformer. On the other hand, for complex examples, the resolution based theorem prover seems to flounder and the overall backward analysis can take much longer than the forward one. This is rather surprising, as backward predicate transformers have the reputation of being more efficient than their forward counterpart, and resolution has the reputation of being more efficient than the tableaux method.

6 Method correction

The natural counterpart of safety detection is that of method correction. The backward predicate transformer is used to produce a condition which, when included into the code of a method, will ensure its safety with respect to a specific constraint. As opposed to the approach we have already presented, the advantages of automatic method correction are unclear, and have to be further assessed. The following definition provides a very general method to alter methods in order to make them safe.

Definition 4. Let C a constraint and m be a method defined as follows:

> method m (*parameters*) in class κ
>   *body*

The corrected version of m with respect to C, written m_C, is defined as follows:

> method m_C (*parameters*) in class κ
>   {if $\overleftarrow{m}$ (C)
>   then *body*}

Theorem 6. *Let m be a method and C a constraint. m_C is safe with respect to C.*

This technique of method correction is sound, but many questions put its applicability in doubt. A first problem will occur if we apply method correction to a method which is safe but cannot be proven so. In that case, the correction is unnecessary, and will certainly burden the original code with redundant tests. A second problem is in assessing the gain that method correction brings in terms of the efficiency of the system. The idea of method correction is just to undertake a preliminary test on the database before undertaking the original update. In any case, this technique prevents the system from having to undertake expensive roll-backs when a constraint is violated. However, this preliminary test can be in itself very expensive, as the predicate transformers generate formulae that are far bigger than their input formulae. So, undertaking systematic method correction might be the best way of ensuring very low system performances.

7 Related work

The study of integrity constraints in database systems has been a topic of large interest [34, 28, 19, 10, 26, 22, 9, 24, 20, 35, 8, 32, 25].

Several works concern the optimisation of checking: [28, 22] for relational databases, [9] for deductive databases, [4] for object-oriented databases, and [25] for deductive object-oriented databases.

The subject of finding consistency proofs for database programs is not new: [19, 10, 29] give some indications on how Hoare's logic could be used for that purpose. Unlike our approach, the invariance of integrity constraints is proven, by hand.

[30] asserts that conventional methods are not suited to automatic transaction safety verification and takes the opposite direction of *transaction synthesis*.

More recently, [25] has defined a way to obtain some *weakest-preconditions* for a very simple language, in the context of deductive and object oriented databases. The choice of that language is somewhat unrealistic as it does not allow basic constructs such as if's. His work focuses on checking the constraints at run-time, rather than proving at compile-time that constraints will be preserved by transactions.

[32] is, to our knowledge, the most in-depth application of the axiomatic method to our problem. It uses a complex theorem prover that uses Boyer-Moore's computational logic, based on higher-order recursive functions. Their theorem prover is in fact an expert system which uses a knowledge base where some properties of database constructs are kept. Their knowledge base is first filled with axioms about basic language constructs. The main problem with this approach is that the consistency of those axioms is not guaranteed, particularly in the case of classical set theory (as mentioned by the authors). If those axioms are not consistent, then the expert system could prove just anything. Their approach is based on the confidence that no "surprising" properties can be derived from the axioms and is therefore not formally founded.

8 Conclusions

We have presented an approach based on combined abstract interpretation and automated theorem proving techniques to statically deal with integrity constraints in object-oriented database programming languages that provide integrated facilities, as the extended version of O_2. This approach focuses on a compile-time checking of constraints. No human intervention is needed, therefore the whole process is fully automatic.

Ongoing experimentation focuses on the refinement and optimisation of the method. It should also give more information about the cost of this method.

We plan to apply our method to dynamic (temporal) constraints. To this end we shall define temporal-logic based predicate transformers and explore the domain of temporal theorem proving techniques.

Acknowledgements

We are thankful to Giorgio Ghelli and Atsushi Ohori who first recommended us to study abstract interpretation theory. We are very grateful to Giuseppe Castagna for his suggestions and many valuable comments for improving this paper. We also would like to thank Serenella Cerrito for reading an early version of this paper. Patrick Cousot deserves a special acknowldgement there, in assuring us that this work was far from a trivial application of abstract interpretation he gave us a tremendous confidence.

References

1. S. Abiteboul and A. Bonner. Objects and views. In *ACM International Conference on Management of Data (SIGMOD)*, pages 238–248, Denver, Colorado, USA, May 1991.
2. A. Albano, R. Bergamini, G. Ghelli, and R. Orsini. An object data model with roles. In *International Conference on Very Large Databases*, pages 39–52, 1993.
3. A. Albano, R. Bergamini, G. Ghelli, and R. Orsini. Fibonacci: a programming language for object databases. *VLDB Journal*, 4(3):403–444, July 95.
4. V. Benzaken and A. Doucet. Thémis: A Database Programming Language Handling Integrity Constraints. *VLDB Journal*, 4(3):493–518, 1995.

5. V. Benzaken and X. Schaefer. Forward and backward analysis of object-oriented database programming languages: an application to static integrity management. Technical report, L.R.I, 1997. Available by ftp at `ftp.lri.fr/LRI/articles/benzaken/report.ps.gz`.
6. V. Benzaken and X. Schaefer. Static integrity constraint management in object-oriented database programming languages via predicate transformers. *European Conference on Object-Oriented Programming (ECOOP'97)*, number 1241 in LNCS,Springer-Verlag, 1997.
7. John Boyland and Giuseppe Castagna. Type-safe compilation of covariant specialization: a practical case. In *ECOOP'96*, number 1008 in LNCS, Springer, 1996.
8. F. Bry, H. Decker, and R. Manthey. A Uniform Approach to Constraint Satisfaction and Constraint Satisfiability in Deductive Databases. *EDBT'88*, LNCS 303, Springer, 1988.
9. F. Bry and R. Manthey. Checking Consistency of Database Constraints: A Logical Basis. In *Proceedings of the VLDB International Conference*, pages 13–20, August 1986.
10. M. A. Casanova and P. A. Bernstein. A formal system for reasonning about programs accessing a relational database. *ACM Trans. on Database Systems*, 2(3):386–414, 1980.
11. Giuseppe Castagna. *Object-Oriented Programming: A Unified Foundation*. Progress in Theoretical Computer Science. Birkäuser, Boston, 1996. ISBN 3-7643-3905-5.
12. E. M. Clarke. Programming languages constructs for which it is impossible to obtain good hoare axiom systems. *Journal of the ACM*, 26(1):129–147, January 79.
13. P. Cousot and R. Cousot. Abstract Interpretation: A Unified Lattice Model for Static Analysis of Programs by Construction or Approximation of Fixpoints. In *4th POPL*, 1977.
14. P. Cousot and R. Cousot. Systematic design of program analysis frameworks. In *6th POPL*, 1979.
15. O. Deux. The Story of O_2. *IEEE Transaction on Knowledge and Data Engineering*, 2(1), March 1990.
16. E. W. Dijkstra. *A Discipline of Programming*. Prentice-Hall, 1976.
17. E. W. Dijkstra and C. S. Scholten. *Predicate Calculus and Program Semantics*. Texts and Monographs in Computer Science. Springer-Verlag, 1990.
18. Melvin Fitting. *First-order logic and automated theorem proving*. Springer, 1990.
19. G. Gardarin and M. Melkanoff. Proving the Consistency of Database Transactions. In *VLDB International Conference*, pages 291–298, Rio, Brasil, October 1979.
20. L. Henschen, W. Mc Cune, and S. Naqvi. Compiling constraint checking programs from first order formulas. *Advances in Database Theory*, volume 2. Plenum, 1984.
21. C.A.R. Hoare. An axiomatic basis for computer programming. *Comm. ACM*, 12, 1969.
22. A. Hsu and T. Imielinski. Integrity Checking for Multiple Updates. In *Proceedings of the ACM SIGMOD International Conference*, pages 152–168, 1985.
23. N. D. Jones and F. Nielson. Abstract interpretation. *Semantic Modelling*, volume 4 of *Handbook of Logic in Computer Science*, chapter 5, pages 527–636. Oxford Science Publication, 1995.
24. R. Kowalski, F. Sadri, and P. Soper. Integrity Checking in Deductive Databases. In *Proceedings of the VLDB International Conference*, pages 61–70, 1987.
25. Michael Lawley. Transaction safety in deductive object-oriented databases. In *Proceedings of the Fourth DOOD*, number 1013 in LNCS, Springer 1995.
26. J. W. Lloyd and R. W. Topor. A basis for deductive database systems. *Journal of Logic Programming*, 2(2), 1985.
27. William W. McCune. *OTTER 3.0 Reference Manual aud Guide*. Argonne National Laboratory. available at http://www.mcs.anl.gov/home/mccune/ar/otter.
28. J.M. Nicolas. Logic for Improving Integrity Checking in Relational Databases. Technical report, ONERA-CERT, 1979.
29. Xiaolei Qian. An axiom system for database transactions. *Information Processing Letters*, 36:183–189, November 1990.
30. Xiaolei Qian. The deductive synthesis of database transactions. *ACM Transactions on Database Systems*, 18(4):626–677, December 1993.
31. X. Schaefer. *Bases de données orientées objet, contraintes d'intégrité et analyse statique*. PhD thesis, Université de Paris 1 - Panthéon - Sorbonne, 1997.
32. T. Sheard and D. Stemple. Automatic Verification of Database Transaction Safety. *ACM Trans. on Database Systems*, 14(3):322–368, September 1989.
33. C. Sousa, C. Delobel, and S. Abiteboul. Virtual schemas and bases. *International Conference on Extending Database Technology*, number 779 in LNCS, Springer-Verlag, 1994.
34. M. Stonebraker. Implementation of Integrity Constraints and Views by Query Modification. In *ACM SIGMOD International Conference*, San Jose, California, May 1975.
35. W. Weber, W. Stugky, and J. Karzt. Integrity Checking in database systems. *Information Systems*, 8(2):125–136, 1983.

OCB: A Generic Benchmark to Evaluate the Performances of Object-Oriented Database Systems

Jérôme Darmont
Bertrand Petit
Michel Schneider

Laboratoire d'Informatique (LIMOS)
Université Blaise Pascal – Clermont-Ferrand II
Complexe Scientifique des Cézeaux
63177 Aubière Cedex
FRANCE
darmont@libd1.univ-bpclermont.fr

Abstract. We present in this paper a generic object-oriented benchmark (the Object Clustering Benchmark) that has been designed to evaluate the performances of clustering policies in object-oriented databases. OCB is generic because its sample database may be customized to fit the databases introduced by the main existing benchmarks (e.g., OO1). OCB's current form is clustering-oriented because of its clustering-oriented workload, but it can be easily adapted to other purposes. Lastly, OCB's code is compact and easily portable. OCB has been implemented in a real system (Texas, running on a Sun workstation), in order to test a specific clustering policy called DSTC. A few results concerning this test are presented.
Keywords: object-oriented databases, clustering, performance evaluation, benchmarking, DSTC.

1 Introduction

This study originates from the design of clustering algorithms to improve the performance of object-oriented databases. The principle of clustering is to store related objects close together on secondary storage, so that when an object is accessed from disk, all its related objects are also loaded into the main memory. Subsequent accesses to these related objects are thus main memory accesses, instead of much slower I/Os.

But clustering involves some overhead (to gather and maintain usage statistics, to reorganize the database...), so it is not easy to determine the real impact of a given clustering heuristic on the overall performances. Hence, clustering algorithms are validated only if performance tests demonstrate their actual value.

The validation of clustering methods can be achieved by several ways. First, mathematical analysis can be used to ascertain the complexity of a clustering algorithm [7]. Although mathematical analysis provides exact results, it is very difficult to take into account all the parameters defining a real system. Hence, simplification hypothesis are made, and results tend to differ from reality. Simulation may also be used, and offers several advantages [8]. First, clustering algorithms that are possibly implemented on different OODBs and/or operating systems can be compared within the same environment, and thus on the same basis. A given algorithm can also be tested on different platforms to determine how its behavior might be influenced by its host system. Simulation also allows the *a priori* modeling of research prototypes before they are actually implemented in an OODB. Eventually, the most customary mean to measure the performances of DBMSs in general is the use of benchmarks, that directly gauge the response of an existing system, and, *a fortiori*, the performances of a clustering algorithm implemented in an existing system. However, the usual general purpose benchmarks are not well suited to the evaluation of clustering algorithms, that are very data dependent.

Some authors propose dedicated tools to evaluate the performances of their own clustering heuristic. We preferred to design generic tools, in order to be able to compare different algorithms on the same basis, using standard and easy to implement metrics. It is actually interesting to compare clustering policies together, instead of comparing them to a non-clustering policy. We can also use different platforms to test a given algorithm. We are actually involved in the development of both simulation models and a benchmark. We focus in this paper on the latter, a generic, clustering-oriented benchmark called the Object Clustering Benchmark (OCB).

The remainder of this paper is organized as follows. Section 2 presents the most popular benchmarks for evaluating the performances of OODBs. Our own benchmark, OCB, is then described in Section 3. Section 4 presents experiments we performed to validate our benchmark. Section 5 eventually concludes this paper and provides future research directions.

2 Related Work

Benchmarking the performances of an OODB consists of performing a set of tests in order to measure the system response under certain conditions. Benchmarks are used to compare the global performances of OODBs, but also to illustrate the advantages of one system or another in a given situation, or to determine an optimal hardware configuration (memory buffer size, number of disks...) for a given OODB and/or application. Several well-known standard object-oriented benchmarks are used nowadays. The presentation of three of them (OO1, HyperModel, and OO7) follows.

Typically, a benchmark is constituted of two main elements:

- a database (a conceptual schema, and a database generation method);
- a workload (a set of operations to perform on the database, e.g., different kind of queries; and a protocol detailing the execution of these operations).

2.1   OO1

OO1 (Objects Operations 1), sometimes called the "Cattell Benchmark" [6], is customarily used to evaluate the performances of both relational and object-oriented DBMSs.

OO1 Database: OO1's database is based on two classes: *Part*, and *Connection*. The parts are composite elements that are connected (through *Connection* objects) to three other parts. Each connection references two parts: the source (*From*), and the destination part (*To*).

The database is generated the following way:

1. create all the *Part* objects and store them into a dictionary;
2. for each part, randomly choose three other parts and create the associated connections.

The locality of reference (objects are often linked to relatively close objects) is simulated by a reference zone. I.e., *Part* #i is randomly linked to parts which *Id* are in the interval [*Id-RefZone*, *Id+RefZone*]. The probability that the links are determined this way is 0.9. Otherwise, the linked parts are chosen totally at random.

OO1 Workload: OO1 performs three types of operations. Each of them is run 10 times. Response time is measured for each run.

- *Lookup:* access to 1000 randomly selected parts.
- *Traversal:* randomly select a root part, then explore the corresponding part tree (in depth first) through the *Connect* and *To* references, up to seven hops (total of 3280 parts, with possible duplicates). Also perform a *reverse traversal* by swapping the *To* and *From* directions.
- *Insert:* add 100 parts, and the corresponding connections, to the database. Commit the changes.

Comments: OO1 is a simple benchmark, and hence is very easy to implement. It was used to test a broad range of systems, including object-oriented DBMSs, relational DBMSs, and other systems like Sun's INDEX (B-tree based) system. Its visibility and simplicity actually make of OO1 a standard for OODB benchmarking. However, its data model is too elementary to measure the elaborate traversals that are common in many types of applications, like engineering applications. Furthermore, OO1 only supports simple navigational and update tasks, and has no notion of complex objects (e.g., composite objects).

2.2   The HyperModel Benchmark

The HyperModel Benchmark (also called the Tektronix Benchmark in the literature) [1][2] offers a more complex database than OO1. Furthermore, it is recognized for the richness of the tests it proposes.

HyperModel Database: The HyperModel Benchmark is based on an extended hypertext model. Hypertext is a generic graph structure consisting of nodes and links. The main characteristic of this database is the various relationships existing between classes: *inheritance* (the attributes of a *Node* object may be inherited from another *Node* object), *aggregation* (an instance of the *Node* class may be composed of one or several other instances), and eventually *association* (two *Node* objects may be bound by an oriented link).

HyperModel Workload: The benchmark consists of 20 operations. To measure the time to perform each operation, the following sequence is followed.

1. *Setup:* prepare 50 inputs to the operations (the setup is not timed);
2. *Cold run:* run the operation 50 times, on the 50 inputs precomputed in the setup phase; then, if the operation is an update, commit the changes once for all 50 operations;
3. *Warm run:* repeat the operation 50 times with the same input to test the effect of caching; again, perform a commit if the operation was an update.

The 20 possible operations belong to seven different kinds:

– *Name Lookup:* retrieve one randomly selected node;
– *Range Lookup:* retrieve the nodes satisfying a range predicate based on an attribute value;
– *Group Lookup:* follow the relationships one level from a randomly selected starting node;
– *Reference Lookup:* reverse Group Lookup;
– *Sequential Scan:* visit all the nodes;
– *Closure Traversal:* Group Lookup up to a predefined depth;
– *Editing:* update one node.

Comments: The HyperModel Benchmark possesses both a richer schema, and a wider extent of operations than OO1. This renders HyperModel potentially better than OO1 to measure the performances of engineering databases. However, this added complexity also makes HyperModel harder to implement, especially since its specifications are not as complete as OO1's. Lastly, the HyperModel Benchmark still has no notion of complex object.

2.3 OO7

OO7 [5] is a more recent benchmark than OO1 and HyperModel, and hence uses the structures described in the previous paragraphs to propose a more complete benchmark, and to simulate various transactions running on a diversified database.

OO7 Database: OO7's database is based on a conceptual model that is very close to the HyperModel Benchmark's, though it contains a higher number of classes. Four kinds of links are also supported (IS-A, 1-1, 1-N, M-N). There are three sizes of the OO7 database: small, medium, and large.

OO7 Workload: The range of transactions offered by OO7 is also close to HyperModel's. Three main groups may be identified:

- *Traversals* browse the object graph using certain criteria. These traversals are very close to OO1's. There are ten different operations that apply depending on the database characteristics (basically, its size);
- *Queries* retrieve objects chosen in function of various criteria. There are eight kinds of queries;
- *Structural Modification Operations* deal with object insertion and deletion (two operations).

Comments: OO7 attempts to correct the flaws of OO1, and HyperModel. This is achieved with a rich schema and a comprehensive set of operations. However, if OO7 is a good benchmark for engineering applications (like CAD, CAM, or CASE), it might not be the case for other types of applications based on objects. Since its schema is static, it cannot be adapted to other purposes. Eventually, OO7 database structure and operations are nontrivial, hence making the benchmark difficult to understand, adapt, or even implement (yet, to be fair, OO7 implementations are available by anonymous FTP).

3 The Object Clustering Benchmark

OCB's first purpose is to test the performances of clustering algorithms within object-oriented systems. Hence, it is structured around a rich object base including many different classes (and thus many different object sizes, numbers of references, etc.), and numerous types of references (allowing the design of multiple interleaved hierarchies). OCB's workload is purposely clustering-oriented, but can be easily extended to be fully generic as well.

OCB's flexibility is also achieved through an extensive set of parameters that allow the benchmark to be very adaptive. Many different kinds of object bases can be modeled with OCB, as well as many different kinds of applications running on these databases. Since there exists no canonical OODB application, this is an important feature. Eventually, the great majority of these parameters are very easy to settle.

3.1 OCB Justification

We initially felt the need for a clustering-oriented benchmark because the existing benchmarks are not adapted to test the performances of most kinds of clustering algorithms, including semantic clustering algorithms. General purpose benchmarks are useful when testing the performances of an OODBMS as a whole, but inherently do not model any specific application, even if most existing benchmarks were designed in a CAD/CAM/CASE context. Hence, they are not well suited to benchmark the performances of clustering algorithms. Some of their queries simply cannot benefit from any clustering, e.g., queries that scan through the whole database, or random accesses. Furthermore, clustering is very data dependent, what is not taken into account by the synthetic benchmarks, that all adopt a somewhat simple database schema. Consequently, we designed a rich and complex database (though very easy to code and generate), and a set of adapted queries.

OCB's main characteristic is indeed its double aptitude to be both generic and clustering-oriented. The clustering orientation definitely comes from the workload, but the set of transactions we use can be easily extended to achieve full genericity. On the other hand, OCB's database is wholly generic. OCB can be easily either parameterized to model a generic application, or dedicated to a given type of object base and/or application.

The last version of OCB (currently in development) also supports multiple users, in a very simple way (using processes), which is almost unique. As far as we know, only OO7 has a multi-user version also in development. OO1 was designed as multi-user, but the published results only involve one single user.

Eventually, OCB's code is very compact, and easy to implement on any platform. OCB is currently implemented to benchmark the Texas persistent storage system for C++, coupled with the DSTC clustering technique. The C++ code is less than 1,500 lines long. OCB is also being ported into a simulation model designed with the QNAP2 simulation software, that supports a non object-oriented language close to Pascal. The QNAP2 code dealing with OCB is likely to be shorter than 1,000 lines.

3.2 OCB Database

OCB's database is both rich and simple to achieve, very tunable, and thus highly generic. The database is constituted of a predefined number of classes (NC), all derived from the same metaclass (Fig. 1). A class is defined by two parameters: $MAXNREF$, the maximum number of references present in the class' instances; and $BASESIZE$, the class' basic size (increment size used to compute the *InstanceSize* after the inheritance graph is processed during the database generation). Note that, on Fig. 1, the Unified Modeling Language (UML) "bind" clause indicates that classes are instanciated from the metaclass using the parameters between brackets. Since different references can point to the same class, 0-N, 1-N, and M-N links are implicitly modeled. Each reference has a type. There are $NREFT$ different types of reference. A reference type can be, for instance, a type of inheritance, aggregation, user association, etc. After instanciation of the database schema, an object points to at most $MAXNREF$ objects from the iterator of the class referenced by this object's class.

The database generation proceeds through three chief steps.

1. Instanciation of the $CLASS$ metaclass into NC classes: creation of the classes without any reference, then selection of the classes referenced by each class. The type of the references ($TRef$) can be either randomly chosen according to the $DIST1$ random distribution, or fixed *a priori*. The referenced classes belong to an [$INFCLASS$, $SUPCLASS$] interval that models a certain locality

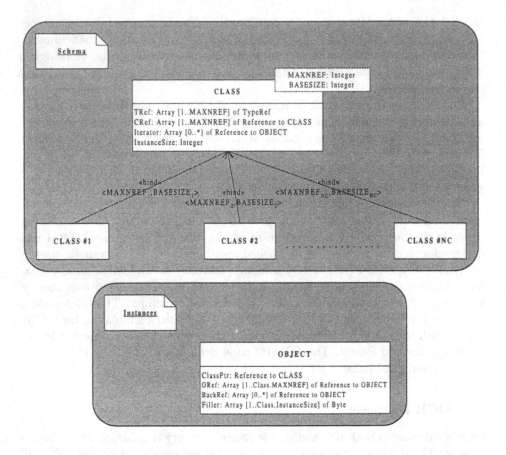

Fig. 1. OCB database schema (UML Static Structure Diagram)

of reference at the class level. The class reference selection can be either performed at random according to the *DIST2* random distribution, or set up *a priori*. NIL references are possible.

2. Check-up of the database consistency: suppression of all the cycles and discrepancies within the graphs that do not allow them (e.g., the inheritance graph, or composition hierarchies).

3. Instanciation of the *NC* classes into *NO* objects: creation of the objects, first without any reference (their class is randomly determined according to the *DIST3* random distribution), then random selection of the objects referenced by each object. The referenced objects belong to an [*INFREF*, *SUPREF*] interval that models the locality of reference as introduced by OO1. The object reference random selection is performed according to the *DIST4* random distribution. Reverse references (*BackRef*) are instanciated at the same time the direct links are.

The full database generation algorithm is provided in Fig. 2.

```
// Schema: Classes
For i = 1, NC do
  For j = 1, MAXNREF (i) do
    Class (i).TRef (j) = RAND (DIST1, 1, NREFT)
  End for
  Class (i).InstanceSize = BASESIZE (i)
End for

// Schema: Inter-classes references
For i = 1, NC do
  For j = 1, MAXNREF (i) do
    Class (i).CRef (j) = RAND (DIST2, INFCLASS, SUPCLASS)
  End for
End for

// Schema: Graph consistency for hierarchies without cycles
For i = 1, NC do
  For j = 1, MAXNREF (i) do
    If In_No_Cycle (Class (i).TRef (j)) then
      // Browse through class CRef (j) graph,
      // following the TRef (j) references
      If Class (i) belongs to the graph or a cycle is detected then
        Class (i).CRef (j) = NULL
      Else
        If Is_Inheritance (Class (i).TRef (j)) then
          // Browse through class CRef (j) inheritance graph
          // and add BASESIZE (i) to InstanceSize for each subclass
        End if
      End if
    End if
  End for
End for

// Instances: Objects
For i = 1, NO do
  Object (i).ClassPtr = RAND (DIST3, 1, NC)
  Object (i).ClassPtr.Add_Object_Into_Iterator (Object (i))
End for

// Instances: Inter-objects references
For i = 1, NC do
  For j = 1, Class (i).Get_Iterator_Count() do
    For k = 1, MAXNREF (i) do
      l = RAND (DIST4, INFREF, SUPREF)
      Iterator (i).Object (j).ORef (k) = Class (CRef(k)).Iterator (l)
      Add_BackRef (Class (CRef(k)).Iterator (l), Iterator (i).Object (j))
    End for
  End for
End for
```

Fig. 2. OCB database generation algorithm

Note: The random numbers used in the database creation are generated by the Lewis-Payne random generator.

The database parameters are summarized in Table 1.

3.3 OCB Workload

Since benchmarking the performances of clustering algorithms is our main goal, we focused OCB's workload on a set of transactions that explore the effects

Name	Parameter	Default value
NC	Number of classes in the database	20
MAXNREF (i)	Maximum number of references, per class	10
BASESIZE (i)	Instances base size, per class	50 bytes
NO	Total number of objects	20000
NREFT	Number of reference types	4
INFCLASS	Inferior bound, set of referenced classes	1
SUPCLASS	Superior bound, set of referenced classes	NC
INFREF	Inferior bound, set of referenced objects	1
SUPREF	Superior bound, set of referenced objects	NO
DIST1	Reference types random distribution	Uniform
DIST2	Class references random distribution	Uniform
DIST3	Objects in classes random distribution	Uniform
DIST4	Objects references random distribution	Uniform

Table 1. OCB database parameters

of clustering. Hence, we excluded at once some kinds of queries that simply cannot benefit from any clustering effort, e.g., creation and update operations, or HyperModel Range Lookup and Sequential Scan [8].

To model an appropriate workload for our needs, we used the types of transactions identified by [4] and [10] (Fig. 3). These operations are at the same time well suited to explore the possibilities offered by clustering, and they can be tailored to model different kinds of applications. They are basically divided into two types: set-oriented accesses, and navigational accesses, that have been empirically found by [10] to match breadth-first and depth-first traversals, respectively. Navigational accesses are further divided into simple, depth first traversals, hierarchy traversals that always follow the same type of reference, and finally stochastic traversals that select the next link to cross at random. Stochastic traversals approach Markov chains, that simulate well the access patterns caused by real queries, according to [12]. At each step, the probability to follow reference number N is $p(N) = 1/2^N$. Each type of transaction proceeds from a randomly chosen root object (according to the *DIST5* random distribution), and up to a predefined depth depending on the transaction type. All these transactions can be reversed to follow the links backwards ("ascending" the graphs).

The execution of the transactions by each client (the benchmark is to be multi-user) is organized according to the following protocol:

1. cold run of *COLDN* transactions which types are determined randomly, according to predefined probabilities. This step's purpose is to fill in the cache in order to observe the real (stationary) behavior of the clustering algorithm implemented in the benchmarked system;
2. warm run of *HOTN* transactions.

A latency time *THINK* can be introduced between each transaction run. The OCB workload parameters are summarized in Table 2.

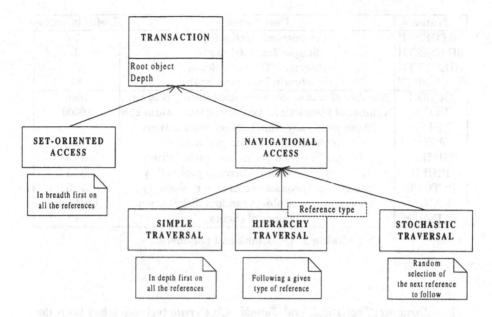

Fig. 3. OCB transaction classes (UML Static Structure Diagram)

The metrics measured by OCB are basically the database response time (global, and per transaction type), the number of accessed objects (still globally, and per transaction type), and the number of I/O performed. We distinguish the I/Os necessary to execute the transactions, and the clustering I/O overhead (I/Os needed to cluster the database).

4 Validation Experiments

The Object Clustering Benchmark has been used to measure the performances of the DSTC clustering technique, that is implemented in the Texas system, running on a Sun workstation. The efficiency of DSTC had already been evaluated with another benchmark called DSTC-CluB [3], that was derived from OO1. Hence, some comparisons are possible.

4.1 Texas and the DSTC Clustering Technique

Texas is a persistent storage for C++, designed and developed at the University of Texas, Austin [11]. Texas is a virtual memory mapped system, and is hence very efficient. Memory data formats are those of C++. Persistent objects are stored on disk using this same format. Thus, when a disk page is loaded into memory, all the disk addresses towards referenced objects are swizzled to virtual memory addresses, and vice versa, when a page is trashed from the virtual memory.

Name	Parameter	Default value
SETDEPTH	Set-oriented Access depth	3
SIMDEPTH	Simple Traversal depth	3
HIEDEPTH	Hierarchy Traversal depth	5
STODEPTH	Stochastic Traversal depth	50
COLDN	Number of transactions executed during cold run	1000
HOTN	Number of transactions executed during warm run	10000
THINK	Average latency time between transactions	0
PSET	Set Access occurrence probability	0.25
PSIMPLE	Simple Traversal occurrence probability	0.25
PHIER	Hierarchy Traversal occurrence probability	0.25
PSTOCH	Stochastic Traversal occurrence probability	0.25
RAND5	Transaction root object random distribution	Uniform
CLIENTN	Number of clients	1

Table 2. OCB workload parameters

The *Dynamic, Statistical, and Tunable Clustering* technique has been developed at Blaise Pascal University (Clermont-Ferrand II) as a Ph.D. project [4]. DSTC is heavily based on the observation of database usage (basically, inter-object links crossings). It utilizes run-time computed statistics to dynamically reorganize the database whenever necessary. The DSTC strategy is subdivided into five phases.

1. *Observation Phase:* During a predefined Observation Period, data related to the transactions execution is collected and stored in a transient Observation Matrix.
2. *Selection Phase:* Data stored in the Observation Matrix are sorted. Only significant statistics are saved.
3. *Consolidation Phase:* The results of the Selection Phase are used to update the data gathered during the previous Observation Periods, that are stored in a persistent Consolidated Matrix.
4. *Dynamic Cluster Reorganization :* The Consolidated Matrix statistics are used either to build new Clustering Units, or to modify existing Clustering Units.
5. *Physical Clustering Organization:* Clustering Units are eventually applied to consider a new object placement on disk. This phase is triggered when the system is idle.

4.2 Material Conditions

DSTC is integrated in a Texas prototype (version 0.2.1) running on a Sun SPARC/ELC workstation. The operating system is SUN OS version 4.3.1. The available main memory is 8 Mb, plus 24 Mb of disk swap. The disk is set up with pages of 4 Kb. Texas and the additional DSTC modules are compiled using the GNU C++ (version 2.4.5) compiler.

4.3   Experiments and Results

These results are not the outcome of extensive tests performed on the Texas / DSTC couple. They are rather significant experiments to demonstrate OCB's feasibility, validity, and functionality.

Object Base Creation Time: The aim of this series of tests is to demonstrate the mere feasibility of OCB. Since we recommend the use of a complex object base, we had to check if our specifications were possible to achieve. Figure 4 presents the database average generation time depending on the database size, with a 1-class schema, a 20-class schema, and a 50-class schema. The time required to create the object base remains indeed reasonable, even for the biggest OCB database (about 15 Mb) used with Texas. The number of classes in the schema influences the database generation time because the inheritance graph consistency is rendered more complex by a high number of classes.

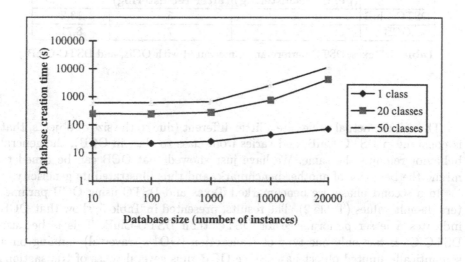

Fig. 4. Database average creation time, function of the database size

I/O Cost: We obtained a first validation for our benchmark by comparing the results achieved by DSTC-CluB (the DSTC Clustering Benchmark) [3] with those achieved by OCB. First, we tuned OCB's database so that it approximates DSTC-CluB's (the OCB database parameters values are provided by Table 3). The results, in terms of I/O cost, are sum up in Table 4. Note that DSTC-CluB measures the number of transaction I/Os before, and after the DSTC algorithm reorganizes the database.

Name	Parameter	Value
NC	Number of classes in the database	2
MAXNREF	Maximum number of references, per class	3
BASESIZE	Instances base size, per class	50 bytes
NO	Total number of objects	20000
NREFT	Number of reference types	3
INFCLASS	Inferior bound, set of referenced classes	0
SUPCLASS	Superior bound, set of referenced classes	NC
INFREF	Inferior bound, set of referenced objects	PartId - RefZone
SUPREF	Superior bound, set of referenced objects	PartId + RefZone
DIST1	Reference types random distribution	Constant
DIST2	Class references random distribution	Constant
DIST3	Objects in classes random distribution	Constant
DIST4	Objects references random distribution	Special

Table 3. OCB database parameters in order to approximate DSTC-CluB's database

Benchmark	Number of I/Os (before reclustering)	Number of I/Os (after reclustering)	Gain Factor
DSTC-CluB	66	5	13,2
OCB	61	7	8,71

Table 4. Texas/DSTC performance, measured with OCB, and DSTC-CluB

Though the actual values are a little different (due to the size of objects, that is constant in DSTC-CluB, and varies from class to class in OCB), the general behavior remains the same. We have just showed that OCB can be tuned to mimic the behavior of another benchmark, and thus illustrated its genericity.

In a second phase, we benchmarked Texas and DSTC using OCB parameters default values (Table 2). The results, presented in Table 5, show that OCB indicates a lesser performance for DSTC than DSTC-CluB. This is because DSTC-CluB has only one type of transaction (OO1's traversal) running on a semantically limited object base. Since OCB runs several types of transactions on the database (thus more closely modeling a real transaction workload), the access patterns, and the associated usage statistics, are much less stereotyped. Hence, clustering with DSTC is demonstrated not to be as good as stated in [3]. It though remains an excellent choice, since it still improves Texas' performances by a 2.5 factor.

5 Conclusions and Future Research

OCB has been demonstrated to be valid to benchmark the performances of clustering algorithms in OODBs. We have indeed proved that, properly customized, OCB could confirm results obtained with the previous benchmark DSTC-CluB,

Benchmark	Number of I/Os (before reclustering)	Number of I/Os (after reclustering)	Gain Factor
OCB	31	12	2,58

Table 5. Texas/DSTC performance, measured with OCB

and even provide more insight about clustering policies performance than DSTC-CluB (and, *a fortiori*, OO1).

OCB's main qualities are its richness, its flexibility, and its compactness. OCB indeed offers an object base which complexity has never been achieved before in object-oriented benchmarks. Furthermore, since this database, and likewise, the transactions running on it, are wholly tunable through a set of comprehensive (but easily set) parameters, OCB can be used to model any kind of object-oriented database application. Lastly, OCB's code is short, reasonably easy to implement, and easily portable, even in non object-oriented environments like

The perspectives opened by this study are numerous. First, we have mentioned that OCB could be easily enhanced to become a fully generic object-oriented benchmark. Since OCB's object base is already generic, this goal can be achieved by extending the transaction set so that it includes a broader range of operations (namely operations we discarded in the first place because they couldn't benefit from clustering). We think too, that existing benchmark databases might be approximated with OCB's schema, tuned by the appropriate parameters.

Another obvious future task is the actual exploitation of OCB: the benchmarking of several different clustering techniques for the sake of performance comparison, and possibly each time on different systems (OODB/OS couple). We also plan to integrate OCB into simulation models, in order to benefit from the advantages of simulation (platform independence, *a priori* modeling of non-implemented research prototypes, low cost).

Eventually, when designing our benchmark, we essentially focused on performance. However, though very important, performance is not the only factor to consider. Functionality is also very significant [2]. Hence, we plan to work in this direction, and add a qualitative element into OCB, a bit the way [9] operated for the CAD-oriented OCAD benchmark. For instance, we could evaluate if a clustering heuristic's parameters are easy to apprehend and set up, if the algorithm is easy to use, or transparent to the user, etc.

References

1. T.L. Anderson, A.J. Berre, M. Mallison, H.H. Porter III, B. Scheider: The Hyper-Model Benchmark. International Conference on Extending Database Technology, Venice, Italy, March 1990, pp. 317-331
2. A.J. Berre, T.L. Anderson: The HyperModel Benchmark for Evaluating Object-Oriented Databases. In "Object-Oriented Databases with Applications to CASE, Networks and VLSI CAD", Edited by R. Gupta and E. Horowitz, Prentice Hall Series in Data and Knowledge Base Systems, 1991, pp. 75-91
3. F. Bullat, M. Schneider: Dynamic Clustering in Object Database Exploiting Effective Use of Relationships Between Objects. ECOOP '96, Linz, Austria, July 1996; Lecture Notes in Computer Science No. 1098, pp. 344-365
4. F. Bullat: Regroupement dynamique d'objets dans les bases de données. PhD Thesis, Blaise Pascal University, Clermont-Ferrand II, France, January 1996
5. M.J. Carey, D.J. Dewitt, J.F. Naughton: The OO7 Benchmark. Technical report, University of Wisconsin-Madison, January 1994
6. R.G.G. Cattell: An Engineering Database Benchmark. In "The Benchmark Handbook for Database Transaction Processing Systems", Edited by Jim Gray, Morgan Kaufmann Publishers, 1991, pp. 247-281
7. S. Chabridon, J.-C. Liao, Y. Ma, L. Gruenwald: Clustering Techniques for Object-Oriented Database Systems. 38th IEEE Computer Society International Conference, San Francisco, February 1993, pp. 232-242
8. J. Darmont, A. Attoui, M. Gourgand: Simulation of clustering algorithms in OODBs in order to evaluate their performance. Simulation Practice and Theory, No. 5, 1997, pp. 269-287
9. J. Kempe, W. Kowarschick, W. Kießling, R. Hitzelberger, F. Dutkowski: Benchmarking Object-Oriented Database Systems for CAD. 6th International Conference on Database and Expert Systems Applications (DEXA 95), London, UK, 1995; LNCS Vol. 978 (Springer), pp. 167-176
10. W.J. Mc Iver Jr., R. King: Self-Adaptive, On-Line Reclustering of Complex Object Data. ACM SIGMOD Conference, Minneapolis, Minnesota, 1994, pp. 407-418
11. V. Singhal, S.V. Kakkad, P.R. Wilson: Texas: An Efficient, Portable Persistent Store. 5th International Workshop on Persistent Object Systems, San Miniato, Italy, 1992
12. M.M. Tsangaris, J.F. Naughton: On the Performance of Object Clustering Techniques. ACM SIGMOD International Conference on Management of Data, San Diego, California, June 1992, pp. 144-153

A Path Removing Technique
for Detecting Trigger Termination

Sin Yeung LEE & Tok Wang LING
Department of Information Systems and Computer Science
National University of Singapore
Lower Kent Ridge Road, Singapore 119260, Singapore.
email : jlee@iscs.nus.edu.sg, lingtw@iscs.nus.edu.sg

Abstract Termination decision in trigger systems is to ensure that any rule execution does not result in an infinite loop. Generally, this is an undecidable task. Several recent works have been proposed to prove termination under certain situations. However, most of these existing methods make use of the trigger conditions only in a limited way. In particular, overall conditions of long trigger sequences are not fully used to decide termination. In this paper, we will introduce the activation formula, which considers the overall conditions of long trigger sequences and hence covers many previous works. With this extension, traditional trigger edge elimination methods are no longer sufficient. We will then present a path elimination method called the node splitting method. Using this new approach, more termination situations than existing works can be detected.

1 Introduction

Recently, there is an increasing interest in providing rule processing to database systems so that they are capable of automatic updating as well as enforcing database integrity. One of the most popular approaches is the ECA rules [5, 6]. Although ECA rules are very powerful, the way to specify them is unstructured. The final database state depends greatly on the rule execution order. Furthermore, rules may activate each other indefinitely causing the system not to terminate. For example, consider the following wrongly written trigger rules:

```
r1 :: [BEFORE] ACC.withdraw(Amt)
      IF (Amt < 10)  ACC.serviceCharge();
r2 :: [BEFORE] ACC.serviceCharge()
      IF (ACC.balance>11)  ACC.withdraw(1);
                    else  Rollback;
```

The original intention of these two trigger rules is to implement the policy that any withdrawal below ten dollars shall incur a dollar service charge. Obviously, the two rules can reactivate each other. Since the two rules are BEFORE rules, i.e., the trigger conditions are checked before the update, once an account has more than 11 dollars, the execution of these two rules will not terminate.

This non-termination decision problem makes developing even a simple application a difficult task. Hence, it is important to have some analysis methods on the set of trigger rules to predict its behavior in advance. Although it is undecidable whether the execution of any given set of trigger rules will finally terminate, it is still beneficial to detect those trigger rules which terminate and those rules which may not terminate. This can assist the rule programmers so that they need only to verify a smaller subset of the trigger rules.

There are many recent works on this termination problem. In particular, [1] first introduces the trigger graph method. In a trigger graph, each node represents a rule, and each edge represents the possibility that one rule may trigger the execution of another rule. An obvious sufficient condition of termination is that the trigger graph is acyclic. This is a simple syntactical analysis. However, it may conservatively ignore a lot of termination conditions. Later works such as [3, 8] improve this idea. [8] proposes a refinement method. To decide if one rule r can actually trigger another rule r', [8] constructs a conjunct based on the trigger conditions of the two rules. If the conjunct is not satisfiable, then the edge between the two rules is removed. On the other hand, [3] augments a trigger graph with an activation graph. An edge is removed unless it is in a cycle and can be re-activated after a self-deactivation [3].

Nonetheless, there are still many terminating situations which are not detected by any of the above methods. On closer examination, we identify two inadequancies:

1. Inadequacy of single-edge analysis

   Most existing methods [3, 8] analyze edges of the trigger graph and eliminates only a single edge one at a time, many terminating conditions therefore cannot be detected. For example, consider the following three rules:

   > r1 :: $e1(X,Y)$ IF $X > 5$ DO $e2(X,Y)$
   > r2 :: $e2(X,Y)$ IF $Y = 1$ DO $e3(X,Y)$
   > r3 :: $e3(X,Y)$ IF $X < 5$ DO $e1(X,Y)$

   where $e1, e2$ and $e3$ are some parameterized events. They can be methods of an OODBMS, or updates in a RDBMS. Carefully inspecting the conditions of rule r1 and rule r3, we see that the execution sequence: r1, r2 and finally r3 cannot be executed. Hence, the path ≪r1,r2,r3≫ can be removed from the trigger graph. The new graph is acyclic and this trigger system will terminate.

   However, since ≪r1,r2≫ and ≪r2,r3≫ are both executable edges, [8] cannot remove any edge and thus cannot detect termination. Similarly, [1, 3] do not offer any better answer. All these edge analyses fail to conclude termination. In Section 4, we shall extend the idea of edge analysis to a more general path analysis.

2. Inadequacy of ignoring updatable predicates/attributes

   Trigger termination methods differ from other rule termination and local stratifiability methods [10, 11] in that predicates can be updated during the execution of the trigger rules. To take the trigger actions into consideration, much more complex algorithm is needed. [3, 9] explicitly make use of the effect of the trigger actions upon the trigger conditions to improve the termination decision. On the other hand, [8] selects only attribute values that will not be updated to detect termination. This makes some useful termination conditions undetected. For example, consider the following three rules:

   > r1 :: $e1(X,Y)$ IF $X.v < 1$ DO $e2(X,Y)$
   > r2 :: $e2(X,Y)$ IF $X.v > 2$ DO $e1(X,Y)$
   > r3 :: $e3(X,Y)$ DO SET $X.v$ TO Y;

[8] argues that value of attribute v may be changed between the execution of r1 and r2, hence, it is not correct to directly conjunct the two trigger conditions of r1 and r2 together. Hence, [8] does not use the attribute v to detect termination. However, with a more careful investigation, since r3 only executes finitely in the given trigger system, eventually the attribute v will not be updated any more, and the conditions of r1 and r2 can still conclude termination. Using this idea, we propose a new concept called finitely-updatable predicate to improve [8].

The main contribution of this paper is to handle the above deficiencies:
1. Our method considers an overall condition of a long rule sequence, and
2. is capable to make use of more predicates to decide termination.

In the next section, we outline the background setting of the trigger architecture used in the discussion. Section 3 will introduce the *activation formula* of an execution sequence $\ll r_1, \ldots, r_n \gg$, which is the necessary condition that rule r_1 will eventually trigger rule r_n via rules $r_2, \ldots, r_{n-1}$. Since traditional methods cannot remove trigger path, Section 4 will introduce the *node splitting method.* to remove path from a trigger graph. Section 5 will show how our proposed finitely-updatable predicate idea improves existing methods. Section 6 will cite some related works, and Section 7 will conclude the paper.

2 Trigger Architecture

We assume a general abstract architecture of the underlying active databases that does not depend on any particular architecture. The underlying database can be an active OODB, or just a simple RDB. Each trigger rule takes the following form:

$rule\_name$ :: *event* IF *condition* DO $action_1, \ldots, action_n$

where *rule_name* is the name of the trigger rule. The *event* and $action_i$ in the trigger rules are abstracted to take the following form,

$event\_name(variable\_list)$

condition is a conjunction of positive literals, negative literals and/or evaluable predicates. Any variable which appears in the variable list of any $action_i$ must either appear in the *event* or in the *condition*. Furthermore, in order that the evaluation of *condition* is safe, any variable that appears in any negative literal or an evaluable predicate in *condition* should also appear in either *event* or in a positive literal in *condition*. We shall call those variables that appear in *condition* but not in *event* as *local variables*. Throughout this paper, we will also refer *event* as $rule\_name.\text{E\scriptsize VENT}$ and *condition* as $rule\_name.\text{C\scriptsize OND}$.

Example 2.1 The following specifies that an increase of an employee salary should also trigger an increase of the salary of his/her manager by the same amount:

$incr\_salary\_rule$ :: $incr\_salary(EmpID,IncrAmt)$

  IF $emp(EmpID,MgrID,Salary)$ DO $incr\_salary(MgrID,IncrAmt)$ □

As our proposed method is independent on the rule execution order, we need no assumption on the model of execution.

3 Activation Formula

[8] introduces the trigger formula, which is a more refined condition to decide if a rule r_1 can trigger another rule r_2. The trigger formula is constructed by conjuncting the trigger conditions of trigger rules r_1 and r_2 in a selective way. If the trigger formula is unsatisfiable, then the corresponding trigger edge between r_1 and r_2 in the trigger graph is removed. If the final graph is acyclic, then the trigger system will terminate. For example, given the following two trigger rules:

r1 :: $e1(X)$ IF $(X > 1)$ DO $e2(X)$
r2 :: $e2(X)$ IF $(X < 1)$ DO $e1(X)$

[8] constructs the trigger formulae as,

$(X > 1) \wedge (X < 1)$

This formula is unsatisfiable, therefore, the edge «r1,r2» is removed from the trigger graph. Since the resultant graph is acyclic, this trigger system will terminate.

A direct generalization is to consider more than one edge by conjuncting more conditions together. If the resultant condition is a contradiction, then the sequence of rules cannot be executed at all. This guarantees termination. For example,

r1 :: $e1(X)$ IF $(X > 1)$ DO $e2(X)$
r2 :: $e2(X)$ IF $(X > 5)$ DO $e3(X)$
r3 :: $e3(X)$ IF $(X < 1)$ DO $e1(X)$

The conjunction of conditions of the rules from the execution sequence «r1,r2,r3» is

$(X > 1) \wedge (X > 5) \wedge (X < 1)$

which is clearly unsatisfiable. Hence, r1 cannnot trigger r3 via r2 during run time.

However, this generalization of conjuncting conditions is far from trivial, there are two major considerations to be handled:

1. Conflict of variables.

   The scope of the variables used in a trigger condition is only within the rule itself. When the conditions from several trigger rules are conjuncted together, conflict of variables may occur. For example, the variable X of the following two rules belongs to a different scope:

   r1 :: $e1(X)$ IF $(X > 1) \wedge p(X,Y)$ DO $e2(Y)$
   r2 :: $e2(X)$ IF $(X < 1)$ DO $e1(X)$

   Hence we cannot directly conjunct the trigger conditions of these two rules together. The solution adopted by [8] requires that each variable used in each trigger rule has a different name. This solution has an obvious problem. The variable conflict still occurs if the condition from the same rule appears at least twice in the conjunction. For example, consider another trigger rule:

   r3 :: $e3(X,Y)$ IF $(X > Y)$ DO $e3(Y,X)$

   A simple conjunction of r3 with r3 gives a wrong formula:

   $(X > Y) \wedge (X > Y)$

2. Process to eliminate trigger edges.

   Even if we can prove that a sequence of rules cannot be executed, it is possible that no edge can be removed from the trigger graph. For example, consider the following graph, even if we prove that rule r1 cannot trigger r4 via r2, no edge can be immediately removed from the trigger graph without destroying other cycle.

In Section 4, we propose a method to eliminate a path instead of an edge from a trigger graph.

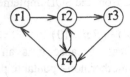

3.1 Predicate Selection Procedure

Our method investigates the conjunction of the trigger conditions in each trigger rule in a given execution sequence. However, as shown in [8], we cannot include every predicate in the trigger conditions, we need a *predicate selection procedure* to select the correct predicates to be included in the conjunction of the trigger conditions. We propose two possible predicate selection procedures:
1. Non-Updatable predicate selection procedure
2. Finitely updatable predicate selection procedure

The first selection procedure is a simplified version of the second selection procedure, and is used for the ease of discussion. The second procedure — finitely updatable predicate selection procedure, will be used in the final termination decision algorithm. Section 5 will discuss the algorithm making use of the latter selection procedure. The two selection procedures are further elaborated as follows:

3.1.1 Non-Updatable predicate procedure

This selection procedure only selects predicates that cannot be updated by any trigger execution. Non-updatable predicates fall into the following categories:
1. Evaluable function
2. Predicate/attribute that is not modified, whether directly or indirectly, by any action of some trigger rules.

Example 3.1 Given a bank database which contains the following relations:
1. $acc(Acc\#, Owner, Bal)$
   $Acc\#$ is the account number owned by *Owner* with amount *Bal*.
2. $bankcard(Card\#, Acc\#)$
   The bankcard $Card\#$ is associated with the account $Acc\#$. One account can have many bankcards, but each bankcard can only be associated with one account.

In this database, two trigger rules are specified,

```
// If a bankcard is lost, debit into the owner's account
// a service charge of 10 dollars.
```
r1 :: replace_lost_card($Card\#$) IF $bankcard(Card\#, Acc\#)$ DO debit($Acc\#, 10$)
```
// If an account has insufficient fund during debit,
// alert the owner, but allow overdraft.
```
r2 :: debit($Acc\#, Amt$) IF $acc(Acc\#, Owner, Bal) \wedge (Bal < Amt)$ DO
         alert($Owner, Acc\#$, 'Overdraft')

The trigger events update the databases in the following ways:
1. The event *replace_lost_card* will issue a new bankcard to its owner. It will not update the relations *acc* and *bankcard*.

2. The event *debit* is to update the *Bal* of *Owner*'s account in the relation *acc*.

3. The event *alert* does not update the database.

Note that all these information can be easily extracted from the SQL implementation. Now consider the following formula,

$$bankcard(Card\#,Acc\#) \land acc(Acc\#,Owner,Bal) \land (Bal < 10)$$

the predicate $(Bal < 10)$, is a non-updatable predicate because it is an evaluable function. The predicate $bankcard(Card\#,Acc\#)$ is another non-updatable predicate as no trigger action updates the relation *bankcard*. On the other hand, the predicate $acc(Acc\#,Owner,Bal)$ is an updatable predicate as it can be updated by the action *debit* in trigger rule r1. Therefore, using our non-updatable predicate selection procedure, the formula

$$bankcard(Card\#,Acc\#) \land acc(Acc\#,Owner,Bal) \land (Bal < 10)$$

is modified to be,

$$bankcard(Card\#,Acc\#) \land (Bal < 10)$$

As the variable *Bal* appears once in the above condition, hence $Bal < 10$ is trivially satisfiable. Now, the final condition is simplified to,

$$bankcard(Card\#,Acc\#) \qquad \square$$

3.1.2 Finitely Updatable predicate procedure

In practice, it is unlikely to include many predicates in the conjunction of the trigger conditions, as relations/objects are often targets of update. The *finitely-updatable predicate selection* is therefore an improvement on it. Instead of including only predicates which are not updated by any trigger action, this predicate selection procedure includes predicates that are not updated indefinitely by any trigger action. However, to decide which predicate is updated only finitely is as hard as the original termination problem. In this case, we need to incorporate a much more complex incremental algorithm for termination detection. We will discuss this further in Section 5. Meanwhile, to clarify the basic concept, we employ the non-updatable predicate selection procedure as our default predicate selection procedure.

3.2 Construction of Activation Formula

Definition 3.1 Given an execution sequence $\ll r_1, \ldots, r_n \gg$, an *activation formula* $F_{act}(\ll r_1, \ldots, r_n \gg)$ is a necessary condition for rule r_1 to eventually trigger rule r_n via rules $r_2, \ldots, r_{n-1}$. $\qquad \square$

Example 3.2 Consider the following trigger rules,

> r1 :: $e1(X,Y)$ IF $X > 3$ DO $e2(X,Y)$
> r2 :: $e2(X,Y)$ IF $X < 1$ DO $e1(X,Y)$

An activation formula of path $\ll r1, r2 \gg$ is $(X > 3) \land (X < 1)$. Events such as $e1(4,2)$ cannot trigger another event $e1$ via the trigger sequence r1, r2. Note that since an activation formula gives only the necessary condition, therefore, it is not necessarily unique. Another weaker activation formula is $(X < 1)$. $\qquad \square$

The following algorithm computes an activation formula for a given execution sequence $\ll r_1, \ldots, r_n \gg$:

Algorithm 3.1 Given an execution sequence $\ll r_1, \ldots, r_n \gg$, and a predicate selection procedure *PSP*, we compute an activation formula, $F_{act}(\ll r_1, \ldots, r_n \gg)$ as follows,

1. We first compute an intermediate condition C as follows,
2. When $n = 1$, C is set to r_1. *COND*
3. Otherwise, let C' be $F_{act}(\ll r_2, \ldots, r_n \gg)$ subject to the selection procedure *PSP*, and let σ be the substitution unifier between the event of rule r_2 and the triggering action of rule r_1. We perform the following steps,
   i. Rename any local variable in C' that also appears in r_1 to another name to avoid name conflict.
   ii. C is set to r_1. *COND* $\wedge$ $C'\sigma$
4. To compute the final $F_{act}(\ll r_1, \ldots, r_n \gg)$, apply the predicate selection procedure *PSP* to remove any unwanted predicates in the formula C. □

Example 3.3 Consider the following three trigger rules,

r1 :: $e1(X,Y)$ IF $(X > 1)$ DO $\{e2(X,0), e3(1,Y)\}$
r2 :: $e2(X,Y)$ IF TRUE DO $e1(Y,X)$
r3 :: $e3(X,Y)$ IF $X \neq Y$ DO $e2(X,Y)$

Subject to the non-updatable predicate selection procedure, the activation formula for $F_{act}(\ll r_1, r_2, r_1 \gg)$ can be computed as follows,

1. First, we compute $F_{act}(\ll r_2, r_1 \gg)$, which requires to compute $F_{act}(\ll r_1 \gg)$.
2. Now, $F_{act}(\ll r_1 \gg)$ is actually the condition of rule r1 after removing any updatable predicate. This gives the formula $(X > 1)$.
3. To compute $F_{act}(\ll r_2, r_1 \gg)$, we first observe that $\{X/Y, Y/X\}$ is the substitution σ between the event of r_1, $e1(X,Y)$, and the matching action of r_2, $e1(Y,X)$. Applying the algorithm, we have
   TRUE $\wedge$ $(X > 1)\{X/Y, Y/X\}$
   After simplification and elimination of any updatable predicate, we have $(Y > 1)$.
4. Finally, to compute $F_{act}(\ll r_1, r_2, r_1 \gg)$, $\{X/X, Y/0\}$ is the substitution σ between the $e2(X,Y)$, and the matching action $e2(X,0)$. We compute C to be,
   $(X > 1) \wedge ((Y > 1)\{X/X, Y/0\})$
   It can be simplified to FALSE. In other words, the activation formula of the execution sequence from r_1, to r_2, and then back to r_1 is not possible. □

Definition 3.2 An execution sequence $\ll r_1, \ldots, r_n \gg$ where r_i's are trigger rules which are not necessarily distinct, is an *activable path* subject to a predicate selection procedure *PSP* if the activation formulae $F_{act}(\ll r_1, \ldots, r_n \gg)$ subject to *PSP* is satisfiable. Otherwise, the sequence is a *non-activable path*. □

Example 3.4 From Example 3.3, the path $\ll r2, r1 \gg$ is an activable path. The path $\ll r1, r2, r1 \gg$ is a non-activable path. □

Definition 3.3 A *simple cycle* is denoted by $\ll r_1, \ldots, r_n \gg^+$ where r_i's are all distinct. It indicates the cyclic execution that rule r_1 triggers r_2, which then triggers r_3 and so on until r_n, which triggers back r_1.

Theorem 3.1 Given a trigger graph G, and if each simple cycle Γ contains a non-activable path, then the trigger system can terminate. □

Example 3.5 Consider the following five rules:
r1 :: $e1(X,Y)$ IF $X>1$ DO $\{e2(X,Y),e3(X,Y)\}$
r2 :: $e2(X,Y)$ IF $Y<1$ DO $e1(Y,X)$
r3 :: $e2(X,Y)$ IF $X<2$ DO $e3(X,Y)$
r4 :: $e3(X,Y)$ IF $X<Y$ DO $e4(Y+1,X)$
r5 :: $e4(X,Y)$ IF $X<Y$ DO $e1(X,Y)$

There are three simple cycles: $\ll$r1,r2$\gg^+$, $\ll$r1,r4,r5$\gg^+$ and $\ll$r1,r3,r4,r5$\gg^+$. Each of these cycles contains at least one non-activable path. For instance, the cycle $\ll$r1,r2$\gg^+$ contains a non-activable path $\ll$r1,r2,r1$\gg$. Hence, from Theorem 3.1, the trigger system can terminate.

Now consider the cycles $\ll$r1,r4,r5$\gg^+$ and $\ll$r1,r3,r4,r5$\gg^+$. Proving that these two cycles contain non-activable paths requires us to examine the same non-activable path $\ll$r4,r5,r1$\gg$ twice. To eliminate this re-examination, we propose to remove the path from the trigger graph once we find it. In this example, after the path $\ll$r4,r5,r1$\gg$ is removed, the trigger graph is greatly reduced. The only cycle left is $\ll$r1,r2$\gg^+$. □

4 Path removal by node-splitting method

As described in section 3, knowing that, say, $\ll r_1,r_2,r_3\gg$ is a non-activable path does not necessarily mean that any edge can be removed from the given trigger graph. We therefore need an operation that will eliminate paths instead of just edges from a trigger graph. Formally, we need an operation $remove(G,\pi)$ described as,

Definition 4.1 The operation $remove(G,\pi)$ where G is a trigger graph and π is a path in G generates a new graph G' such that
1. the path π is not represented in G', and
2. all other paths in G which do not contain the subpath π are represented in G'. □

To eliminate a path $\ll r_1,r_2,r_3\gg$ from a trigger graph, we propose a path removing method called *node-splitting* method. The main idea of the node-splitting method is to split the node r_2 into two almost equivalent nodes: r_2 and r'_2. Furthermore, all the edges from r_2 are duplicated for r'_2 except that r_1 has an edge to r'_2 but not to r_2, and r_3 has an edge from r_2 but not from r'_2. Now that r_1 can still trigger r'_2, and r_2 can still trigger r_3. However, it is no longer possible for rule r_1 to trigger r_3 via either r_2, or r'_2. This idea is summarized in the following diagram:

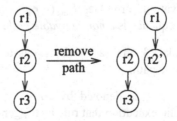

Figure 4.1

The following gives a formal algorithm on how the operation $remove(G,\pi)$ can be implemented by using the node-splitting method:

Algorithm 4.1 *(Path removing algorithm)* Consider a trigger graph G and any path $\ll r_1,\ldots,r_n\gg$ where $n\geq 3$ and $r_1,\ldots,r_{n-1}$ are distinct. However, r_n can be the same node as r_1, or just another node. The operation $remove(G,\ll r_1,\ldots,r_n\gg)$ is done as follows,

1. Duplicate all the nodes $r_2,\ldots,r_{n-1}$, and name the new nodes as $r'_2,\ldots,r'_{n-1}$ respectively.
2. For $2\leq i\leq n-2$, insert the edge $\ll r'_i,r'_{i+1}\gg$.
3. For each outgoing edge $\ll r_i,t\gg$ of node r_i, except the edge $\ll r_i,r_{i+1}\gg$ where $2\leq i\leq n-1$, insert the edge $\ll r'_i,t\gg$ in the graph.
4. Insert the edge $\ll r_1,r'_2\gg$ and remove the edge $\ll r_1,r_2\gg$. □

Example 4.1 Given the trigger graph in Figure 4.2, if we want to remove the path $\ll r_2,r_3,r_4,r_2\gg$ from the graph, we apply Algorithm 4.1. The new trigger graph is shown in Figure 4.3. Note that the path $\ll r_2,r_3,r_4,r_2\gg$ no longer appears in the split graph. So our splitting method does remove the path from the graph. Other paths in G such as $\ll r_1,r_2,r_3,r_1\gg$ do has a corresponding path $\ll r_1,r_2,r'_3,r_1\gg$ in G'. Indeed, our method does not remove any other path that does not contain a subpath of $\ll r_2,r_3,r_4,r_2\gg$. The proof of its correctness can be found in the subsection 4.1.

The resultant graph seems to be more complex. However, in the context of termination decision, it is easily shown that r_3 cannot be part of any cycle and thus can be removed. This removal causes r_4 to have only outgoing edges, and thus cannot be part of any cycle. After r_4 is removed, the simplified graph is shown in Figure 4.4.

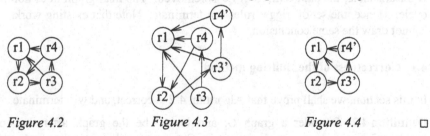

Figure 4.2   *Figure 4.3*   *Figure 4.4*   □

Using Algorithm 4.1 to remove a path from a trigger graph, we can construct a new termination decision algorithm as follows,

Algorithm 4.2 Given a trigger system *TS*, we decide if it terminates as follows,
1. Construct a trigger graph G for *TS*.
2. Remove any node which is not inside any cycle in the current trigger graph.
3. Remove any edge $\ll s,t\gg$ if its activation formula is unsatisfiable.
4. If the graph is acyclic, then conclude that "Terminate" and exit the algorithm.
5. Pick up one of the smallest cycles in the current trigger graph. If it contains no non-activable path, then return "May not terminate" and exit the algorithm.
6. Otherwise, remove this path according to Algorithm 4.1. The new graph is now the current trigger graph. Repeat step 2 again. □

Example 4.2 Given the following trigger sets,

r1 :: $e1(X,Y)$ IF $X>1$ DO $\{e2(X,Y),e5(X,Y)\}$
r2 :: $e2(X,Y)$ IF $a(Y,Z)$ DO $e3(Z,1)$
r3 :: $e3(X,Y)$ IF $b(X,Y)$ DO $\{e1(Y,X),e4(X,Y)\}$
r4 :: $e4(X,Y)$ IF $\neg b(X,1)$ DO $e2(X,Y)$
r5 :: $e5(X,Y)$ IF T$_{RUE}$ DO $e2(X,Y)$

We assume no event updates the relation b. We apply Algorithm 4.2 to decide if the set of rules will terminate. The frist step is to construct a trigger graph as in Figure 4.5. In step 2, we eliminate any node which is not inside any cycle. No such node is found from the current graph. Similarly, no edge can be removed at step 3.

In step 5 of Algorithm 4.2, we pick one of the smallest cycles, say, $\ll$r1,r2,r3$\gg^{+}$ in the graph. It contains a non-activable path $\ll$r2,r3,r1$\gg$. To remove this path, we apply Algorithm 4.1 to split node r3 into r3 and r3$'$. The resultant graph is shown in Figure 4.6. Repeat from step 2 of Algorithm 4.2, nodes r3,r1 and r5 are removed, as they are not part of any cycle in the new graph. The resultant graph is shown in Figure 4.7.

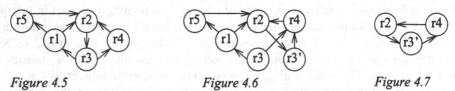

Figure 4.5   *Figure 4.6*   *Figure 4.7*

Only one cycle remains. Finally, as $F_{act}(\ll$r2,r3$'$,r4$\gg)$ is,

$$a(Y,Z) \wedge b(Z,1) \wedge \neg b(Z,1)$$

is unsatisfiable, the path $\ll$r2,r3$'$,r4$\gg$ is removed. The final graph does not have any cycle. Hence, the set of trigger rules can terminate. Note that existing works [3, 4, 8] cannot draw the same conclusion.   □

4.1 Correctness of the splitting method

In this section, we shall prove that Algorithm 4.2 is correct, and will terminate.

Definition 4.2 Consider a graph G, and let G' be the graph after the operation $remove(G,\ll r_1,\ldots,r_n\gg)$. A node r in G' *corresponds* to another node s in G if either r is s, or r is a split node duplicated from s. A path $P' \ll s_1,\ldots,s_n\gg$ in G' *corresponds* to a path $P \ll r_1,\ldots,r_n\gg$ in G if s_i corresponds to r_i for every i $(1 \leq i \leq n)$. □

Example 4.3 Refering to Figure 4.1, let G be the given graph, and G' be the split graph. The path $\ll r_1,r'_2\gg$ in G' corresponds to the path $\ll r_1,r_2\gg$ in G. and the path $\ll r_2,r_3\gg$ in G' corresponds to the path $\ll r_2,r_3\gg$ in G. However, no path in G' corresponds to the path $\ll r_1,r_2,r_3\gg$ in G.   □

The above example shows that it is possible to have a path in the original graph without having a corresponding path in the new graph. The following theorem states exactly which path in the original graph is removed after the split process.

Lemma 4.1 Consider a graph G, and let G' be the graph after the operation $remove(G, \ll r_1, \ldots, r_n \gg)$. A path P in G has no corresponding path in G' if and only if P contains the subpath $\ll r_1, \ldots, r_n \gg$. □

Lemma 4.2 Consider a set of trigger rules T, and let G be its trigger graph. Let π be a non-activable path in G, and G' be the resultant graph of $remove(G, \pi)$, we have:

If a path $\ll r_1, \ldots, r_n \gg$ in G can be executed, then $\ll r_1, \ldots, r_n \gg$ has a corresponding path in G'.

PROOF (*by contradiction*) Assume a path $\ll r_1, \ldots, r_n \gg$ in G can be executed but does not have a corresponding path in G'. According to Lemma 4.1, any path eliminated from G by the split process always contains the path π. Furthermore, no other path can be removed. Hence, if the path $\ll r_1, \ldots, r_n \gg$ is eliminated from G, it must contain the non-activable path π. Since π is non-activable, $\ll r_1, \ldots, r_n \gg$ cannot be executed in run time. A contradiction occurs. □

In other words, our node splitting will not remove any rule sequence that is executable. With this, we have the following theorem concerning the trigger termination.

Theorem 4.1 Let T be a set of trigger rules, and G_1 be its trigger graph. Let G_{i+1} be the resultant graph of $remove(G_i, \pi_i)$ where π_i is a non-activable path in G_i. If there is a G_k ($k \geq 1$) which is acyclic, then the set of trigger rules T will terminate. □

The above theorem states that if Algorithm 4.2 concludes termination, then the trigger system indeed terminates. However, as the Algorithm 4.2 introduces new nodes, it may be argued that new cycles may be created/duplicated and the algorithm may keep on introducing new cycles and may not terminate. Fortunately, the following two lemmas guarantee that no new cycle is created by Algorithm 4.2.

Lemma 4.3 Let G' be the result of $remove(G, \pi)$. Every cycle in G' has a corresponding cycle in G. □

This lemma states that when new nodes are introduced by the operation $remove(G, \pi)$, no new cycle will be introduced that has no corresponding cycle in G. The next lemma further states that if π is in one of the shortest cycles, then every cycle in G has at most one cycle in G' that corresponds to it. Hence, the number of cycles will not increase after each $remove$ operation.

Lemma 4.4 Let G' be the result of $remove(G, \pi)$. If no subset of the nodes used in π forms a cycle in G, then for any cycle Γ in G, there is at most one cycle in G' which corresponds to Γ.

PROOF Assume it is otherwise, given a cycle Γ, $\ll s_1, \ldots, s_n \gg^+$, and a path π, $\ll r_1, \ldots, r_m \gg$ in G, it is possible to have two cycles Γ_1 and Γ_2 in G' which correspond to Γ. Obviously, the cycle Γ must use at least one of the split nodes, say, s_k. After $remove(G, \pi)$, without loss of generality, we assume Γ_1 uses the original node s_k and Γ_2 uses the duplicated node s'_k. Consider the node s_{k-1} in Γ, an edge $\ll s_{k-1}, s_k \gg$ can only be one of the following cases:

1. $\ll s_{k-1}, s_k \gg$ corresponds to an edge in the split path π, but s_{k-1} is not the first node r_1. In other words, s_{k-1} corresponds to r_{i-1} for some $i \leq 2$, and s_k corresponds to r_i.
2. $\ll s_{k-1}, s_k \gg$ corresponds to an edge in π, and s_{k-1} is also the first node, r_1.

3. $\ll s_{k-1}, s_k \gg$ does not correspond to any edge in the split path π.

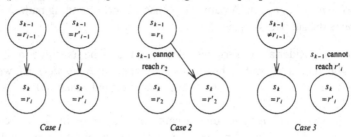

Case 1   Case 2   Case 3

If this is the first case, we can replace k by $(k+n-1) \bmod n$ and repeat the argument. Since no subset of r_i forms a cycle, after repeatedly reducing the value of k, either case 2 or case 3 must occur. If finally, case 2 occurs, since the first node of the path π, r_1, has an edge only to r'_2 and not to r_2, hence Γ_1 has one edge missing from Γ and is no longer a corresponding path of Γ. Contradiction occurs. If it is case 3, then since the only incoming edge to r'_i is r'_{i-1}, and no other node has an incoming edge which leads to r'_i, Γ_2 has one edge missing from Γ and is again no longer a corresponding path of Γ. Since either case 2 or case 3 will occur, at least one of the Γ_1 and Γ_2 does not correspond to Γ, we cannot have two cycles in G' corresponding to the same cycle in G. □

Lemma 4.5 Let G be a trigger graph which contains at least one cycle. Let G' be the resultant graph after the operation $remove(G,\pi)$ described in Algorithm 4.1. If π is contained in one of the smallest cycle, then the total number of cycles in G' is always less than that in G. □

Theorem 4.2 Algorithm 4.1 is correct and will terminate. □

4.2 Efficiency of the splitting method

Although our method can decide much more terminating cases which are undecidable using existing methods [8], the worst case run-time complexity of this method is exponential. It is however unavoidable if we analyze a trigger graph by path instead of edge. This is illustrated by the following theorem:

Theorem 4.3 To test whether there is an activable path between two rules in a trigger graph is NP-complete, even if the trigger conditions use only propositional logic. □

Our method may run into exponential time, nevertheless, it is still an effective method for the following reasons:

1. For any method that detects all our termination cases, it is unavoidable that it must be at least NP-complete as stated in Theorem 4.3.
2. Worst case performance only appears in some artificially designed cases. In practice, our method still performs reasonably well.
3. More importantly, any termination case that can be detected by methods [1, 8] can also be detected within the first four steps of Algorithm 4.2 with the same time complexity.

5 Finitely-updatable predicate

One of the limitations of using non-updatable predicates is that usually very few predicates can be used in an activation formula. To include more predicates in the activation formula, and thus detect more termination conditions, we propose to use a more powerful predicate selection procedure during the computation of activation formula. The idea is to take not only non-updatable predicate, but also finitely updatable predicate. As described in Section 3.1.2, a finitely-updatable predicate is a predicate which can be updated only finitely during a trigger session. Since to decide exactly the set of finitely-updatable predicates is as hard as to prove trigger termination, we can only approximate this set by maintaining a set of predicates which are definitely finitely-updatable, but we have no conclusion on those predicates that are not in the set. The following algorithm describes how to incorporate finitely-updatable predicates in our termination decision algorithm, as well as other existing methods.

Algorithm 5.1 Given a trigger graph, we detect termination by the following steps,
1. Initialize the set of finitely updatable predicates S to be the set of predicates that are not updated by any action of any trigger rule.
2. Treat every element in S as if it is not updated by the trigger system, apply any existing termination detection method to decide termination.
3. If termination is proven, report "termination" and exit.
4. Otherwise, we mark the following rules as possiblely infinitely execution rules:
   i. Rules that are in any unresolved cycle, i.e., cycle which has not been proven to terminate, and
   ii. rules that are reachable from some unresolved cycles in the trigger graph.
   Let T be the set of predicates that are updated by some actions of some possiblely infinitely execution rules. We update S to contain all other predicates used in the databases except those in T.
5. If any new element is introduced into S, then repeat the process from step 2.
6. Otherwise, S is unchanged. Exit the process and report "no conclusion". □

The following example demonstrates how [8] can be improved with the finitely-updatable predicate concept:

Example 5.1 Given the following three trigger rules in an OODB environment:
   r1 :: *incr_salary*($EMP1$) IF $EMP1 \neq me$ DO *incr_salary*(me)
   r2 :: $e2(EMP2)$ IF $EMP2.salary > 1000$ DO $e3(EMP2)$
   r3 :: $e3(EMP3)$ IF $EMP3.salary < 1000$ DO $e2(EMP3)$
Since the *salary* property of an EMPLOYEE class can be updated by rule r1, [8] will not make use of any predicate that used the attribute "salary". The "qualified connecting formula" of the edge $\ll r2,r3\gg$ is therefore a simple T$_{RUE}$. Hence, [8] can only conclude that the rules set may not terminate.

On the other hand, our concept of finitely-updatable predicate improves this situation. Using the activation formula, $\ll r1,r1 \gg$ is not an activable path, and hence it can only be finitely executed. The salary is only updated finitely. After the set of finitely updatable set is incrementally refined, we return to step 2 of Algorithm 5.1 and apply [8]. We improve [8] to construct a more useful formula,

$(EMP2.salary > 1000) \wedge (EMP2 = EMP3) \wedge (EMP3.salary < 1000)$

As this formula is unsatisfiable, termination therefore is detected.

6 Related Works

One of the common approaches to decide termination is based on the trigger graph introduced in [1]. Other researches [2, 3, 4, 8, 9] are all based on the trigger graph approach. These methods prove termination by showing that the graph is acyclic. [3, 4] augment the trigger graph with an activation graph so that if any rule in a cycle is not re-activated again, then the rule should only be executed once. In this case, that cycle can terminate. [9] enhances [4] by removing some of its restrictions, and constructs a stronger condition for termination decision. [8] refines the graph by using "trigger formula" to decide if a rule will in fact activate another rule during run-time. These methods can be improved as they only make use of the trigger conditions in a limited way. We propose the node-splitting method to detect more termination conditions than these existing works.

Beside using trigger graph, [7] takes a different approach. ECA rules are reduced to term rewriting systems. After then, known techniques for termination analysis are applied. However, proving termination requires the definition of a well-founded term rewriting system. [11] gives a different approach by computing a durable-change semantics model using Datalog^{1S}. However, the method is still incomplete as it needs to decide if a given Datalog^{1S} program is eventually cyclic.

Finite execution has also been considered in other research areas such as expert systems and deductive databases. In particular, [10] is to prove local stratifiablity of a given set of deductive rules. Although our method and [10] are similar as they both construct a conjunction and show that it is not satisfiable within a cyclic execution, however, there are some subtle differences:

1. To detect termination, [10] needs to show that a tuple instance will not appear again via negation during evaluation. However, in trigger systems, duplicate event instances often occur. For example, the event to update of a project's budget can be invoked a few times for the same project within a transaction.
2. [10] does not allow database update. and hence cannot directly be applied to a trigger system. As shown in [8], it is wrong to simply conjunct two trigger conditions as they may be evaluated under different database states. On the other hand, our finitely-updatable predicate selection procedure is able to decide termination even if the database is updated by the trigger actions.

7 Conclusion

We have described the idea of non-activable path and proposed the node-splitting method to detect more termination situations for an ECA-rule active database model. Our method is designed for a general architecture, and hence, it will be equally applicable to different trigger variations such as active OODB and priority rule sets.

Our method gives a much better sufficient conditions than many previous works. In particular, the proposed activation formula considers trigger conditions along an execution path, instead of just one single edge between two rules. Therefore, all the termination situations detected by [1, 7, 8] can also be detected by our method. Finally, we have also explored different predicate selection procedures. In particular, the finitely-updatable predicate selection procedure can be used also to improve other existing methods [8].

REFERENCE

[1]   A.Aiken, J.Widom and J.M.Hellerstein, "Behavior of database production rules: Termination, confluence, and observable determinism", *Proc ACM SIGMOD International Conf on the Management of Data*, 59-68, 1992.

[2]   E.Baralis, S.Ceri and J.Widom, "Better Termination Analysis for Active Databases", *Proc of the 1st Int. Workshop on Rules in Database Syst.*, 163-179, 1993.

[3]   E.Baralis, S.Ceri and S.Paraboschi, "Improved Rule Analysis by Means of Triggering and Activation Graphs", *RIDS'95*, 165-181.

[4]   E.Baralis, S.Ceri and S.Paraboschi, "Run-Time Detection of Non-Terminating Active Rule Systems", *DOOD*, 38-54, 1995.

[5]   U.Dayal, "Active Database Systems", *Proc 3rd International Conf on Data and Knowledge Bases*, Jerusalem Israel, Jun 1988.

[6]   O.Diaz, N.Paton and P.Gray, "Rule management in object-oriented databases: A uniform approach", *Proc 17th International Conf on VLDB*, Barcelona, Spain, Sept 1991.

[7]   A.P. Karadimce and S.D. Urban, "Conditional term rewriting as a formal basis for analysis of active database rules", *4th International Workshop on Research Issues in Data Engineering (RIDE-ADS'94)*, Feb 1994.

[8]   A.P.Karadimce, S.D.Urban, "Refined Trigger Graphs: A Logic-Based Approach to Termination Analysis in an Active Object-Oriented Database", *ICDE'96*, 384-391.

[9]   S.Y.Lee, T.W.Ling, "Refined Termination Decision in Active Databases", *DEXA'97*, 182-191, Sept 1997.

[10]   K.A.Ross, "Structural Totality and Constraints Stratification", *PODS*, 184-185, 1995.

[11]   C.Zaniolo, "Active Database Rules with Transaction-Conscious Stable-Model Semantics", *DOOD'95*, 55-72, Dec 1995.

View Maintenance and Integrity

The CVS Algorithm for View Synchronization in Evolvable Large-Scale Information Systems*

Anisoara Nica[1], Amy J. Lee[1] and Elke A. Rundensteiner[2]

[1] Department of EECS, University of Michigan
Ann Arbor, MI 48109-2122
[2] Department of Computer Science
Worcester Polytechnic Institute, Worcester, MA 01609-2280

Abstract. Current view technology supports only *static views* in the sense that views become undefined and hence obsolete as soon as the underlying information sources (ISs) undergo capability changes. We propose to address this new view evolution problem - which we call *view synchronization* - by a novel solution approach that allows affected view definitions to be dynamically evolved to keep them in synch with evolving ISs. We present in this paper a general strategy for the view synchronization process that guided by constraints imposed by the view evolution preferences embedded in the view definition achieves view preservation (i.e., view redefinition). We present the formal correctness, the CVS algorithm, as well as numerous examples to demonstrate the main concepts.

1 Introduction

Advanced applications such as web-based information services, digital libraries, and data mining typically operate in an information space populated with a large number of dynamic information sources (ISs) such as the WWW [14]. In order to provide easy access to information in such environments, relevant data is often retrieved from several sources, integrated as necessary, and then materialized at the user site as what's called a *view* (or data warehouse). The ISs in such environments are however dynamic, updating not only their content but also their capabilities, and joining or leaving the environment frequently.

Views in such environments thus introduce new challenges to the database community [14]. In our prior work [12, 4], we have identified view evolution caused by capability changes of one or several of the underlying ISs as a critical new problem faced by these applications. Current view technology is insufficient for supporting *flexible* view definitions. That is views are *static*, meaning views are assumed to be specified on top of a fixed environment and once the underlying ISs change their capabilities, the views defined upon them become undefined.

In our prior work, we have proposed a novel approach to solve this view inflexibility problem [12, 5, 8], called EVE (Evolveable View Environment). EVE

---
* This work was supported in part by the NSF NYI grant #IRI 94-57609. We would also like to thank our industrial sponsors, in particular IBM for the IBM Partnership Award and our collaborators at IBM Toronto for their support.

"preserves as much as possible" of the view instead of completely disabling it with each IS change. While the evolution of views is assumed to be implicitly triggered by capability changes of (autonomous) ISs in our work, previous work [3, 7] assumed that view redefinition was explicitly requested by the view developer at the view site, while the ISs remained unchanged. They [3, 7] thus focused on the maintenance of the materialized views after such view redefinition and not on the modification of the view definitions themselves as done in our work. One key component of our EVE framework is E-SQL (SQL extended with view evolution preferences) that allows the view definer to control the view evolution process by indicating the criticality and dispensability of the different components of the view definition. A second key component of our EVE framework is a language called MISD for capturing descriptions of the content, capabilities as well as semantics interrelationships of all ISs in the system. Descriptions of ISs expressed in this language are maintained in a meta-knowledge base (MKB), thus making a wide range of resources available to the view synchronizer during the view evolution process.

Given a view defined in E-SQL and a MKB, we present in this paper a formal foundation for the concept of *legal rewritings* of a view affected by capability changes. This includes properties characterizing all MKB constraints must be obeyed, as well as that maximal preservation of the E-SQL evolution preferences must be achieved. Based on this formal foundation, we then propose a general strategy for solving the view synchronization problem. Our algorithm, called CVS (Complex View Synchronization), finds valid replacements for affected (deleted) components of the existing view definitions based on the semantic constraints captured in the MKB. For this, rather than just providing simple so-called 'one-step-away' view rewritings [4, 12], our solution succeeds in determining possibly complex view rewrites through multiple join constraints given in the MKB. To demonstrate our approach, we present algorithms for handling the most difficult capability change operator, namely, the delete-relation operator, in depth in this paper. The proposed strategy is shown to find a new valid definition of a view in many cases where current view technology (as well as our initial simple solution [4, 12]) would have simply disabled the view.

The remainder of the paper is structured as follows. In Sections 2 and 3 we present the IS description language and E-SQL, respectively. Section 4 describes the formal basis for correct view synchronization, while Section 5 introduces our CVS algorithm for synchronizing views based on this formal model. Sections 6 and 7 conclude the paper.

2   MISD: Model for Information Source Description

While individual ISs could be based on any data model, the schema exported by an IS is described by a set of relations $IS.R_1$, $IS.R_2$, ..., $IS.R_n$. A relation description contains three types of information specifying its data structure and content, its query capabilities as well as its relationships with exported relations from other ISs that semantically express the operations allowed between ISs.

The descriptions of the ISs are stored in the meta knowledge base (MKB) and are used in the process of view evolution [5].

Name	Syntax
Type Integrity Constraint	$\mathcal{TC}_{R.A_i} = (R(A_i) \subseteq Type_i(A_i))$
Order Integrity Constraint	$\mathcal{OC}_R = (R(A_1,\ldots,A_n) \subseteq \mathcal{C}(A_{i_1},\ldots,A_{i_k}))$
Join Constraint	$\mathcal{JC}_{R_1,R_2} = (C_1\ AND\ \cdots\ AND\ C_l)$
Partial/Complete Constraint	$\mathcal{PC}_{R_1,R_2} = (\pi_{\bar{A}_1}(\sigma_{C(\mathcal{B}_1)}R_1)\ \theta\ \pi_{\bar{A}_2}(\sigma_{C(\mathcal{B}_2)}R_2))$ $\theta \in \{\subset, \subseteq, \equiv, \supseteq, \supset\}$

Fig. 1. Semantic Constraints for IS Descriptions.

Example 1. We will use the following example in the rest of the paper. Consider a large travel agency which has a headquarter in Detroit, USA, and many branches all over the world. It helps its customers to arrange flights, car rentals, hotel reservations, tours, and purchasing insurances. A part of relevant IS descriptions is summarized in Fig. 2 in MISD format described below.

We introduce below MISD constraints that are used in the remainder of this paper. All MISD constraints are summarized in Fig. 1 [4, 8].
A relation R is described by specifying its information source and its set of attributes as $IS.R(A_1,\ldots,A_n)$. Each attribute A_i is given a name and a data type to specify its domain of values. This information is specified by using a *type integrity constraint* of of the format $R(A_1,\ldots,A_n) \subseteq Type_1(A_1),\ldots,Type_n(A_n)$. It says that an attribute A_i is of type $Type_i$, for $i = 1,\ldots,n$. If two attributes are exported with the same name, they are assumed to have the same type.
A *join constraint* is used to specify a meaningful way to combine information from two ISs. The join constraint is a conjunction of primitive clauses (not necessarily equijoin) of the form $\mathcal{JC}_{R_1,R_2} = (C_1\ AND\ \cdots\ AND\ C_l)$ where $C_1,\ldots,C_l$ are primitive clauses over the the attributes of R_1 and R_2. The join constraint gives a default join condition that could be used to join R_1 and R_2, specifying that the join relation $J = R_1 \bowtie_{(C_1\cdots\ AND\ \cdots C_l)} R_2$ is a meaningful way of combining the two relations. The MISD *attribute function-of constraint* relates two attributes by defining a function to transform one of them into another. This constraint is specified by $\mathcal{F}_{R_1.A,R_2.B} = (\ R_1.A = f(R_2.B)\ )$ where f is a function. $\mathcal{F}_{R_1.A,R_2.B}$ specifies that if there exists a meaningful way of combining the two relations R_1 and R_2 (e.g., using join constraints) then for any tuple t in that join relation we have $t[R_1.A] = f(t[R_2.B])$.

Example 2. For our running example, some join constraints and function-of constraints are given in Fig. 2 (underlined names are the relations for which the join constraints are defined).

IS #	Descriptions
IS 1	Customer(Name, Addr, Phone, Age)
IS 2	Tour(TourID, TourName, Type, NoDays)
IS 3	Participant(Participant, TourID, StartDate, Loc)
IS 4	FlightRes(PName, Airline, FlightNo, Source, Dest, Date)
IS 5	Accident−Ins(Holder, Type, Amount, Birthday)
IS 6	Hotels(City, Address, PhoneNumber)
IS 7	RentACar(Company, City, PhoneNumber, Location)

$\mathcal{JC}$	Join Constraint
JC1	Customer.Name = FlightRes.PName
JC2	Customer.Name = Accident−Ins.Holder AND Customer.Age > 1
JC3	Customer.Name = Participant.Participant
JC4	Participant.TourID = Tour.TourID
JC5	Hotels.Address = RentACar.Location
JC6	FlightRes.PName = Accident−Ins.Holder

$\mathcal{F}$	Function-of Constraints
F1	Customer.Name = FlightRes.PName
F2	Customer.Name = Accident−Ins.Holder
F3	Customer.Age = (today - Accident−Ins.Birthday)/ 365
F4	Customer.Name = Participant.Participant
F5	Participant.TourID = Tour.TourID
F6	Hotels.Address = RentACar.Location
F7	Hotels.City = RentACar.City

Fig. 2. Content Descriptions, Join and Function-of Constraints for Ex. 1

3 Extending SQL for Flexible View Synchronization

In this section, we present E-SQL, which is an extension of SELECT-FROM-WHERE SQL augmented with specifications for how the view definition may be synchronized under IS capability changes. Evolution preferences, expressed as *evolution parameters*, allow the user to specify criteria based on which the view will be transparently evolved by the system under capability changes at the ISs. As indicated in Fig. 3, each component of the view definition (i.e., attribute, relation or condition) has attached two evolution parameters. One, the *dispensable parameter* (notation $\mathcal{X}D$, where $\mathcal{X}$ could be $\mathcal{A}$, $\mathcal{R}$ or $\mathcal{C}$) specifies if the component could be dropped (*true*) or must be present in any evolved view definition (*false*). Two, the *replaceable parameter* (notation $\mathcal{X}R$) specifies if the component could be replaced in the process of view evolution (*true*) or must be left unchanged as defined in the initial view (*false*). In Fig. 3, each type of evolution parameter used by E-SQL is represented by a row in that table, column one gives the parameter name and its abbreviation while column two lists the possible values each parameter can take (default values are underlined). The example below demonstrates the integrated usage of these evolution parameters (a detailed description of E-SQL can be found in [5]).

Evolution Parameter	Semantics
Attribute- dispensable ($\mathcal{A}D$)	*true:* the attribute is dispensable
	false: the attribute is indispensable
replaceable ($\mathcal{A}R$)	*true:* the attribute is replaceable
	false: the attribute is nonreplaceable
Condition- dispensable ($\mathcal{C}D$)	*true:* the condition is dispensable
	false: the condition is indispensable
replaceable ($\mathcal{C}R$)	*true:* the condition is replaceable
	false: the condition is nonreplaceable
Relation- dispensable ($\mathcal{R}D$)	*true:* the relation is dispensable
	false: the relation is indispensable
replaceable ($\mathcal{R}R$)	*true:* the relation is replaceable
	false: the relation is nonreplaceable
View- extent ($\mathcal{V}E$)	$\equiv$: the new extent is equal to the old extent
	$\supseteq$: the new extent is a superset of the old extent
	$\subseteq$: the new extent is a subset of the old extent
	$\approx$: the new extent could be anything

Fig. 3. View Evolution Parameters of E-SQL Language.

Example 3. Let's assume a web-based travel agency TRAV has a promotion for its customers who travel to Asia by air. TRAV will either going to send promotion letters to these customers or call them by phone. Therefore, it needs to find the customers' names, addresses, and phone numbers. Since an SQL view definition is static, we formulate this view in Eq. (1) using E-SQL, setting the view evolution parameters so that the view **Asia-Customer** may survive in a changing environment. Assume the company is willing to put off the phone marketing strategy, if the customer's phone number cannot be obtained, e.g., the information provider of the **Customer** relation decides to delete **Phone**. This preference is stated in the SELECT clause of Eq. (1) by the *attribute-dispensable parameter* $AD = true$ for the attribute **Phone**. In addition, if the travel agent is willing to accept the customer information from other branches, we set the *relation-replaceable parameter* $\mathcal{R}R$ in the FROM clause to true for the relation **Customer**. Further, let's assume TRAV is willing to offer its promotion to *all* the customers who travel by air, if identifying who travels to Asia is impossible (i.e., the second WHERE condition cannot be verified). This preference can be explicitly specified by associating the *condition-dispensable parameter* $CC = true$ with that condition in the WHERE clause.

CREATE VIEW **Asia-Customer** ($\mathcal{V}E = \supseteq$) AS
SELECT **C.Name** ($\mathcal{A}R = true$), **C.Addr** ($\mathcal{A}R = true$),
　　　　　C.Phone ($AD = true$, $\mathcal{A}R = false$)
FROM **Customer C** ($\mathcal{R}R = true$), **FlightRes F** $\qquad$ (1)
WHERE **(C.Name = F.PName)** AND **(F.Dest = 'Asia')** ($CD = true$)

4 Formal Foundation for View Synchronization

We propose in [8] a three-step strategy for the view synchronization:

Step 1. Given a capability change ch, EVE system will first evolve the meta knowledge base MKB into MKB' by detecting and modifying the affected MISD descriptions found in the MKB.

Step 2. EVE detects all views affected either directly or indirectly (due to MKB evolution) by the capability change ch.

Step 3. Lastly, for affected yet potentially curable views we apply some view synchronization algorithm to find legal rewritings guided by constraints imposed by E-SQL evolution preferences from the view definition.

Due to limited space, the rest of the paper concentrates on the most difficult step of the view synchronization process, namely, the third one. In the remainder of this section, we introduce and formally define the concept of a *legal rewriting* for an affected view. In Section 5, we present an algorithm for view synchronization, referred to as Complex View Synchronization (or short, CVS) algorithm.

We assume SELECT-FROM-WHERE E-SQL views defined such that all *distinguished* attributes (i.e., the attributes used in the WHERE clause in an indispensable condition) are among the *preserved* attributes (i.e., the attributes in the SELECT clause). Plus, we assume that a relation appears at most once in the FROM clause of a view.

Definition 1. Let ch be a capability change, and MKB and MKB' be the state of the meta knowledge base containing the IS descriptions right before and right after the change ch, respectively. We say that a view V' is a **legal rewriting** of the view V under capability change ch if the following properties hold:

P1. The view V' is **no longer affected** by the change ch.

P2. The view V' can be **evaluated** in the new state of the information space (i.e., the view V' contains only elements defined in MKB').

P3. The **view extent parameter** VE_V of V (Fig. 3) is satisfied by the view V'. I.e., if $\bar{B}_V$ and $\bar{B}_{V'}$ are the attributes of interfaces of V and V', respectively, then

$$\pi_{\bar{B}_V \cap \bar{B}_{V'}}(V') \ VE_V \ \pi_{\bar{B}_V \cap \bar{B}_{V'}}(V) \tag{2}$$

is satisfied for any state of the underlying information sources.

P4. All **evolution parameters** attached to the view elements such as attributes, relations or conditions of the view V are satisfied by the view V'. For example, any legal rewriting V' of the view V must have in the interface all indispensable attributes (i.e., the ones having $AD = false$ in V) [3].

Example 4. Let an E-SQL view be defined as in Eq. (3) and the change ch is "delete attribute **Customer.Addr**".

---

[3] See [8] for a discussion of how evolution parameters are set for new components

CREATE VIEW **Asia-Customer (AName, AAddr, APh)** $(\mathcal{V}E = \supseteq)$AS
SELECT   **C.Name, C.Addr**($AD = false, AR = true$)**, C.Phone**
FROM   **Customer C, FlightRes F**   (3)
WHERE   **(C.Name = F.PName) AND (F.Dest = 'Asia')**

CREATE VIEW **Asia-Customer' (AName, AAddr, APh)** $(\mathcal{V}E = \supseteq)$AS
SELECT   **C.Name, P.PAddr** ($AD = false, AR = true$)**, C.Phone**
FROM   **Customer C, FlightRes F, <u>Person P</u>**   (4)
WHERE   **(C.Name = F.PName) AND (F.Dest = 'Asia')**
         <u>**AND (P.Name = C.Name)**</u>

We have to find a replacement for this attribute that could be obtained using constraints defined in MKB. Let's assume we have defined the following constraints in MKB:

(i) The relation **Person** is defined by **Person(Name, SSN, PAddr)**;

(ii) $\mathcal{JC}$**Customer, Person** $= ($ **Customer.Name = Person.Name** $)$;

(iii) $\mathcal{F}$**Customer.Addr, Person.PAddr** $= ($ **Customer.Addr = Person.PAddr** $)$;

(iv) $\mathcal{PC}$**Customer, Person** $= (\pi_{\text{Name, PAddr}}(\text{Person}) \supseteq \pi_{\text{Name, Addr}}(\text{Customer}))$.

It is easily verifiable that the new view definition **Asia-Customer'** defined in Eq. (4) is a legal rewriting (new elements are underlined) conform to Def. 1.

We use $\mathcal{JC}$**Customer, Person** (defined in (ii)) to obtain the address from the relation **Person** by using in the WHERE clause the join relation (**Customer** $\bowtie_{\mathcal{JC}\text{Customer, Person}}$ **Person**), and the function-of constraint defined in (iii). We can prove that the the extent parameter "$\mathcal{V}E = \supseteq$" is satisfied given the $\mathcal{PC}$ constraint from (iv). I.e., for any state of the relations **Customer**, **Person** and **FlightRes, Asia-Customer'** $\supseteq$ **Asia-Customer**.

5 View Synchronization: The CVS Algorithm

We now describe our solution for the third step of the view synchronization process given in Section 4, namely, the actual rewriting of an affected view definition. Four of the six capability change operations we consider can be handled in a straightforward manner. Namely, *add-relation*, *add-attribute*, *rename-relation* and *rename-attribute* capability changes do not cause any changes to existing (and hence valid) views.

However, the two remaining capability change operators, i.e., *delete-attribute* and *delete-relation*, cause existing views to become invalid and hence need to be addressed by the view synchronization algorithm. Below, we present the algorithm for handling the most difficult operator, namely, the *delete-relation* operator, in depth. The algorithm for the *delete-attribute* operator is a simplified version of it and is omitted in this paper due to space limitations.

We start by giving definitions of concepts needed to characterize valid replacements of view components (the assumptions made in Section 4 about view definitions are still valid here).

Example 5. To illustrate the steps of our approach for rewriting, we will use the view defined by Eq. (5) and the change operator "delete relation **Customer**" defined in the context of our Ex. 1. The view **Customer-Passengers-Asia** defines (*passenger, participant*) pairs of passengers flying to Asia and participants to a tour in Asia that fly and start the tour at the same day, respectively. Such a view could be used to see what participants of a tour are flying to "Asia" on the same day as the tour starts.

CREATE VIEW **Customer-Passengers-Asia** $(\mathcal{V}E_V)$ AS
SELECT   **C.Name** (*false, true*), **C.Age** (*true, true*),
           P.Participant (*true, true*), **P.TourID** (*true, true*)
FROM   **Customer C** (*true, true*), **FlightRes F** (*true, true*),   (5)
           Participant P (*true, true*)
WHERE   (**C.Name=F.PName**)(*false, true*)AND(**F.Dest=**'Asia')
           (**P.StartDate = F.Date**) AND (**P.Loc = 'Asia'**)

Generally, a database schema can be represented as a hypergraph whose nodes are the attributes and whose hyperedges are the relations. We extent this representation for the MISD descriptions (relations, attributes, constraints) described in MKB by defining the hypergraph
$$\mathcal{H}(MKB) = \{ (\mathcal{A}(MKB)), (\mathcal{J}(MKB), \mathcal{S}(MKB), \mathcal{F}(MKB)) \}$$
whose components correspond to the set of attributes as hypernodes, and the set of join constraints, relations, and function-of constraints as hyperedges, respectively.

Example 6. Fig. 4 depicts the hypergraph for our travel agency example with:
$\mathcal{A}(MKB) = \{$ **Name, Addr, Phone, Age, Tour.TourID, TourName, Tour.Type, NoDays, Participant, TourID, StartDate, Loc, PName, Airline, FlightNo, Source, Dest, Data, Holder, Type, Amount, Birthday, Hotels.City, Hotels.Address, Hotels.PhoneNumber, Company, City, PhoneNumber, Location** $\}$ (see Fig. 2);
$\mathcal{J}(MKB) = \{$ **JC1, JC2, JC3, JC4, JC5, JC6** $\}$ (see Fig. 2);
$\mathcal{S}(MKB) = \{$ **Customer, Tour, Participant, FlightRes, Accident-Ins, Hotels, RentACar** $\}$ (see Fig. 2);
$\mathcal{F}(MKB) = \{$ **F1, F2, F3, F4, F5, F6, F7** $\}$ (see Fig. 2).

We say that a hypergraph is disconnected if one can partition its hyperedges into nonempty sets such that no hypernode appears in hyperedges of different sets. If such partition doesn't exist, then we say that the hypergraph is connected. Using these definitions, one can define connected sub-hypergraphs of a disconnected hypergraph as being its maximal connected components. For our problem, we are interested in finding the connected sub-hypergraph that contains a given relation R denoted by $\mathcal{H}_R(MKB)$. Note that because $\mathcal{J}C$-nodes are the only shared nodes between relation-edges in $\mathcal{H}(MKB)$ and because $\mathcal{H}_R(MKB)$ is a connected sub-hypergraph, we have: $\forall S_1, S_2 \in \mathcal{S}_R(MKB)$, there exists a sequence of join constraints $\mathcal{J}C_{S_1,R_1}, \ldots, \mathcal{J}C_{R_n,S_2}$ defined in MKB, with $R_1, \ldots, R_n \in \mathcal{S}_R(MKB)$ such that the following join relation can be defined $S_1 \bowtie_{\mathcal{J}C_{S_1,R_1}} R_1 \cdots \bowtie \cdots \bowtie_{\mathcal{J}C_{R_n,S_2}} S_2$.

Example 7. Fig. 4 depicts two connected sub-hypergraphs for the hypergraph $\mathcal{H}$(MKB) for Ex. 1. E.g., the connected sub-hypergraph $\mathcal{H}_{\text{Customer}}(MKB)$ is the connected sub-hypergraph drawn on the top left of the Fig. 4.

Given a view definition referring to a relation R and an MKB, we want to determine which parts of the view need to be replaced when R is dropped. To find possible replacements, we look in the MKB for join constraints related to the relation R that are also used in the view definition. That is, the view could be seen as a join between a join relation defined using only join constraints from MKB and some other relations (the rest of the view definition). As we will show later, if R is to be dropped, our synchronization algorithm will try to substitute the affected part of the view definition with another join relation defined using join constraints from MKB. Def. 2 formally defines this relationship between a view definition and the (default) join constraints in MKB.

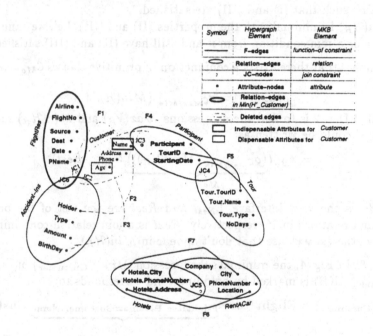

Fig. 4. The Hypergraphs $\mathcal{H}$(MKB) and $\mathcal{H}'$(MKB') for Ex. 1.

Definition 2. R-mapping of a view V into sub-hypergraph $\mathcal{H}_R(MKB)$.
We define the R-mapping of V into $\mathcal{H}_R(MKB)$ by R-mapping(V, $\mathcal{H}_R(MKB)$) $= (Max(V_R), Min(\mathcal{H}_R))$ to be a pair of two subexpressions one constructed from the view V and the second one constructed from the connected sub-hypergraph $\mathcal{H}_R(MKB)$ such that the following must hold:
(I) The expression $Max(V_R)$ is of the form:

$$Max(V_R) = R_{v_1} \bowtie_{C_{R_{v_1}.R_{v_2}}} \cdots \bowtie_{C_{R_{v_{l-1}}.R_{v_l}}} R_{v_l} \tag{6}$$

such that relations $\{R_{v_1}, \ldots, R_{v_l}\}(\ni R)$ are from the FROM clause of V, and $\{C_{R_{v_1}, R_{v_2}}, \ldots, C_{R_{v_{l-1}}, R_{v_l}}\}$ are conjunctions of primitive clauses from the WHERE clause of V. A conjunction $C_{R_{v_{s-1}}, R_{v_s}}$ contains all the primitive clauses that use only attributes of relations $R_{v_{s-1}}$ and R_{v_s}.

(II) The expression $Min(\mathcal{H}_R)$ is of the form:

$$Min(\mathcal{H}_R) = R_{v_1} \bowtie_{JC_{R_{v_1}, R_{v_2}}} \cdots \cdots \bowtie_{JC_{R_{v_{l-1}}, R_{v_l}}} R_{v_l} \tag{7}$$

with $\{R_{v_1}, \ldots, R_{v_l}\} \subseteq S_R(MKB)$, $\{JC_{R_{v_1}, R_{v_2}}, \ldots, JC_{R_{v_{l-1}}, R_{v_l}}\} \subseteq J_R(MKB)$.

(III) The relation $Max(V_R)$ is *contained* in the relation $Min(\mathcal{H}_R)$:

$$Max(V_R) \subseteq Min(\mathcal{H}_R) \tag{8}$$

(IV) $Max(V_R)$ is maximal with the properties (I) and (III). I.e., there is no other relations from the FROM clause and primitive clauses from the WHERE clause of the view V that could be added to it and still be able to find a subexpression in $\mathcal{H}_R(MKB)$ such that (I) and (III) are satisfied.

(V) $Min(\mathcal{H}_R)$ is minimal with the properties (II) and (III). I.e., we cannot drop a relation or a join condition from it and still have (II) and (III) satisfied.

Def. 2 implies that there exists a conjunction of primitive clauses $C_{Max/Min}$ such that

$$Max(V_R) = \sigma_{C_{Max/Min}} (Min(\mathcal{H}_R)) \tag{9}$$

The goal of Def. 2 is to find the expressions $Max(V_R)$ and $Min(\mathcal{H}_R)$ such that the view V could be written as:

$$V = \pi_{\bar{B}_V}(\underbrace{(\sigma_{C_{Max/Min}} (Min(\mathcal{H}_R)))}_{Max(V_R)} \bowtie_{C_{Rest}} Rest) \tag{10}$$

where $\bar{B}_V$ is the view interface, C_{Rest} and $Rest$ are the rest of the primitive clauses and relations in V, respectively. $Rest$ is a join relation containing relations from the FROM clause that don't appear in $Min(\mathcal{H}_R)$.

Example 8. In Fig. 4, the minimal subexpression $Min(\mathcal{H}_{\text{Customer}})$ of $\mathcal{H}_{\text{Customer}}(MKB)$ is marked by bold lines and corresponds to:

$$Min(\mathcal{H}_{\text{Customer}}) = \textbf{FlightRes} \underbrace{\bowtie_{\textbf{FlightRes.PName=Customer.Name}}}_{JC1} \textbf{Customer}$$

$$\tag{11}$$

The maximal subexpression $Max(\textbf{Customer-Passenger-Asia}_{\text{Customer}})$ of the view defined by Eq. (5) and the relation **Customer** is:

$$Max(\textbf{Customer-Passenger-Asia}_{\text{Customer}}) = \tag{12}$$

$$= \textbf{FlightRes} \bowtie \underbrace{\begin{pmatrix} \textbf{(FlightRes.PName= Customer.Name)} \\ \text{AND (FlightRes.Dest='Asia')} \end{pmatrix}}_{{}^C\textbf{FlightRes, Customer}} \textbf{Customer}$$

$$= \underbrace{\sigma_{\textbf{FlightRes.Dest='Asia'}}}_{C_{Max/Min}} (Min(\mathcal{H}_R))$$

The relation defined in Eq. (12) is contained in the relation defined by Eq. (11) and they are maximal and minimal, respectively, with this property (conform with Def. 2).

To find two expressions $Max(V_R)$ and $Min(\mathcal{H}_R)$ with the properties from Def.. 2 it is sufficient to have each join constraint $\mathcal{J}C_{S,S'}$ of expression $Min(\mathcal{H}_R)$ (Eq. (7)) implied by the corresponding join condition $C_{S,S'}$ of expression $Max(V_R)$ (Eq. (6)), where $S, S' \in \{R_{v_1}, \dots, R_{v_l}\}$. The algorithm for computing the R-mapping is straightforward and it is omitted here (see [8]).

Intuitively, we now have found the maximal part of the view definition that "relates" to our MKB (Def. 2). So now we can ask how this part (i.e., $Max(V_R)$) is affected by the relation R being dropped. And, further, we need to determine how we can find new join relations from the MKB that can replace affected view components in the view definition (i.e., $Max(V_R)$). The next definition identifies what are the most useful candidates for such replacement constructed using join constraints defined in MKB. At this point we don't worry about the relationship between the R-mapping and the potential candidates (e.g., subset, equivalent or superset). Our goal is to find all possible replacements for the relation $Max(V_R)$ (Eq. (10)). Only after that, when given the view-extent parameter $\mathcal{V}E_V$ (Section 3) and the $\mathcal{P}C$ constraints from MKB (Section 2), we want to choose the ones that satisfy the property P3 from Def. 1.

Definition 3. R-replacement$(V, \mathcal{H}_R(MKB))$. For a view V and the MKB, we compute a set of expressions constructed from $\mathcal{H}_R(MKB)$ that don't contain R and could be used to meaningfully replace the maximal subexpression $Max(V_R)$ in V. Let MKB' be the meta knowledge base evolved from MKB when relation R is dropped; and $\mathcal{H}'_R(MKB')$ be the sub-hypergraph of $\mathcal{H}_R(MKB)$ obtained by erasing relation-edge R. We define R-replacement$(V, \mathcal{H}_R(MKB))$ $= \{Max(V_{1,R}), \dots, Max(V_{l,R})\}$ to be a set of subexpressions constructed from $\mathcal{H}'_R(MKB')$ and $Max(V_R)$ such that $Max(V_{j,R})$ has the following properties:

(I) $Max(V_{j,R}) = \sigma_{C'_{Max/Min}} \left(R_1 \bowtie_{\mathcal{J}C_{R_1,R_2}} \cdots \bowtie_{\mathcal{J}C_{R_{k-1},R_k}} R_k \right)$ with $R_1, \dots, R_k$ and $\mathcal{J}C_{R_1,R_2}, \dots, \mathcal{J}C_{R_{k-1},R_k}$ in $\mathcal{H}'_R(MKB')$.

(II) R doesn't appear in $Max(V_{j,R})$. I.e., R is not among $R_1, \dots, R_k$.

(III) The expression $Min(\mathcal{H}_R)$ without R, $Min(\mathcal{H}'_R)$, could be mapped into $Max(V_{j,R})$. That is, if $Min(\mathcal{H}_R)$ is given by the Eq. (7) then: $\{R_{v_1}, \dots, R_{v_l}\} \setminus \{R\}$ $\subseteq \{R_1, \dots, R_k\}$ and $\{\mathcal{J}C_{R_{v_1},R_{v_2}}, \dots \mathcal{J}C_{R_{v_{l-1}},R_{v_l}}\} \setminus \{\mathcal{J}C_{S,S'} \mid S = R \text{ or } S' = R\}$ $\subseteq \{\mathcal{J}C_{R_1,R_2,\dots}\mathcal{J}C_{R_{k-1},R_k}\}$. I.e., the expression $Max(V_{j,R})$ must contain all the elements of the expression $Min(\mathcal{H}_R)$ unaffected by dropping relation R.

(IV) For any attribute $A \in R$ that is indispensable and replaceable in the view definition, the expression $Max(V_{j,R})$ contains a relation $S \in \{R_1, \dots, R_k\}$ such that there exists a function-of constraint $\mathcal{F}_{R.A,S.B} = (R.A = f(S.B))$ in MKB. We call the relation S a **cover** for the attribute A and the attribute $f(S.B)$ a **replacement** for the attribute A in $Max(V_{j,R})$.

(V) The conjunction $C'_{Max/Min}$ is obtained from conjunction $C_{Max/Min}$ by substituting the attributes of R with their **replacements** (see (IV)) if any, or dropping primitive clauses that are dispensable and for which no replacement was found for their attributes.

Erasing R from the connected sub-hypergraph $\mathcal{H}_R(MKB)$ could lead to a disconnected sub-hypergraph $\mathcal{H}'_R(MKB')$. If $\mathcal{H}'_R(MKB')$ is disconnected and the relations left in $Min(\mathcal{H}'_R)$ are in disconnected components then the set R-replacement$(V, \mathcal{H}_R(MKB))$ is empty. If relations left in $Min(\mathcal{H}'_R)$ are in a connected component of $\mathcal{H}'_R(MKB')$, the construction algorithm of the set $\{Max(V_{1,R}), \ldots, Max(V_{k,R})\}$ is following directly from Def. 3 (see [8]).

Example 9. In Fig. 4, the expression $Min(\mathcal{H}'_{\text{Customer}})$ defined by Eq. (11) is marked with bold lines: $Min(\mathcal{H}'_{\text{Customer}}) = (\textbf{FlightRes})$. We give now an example of R-replacements for the view defined by Eq. (5) and $R = \textbf{Customer}$. $\mathcal{H}'(MKB')$ is depicted in Fig. 4.

Step 1. In our example, using the hypergraph depicted in Fig. 4, we find:
$\overline{Cover}(\textbf{Customer.Name}) =$
$\{$ ($\textbf{Accident-Ins}$, $\textbf{F2} = (\textbf{Customer.Name} = \textbf{Accident-Ins.Holder}))$,
($\textbf{Participant}$, $\textbf{F4} = (\textbf{Customer.Name} = \textbf{Participant.Participant})$),
($\textbf{FlightRes}$, $\textbf{F1} = (\textbf{Customer.Name} = \textbf{FlightRes.PName})$) $\}$.
Step 2. From Def. 3 (V), $C'_{Max/Min} = (\textbf{FlightRes.Dest} = \text{'Asia'})$. Let's now construct the candidate expressions $Max(\textbf{Customer-Passenger-Asia}_{j,\textbf{Customer}})$ and define what is the replacement for the attribute $\textbf{Customer.Name}$.
(1) For the cover $(\textbf{Accident-Ins}, (\textbf{Customer.Name} = \textbf{Accident-Ins.Holder}))$ the expression below has all the properties from Def. 3. Similarly, we can construct $Max(\textbf{Customer-Passenger-Asia}_{2,\textbf{Customer}})$ from the third cover.

$$Max(\textbf{Customer-Passenger-Asia}_{1,\textbf{Customer}}) = \sigma_{\underbrace{(\textbf{FlightRes.Dest} = \text{'Asia'})}_{C'_{Max/Min}}}$$

$$\left(\underbrace{\textbf{FlightRes}}_{Min(\mathcal{H}'_{\textbf{Customer}})} \bowtie_{\underbrace{(\textbf{FlightRes.PName} = \textbf{Accident-Ins.Holder})}_{JC6}} \underbrace{\textbf{Accident-Ins}}_{Cover(\textbf{Customer.Name})} \right)$$

(2) The cover $(\textbf{Participant},(\textbf{Customer.Name} = \textbf{Participant.Participant}))$ cannot be used as replacement as there is no connected path in $\mathcal{H}'(MKB')$ (Fig. 4) that contains both the cover and the relation $\textbf{FlightRes}$.

Now we are ready to give the **Complex View Synchronization (CVS)** algorithm that has as input a view definition V, the MKB and a change "delete relation R", and returns all legal rewritings (see Def. 1) of the view V.
$\textbf{CVS}(V, ch = \text{delete-relation } R, \textbf{MKB}, \textbf{MKB'})$
INPUT: a SELECT-FROM-WHERE E-SQL view definition V;
change $ch = delete\text{-}relation$ R;
MKB represented by the hypergraph $\mathcal{H}(MKB)$;
evolved MKB' represented by the hypergraph $\mathcal{H}'(MKB')$.
OUTPUT: A set of legal rewritings $V_1, \ldots V_l$ of V.
Step 1. Construct the sub-hypergraph $\mathcal{H}_R(MKB)$.
Step 2. Compute R-mapping$(V, \mathcal{H}_R(MKB)) = (Max(V_R), Min(\mathcal{H}_R))$ (Def. 2).

Step 3. Compute R-replacement$(V, \mathcal{H}'_R(MKB')) = \{Max(V_{1,R}), \ldots, Max(V_{k,R})\}$ as defined in Def. 3. If R-replacement$(V, \mathcal{H}'_R(MKB') = \emptyset$ then the algorithm fails to find an evolved view definition for the view V.

Step 4. A synchronized view definition V' is found by replacing $Max(V_R)$ with $Max(V_{j,R})$ in Eq. (10); and then by substituting the attributes of R in V with the corresponding replacements found in $Max(V_{j,R})$. Because some more conditions are added in the WHERE clause (corresponding to the join conditions in $Max(V_{j,R})$), we have to check if there are no inconsistencies in the WHERE clause.

Step 5. Set the E-SQL evolution parameters for all V' obtained at Step 4.

Step 6. All the rewritings obtained by Step 4 have properties P1, P2, and P4 from Def. 1, Section 4. At this step, we have to check for which rewriting V' obtained in Step 4 the extent parameter VE_V of the view V is satisfied (property P3 from Def. 1) This problem is similar to the problem of answering queries using views which was extensively studied in the database community [6, 13]. However, our rewritings are not necessarily equivalent to the initial view, the relationship among them being imposed by the view-extent evolution parameter. We use the partial/complete information constraints defined in MKB' to compare the extents of the initial view V and the evolved view V'. This development is beyond the scope of current paper and it is part of our future work.

Example 10. For our view **Customer-Passenger-Asia** defined by Eq. (5), we now show how to apply Steps 4 and 5 from the algorithm CVS and find replacement under the change "delete relation **Customer**".

$Max(\textbf{Customer-Passenger-Asia}_{\textbf{Customer}}) =$
$\textbf{FlightRes} \bowtie_{\left(\begin{array}{c}(\text{FlightRes.PName} = \text{Customer.Name}) \text{ AND}\\ (\text{FlightRes.Dest} = \text{'Asia'})\end{array}\right)} \textbf{Customer}$

(Ex. 8, Eq. (12)) could be replaced, for example, with the following expression found at Step 3 of **CVS** (the second solution is similarly obtained from $Max(\textbf{Customer-Passenger-Asia}_{2,\textbf{Customer}})$):

(1) $Max(\textbf{Customer-Passenger-Asia}_{1,\textbf{Customer}}) =$
$\sigma_{(\text{FlightRes.Dest} = \text{'Asia'})}(\text{ } \textbf{FlightRes} \bowtie_{(\text{FlightRes.PName} = \text{Accident-Ins.Holder})}$
Accident−Ins).

```
CREATE VIEW Customer-Passengers-Asia₁ AS
SELECT     A.Holder (false, true), f(A.Birthday) (true, true),
           P.Participant (true, true), P.TourID (true, true)
FROM       Accident−Ins A(true, true), FlightRes F (true, true),   (13)
           Participant P (true, true)
WHERE      (F.PName=A.Holder)(false, true)AND(F.Dest='Asia')
           (P.StartDate = F.Date) AND (P.Loc = 'Asia')
```

For this particular case, we see that the attribute **Customer.Age** is also covered by the relation **Accident−Ins** with the function-of constraint $F3 = ($Customer.Age $= (today - $**Accident−Ins.Birthday**$)/365)$. In this case, we can replace the attribute **Customer.Age** in the view, too. A new rewriting of Eq. (5) using this substitution is given in Eq. (13).

6 Related Work

While no one has addressed the view synchronization problem itself before, there are several issues we address for EVE that relate to work done before in other contexts as outlined below.

Gupta et al. [3] and Mohania et al. [7] address the problem of materialized view maintenance after a view redefinition explicitly initiated by the user takes place. They study under which conditions this view maintenance can take place without requiring access to base relations, i.e., the self-maintainability issue.

The EVE system can be seen as an information integration system using view technology to gather and customize data across heterogeneous ISs [4, 12, 5, 8]. On this venue, related work that addresses the problem of information integration are among others the SIMS [1] and SoftBot [2] projects. In the SIMS project, the user interaction with the system is via queries posed against a unified schema. The SoftBot project has a very different approach to query processing as the system discovers the "link" among data sources. None of the two projects addresses the particular problem of evolution under IS changes.

Much research has been done on query reformulation using materialized views. For example, Levy et. al. [6, 13] consider the problem of replacing a query with a new query expression containing view definitions such that the new query is *equivalent* to the old one. To the best of our knowledge, there is no work done that has as purpose query reformulation without *equivalence* (e.g., the new query definition is a subset of the original view). We, on the other hand, have extended the notion of query reformulation by using E-SQL to specify constraints on query reformulation. Thus, when in compliance to those constraints, we allow the view redefinitions to be a subset or a superset of the original view.

7 Conclusion

To our knowledge, we are the first to study the problem of view synchronization caused by capability changes of participating ISs. In [12], we establish a taxonomy of view adaptation problems which distinguishes our new view synchronization problem, while in [4, 5] we lay the basis for the EVE solution framework. Formal criteria of correctness for view synchronization as well as actual algorithms for achieving view synchronization are the key contributions of this current work. To summarize, the main contributions of this paper are:

− We have formally presented the properties for *legal rewritings*.

− We have designed a solution approach for view synchronization that achieves view rewriting by exploiting chains of *multiple join constraints* given in the MKB.

− To demonstrate our solution approach, we have presented the *Complex View Synchronization (CVS)* algorithm for handling the most difficult capability change operator, namely, the "delete-relation" operator.

This work has opened a new problem domain important for a wide range of modern applications, and we thus expect that much future research will be conducted within the context of our proposed framework. Examples of work to be done include the exploration of alternative view evolution preference models, MKB evolution and cost models for maximal view preservation.

References

1. Y. Arens, C. A. Knoblock, and W.-M. Shen. Query Reformulation for Dynamic Information Integration. *J. of Intelligent Information Systems*, 6:99–130, 1996.
2. O. Etzioni and D. Weld. A Softbot-Based Interface to the Internet. *Communication of ACM*, 1994.
3. A. Gupta, I.S. Mumick, and K.A. Ross. Adapting Materialized Views after Redefinition. In *Proc. of ACM SIGMOD Int. Conf. on Management of Data*, 1995.
4. A. J. Lee, A. Nica, and E. A. Rundensteiner. Keeping Virtual Information Resources Up and Running. In *Proc. of IBM Centre for Advanced Studies Conf. CASCON97, Best Paper Award*, pages 1–14, November 1997.
5. A. J. Lee, A. Nica, and E. A. Rundensteiner. The EVE Framework: View Evolution in an Evolving Environment. Technical Report WPI-CS-TR-97-4, Worcester Polytechnic Institute, Dept. of Computer Science, 1997.
6. Alon Y. Levy, Anand Rajaraman, and Jeffrey D. Ullman. Answering queries using limited external processors. In *Proc. of the Fifteenth ACM SIGACT-SIGMOD-SIGART Symposium on Principles of Database Systems*, pages 227–237, 1996.
7. M. Mohania and G. Dong. Algorithms for Adapting Materialized Views in Data Warehouses. *Int. Symposium on Cooperative Database Systems for Advanced Applications*, December 1996.
8. A. Nica, A.J. Lee, and E. A. Rundensteiner. View Synchronization with Complex Substitution Algorithms. Technical Report WPI-CS-TR-97-8, Worcester Polytechnic Institute, Dept. of Computer Science, 1997.
9. A. Nica and E. A. Rundensteiner. On Translating Loosely-Specified Queries into Executable Plans in Large-Scale Information Systems. In *Proc. of Second IFCIS Int. Conf. on Cooperative Information Systems CoopIS*, pages 213–222, 1997.
10. A. Nica and E. A. Rundensteiner. Loosely-Specified Query Processing in Large-Scale Information Systems. *Int. Journal of Cooperative Information Systems*, 1998.
11. Y. G. Ra and E. A. Rundensteiner. A transparent schema-evolution system based on object-oriented view technology. *IEEE Transactions on Knowledge and Data Engineering*, September 1997.
12. E. A. Rundensteiner, A. J. Lee, and A. Nica. On Preserving Views in Evolving Environments. In *Proc. of 4th Int. Workshop on Knowledge Representation Meets Databases (KRDB'97): Intelligent Access to Heterogeneous Information*, pages 13.1–13.11, Athens, Greece, August 1997.
13. D. Srivastava, S. Dar, H.V. Jagadish, and A.Y. Levy. Answering Queries with Aggregation Using Views. In *Proc. of Int. Conf. on Very Large Data Bases*, 1996.
14. J. Widom. Research Problems in Data Warehousing. In *Proc. of Int. Conf. on Information and Knowledge Management*, pages 25–30, November 1995.

Integration of Incremental View Maintenance into Query Optimizers

Dimitra Vista

AT&T Labs – Research
180 Park Avenue, Bldg 103, Rm B-155
Florham Park, NJ, 07932-0971, USA *

Abstract. We report on our experiences in integrating view maintenance policies into a database query optimizer. We present the design,
implementation and use of the RHODES query optimizer. RHODES is
responsible for the generation of the maintenance expressions to be used
for the maintenance of views, as well as for the generation of execution plans for their execution. We also discuss a variety of optimizations
that RHODES applies during view maintenance and change propagation. We demonstrate the effectiveness of the proposed optimizations by
experiments performed on the TPC-D database. The experiments also
demonstrate the cost tradeoffs amongst multiple maintenance policies
for a view.

1 Introduction

In the recent years, there has been a tremendous interest in the design and
use of incremental techniques to improve the performance of view maintenance
[BC79, BLT86, CGL+96, CW91, GL95, GM95, GMS93, MQM97, QGMW96,
QW91, ZGMHW95]. Typically, the objective of these techniques is to find the
new value of a materialized view, after some update, by first computing the
changes to the view and then incorporating these changes into the view's stored
value. To compute the changes to a view's value, the so called *maintenance
expressions* of the view are used. The specification of these expressions may depend on a number of factors, including the definition of the view, the incremental
maintenance strategy used (immediate, deferred, etc.), the actual updates, and
so on. The changes to a view computed by the maintenance expressions are
called *incremental insertions* and *deletions*.

In this paper we propose to integrate view maintenance policies into existing query optimizers. The concept that maintenance expressions need to be
optimized is, of course, not new. However, when it comes to view maintenance,
there are a number of questions we must address:

1. Should we use an incremental method for the maintenance of the view or
   should we use re-evaluation? This question has been raised before and some

---

* This work was performed while the author was a student at the University of Toronto.

analysis and experimentation supports the predominant view that incremental methods are more efficient than their non-incremental counterparts [Han87, BM90, SR88, Rou91]. Tools to determine if views must be materialized or not typically operate outside of a traditional query optimizer.

2. Even if it was guaranteed that the view is to be maintained incrementally, which one of the many available incremental methods should we use? To our knowledge, there is no framework available that allows us to easily combine various existing proposals in a unifying framework.

3. For most views, there is a choice amongst multiple possible maintenance expressions, even within the same delta algebra. Which one is likely to be more efficient? The *choice* of which maintenance expressions to use depends both on the system aspects of the database and on the specific update.

We see the incremental view maintenance problem as an optimization problem. The objective is to minimize the cost to perform view maintenance. The decision involves which maintenance strategy to choose, among incremental maintenance and re-computation, for each materialized view, and each update and, if choosing incremental view maintenance which maintenance expressions to chose. The knowledge available is the database schema, the definition of views, the update, the cardinalities of the relations in the database and their updates, the distribution of data values, and the physical design of the database system.

In this paper, we report on the design, implementation and experiences of using the RHODES database query optimizer, that we have built using the Volcano optimizer generator [GM93]. RHODES operates on a multiset algebra consistent with SQL (duplicate semantics) and minimizes the estimated I/O necessary to maintain a view. In particular, it address all issues discussed above and utilizes several special optimizations amenable to maintenance expressions. Note that with proposing RHODES we are saying something more than that maintenance expressions be optimized. We are saying that the choice of which maintenance expressions to use affects the performance of view maintenance. And, that the optimizer of the DBMS should be responsible for making this choice, because it has access to and knowledge of all of the parameters that affect it.

The rest of the paper is organized as follows. Section 2 presents a motivating example. Section 3 describes how RHODES supports incremental view maintenance. Section 4 presents the optimizations performed by RHODES. Section 5 presents experimental results supporting our claims and our proposed optimizations. Finally, Section 6 concludes the paper.

2 Motivating Example

$$P : \text{PART(P\_PARTKEY}, \ldots).$$
$$PS : \text{PARTSUPP(PS\_PARTKEY, PS\_SUPPKEY}, \ldots).$$
$$S : \text{SUPPLIER(S\_SUPPKEY}, \ldots).$$

Let us assume the above database relations from the TPC-D database [TPC95] and a view V defined as *select* * *from* P, PS, S *where* PS.PS_PARTKEY = P.P_PARTKEY *and* PS.PS_SUPPKEY = S.S_SUPPKEY.

Equivalently, we can specify the same view as $V = P \bowtie PS \bowtie S$ (ignoring arguments). Suppose, now, that each of the P, PS and S relations lose a number of tuples specified by $\delta_P^-, \delta_{PS}^-$ and δ_S^-, resp. There exists an algebraic equation that defines the deletions from a join expression given the tables being joined and the deletions from these tables. Let δ_A^- be the deletions from $P \bowtie PS$; δ_B^- the deletions from $PS \bowtie S$; and, δ_V^- the deletions from V. There are a number of different ways to compute δ_V^-. Assuming immediate update propagation where the incremental expressions are evaluated in the old state of the database we can:

1. compute the deletions from $P \bowtie PS$ and propagate them to V:

$$\delta_V^- = \delta_A^- \bowtie S \ \cup \ P \bowtie PS \bowtie \delta_S^- \ - \ \delta_A^- \bowtie \delta_S^-, \text{ where}$$
$$\delta_A^- = \delta_P^- \bowtie PS \ \cup \ P \bowtie \delta_{PS}^- \ - \ \delta_P^- \bowtie \delta_{PS}^-.$$

2. or compute the deletions from $PS \bowtie S$ and propagate them to V:

$$\delta_V^- = P \bowtie \delta_B^- \ \cup \ \delta_P^- \bowtie PS \bowtie S \ - \ \delta_P^- \bowtie \delta_B^-, \text{ where}$$
$$\delta_B^- = \delta_{PS}^- \bowtie S \ \cup \ PS \bowtie \delta_S^- \ - \ \delta_{PS}^- \bowtie \delta_S^-.$$

A number of other alternatives are also possible. Our objective with this example is not to list them all. The point that we are trying to make is that there may be more than one alternative equivalent maintenance expressions to compute the deletions from a view V. The *choice* of the alternative may affect both the performance of incremental view maintenance and the optimizations that are possible in the optimizer.

If a database optimizer is given one of the alternatives to optimize, it might not be able to transform it into the other alternative and may, thus, miss a better execution plan. The main reason for failing to make the connection (in this case) is that set difference is *not* distributive. Also, although seemingly very alike, the two alternatives are amenable to different optimizations. Suppose, for example, that there is a foreign key reference from P to PS. Then, tuples deleted from PS can only join with tuples deleted from P because, otherwise, the foreign key reference would not be satisfied after the database update. Thus, we can use the equivalence $P \bowtie \delta_{PS}^- = \delta_P^- \bowtie \delta_{PS}^-$ and we can rewrite the first alternative as

$$\delta_V^- = \delta_A^- \bowtie S \ \cup \ P \bowtie PS \bowtie \delta_S^- \ - \ \delta_A^- \bowtie \delta_S^-, \text{ where}$$
$$\delta_A^- = \delta_P^- \bowtie PS$$

while the second alternative cannot be rewritten using the equivalence.

Thus, by adopting the fist alternative, we were able to reduce access to the database relations and the total number of joins, and, therefore, increase the likelihood that the performance of the incremental approach be better than re-evaluation. It is not clear that a database optimizer could easily have incorporated that kind of optimization if it was given the second alternative rather than the first[2].

---

[2] Note that it does not suffice that the database optimizer be given the unfolded expressions, instead of the ones presented here. Simple unfolding is common in DBMS's but different maintenance expressions result in different unfolded expressions. The reason is that the set difference operation is not distributive.

3 The RHODES Database Optimizer

In this section, using RHODES as an example, we show how a database query optimizer can be extended to support the decisions associated with materialized view maintenance. The proposed extensions are simple enough to be incorporated into any optimizer.

RHODES is a relational query optimizer that supports traditional optimization techniques, including join re-orderings, general query transformation, selective use of indices and cost-based plan selection. It utilizes a *system catalog* containing all information necessary for plan cost estimation, including information about the database updates (in a data warehouse, for instance, updates received at the warehouse are stored until the warehouse is ready to propagate them to its views). To support the new functionality, the basic set of logical operators supported is extended with five new operators:

- NEW(V): the NEW logical operator takes a query expression V as its argument and returns the value the expression V would have under the database resulting from incorporating any (delayed or non-committed) updates. If no updates are recorded in the catalog, the result of NEW(V) is the same as the value of V.
- $\delta^-(V), \delta^+(V)$: these logical operators take a query expression V as argument and return *exactly* the set of tuples that must be deleted (δ^-) or added (δ^+) from the old value of V (as if V was materialized), when the database changes are merged with the old database.
- $\Delta^-(V), \Delta^+(V)$: these logical operators take a query expression V as argument and return *one over-estimation* of the set of tuples to be deleted (Δ^-) or added (Δ^+) from the value of V (as if V was materialized).

Griffin and Libkin [GL95] formalized that the incremental maintenance problem in the immediate update propagation case consists of finding a solution to the equation $V^v = (V - \delta_V^-) \cup \delta_V^+$. Any solution satisfying 1) $\delta_V^- \subseteq V$ and 2) $\delta_V^- \cap \delta_V^+ = \emptyset$ is a *strongly minimal solution*, and defines the exact changes to V. Any solution satisfying only 1 is a *weakly minimal solution*, and defines one over-estimation of the changes. Griffin and Libkin proposed the use of weakly minimal solutions (Δ_V^- and Δ_V^+) [GL95] for supporting deferred updates more efficiently. We make the observation that using weakly minimal solutions has the potential to improve the performance of any view maintenance, including immediate update. The relationships between strongly minimal solutions and weakly minimal solutions are:

1. strongly minimal solutions are the net effect of weakly minimal solutions, i.e., $\delta_Q^- = \Delta_Q^- - \Delta_Q^+$ and $\delta_Q^+ = \Delta_Q^+ - \Delta_Q^-$;
2. each weakly minimal solution contains the strongly minimal solution and an excess of tuples Δ (possibly empty), i.e., there exists a multiset of tuples Δ such that $\Delta_Q^- = \delta_Q^- \cup \Delta$, $\Delta_Q^+ = \delta_Q^+ \cup \Delta$, and $\Delta = \Delta_Q^- \cap \Delta_Q^+$.

Supporting the new operators in RHODES does not require any change in the physical algebra of the database system, neither does it require special algorithms or specialized data structures to be built on top of an existing DBMS. In fact, transformation rules are used in RHODES to *expand* the definition of each of the new logical operators, as discussed below.

3.1 The New Operators

The NEW operator: There are 3 different ways to compute the new value of V:

- by re-evaluating V using the transformation rules:
  $\text{NEW}(V) = \text{NEW}(A) \odot \text{NEW}(B)$, if $V = A \odot B$, $\odot \in \{\times, \bowtie, -, -^d, \cup, \cup^d, \cap, \cap^d, \text{etc}\}$
  $\text{NEW}(V) = \odot(\text{NEW}(A))$, if $V = \odot(V)$, $\odot \in \{\text{GET}, \pi, \pi^d, \sigma, \text{etc}\}$
- by incremental computation using the maintenance expressions of V:
  $\text{NEW}(V) = [V - \delta^-(V)] \cup \delta^+(V)$
- and, by incremental computation using over-estimations:
  $\text{NEW}(V) = [V - \Delta^-(V)] \cup \Delta^+(V)$

The refresh function [CGL+96, MQM97], which separates change computation from view update, is another alternative to the ones presented here. RHODES does not currently support it, but it is easy to have another transformation rule that uses the refresh function, assuming the cost associated with each refresh can be estimated adequately.

The δ^- and δ^+ operators: There are 2 different ways to compute incrementally the deletions and insertions of a view V:

- by using the maintenance expression given by the transformation rules $\delta_V^- = \Delta_V^- - \Delta_V^+$ and $\delta_V^+ = \Delta_V^+ - \Delta_V^-$;
- and, by using your favorite maintenance expressions. Currently, RHODES supports the algorithm of Griffin and Libkin [GL95] as well as the algorithms described in [QW91, GLT]. In principle, we can have multiple delta algebra expressions with the intention of letting the optimizer decide amongst different algorithms proposed in the literature.

The Δ^- and Δ^+ operators: There is one transformation rule per logical operator that defines over-estimations for deletions and insertions. Currently, these correspond to the weakly minimal solutions of Colby et al. [CGL+96]. Note that, unlike the case of exact changes, only one definition for over-estimations may exist, as each over-estimation may define a different relation and simultaneous use of different over-estimations may result in incorrect answers.

All transformations discussed assume immediate update propagation. In a data warehouse where the updates are propagated in a deferred fashion, the equations are slightly different but they are described in a similar fashion.

4 View Maintenance Specific Optimization

Maintenance expressions are amenable to a number of simplifications. Each one of these simplifications is expressed in RHODES as a transformation rule. We propose three classes of simplifications:

1. **Simplifications when foreign key references are defined.**
   Suppose that the relations A and B are joined and the join condition is a conjunctive condition containing $X_A = X_B$, where X_A is an attribute of A and X_B is the primary key attribute of B. If there is a foreign key reference from X_A to B, tuples inserted into B do not join with tuples from the old value of A, because the X_A values in A before the update already appear in the domain of X_B in B before the update. Since B has at least one key, if $t \in \delta_B^+$, then $t \notin B$. The following equivalences have been defined in RHODES (θ stands for a join condition of the form discussed above):

$$
\begin{aligned}
&1.\ A \bowtie_\theta \delta_B^+ && = \emptyset \\
&2.\ \delta_A^- \bowtie_\theta \delta_B^+ && = \emptyset \\
&3.\ (A - \delta_A^-) \bowtie_\theta \delta_B^+ && = \emptyset \\
&4.\ A^v \bowtie_\theta \delta_B^+ && = \delta_A^+ \bowtie_\theta \delta_B^+
\end{aligned}
$$

Also, tuples deleted from B either do not join with the value of A before the update, or they join with tuples deleted from A, or else the foreign key constraint would not be satisfied after the update[3]. For the same reason, tuples deleted from B do not join with tuples inserted into A. Therefore, the following equivalences also hold:

$$
\begin{aligned}
&5.\ \delta_A^+ \bowtie_\theta \delta_B^- && = \emptyset \\
&6.\ \delta_A^+ \bowtie_\theta (B - \delta_B^-) && = \delta_A^+ \bowtie_\theta B \\
&7.\ A \bowtie_\theta \delta_B^- && = \delta_A^- \bowtie_\theta \delta_B^- \\
&8.\ A^v \bowtie_\theta \delta_B^- && = \delta_A^- \bowtie_\theta \delta_B^-
\end{aligned}
$$

Using foreign keys for simplification of incremental expressions has also been recognized by Quass et al. [QGMW96]. The purpose of that work is to use the knowledge about keys and foreign keys, in order to make a set of views self-maintainable. The equivalences presented above complete the ones discussed by Quass et al., who studied a generalization to many relations of equation 1. We do not need to have this generalization because all possible join reorderings are generated by the optimizer and the applicability of each of these simplifications is tested against every possible 2-way join.

Example

Let us assume again the schema and view of Section 2. For referential integrity, all the values appearing in the PS_PARTKEY of PARTSUPP (PS) must appear in the P_PARTKEY of PART (P), and all the values appearing in the

---

[3] The constraint may be violated before a transaction commits, but we assume that the optimizer is called at some point where the constraints are known to be satisfied.

PS_SUPPKEY must appear in the S_SUPPKEY of SUPPLIER (S), so that all the parts supplied by a supplier are valid parts, and all the suppliers supplying parts are valid suppliers.

Tuples that are deleted from PS can only join with tuples deleted from P or tuples deleted from S because, otherwise, the foreign key references would not be satisfied after the database update. Thus, we can use:

$$PS \bowtie \delta_P^- = \delta_{PS}^- \bowtie \delta_P^-$$
$$PS \bowtie \delta_S^- = \delta_{PS}^- \bowtie \delta_S^-$$

and we can rewrite δ_A^- as

$$\delta_A^- = P \bowtie \delta_{PS}^-$$

and simplify the maintenance expression as

$$
\begin{aligned}
\delta_V^- &= \delta_A^- \bowtie S \;\cup\; P \bowtie PS \bowtie \delta_S^- \;-\; \delta_A^- \bowtie \delta_S^- \\
&= \delta_A^- \bowtie S \;\cup\; P \bowtie \delta_{PS}^- \bowtie \delta_S^- \;-\; \delta_A^- \bowtie \delta_S^- \\
&= P \bowtie \delta_{PS}^- \bowtie S \;\cup\; P \bowtie \delta_{PS}^- \bowtie \delta_S^- \;-\; P \bowtie \delta_{PS}^- \bowtie \delta_S^- \\
&= P \bowtie \delta_{PS}^- \bowtie S
\end{aligned}
$$

Thus, using this optimization, we were able to reduce accesses to the database relations from 5 to 2; accesses to the delta relations from 8 to 1; and, the total number of joins from 7 to 2. Consequently, we increased the likelihood that the performance of the maintenance expression will be very good.

2. **Simplifications when the relations do not to contain duplicates.**
   When the relations are known not to contain duplicates, instead of using the complicated expressions of the multiset algebra [GL95], we can use the much simpler ones for the relational algebra [QW91, GLT]. RHODES uses knowledge about keys in relations to map expressions of the multiset algebra into relational algebra. To verify that a relation does not contain duplicates, RHODES uses the sufficient (but not necessary) condition that a relation does not contain duplicates, if it contains at least one key. In RHODES, keys for a (derived) relation are generated from the inputs to the operators computing the relation and their keys, using an algorithm similar to the one of Bhargava et. al [BGI95].

3. **Simplifications due to empty relations.**
   During view maintenance many maintenance expressions evaluate to empty. For example, if a relation A is not updated during a transaction, both its δ_A^- and δ_A^+ are empty. It is important to detect such expressions. RHODES uses transformation rules governing the empty set to achieve the simplifications [Vis97].

5 Experiments

In this section, we present experimental evidence that different maintenance expressions for a view result in differences in the performance of computing the view changes. These performance differences are big enough to justify our

Relation	Primary Key	Index Type	No. tuples	No. pages
P	P_PARTKEY	P	25000	955
PS	{PS_PARTKEY, PS_SUPPKEY}	DS, DS	100000	4015
S	S_SUPPKEY	P	1250	61

Table 1. Information about the TPC-D relations

claim that an intelligent component of the DBMS is needed to decide among the different choices. We also show the benefits of our proposed optimizations.

All experiments are run on the TPC-D database benchmark relations [TPC95] using the DB2 PE parallel edition. Table 1 contains information about some of the relations in the database, such as primary keys, indices on attributes, cardinality, and memory pages. A primary index (denoted with P) is defined on the P_PARTKEY attribute of PART (P) and on the S_SUPPKEY attribute of SUPPLIER (S). A dense secondary index (denoted with DS) has been defined on each of the PS_PARTKEY and PS_SUPPKEY attributes of the PARTSUPP (PS) relation. The distribution of attribute values is uniform.

We conduct a number of independent experiments. This means that before an experiment is conducted, the buffer of the database is cleared of its contents so that the result of an experiment does not depend on the hit-ratio resulting from previously cached pages.

On top of the database, we define three views:

J1 : select * from P, PS where P_PARTKEY = PS_PARTKEY
J2 : select * from PS, S where PS_SUPPKEY = S_SUPPKEY
J3 : select * from P, PS, S where P_PARTKEY = PS_PARTKEY and
      PS_SUPPKEY = S_SUPPKEY

We measure the logical I/O necessary to perform change propagation, which we get by a monitor program that takes "snapshots" of the DBMS state. Each state contains, among other things, counters that record the activity of the DBMS since the last time a "reset" of the counters was issued.

5.1 Using Different Incremental Queries

These experiments compare the performance of different equivalent maintenance expressions for a view.

Experiment 1.a: In this experiment, we delete one tuple from S, a portion of P ranging from 0.1% to 10% of P, and all related PS facts and we monitor the propagation of incremental deletions to J3. We use two different queries to compute the incremental deletions: the first is to propagate the database

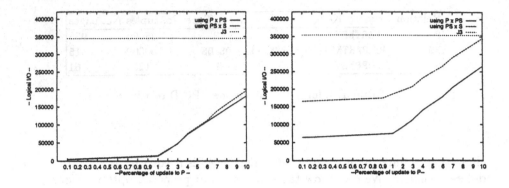

Fig. 1. Exp. 1.a: Incremental deletions to J3 with the index on PS_PARTKEY and Exp. 1.b: Incremental deletions to J3 without the index on PS_PARTKEY

deletions through P ⋈ PS and the second is to propagate the database deletions through PS ⋈ S. We also compare the results with computing J3. Figure 1.a shows the results. As we can see, the performance of both incremental methods is much better than initial view computation.

The plan chosen by DB2 to compute J3 in this experiment is as follows: first the join between PS and S is performed by scanning the S relation and looking-up, using the index on the PS_SUPPKEY of PS, the corresponding tuples in PS (nested-loops join). Then, for each tuple in the intermediate join, the corresponding tuples in the P relation are found (merge join). Therefore, the index on PS_PARTKEY of PS is *not used* during the evaluation.

Next, we repeat the same experiment, only in this case, we drop the index on the PS_PARTKEY attribute of PS. We want to see if an index that is not relevant to view computation is important for the incremental maintenance of that view.

Experiment 1.b: We use the same updates as before and monitor the propagation of incremental deletions to J3 using the two different ways described above. This time, no index exists on the PS_PARTKEY attribute of P. Figure 1.b shows the results. The performance difference between choosing to propagate through P ⋈ PS or through PS ⋈ S is rather big. In fact, to compute the incremental changes through P ⋈ PS the time[4] ranges from 54 sec to 3 min, while through PS ⋈ S the time ranges from 26 min to 28 min. Computing J3 requires approximately 34 min.

Experiment 2.a: We add a portion of P and related PS facts as well as one new supplier. We monitor propagation of incremental insertions to J3. Figure 2.a shows the results. All defined indices are available during evaluation. Note that, in contrast to propagating the deletions, the two methods of propagating insertions have a slight difference in performance.

---

[4] This refers to real time, not cpu or system time.

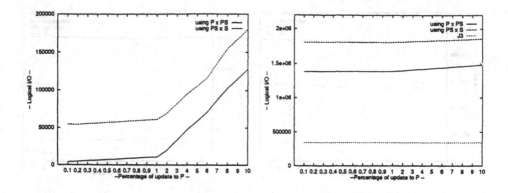

Fig. 2. Exp. 2.a: Incremental insertions to J3 (due to insertions only) and Exp. 2.b: Incremental insertions to J3 (due to insertions and deletions)

Experiment 2.b: We delete a portion of P, one tuple from S and all related PS facts. We also add a portion to P, one tuple to S, and related PS facts. We monitor propagation of incremental insertions to J3. Figure 2.b shows the results. As we see, one incremental method is better than view evaluation but the other is not. In fact, the time to compute the incremental insertions through P ⋈ PS ranges from 12.5 min to 14 min while to compute them through PS ⋈ S the time ranges from 53 min to 54 min.

In this set of experiments, we used optimized queries to propagate incremental changes through P ⋈ PS and through PS ⋈ S. The only optimization that was *not* applied during these experiments is the optimization due to foreign key references. As we see later, this optimization greatly improves performance.

5.2 Using the Key Constraint Optimizations

In this section, we present examples where we compare the optimized change propagation queries (where all optimizations except the foreign key reference optimization are active) to the non-optimized change propagation queries (the ones derived by the method of Griffin and Libkin [GL95]).

Experiment 3.a: We add and delete a portion of P ranging from 0.1% to 10% of P, we add and delete one tuple from S and we add and delete related PS facts. We monitor propagation of incremental insertions to J3. Figure 3.a shows the results.

Experiment 3.b: We use the same update as in 3.a but we measure the propagation of incremental deletions to join J3. Figure 3.b shows the results.

In the above two examples, the optimized queries that maintain the view coincide with the over-estimations of the changes for these views. This shows that using over-estimations of changes in place of their actual changes has the potential to improve the performance of change propagation.

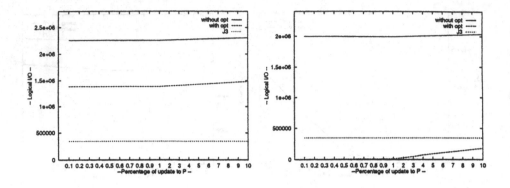

Fig. 3. Exp. 3.a: Incremental insertions to J3 with and without key optimization and Exp. 3.b: Incremental deletions to J3 with and without key optimization

5.3 Using the Foreign Key Constraint Optimizations

The experiments presented here show the benefit of using the new foreign key constraint optimizations proposed. We take a number of updates and monitor propagating these updates to each of the three defined views J1, J2 and J3. In this database schema, there is a foreign key reference from PS_PARTKEY of PS to P_PARTKEY of P and one foreign key reference from PS_SUPPKEY of PS to S_SUPPKEY of S.

We use two different ways to propagate the updates: one uses all available optimizations except the optimization due to the foreign key references and the other also uses this additional optimization as well. We use RHODES to derive the expressions before submitting them to DB2. In the figures that follow, "without fk opt" means that all optimizations but the one due to the foreign key references are on while running RHODES, while "with fk opt" refers to all optimizations being active.

Experiment 4.a: We delete a portion of P, one tuple from S and all related PS facts and monitor the changes to J1. Figure 4.a shows the results. As we see, the additional optimization greatly improves performance. The optimized query due to the foreign key is $\delta^-(\text{PS}) \bowtie \text{P}$.

Experiment 4.b: We use the same updates as before, only now we look at the propagation of incremental changes to J2. Figure 4.b shows the results. The optimized query is $\delta^-(\text{PS}) \bowtie \text{S}$. One may be wondering why the cost is so high for propagating changes to this join since only one tuple changes from S (which in this case joins with about 80 tuples from PS). With no index on the changes of PS, scanning the changes to PS is the most important factor that affects the performance.

Experiment 5.a: We add a portion to the P relation ranging from 0.1% to 10% of P and related PS facts. We monitor propagating the incremental insertions

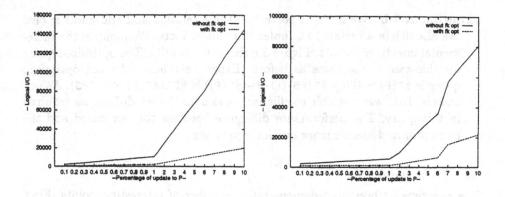

Fig. 4. Exp. 4.a: Incremental deletions to J1 with and without foreign key optimization and Exp. 4.b: Incremental deletions to J2 with and without foreign key optimization

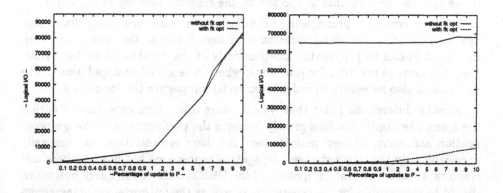

Fig. 5. Exp. 5.a: Incremental insertions to J1 when both P and PS get insertions, with and without foreign key optimization and Exp. 5.b: Incremental insertions to J1 when both P and PS get insertions and deletions, with and without foreign key optimization

to J1. Figure 5.a shows the results. The non-optimized maintenance query is $\delta^+(P) \bowtie PS \cup P \bowtie \delta^+(PS) \cup \delta^+(P) \bowtie \delta^+(PS)$. The optimized query is $\delta^+(PS) \bowtie P \cup \delta^+(PS) \bowtie \delta^+(P)$. As we see the only difference between the two queries is the extra factor of $\delta^+(P) \bowtie PS$ which evaluates to empty. The DB2 system was able to understand this by simply accessing the index on PS_PARTKEY of PS without accessing the PS data at all. Thus, the optimized and the non-optimized queries have almost the same run time performance. However, this is because the two relations change by insertions only. Next, we repeat the same experiment, only in this case we allow deletions as well as insertions to the two relations.

Experiment 5.b: We delete a portion to the P relation and add another one. We also delete all related PS tuples and add PS facts. We monitor the incremental insertions into J1. Figure 5.b shows the results. The optimized query for this case is the same as before (Experiment 5.a). The non-optimized query is $\delta^+(P) \bowtie (PS - \delta^-(PS)) \cup (P - \delta^-(P)) \bowtie PS \cup \delta^+(P) \bowtie \delta^+(PS)$. As one can see, DB2 was not able to efficiently evaluate the set differences required in this query. The performance difference between the optimized and the non-optimized maintenance queries is very big.

5.4 Discussion

The experiments presented demonstrate a number of interesting points. First, they show that it is indeed possible for different change propagation strategies to result in significant performance differences. Second, they show that having indices defined on the database data is very helpful during change propagation, even in the case where these indices do not participate in view creation (see experiment 1.b). Although, this is not a surprising result, it is still interesting to see how the performance is affected by the creation and use of the index.

It also seems that propagating deletions is less time consuming than propagating insertions. For database data with keys (such as the ones used here), the deletions can be propagated independently of the database insertions. However, the same is not true for insertions, where access and manipulation of the deletions is also necessary in order to correctly propagate the insertions.

Another interesting point that we can make from these experiments is that the foreign key optimizations greatly improve the performance of change propagation and, thus, of view maintenance. As these optimizations are generally applicable only to certain change propagation expressions but not to others, our claim that "an intelligent component of the DBMS, such as the query optimizer, should be responsible for the generation as well as the optimization of incremental and change propagation queries" is strongly supported by the results of these experiments.

Looking at the experiments, we can also see that even for small updates, where relations change by no more than 10% of their original sizes, the performance of change propagation may be comparable to the performance of view computation. Incremental view maintenance involves the computation of *both* insertions and deletions before incremental changes can be incorporated into the old values of the views. If one adds the cost to compute both insertions and deletions and the cost of incorporating these insertions and deletions to the old value of the view (even using **refresh**), one can see that it is not at all clear that incremental view maintenance is going to be always better than view re-evaluation, but wins greatly in many cases.

6 Conclusions

One primary contribution in this paper is that we provide a different perspective to address view maintenance and change propagation. We can summarize this perspective with:

"both the choice of incremental view maintenance versus non-incremental view maintenance as well as the choice of an appropriate propagation strategy are best left to the database query optimizer to make."

We showed how one can take their favorite algorithm(s) for incremental view maintenance and incorporate it into the database query optimizer. As a proof of concept that it is easy to extend an optimizer to support this, we have built the RHODES database optimizer that supports both incremental view maintenance and change propagation. The implementation of RHODES is such that each view is examined independently of the other views.

If RHODES is invoked at the end of each updating transaction, there is an increase in time and system resource usage during view maintenance due to optimization. Many query expressions are examined for the maintenance of each view, and, if there are a lot of views to be maintained, this may result in some performance degradation. The view maintenance optimization time and resource consumption is influenced by the complexity of each view expression, especially by the number of joins and subqueries the view expressions contain. Decision support queries or end-of-the-month queries, however, are good examples of complex queries, where the increase in the optimization time may not affect the overall performance of the system very much.

All experiments conducted were on data with uniform distributions. It would be interesting to see how the performance results would be affected under different distributions of data values. See [Vis97] for more details and a thorough validation of RHODES.

References

[BC79]   O.P. Buneman and E.K. Clemons. Efficiently Monitoring Relational Databases. *ACM Transactions on Data Base Systems*, 4(3):368–382, 1979.

[BGI95]   G. Bhargava, P. Goel, and B. Iyer. Simplification of Outer Joins. In *Proceedings of the 1995 IBM CASCON Conference*, pages 63–13, 1995.

[BLT86]   J.A. Blakeley, P-A. Larson, and F.W. Tompa. Efficiently Updating Materialized Views. In *Proceeding of ACM-SIGMOD Conference on Management of Data*, pages 61–71, 1986.

[BM90]   J.A. Blakeley and N.L. Martin. Join Index, Materialized View, and Hybrid-Hash Join: A Performance Analysis. In *Proceedings of the 6th International Conference on Data Engineering*, pages 256–263, 1990.

[CGL+96]   L.S. Colby, T. Griffin, L. Libkin, I.S. Mumick, and H. Trickey. Algorithms for Deferred View Maintenance. In *Proceeding of ACM-SIGMOD Conference on Management of Data*, pages 469–480, 1996.

[CW91]   S. Ceri and J. Widom. Deriving Production Rules for Incremental View Maintenance. In *Proceeding of the 17th International Conference on Very Large Data Bases*, pages 577–589, 1991.

[GL95]   T. Griffin and L. Libkin. Incremental Maintenance of Views with Duplicates. In *Proceeding of ACM-SIGMOD Conference on Management of Data*, pages 328–339, 1995.

[GLT]   T. Griffin, L. Libkin, and H. Trickey. A Correction to "Incremental Recomputation of Active Relational Expressions" by Qian and Wiederhold. To Appear in IEEE Transactions on Knowledge and Data Engineering.

[GM93]   G. Graefe and W. J. McKenna. The Volcano Optimizer Generator: Extensibility and Efficient Search. In *Proceedings of the 9th International Conference on Data Engineering*, pages 209–218. IEEE Computer Society Press, 1993.

[GM95]   A. Gupta and I.S. Mumick. Maintenance of Materialized Views: Problems, Techniques and Applications. *Data Engineering, Special Issue on Materialized Views and Data Warehousing, IEEE Computer Society*, 18(2):3–18, 1995.

[GMS93]   A. Gupta, I.S. Mumick, and V.S. Subrahmanian. Maintaining Views Incrementally. In *Proceeding of ACM-SIGMOD Conference on Management of Data*, pages 157–166, 1993.

[Han87]   E.N. Hanson. A Performance Analysis of View Materialization Strategies. In *Proceeding of ACM-SIGMOD Conference on Management of Data*, pages 440–453, 1987.

[MQM97]   I. S. Mumick, D. Quass, and B. S. Mumick. Maintenance of Data Cubes and Summary Tables in a Warehouse. In *Proceeding of ACM-SIGMOD Conference on Management of Data*, 1997.

[QGMW96]   D. Quass, A. Gupta, I.S. Mumick, and J. Widom. Making Views Self-Maintainable for Data Warehousing (Extended Abstract). In *Proceedings of the Conference on Parallel and Distributed Information Systems*, 1996.

[QW91]   X. Qian and G. Wiederhold. Incremental Recomputation of Active Relational Expressions. *IEEE Transactions on Knowledge and Data Engineering*, 3(3):337–341, September 1991.

[Rou91]   N. Roussopoulos. An Incremental Access Method for ViewCache: Concept, Algorithms, and Cost Analysis. *ACM Transactions on Data Base Systems*, 16(3):535–563, 1991.

[SR88]   J. Srivastava and D. Rotem. Analytical Modeling of Materialized View Maintenance. In *Proceedings of the ACM SIGACT-SIGMOD Symposium on Principles of Database Systems*, pages 126–134, 1988.

[TPC95]   Transaction Processing Performance Council TPC. Benchmark D. Standard Specification, Revision 1.0, 1995.

[Vis97]   D. Vista. *Optimizing Incremental View Maintenance Expressions in Relational Databases*. PhD thesis, University of Toronto, Dept. of Computer Science, 1997.

[ZGMHW95]   Y. Zhuge, H. Garcia-Molina, J. Hammer, and J. Widom. View Maintenance in Warehousing Environment. In *Proceeding of ACM-SIGMOD Conference on Management of Data*, pages 316–327, 1995.

Maintaining Temporal Views
over Non-temporal Information Sources
for Data Warehousing*

Jun Yang and Jennifer Widom

Computer Science Department
Stanford University
e-mail: {junyang,widom}@db.stanford.edu

Abstract. An important use of data warehousing is to provide temporal views over the history of source data that may itself be non-temporal. While recent work in view maintenance is applicable to data warehousing, only non-temporal views have been considered. In this paper, we introduce a framework for maintaining temporal views over non-temporal information sources in a data warehousing environment. We describe an architecture for the temporal data warehouse that automatically maintains temporal views over non-temporal source relations, and allows users to ask temporal queries using these views. Because of the dimension of time, a materialized temporal view may need to be updated not only when source relations change, but also as time advances. We present incremental techniques to maintain temporal views for both cases.

1 Introduction

A data warehouse is a repository for efficient querying and analysis of integrated information from a wide variety of sources. The warehouse effectively maintains materialized views over base relations at the sources [20]. Clients of the warehouse may not only be interested in the most up-to-date information, but also the history of how the source data has evolved. It is therefore important that the warehouse supports temporal queries. On the other hand, underlying information sources often are non-temporal, *i.e.*, only the current state of the data is available. Thus, we are interested in techniques by which the warehouse can materialize relevant temporal views over the history of non-temporal source data. Many applications will benefit from such a temporal data warehouse. For example, a warehouse that stores daily bank account balances can provide audit logs for financial analysts. A company may use a temporal warehouse to keep track of periodic marketing and income figures, personnel transfers, and the history of relevant corporate partnerships.

---

* This work was supported by Rome Laboratories under Air Force Contract F30602-96-1-0312, and by the Advanced Research and Development Committee of the Community Management Staff as a project in the MDDS Program.

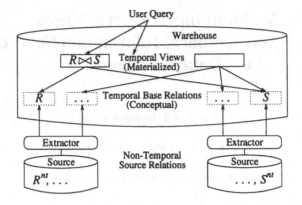

Fig. 1. A simple temporal data warehouse architecture.

There has been little research work to date on the temporal view maintenance problem, in the warehousing context or otherwise. Meanwhile, since applications do often require temporal support, most commercial systems store time information as normal attributes in the standard relational model, and query it using SQL. However, as pointed out by the temporal database community, writing temporal queries in the absence of a temporal data model can be extremely cumbersome and error-prone. Users cannot easily express queries whose interpretation changes over time, let alone specifying them as views to be maintained automatically. Furthermore, when time is treated as a normal attribute, it is difficult for these systems to exploit the semantics of time for view maintenance; input from the warehouse administrator is usually required.

To overcome these limitations, we introduce a framework for maintaining temporal views over non-temporal information sources. We present an algorithm to incrementally maintain temporal views as time advances and source relations undergo changes. The temporal view definition language we consider is equivalent to a subset of TSQL2 [3] including a class of commonly used aggregates termed *moving-window aggregates* [12].

Fig. 1 depicts a simple temporal data warehouse architecture. Each data source contains a number of non-temporal source relations which are monitored and exported by an *extractor* [20]. When a non-temporal source relation is updated, the extractor notifies the warehouse with the content of the update. Conceptually, for each non-temporal source relation R^{nt}, the warehouse maintains a temporal relation R, which encodes the complete history of R^{nt}. R can then be used as a base relation to construct definitions for materialized temporal views. Users formulate queries over the temporal views exported by the warehouse. It is important to note that the temporal base relations serve primarily as *conceptual* base relations to define views; they are not necessarily materialized.

The full version of this paper [22] contains a more detailed and formal presentation of the subject with a complete set of theorems and proofs, as well as discussion of the implementation of our work.

2 Related Work

The view maintenance problem has been studied extensively; see [7] for a survey. However, most work to date considers only non-temporal views. Although temporal view maintenance introduces many problems that are not present for non-temporal views, a number of techniques developed for maintaining non-temporal views are still applicable. For example, we adopt the algebraic approach of [6, 15] for propagating source changes (Section 4.2), and we apply methods for maintaining non-temporal aggregate views from [16].

Numerous temporal data models and query languages have been proposed; see [13] for a survey. We have chosen BCDM [10], the underlying data model for TSQL2 [3], as a basis for our work. Our concept of τ-reducibility (Section 3.2) is essentially that of *snapshot reducibility* discussed in [18]. We use a different name in order to avoid potential confusion with the SNAPSHOT construct in TSQL2.

A number of papers are related to temporal view maintenance to some degree. Reference [8] addresses the view maintenance problem in the *chronicle* data model. Under that model, each tuple is timestamped with a single time instant rather than a set; consequently, their algebra is weaker than ours, and more efficient algorithms are possible. Reference [9] presents techniques to incrementally maintain views defined using non-temporal operators over arbitrary snapshots of base relations, rather than temporal views over the complete history. In order to access the complete history, *backlogs* must be queried explicitly. The *differential operators* they introduce are closely related to our change propagation through τ-reducible operators (Section 4.2). Reference [1] considers the maintenance of relational queries whose selection predicates may refer to the symbol NOW, the current time. We consider a more expressive temporal query language and also handle NOW stored in data. References [4] and [14] explore the related problem of monitoring temporal integrity constraints. The languages they use are logical rather than algebraic, and are generally less expressive. Furthermore, the problem of detecting constraint violations is a strict subset of the problem of maintaining views. Finally, reference [11] develops a framework for system-managed expiration of warehouse data, which can be used to vacuum historical data for a restricted class of temporal views.

3 Preliminaries

3.1 Data Model and View Definition Language

The temporal data model we use is essentially BCDM (*Bitemporal Conceptual Data Model* [10]) restricted to transaction time. The time domain $\mathbb{T} = \{t_0, t_1, ...\}$ is a finite, non-empty set of *time instants* (also known as *chronons*) with $<$ as the total order relation. A temporal relation schema has the form $(A_1, A_2, ..., A_m, \mathbb{T})$, where the A_i's are *explicit attributes* and $\mathbb{T}$ is the implicit *timestamp attribute*. Values for explicit attributes come from regular value domains; the value for the timestamp attribute is a non-empty set whose elements are either time instants from $\mathbb{T}$ or a special symbol NOW. Explicit attributes form

id	dept	name	office	phone	T
123456	Research	Amy	121	1-2345	[01/01/91, 05/01/92], [01/01/94, 06/01/96)
123456	Research	Amy	151	1-5432	[06/01/96, 12/31/96]
700000	Development	Ben	B07	7-0000	[11/01/96, 05/01/97]
714285	Development	Coy	B17	7-1428	[11/01/96, NOW]

Fig. 2. Contents of temporal relation R on 09/30/97.

a key, *i.e.*, $A_1, A_2, ..., A_m \to$ T. Suppose t_{now} is the current (transaction) time of the database. For any tuple r in a temporal relation, $\forall t \in r.$T: $t \leq t_{now}$ or t is the symbol NOW; furthermore, $t_{now} \in r.$T iff NOW $\in r.$T.

A tuple $\langle a_1, a_2, ..., a_m, c \rangle$ is interpreted as follows: The non-temporal tuple $\langle a_1, a_2, ..., a_m \rangle$ is present in the database snapshot at time t iff $t \in c$. Each snapshot is purely relational and contains no duplicates. When NOW appears in $r.$T, it means that r will continue to "stay alive", so conceptually the database will need to update $r.$T to include new time instants as time advances. In practice, such updates need not be done explicitly, because T can be implemented by storing start and end times for the set of maximal, non-overlapping periods encoding T. One of the end times may store the symbol NOW, which "automatically" extends T as time advances. We assume this implementation in some later discussions. For a detailed discussion of NOW in temporal databases, please refer to [5]. Fig. 2 shows a temporal relation R(id, dept, name, office, phone, T) that stores employee directory information for a company, with T encoded as a set of periods.

Views in the warehouse are constructed from the conceptual temporal base relations (recall Fig. 1) using temporal algebra operators. To simplify the initial presentation, we introduce the aggregate operator separately in Section 5. In the following, R, R_i, S are temporal relations, r, r_i, s are tuples from the respective relations, and A_R, A_{R_i}, A_S denote the sets of explicit attributes in their schemas. Let $r.A$ denote the part of r containing values for the attributes in a set A. To facilitate definition, we also define $h(R, r', A) \stackrel{\text{def}}{=} \{t \mid \exists r \in R : r.A = r'.A \wedge t \in r.T\}$, which returns the union of the timestamps of all the tuples in R that agree with r' on attributes in A. The five non-aggregate operators are:

- **(Difference)** $R - S \stackrel{\text{def}}{=} \{\langle r.A_R, c \rangle \mid r \in R \wedge c = r.T - h(S, r, A_R) \wedge c \neq \varnothing\}$.
- **(Union)** $R \cup S \stackrel{\text{def}}{=} \{\langle u, c \rangle \mid (\exists r \in R : u = r.A_R \wedge c = r.T \cup h(S, r, A_R)) \vee (\exists s \in S : u = s.A_R \wedge c = s.T \cup h(R, s, A_R))\}$.
- **(Projection)** $\pi_{A'}(R) \stackrel{\text{def}}{=} \{\langle r.A', c \rangle \mid r \in R \wedge c = h(R, r, A')\}$.
- **(Selection)** $\sigma_p(R) \stackrel{\text{def}}{=} \{r \mid r \in R \wedge p(r)\}$.
- **(Join)** $\bowtie_p (R_1, ..., R_n) \stackrel{\text{def}}{=} \{\langle r_1.A_{R_1}, ..., r_n.A_{R_n}, c \rangle \mid r_1 \in R_1 \wedge ... \wedge r_n \in R_n \wedge p(r_1, ..., r_n) \wedge c = r_1.T \cap ... \cap r_n.T \wedge c \neq \varnothing\}$.

Intersection is defined as: $R \cap S \stackrel{\text{def}}{=} R - (R - S)$. Selection and join predicates may reference explicit attributes, constants, and standard comparison and arithmetic operators, as well as referencing the timestamp attribute T, time constants (including NOW), and built-in functions and predicates such as start(T) (returns the smallest element in T), end(T) (returns the largest element in T), length(T), contains($1.T, $2.T)[1], overlaps($1.T, $2.T), *etc.*, with the expected interpretation. The exact predicate language does not affect our algorithms, although we do assume that predicates are closed under conjunction and complement.

Our treatment of NOW deserves further explanation. During query evaluation, all predicates are evaluated with the implicit binding of $NOW = t_{now}$, where t_{now} is the current time (a constant in $\mathbb{T}$). However, when computing result timestamps, the NOW stored in input tuples cannot simply be replaced with t_{now}. NOW is still treated as a distinct symbol, and thus may appear in the result timestamps. This approach is different from the TSQL2 approach proposed in [3], in which all occurrences of NOW in the query and input relations are replaced with t_{now} during query evaluation. Under that approach, NOW would never appear in a result relation, which is not a problem in general for query results. However, the information about whether a result tuple has the potential to "stay alive" as time advances is lost, which does pose a problem for view maintenance. Thus our slightly different treatment of NOW seems to be necessary.

3.2 Classification of Temporal Operators

In this section we consider how temporal relations and operators can be reduced to their non-temporal counterparts. This allows us to reason with temporal relations by reducing the problem to a simpler one that deals only with non-temporal relations, enabling intuitive reasoning and formal proofs. By exploiting the properties preserved in the reduction, we can reuse some techniques developed for non-temporal view maintenance. For temporal operators that do not reference time explicitly, it is easy to find their non-temporal counterparts; for others, the reduction is more complicated and does not preserve all desirable properties. This leads to the classification into τ-*reducible* and θ-*reducible* operators.

τ-Reducible Operators. We formalize the notion of snapshots by defining the operator τ on a temporal relation R as: $\tau_t(R) \stackrel{\text{def}}{=} \{\langle r.A_R \rangle \mid r \in R \wedge t \in r.\text{T}\}$. Intuitively, $\tau_t(R)$ returns a non-temporal relation containing tuples "alive" in the snapshot of R at time t. Let $R_1, ..., R_n$ be relations in a temporal database with current time t_{now}. A temporal operator op is τ-*reducible* with respect to its non-temporal counterpart op^{nt} if $\forall t, t_0 \leq t \leq t_{now}$: $\tau_t(op(R_1, ..., R_n)) =_{nt} op^{nt}(\tau_t(R_1), ..., \tau_t(R_n))$, where $=_{nt}$ is the standard relational equality. (Note the correspondence with *snapshot reducibility* [18].) It can be shown that two temporal relational expressions defined using only τ-reducible operators are equivalent if their non-temporal counterparts are equivalent in set-based relational algebra. This property allows us to reuse many known non-temporal equalities.

Operators that contain no explicit references to time are τ-reducible: $-$, $\cup$, $\pi_{A'}$, σ_p, and $\bowtie_p$, where p contains no references to NOW or T.

---

[1] We use $\$i$ to denote the i-th argument of a join operator.

θ-Reducible Operators. Temporal selection and join may make explicit references to time in their predicates. Consequently, finding non-temporal counterparts requires a different mapping. Intuitively, we want to be able to treat T as a normal attribute in a non-temporal relation. For this purpose, we define the operator θ as follows: $\theta(R) \stackrel{\text{def}}{=} \{\langle r.A_R, r.\text{T}\rangle \mid r \in R\}$. Here, R is a temporal relation, and $\theta(R)$ returns a non-temporal relation whose schema is the same as R, except that attribute T is converted to an explicit attribute, encoded to adhere to 1NF. As a concrete example for this encoding, we may represent T by a bit vector of length $|\text{T}|$. A time instant $t_i \in \text{T}$ iff the i-th bit of the vector is 1; $\text{NOW} \in \text{T}$ iff $t_{now} \in \text{T}$. Since $|\text{T}|$ is huge, this scheme serves no practical purpose. We only need to demonstrate its existence in order to develop our theory; θ is never used in any maintenance expressions that we present later.

A temporal predicate p over R can be converted into a non-temporal predicate over $\theta(R)$ by replacing, in p, all timestamp constants and all built-in functions and predicates on timestamps with non-temporal counterparts based on the encoding used for T. We will abuse notation by omitting this bijective conversion function, since the intended interpretation is always clear from the context.

Operator σ_p, where p is a selection predicate on R that references NOW and/or T, is θ-*reducible* with respect to the non-temporal selection operator σ_p^{nt} in the sense that: $\theta(\sigma_p(R)) =_{nt} \sigma_p^{nt}(\theta(R))$. Operator $\bowtie_p$, where p is a join predicate that references NOW and/or T, is θ-*reducible* with respect to $\pi_{A'}^{nt} \circ \bowtie_{p'}^{nt}$ in the sense that: $\theta(\bowtie_p(R_1,...,R_n)) =_{nt} \pi_{A'}^{nt}(\bowtie_{p'}^{nt}(\theta(R_1),...,\theta(R_n)))$. Here $A' = \{\$1.A,...,\$n.A,\$1.\text{T} \cap ... \cap \$n.\text{T}\}$ and p' denotes $(p \wedge \$1.\text{T} \cap ... \cap \$n.\text{T} \neq \varnothing)$.

3.3 Example

Consider a non-temporal relation $R^{nt}(\text{id}, \text{dept}, \text{name}, \text{office}, \text{phone})$ that stores employee directory information for a company. Another non-temporal relation $S^{nt}(\text{id}, \text{project}, \text{supervisor})$ records current project assignments for all employees. At the temporal data warehouse, there will be two conceptual temporal base relations, $R(\text{id}, \text{dept}, \text{name}, \text{office}, \text{phone}, \text{T})$ and $S(\text{id}, \text{project}, \text{supervisor}, \text{T})$, which encode the history of R^{nt} and S^{nt}, respectively. Our previous Fig. 2 depicts the state of R on 09/30/97.

Suppose we are interested in a warehouse view that provides the project assignment history of all employees who joined the Development department within the past year but are no longer employed within that department now. We define:

$$V \stackrel{\text{def}}{=} \bowtie_{(\$1.\text{id}=\$2.\text{id}) \wedge (\text{start}(\$1.\text{T}) \geq \text{NOW}-1\text{year}) \wedge (\text{end}(\$1.\text{T}) < \text{NOW})}$$
$$\left(\pi_{\{\text{id}\}}(\sigma_{\text{dept}=\text{"Development"}}(R)), \; S\right).$$

Here $\pi_{\{\text{id}\}}$ is necessary because there may be multiple tuples in R with the same values for id but different values for office or phone, if someone changes office or phone number (*e.g.*, Amy in Fig. 2).

On 09/30/97, only the Ben tuple satisfies the join predicate, so V only contains the project assignment history of employee 700000. Suppose that on

id	dept	name	office	phone	T
123456	Research	Amy	121	1-2345	[01/01/91, 05/01/92], [01/01/94, 06/01/96)
123456	Research	Amy	151	1-5432	[06/01/96, 12/31/96]
700000	Development	Ben	B07	7-0000	[11/01/96, 05/01/97], [10/01/97, NOW]
714285	Development	Coy	B17	7-1428	[11/01/96, 10/01/97)

Fig. 3. Contents of temporal relation R on and after 10/01/97.

10/01/97, Ben returns to the company and is assigned the same employee ID, office, and phone: $\langle 700000, \text{Development}, \text{Ben}, \text{B07}, 7\text{-}0000 \rangle$ is inserted into R^{nt} and a tuple recording Ben's new project assignment is inserted into S^{nt}. Also, Coy leaves the company on the same day: $\langle 714285, \text{Development}, \text{Coy}, \text{B17}, 7\text{-}1428 \rangle$ is deleted from R^{nt} and the corresponding tuples are deleted from S^{nt}. After the update, R should contain the tuples shown in Fig. 3. For brevity, we do not specify the contents of S, since they are not needed to understand the example.

Let us consider how V is affected. Ben's return changes the timestamp of the temporal Ben tuple to $\{[11/01/96, 05/01/97], [10/01/97, \text{NOW}]\}$, which no longer satisfies end($1.T$) < NOW. As a result, the project assignment history of employee 700000 is removed from V. On the other hand, Coy's departure makes the Coy tuple's T now satisfy the join predicate, so the project assignment history of employee 714285 is added to V. An important observation here is that θ-reducible temporal operators, such as the join in our example, do not preserve the monotonicity of their non-temporal counterparts. That is, we cannot guarantee $op(..., R, ...) \subseteq op(..., R \cup \triangle R, ...)$; in other words, "insertions" into base relations may cause not only insertions, but also deletions, to the view. Monotonicity fails for θ-reducible operators because under θ-reduction, $R \cup \triangle R$ can act as a modification of the attribute T, rather than as a pure insertion, as illustrated above by the Ben tuple. Deletion $R - \triangledown R$ also can result in modification, as illustrated by the Coy tuple.

A temporal view may change even without source updates, due to the dimension of time. Tuple timestamps containing NOW extend as time advances; for example, length(T) may increase over time. Moreover, the interpretation of predicates that reference NOW also changes over time. For example, suppose that R^{nt} and S^{nt} stay the same after 10/01/97. If we evaluate V two months later, on 12/01/97, we notice that V no longer contains the project assignment history for Coy, because the predicate start(T) $\geq$ NOW $-$ 1year is no longer satisfied when the binding for NOW changes from 10/01/97 to 12/01/97. There is no non-temporal analogy for this phenomenon, so we cannot apply known techniques for non-temporal view maintenance in this case.

4 Maintaining Temporal Views

As shown in Section 3.3, temporal views need to be maintained on two occasions: when source relations are updated (we call this *change propagation*), and when the temporal database's current time advances (we call this *view refresh*). We adopt an "eager" approach for change propagation: Source changes are immediately propagated through all the affected views. On the other hand, we adopt a "lazy" approach for view refresh: We refresh a view with respect to advanced time only when it is required for computation. A view is required for computation if it is affected by a source update, or if it is referenced in a user query. Note that a lazy approach for refreshing views is essential to performance. It is unacceptable if the warehouse has to refresh all its materialized views every time the clock ticks. The complete algorithm for temporal view maintenance is outlined as follows:

1. When some extractor (recall Fig. 1) reports a source update at t_{now} that affects the conceptual temporal base relation R:
   - Step 1.1: Convert the source update to an update on R in the form of *deltas* ∇R and $\triangle R$, in the same style as [6, 15]. This step is discussed in Section 4.1.
   - Step 1.2: Refresh all views whose definitions reference R so that they are current with respect to t_{now}. This step is discussed in Section 4.3.
   - Step 1.3: Propagate ∇R and $\triangle R$ through all the affected views. This step is discussed in Section 4.2.
2. When the user presents a query to the warehouse at time t_{now}:
   - Step 2.1: Refresh all views referenced in the user query so that they are current with respect to t_{now}, as in Step 1.2.
   - Step 2.2: Compute the query using the refreshed views.

4.1 Maintaining Conceptual Temporal Base Relations

For each non-temporal source relation R^{nt}, the warehouse conceptually maintains a temporal relation R which encodes the history of R^{nt}. Suppose the extractor reports the source update $R^{nt} \leftarrow R^{nt} -^{nt} \nabla R^{nt} \cup^{nt} \triangle R^{nt}$ at time t_{now}. We wish to find ∇R and $\triangle R$ such that $R \leftarrow R - \nabla R \cup \triangle R$ will continue to faithfully encode the history of R^{nt}. It turns out that we can obtain the desired deltas simply by timestamping ∇R^{nt} and $\triangle R^{nt}$ with $\{t_{now}, \text{NOW}\}$. Formally, $\nabla R = \{\langle r^{nt}, \{t_{now}, \text{NOW}\}\rangle \mid r^{nt} \in \nabla R^{nt}\}$ and $\triangle R = \{\langle r^{nt}, \{t_{now}, \text{NOW}\}\rangle \mid r^{nt} \in \triangle R^{nt}\}$. Intuitively, the effect of ∇R is to terminate the NOW-ending timestamp right before t_{now} for each tuple in ∇R^{nt}. The effect of $\triangle R$ is to create a NOW-ending timestamp for each tuple in $\triangle R^{nt}$, which will extend automatically from t_{now}. Note again that we do not require R to be materialized at this point. The sole purpose of this procedure is to generate ∇R and $\triangle R$, which are then used to initiate change propagation discussed in Section 4.2. There are several options for the exact point at which base relation deltas are timestamped, depending on the capabilities of the sources and on the warehousing environment; see the full version of this paper [22] for a discussion.

4.2 Propagating Changes

Given an update to the temporal base relation R, we need to propagate its effect through all views whose definitions reference R. This is achieved by repeatedly applying a set of *change propagation equations* to factor out the base relation deltas from the expressions defining the views [6, 15]. Change propagation equations for a temporal operator *op* have the following forms:

$$op(R_1, ..., R_i - \nabla R_i, ..., R_n) = op(R_1, ..., R_i, ..., R_n) - \nabla^- \mathcal{E} \cup \Delta^- \mathcal{E}$$

$$op(R_1, ..., R_i \cup \Delta R_i, ..., R_n) = op(R_1, ..., R_i, ..., R_n) - \nabla^+ \mathcal{E} \cup \Delta^+ \mathcal{E}$$

where $\nabla^- \mathcal{E}$ and $\Delta^- \mathcal{E}$ (respectively, $\nabla^+ \mathcal{E}$ and $\Delta^+ \mathcal{E}$) are expressions possibly containing $R_1, ..., R_n$ and ∇R_i (respectively, ΔR_i), or may be empty.

Since τ reduction preserves relational equalities, change propagation equations for τ-reducible operators can be derived directly from the corresponding equalities in non-temporal relational algebra, as in, *e.g.*, [15]. The equations are identical in form to their non-temporal counterparts, except that all operators are temporal. In the following, p contains no references to NOW or T:

(c.1) $(R - \nabla R) - S = (R - S) - (\nabla R - S)$

(c.2) $(R \cup \Delta R) - S = (R - S) \cup (\Delta R - S)$

(c.3) $R - (S - \nabla S) = (R - S) \cup (R \cap \nabla S)$

(c.4) $R - (S \cup \Delta S) = (R - S) - (R \cap \Delta S)$

(c.5) $(R - \nabla R) \cup S = (R \cup S) - (\nabla R - S)$

(c.6) $(R \cup \Delta R) \cup S = (R \cup S) \cup (\Delta R - S)$

(c.7) $\pi_{A'}(R - \nabla R) = \pi_{A'}(R) - (\pi_{A'}(R) - \pi_{A'}(R - \nabla R))$

(c.8) $\pi_{A'}(R \cup \Delta R) = \pi_{A'}(R) \cup (\pi_{A'}(\Delta R) - \pi_{A'}(R))$

(c.9) $\sigma_p(R - \nabla R) = \sigma_p(R) - \sigma_p(\nabla R)$

(c.10) $\sigma_p(R \cup \Delta R) = \sigma_p(R) \cup \sigma_p(\Delta R)$

(c.11) $\bowtie_p(R_1, ..., R_i - \nabla R_i, ...) = \bowtie_p(R_1, ..., R_i, ...) - \bowtie_p(R_1, ..., \nabla R_i, ...)$

(c.12) $\bowtie_p(R_1, ..., R_i \cup \Delta R_i, ...) = \bowtie_p(R_1, ..., R_i, ...) \cup \bowtie_p(R_1, ..., \Delta R_i, ...)$

Under θ reduction, deltas sometimes behave like (timestamp) modifications rather than deletions and insertions, as motivated in Section 3.3. Therefore, we cannot simply reuse the non-temporal change propagation equations for θ-reducible operators. Instead, we provide a way to transform arbitrary deltas into *pure deltas*, *i.e.*, deltas that do not behave like modifications under θ reduction. Then the known non-temporal equalities can be reused.

First, we define the temporal semijoin operator $\ltimes_p$: $\ltimes_p(R_1, R_2, ..., R_n) \stackrel{\text{def}}{=}$ $\{r_1 \mid \exists r_2, ..., r_n : r_1 \in R_1 \wedge r_2 \in R_2 \wedge ... \wedge r_n \in R_n \wedge p(r_1, r_2, ..., r_n)\}$. Suppose $\nabla_1 R$ and $\Delta_1 R$ are arbitrary deltas on R. Let $\nabla_2 R = \ltimes_{\$1.A_R = \$2.A_R}(R, \nabla_1 R \cup \Delta_1 R)$ and $\Delta_2 R = \nabla_2 R - \nabla_1 R \cup \Delta_1 R$. Then: (i) $R - \nabla_1 R \cup \Delta_1 R = R - \nabla_2 R \cup \Delta_2 R$; (ii) $\theta(R - \nabla_2 R) =_{nt} \theta(R) -^{nt} \theta(\nabla_2 R)$; (iii) $\theta(R - \nabla_2 R \cup \Delta_2 R) =_{nt} \theta(R - \nabla_2 R) \cup^{nt}$ $\theta(\Delta_2 R)$. Intuitively, we use semijoin in the definition for $\nabla_2 R$ to obtain all the complete tuples in R affected by deltas. $\Delta_2 R$ is the result of applying deltas to these tuples. The notion of pure deltas is captured by Conditions (ii) and (iii). Condition (ii) ensures that $\nabla_2 R$ will remove tuples completely, instead of just shrinking their timestamps. Condition (iii) guarantees that $\Delta_2 R$ only contains tuples that do not agree with any existing tuple on the set of explicit attributes, so that it cannot possibly expand any existing tuple's timestamp.

Change propagation equations for θ-reducible operators are presented below. Again, the equations are identical to their non-temporal counterparts, but with an important requirement that ∇R and $\triangle R$ must be pure deltas (similarly for ∇R_i and $\triangle R_i$). Before applying the following change propagation equations, we may need to first apply the transformation discussed above, if the pure delta requirement is not already satisfied. Here, p may reference NOW and/or T:

(c.13) $\quad \sigma_p(R - \nabla R) = \sigma_p(R) - \sigma_p(\nabla R)$

(c.14) $\quad \sigma_p(R \cup \triangle R) = \sigma_p(R) \cup \sigma_p(\triangle R)$

(c.15) $\quad \bowtie_p(R_1, ..., R_i - \nabla R_i, ...) = \bowtie_p(R_1, ..., R_i, ...) - \bowtie_p(R_1, ..., \nabla R_i, ...)$

(c.16) $\quad \bowtie_p(R_1, ..., R_i \cup \triangle R_i, ...) = \bowtie_p(R_1, ..., R_i, ...) \cup \bowtie_p(R_1, ..., \triangle R_i, ...)$

It is also possible to develop change propagation equations for θ-reducible operators without requiring pure deltas. However, doing so significantly complicates the expressions. Furthermore, for the change propagation equations above, it can be shown that the deltas generated by the right-hand sides are indeed pure themselves. If they need to be propagated further through enclosing θ-reducible operators, it is more efficient to use these simple change propagation equations where the requirement of pure deltas is already met.

As a concrete example, consider $V \stackrel{\text{def}}{=} \bowtie_p\big(\pi_{\{\text{id}\}}(\sigma_q(R)), S\big)$ defined in Section 3.3, where p denotes the join predicate ($\$1.\text{id} = \$2.\text{id}$) $\wedge$ ($\text{start}(\$1.\text{T}) \geq$ NOW $-$ 1year) $\wedge$ ($\text{end}(\$1.\text{T}) <$ NOW), and q denotes the selection predicate $\text{dept} =$ "Development". We show how to derive the maintenance expression for V when ∇R^{nt} is deleted from R^{nt} (the case for $\triangle R^{nt}$ is similar). First we obtain the temporal delta $\nabla R = \{\langle r^{nt}, \{t_{now}, \text{NOW}\}\rangle \mid r^{nt} \in \nabla R^{nt}\}$ as discussed in Section 4.1. Then,

$$\bowtie_p\big(\pi_{\{\text{id}\}}(\sigma_q(R - \nabla R)), \ S\big) \tag{1}$$

$$\stackrel{(c.9)}{=} \bowtie_p\big(\pi_{\{\text{id}\}}(\sigma_q(R) - \sigma_q(\nabla R)), \ S\big)$$

$$\stackrel{(c.7)}{=} \bowtie_p\Big(\pi_{\{\text{id}\}}(\sigma_q(R)) - \big(\pi_{\{\text{id}\}}(\sigma_q(R)) - \pi_{\{\text{id}\}}(\sigma_q(R) - \sigma_q(\nabla R))\big), \ S\Big).$$

As a shorthand, let $U = \pi_{\{\text{id}\}}(\sigma_q(R)) - \pi_{\{\text{id}\}}(\sigma_q(R) - \sigma_q(\nabla R))$. Since $\bowtie_p$ is a θ-reducible operator, we must first transform U into pure deltas:

$$U_1 = \bowtie_{\$1.\text{id}=\$2.\text{id}}\big(\pi_{\{\text{id}\}}(\sigma_q(R)), \ U\big), \text{ and } U_2 = U_1 - U.$$

Then we continue applying change propagation equations:

$$(1) \quad = \quad \bowtie_p\big(\pi_{\{\text{id}\}}(\sigma_q(R)) - U_1 \cup U_2, \ S\big)$$

$$\stackrel{(c.16),(c.15)}{=} \bowtie_p\big(\pi_{\{\text{id}\}}(\sigma_q(R)), \ S\big) - \bowtie_p(U_1, S) \cup \bowtie_p(U_2, S).$$

In the above, $\bowtie_p\big(\pi_{\{\text{id}\}}(\sigma_q(R)), S\big)$ is exactly the contents of V before the source update; $\bowtie_p(U_1, S)$ and $\bowtie_p(U_2, S)$ represent the incremental changes to V.

4.3 Refreshing Views

Before we describe the procedure for refreshing views with respect to time, we need some additional notation: Let $\mathcal{E}$ be a temporal relational expression, and let $[\mathcal{E}]_t$ denote the result of evaluating $\mathcal{E}$ in the temporal database state at time

t. We omit the bracket notation for $t = t_{now}$, i.e., $[\mathcal{E}]_{t_{now}} = \mathcal{E}$. We use $\varphi([\mathcal{E}]_t)$ to denote the result of refreshing $[\mathcal{E}]_t$ with respect to t_{now}; thus, $\varphi([\mathcal{E}]_t) = \mathcal{E}$. We also define a special operator ψ_t as: $\psi_t(R) \stackrel{\text{def}}{=} \{\langle r.A_R, c\rangle \mid r \in R \wedge ((\texttt{NOW} \notin r.\texttt{T} \wedge c = r.\texttt{T}) \vee (\texttt{NOW} \in r.\texttt{T} \wedge c = r.\texttt{T} \cup c'))\}$, where R is a temporal relation and $c' = \{t' \mid t' \in \texttt{T} \wedge t < t' \leq t_{now}\}$. Intuitively, ψ_t adds the missing time instants between t and t_{now} to tuple timestamps containing $\texttt{NOW}$. This operator is introduced primarily for the purpose of our discussion. As discussed earlier, in reality the timestamp attribute would be implemented as a set of maximal, non-overlapping time periods, and a period ending with $\texttt{NOW}$ requires no update as time advances. Therefore, ψ_t is the identity operator in practice.

The procedure for refreshing views works as follows: Suppose $\mathcal{E}$ defines a temporal view which was last refreshed at time t. We derive expressions $\nabla\mathcal{E}$ and $\Delta\mathcal{E}$ such that $\varphi([\mathcal{E}]_t) = \psi_t([\mathcal{E}]_t) - \nabla\mathcal{E} \cup \Delta\mathcal{E}$. To refresh the view, we simply compute $\nabla\mathcal{E}$ and $\Delta\mathcal{E}$ and apply them to the already materialized $[\mathcal{E}]_t$. $\nabla\mathcal{E}$ and $\Delta\mathcal{E}$ are derived by induction on the structure of $\mathcal{E}$. The base case is trivial: $\varphi([R]_t) = \psi_t([R]_t) - \varnothing \cup \varnothing$ for any base relation R. Suppose that $\mathcal{E} = op(..., \mathcal{E}_i, ...)$. The inductive hypothesis is $\forall i : \varphi([\mathcal{E}_i]_t) = \psi_t([\mathcal{E}_i]_t) - \nabla\mathcal{E}_i \cup \Delta\mathcal{E}_i$. Then,

$$\varphi([\mathcal{E}]_t) = op(..., \varphi([\mathcal{E}_i]_t), ...) = op(..., \psi_t([\mathcal{E}_i]_t) - \nabla\mathcal{E}_i \cup \Delta\mathcal{E}_i, ...).$$

By repeatedly applying the change propagation equations for op given in Section 4.2, we factor out $\nabla\mathcal{E}_i$'s and $\Delta\mathcal{E}_i$'s and combine them into $\nabla\mathcal{E}'$ and $\Delta\mathcal{E}'$:

$$\varphi([\mathcal{E}]_t) = op(..., \psi_t([\mathcal{E}_i]_t), ...) - \nabla\mathcal{E}' \cup \Delta\mathcal{E}'.$$

We then apply the *view refresh equations* to be given later, and arrive at:

$$\varphi([\mathcal{E}]_t) = (\psi_t([op(..., \mathcal{E}_i, ...)]_t) - \nabla\mathcal{E}'' \cup \Delta\mathcal{E}'') - \nabla\mathcal{E}' \cup \Delta\mathcal{E}' = \psi_t([\mathcal{E}]_t) - \nabla\mathcal{E} \cup \Delta\mathcal{E},$$

where $\nabla\mathcal{E} = \nabla\mathcal{E}'' \cup (\nabla\mathcal{E}' - \Delta\mathcal{E}'')$ and $\Delta\mathcal{E} = (\Delta\mathcal{E}'' - \nabla\mathcal{E}') \cup \Delta\mathcal{E}'$.

Since τ-reducible operators make no explicit references to time, we would expect it to be easy to refresh views whose definitions contain only these operators. Indeed, as shown by the following view refresh equation (r.1), refreshing such views involves nothing more than applying ψ_t to the previously materialized views, and no deltas are generated. Here op is any τ-reducible operator:

$$(\text{r.1}) \quad op(\psi_t([\mathcal{E}_1]_t), ..., \psi_t([\mathcal{E}_n]_t)) = \psi_t([op(\mathcal{E}_1, ..., \mathcal{E}_n)]_t)$$

On the other hand, refreshing a view whose definition contains θ-reducible operators sometimes requires updating the previously materialized result, because the truth value of a temporal predicate can change as time advances. In the following, p may reference $\texttt{NOW}$ and/or $\texttt{T}$. In (r.3), q denotes the predicate $\$1.\texttt{T} \cap ... \cap \$n.\texttt{T} \neq \varnothing$. The temporal semijoin operator $\ltimes_p$ was defined in Section 4.2.

$$(\text{r.2}) \quad \sigma_p(\psi_t([\mathcal{E}]_t)) = \psi_t([\sigma_p(\mathcal{E})]_t) - \sigma_{\neg p}\Big(\psi_t([\sigma_p(\mathcal{E})]_t)\Big) \cup \sigma_p\Big(\psi_t([\sigma_{\neg p}(\mathcal{E})]_t)\Big)$$

$$(\text{r.3}) \quad \ltimes_p(\psi_t([\mathcal{E}_1]_t), ..., \psi_t([\mathcal{E}_n]_t)) = \psi_t([\ltimes_p(\mathcal{E}_1, ..., \mathcal{E}_n)]_t)$$
$$- \ltimes_{\neg p}\Big(\psi_t([\ltimes_{p \wedge q}(\mathcal{E}_1, \mathcal{E}_2, ..., \mathcal{E}_n)]_t), ..., \psi_t([\ltimes_{p \wedge q}(\mathcal{E}_n, \mathcal{E}_1, ..., \mathcal{E}_{n-1})]_t)\Big)$$
$$\cup \ltimes_p\Big(\psi_t([\ltimes_{\neg p \wedge q}(\mathcal{E}_1, \mathcal{E}_2, ..., \mathcal{E}_n)]_t), ..., \psi_t([\ltimes_{\neg p \wedge q}(\mathcal{E}_n, \mathcal{E}_1, ..., \mathcal{E}_{n-1})]_t)\Big)$$

Intuitively, to obtain tuples that satisfy p at t_{now} given the result materialized at t, we first delete tuples that satisfy p at t but not at t_{now}, and then insert tuples that satisfy p at t_{now} but not at t. In (r.3), we use semijoins to retain individual tuple timestamps in order to reevaluate the join predicate at t_{now}. Without semijoins, we will lose track of these individual timestamps, since temporal join stores in the result only the intersection of timestamps from joining tuples.

The updates generated by (r.2) and (r.3) appear quite complicated. However, by making compile-time analysis of the predicates, it is possible to determine if certain terms are guaranteed to be empty regardless of the database instance. If an update is guaranteed to be empty, it does not have to be computed or applied at run-time. For example, consider the deletion $\sigma_{\neg p}(\psi_t([\sigma_p(\mathcal{E})]_t))$ generated by (r.2). Since we assume an implementation in which a timestamp is encoded by a set of periods using NOW, ψ_t can be eliminated. Let $[p]_t$ denote the predicate p evaluated at time t, i.e., with the implicit binding NOW $= t$. The deletion can be rewritten as $\sigma_{[\neg p]_{t_{now}} \wedge [p]_t}([\mathcal{E}]_t)$. Similarly, it is easy to verify that the deletion in (r.3) can be rewritten as $\bowtie_{[\neg p]_{t_{now}} \wedge [p]_t}([\mathcal{E}_1]_t, ..., [\mathcal{E}_n]_t)$. The problem of determining whether these terms are guaranteed to be empty is reduced to that of testing whether the predicate $[\neg p]_{t_{now}} \wedge [p]_t \wedge t < t_{now}$ is unsatisfiable. If we impose a further restriction that T can be encoded by just one start time TS and one end time TE (such an assumption often holds for a transaction time relation), then any temporal predicate, including any built-in function or predicate such as start, length, or overlaps, can be rewritten as an ordinary boolean expression involving TS, TE, $+$, $-$, $=$, $>$, $<$. Then, existing algorithms [2] can be used to test for satisfiability. This is illustrated in the example below.

We now demonstrate how to derive the expression for refreshing a temporal view as time advances. We use the same view $V \stackrel{\text{def}}{=} \bowtie_p(\pi_{\{id\}}(\sigma_q(R)), S)$ as in Section 3.3. In the following, the operator ψ_t is omitted because we assume an implementation in which a timestamp is encoded by a set of periods using NOW.

$$\varphi([\bowtie_p(\pi_{\{id\}}(\sigma_q(R)), S)]_t) \qquad (2)$$
$$= \bowtie_p(\varphi([\pi_{\{id\}}(\sigma_q(R))]_t), \varphi([S]_t))$$
$$\stackrel{(r.1)}{=} \bowtie_p([\pi_{\{id\}}(\sigma_q(R))]_t, [S]_t)$$
$$\stackrel{(r.3)}{=} [\bowtie_p(\pi_{\{id\}}(\sigma_q(R)), S)]_t - \bowtie_{[\neg p]_{t_{now}} \wedge [p]_t}([\pi_{\{id\}}(\sigma_q(R))]_t, [S]_t)$$
$$\cup \bowtie_{[p]_{t_{now}} \wedge [\neg p]_t}([\pi_{\{id\}}(\sigma_q(R))]_t, [S]_t).$$

In order to test whether the updates generated by (r.3) are empty, we have rewritten them using the $[]_t$ notation for predicates. It can be shown easily that the join predicate for the insertion, $[p]_{t_{now}} \wedge [\neg p]_t$, is unsatisfiable because $(\text{start}(\$1.\text{T}) \geq t_{now} - 1\text{year}) \wedge (\text{start}(\$1.\text{T}) < t - 1\text{year}) \wedge t < t_{now}$ is unsatisfiable. Therefore, we can simplify (2) into:

$$[\bowtie_p(\pi_{\{id\}}(\sigma_q(R)), S)]_t - \bowtie_{[\neg p]_{t_{now}} \wedge [p]_t}([\pi_{\{id\}}(\sigma_q(R))]_t, [S]_t)$$
$$= [\bowtie_p(\pi_{\{id\}}(\sigma_q(R)), S)]_t$$
$$- \bowtie_{\neg p}([\bowtie_{p \wedge \$1.T \cap \$2.T \neq \varnothing}(\pi_{\{id\}}(\sigma_q(R)), S)]_t, [\bowtie_{p \wedge \$1.T \cap \$2.T \neq \varnothing}(S, \pi_{\{id\}}(\sigma_q(R)))]_t).$$

From this equation, we see that tuples are automatically "expired" from V as time advances. The deletions can be computed from the old V, plus individual timestamps of the joining tuples (this is the purpose of the semijoins). If we materialize semijoin results or simply record individual timestamps of the joining tuples, there is no need to access the complete source history in R and S.

5 Maintaining Temporal Aggregates

We briefly outline our approach for maintaining a class of commonly used temporal aggregate views called *moving-window aggregates* [12]. A complete discussion appears in the full version of this paper [22]. We use $\Pi_{A',w}$ to denote the aggregate operator, where A' contains both group-by and aggregated attributes, and $w \geq 0$ is the *window*. To formally define $\Pi_{A',w}$, we extend τ_t with an additional parameter for window length: $\tau_{t,w}(R) \stackrel{\text{def}}{=} \{\langle r.A_R \rangle \mid r \in R \land (\exists t' \in r.T : t - w \leq t' \leq t)\}$. In other words, $\tau_{t,w}(R)$ returns a non-temporal relation containing all tuples valid at some point during the period $[t - w, t]$. Now, we define $\Pi_{A',w}(R)$ as a temporal relation with the property that for any $t \leq t_{now}$, $\tau_t(\Pi_{A',w}(R)) = \Pi_{A'}^{nt}(\tau_{t,w}(R))$. Here $\Pi_{A'}^{nt}$ is the standard non-temporal grouping and aggregate operator [16]. Intuitively, the result of a temporal aggregate is a sequence of values generated by moving a window of given length along the time line, and computing the non-temporal aggregate from all tuples valid in the current window. For detailed discussion on temporal aggregates please refer to [19].

An aggregate with $w = 0$ is termed *instantaneous* because its value at time t is computed only from the tuples valid at time t. $\Pi_{A',0}$ is τ-reducible: $\tau_t(\Pi_{A',0}(R)) = \Pi_{A'}^{nt}(\tau_{t,0}(R)) = \Pi_{A'}^{nt}(\tau_t(R))$. Thus, for $\Pi_{A',0}$ we may simply reuse the change propagation equations developed for non-temporal aggregates [16], and use (r.1) for view refresh.

In the general case where $w > 0$, $\Pi_{A',w}$ is not τ-reducible. It is termed *cumulative* since its value at time t may depend on tuples that have been valid in the past, as well as those valid at t. A possible approach is to θ-reduce $\Pi_{A',w}$ and require pure deltas as in Section 4.2. However, this would cause the aggregate to be recomputed for *all* valid periods of the affected tuples. This is both inefficient and unnecessary, because during those periods that are more than w away from the delta timestamps, the aggregate result cannot be affected. Therefore, we take a different approach based on the key observation that $\Pi_{A',w}(R) = \Pi_{A',0}(\text{EX}_w(R))$. Here, $\text{EX}_w(R) \stackrel{\text{def}}{=} \{\langle r.A_R, c \rangle \mid r \in R\}$, where $c = \{t \mid (t \in \mathbb{T} \land t \leq t_{now} \land (\exists t' \in r.T : 0 \leq t - t' \leq w)) \lor (t = \text{NOW} \land (\exists t' \in r.T : 0 \leq t_{now} - t' \leq w))\}$. Intuitively, assuming a timestamp is implemented as a set of periods, EX_w extends the end time of each period in a timestamp by w units, and merges adjacent periods together if they become overlapped.

Now, the problem of propagating changes through $\Pi_{A',w}$ can be reduced to first propagating changes through EX_w, and then through $\Pi_{A',0}$. For example:

$$\Pi_{A',w}(R \cup \Delta R) = \Pi_{A',0}(\text{EX}_w(R \cup \Delta R)) = \Pi_{A',0}(\text{EX}_w(R) \cup (\text{EX}_w(\Delta R) - \text{EX}_w(R))).$$

Applying the change propagation equations for $\Pi_{A',0}$, we will obtain the term $\Pi_{A',0}(\mathsf{EX}_w(R))$, which is exactly $\Pi_{A',w}(R)$, the view we are maintaining. The remaining terms are the incremental changes. Propagating ∇R is similar.

Now we turn to the problem of refreshing cumulative aggregate views with respect to the current time. Unlike the τ-reducible instantaneous aggregates, the value of a cumulative aggregate at time t_{now} may not stay the same as time advances, even if there are no updates. Intuitively, for each tuple valid at NOW in the materialized aggregate result, we terminate its timestamp at t. Then, we compute the new values of the aggregate for the period $[t+1, \mathrm{NOW}]$ using the contents of $\mathcal{E}$ during $[t+1-w, \mathrm{NOW}]$, and append them to the result. In the following view refresh equation, $\mathsf{FR}_d(R)$ returns the fragment of R in the period d. It is just a shorthand for $\pi_{\$1.A}(\bowtie_{\mathtt{true}}(R, D))$, where D is a temporal relation containing a single tuple with timestamp $\{d\}$.

$$
\begin{aligned}
(\text{r.4}) \quad \Pi_{A',w}(\psi_t([\mathcal{E}]_t)) =\ & \psi_t([\Pi_{A',w}(\mathcal{E})]_t) \\
& - \mathsf{FR}_{[t+1,\mathrm{NOW}]}\Big(\sigma_{\mathrm{NOW}\in T}\big(\psi_t([\Pi_{A',w}(\mathcal{E})]_t)\big)\Big) \\
& \cup \mathsf{FR}_{[t+1,\mathrm{NOW}]}\Big(\Pi_{A',w}(\mathsf{FR}_{[t+1-w,\mathrm{NOW}]}(\psi_t([\mathcal{E}]_t)))\Big)
\end{aligned}
$$

6 Conclusion and Future Work

Providing temporal views over non-temporal source data is a very useful feature of a data warehouse. In this paper, we have presented a systematic approach to maintaining temporal views. Our framework is useful not only in data warehousing, but also in other settings where the temporal view maintenance problem arises.

We are currently in the process of implementing our algorithm and studying its performance within the WHIPS warehousing prototype [21]; see the full version of this paper [22] for a discussion. We are also investigating the *self-maintenance* problem [17] for temporal views. Another possible enhancement to our framework is to allow different degrees of "laziness" or "eagerness" in propagating source updates and refreshing views. This flexibility will complicate the algorithm, but it may yield better performance because multiple updates can be combined in batch and processed more efficiently.

References

1. L. Bækgaard and L. Mark. Incremental computation of time-varying query expressions. *IEEE Trans. on Knowledge & Data Eng.*, 7(4):583–590, 1995.
2. J. A. Blakeley, N. Coburn, and P.-Å. Larson. Updating derived relations: Detecting irrelevant and autonomously computable updates. *ACM Trans. on Database Systems*, 14(3):369–400, 1989.
3. M. H. Böhlen, C. S. Jensen, and R. T. Snodgrass. Evaluating the completeness of TSQL2. In *Proc. of the Intl. Workshop on Temporal Databases*, pages 153–174, 1995.
4. J. Chomicki and D. Toman. Implementing temporal integrity constraints using an active DBMS. *IEEE Trans. on Knowledge & Data Eng.*, 7(4):566–581, 1995.

5. J. Clifford, C. E. Dyreson, T. Isakowitz, C. S. Jensen, and R. T. Snodgrass. On the semantics of "NOW" in databases. *ACM Trans. on Database Systems*, 22(2):171–214, 1997.

6. T. Griffin and L. Libkin. Incremental maintenance of views with duplicates. In *Proc. of the 1995 ACM SIGMOD Intl. Conf. on Management of Data*, pages 328–339, 1995.

7. A. Gupta and I. S. Mumick. Maintenance of materialized views: Problems, techniques, and applications. *IEEE Data Eng.*, 18(2):3–18, 1995.

8. H. V. Jagadish, I. S. Mumick, and A. Silberschatz. View maintenance issues for the chronicle data model. In *Proc. of the 1995 ACM Symp. on Principles of Database Systems*, pages 113–124, 1995.

9. C. S. Jensen and L. Mark. Differential query processing in transaction-time databases. In *Temporal Databases: Theory, Design, and Implementation*, chapter 19, pages 457–491. Benjamin/Cummings, 1993.

10. C. S. Jensen, M. D. Soo, and R. T. Snodgrass. Unifying temporal models via a conceptual model. *Information Systems*, 19(7):513–547, 1994.

11. W. Labio and H. Garcia-Molina. Expiring data from the warehouse. Technical report, Computer Science Dept., Stanford Univ., 1997. http://www-db.stanford.edu/pub/papers/expire.ps.

12. S. B. Navathe and R. Ahmed. A temporal relational model and a query language. *Information Sciences*, 49(1):147–175, 1989.

13. G. Özsoyoğlu and R. Snodgrass. Temporal and real-time databases: A survey. *IEEE Trans. on Knowledge & Data Eng.*, 7(4):513–532, 1995.

14. D. Plexousakis. Integrity constraint and rule maintenance in temporal deductive knowledge bases. In *Proc. of the 1993 Intl. Conf. on Very Large Data Bases*, pages 146–157, 1993.

15. X. Qian and G. Wiederhold. Incremental recomputation of active relational expressions. *IEEE Trans. on Knowledge & Data Eng.*, 3(3):337–341, 1991.

16. D. Quass. Maintenance expressions for views with aggregation. In *Proc. of the ACM Workshop on Materialized Views: Techniques & Applications*, pages 110–118, 1996.

17. D. Quass, A. Gupta, I. S. Mumick, and J. Widom. Making views self-maintainable for data warehousing. In *Proc. of the 1996 Intl. Conf. on Parallel & Distributed Information Systems*, 1996.

18. R. T. Snodgrass. The temporal query language TQuel. *ACM Trans. on Database Systems*, 12(2):247–298, 1987.

19. R. T. Snodgrass, S. Gomez, and L. E. McKenzie. Aggregates in the temporal query language TQuel. *IEEE Trans. on Knowledge & Data Eng.*, 5(5):826–842, 1993.

20. J. Widom. Research problems in data warehousing. In *Proc. of the 1995 Intl. Conf. on Information & Knowledge Management*, pages 25–30, 1995.

21. J. L. Wiener, H. Gupta, W. J. Labio, Y. Zhuge, H. Garcia-Molina, and J. Widom. A system prototype for warehouse view maintenance. In *Proc. of the ACM Workshop on Materialized Views: Techniques & Applications*, pages 26–33, 1996.

22. J. Yang and J. Widom. Maintaining temporal views over non-temporal information sources for data warehousing. Technical report, Computer Science Dept., Stanford Univ., 1998. http://www-db.stanford.edu/pub/papers/yw-tempview.ps.

Referential Actions: From Logical Semantics to Implementation

Bertram Ludäscher   Wolfgang May

Institut für Informatik, Universität Freiburg, Germany
{ludaesch,may}@informatik.uni-freiburg.de

Abstract. Referential actions (*rac*'s) are specialized triggers used to automatically maintain referential integrity. While their local effects can be grasped easily, it is far from obvious what the global semantics of a set *RA* of interacting *rac*'s should be. To capture the intended meaning of *RA*, we first present an abstract non-constructive semantics. By formalizing *RA* as a logic program P_{RA}, a constructive semantics is obtained. The equivalence of the logic programming semantics and the abstract semantics is proven using a game-theoretic characterization, which provides additional insight into the meaning of *rac*'s. As shown in previous work, for general *rac*'s, it may be infeasible to compute all *maximal admissible* solutions. Therefore, we focus on a tractable subset, i.e., *rac*'s without modifications. We show that in this case a unique maximal admissible solution exists, and derive a PTIME algorithm for computing this solution. In case a set $U_\triangleright$ of user requests is not admissible, a maximal admissible subset of $U_\triangleright$ is suggested.

1 Introduction

We study the following problem: Given a relational database D, a set of user-defined update requests $U_\triangleright$, and a set of referential actions RA, find those sets of updates Δ which (i) preserve referential integrity in the new database D', (ii) are maximal wrt. $U_\triangleright$, and (iii) reflect the intended meaning of RA. This notion of intended "optimal" updates will be formalized using so-called *maximal admissible* sets of updates.

The problem is important both from a practical and theoretical point of view: *Referential integrity constraints* (*ric*'s) are a central concept of the relational database model and frequently used in real world applications. *Referential actions* (*rac*'s) are specialized triggers used to automatically enforce integrity, thereby relieving the user from the burden of enumerating all induced updates which arise from an initial user request $U_\triangleright$.

Due to their practical importance, *rac*'s have been included in the SQL2 standard and SQL3 proposal [ISO92, ISO95]. In [DD94] and [Dat90], the problem of unpredictable behavior, i.e., ambiguities in determining the above Δ and D', in certain situations is addressed. In [Hor92, CPM96], a solution is presented, based on a rather ad-hoc run-time execution model. In a different approach, [Mar94] presents safeness conditions which aim at avoiding ambiguities at the schema level. However, as shown in [Rei96], it is in general undecidable whether a database schema with *rac*'s is ambiguous. Summarizing, from a theoretical point of view, the problem has not been solved in a satisfactory way.

In this paper, we continue our work on declarative semantics for referential actions. First results have been reported in [LMR96]. In [LML97a], it is shown that for rac's with modifications, it may be infeasible to compute all maximal admissible solutions (intuitively, there are several equally justified ways how to propagate the combined effect of modifications, leading to an exponential blow up, both in the number of rules for integrity maintenance and in the number of solutions). Here, we therefore restrict to the tractable class of rac's without modifications. This guarantees the existence of a unique optimal solution which can be efficiently computed.

In Section 2, we introduce the basics of referential integrity and illustrate the problem of ambiguity. In Section 3.1, we identify and formalize desirable abstract properties of updates which lead to a non-constructive global semantics of rac's. A constructive definition providing a global semantics is obtained by formalizing a set of referential actions RA as a logic program P_{RA} (Section 3.2). The correctness of this characterization is proven via an equivalent game-theoretic characterization (Section 3.3) which allows intelligible proofs on a less technical level (Section 4). From the logic programming characterization, an algorithm for computing the maximal admissible solution is derived (Section 5).

2 Referential Integrity

Notation and Preliminaries. A relation schema consists of a relation name R and a vector of attributes $(A_1, \ldots, A_n)$. We identify attribute names A_i of R with the integers $1, \ldots, n$. By $\vec{A} = (i_1, \ldots, i_k)$ we denote a vector of $k \leq n$ distinct attributes (usually $\vec{A}$ will be some key).

Tuples of R are denoted by first-order atoms $R(\vec{X})$ with n-ary relation symbol R, and vector $\vec{X}$ of variables or constants from the underlying domain. To emphasize that such a vector is ground, i.e., comprises only constants, we write $\bar{x}$ instead of $\vec{X}$. The *projection* of tuples $\vec{X}$ to an attribute vector $\vec{A}$ is denoted by $\vec{X}[\vec{A}]$: e.g., if $\bar{x} = (a, b, c)$, $\vec{A} = (1, 3)$, then $\bar{x}[\vec{A}] = (a, c)$. Deletions are denoted by del:$R(\bar{x})$.

For a relation schema R with attributes $\vec{A}$, a minimal subset $\vec{K}$ of $\vec{A}$ whose values uniquely identify each tuple in R is a *candidate key*. In general, the database schema specifies which attribute vectors are keys. A candidate key $R.\vec{K}$ has to satisfy the first-order sentence φ_{key} for every database instance D:

$$\forall \vec{X}_1, \vec{X}_2 \ (R(\vec{X}_1) \wedge R(\vec{X}_2) \wedge \vec{X}_1[\vec{K}] = \vec{X}_2[\vec{K}] \rightarrow \vec{X}_1 = \vec{X}_2) \ . \qquad (\varphi_{key})$$

Referential Integrity Constraints. A *referential integrity constraint* (ric) is an expression of the form

$$R_C.\vec{F} \rightarrow R_P.\vec{K} \ ,$$

where $\vec{F}$ is a *foreign key* of the *child relation* R_C, referencing a candidate key $\vec{K}$ of the *parent relation* R_P. A ric $R_C.\vec{F} \rightarrow R_P.\vec{K}$ is *satisfied* by a given database D, if for every child tuple $R_C(\bar{x})$ with foreign key values $\bar{x}[\vec{F}]$, there exists a tuple $R_P(\bar{y})$ with matching key value, i.e., $\bar{x}[\vec{F}] = \bar{y}[\vec{K}]$. Thus, for a database instance D, a *ric* is satisfied if $D \models \varphi_{ric}$:

$$\forall \bar{X} \ (\ R_C(\bar{X}) \rightarrow \exists \bar{Y} \ (R_P(\bar{Y}) \wedge \bar{X}[\vec{F}] = \bar{Y}[\vec{K}]) \ ) \ . \qquad (\varphi_{ric})$$

A *ric* is *violated* by D if it is not satisfied by D.

Referential Actions. Rule-based approaches to referential integrity maintenance are attractive since they describe how *ric*'s should be enforced using "local repairs": Given a *ric* $R_C.\vec{F} \rightarrow R_P.\vec{K}$ and an update operation insert, delete,
or modify on R_P or R_C, a *referential action* (*rac*) defines some local operation
on R_C or R_P, respectively. It is easy to see from the logical implication in (φ_{ric})
that insert into R_P and delete from R_C cannot introduce a violation of a *ric*,
whereas the other updates can. For these, there are two strategies to maintain
referential integrity by *local* actions:

- CASCADE: propagate the update from the parent to the child,
- REJECT: reject an update on the parent if there exists a referencing tuple.

The Problem of Ambiguity. With this *local* specification of behavior, there
may be ambiguities wrt. the *global* semantics, leading to different final states.
A relational database *schema* S with *rac*'s RA is ambiguous, if there is some
database instance D and some set of user requests $U_\triangleright$ s.t. there are different
final states D' depending on the execution order of referential actions. As shown
in [Rei96], it is in general undecidable whether a schema with *rac*'s is ambiguous
(given D and $U_\triangleright$, the problem becomes decidable). The following example from
[Rei96] illustrates the problem:

Example 1 Consider the database with *rac*'s depicted in Fig. 1. Solid arcs represent *ric*'s and point from R_C to R_P, *rac*'s are denoted by dashed (CASCADE)
or dotted (REJECT) arcs. Let $U_\triangleright = \{\text{del}:R_1(a)\}$ be a user request to delete the
tuple $R_1(a)$. Depending on the order of execution of *rac*'s, one of two different
final states may be reached:

1. If execution follows the path R_1-R_3-R_4, the tuple $R_3(a, y)$ cannot be deleted:
   Since $R_4(a, x, y)$ references $R_3(a, y)$, the *rac* for R_4 forbids the deletion of
   $R_3(a, y)$. This in turn forbids the deletion of $R_1(a)$. Thus, the user request
   del:$R_1(a)$ is rejected, and the database remains unchanged, i.e., $D' = D$.

2. If execution follows the path R_1-R_2-R_4, the tuples $R_2(a, x)$ and $R_4(a, x, y)$
   are requested for deletion. Hence, the *rac* for $R_4.(1, 3) \rightarrow R_3.(1, 2)$ can assume
   that $R_4(a, x, y)$ is deleted, thus no referencing tuple exists in R_4. Therefore,
   all deletions can be executed, resulting in a new database state $D' \neq D$.

We argue that (2) is preferable to (1), since it accomplishes the desired user
request without violating referential integrity. □

2.1 Disambiguating Strategies

The ambiguity in Example 1 can be eliminated by specifying that *rac*'s of type
REJECT are always evaluated wrt. the database state either *before* starting the
transaction or *after* the complete transaction, leading to the following strategies
to maintain referential integrity by referential actions:

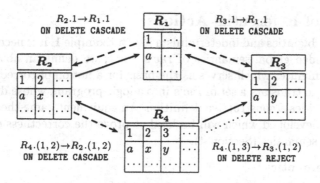

Fig. 1. Database with referential actions

- CASCADE: propagate the update from the parent to the child,
- RESTRICT: (i) reject an update on the *parent* if there exists a child referencing it in the *original* database state, or (ii) reject an update on the *child* if there is no tuple with the respective parent key in the *original* database state,
- NO ACTION: similar to RESTRICT, but look at the database state *after* (hypothetically) applying all updates (in active database terminology, this corresponds to change *immediate coupling* of referential actions into *deferred coupling*).

Since the final state depends on the updates to be executed, and these may in turn depend on the final state via NO ACTION, there is a cyclic dependency. In Section 3, we show how to solve this semantical problem using different (logical and game-theoretic) characterizations of *rac*'s.

In SQL, referential actions for a given *ric* $R_C.\vec{F} \to R_P.\vec{K}$ are specified with the definition of the child relation:

```
{CREATE | ALTER} TABLE R_C
  ...
  FOREIGN KEY F REFERENCES R_P K
  [ON UPDATE {NO ACTION | CASCADE | RESTRICT | SET NULL | SET DEFAULT}]
  [ON DELETE {NO ACTION | CASCADE | RESTRICT | SET NULL | SET DEFAULT}]
  ...
```

(RESTRICT is not contained in SQL2, but in the SQL3 proposal.)

Due to lack of space, we do not consider insertions in the sequel. Note however, that insertions can be handled in a straightforward way by rejecting updates which aim to insert a child tuple whose corresponding parent does not exist (this is also the SQL strategy), and all results can be directly extended to incorporate insertions (cf. [LML97a, LML97b]). Moreover, as mentioned above, we deliberately exclude modifications (i.e., ON UPDATE triggers and SET NULL/DEFAULT actions, the latter being a special case of modifications), since this problem is intractable in general [LML97a].

Thus, in this work, we investigate *rics* $R_C.\vec{F} \to R_P.\vec{K}$ with corresponding *rac*'s of the form $R_C.\vec{F} \to R_P.\vec{K}$ ON DELETE {CASCADE | RESTRICT | NO ACTION}.

3 Semantics of Referential Actions

In order to avoid ambiguities and indeterminism like in Example 1, it is necessary to specify the intended global semantics of rac's. First, we define an abstract, non-constructive semantics which serves as the basis for a notion of correctness. Next, we show how to translate a set of rac's into a logic program, whose declarative semantics provides a constructive definition. An equivalent game-theoretic characterization is developed which will be used to prove the correctness of the logic programming semantics (Section 4).

3.1 Abstract Semantics

Let D be a database represented as a set of ground atoms, RA a set of rac's, and $U_\rhd = \{\text{del}:R_1(\bar{x}_1), \ldots, \text{del}:R_n(\bar{x}_n)\}$ a set of (external) *user delete requests* which are passed to the system. D and RA define three graphs $\mathcal{DC}$ (ON DELETE CASCADE), $\mathcal{DR}$ (ON DELETE RESTRICT), and $\mathcal{DN}$ (ON DELETE NO ACTION) corresponding to the different types of references:

$$\mathcal{DC} := \{(R_C(\bar{x}), R_P(\bar{y})) \in D \times D \mid$$
$$R_C.\vec{F} \rightarrow R_P.\vec{K} \text{ ON DELETE CASCADE} \in RA \text{ and } \bar{x}[\vec{F}] = \bar{y}[\vec{K}]\},$$

$\mathcal{DR}$ and $\mathcal{DN}$ are defined analogously. $\mathcal{DC}^*$ denotes the reflexive transitive closure of $\mathcal{DC}$. Note that the graphs describe *potential* interactions due to rac's, independent of the given user requests $U_\rhd$. To capture the intended semantics, $U_\rhd$ has to be considered:

Definition 1 Given RA, D, and $U_\rhd$, a set Δ of delete requests is called

- *founded*, if $\text{del}:R(\bar{x}) \in \Delta$ implies $(R(\bar{x}), R'(\bar{x}')) \in \mathcal{DC}^*$ for some $\text{del}:R'(\bar{x}') \in U_\rhd$,
- *complete*, if $\text{del}:R_P(\bar{y}) \in \Delta$ and $(R_C(\bar{x}), R_P(\bar{y})) \in \mathcal{DC}$ implies $\text{del}:R_C(\bar{x}) \in \Delta$,
- *feasible*, if
  - $(R_C(\bar{x}), R_P(\bar{y})) \in \mathcal{DR}$ implies $\text{del}:R_P(\bar{y}) \notin \Delta$, and
  - $\text{del}:R_P(\bar{y}) \in \Delta$ and $(R_C(\bar{x}), R_P(\bar{y})) \in \mathcal{DN}$ implies $\text{del}:R_C(\bar{x}) \in \Delta$,
- *admissible*, if it is founded, complete, and feasible. □

Foundedness guarantees that all deletions are "justified" by some user request, completeness guarantees that no cascading deletions are "forgotten", and feasibility ensures that RESTRICT/NO ACTION rac's are "obeyed".

Definition 2 (Maximal Admissible Sets, Intended Semantics)
Let RA, D, and $U_\rhd$ be given.

- The set of *induced updates* $\Delta(U)$ of a set of user requests $U \subseteq U_\rhd$ is the least set Δ which contains U and is complete.

- A set of user requests $U \subseteq U_\rhd$ is *admissible* if $\Delta(U)$ is admissible, and *maximal admissible* if there is no other admissible U', s.t. $U \subsetneq U' \subseteq U_\rhd$.

- The *intended semantics* are the maximal admissible subsets of $U_\rhd$. □

Proposition 1 (Correctness)
a) If $U \subseteq U_\rhd$, then $\Delta(U)$ is founded and complete.
b) If Δ is complete and feasible, then $D' := D \pm \Delta(U)$ satisfies all rics. □

PROOF *a)* $\Delta(U)$ is defined as the *least* complete set. It follows that $\Delta(U)$ is founded. *b)* Completeness guarantees that all *ric*'s labeled with ON DELETE CASCADE in RA are satisfied, feasibility guarantees that all *ric*'s labeled with ON DELETE RESTRICT/NO ACTION are satisfied. ∎

Theorem 2 (Uniqueness)
Given RA, D, and $U_\triangleright$, there is exactly one maximal admissible $U_{\max} \subseteq U_\triangleright$.

PROOF Observe that $U_1 \cup U_2$ is admissible if $U_1, U_2 \subseteq U_\triangleright$ are admissible. Thus, the union of all admissible subsets of $U_\triangleright$ yields $U_{\max}$. ∎

3.2 Logic Programming Characterization

We show how a set RA of *rac*'s is compiled into a logic program P_{RA} whose rules specify their local behavior. The advantage of this logical formalization is that the declarative semantics of P_{RA} defines a precise *global* semantics.

The following rule derives for every user request del:$R(\bar{x}) \in U_\triangleright$ an *internal delete request* req_del:$R(\bar{x})$, provided there is no *blocking* blk_del:$R(\bar{x})$:

$$\text{req\_del}{:}R(\bar{X}) \leftarrow \text{del}{:}R(\bar{X}), \neg\text{blk\_del}{:}R(\bar{X}). \qquad (I)$$

Referential actions are specified as follows:

- $R_C.\vec{F} {\rightarrow} R_P.\vec{K}$ ON DELETE CASCADE is encoded into two rules: the first one propagates internal delete requests downwards from the parent to the child:

$$\text{req\_del}{:}R_C(\bar{X}) \leftarrow \text{req\_del}{:}R_P(\bar{Y}),\ R_C(\bar{X}),\ \bar{X}[\vec{F}] = \bar{Y}[\vec{K}]. \qquad (DC_1)$$

Additionally, blockings are propagated upwards, i.e., when the deletion of a child is blocked, the deletion of the referenced parent is also blocked:

$$\text{blk\_del}{:}R_P(\bar{Y}) \leftarrow R_P(\bar{Y}),\ \text{blk\_del}{:}R_C(\bar{X}),\ \bar{X}[\vec{F}] = \bar{Y}[\vec{K}]. \qquad (DC_2)$$

- $R_C.\vec{F} {\rightarrow} R_P.\vec{K}$ ON DELETE RESTRICT blocks the deletion of a parent tuple if there is a corresponding child tuple:

$$\text{blk\_del}{:}R_P(\bar{Y}) \leftarrow R_P(\bar{Y}),\ R_C(\bar{X}),\ \bar{X}[\vec{F}] = \bar{Y}[\vec{K}]. \qquad (DR)$$

- $R_C.\vec{F} {\rightarrow} R_P.\vec{K}$ ON DELETE NO ACTION blocks the deletion of a parent tuple if there is a corresponding child tuple which is not requested for deletion:

$$\text{blk\_del}{:}R_P(\bar{Y}) \leftarrow R_P(\bar{Y}),\ R_C(\bar{X}),\ \neg\text{req\_del}{:}R_C(\bar{X}),\ \bar{X}[\vec{F}] = \bar{Y}[\vec{K}]. \qquad (DN)$$

Due to the negative cyclic dependency req_del $\overset{\sim}{\rightarrow}$ blk_del $\overset{\sim}{\rightarrow}$ req_del , P_{RA} is in general not stratified.

Well-Founded Semantics. The well-founded model [VGRS91] is widely accepted as a (skeptical) declarative semantics for logic programs. The well-founded model $\mathcal{W}_{RA}$ of $P_{RA} \cup D \cup U_\triangleright$ assigns a third truth value *undefined* to atoms whose truth cannot be determined using a "well-founded" argumentation.

Often, even if not all requested updates can be accomplished, it is still possible to execute some of them while postponing the others. Thus, the information which tuple or update really causes problems is valuable for preparing a refined update that realizes the intended changes *and* is acceptable:

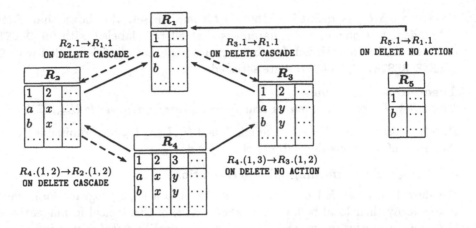

Fig. 2. Extended database with modified *rac*'s

Example 2 Consider the database with *rac*'s in Fig. 2, and the user request $U_\triangleright = \{\mathsf{del}\!:\!R_1(a), \mathsf{del}\!:\!R_1(b)\}$. $\mathsf{del}\!:\!R_1(b)$ is not admissible since it is blocked by $R_5(b)$. However, the other request, $\mathsf{del}\!:\!R_1(a)$, can be executed without violating any *ric* by deleting $R_1(a)$, $R_2(a, x)$, $R_3(a, y)$, and $R_4(a, x, y)$. Thus, the extended set $U'_\triangleright = \{\mathsf{del}\!:\!R_1(a), \mathsf{del}\!:\!R_1(b), \mathsf{del}\!:\!R_5(b)\}$ is a candidate for a refined update request which accomplishes the deletion of $R_1(a)$ and $R_1(b)$.

The well-founded semantics reflects the different status of the single updates:

Given the user request $U_\triangleright = \{\mathsf{del}\!:\!R_1(a)\}$, the delete requests req_del for $R_1(a)$, $R_2(a, x)$, $R_3(a, y)$, $R_4(a, x, y)$, as well as the blockings blk_del for $R_1(a)$ and $R_3(a, y)$ will be *undefined* in the well-founded model.

For the user request $U'_\triangleright = \{\mathsf{del}\!:\!R_1(b)\}$, blk_del is *true* for $R_1(b)$ due to the referencing tuple $R_5(b)$. Thus, req_del:$R_1(b)$ is *false*, and $\mathsf{del}\!:\!R_1(b)$ is not admissible; hence there are no cascaded delete requests. Due to the referencing tuple $R_4(b, x, y)$ which cannot be deleted in this case, blk_del:$R_3(b, y)$ is also *true*. □

$\mathcal{W}_{RA}$ contains some ambiguities which can be interpreted constructively as *degrees of freedom*: The blockings and deletions induced by $U_\triangleright = \{\mathsf{del}\!:\!R_1(a)\}$ in Example 2 are undefined due to the dependency req_del $\rightsquigarrow$ blk_del $\rightsquigarrow$ req_del. This freedom may be used to define different global policies by giving priority either to deletions or blockings (cf. Theorems 10 and 11).

3.3 Triggers as Games

The following game-theoretic formalization provides an elegant characterization of *rac*'s yielding additional insight into the well-founded model of P_{RA} and the intuitive meaning of *rac*'s.

The game is played with a pebble by two players, I (the *"Deleter"*) and II (the *"Spoiler"*), who argue whether a tuple may be deleted. The players move alternately in *rounds*; each round consists of two *moves*. A player who cannot move loses. The set of *positions* of the game is $D \cup U_\triangleright \cup \{\text{restricted}\}$. The possible moves of I and II are defined below. Note that I moves from D to $U_\triangleright$, while II moves from $U_\triangleright$ to $D \cup \{\text{restricted}\}$. Initially, the pebble is placed on some tuple in D (or $U_\triangleright$) and I (or II) starts to move. If II starts the game, the first round only consists of the move by II.

By moving the pebble from $R(\bar{x}) \in D$ to some del:$R'(\bar{x}') \in U_\triangleright$ which cascades down to $R(\bar{x})$, I claims that the deletion of $R(\bar{x})$ is "justified" (i.e., founded) by del:$R'(\bar{x}')$. Conversely, II claims by her moves that del:$R'(\bar{x}')$ is not feasible. II can use two different arguments: Assume that the deletion of $R'(\bar{x}')$ cascades down to some tuple $R_P(\bar{x}_P)$. First, if the deletion of $R_P(\bar{x}_P)$ is restricted by a referencing child tuple $R_C(\bar{x}_C)$, then II may force I into a lost position by moving to restricted (since I cannot move from there). Second, II can move to a child tuple $R'_C(\bar{x}'_C)$ which references $R_P(\bar{x}_P)$ with a NO ACTION trigger. With this move, II claims that this reference to $R_P(\bar{x}_P)$ will remain in the database, so $R_P(\bar{x}_P)$ and, as a consequence, $R'(\bar{x}')$ cannot be deleted. In this case, I may start a new round of the game by finding a justification to delete the referencing child $R'_C(\bar{x}'_C)$. More precisely:

Player I can move from $R(\bar{x})$ to del:$R'(\bar{x}')$ if $(R(\bar{x}), R'(\bar{x}')) \in \mathcal{DC}^*$ and there is no $R_C(\bar{x}_C) \in D$ s.t. $(R_C(\bar{x}_C), R(\bar{x})) \in \mathcal{DR}$.

Player II can move from del:$R'(\bar{x}')$

- to restricted if there are $R_P(\bar{x}_P)$ and $R_C(\bar{x}_C)$ s.t. $(R_P(\bar{x}_P), R'(\bar{x}')) \in \mathcal{DC}^*$ and $(R_C(\bar{x}_C), R_P(\bar{x}_P)) \in \mathcal{DR}$.
- to $R'_C(\bar{x}'_C)$, if $(R_P(\bar{x}_P), R'(\bar{x}')) \in \mathcal{DC}^*$ and $(R'_C(\bar{x}'_C), R_P(\bar{x}_P)) \in \mathcal{DN}$.

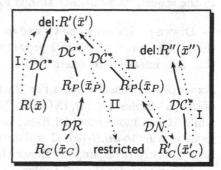

Lemma 3 (Claims of I and II)

1. *If I can move from $R(\bar{x})$ to del:$R'(\bar{x}')$, then deletion of $R'(\bar{x}')$ induces the deletion of $R(\bar{x})$.*

2. *If II can move from del:$R(\bar{x})$ to restricted, then deletion of $R(\bar{x})$ is forbidden in the original database state.*

3. *If II can move from del:$R(\bar{x})$ to $R'(\bar{x}')$, then deletion of $R(\bar{x})$ is only admissible if $R'(\bar{x}')$ is also deleted.* □

PROOF 1. The move of I implies that $(R(\bar{x}), R'(\bar{x}')) \in \mathcal{DC}^*$.
The move of II means that either

2. there are $R_P(\bar{x}_P), R_C(\bar{x}_C)$ s.t. $(R_P(\bar{x}_P), R(\bar{x})) \in \mathcal{DC}^*$ and $(R_C(\bar{x}_C), R'(\bar{x}')) \in \mathcal{DR}$. Then, by (1), deletion of $R(\bar{x})$ induces the deletion of $R_P(\bar{x}_P)$, but the deletion of $R_P(\bar{x}_P)$ is restricted by $R_C(\bar{x}_C)$, or

3. $(R'(\bar{x}'), R(\bar{x})) \in \mathcal{DN} \circ \mathcal{DC}^*$, i.e., there is a $R_P(\bar{x}_P)$ s.t. $(R_P(\bar{x}_P), R(\bar{x})) \in \mathcal{DC}^*$ and $(R'(\bar{x}'), R_P(\bar{x}_P)) \in \mathcal{DN}$. Hence, by (1), deletion of $R(\bar{x})$ induces deletion of $R_P(\bar{x}_P)$, which is only allowed if $R'(\bar{x}')$ is also deleted.[1] ∎

Lemma 4 *The moves are linked with the logical specification as follows:*

---

[1] $\mathcal{DN} \circ \mathcal{DC}^* := \{(x, y) \mid \exists z : (x, z) \in \mathcal{DN} \text{ and } (z, y) \in \mathcal{DC}^*\}$.

- *The moves of I correspond to rule (DC$_1$): I can move from $R(\bar{x})$ to del:$R'(\bar{x}')$ if, given the fact req_del:$R'(\bar{x}')$, req_del:$R(\bar{x})$ can be derived using (DC$_1$).*
- *The moves by II are reflected by the rules (DC$_2$) and (DR)/(DN):*
- *II can move from del:$R(\bar{x})$ to restricted if blk_del:$R(\bar{x})$ is derivable using (DR) and (DC$_2$) only, or*
- *II can move from del:$R(\bar{x})$ to $R'(\bar{x}')$ if blk_del:$R(\bar{x})$ is derivable using (DC$_2$) and an instance of (DN) if req_del:$R'(\bar{x}')$ is assumed to be false.*
- *The negative dependencies in (I), req_del $\rightsquigarrow$ ¬blk_del, and (DN), blk_del $\rightsquigarrow$ ¬req_del, mirror the alternation of moves between I and II, respectively.* □

Definition 3 A position $R(\bar{x}) \in D$ is *won (for I)*, if I can win the game starting from $R(\bar{x})$ no matter how II moves; del:$R(\bar{x}) \in U_\triangleright$ is *won for II*, if II can always win the game starting from del:$R(\bar{x})$. If $p \in D \cup U_\triangleright$ is won (lost) for a player, p is lost (won) for the opponent. A position which is neither lost nor won is *drawn*. In the sequel, "is won/lost" stands for "is won/lost for I". □

Drawn positions can be viewed as ambiguous situations. For the game above, this means that neither can I prove that $R(\bar{x})$ has to be deleted, nor can II prove that it is infeasible to delete $R(\bar{x})$.

Example 3 Consider again Fig. 2 with $U_\triangleright = \{$del:$R_1(a)$, del:$R_1(b)\}$. From each of the "a"-tuples, $\{R_1(a), R_2(a, x), R_3(a, y), R_4(a, x, y)\}$, I can move to del:$R_1(a)$, while II can move from del:$R_1(a)$ to $R_4(a, x, y)$. Thus, after I has started the game moving to del:$R_1(a)$, II will answer with the move to $R_4(a, b, c)$, so I moves back to del:$R_1(a)$ again, etc. Hence the game is drawn for each of the "a"-tuples.

In contrast, for the "b"-tuples, there is an additional move from del:$R_1(b)$ to $R_5(b)$ for II, who now has a winning strategy: by moving to $R_5(b)$, there is no possible answer for I, so I loses. □

Theorem 5 (Game Semantics) *For every tuple $R(\bar{x}) \in D$:*

- *$R(\bar{x})$ is won $\Leftrightarrow$ there is a sequence of user requests from $U_\triangleright$ which deletes $R(\bar{x})$, and if this sequence is executed serially (independent from the order of execution of cascaded deletions), at no stage any ric is violated.*
- *$R(\bar{x})$ is won or drawn $\Leftrightarrow$ simultaneous execution of all user delete requests del:$R'(\bar{x}')$ which are won or drawn does not violate any ric and deletes $R(\bar{x})$.*
- *$R(\bar{x})$ is lost $\Leftrightarrow$ it is not possible with the given set of user delete requests to delete $R(\bar{x})$ without violating a ric.*

PROOF Note that if $R(\bar{x})$ is won or drawn, then $(R_C(\bar{x}_C), R(\bar{x})) \notin \mathcal{DR}$ for any $R_C(\bar{x}_C) \in D$ (otherwise, if I moves from $R(\bar{x})$ to some $R_d(\bar{x}_d)$, II moves to restricted since $(R_C(\bar{x}_C), R_d(\bar{x}_d)) \in \mathcal{DR} \circ \mathcal{DC}^*$ and wins). Thus, no ric of the form ON DELETE RESTRICT is violated when deleting some won or drawn tuple.

- Let $U_{\triangleright,n} := \{u \in U_\triangleright \mid u$ is won in n rounds$\}$. Let $R(\bar{x})$ be won in n rounds:
  - I can move from $R(\bar{x})$, thus there exists a del:$R_d(\bar{x}_d) \in U_{\triangleright,n}$ such that $(R(\bar{x}), R_d(\bar{x}_d)) \in \mathcal{DC}^*$. Hence, executing $U_{\triangleright,n}$ also deletes $R(\bar{x})$.

- For every $R'(\bar{x}')$: if $(R'(\bar{x}'), R(\bar{x})) \in \mathcal{DC}$, then also $(R'(\bar{x}'), R_d(\bar{x}_d)) \in \mathcal{DC}^*$ and $R'(\bar{x}')$ is won in n rounds, and will also be deleted. Thus, no rac ON DELETE CASCADE is violated when executing $U_{\triangleright,n}$.

- For every $R'(\bar{x}')$ s.t. $(R'(\bar{x}'), R(\bar{x})) \in \mathcal{DN}$, $(R'(\bar{x}'), R_d(\bar{x}_d)) \in \mathcal{DN} \circ \mathcal{DC}^*$, thus Π can move from del:$R_d(\bar{x}_d)$ to $R'(\bar{x}')$ which then must be won in $n{-}1$ rounds, thus it is already deleted when executing $U_{\triangleright,n-1}$. Thus, no ric of the form ON DELETE NO ACTION is violated when executing $U_{\triangleright,n}$.

- Let E_i be some enumeration of $U_{\triangleright,i}$. $(E_1, E_2, \ldots)$ can be executed sequentially and at no stage any ric is violated.

• Let $R(\bar{x})$ be won or drawn. Then there is a user request del:$R_d(\bar{x}_d)$ where I can move to (i.e., $(R(\bar{x}), R_d(\bar{x}_d)) \in \mathcal{DC}^*$), which is also won or drawn. Thus, when executing del:$R_d(\bar{x}_d)$, $R(\bar{x})$ is deleted. Since all tuples $R'(\bar{x}')$ s.t. $(R'(\bar{x}'), R(\bar{x})) \in \mathcal{DC} \cup \mathcal{DN}$ are also won or drawn (since Π can move from $R_d(\bar{x}_d)$ to $R'(\bar{x}')$), they will also be deleted. Thus, no ric ON DELETE CASCADE/NO ACTION is violated.

• A tuple $R(\bar{x})$ is lost in n rounds if either

- ($n = 0$) there is no user request del:$R_d(\bar{x}_d)$ s.t. $(R(\bar{x}), R_d(\bar{x}_d)) \in \mathcal{DC}^*$, i.e., the deletion of $R(\bar{x})$ is unfounded, or

- ($n > 0$) every user request del:$R_d(\bar{x}_d)$ s.t. $(R(\bar{x}), R_d(\bar{x}_d)) \in \mathcal{DC}^*$ is lost in $\leq n$ rounds, i.e., either Π can move from del:$R_d(\bar{x}_d)$ to restricted (in this case, by Lemma 3(2), del:$R_d(\bar{x}_d)$ is forbidden), or there is some tuple $R'(\bar{x}')$ s.t. Π can move from del:$R_d(\bar{x}_d)$ to $R'(\bar{x}')$ and which is lost in $\leq n{-}1$ rounds. By induction hypothesis, $R'(\bar{x}')$ cannot be deleted, but by Lemma 3(3), it must be deleted if $R(\bar{x})$ is be deleted. Thus, $R(\bar{x})$ cannot be deleted. ∎

Theorem 6 (Correctness)
The game-theoretic characterization is correct wrt. the abstract semantics:

• $U_w := \{u \in U_\triangleright \mid u \text{ is won}\}$ and $U_{w,d} := \{u \in U_\triangleright \mid u \text{ is won or drawn}\}$ are *admissible*,

• $U_{w,d} = U_{\max}$,

• $\Delta(U_w) = \{\text{del:}R(\bar{x}) \mid R(\bar{x}) \text{ is won}\}$ and
  $\Delta(U_{\max}) = \Delta(U_{w,d}) = \{\text{del:}R(\bar{x}) \mid R(\bar{x}) \text{ is won or drawn}\}$.

4 Equivalence and Correctness

We show that the logical characterization is equivalent to the game-theoretic one. Thus, the correctness of the logical characterization reduces to the correctness of the game-theoretic one proven above.

4.1 Well-Founded Semantics

The *alternating fixpoint computation* (AFP) is a method for computing the well-founded model based on successive rounds [VG93]. This characterization finally leads to an algorithm for determining the maximal admissible subset of a given set $U_\triangleright$ of user requests. We introduce AFP using

Statelog, a state-oriented extension of Datalog which allows to integrate active and deductive rules [LML96]. It can be seen as a restricted class of logic programs where every predicate contains an additional distinguished argument for *state terms* of the form $[S+k]$. Here, S is the distinguished *state variable* ranging over $\mathbb{N}_0$. Statelog rules are of the form

$$[S+k_0] \, H(\bar{X}) \leftarrow [S+k_1] \, B_1(\bar{X}_1), \ldots, [S+k_n] \, B_n(\bar{X}_n) ,$$

where the head $H(\bar{X})$ is an atom, $B_i(\bar{X}_i)$ are atoms or negated atoms, and $k_0 \geq k_i$, for all $i \in \{1, \ldots, n\}$. A rule is *local*, if $k_0 = k_i$, for all $i \in \{1, \ldots, n\}$.

In Statelog, AFP is obtained by attaching state terms to the given non-stratified program P such that all positive literals refer to $[S+1]$ and all negative literals refer to $[S]$. The resulting program P_{AFP} computes the alternating fixpoint of P:

$$[S+1] \, \mathsf{req\_del}{:}R(\bar{X}) \leftarrow \mathsf{del}{:}R(\bar{X}), \, [S] \, \neg\mathsf{blk\_del}{:}R(\bar{X}). \tag{I^A}$$

% $R_C.\vec{F} \rightarrow R_P.\vec{K}$ ON DELETE CASCADE:
$$[S+1] \, \mathsf{req\_del}{:}R_C(\bar{X}) \leftarrow R_C(,\bar{X}), \, \bar{X}[\vec{F}] = \bar{Y}[\vec{K}], \, [S+1] \, \mathsf{req\_del}{:}R_P(\bar{Y}). \tag{DC_1^A}$$
$$[S+1] \, \mathsf{blk\_del}{:}R_P(\bar{Y}) \leftarrow R_P(\bar{Y}), \, \bar{X}[\vec{F}] = \bar{Y}[\vec{K}], \, [S+1] \, \mathsf{blk\_del}{:}R_C(\bar{X}). \tag{DC_2^A}$$

% $R_C.\vec{F} \rightarrow R_P.\vec{K}$ ON DELETE RESTRICT:
$$[S+1] \, \mathsf{blk\_del}{:}R_P(\bar{Y}) \leftarrow R_P(\bar{Y}), \, R_C(\bar{X}), \, \bar{X}[\vec{F}] = \bar{Y}[\vec{K}]. \tag{DR^A}$$

% $R_C.\vec{F} \rightarrow R_P.\vec{K}$ ON DELETE NO ACTION: $\qquad\qquad\qquad (DN^A)$
$$[S+1] \, \mathsf{blk\_del}{:}R_P(\bar{Y}) \leftarrow R_P(\bar{Y}), \, R_C(\bar{X}), \, \bar{X}[\vec{F}] = \bar{Y}[\vec{K}], \, [S] \, \neg\mathsf{req\_del}{:}R_C(\bar{X}).$$

P_{AFP} is locally stratified, thus there is a unique *perfect model* [Prz88] $\mathcal{M}_{AFP}$ of $P_{AFP} \cup D \cup U_\triangleright$. $\mathcal{M}_{AFP}$ mimics the alternating fixpoint computation of $\mathcal{W}_{RA}$: even-numbered states $[2n]$ correspond to the increasing sequence of underestimates of true atoms, while odd-numbered states $[2n+1]$ represent the decreasing sequence of overestimates of true or undefined atoms. The *final state* n_f of the computation is reached if $\mathcal{M}[2n_f] = \mathcal{M}[2n_f+2]$. Then, for all relations R, the truth value of atoms $R(\bar{x})$ in $\mathcal{W}_{RA}$ can be determined from $\mathcal{M}_{AFP}$ as follows:

$$\mathcal{W}_{RA}(\mathsf{req\_del}{:}R(\bar{x})) = \begin{cases} true & \text{if } \mathcal{M}_{AFP} \models [2n_f] \, \mathsf{req\_del}{:}R(\bar{x}) , \\ undef & \text{if } \mathcal{M}_{AFP} \models [2n_f] \, \neg\mathsf{req\_del}{:}R(\bar{x}) \wedge \\ & \qquad [2n_f+1] \, \mathsf{req\_del}{:}R(\bar{x}) , \\ false & \text{if } \mathcal{M}_{AFP} \models [2n_f+1] \, \neg\mathsf{req\_del}{:}R(\bar{x}) . \end{cases}$$

Theorem 7 (Equivalence)
The well-founded model is equivalent to the game-theoretic characterization:
- $R(\bar{x})$ *is won/lost/drawn* $\Leftrightarrow$ $\mathcal{W}_{RA}(\mathsf{req\_del}{:}R(\bar{x})) = true/false/undef$.

PROOF The proof is based on a lemma which is easy to prove from Lemma 4:

Lemma 8
- *I wins at $R(\bar{x})$ within $\leq n$ rounds iff $\mathcal{M}_{AFP} \models [2n] \, \mathsf{req\_del}{:}R(\bar{x})$.*
- *II wins at $R(\bar{x})$ within $\leq n$ rounds iff $\mathcal{M}_{AFP} \models [2n+1] \, \neg\mathsf{req\_del}{:}R(\bar{x})$.* $\qquad\square$

From this, Theorem 7 follows directly: The nth overestimate excludes deletions provably non-admissible in n rounds, whereas the nth underestimate contains all deletions which can be proven in n rounds. Thus, there is an n such that $\mathcal{M}_{AFP} \models [2n]$ req_del:$R(\bar{x})$ iff $\mathcal{W}_{RA}($req_del:$R(\bar{x})) = true$, and there is an n such that $\mathcal{M}_{AFP} \models [2n+1] \neg$req_del:$R(\bar{x})$ iff $\mathcal{W}_{RA}($req_del:$R(\bar{x})) = false$.

The game is drawn at $R(\bar{x})$ if for every tuple $R'(\bar{x}')$ which Π chooses, I can find a user request which deletes it, and conversely, Π has a witness against each of those user requests. Thus, no player has a "well-founded" proof for or against deleting those tuples. ∎

With Theorem 6, the correctness of the logic programming formalization follows:

Theorem 9 (Correctness)
The logic programming characterization is correct wrt. the abstract semantics:

- $U_t := \{del{:}R(\bar{x}) \in U_\triangleright \mid \mathcal{W}_{RA}(req\_del{:}R(\bar{x})) = true\}$ *and*
  $U_{t,u} := \{del{:}R(\bar{x}) \in U_\triangleright \mid \mathcal{W}_{RA}(req\_del{:}R(\bar{x})) \in \{true, undef\}\}$ *are admissible,*
- $U_{t,u} = U_{\max}$, *and*
- $\Delta(U_{\max}) = \Delta(U_{t,u}) = \{del{:}R(\bar{x}) \mid \mathcal{W}_{RA}(req\_del{:}R(\bar{x})) \in \{true, undef\}\}$.

In the following section, it is shown that the maximal admissible subset of $U_\triangleright$, $U_{t,u}$, also corresponds to a total semantics of P.

4.2 Stable Models

The undefined atoms in the well-founded model leave some scope for further interpretation. This is carried out by *stable models*:

Definition 4 (Stable Model) [GL88] Let M_P denote the minimal model of a positive program P. Given an interpretation I, and a ground-instantiated program P, P/I denotes the reduction of P wrt. I, i.e., the program obtained by replacing every negative literal of P by its truth-value wrt. I. An interpretation I is a *stable model* if $M_{P/I} = I$. □

Every stable model S extends the well-founded model W wrt. true and false atoms: $S^{true} \supseteq W^{true}$, $S^{false} \supseteq W^{false}$. Not every program has a stable model.

Theorem 10 *Let S_{RA} be defined by*

$$S_{RA} := D \cup U_\triangleright \cup \{req\_del{:}R(\bar{x}) \mid \mathcal{W}_{RA}(req\_del{:}R(\bar{x})) \in \{true, undef\}\}$$
$$\cup \{blk\_del{:}R(\bar{x}) \mid \mathcal{W}_{RA}(blk\_del{:}R(\bar{x})) = true\} .$$

Then, S_{RA} is a total stable model of $P_{RA} \cup D \cup U_\triangleright$.

S_{RA} is the "maximal" stable model in the sense that it contains all delete requests which are true in some stable model. Consequently, deletions have priority over blockings (cf. Example 2).

Theorem 11 (Correctness) *Let S be a stable model of $P_{RA} \cup D \cup U_\triangleright$. Then*

- $U_S := \{del{:}R(\bar{x}) \mid S \models req\_del{:}R(\bar{x})\} \cap U_\triangleright$ *is admissible and*
  $\Delta(U_S) = \{del{:}R(\bar{x}) \mid S \models req\_del{:}R(\bar{x})\}$.
- $U_{\max} = U_{S_{RA}}$ *and* $\Delta(U_{\max}) = \{del{:}R(\bar{x}) \mid S_{RA} \models req\_del{:}R(\bar{x})\}$.

PROOF *Foundedness*: follows directly from the fact that S is stable (unfounded req_del:$R(\bar{x})$ would not be stable).

Completeness: For every ric $R_C.\vec{F} \rightarrow R_P.\vec{K}$ ON DELETE CASCADE, if $S \models R_C(\bar{x}) \wedge$ req_del:$R_P(\bar{y}) \wedge \bar{x}[\vec{F}] = \bar{y}[\vec{K}]$, then, due to (DC_1), $S = M_{P/S} \models$ req_del:$R_C(\bar{x})$.

Feasibility: Suppose a ric $R_C.\vec{F} \rightarrow R_P.\vec{K}$ ON DELETE RESTRICT or $R_C.\vec{F} \rightarrow R_P.\vec{K}$ ON DELETE NO ACTION would be violated: Then $S \models$ req_del:$R_P(\bar{y}) \wedge R_C(\bar{x}) \wedge \bar{x}[\vec{F}] = \bar{y}[\vec{K}]$ (for NO ACTION also $S \models \neg$req_del:$R_C(\bar{x})$), and thus because of (DR) resp. (DN), $S = M_{P/S} \models$ blk_del:$R_P(\bar{y})$. Thus, by (DC_2), for the founding delete request del:$R(\bar{z})$, $S \models$ blk_del:$R(\bar{z})$, and by (I), $S \models \neg$req_del:$R(\bar{z})$ which is a contradiction to the assumption that del:$R(\bar{z})$ is the founding delete request. $\Delta_S \subseteq \Delta(U_S)$ follows from foundedness, and $\Delta_S \supseteq \Delta(U_S)$ follows from completeness. ∎

5 A Procedural Translation

Another, more "algorithmic" implementation in Statelog is obtained by "cutting" the cyclic dependency at one of the possible points, i.e., at the rules (I) and (DN).

Cutting in (DN) implements the definition of S_{RA}, corresponding to the observation that S_{RA} takes exactly the blockings from the underestimate and the internal delete requests from the overestimate.

The rules (DC_1), (DC_2) and (DR) are already local rules:

$$[S] \text{ req\_del}:R_C(\bar{X}) \leftarrow R_C(\bar{X}), \bar{X}[\vec{F}] = \bar{Y}[\vec{K}], [S] \text{ req\_del}:R_P(\bar{Y}). \qquad (DC_1^S)$$
$$[S] \text{ blk\_del}:R_P(\bar{Y}) \leftarrow R_P(\bar{Y}), \bar{X}[\vec{F}] = \bar{Y}[\vec{K}], [S] \text{ blk\_del}:R_C(\bar{X}). \qquad (DC_2^S)$$
$$[S] \text{ blk\_del}:R_P(\bar{Y}) \leftarrow R_P(\bar{Y}), R_C(\bar{X}), \bar{X}[\vec{F}] = \bar{Y}[\vec{K}]. \qquad (DR^S)$$

The rule (I) is also translated into a local rule:

$$[S] \text{ req\_del}:R(\bar{X}) \leftarrow \text{ del}:R(\bar{X}), [S] \neg\text{blk\_del}:R(\bar{X}). \qquad (I^S)$$

(DN) incorporates the state leap and is augmented to a *progressive* rule (DN^S):

$$[S+1] \text{ blk\_del}:R_P(\bar{Y}) \leftarrow R_P(\bar{Y}), R_C(\bar{X}), \bar{X}[\vec{F}] = \bar{Y}[\vec{K}], [S] \neg\text{req\_del}:R_C(\bar{X}).$$

In the following, we refer to this program as P_S.

P_S is *state-stratified*, which implies that it is locally stratified, so there is a unique perfect model $\mathcal{M}_S$ of $P_S \cup D \cup U_\triangleright$. The state-stratification $\{$blk_del:$R\} \prec \{$req_del:$R\}$, mirrors the stages of the algorithm: First, the blockings are computed by (DN^S) (the only progressive rule; for the initial state, this rule does not fire) and (DR^S), the induced blockings are derived by (DC_2^S), also determining the blocked user delete requests. The remaining user delete requests raise internal delete requests (I^S) which are cascaded by (DC_1^S). From these, the resulting blockings for the next iteration are computed.

Lemma 12 $\mathcal{M}_{AFP}$ *corresponds to* $\mathcal{M}_S$ *as follows*:

1. $\mathcal{M}_{AFP} \models [2n]$ blk_del:$R(\bar{x}) \Leftrightarrow \mathcal{M}_S \models [n]$ blk_del:$R(\bar{x})$.
2. $\mathcal{M}_{AFP} \models [2n+1]$ req_del:$R(\bar{x}) \Leftrightarrow \mathcal{M}_S \models [n]$ req_del:$R(\bar{x})$. □

PROOF P_S and P_{AFP} differ in the rules (I^S) and (I^A): In every iteration, P_S takes the blockings from the underestimate and the delete requests from the overestimates, resulting in S_{RA}. ∎

Theorem 13 (Termination) *For every database D and every set $U_{\rhd}$ of user delete requests, the program reaches a fixpoint, i.e., there is a least $n_f \leq |U_{\rhd}|$, s.t. $\mathcal{M}_S[n_f] = \mathcal{M}_S[n_f+1]$.*

PROOF A fixpoint is reached if the set of blocked user delete requests becomes stationary. Since this set is nondecreasing, there are at most $|U_{\rhd}|$ iterations. ∎

From Lemma 12 and Theorem 10, the correctness of P_S follows:

Theorem 14 (Correctness)
The final state of $\mathcal{M}_S$, $\mathcal{M}_S[n_f]$, represents $U_{\max}$ and $\Delta(U_{\max})$:

- $\mathcal{M}_S[n_f] = S_{RA}$,
- $U_{\max} = \{del{:}R(\bar{x}) \mid \mathcal{M}_S[n_f] \models req\_del{:}R(\bar{x})\} \cap U_{\rhd}$, *and*
- $\Delta(U_{\max}) = \{del{:}R(\bar{x}) \mid \mathcal{M}_S[n_f] \models req\_del{:}R(\bar{x})\}$.

5.1 Implementation in a Procedural Programming Language

The Statelog formalization P_S can be easily translated into the following algorithm **Alg$_S$**:

Input: A consistent database D and a set $U_{\rhd}$ of user delete requests.
$B := \{$all blockings which result from ON DELETE RESTRICT triggers$\}$.
1. (Re)Compute the set of induced blockings B^*, which result from B by propagating blockings upwards the ON DELETE CASCADE chain.
2. (Re)Compute the set U^* of internal requests which result from user cascading delete requests $U_{\rhd}$ which are not blocked: $U^* := (U_{\rhd} \setminus B^*)^*$.
3. Add to B all blockings which are issued by ON DELETE NO ACTION triggers from tuples not in U^*, i.e., which are not requested for deletion.
4. If $B \setminus B^* \neq \emptyset$ then goto 1 else execute requests from U^*.
Output: The new consistent database after executing $U_{\max}$ and the sets $U_{\max}$ of committed and $U_{\rhd} \setminus U_{\max}$ of aborted user requests.

Initially, it is assumed that there are only those blockings which result directly from ON DELETE RESTRICT triggers. Then, blockings are propagated upwards the ON DELETE CASCADE chains, finally blocking the triggering user requests. For the remaining unblocked user requests, the cascaded requests are recomputed. Thus, some more tuples will remain in the database, which could block other requests. In the next step, all blockings are computed which are caused by ON DELETE NO ACTION triggers from tuples which are not reachable via cascaded deletions. These steps are repeated until a fixpoint is reached. Observe that each iteration corresponds to the evaluation of a query with PTIME data complexity. Moreover, since the fixpoint is reached after at most $|U_{\rhd}|$ iterations (Theorem 13), the overall algorithm also has polynomial data complexity.

Theorem 15 *Algorithm $\textbf{Alg}_S$ is correct: $U_{\max} = U^* \cap U_\triangleright$ and $\Delta(U_{\max}) = U^*$.*

PROOF In the nth iteration, $B^* = \{\text{blk\_del}:R(\bar{x}) \mid \mathcal{M}_S \models [n]\ \text{blk\_del}:R(\bar{x})\}$, and $U^* = \{\text{req\_del}:R(\bar{x}) \mid \mathcal{M}_S \models [n]\ \text{req\_del}:R(\bar{x})\}$. ∎

For given D, $U_\triangleright$, and RA, the above algorithm computes the maximal subset $U_{\max}$ of $U_\triangleright$ which can be executed without violating any *ric*, and the set U^* of internal deletions which are induced by it. In case $U_\triangleright$ is not admissible, $U_\triangleright \setminus U_{\max}$ contains the rejected update requests, and by following the chains of blockings from them, the tuples which cause the rejection can be determined. Additionally, by investigating the stages of the algorithm, it can be determined if the blocking is due to the rejection of another request.

References

[CPM96] R. Cochrane, H. Pirahesh, and N. Mattos. Integrating Triggers and Declarative Constraints in SQL Database Sytems. In *Proc. VLDB*, pp. 567–578, Mumbai (Bombay), India, 1996.

[Dat90] C. Date. *Relational Database Writings 1985-1989*. Addison-Wesley, 1990.

[DD94] C. Date and H. Darwen. *A Guide to the SQL Standard: A User's Guide to the Standard Relational Language SQL*. Addison-Wesley, 1994.

[GL88] M. Gelfond and V. Lifschitz. The Stable Model Semantics for Logic Programming. In *Proc. ICLP*, pp. 1070–1080, 1988.

[Hor92] B. M. Horowitz. A Run-Time Execution Model for Referential Integrity Maintenance. In *Proc. Intl. Conf. on Data Engineering*, pp. 548–556, 1992.

[ISO92] ISO/IEC JTC1/SC21. Information Technology – Database Languages – SQL2, July 1992. ANSI, 1430 Broadway, New York, NY 10018.

[ISO95] ISO/ANSI Working draft. *Database Languages – SQL3*, October 1995.

[LML96] B. Ludäscher, W. May, and G. Lausen. Nested Transactions in a Logical Language for Active Rules. In *Proc. Intl. Workshop on Logic in Databases (LID)*, LNCS 1154, pp. 196–222, 1996. Springer.

[LML97a] B. Ludäscher, W. May, and G. Lausen. Referential Actions as Logical Rules. In *Proc. PODS'97*, pp. 217–224, 1997.

[LML97b] B. Ludäscher, W. May, and G. Lausen. Triggers, Games, and Stable Models. Technical report, Institut für Informatik, Universität Freiburg, 1997.

[LMR96] B. Ludäscher, W. May, and J. Reinert. Towards a Logical Semantics for Referential Actions in SQL. In *Proc. 6th Intl. Workshop on Foundations of Models and Languages for Data and Objects: Integrity in Databases*, Dagstuhl, Germany, 1996.

[Mar94] V. M. Markowitz. Safe Referential Integrity and Null Constraint Structures in Relational Databases. *Information Systems*, 19(4):359–378, 1994.

[Prz88] T. C. Przymusinski. On the Declarative Semantics of Deductive Databases and Logic Programs. In J. Minker, editor, *Foundations of Deductive Databases and Logic Programming*, pp. 191–216. Morgan Kaufmann, 1988.

[Rei96] J. Reinert. Ambiguity for Referential Integrity is Undecidable. In *Constraint Databases and Applications*, LNCS 1034, pp. 132–147. Springer, 1996.

[VG93] A. Van Gelder. The Alternating Fixpoint of Logic Programs with Negation. *Journal of Computer and System Sciences*, 47(1):185–221, 1993.

[VGRS91] A. Van Gelder, K. Ross, and J. Schlipf. The Well-Founded Semantics for General Logic Programs. *Journal of the ACM*, 38(3):620 – 650, July 1991.

Databases and the Web

A Conceptual Model and a Tool Environment for Developing More Scalable, Dynamic, and Customizable Web Applications

Piero Fraternali and Paolo Paolini

Dipartimento di Elettronica e Informazione, Politecnico di Milano
Piazza Leonardo da Vinci 32, I-20133 Milano, Italy
`fraterna/paolini@elet.polimi.it`

Abstract. This paper introduces a methodology for the development of applications for the WWW. Web applications are modelled at the conceptual level by using HDM-lite, a design notation supporting the specification of the structural, navigational, and presentation semantics of the application. Conceptual specifications are transformed into a logical-level representation, which enables the generation of the application pages from content data stored in a repository. The proposed approach is substantiated by the implementation of the Autoweb System, a set of software tools supporting the development process from conceptual modelling to the deployment of the application pages on the Web. Autoweb can be used both for developing new applications and for reverse engineering existing applications based on a relational representation of data.

1 Motivations

The great success of the World Wide Web as a personal, social, and business communication medium has spawned an impressive rush in the users' community to develop new applications or port existing software to the Web. As a consequence, the applications found today on the Web cover a very large spectrum of typologies, going from individual hypertexts and hypermedia, like personal homepages or virtual art galleries, to very large and dynamic transactional applications, like electronic commerce systems. At the same time, we assist to a growing interest of the software vendors to offer novel solutions for making Web development more cost-effective and increase the quality of the resulting applications.

From the users' perspective, choosing the appropriate tools and architecture for developing a Web application is a critical decision, which involves at least the following dimensions of the expected application:

- the size of the "information base";
- its dynamicity, i.e., the frequency of changes;
- the need of personalization, i.e., of presenting the same content in different ways (e.g., to different users or to the same user at different times);
- the overall quality of the interface, including graphical quality and control over the display of multimedia data.

The last two points are quite peculiar to Web applications, which have accostumed users to consider the navigation and presentation quality of an application of the same importance as the quality of the information content.

Increasing performance with respect to all the above dimensions, while keeping development costs to a minimum, is clearly a problematic issue: for example, high graphical quality and customization are easily achieved by hand-writing the application pages, but this approach does not ensure scalability and responsiveness to frequent changes. Conversely, using an automatic HTML generator delivering application pages from data stored in a database enables scalability and quick content updates, but limits personalisation and interface quality.

In this paper we propose an approach and a set of software tools for reconciliating the abovementioned application dimensions, which leverage automated software production for reducing the overall development effort.

The key points of our proposals are:

- starting Web application development from conceptual modeling, but using the right model, i.e., one where navigation and presentation have a peer role with respect to the structural view of the application[1].
- transforming conceptual specifications into logical schemas, used for structuring a repository of application data, so to isolate application content from presentation and navigation and enable content dynamicity and customization (same content ⇒ different presentations and/or navigations);
- storing in logical level structures also meta-data about navigation and presentation, so to enable the dynamic update of application navigation and look-and-feel;
- automatically generating application pages from the logical representation, so to enable a higher level of scalability, where not only content can scale, but also the schema of the application.

In a nutshell, the core results of our work are:

- *HDM-lite*, a conceptual model for Web applications; HDM-lite is an evolution of HDM [8], a model for generic hypermedia applications, which we have adapted to the specificity of the Web context.
- *The Autoweb System*, a set of software tools for editing HDM-lite conceptual specifications, transforming them into logical schemas, and automatically producing applications pages. Presently, Autoweb demonstrates the generation of pages both in HTML and Java, but in principle it could be extended to any network language (e.g., ActiveX and TCL/TK).

Throughout the paper, we will use the following small-scale running example to demonstrate the features of HDM-lite and of the Autoweb System.

ACME Furniture Inc. is an aggressive company thriving in the postal market business. To enlarge its customer base, ACME has decided to put part of its

---

[1] Some database vendors also provide conceptual modelling of Web applications, but start from the Entity-Relationship model, which is a conceptual model for database design, not for hypermedia applications.

catalog on the Internet. The catalog advertises various types of furniture, e.g., chairs, tables, lamps, and so on, and also contains special combinations of items sold at a discounted price. Individual items are described by an image, a textual description, their price, and a set of technical features (dimensions, available colors, ...). Combinations are illustrated by a captivating photograph, advertising text, and the discounted price. Since ACME has a number of stores throughout the world, information about the store locations is also made available, including the address and contact information, an image of the store, and a map.

Users are expected to visit the ACME home page containing a logo of the company and some advertising stuff; from there they can browse the list of special offers, and the item catalog. From the page describing a combination, the individual items forming the combination can be accessed, and conversely, it is possible to navigate from an item to the combinations including it. From the home page, the list of stores can also be reached.

A second category of users is also expected: inventory managers. These must directly access the inventory records of the various items at the different stores, either from a store list or from an item list. Their application pages should be textual for network speed and should exclude all customer-oriented advertising.

The rest of the paper is organised as follows: in Section 2 we introduce HDM-lite, presenting its modeling primitives; in Section 3 we discuss the general framework for transforming a HDM-lite conceptual specification into implementation-level application pages; Section 4 illustrates the Autoweb System, a set of software tools that implement the proposed transformations; in Section 5 we enlighten the original features of our proposal with respect to existing related work; finally, Section 6 draws the conclusions and introduces the future work.

2 HDM-lite: a Conceptual Model for Web Applications

At the base of the proposed approach to the development of Web applications there is HDM-lite, a conceptual model for the specification of applications for the WWW. HDM-lite is a Web-specific evolution of HDM (Hypermedia Design Model [8]), a model that has been used by several organizations to design hypermedia applications in different areas. HDM has been proved a valid tool to design traditional hypermedia applications, i.e., those commonly found in CD-ROMs, kiosks, information points, digital libraries, and has influenced a number of subsequent proposals, e.g., [16, 17, 21]. An application is specified in HDM-lite by defining its structure, navigation and presentation, which are formalized in the hyperbase, access, and presentation schema, respectively.

2.1 The Hyperbase Schema

The *hyperbase schema* describes the structure of the information managed by the application, in terms of the main abstractions and their semantic connections. An HDM-lite hyperbase schema is an extended Entity-Relationship model [4] featuring: entitities substructured into a tree of components, typed attributes of components, semantic links between entities and components, and cardinality constraints. Collectively, the application objects and their semantic links constitute the information base of the application, called *hyperbase*.

Figure 1 shows the hyperbase schema of the ACME application, which contains four entity types: items, combinations, stores, and inventory records.

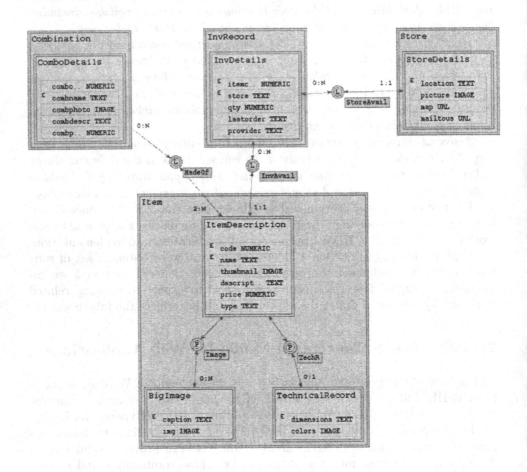

Fig. 1. The Hyperbase Schema of ACME Applications

An item is an aggregate entity consisting of a root component, called *ItemDescription*, containing two subcomponents, called *BigImage*, and *TechnicalRecord*. The two part-of relationships connecting a component to its subcomponents (shown as edges labelled with a P) have cardinality constraints prescribing that an item description contain zero or more big images, and at most one piece of technical data. The information content of each component is determined by its attributes (called *slots* in the HDM-lite jargon). For example, the description of an item consists of a code of type integer, a name of type text, a thumbnail of type image, a description of type text, a price of type integer, and a type of type text. Slots labelled by a capital E belong to the *external name* of the component, that is they are used to denote instances of the component in indexes, lists and so on.

Components and entities are connected by semantic links (shown as edges labelled with an L), analogous to E/R relationships. A link to an entity is equivalent to a link to the entity's topmost component. In the ACME hyperbase schema, a link named *MadeOf* connects combinations to items and has a 0:N cardinality constraint on the participations of an item and a 2:N cardinality constraint on the connections of a combination. Two links named *ItemAvailability* and *StoreAvailability* connect inventory records to items and stores. A store or an item can have zero or more inventory records and an inventory record is linked to exactly one store or item.

2.2 The Access Schema

The *access schema* specifies the way in which the information described by the hyperbase schema is accessed, in terms of the navigation paths between objects and of the entry points to the hyperbase. Multiple access schemas can be attached to the same hyperbase schema, for specifying different access semantics for different application purposes.

An access schema consists of *traversals*, that is, directed navigation paths from a source object to a target set of objects, and *collections*, that is, (possibly hierarchical) indexes over the hyperbase objects. Traversals are based on the semantic relationships of the hyperbase schema; it is possible to navigate only along semantic links and part-of connections specified in the hyperbase schema. Both traversals and collections have a *navigation mode*, which dictates the navigation facilities available to browse objects belonging to the target set of a traversal or to a collection. Supported navigation modes are:

- *index:* when the traversal is traversed or the collection is accessed a list is presented from which one object can be selected. When an individual object is displayed, a command to return to the list is made available.
- *Guided Tour:* when the traversal is traversed or the collection is accessed, one object is directly presented, and then guided tour commands (first, last, next, previous) are made available for accessing other objects.
- *Indexed Guided Tour:* both the initial list and the guided tour commands are made available.
- *Showall:* all objects are presented together.

The above navigation modes assume that objects can be ordered; the default order is nondeteministic, but the user can specify component-specific ordering, or even traversal- and collection-specific ordering.

Since collections tend to be numerous to enrich the available access paths, HDM-lite includes simple scoping rules to let the designer enable the access to a collection in selected portions of the application. More precisely, a collection can be:

- *Global*: it is visible in any part of the application.
- *Local to an entity*: it is visible only from the instances of any component within the boundary of a given entity.
- *Local to a component*: it is visible only from the instances of a specific component.
- *Local to a set of objects*: it is visible only from a specific set of objects.

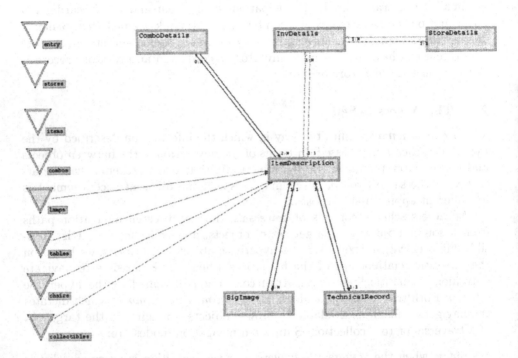

Fig. 2. The Access Schema of the ACME Customer Application

Figure 2 shows the access schema for the ACME customers. Traversals are shown as solid arrows, and collections as labelled triangles. Dotted arrows represent traversals that, although possible due to the part-of and semantic links present in the hyperbase schema, have been disabled by the designer. There are 8 different collections:

- *Entry*: this is a collection of collections elected as the home page of the application. Its visibility is set to global to let customers go back to the home page from any point of the application. The navigation mode is index so that the home page will contain a list of all the members of the Entry collection.
- *Stores, Combos*: these are global collections, ranging over all stores and combinations, respectively. Their navigation mode is set to indexed guided tour.

From any point of the application it will be possible to reach either the store or the combination list, and from a store or a combination the "previous" or "next" one can be accessed.

- *AllItems*: this collection is similar to the previous two but for a fact: a *filtering* clause is specified to select at run-time the objects that will appear in the collection's index. This feature is useful when the number of elements of a collection (or of objects reached by a traversal) is large. The filtering clause is translated at run-time in a query form whereby the user can specify slot values used to filter out undesired objects. In the present case, the filtering condition produces a form permitting the customer to enter desired values for the code, name, and type fields to focus the search on specific items or item types.
- *Lamps, Tables, Chairs, Accessories*: these collections range over sets of items and have visibility local to a set of istances. The idea is to let the customer access the list of all lamps only when he is looking at a lamp.

When an object is accessed, traversals dictate the available navigation paths to other related objects. ACME customers can browse 6 different traversals (see Figure 2): from an item's description to its big images and back; from an item's description to its technical record and back; from an item to the combinations including it, and from a combination to the individual items it contains.

Due to the cardinality constraints expressed in the hyperbase schema, only three of the six traversals may lead to multiple objects: we select the showall mode for displaying the big images of an item one after the other in sequence[2], and the indexed guided tour mode for the two traversals between items and combinations to let customers see an index of the items of a combination, access one item, and then go to the "next" element of the combination (or see the combinations an item belongs to, access one combination, and then step to the "next" combination).

Note that the access schema for the customer application will not permit ACME customers to reach objects of type InventoryRecord.

The access schema for the inventory manager (visible at URL http://www.ing.unico.it/autoweb/ACME) is simpler: he can enter the application by selecting an item or a store using two global collections. Then, he can obtain the list of inventory records of a given store or item.

2.3 The Presentation Schema

The *presentation schema* is a collection of *style sheets*, which are textual descriptions (written in a SGML-like syntax) of the appearance of application pages. More than a presentation schema can be attached to the same ⟨ hyperschema, access schema⟩ pair.

The basic unit of presentation is the *page*; there are three types of pages: *component pages* describe how entities and their sub-components are rendered,

---

[2] We expect big images of an item not to be too numerous.

traversal pages specify the visualization of N-ary traversals requiring an index, and *collection pages* are associated to collections. A style sheet dictates the appearance of a specific type of page (e.g., the page representing objects of type Store), and is logically organised in two levels:

- *the layout level* describes the page layout: each page is modelled as a grid, whose cells may contain presentation elements;
- *the element level* is used to specify elements appearing in the page grid. Two types of elements exists: built-in and user-defined.

Built-in elements are predefined presentation abstractions provided by HDM-lite to support the visualization of the main concepts of the hyperbase and access schema: entities, components, part-of, links, and collections. They can be freely intermixed in the page grid with user-defined elements provided by the graphic designer (e.g., banners, applets, and so on).

There are different categories of built-in elements.

- *Component elements* appear in style sheets for component pages. They include: the *slot panel*, an area dedicated to the presentation of the slot values of a component; the *component heading panel*, an element containing the header information of a component; the *outgoing links panel*, which collects the anchors of the outgoing links of the component.
- *Entity elements* are used in the style sheets of component pages to describe the structure of entities. They include: the *part-of panel*, an area for the presentation of the part-of connections of a component; the *context panel*, used in the presentation of a non-root component of an entity, to recall the external name slots of the component instances containing the sub-component.
- *Navigation elements* represent the various navigational features of part-ofs, links and collections. They include: the *index panel*, an area containing the list of members of a collection or the external names of objects of a N-ary traversal; the *show panel*, containing the actual objects of a N-ary traversal navigated in the showall mode; the *filter panel*, which is a fill-in form restricting the set of entries to be shown in an index; the *navigation console panel*, an area providing commands (first, last, previous, next, up_to_index) to navigate through objects belonging to traversals and collections.

Figure 3 shows the component page of ItemDescription objects in the ACME Customer Application. In the central area, below a user-defined element containing the company's motto, there are the part-of and link panels, both rendered with an iconic style (the magnification lens icon leads to the items's big images, the nut&bolt icon to the technical record, and the bundle icon to the combinations the item is included in). Below this region, the heading panel displays the component's name and is followed by the slot panel, where the item's attributes are presented. The region to the left of the slot panel displays the navigation panels of the collections reachable from the item: the Entry collection, the global collections of all items, stores, and combinations, and the collections of lamps, which is visible only from a lamp's page.

The interested reader may peruse the ACME example starting from the URL http://www.ing.unico.it/autoweb/ACME, which demonstrates three different applications on the same hyperbase, respectively targeted to customers, inventory managers and the ACME database administrator.

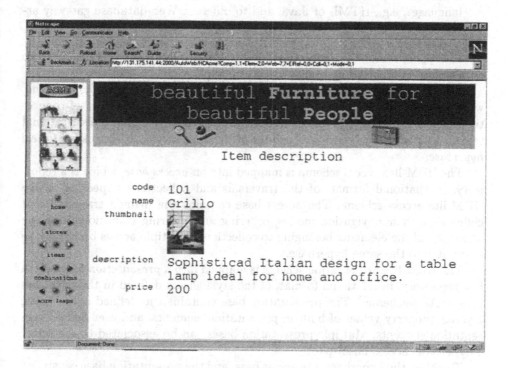

Fig. 3. The HTML Page Generated for Rendering an Instance of ItemDescription

3 Generating Application Pages from Conceptual Specifications

In this Section we introduce the general principles of application generation from HDM-lite, in particular motivating the need of an additional layer of description (the logical schema). Then, in the next Section, we will illustrate an implementation of the application generation process.

The proposed framework for application generation has been designed with the following goals in mind:

- Isolation of content, navigation, and presentation: content data should be maintained independently of navigation paths and presentation semantics, so that it should be possible to present the same content in multiple ways without major re-design and re-implementation efforts.

– Dynamicity and evolvability: it should be possible to update content, navigation, and presentation independently, either at run-time (e.g., for fine tuning the application based on user tracking), or at re-design time (e.g., to respond to changes in the requirements).
– Independence of the interface language and of the software architecture: it should be possible to map the same conceptual design to different Web languages, e.g., HTML or Java, and to different Web-database gateway architectures, e.g., server APIs, CGI gateways, or JDBC.

To support these objectives, an HDM-lite conceptual model is translated into an intermediate *logical* representation of the application.

The HDM-lite hyperbase schema is mapped into a *logical hyperbase schema*, which is a relational representation of the entities, components, part-of connections, and links appearing in the HDM-lite hyperbase schema. This relational schema is used to structure a repository of the application objects called *logical hyperbase*.

The HDM-lite access schema is mapped into an *access base*, which is a repository, in relational format, of the traversals and collections appearing in the HDM-lite access schema. The access base contains the defined traversals and collections, their navigation modes, ordering and filtering conditions, and the identifiers of the elements belonging to collections. Multiple access bases may be associated to the same hyperbase.

The HDM-lite presentation schema is mapped into a *presentation base*, which is a repository, in relational format, of the style sheets defined in the HDM-lite presentation schema.[3] The presentation base contains the defined style sheets, layouts, property values of built-in presentation elements, and user-defined presentation elements. Multiple presentation bases can be associated to the same ⟨ hyperbase, access base⟩ pair.

Together, the hyperbase, the access base, and the presentation base constitute an intermediate representation of the application, which is persistent, updatable, and implementation-independent. This characteristic is not found in other Web-database solutions, where only the application content is organised into a repository. Providing a logical model and a repository also for the navigation and the presentation affects content isolation, evolvability, and implementation-independence in the following ways:

– The different features of the application can be populated selectively, through different interfaces. Typically, the access base and the presentation base are filled in automatically by software tools processing HDM-lite conceptual specifications, whereas the hyperbase is populated by the application content providers.
– Not only the content, but also the navigation and the presentation data can be easily changed, even at run-time, making the application more flexible and durable.

---

[3] Presently style sheets are stored as files; work is ongoing to store them in the database.

– Different network languages and gateway architectures can be addressed, by defining different mappings from the hyperbase, access base, and presentation base to different implementation platforms.

4 The Autoweb System

The two-steps generation process described in the previous Section (from conceptual specification to logical structures, and from these to physical pages) is supported by the *Autoweb System*, a software environment which consists of two components: Visual HDM (VHDM), a CASE tool assisting the input of HDM-lite conceptual schemas and their transformation into relational structures, and the Autoweb Page Generator, which generates application pages from logical structures.

4.1 Visual HDM

The Visual-HDM Diagram Editor/Logical Schema Generator accepts as input the conceptual specification of a Web application in HDM-lite, and automatically produces the logical schema of the hyperbase, the access base, and the presentation base[4].

Diagram editing facilities are supported (multiple diagrams, cut&paste, undo, customizable editing and visual preferences) and output generation may be targeted to different relational platforms (presently, Oracle 7 and MiniSQL). A test data generation function permits the designer to instantly produce a rapid prototype of the conceptual specification, so to assess as early as possible the adequacy of structure, navigation and presentation.

The mapping of the conceptual hyperbase schema into its logical counterpart is a straightforward task, similar to the logical design of an Entity-Relationship conceptual model. The only critical aspect is the loss of semantics in the passage from the conceptual to the logical model (e.g., cardinality and HDM-lite implicit referential integrity constraints are not supported in the relational model), which requires extra mechanisms for integrity checking. Since these mechanisms are implementation-dependent, the designer can choose among enforcement on the client-side (in which case VHDM does nothing and integrity is enforced via controls added by the Autoweb Page Generator to all data entry pages), and enforcement on the server-side, which requires VHDM to generate additional DBMS-dependent SQL code (typically, foreign key clauses and triggers).

The generation of the access base and of the presentation base is done in a reflexive way: the logical schema of the access base and of the presentation base are fixed, and are defined by reflexively modelling traversals, collections, and styles in HDM-lite and then mapping the resulting conceptual hyperbase schema into relational structures, in the same way as for normal applications.

---

[4] The actual output is a set of files containing SQL DDL statements for creating the logical schema of the hyperbase, and SQL DML statements for creating the access base(s) and the presentation base(s).

Then, each HDM-lite access schema and style sheet is tranformed into a set of tuples of the access base and of the presentation base. In this way, the access base and the presentation base can be browsed and updated by means of application pages automatically generated by the Autoweb Page Generator.

4.2 The Autoweb Page Generator

The Autoweb Page Generator is a software tool producing application pages (presently, both in HTML and Java) from data stored in the hyperbase, access base and presentation base.

In the present implementation the Page Generator is a runtime component acting as a gateway between the HTPP server managing the dialogue with clients and one or more DBMS engines storing the application hyperbase. The Page Generator presents itself to its clients with an object oriented interface providing services for:

- opening and closing the connection to a database containing one of more applications. Several connections to different databases can be open simultaneosly.
- Serving read and write requests from clients; several applications can be up and running simoultaneously and the Page Generator can concurrently interact with clients browsing the same application or different applications. Mutual exclusion of read and write requests is enforced by the concurrency manager of the underlying DBMS.
- Bootstrapping an application; to increase efficiency, the access and presentation base may be loaded into main memory at the bootstrap, so that subsequent client requests can be served without querying the access and presentation base.

5 Comparison with Related Work

In the hypertext and hypermedia community several methodologies have appeared for the structured develompment of hypertext and hypermedia applications [3, 8, 11, 7, 9, 16, 17, 21], and also a few tools have been implemented for the automatic development of WWW applications [5, 19, 21].

Our approach descends from HDM [8], an early proposal for hypermedia design, which we have adapted to the Web context and to the needs of automatic implementation, by constraining the structural and access models to enable application generation, and by introducing the presentation model.

The navigational features of HDM-lite can also be traced to investigations on hypertext navigation semantics [2, 13, 11, 18], where several useful navigation abstractions (like hierarchical guided tours, graphical history navigation, and stateful indexes) have been experimented to enhance Web access.

With respect to the Autoweb System, existing research tools, like RMC and HSDL [5, 19], do not rely on a database-centered architecture and do not provide an explicit, updatable representation of navigation and presentation.

The architecture of the Autoweb System and its page generation technique has been influenced by research on the integration of database and Web technology [6, 15, 20], where several alternatives are discussed for the smooth integration of Web languages and database query languages.

Very recently, the Araneus Project [1] has proposed an approach for the development of data-intensive Web sites with objectives comparable to those of our work. Araneus advocates a methodology where Web development follows a double track: on one side, the database is designed and implemented top-down in a traditional way, using conceptual design first (with the Entity Relationship model), followed by logical design in the relational model. On the other side, a Web site is designed bottom up: the conceptual hyperbase schema (based on a model called NCM) is designed from the ER schema, then is translated into a logical design (based on a model called ADM), and finally implemented.

An extensive review has been conducted to compare the Autoweb approach to commercial products for Web development, including: Web-DB gateways (e.g., StoryServer [22], Cold Fusion [10]), Web form and application generators (e.g., Microsoft Access'97 form generator, Oracle Developer 2000 [14]), CASE environments for the Web (e.g., Oracle Designer 2000 [12]), and last-generation authoring tools for hypermedia documents exportable to the Web (e.g., Macromedia Director, Asymetrix Toolbook II). With respect to these products, Autoweb has the unique feature of integrating a modelling notation originally conceived for hypermedia applications[5] with a software architecture and a structured development process capable of supporting the development of data intensive applications. As a result, Autoweb offers the same advantages in terms of reduced development effort and evolvability as state-of-the-practice systems for Web-DB integration, but overcomes the limitations of these products in the customization and dynamic redefinition of the navigation and presentation semantics.

6 Conclusions and Future Work

In this paper we have introduced and discussed a conceptual model and a set of tools for the model-driven development of Web applications, which aim at unifying into a coherent framework, tailored to Web development, concepts and techniques coming from Information System and hypermedia development. The HDM-lite model has been proposed to support the specification of Web applications not only in terms of structure, but also of navigation and presentation semantics. HDM-lite overcomes the deficiencies of database conceptual models (e.g., the Entity/Relationship model), which have no provision for describing the access paths to the application objects and the visual rendering of application objects and of navigation primitives, which are essential aspects of Web

---

[5] The only commercial tool of which we are aware that supports conceptual modelling and automatic implementation of Web applications is Oracle Designer 2000, which starts from the Entity Relationship model and has very basic capabilities for customizing navigation and presentation.

development. HDM-lite also extends existing models for hypermedia applications, by introducing the presentation schema as an independent specification layer. HDM-lite is supported by the Autoweb System, a CASE environment for specifying and implementing Web applications.

The Autoweb System gives the following benefits to Web developers:

- *Scalability:* Autoweb shares with Web-database products the capability of scaling the dimension of the information base without the need of application re-design or re-implementation.
- *Dynamicity:* Autoweb permits the update not only of the content of an application, but also of the navigation and presentation semantics; this enables the tuning of the navigational aids and of the look-and-feel of the application at run-time, for example based on the tracking of the user's behavior.
- *Personalization:* Autoweb has unique features in terms of personalization: by separating content from both navigation and presentation and permitting multiple presentation/navigation layers on top of the same content, customized applications can be deployed very easily.
- *Interface Quality:* although the output of Autoweb is not comparable to what can be obtained with manual authoring or with hypermedia authoring tools, the flexibility of presentation styles greatly enhances the quality of the interface with respect to current Web-database application generators; interface quality benefits also from the coherence and uniformity induced by the presence of a conceptual model of structure and navigation.
- *Reduction of Development Effort:* the above advantages coexist with an overall reduction of the development costs thanks to the code generation approach; as in any other software field, this gain is somewhat counterbalanced by the extra effort spent in conceptual modelling, so that cost reduction is achieved only when the application complexity is above a threshold. We claim that more and more Web applications in the near future will exhibit such a complexity.

The ongoing and future work concentrates on adding knowledge representation facilities, and in particular a query language, to HDM-lite and to the Autoweb System. This extension will permit:

- The specification of derived information: derived slots and links, intensional collections, entities and components. From these building blocks, hyperviews could be defined, to adapt also the structure of an application to user-specific needs.
- The specification and enforcement of integrity properties: generic constraints on the allowed structure and navigation could be stated in a declarative way and enforced upon modification of the hyperbase.
- Reactive capabilities: well-known concepts like triggers and business rules could be experimented in the Web context, for example by coupling database reaction and Web push-technology to selectively inform users about changes in the application content.

References

1. P. Atzeni, G. Mecca, and P. Merialdo. To Weave the Web. In *Proc. 23rd Conference on Very Large Databases*, pages 206–215, Athens, Greece, Aug. 26-29, 1997.
2. E. Z. Ayers and J. T. Stasko. Using Graphic Hystory in Browsing the World Wide Web. In *Proc. Fourth Int. WWW Conf.*, Boston, Mass., Dec. 11-14, 1995.
3. V. Balasubramanian, B. M. Ma, and J. Yoo. A systematic approach to designing a WWW application. *CACM*, 38(8):47–48, 1995.
4. P. P. Chen. The entity-relationship model: toward a unified view of data. *ACM TODS*, 1(1):9–36, 1976.
5. A. Daz, T. Isakowitz, V. Maiorana, and G. Gilabert. RMC: A tool to design WWW applications. In *Proc. Fourth Int. WWW Conf.*, pages 11–14, Boston, Mass., 1995.
6. D. Eichmann, T. McGregor, and D. Danley. Integrating structured databases into the Web: The MORE system. *Computer Networks and ISDN Systems*, 27(2):281–288, 1994.
7. F.Garzotto, L. Mainetti, and P. Paolini. Hypermedia design, analysis, and evaluation issues. *Communications of the ACM*, 38(8):74–86, 1995.
8. F.Garzotto, P.Paolini, and D.Schwabe. HDM-A model-based approach to hypertext application design. *ACM TOIS*, 11(15):1–26, 1993.
9. F.G.Halasz and M.Schwarz. The dexter hypertext reference model. *Communications of the ACM*, 37(2):30–39, 1994.
10. B. Forta and al. *The Cold Fusion Web Database Kit*. QUE Corp., 1997.
11. F. Garzotto, L. Mainetti, and P. Paolini. Navigation in hypermedia applications: Modeling and semantics. *Journal of Organizational Computing*, 1996.
12. M. Gwyer. Oracle Designer/2000 WebServer Generator Technical Overview (version 1.3.2). Technical report, Oracle Corporation,, Sept. 1996.
13. F. J. Hauch. Supporting hierarchical guided tours in the World Wide Web. In *Proc. Fifth International World Wide Web Conference*, Paris, France, May 1996.
14. I. V. Hoven. Deploying Developer/2000 applications on the Web, Oracle white paper. Technical report, Oracle Corporation, Feb. 1997.
15. A. Hunter, I. Ferguson, and S. Hedges. SWOOP: An application generator for Oracle WWW systems. In *Proc. Fourth Int. WWW Conference*, Boston, Mass., 1995.
16. T. Isakowitz, E.A.Sthor, and P.Balasubranian. RMM: a methodology for structured hypermedia design. *Communications of the ACM*, 38(8):34–44, 1995.
17. J.Nanard and M.Nanard. Hypertext design environments and the hypertext design process. *Communications of the ACM*, 38(8):45–46, 1995.
18. K. L. Jones. NIF-T-NAV: a hierarchical navigator for WWW pages. In *Proc. Fifth International World Wide Web Conference*, Paris, France, 1996.
19. M. Kesseler. A schema-based approach to HTML authoring. In *Proc. Fourth Int. WWW Conf.*, Boston, Mass., 1995.
20. T. Nguyen and V. Srinivasan. Accessing relational databases from the World Wide Web. In *Proc. ACM SIGMOD Conference*, pages 529–540, 1996.
21. D. Schwabe and G. Rossi. The object-oriented hypermedia design model. *Communications of the ACM*, 38(8):45–46, 1995.
22. Vignette. StoryServer Overview. Technical report, Vignette Corp., March 1997.

Design and Maintenance
of Data-Intensive Web Sites

Paolo Atzeni,[1] Giansalvatore Mecca,[2] Paolo Merialdo[1*]

[1] Dip. Informatica e Automazione, Università di Roma Tre, Italy
[2] DIFA, Università della Basilicata, Potenza, Italy

{atzeni,mecca,merialdo}@dia.uniroma3.it

Abstract. A methodology for designing and maintaining large Web sites is introduced. It would be especially useful if data to be published in the site are managed using a DBMS. The design process is composed of two intertwined activities: database design and hypertext design. Each of these is further divided in a conceptual phase and a logical phase, based on specific data models, proposed in our project. The methodology strongly supports site maintenance: in fact, the various models provide a concise description of the site structure; they allow to reason about the overall organization of pages in the site and possibly to restructure it.

1   Introduction

Because of the popularity of the World Wide Web (Web), the need to organize large amounts of data in hypertextual form is increasing. In fact, since the Web is becoming a major computing platform and a uniform interface for sharing data, many organizations have found interest in delivering information through the Web, both in Internet and in intranet environments. Due to this growth of interest, many Web sites now contain valuable pieces of information, which can represent a precious resource for their owners. However, in most cases this is not properly exploited: limitations appear in the organization of data, clearly due to casual or even chaotic development: data is often difficult to find and correlate, and so users waste there time in inefficient and ineffective browsing. Similarly, many Web sites, after being established, are almost completely abandoned, in the sense that they present numerous errors and inconsistencies due to poor maintenance; also, their information is often obsolete. We believe that the life-cycle of a Web site should be supported by a sound methodological approach, similar to that used for traditional databases and information systems. A first step in this direction is represented by some methodologies that have been recently proposed in the context of hypermedia design [4, 5, 7, 8]. They provide specific data models and methodological steps to assist in the process of designing a hypermedia application. However, they do not take into account the major importance that data and databases should have in this framework. In fact, we believe that whenever a site is to contain significant amounts of data, its

---

* Work in part done while visiting the University of Toronto.

design and maintenance should consider and coordinate two aspects. On the one hand, there are features of the design process that strictly concern data management; this is especially true when it is necessary to manage large collections of data, possibly coming from databases and corporate information systems. On the other hand, the hypertext structure should be carefully designed in order to provide a page organization to be effectively browsed by the users.

As a response to these needs, this paper presents the ARANEUS *Web Design Methodology*, a thorough and systematic design process to organize and maintain large amounts of data in a Web hypertext. This is part of the ARANEUS Project [1, 2] at Università di Roma Tre with the goal of developing tools for managing Web data. The overall methodology is based on two well distinguished and yet tightly interconnected processes: the *database design* process and the *hypertext design* process. For each of these processes, we distinguish a *conceptual* and *logical* design phase, in the spirit of databases [3]. This allows to isolate system features from higher-level perspectives, and facilitates the restructuring and maintenance process: there is in fact a high degree *hypertext data independence* from one level to the other, and also with respect to the database. For example, one can change the hypertext logical scheme without changing the database scheme, or reorganizing the physical appearance of the hypertext without changing its conceptual or logical scheme.

The methodology would be profitably complemented by tools for the deployment of the pages of a Web site, starting from a database or another structured source. In fact, within the ARANEUS project, we have developed PENELOPE [2], a tool for the generation of static and dynamic pages from a relational database. However, the modularity of the methodology would allow for the use of any other tool, including those offered by database vendors for building Web interfaces to their systems.

The rest of the paper is organized as follows. Section 2 contains a general description of the methodology. Section 3 introduces the *Navigation Conceptual Model* (NCM) and the hypertext conceptual design phase. The hypertext logical design phase, based on the ARANEUS Data Model (ADM), is then discussed in Sections 4 and 5, respectively devoted to the "translation" from NCM to ADM and to restructuring in ADM.

2 The ARANEUS Design Methodology: Major Features

In this section, we give an overview of the original aspects of our approach. We first motivate and comment the distinction of different steps in the design of hypertexts and then illustrate the consequent organization of the methodology.

It is now widely accepted that essentially every application needs a precise and implementation independent description of the data of interest, and that this description can be effectively obtained by using a database conceptual model, usually a version of the Entity-Relationship (ER) model [3]. Since most hypertexts offered on the Web, and especially those we are mainly interested in, contain information that is essentially represented (and stored) as data, our

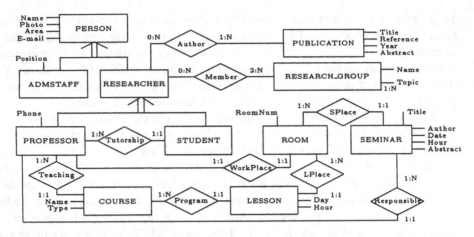

Fig. 1. Department ER scheme

methodology starts with conceptual database design and uses the conceptual scheme also as the basis for hypertext design (following previous proposals in this respect, in particular RMM [7]). At the same time, departing in this from existing approaches, we believe that the distance between the ER model, which is a tool for the representation of the essential properties of data in an abstract way, and HTML is indeed great. There are in fact many types of differences. We illustrate them by referring to an example application that will be used throughout the paper. It concerns a (simplified version of) a university department; its ER scheme, as produced by a conceptual design phase is shown in Figure 1. A first important point is that a conceptual representation of data always separates the various concepts in a scheme, whereas in hypertexts it is reasonable to show distinct concepts together (adding nested structures, in database terms), for the sake of clarity and effectiveness in the presentation. In the example, the hypertext will likely include pages corresponding to entity COURSE, but not to LESSON nor ROOM, whose data can profitably be absorbed within COURSE, with nested structures.

Moreover, a conceptual model has links between entities only when there are semantically relevant (and non-redundant) relationships, whereas hypertexts usually have additional links (and nodes) that serve as access paths. Specifically, each hypertext has an entry point (the home-page, in Web terminology), and other additional pages that are essential for the navigation. Also, relationships in the ER model are undirected, whereas hypertextual navigation is conceptually directed (often, but not always, bidirectional).

Additional issues follow from the way collections of homogeneous entities are actually represented in hypertexts. In fact, there are two different basic forms: to have a different page for each instance of the entity, and so a set of similar pages or to have just one page for all instances, with a list of homogeneous elements. In the example, we could decide to have just one page for the entity SEMINAR, with a list of all data concerning the various seminars, whereas for the entity

PROFESSOR it would be better to have one page for each instance.

Then, there are specific issues related to features of the hypertext language (HTML, in our case) that could be useful to represent at a level that is more abstract than the language itself but too detailed for being relevant together with the initial descriptions of links. For example, a list could suffice to access professors, since there are a few dozens, whereas students need a direct access: HTML has the form construct that could be useful in this respect. This distinction is clearly not relevant at the conceptual level, but it is certainly important to specify it well before going down to HTML code.

Finally, there are features that are related only to the presentation of data, and not to their organization: the actual layout of an HTML page corresponds to one of the possible "implementations" of the logical structure of the involved data.

Our methodology takes these issues into account by offering three different levels (and models) for the definition of hypertexts, by separating the various features, from the most abstract to the concrete ones. At the highest level of abstraction we have the *hypertext conceptual* level, rather close to the database conceptual level: hypertexts are defined by means of the *Navigation Conceptual Model* (NCM), a variant of the ER model; beside ER concepts, it allows the specification of access paths and directions of relationships as well as nested reorganizations of data. Then, we have the *hypertext logical* level, where the data contained in the hypertext are described in terms of pages and their types (*page schemes*); here we use the ARANEUS *Data Model* (ADM) we have recently proposed [2]. Finally, the organization of data in pages, the layout, and the final appearance are issues that do not influence data except in the presentation. Therefore we propose that there is a *presentation level* concerned with HTML templates (prototypical pages) associated with page schemes.

The issues discussed above motivate the organization of the ARANEUS Design Methodology. Figure 2 shows the phases, the precedences among them, and their major products. Let us briefly comment on each of them. Given the central role data have in the Web sites we consider and the maturity of database methodologies [3], our Phases 1 and 2 involve the standard conceptual and logical design activities for databases. The database conceptual scheme is the major input to Phase 3, where it is "transformed" into an NCM hypertext conceptual scheme. Then, Phase 4 receives an NCM scheme as input and produces an ADM (logical) scheme. Phase 5, given the ADM scheme, associates an HTML template with each of its page schemes. Finally, Phase 6 makes use of the logical database scheme (produced in Phase 2) and of the hypertext logical scheme and the associated templates, in order to generate actual HTML pages.

The organization of the methodology is modular, since the phases interact only via the respective products. This means that it is possible to adapt the methodology to specific contexts: for example, although we proceed as if the database and the hypertext are designed in parallel, it may be the case that the database already exists, and so Phases 1 and 2 are not needed (assuming that the conceptual scheme exists, otherwise a reverse engineering activity could

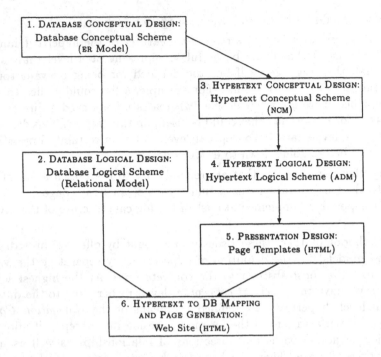

Fig. 2. The ARANEUS Design Methodology

be needed). Also, the methodology can be profitably adapted to support maintenance activities, especially if the modifications concern only the hypertext:
the conceptual and logical description of the site represent an essential documentation, based on which the overall quality of the chosen structure can be
evaluated, both in terms of effectiveness and performance, possibly allowing for
re-organizations. In the subsequent sections we discuss in some detail the phases
of the methodology mainly concerned with the modeling aspects of hypertext
design.

3 Hypertext Conceptual Design

3.1 NCM: The Navigational Conceptual Model

As we argued in Section 2, a conceptual representation of hypertexts should concern the entities of interest, the relevant paths among them, and the additional
(high level representation of) access paths. These issues are at the basis of NCM,
our data model for the conceptual description of hypertexts.

Figure 3 shows the graphical representations for NCM constructs. We now
discuss the constructs in detail, first macroentities, union nodes, and directed

relationships, which are used to give a hypertextual view of the domain of interest, and then aggregations, which allow a conceptual description of the hypertext access structure. All examples refer to the Department application, whose NCM scheme is shown in Figure 4.

Macroentities Macroentities are intensional descriptions of classes of real world objects to be presented in the hypertext. They indicate the smallest autonomous pieces of information which have an independent existence in the hypertext. As we discussed in Section 2, macroentities are the NCM counterpart to ER entities, because of the common correspondence to real-world objects, with the difference that macroentities have to be relevant from the hypertextual point of view, in the sense that we want to have hypertext elements derived from them, which need not be the case for all ER entities. Examples of macroentities, in our department Web site are **STUDENT** and **COURSE**. Similarly to ER entities, NCM macroentities have attributes and keys, however with some differences with respect to most versions of the ER model. In fact, since a macroentity may involve multiple concepts, it is essential to specify, for each of its *attributes*, whether it is *simple* (atomic) or *complex* (structured), with possible nesting, and its *cardinality* (that is, whether it is monovalued or multivalued [3]). In the example in Figure 4 all attributes are simple and monovalued except for the structured and multivalued attribute of **COURSE** that represents the information (day, hour, and room) of interest for the various meetings of each course. With respect to identification, we have a notion of *descriptive key*, a set of attributes with two properties: *(i)* to be a superkey (in the usual sense) and *(ii)* to be explicative about the corresponding instance, i.e., the user should directly infer the meaning of its values. In the Department Example, a descriptive key for a **SEMINAR** macroentity is made of the **Title** and the **Author** of the seminar: although the title alone would suffice to identify a seminar, it does not convey enough meaning about the corresponding seminar itself, so that also the name of the author is needed to satisfy the second property.

Directed Relationships In NCM *directed relationships* describe how it is possible to navigate in the hypertext from a source node (a macroentity) to a

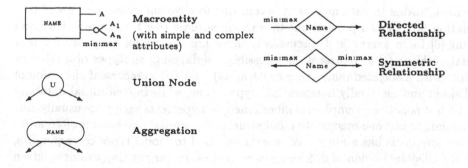

Fig. 3. Graphical Representation of NCM Constructs

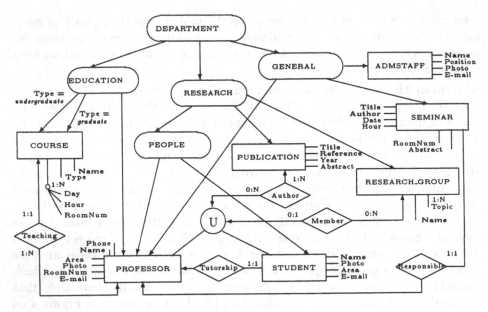

Fig. 4. The Department NCM scheme

destination node (a macroentity again or a union node, see below) based on their conceptual relationships. There are two major differences with respect to ER relationships: first the notion of direction of traversal, and second the fact that, whereas in the ER "redundant" relationships are usually not represented (since they can be obtained by composition), here redundancy can be relevant, if it corresponds to an interesting connection. Each directed relationship has a *cardinality constraint* that specifies the (minimum and maximum) number of instances of the destination node associated with one instance of the source node. We also have *symmetric* directed relationships, that can be seen as composed of two asymmetric directed relationship, being one the inverse of the other. They are used to indicate that navigation between the two nodes can proceed in both ways.

Union Nodes In data models, it is common to have one or more forms of IS-A relationships [3]. As pointed out by various authors (see for example Hull and King [6] for a survey and discussion), there are two major purposes for IS-A relationships: *(i)* to represent the (possibly overlapping) subtypes of a relevant type (with associated inheritance constraints), and *(ii)* to represent the union of (disjoint and essentially independent) types. Now, while in conceptual database models it is better to emphasize inheritance, in hypertexts each page usually corresponds to just one macroentity, but structurally similar navigations often arise. Therefore, NCM has a *union node* construct, used to model types corresponding to the (disjoint) union of different macroentities. In our running example, given that macroentities **PROFESSOR** and **STUDENT** are defined, since both professors and students can author publications and we want to describe authorship only once, we would include a union node for them, reachable from publication via a directed relationship.

Aggregations Aggregation is the NCM primitive that allows to model the hypertext access structure. An aggregation node is a means to reach the involved concepts, which are macroentities or, in turn, other aggregations. Possible aggregations in our example would be a DEPARTMENT concept (modeling the homepage of the site), leading to other aggregation nodes (essentially another page with a menu) such as EDUCATION and RESEARCH; the latter could in turn lead to macroentities PUBLICATION and RESEARCH_GROUP.

Sometimes, the participation of a macroentity to an aggregation is only partial, in the sense that only a subset of instances of the macroentity is involved; this can be modeled in NCM by attaching *labels* to aggregation links; each label is associated with a predicate on instances of the destination node and is used to specify that only instances satisfying the predicate are considered as part of the aggregation. In our running example, we may think of aggregating macroentities COURSE and PROFESSOR under the name EDUCATION. However, it is reasonable to distinguish graduate courses from undergraduate ones; links with different labels ("undergraduate" and "graduate") are used to this end (see Figure 4).

3.2 From ER Schemes to NCM Schemes

As we saw, there is a rather close correspondence between NCM and the ER model. Therefore, the hypertext NCM scheme is derived from the database conceptual scheme, by means of a process that takes into account, in turn, the specific differences. It is organized according to the three steps: the first produces macroentities, the second directed relationships, and the third union nodes and aggregations. In each case, the basic rule is to follow the definition of the construct and the motivations for it. For the sake of space, we only comment on the major issues, mainly referring to the example.

Step 3.1: Selecting Macroentities Following the definition, macroentities are naturally derived from ER entities or, in some cases, from compositions of entities and relationships. Each entity representing objects that are considered relevant and independent in the hypertext, originates a macroentity. In our example, STUDENT, PUBLICATION, ADMSTAFF and RESEARCH_GROUP macroentities are derived from the corresponding ER entities. Other ER entities are absorbed by more relevant ones; as an example, consider the fragment of scheme about courses, lessons, and rooms; here, ROOM and LESSON are not considered as autonomous concepts in the hypertext design. Thus, we choose to incorporate them in macroentities corresponding to courses, seminars, and professors. Clearly, this process may give rise to multivalued attributes, for example to model all lessons associated with an instance of macroentity COURSE.

With respect to IS-A relationships, as a general rule, if the children (or leaves, in case of a multilevel hierarchy) are relevant, then only them give rise to NCM macroentities. The other entities are temporarily ignored, to be considered later in Step 3.3. In the example, in the ER scheme in Figure 1 there is the IS-A hierarchy over persons and in the NCM scheme in Figure 4 we have macroentities only for the three leaf nodes (PROFESSOR, STUDENT, and ADMSTAFF).

Step 3.2: Designing Directed Relationships Directed relationships are usually derived from ER relationships, with the specification of the direction. In our example, a directed relationship from macroentity SEMINAR and PROFESSOR in the NCM scheme models the fact that it is possible to navigate from seminars to their respective organizers (and not vice versa); similarly, a symmetric directed relationship between PROFESSOR and macroentity COURSE is used to describe that it will be possible to navigate the association between the two concepts in both ways. Additional directed relationships can be introduced, if there are relevant links to be included in the hypertext; in the example (however not shown in the figure) we could include a directed relationship from PROFESSOR to PUBLICATION to provide immediate access to all publications of the group led by the professor.

Step 3.3: Designing Union Nodes and Aggregations As apparent from the examples illustrated so far, both union nodes and aggregations can arise from IS-A hierarchies. Therefore, a major activity in this step is the examination of the IS-A hierarchies in the conceptual scheme.

Specifically, if there is a relationship in the ER scheme involving an entity that is the parent of an IS-A hierarchy whose children have given rise to macroentities, then it should be considered whether a union node could be useful, in order to allow for navigations from (another) macroentity to the various "child" macroentities. In our running example, this is indeed the case for entity RESEARCHER, involved in relationship Author. Let us note that the authorship relationship is intuitively bidirectional; indeed, our model does not allow for union nodes to be sources for directed relationships; however, we indicate in Figure 4 a symmetric relationship Author as a shorthand.

The same intermediate nodes should be considered also as candidates for becoming aggregation nodes: this is the case if it is interesting (from the hypertext point of view) to have a common access path to the sets of instances of the various child macroentities. It is important to note that it may be the case that a parent entity gives rise to both a union node and an aggregation. In fact, in our running example, we also have (beside the union node discussed earlier) PEOPLE as an aggregation of PROFESSOR and STUDENT.

Additional aggregations may be explicitly introduced in order to better organize information inside the hypertext and provide additional access paths. For example, professors, seminars and administrative staff are aggregated under a concept of "general Department matters."

4 Hypertext Logical Design

NCM schemes describe how concepts can be navigated in the target hypertext. On the other side, actual Web hypertexts are essentially graphs of pages: these two ways of organizing information can be rather far away from each other, and specific methodological steps are needed in order to derive the second from the first. The hypertext logical design phase is concerned with these aspects.

It is based on a logical hypertext data model, called ADM [2], which allows to describe in a tight and concise way the structure of HTML pages by abstracting their logical features.

4.1 ADM Page Schemes

The fundamental feature of ADM is the notion of *page scheme*, which resembles the notion of relation scheme in relational databases or class in object-oriented databases: a page scheme is an intensional description of a set of Web pages with common features. An instance of a page scheme is a Web page, which is considered as an object with an identifier (the URL) and a set of attributes. On a page scheme a special constraint can be specified in order to model an important case in this framework: when a page scheme is "unique", it has just one instance, in the sense that there are no other pages with the same structure. Typically, at least the home page of each site falls in this category.

Page features are described by means of *attributes*, which may have simple or complex type. *Simple attributes* are monovalued and correspond to atomic pieces of information, such as *text*, *images* or other multimedia types. *Links* are simple attributes of a special kind, used to model hypertextual links; each link is a pair *(anchor, reference)*, where the *reference* is the URL of the destination page, possibly concatenated to an *offset*, inside the target page scheme, and *anchor* is a text or an image. Anchors for links may either be constant strings, or correspond to tuples of attributes. *Complex attributes* are multivalued and represent (ordered) collections of objects, that is, *lists* of tuples. Component types in lists can be in turn multivalued, and therefore nested lists are allowed. It should be noted that we have chosen lists as the only multivalued type since repeated patterns in Web pages are physically ordered. Attributes may be labeled as "optional" in order to allow null values.

ADM provides two further constructs, particularly relevant in the Web framework. First, ADM, like NCM, also provides a *heterogeneous union* type, in order to provide flexibility in modeling. Moreover, an important construct in Web pages is represented by *forms*. Forms are used to execute programs on the server and dynamically generate pages. ADM provides a *form type*: in order to abstract the logical features of an HTML form, we see it as a *virtual list of tuples*; each tuple has as many attributes as the fill-in fields of the form, plus a link to the resulting page; such lists are virtual since tuples are not stored in the page but are generated in response to the submission of the form. Figure 5 shows the graphical representation of ADM constructs.

The hypertext logical design phase aims at producing an ADM scheme starting from the NCM hypertext conceptual specifications and can be seen as a two-step process: first, a skeleton of the ADM scheme is built by mapping NCM constructs to ADM ones; then, this first ADM scheme can be further restructured in order to improve effectiveness and efficiency. The reason for adopting such a composite process is to emphasize the flexibility of the ADM data model in reorganizing the designed hypertext. Clearly, the need for reorganizations may occur in the site lifetime, and usually require a great effort in order to correspondingly maintain

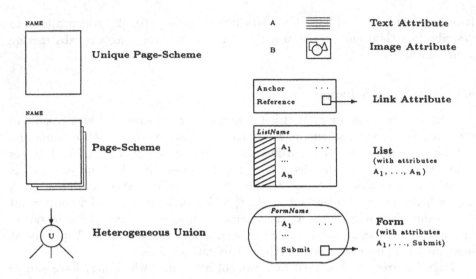

Fig. 5. ADM Constructs

the system. ADM is a natural framework for reasoning about the actual organization of the site, and provides useful support to these activities. We discuss now how NCM constructs can be mapped to page schemes; then, in Section 5, we discuss restructuring, seen also as a maintenance activity.

4.2 From NCM Schemes to ADM Schemes

A translation from NCM to ADM essentially consists in mapping NCM nodes to page schemes and NCM links to ADM link attributes. There are three main methodological steps in this process, as follows.

Step 4.1: Mapping Macroentities There are several ways of organizing the presentation of a macroentity instance using Web pages. The most natural way is to use one page for each macroentity instance. At the opposite end, all instances of particular macroentities may be presented in a single page; although there is no definitive rule, this latter representation seems more appropriate when instances have a particularly concise description. In the former case, a page scheme with the same attributes as the macroentity is generated. In the latter case, the resulting page scheme will consist of a list of tuples having the same attributes as the starting macroentity. Note that, when translating attributes, NCM single valued attributes are mapped to ADM simple attributes and NCM multivalued attributes are mapped to ADM lists. Figures 6 and 7 show the mapping of macroentities **PROFESSOR** and **SEMINAR** into the corresponding ADM page schemes: instances of the former will be presented in separate pages, while instances of the latter will be items of a list.

Step 4.2: Mapping Directed Relationships Directed relationships are mapped to links between page schemes. As a preliminary step, all NCM symmetric

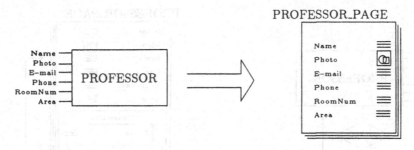

Fig. 6. Step 4.1: Mapping Macroentities to page schemes

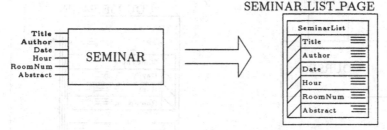

Fig. 7. Step 4.1: Mapping Macroentities to lists

relationships are split in two asymmetric relationships. Then, a new attribute is added to the source page scheme (i.e., the page scheme corresponding to the source macroentity): it is a link attribute, if the maximum cardinality of the relationship is 1, or a list of links, if the cardinality is N. The link anchor is in both cases to be chosen among the descriptive keys of the target macroentity; moreover, if the target macroentity has been mapped to a list, then an offset may be added to the reference in order to point to a specific tuple in the list.

Figure 8 illustrates this process. The symmetric relationship **Teaching** between **PROFESSOR** and **COURSE** is split in two directed relationships: **Teaches** and **TaughtBy**. The former, going from professor to courses, has cardinality N and is mapped to a list of links (**CourseList**) in page scheme **ProfessorPage**: each item in the list points to an instance of **CoursePage**. The latter, **TaughtBy**, goes from each course to the corresponding professor; it has cardinality 1 and is translated adding a link attribute to page scheme **CoursePage**; note that the anchor of these links corresponds to a descriptive key of the target macroentity.

Step 4.3: Mapping Aggregations Each NCM aggregation node is mapped to an ADM unique page scheme. NCM aggregation links correspond to link attributes, with some subtleties: if the destination node is in turn an aggregation or a macroentity mapped to a unique page scheme, a single link to the corresponding page scheme is used; the anchor to be used is a constant string, usually corresponding to the target page scheme name. On the contrary, if the target node is a macroentity mapped to a page scheme or a union node, an ADM list attribute is added to the source page scheme; each item in the list is a link to one instance of the destination page scheme. For instance, in the running example

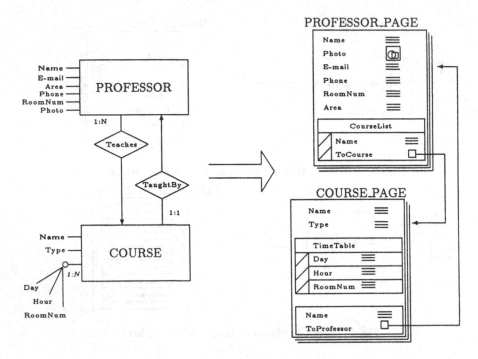

Fig. 8. Step 4.2: Mapping Directed Relationships

aggregation **RESEARCH** is mapped to page scheme **RESEARCH_PAGE**. Since one of the components nodes is an aggregation, **PEOPLE**, this is in turn mapped to page scheme **PEOPLE_PAGE**.

5 Restructuring and Maintaining a Site

Let us discuss the issue of *modifying* an ADM scheme. This can be useful for two reasons. First, the initial scheme, while reflecting the conceptual NCM scheme, may present some limitations. In particular, data may not be sufficiently organized and complex or counterintuitive navigations may be required in order to access information. Second, and more important, it is often the case that the need for changing the organization of an hypertext arises, still with respect to the same conceptual structure. Therefore, the issue of restructuring a scheme is relevant both in a standard design activity and in a maintenance initiative. ADM provides a natural framework to reason about page organization, and to reorganize data without changing the hypertext conceptual structure. We proceed by presenting some meaningful transformations that can be used to restructure and maintain an ADM scheme. The results of them are shown in Figure 9, which also presents the final ADM scheme for the Department example.

Page schemes corresponding to particularly rich macroentities may be split in two (or more) page schemes, each presenting a subset of the attributes of the page scheme. This activity resembles the *slice design* activity in RMM [7] or

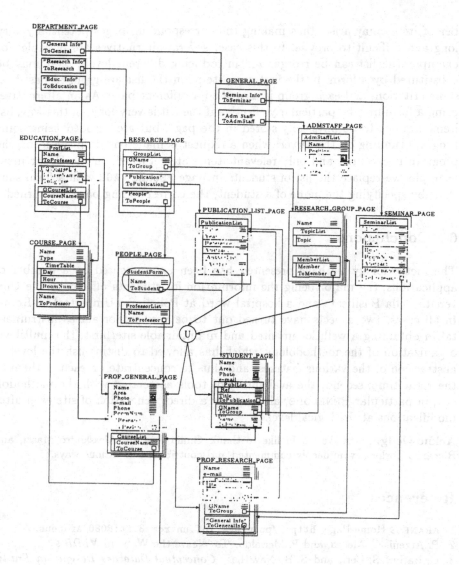

Fig. 9. The Department ADM scheme

partitioning in logical database design [3]. In the running example, page scheme **PROFESSOR_PAGE** results too dense, then we might think of isolating general information (like name, photo, phone, room number, e-mail address, plus the list of courses) from data concerning research; to do this, the original page scheme is split in two, **PROF_GENERAL_PAGE** and **PROF_RESEARCH_PAGE**. Clearly, the two (or more) parts may overlap on some attributes.

When mapping directed relationships to lists of links, lists with a large number of items may arise, thus making the corresponding pages potentially very long and difficult to browse. In this case, several alternatives are possible; for example, the list can be reorganized introducing different levels, or it may be substituted by a form. In the first case, items in the list are grouped based on some criterion, and each group is moved to a different page. As an alternative, using a form may be particularly effective if the list is very long; in this way, list items are not to be physically stored in the page, but are encoded using some program running on the server: when a request is made based on the form, the program is executed and only relevant items are returned. In the Department example, we replace the list of students in page PEOPLE_PAGE with a form such that, by specifying the name of a student, the corresponding page is returned.

6   Conclusions

The methodology we have presented has been experimented on a number of applications, the major being the information for students offered by the Università della Basilicata and a hospital ward at Policlinico Umberto I in Rome. In all cases, two aspects have turned out to be very important as instrumental in obtaining a well documented and maintainable site: first, the multilevel organization of the methodology, which has allowed to distinguish the level of abstraction of the various features, and thus to concentrate on each of them at the right time; second, the availability of tools associated with the methodology, in particular PENELOPE, allowing for a direct generation of site even after modifications at the logical level.

Acknowledgments We would like to thank Giulia Festino, Alessandro Masci, and Riccardo Torlone, who deeply commented and contributed in various ways.

References

1. ARANEUS Home Page. http://poincare.inf.uniroma3.it:8080/Araneus.
2. P. Atzeni, G. Mecca, and P. Merialdo. To Weave the Web. In *VLDB'97*.
3. C. Batini, S. Ceri, and S. B. Navathe. *Conceptual Database Design: an Entity-Relationship Approach*. Benjamin and Cummings Publ. Co., 1993.
4. P. Fraternali and P. Paolini. A conceptual model and a tool environment for developing more scalable, dynamic, and customizable Web applications. This Volume.
5. F. Garzotto, P. Paolini, and D. Schwabe. HDM – a model-based approach to hypertext application design. *ACM TODS*, 11(1):1–26, January 1993.
6. R.B. Hull and R. King. Semantic database modelling: Survey, applications and research issues. *ACM Computing Surveys*, 19(3):201–260, September 1987.
7. T. Isakowitz, E. A. Stohr, and P. Balasubramanian. RMM: A methodology for structured hypermedia design. *Comm. ACM*, 58(8):34–44, August 1995.
8. D. Schwabe and G. Rossi. The Object-Oriented Hypermedia Design Model. *Comm. ACM*, 58(8):45–46, August 1995.

Dynamic and Structured Presentation of Database Contents on the Web

Motomichi Toyama[1]* and Takuhiro Nagafuji[2]

[1] Department of Information and Computer Science, e-mail: `toyama@ics.keio.ac.jp`
[2] Department of Administration Engineering, e-mail: `naf@ae.keio.ac.jp`
Keio University, Yokohama, Japan

Abstract. Attractive presentation of database contents is a key component of Web-based businesses. TFE (Target Form Expression) is a database publishing/presentation extension of SQL that yields a query result presented as a document in any of several target media, for example, HTML, Java, LaTeX. When a Web (HTML) document is the target medium, TFE yields intra-page and inter-page hierarchical structures in arbitrary size and complexity. The inter-page structures are automatically-generated hyper-links which allow the resulting Web document to be browsed in a fashion similar to drill down in a data warehouse. In this paper, we introduce a new primitive of TFE that allows the invocation of another query. Combined with the incremental evaluation of invoked queries, it improves both efficiency and functionality compared to monolithic and static implementations. The improved functionality includes recursive navigation. A small number of query rewriting rules are provided to show the equivalence of a query and its decompositions. Incremental query evaluation gives application system an enhanced capability for designing database/Web applications to meet performance and functionality requirements while retaining simplicity of description. A new diagramming method called Database Presentation Diagram is also introduced to visualize the structures of a set of queries and the presentation produced with them.

1 Introduction

Presentation of database contents is a key component of many Web-based businesses. Within a business, for example, Web technology may be used to distribute corporate data to employees' desktops. Product price lists could be publicized on the Web in electronic commerce applications. Although there are many commercial products like Allaire's Cold Fusion[1] that help users convert database contents into HTML documents, most of them do not have structuring capabilities such as grouping or hyper-link generation[2-4].

TFE (Target Form Expression) is an extended replacement for SQL's target list for database publishing and presentaion[6]; it yields a query result presented

---

* This paper was written while the author was at Oregon Graduate Insitute. The work was partially supported by the DARPA grant on the Continual Queries Project.

Fig. 1. Sample Web Pages Generated with a SQL+TFE Query

as a document, e.g., as a LaTeX document or a Web document (a set of Web pages). When the target media is a Web document[5], it provides both intra-page structuring (nested tables) and inter-page structuring in an integrated manner (Fig. 1). The inter-page structure (automatically-generated hyper-links) allows browsing on the resulting Web document in a fashion similar to drill down in a data warehouse.

In this paper, we introduce a dynamic query invocation capability into TFE. Using dynamic invocation, several queries can cooperate to generate a complex document by invoking one another. Compared to monolithic and static implementations, dynamic invocation provides enhanced functionality and improved efficiency for certain usage patterns. We focus on the benefits of dynamic query invocation when the target medium is a Web document in HTML.

By decomposing a large and complicated SQL+TFE query which yields a complex Web document into several simple sub-queries, an equivalent presentation can be provided in less space. Because the dynamic portion is generated and sent on the fly, the results need not be kept as HTML files. When a presentation is very large and only a small portion is actually accessed, the computational cost can also be reduced because pages are translated into HTML in an on-demand basis. Maintaining consistency between dynamically-generated pages and current database state is another big advantage of dynamic generation.

Dynamic invocation provides enhanced functionality by allowing the resulting Web document to have a more general topology. A Web document which is generated by a single SQL+TFE query is restricted to a rooted-tree topology. A set of queries invoking each other recursively will yield a Web document with an arbitrary network topology. This allows navigation on recursive structures such as a family tree while using a non-recursive-SQL database system as a back-end.

An overview of TFE is presented in the next section. Section 3 introduces the **invoke** function and a diagramming method called DPD. In section 4, we discuss decomposition of a query into a semantically equivalent set of sub-queries. In section 5, the extended topology and recursive navigation are discussed. Implementation details are provided in section 6.

2 An Overview of TFE

We briefly present the original version of TFE , which extends SQL to generate various kinds of structured publishing/presentation documents. Although we concentrate on HTML Web document generation in this paper, the same discussion applies to other target media to various extents.

TFE (Target Form Expression) is an extension of an SQL target list. Unlike an ordinary target list, which is a comma-separated list of attributes, TFE uses new operators (connectors and repeaters) to specify the structure of the document generated as the result of the query. Each connector and repeater is associated with a dimension: when generating a Web document, the first two dimensions are associated with the columns and rows of the <TABLE> structure of HTML and the third dimension is associated with hyper-links.

We have introduced the GENERATE <medium> <TFE> clause to SQL syntax to clarify the distinction with the SELECT <target list> clause. Other target medium designations, which are allowed in the current implementation but not treated in this paper, include LATEX, JAVA, EXCEL, TCLTK, O2C, and SQL.

2.1 Connectors and Repeaters

Binary operators represented by a comma (,), an exclamation point (!) and a percent (%) are used as the connectors of the first three dimensions. Conceptually, they connect the objects generated as their operands horizontally, vertically and in the depth direction, respectively.

A pair of square brackets ([ ]) followed by any of the above connectors is a repeater for that dimension. It will connect multiple instances in its associated dimension repeatedly. For example,

[emp.name, emp.salary]!

will connect name-salary pairs vertically as long as there are such tuples in the query result; it yields the same result as an ordinary target list.

Nesting of repeaters introduces grouping if the inner repeaters are connected to one or more simple attributes. For example,

[store.name, [dept.name ! {[emp.name]!, [item.name]!}]!]%

will group employees and sales items by store and department. Curly braces ({ }) specify the precedence of connections.

Additional features of TFE such as the ornamental operator (@), **verb** function and **imagefile** function are explained in [5].

2.2 Sample Presentation with TFE

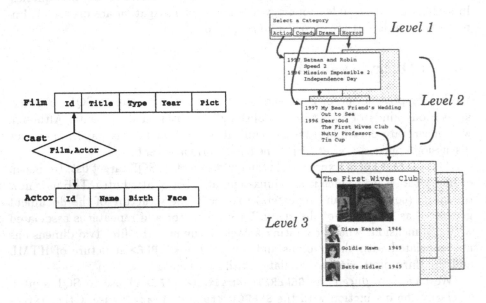

Fig. 2. Movie Database and the Web Pages Generated with a SQL+TFE Query

Fig. 2 shows a sample Web document generated by the following SQL+TFE query against a movie information database; the database schema is depicted on the left. The **type** attribute of **film** specifies a category such as 'action' or 'comedy' and the **pict** attribute provides a still picture. The **face** of the **actor** is also an image attribute[1].

```
GENERATE HTML verb(Select a Category) !
     [f.type %
          [f.year, [f.title %
              {f.title ! imagefile(f.pict) !
                 [imagefile(a.face), a.name, a.birth]!} ]!]! ],
     FROM film f, cast c, actor a
     WHERE f.id=c.film and c.actor=a.id
```

The query generates a three-level hierarchical Web document whose only root page (first level) contains categories of movies. The second-level pages contain movie titles associated with a category, and each third-level page contains a movie title, a still picture from the movie, and a list of actors and actresses appearing in the movie.

---

[1] The database contains the file names of the images; the **imagefile** function of TFE is used to display the images.

3 Dynamic Query Invocation

In this section, we introduce the syntax and semantics of the **invoke** function. As with functions and procedures in a programming language, **invoke** introduces modularity into SQL+TFE queries. In addition, a diagramming method (Database Presentation Diagram) is introduced to visualize the structure of queries and the presentations they generate.

3.1 Syntax

The syntax of the **invoke** function is as follows:

INVOKE(file, string1, att1, string2, att2, ...)

The first argument is the name of a file containing a SQL+TFE query. Pairs of arguments **string1** and **att1**, **string2** and **att2**, ..., form additional conditions to be appended to the invoked query. Each string is a string that is used as-is. The value, in the current context, of each attribute is concatenated to the preceding **string** argument to form a query condition.

3.2 Semantics

In general, an **invoke** function is expected to return a printable object, either an atomic value or a complex hypertext. Unlike other primitives of the original TFE, the returned object is not produced from the materials found in the current query's result. Instead, another query designated by its first argument is executed and returns a printable object. Upon invocation, each pair of arguments is appended to the **WHERE** clause of the invoked query by conjunction[2].

The current implementation allows the **invoke** function to appear only on the right-hand side of a depth connector (%). Therefore, each invocation is associated with an instance of a hyper-link. Under the principle of incremental evaluation, a query invocation takes place when the anchor point of a hyper-link, which is generated as the left operand of a depth connector, is selected on a Web page. The resulting page is sent to the browser on the fly. When an invoked query has one or more depth connectors, and thus generates multiple pages, only the root page is sent on the fly while other pages are temporarily stored as HTML files.

3.3 Example

Example Q0 is a simplified version of the movie application in the previous section. It is *not* using the **invoke** function. The result of Q0 is essentially the same three-level hypertext document shown in Fig. 2, except for the omission of some attributes, intra-page structures and ornaments.

---

[2] Conjunction is assumed to keep syntax simpler for the majority of applications. There are no technical difficulties preventing the extension of **invoke** to allow the use of other logical operators such as disjunction.

Original Query

```
Q0: GENERATE HTML [f.type % [f.title % [a.name, a.birth]!]!]!
    FROM film f, actor a, cast c
    WHERE f.id=c.film and c.actor=a.id
```

We decompose Q0 into a functionally-equivalent pair of queries, Q1a and Q1b, linked by the **invoke** function. The upper two levels of the Web document contain only values drawn from the relation **film**, so these two levels are generated by query Q1a on **film**. When a user has selected a film title from a second-level page, the **id** of the film is passed to Q1b to dynamically generate a third-level page that contains a list of actors (name and birth year) appearing in the selected film. Assuming the **id** of the selected film is `'f0xXyY'`, the condition added to Q1b (**AND c.film='f0xXyY'**) is written in parentheses as follows.

Decomposition 1: Intuitive decomposition

```
Q1a: GENERATE HTML [f.type % [f.title % INVOKE(Q1b,'c.film=',f.id)]!]!
     FROM film f

Q1b: GENERATE HTML [a.name, a.birth]!
     FROM actor a, cast c
     WHERE c.actor=a.id
     (AND c.film='f0xXyY') ; condition dynamically added on invocation
```

Unlike Q0, which generates all three levels of the Web document, Q1a generates only the upper two levels. Third-level pages are dynamically generated by Q1b on demand.

3.4 Performance Comparison

Although Q0 and Q1 (a, b) produce physically different Web documents, they behave identically in the eyes of the viewer. In this section, we develop a cost approximation formula for a query and compare the performances of Q0 and Q1 in two different situations.

Evaluation Formula We assume the time (in seconds) for a query to generate a Web document can be approximated by the following formula, where P is the number of resulting Web pages.

$$C_{query} = C_0 + C_1 \cdot P + C_X$$

C_0 is the data-size-independent cost incurred to execute a query. It includes such costs as DBMS invocation overhead and query compilation. C_1 represents the overhead to create and store an HTML file. When a query is invoked dynamically, and when it generates only a one-page HTML document, P will be zero; the HTML document is sent through the WWW server as a result of a CGI script, hence no file is created. The third term C_X represents the cost of query execution and translation into HTML. This term will be a very complex function of the characteristics of a query and the physical structure of the database such as the avilability of indices.

For the sake of simplicity, where we discuss on the relative performance of queries yielding equivalent results, we replace the third term with a linear expression—certainly oversimplified for a performance discussion in general— that is proportional to the total size of the resulting presentation. The revised formula has variable S representing the size of the presentation in KB (kilo byte):

$$C_{query} = C_0 + C_1 \cdot P + C_2 \cdot S$$

For example, the following empirical values of C_0, C_1, and C_2 are obtained from extensive executions of our software running with mSQL 1.0.16, GNU Common Lisp 2.2.1, and FreeBSD 2.2.2 on a Pentium MMX 166MHz computer:

$$C_0 = 0.38 \text{ [sec]}, \quad C_1 = 0.0133 \text{ [sec/page]}, \quad C_2 = 0.0127 \text{ [sec/KB]}$$

Comparison For this comparison, we will assume the sizes of the database and the resulting Web document as follows. The number of tuples of the three base relations film, actor and cast are 9,000, 7,000 and 40,000, respectively. Also, we assume the size of the resulting presentation, depicted in Fig. 2, as follows: one Web page of 10 KB is in the first level, 20 Web pages of 15 KB are in the second level and 9,000 Web pages of 8 KB each are in the third level.

With these assumptions, the estimated execution time of query Q0, which yields 9021 Web pages totaling 70.6 MB, is calculated as follows.

$$C_{Q0} = 0.38 + 0.0133 \cdot (1 + 20 + 9000) + 0.0127 \cdot (1 \cdot 10 + 20 \cdot 15 + 9000 \cdot 8)$$
$$= 1038.7 \text{ [sec]}$$

The execution time of Q1 is estimated as follows.

$$C_{Q1a} = 0.38 + 0.0133 \cdot (1 + 20) + 0.0127 \cdot (1 \cdot 10 + 20 \cdot 15) = 4.60 \text{ [sec]}$$
$$C_{Q1b} = 0.38 + 0.0133 \cdot 0 + 0.0127 \cdot (1 \cdot 8) = 0.48 \text{ [sec]}$$

We will compare the two versions in two different usage scenarios.
Case 1: Infrequent updates, extremely intensive accesses.

As we could easily imagine with the movie information example, some sorts of information are quite stable and accessed frequently. Assuming that a weekly update is sufficient, a batch maintenance policy makes sense. Weekly execution of Q0 requires 1039 seconds (17 minutes and 19 seconds) to re-generate the whole Web document. And each Web page access will be served as quickly as possible because no database access is required at that time. The cost of building the presentation is fixed at 1039 seconds per week.
Case 2: Frequent updates on leaves, intensive accesses.

A Web-based business may include volatile information on its Web documents. A price list served on the Web, for example, should agree with the prices stored in the company's database. Using Q0 dynamically would be prohibitively expensive because the response time would be in excess of 17 minutes. Dynamic execution of Q1b, however, can ensure realtime consistency of leaves and the database contents at the cost of 0.48 seconds on each access of a leaf page. For a realtime application similar in size to our movie infomation example, the total weekly cost of building the application would be about 5 seconds per week plus about 0.5 seconds per access. The total weekly cost of Q1 exceeds that of Q0 for more than two thousand accesses per week, but Q1 uses much less disk space while ensuring that the presentation is consistent with the underlying database. If the per-access cost of Q1 is reasonable for the application, then, Q1 may be preferable to Q0.

3.5 Database Presentation Diagrams

With dynamic query invocation, an application developer can produce queries and presentations with complex interrelationships. To visualize the structures and behavior of queries using **invoke** and their resulting Web presentation, we introduce a schematic expression called the *Database Presentation Diagram* (DPD). The DPD serves as a map for an entire database/Web application. Fig. 3 shows the DPDs for Q0 and Q1 from subsection 3.3. A DPD consists of two sub-diagrams—a *Query Invocation Diagram* (QID) and a *Hypertext Link Diagram* (HTLD)—with *export arrows* between them. A QID depicts a set of queries and the invocations among them. An HTLD illustrates transitions (i.e. hyper-links) between Web page schemas. These components are explained later.

Query Invocation Diagrams (QID) A Query Invocation Diagram is a directed graph whose nodes represent queries and whose edges represent invocations. An edge is drawn as a bold arrow labeled with the names of attributes passed to the invoked query. Each node is drawn as a query diagram surround by a dotted line. A *query diagram*, which resembles an Entity-Relationship diagram, has nodes that represent relations in the **FROM** clause of a query. An edge in a query graph represents a join term in the **WHERE** clause of the query.

On the left half of Fig. 3b, for example, two nodes represent queries Q1a and Q1b, respectively. The bold arrow indicates that Q1b is invoked by Q1a with **film.id** as an argument. From the query diagram in the QID node for Q1b, we learn that Q1b queries relations **cast** and **actor**.

Hypertext Link Diagrams (HTLD) A Hypertext Link Diagram is an abstraction of a hypertext document represented as a directed graph of hexagonal nodes. Each node represents a page schema and is labeled with the names of database attributes names that are presented on the page. An arrow from one node to another designates a hyper-link between those page schemas. For example, on the right half of Fig. 3b we see that there are three page schemas

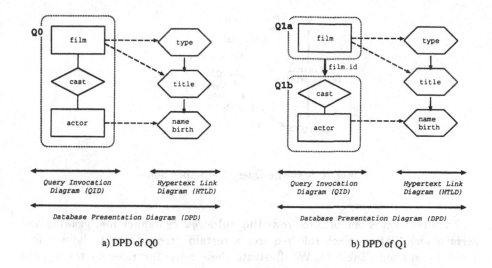

Fig. 3. Database Presentation Diagrams

constituting the hypertext. The root page displays the film's **type** information from the database. A second-level page contains film titles. A third-level page includes the name and birth year of actors in the selected film.

Export Arrows A DPD is obtained by connecting nodes in a QID to nodes in a HTLD with *export arrows*. An arrow in dashed-line is drawn when a query supplies values to a page in the resulting hypertext. Because TFE allows a single query to produce multi-level hypertext, one node in the QID may supply values to several different nodes in the HTLD. No resulting page may gather values from more than one query, however, so each HTLD node has at most one incoming arrow.

4 Equivalence in Query Decomposition

In this section, we discuss the equivalences of a query and its decomposition. A set of query rewriting rules is provided to show the equivalence. These rules are presented informally; future work will include a more rigorous analysis.

4.1 Stepwise Decomposition

In subsection 3.3, we stated that Q1 is equivalent to Q0. The equivalence is not apparent, however, so we show another approach to query decomposition. This approach applies small revisions to the original query so that we can verify the equivalence of query semantics after each revision. Through the revisions Q2, Q3, and Q4, the original query Q0 is eventually rewritten to Q1 (Fig. 4).

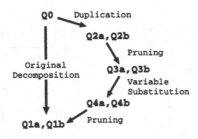

Fig. 4. Stepwise Query Decomposition

Each revision is one of three rewriting rules: *query duplication, pruning* and *variable substitution*. Each rule requires a certain precondition to hold before it can be applied (Table 1). We illustrate these rewriting rules by tracing the stepwise revision of Q0 as depicted in Fig. 4.

Table 1. Query Rewriting Rules

Rule	Description	Precondition
Query Duplication	Duplicate original query on **FROM** and **WHERE** clauses. Adjust TFE of each query.	None
Pruning	Remove unnecessary relations in a query.	Inclusion dependency.
Variable Substitution	Replace a variable in a query with an equivalent one.	Functional dependency. Equivalence in **WHERE** clause.

Decomposition 2: Create linked query by duplication

Q2a and Q2b (Fig. 5) are obtained by applying query duplication to Q0. The **FROM** and **WHERE** clauses of Q2a and Q2b are identical to those of Q0. The differences are found only in their TFE in the **GENERATE** clause, where Q2a has attributes **f.type** and **f.title** and the invocation of Q2b. The values of these attributes are passed to Q2b as arguments which restrict the scope of the subquery to the current tuple's values (for example, **AND type='drama' AND title='AA'**).

We show informally that Q2(a,b) is equivalent to Q0. The **FROM** and **WHERE** clauses of Q0 and Q2a are the same and the TFE of Q2a is the same as that of Q0 for the upper two levels of the tree structure, so the two-level Web document generated with Q2a matches the upper two levels of the Q0 result. A third-level leaf page in the Q0 result should be the same as one generated with Q2b

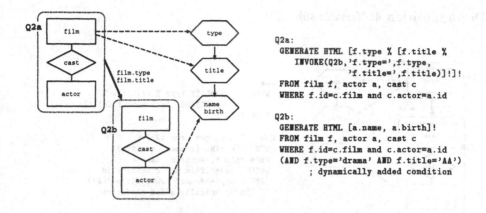

```
Q2a:
  GENERATE HTML [f.type % [f.title %
    INVOKE(Q2b,'f.type=',f.type,
               'f.title=',f.title)]!]!
  FROM film f, actor a, cast c
  WHERE f.id=c.film and c.actor=a.id

Q2b:
  GENERATE HTML [a.name, a.birth]!
  FROM film f, actor a, cast c
  WHERE f.id=c.film and c.actor=a.id
  (AND f.type='drama' AND f.title='AA')
    ; dynamically added condition
```

Fig. 5. Q2: Decomposition by Query Duplication

because the TFE for that part is the same and Q2b is given additional conditions
as arguments that identify a leaf in the tree structure.

Note: We are following the definition of nest operator by Hulin[7] rather than
that by Jaeshke and Schek[8] in our grouping algorithm. Therefore, we can group
each Y_1, Y_2, ..., in $[X\ [Y_1]\ [Y_2]\ ...\ ]$ by X independently of other Ys. As a
consequence, even when we decompose a query into three or more subqueries by
repeated applications of duplication, the equivalence still hold.

Decomposition 3: Prune cast and actor in Q2a by inclusion dependency

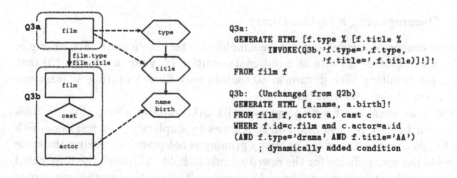

```
Q3a:
  GENERATE HTML [f.type % [f.title %
    INVOKE(Q3b,'f.type=',f.type,
               'f.title=',f.title)]!]!
  FROM film f

Q3b:  (Unchanged from Q2b)
  GENERATE HTML [a.name, a.birth]!
  FROM film f, actor a, cast c
  WHERE f.id=c.film and c.actor=a.id
  (AND f.type='drama' AND f.title='AA')
    ; dynamically added condition
```

Fig. 6. Q3: Rewriting by Pruning

In Decomposition 3, we apply *pruning* to Q2a to produce Q3a; Q3b is the
same as Q2b (Fig. 6). The relations cast and actor in Q2a are pruned because
these relations neither supply outputs nor are they used in the selection condition
of Q2a. This pruning is allowed only if the inclusion dependency π_{film} (cast $\bowtie$
actor) $\supset \pi_{id}$ film holds.

Decomposition 4: Variable substitution

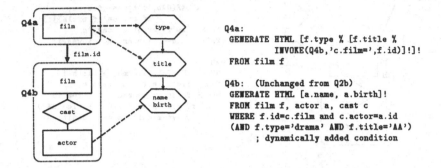

Q4a:
```
GENERATE HTML [f.type % [f.title %
                INVOKE(Q4b,'c.film=',f.id)]!]!
FROM film f

Q4b:  (Unchanged from Q2b)
GENERATE HTML [a.name, a.birth]!
FROM film f, actor a, cast c
WHERE f.id=c.film and c.actor=a.id
(AND f.type='drama' AND f.title='AA')
    ; dynamically added condition
```

Fig. 7. Q4: Rewriting by Variable Substitution

In Decomposition 4, the argument attributes f.type and f.title in Q3a are replaced with f.id in Q4a (Fig. 7). Also, the string concatenated to the value is changed to 'c.film='. The attributes are changed by assuming the functional dependency title→id. Then, based on the identity f.id≡c.film in Q4b, the condition string is replaced. The resulting Q4a is identical to Q1a.

Decomposition 5: Prune film in Q4b

Finally, by pruning film in Q4b, we obtain a query identical to Q1b. This pruning is based on the inclusion dependency π_{id} film $\supset$ π_{film} cast.

4.2 Decomposing a Cyclic Query

Certain classes of queries can not be simplified after duplication. For example, Q0' is a variation of Q0 with an additional condition (f.year-a.birth<13) that limits the resulting Web document to contain only films featuring at least one child actor of age twelve or less.

Q0' is an example of a cyclic query, as its QID contains a loop (Fig. 8). This query can be decomposed into two subqueries by duplication as was done with Q2. Further refinement of the query by pruning is not possible because the cycle prevents the precondition for the rewriting rule to hold. Although the duplicated version could not be further refined by pruning, it can still save disk space over Q0' while providing up-to-date information on the leaf pages.

5 Network Topology and Recursive Navigation

Another benefit of dynamic query invocation is analogous to that of procedures or functions in programming language: recursion. By invoking a query from

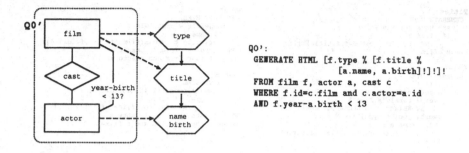

Fig. 8. Q0': Cyclic Query

itself, either directly or indirectly, we can facilitate recursive navigation on Web document browsing.

Suppose the query `Titles` in Fig. 9 is executed. A list of film titles appears on the screen. When a title is selected, `Film` is invoked with the film's id as an argument. In this way, the network of queries depicted in Fig. 9 is invoked when a button is selected on a browser's display. Unrestricted navigation can be done without calculating the transitive closure of the entire structure. Only the relevant nodes are materialized on demand.

6 Implementation

6.1 HTML Invocation Mechanism

The current implementation of the HTML version of the TFE processor allows an `invoke` function to appear as the right-hand side operand of a depth connector. Although general semantics explains what should be done for invocation, an actual implementation has many factors to be decided. An invocation may be designed as either eager or lazy, for example. An eager invocation means that all possible invocations are executed when the invoking query is evaluated, whereas lazy invocation means that the invoked query is executed only when it is referenced. For example, when a user selects a button labeled "Casablanca" on a movie titles page, under lazy invocation an associated query could be invoked with "Casablanca" as an argument. The eager invocation will execute the same query for all of the movie titles before a user makes a selection. Both implementations appear the same to the user.

The current implementation generates HTML code based on a lazy invocation (incremental evaluation) scheme. Therefore, the anchor page (generated by the invoking query) contains anchor points that consists of a HREF to a CGI script with appropriate arguments to be passed. Fig. 10 shows the excerpts from the static and dynamic hyper-link code on the second-level pages of the movie information system as generated by Q0 (static) and Q1a (dynamic), respectively.

It is important to note that the CGI script called `tfe.cgi` is generic to queries. Unlike the common practice of database-Web gateways, where the CGI

```
Titles:                                    Actor:
  GENERATE HTML                              GENERATE HTML
  [verb(November Movies) !                   [imagefile(a.pict,'GIF/'),
    [f.title %                                (a.name !
       INVOKE(film, 'title=',f.title)]!]!       [f.title % INVOKE(film,'f.id=',f.id)]!)]!
  FROM  film f                               FROM actor a, film f, cast c
                                             WHERE f.id=c.film and c.actor=a.id
Film:
  GENERATE HTML                            Theater:
  [f.title !                                 GENERATE HTML
     {imagefile(f.pict,'GIF/'),              [t.name ! imagefile(t.map,'GIF/') !
      {(verb(Stars),[a.name %                  [f.type, [f.title %
       INVOKE(actor,'a.name=',a.name)]!) !        INVOKE(film,'f.id=',f.id)]!]! !]!
      (verb(Type),f.type) !                  FROM theater t, film f, show s
      (verb(Theaters) %                       WHERE s.theater=t.id and s.film=f.id
       INVOKE(theaters,'f.title=',f.title)
     }} !
   }!
  FROM   film f, actor a, cast c
  WHERE f.id=c.film and c.actor=a.id
```

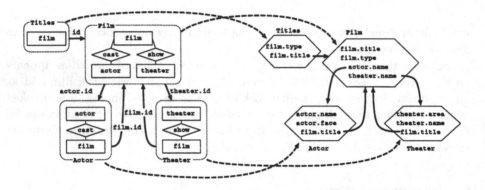

Fig. 9. Recursive Movie Guide

script is hand-crafted for each query, users do not have to write the CGI script themselves. The generic CGI script takes its arguments to form a SQL+TFE query by simple string concatenations and sends it to the query processor to obtain the resulting presentation in HTML.

7 Concluding Remarks

We introduced a new primitive of TFE that allows the invocation of another query. Combined with incremental evaluation of invoked queries, it can be used to reduce the space required to hold complex Web documents, reduce the cost to keep Web documents up-to-date and enable recursive navigation. A new diagramming method called *Database Presentation Diagram* was also introduced to visualize a set of queries and the Web presentation they produce. Finally, a set of query rewriting rules is provided to show the equivalence of the original query and its decompositions.

By integrating dynamic HTML-generation semantics into SQL, the resulting software provides the application system's developers with greater opportunity

Static Links (Q0)

```
<TR><TD>1996</TD><TD><A HREF="Q0_123.html">Dear God</TD></TR>
<TR><TD>      </TD><TD><A HREF="Q0_124.html">The First Wives Club</TD></TR>
<TR><TD>      </TD><TD><A HREF="Q0_125.html">Nutty Professor</TD></TR>
<TR><TD>      </TD><TD><A HREF="Q0_126.html">Tin Cup</TD></TR>
```

Dynamic Links (Q1a)

```
<TR><TD>1996</TD><TD><A HREF="tfe.cgi?Q1b+c.film=+f01234">Dear God</TD></TR>
<TR><TD>      </TD><TD><A HREF="tfe.cgi?Q1b+c.film=+f02432">The First Wives Club</TD></TR>
<TR><TD>      </TD><TD><A HREF="tfe.cgi?Q1b+c.film=+f03398">Nutty Professor</TD></TR>
<TR><TD>      </TD><TD><A HREF="tfe.cgi?Q1b+c.film=+f05432">Tin Cup</TD></TR>
```

Fig. 10. Hyper-links Generated by Static and Dynamic Linking

to design a database/Web application meeting a particular performance and functionality requirement while retaining simplicity of query description.

Our software adding TFE features to an SQL database system supports target media other than HTML. Our future research plans include further development of dynamic query invocation in various target media. Although the merits of dynamic query invocation are most notable when combined with incremental evaluation triggered by a browsing action on a Web system, other applications suggest themselves. For example, a SQL+TFE query generating O2C code could query a relational database and create objects in an O2 object-oriented database.

We are also enhancing our WYSISYG tool to prepare a SQL+TFE query so that it can deal with a set of cooperative queries. It will suggest the user with possible decompositions that yield better performance.

Acknowledgement

The authors are grateful to Calton Pu, David Maier and Karen Ward of OGI, and to the anonymous referees for their helpful comments and suggestions.

References

1. http://www.allaire.com/
2. C. Lang, J. Chow, *Database Publishing on the Web and Intranets*, Coriolis Group Books (1996).
3. P-C. Kim, http://grigg.chungnam.ac.kr/projects/UniWeb/documents/www_dbms.html
4. http://web.ce.utk.edu/DistanceLearningResources/databases.htm
5. T. Seto, T. Nagafuji, M. Toyama, Generating HTML Sources with TFE Enhanced SQL, in *Proc. ACM Symp. on Applied Computing (SAC '97)*, ACM (1997), 96-105.
6. M. Toyama, Three Dimensional Generalization of Target List for Simple Database Publishing and Browsing, in *Research and Practical Issues in Database (Proc. 3rd Australian Database Conference)*, World Scientific Pub. Co. (1992), 139-153.
7. G. Hulin, On Restructuring Nested Relations in Partitioned Normal Form, in *Proc. 16th VLDB Conf.*, (1990), 626-637.
8. G. Jaeshke, H. J. Schek, Remarks on the Algebra of Non First Normal Form Relations, In *Proc. PODS '82*, ACM (1982), 124-138.

Workflow and Scientific Databases

Mining Process Models from Workflow Logs

Rakesh Agrawal[1] and Dimitrios Gunopulos[2] and Frank Leymann[3]

[1] IBM Almaden Research Center, 650 Harry Rd., San Jose, CA 95120, USA,
ragrawal@almaden.ibm.com
[2] IBM Almaden Research Center, 650 Harry Rd., San Jose, CA 95120, USA,
gunopulo@almaden.ibm.com
[3] IBM German Software Development Lab, Hanns-Klemm-Str 45, D-71034
Böblingen, Germany, ley@sdfvm1.ibm.com

Abstract. Modern enterprises increasingly use the workflow paradigm
to prescribe how business processes should be performed. Processes are
typically modeled as annotated activity graphs. We present an approach
for a system that constructs process models from logs of past, unstructured executions of the given process. The graph so produced conforms
to the dependencies and past executions present in the log. By providing
models that capture the previous executions of the process, this technique
allows easier introduction of a workflow system and evaluation and evolution of existing process models. We also present results from applying
the algorithm to synthetic data sets as well as process logs obtained from
an IBM Flowmark installation.

1 Introduction

Organizations typically prescribe how business processes have to be performed,
particularly when activities are complex and involve many people. A *business
process* specifies the way in which the resources of an enterprise are used. The
performance of an enterprise depends on the quality and the accuracy of the
business process. Thus techniques to manage and support business processes are
an active research area. [RW92] [DS93] [GHS95] [LA92] [MAGK95].

In particular, a significant amount of research has been done in the area of
modeling and supporting the execution of business processes. The model generally used is the *workflow* model [Hol94]. Workflow systems assume that a process
can be divided in small, unitary actions, called *activities*. To perform the process,
one must perform the set (or perhaps a subset) of the activities that comprise
it. In addition, there may be *dependencies* between different activities.

The main approach used in workflow systems is to model the process as a
directed graph. The graph vertices represent individual activities and the edges
represent dependencies between them. In other words, if activity A has to be
executed before activity B, an edge appears in the graph from A to B. In practice,
certain executions of the process may include a given activity and others may
not. Each edge $A \to B$ is, therefore, annotated with a Boolean function that
determines whether the control flows from A to B.

Current workflow systems assume that a model of the process is available and
the main task of the system is to insure that all the activities are performed in

the right order and the process terminates successfully [GR97] [LA92]. The user is required to provide the process model. Constructing the desired process model from an unstructured model of process execution is quite difficult, expensive and in most cases require the use of an expert [CCPP96] [Sch93].

Contribution We present a new approach to address the problem of model construction. We describe an algorithm that, given a log of unstructured executions of a process, generates a graph model of the process. The resulting graph represents the control flow of the business process and satisfies the following desiderata:

- *Completeness*: The graph should preserve all the dependencies between activities that are present in the log. It should also permit all the executions of the process present in the log.
- *Irredundancy*: The graph should not introduce spurious dependencies between activities.
- *Minimality*: To clarify the presentation, the graph should have the minimal number of edges.

The work we present has been done in the context of the IBM workflow product, Flowmark [LA92]. However, the process model we consider is quite general and the algorithms we propose are applicable to other workflow systems. The new capability we are proposing can be applied in several ways. A technique that takes logs of existing process executions and finds a model that captures the process can ease the introduction of a workflow management system. In an enterprise with an installed workflow system, it can help in the evaluation of the workflow system by comparing the synthesized process graphs with purported graphs. It can also allow the evolution of the current process model into future versions of the model by incorporating feedback from successful process executions.

The following schema is being adopted in Flowmark for capturing the logs of existing processes in an enterprise that does not yet have an workflow system in place. First, all the activities in a process are identified. But since the control flow is not yet known, all possible activities are presented to the user for consideration through a graphical interface. The user selects the activities that, according to user's informal model of the business process, have to be executed next. Thus the successful executions of the process are recorded.

Related research The specification of dependencies between events has received much attention [Kle91] [ASE+96]. Our dependency model is a simplification of that proposed in [Kle91], and is consistent with the directed graph process model.

In previous work in process discovery [CW95] [CW96], the finite state machine model has been used to represent the process. Our process model is different from the finite state machine model. Consider a simple process graph: $(\{S, A, B, E\}, \{S \rightarrow A, A \rightarrow E, S \rightarrow B, B \rightarrow E\})$, in which two activities A and B can proceed in parallel starting from an initiating activity S and followed by a terminating activity E. This process graph can generate $SABE$ and $SBAE$

as valid executions. The automaton that accepts these two strings is a quite different structure. In an automaton, the activities (input tokens) are represented by the edges (transitions between states), while in a process graph the edges only represent control conditions and vertices represent activities. An activity appears only once in a process graph as a vertex label, whereas the same token (activity) may appear multiple times in an automaton.

The problem considered in this paper generalizes the problem of mining sequential patterns [AS95] [MTV95], but it is applicable in a more restricted setting. Sequential patterns allow only a total ordering of fully parallel subsets, whereas process graphs are richer structures: they can be used to model any partial ordering of the activities and admit cycles in the general setting. On the other hand, we assume that the activities form only one graph structure, whereas in the sequential patterns problem the goal is to discover all patterns that occur frequently.

Organization of the paper The rest of the paper is organized as follows. In Section 2 we describe the process model used in the paper. In Section 3 we present an algorithm to find a process graph, assuming that the graph is acyclic and that each activity appears exactly once in each execution. The algorithm finds the minimal such graph in one pass over the log. In Section 4 we extend this algorithm to handle the case where some activities may not appear in each execution. In Section 5 we consider the case of general directed graphs admitting cycles. In these sections, we make the assumption that the log contains correct executions of the business process. However, this may not be the case in practice, and we outline a strategy to deal with this problem in Section 6. Section 7 presents implementation results using both synthetic datasets and logs from a Flowmark installation. We conclude with a summary in Section 8.

2 Process model

Business processes consist of separate activities. An activity is an action that is a semantical unit at some level. In addition, each activity can be thought of as a function that modifies the state of the process. Business processes are modeled as graphs with individual activities as nodes.

The edges on the graph represent the potential flow of control from one activity to another[4]. Each edge is associated with a Boolean function (on the state of the process), which determines whether the edge will be followed or not. If a vertex (activity) has more than one outgoing edge, the respective Boolean functions are independent from each other.

Definition 1 (Business process). A business process P is defined as a set of activities $V_P = V_1, \ldots, V_n$, a directed graph $G_P = (V_P, E_P)$, an output function $o_P : V_P \to \mathcal{N}^k$, and $\forall (u, v) \in E_P$ a Boolean function $f_{(u,v)} : \mathcal{N}^k \to \{0, 1\}$.

We will assume that G_P has a single source and a single sink. These are the process' activating and terminating activities. If there are no such activities,

---

[4] For the purposes of this paper, we will not differentiate between control flow and data flow, a distinction made in some systems [GR97] [LA92].

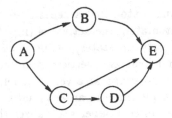

Fig. 1. Example 1

one can add an activating node with edges to the first executed activities in the graph, and a terminating node with edges from the terminating activities of the process. The execution of the business process follows the activity graph: for each activity u that terminates, the output $o(u)$ is computed. Then the functions on the outgoing edges are evaluated on the output. If $f_{(u,v)}(o(u))$ is true, then we test if v can be executed. This test in general is a logical expression involving the activities that point to v in G. When v is ready, the outputs of incoming activities are passed as input to v, and it is inserted into a queue to be executed by the next available agent.

Example 1. Figure 1 gives the graph G_P of a process P. The process consists of five activities $V_P = \{A, B, C, D, E\}$. A is the starting activity and E is the terminating activity. The edges of the graph G_P ($E_P = \{(A, B), (A, C), (B, E),$ $(C, D), (C, E), (D, E)\}$ represent the flow of execution, so that D always follows C, but B and C can happen in parallel. Not shown in Figure 1 are o_P and the Boolean conditions on the edges. Each activity has a set of output parameters that are passed along the edges, $o(A), \ldots, o(E) \in \mathcal{N}^2$. The output parameters are represented as a vector $(o(A)[1], o(A)[2])$. Each edge has a Boolean function on the parameters, such as: $f_{(C,D)} = (o(C)[1] > 0) \wedge (o(C)[2] < o(C)[1]))$. For example an execution of this process will include activity D if $f_{(A,C)}$ and $f_{(C,D)}$ are true.

Each execution of a process is a list of events that record when each activity was started and when it terminated. We can therefore consider the log as a set of separate executions of an unknown underlying process graph.

Definition 2 (Execution log). The log of one execution of a process (or simply execution) is a list of event records (P, A, E, T, O) where P is the name of the process execution, A is the name of the activity, $E \in \{\text{START}, \text{END}\}$ is the type of the event, T is the time the event occured, and $O = o(A)$ is the output of the activity if $E = \text{END}$ and a null vector otherwise.

For notational simplicity, we will not write the process execution name and output in the event records. We assume that the activities are instantaneous and no two activities start at the same time. With this simplification, we can represent an execution as a list of activities. This simplification is justified because if there are two activities in the log that overlap in time, then they must be independent activities. As we will see, the main challenge in inducing a process graph from a log of past executions lies in identifying dependency relationship between activities.

Example 2. Sample executions of the graph in Figure 1 are *ABCE*, *ACDBE*, *ACDE*.

If there exists a dependency between two activities in the real process, then these two activities will appear in the same order in each execution. However only the executions that are recorded in the log are known, and so we define a dependency between two activities with respect to the log. In the model graph, each dependency is represented either as a direct edge or as a path of edges from an activity to another.

Definition 3 (Following). Given a log of executions of the same process, activity B follows activity A if either activity B starts after A terminates in each execution they both appear, or there exists an activity C such that C follows A and B follows C.

Definition 4 (Dependence between activities). Given a log of executions of the same process, if activity B follows A but A does not follow B, then B depends on A. If A follows B and B follows A, or A does not follow B and B does not follow A, then A and B are independent.

Example 3. Consider the following log of executions of some process: $\{ABCE,\ ACDE,\ ADBE\}$. The activity B follows A (because B starts after A in the two executions both of them appear) but A does not follow B, therefore B depends on A. On the other hand, B follows D (because it is recorded after D in the only execution that both are present) and D follows B (because it follows C, which follows B), therefore B and D are independent.

Let us add $ADCE$ to the above log. Now, B and D are no longer independent; rather, B depends on D. It is because B follows D as before, but C and D are now independent, so we do not have D following B via C.

Given a log of executions, we can define the concept of a dependency graph, that is, a graph that represents all the dependencies found in the log.

Definition 5 (Dependency graph). Given a set of activities V and a log of executions L of the same process, a directed graph G_{VL} is a dependency graph if there exists a path from activity u to activity v in G_{VL} if and only if v depends on u.

In general, for a given log, the dependency graph is not unique. In particular, two graphs with the same transitive closure represent the same dependencies.

Every execution of the process recorded in the log may not include all the activities of the process graph. This can happen when not all edges outgoing from an activity are taken (e.g. the execution ACE in Figure 2). An execution R *induces* a subgraph G' of the process graph $G = (V, E)$ in a natural way: $G' = (V', E')$, where $V' = \{v \in V \mid v$ appears in $R\}$ and $E' = \{(v, u) \in E \mid v$ terminates before u starts in $R\}$.

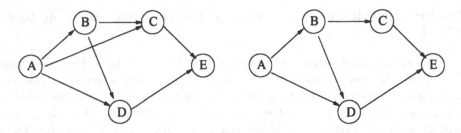

Fig. 2. Example 5

Definition 6 (Consistency of an execution). Given a process model graph $G = (V, E)$ of a process P and an execution R, R is consistent with G if the activities in R are a subset V' of the activities in G, and the induced subgraph $G' = (V', \{(u, v) \in E \mid u, v \in V'\})$ is connected, the first and last activities in R are process' initiating and terminating activities respectively, all nodes in V' can be reached from the initiating activity, and no dependency in the graph is violated by the ordering of the activities in R.

This definition of consistency is equivalent to the following one: R can be a successful execution of P for suitably chosen activity outputs and Boolean edge functions.

Example 4. The execution $ACBE$ is consistent with the graph in Figure 1, but $ADBE$ is not.

Given a log of executions, we want to find a process model graph that preserves all the dependencies present in the log. At the same time, we do not want the graph to introduce spurious dependencies. The graph must also be consistent with all executions in the log. A graph that satisfies these conditions is called a *conformal* graph.

Definition 7 (Conformal graph). A process model graph G is conformal with a log L of executions if all of the following hold:

- *Dependency completeness*: For each dependency in L, there exists a path in G.
- *Irredundancy of dependencies*: There is no path in G between independent activities in L.
- *Execution completeness*: G is consistent with every execution in L.

Example 5. Consider the log $\{ADCE, ABCDE\}$. Both the graphs in Figure 2 are dependency graphs. The first graph is conformal, but the second is not because it does not allow the execution $ADCE$.

Problem statement. We define the following two problems:

Problem 1: Graph mining. Given a log of executions of the same process, find a conformal process graph.

Problem 2: Conditions mining. Given a log of executions of the same process and a corresponding conformal process graph $G = (V, E)$, find the Boolean functions $f_{(u,v)}$, $(u, v) \in E$.

In this paper we will only consider Problem 1. Problem 2 is the subject of ongoing research; some preliminary ideas can be found in [AGL97]. Assume throughout that the process graph has $|V| = n$ vertices, and the log contains m separate executions of the process. Generally, $m \gg n$.

In Sections 3 and 4, we will assume that the process graph is acyclic. This assumption is reasonable in many cases and, in fact, it is also frequently the case in practice [LA92]. We will relax this assumption in Section 5 and allow for cycles in the process graph.

3 Finding directed acyclic graphs

We first consider the special case of finding model graphs for acyclic processes whose executions contain exactly one instance of every activity. For this special case, we can obtain a faster algorithm and prove the following minimality result:

Given a log of executions of the same process, such that each activity appears exactly once in each execution, there exists a unique process model graph that is conformal and minimizes the number of edges.

Lemma 1. *Given a log of executions of the same process, such that each activity appears in each execution exactly once, if B depends on A then B starts after A terminates in every execution in the log.*

Proof. Assume that this is not the case. Then there exists an execution such that B starts before A terminates. From the definition of dependency, there must be a path of followings from A to B. But since all activities are present in each execution, there must be at least one following which does not hold for the execution where B starts before A, a contradiction. □

Lemma 2. *Let G and G′ be graphs with the same transitive closure. Then both graphs are consistent with the same set of executions if each activity appears exactly once in each execution.*

Proof. Since every activity appears in each execution, the induced subgraph for any execution is the original graph. The two graphs have the same transitive closure, so if there is a path between two activities in one, then there is a path between the same activities in the other. It follows that if a dependency is violated in one graph, then it must be violated in the other one. □

Lemma 3. *Given a log of executions of the same process, where all activities appear in each execution once, and a dependency graph G for this log, G is conformal.*

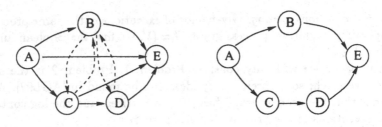

Fig. 3. Example 6

Proof. By definition, the dependency graph preserves all the dependencies present in the log, and none other. For a given execution in the log, the induced subgraph is again the graph G because all activities are present. Further, no dependency is violated because if one was, it would not be in the dependency graph. It follows that G is conformal. □

We can now give an algorithm that finds the minimal conformal graph.

Algorithm 1 (Special DAG). Given a log L of m executions of a process, find the minimal conformal graph G, assuming there are no cycles in the graph and each activity appears in each execution of the process.

1. Start with the graph $G = (V, E)$, with V being the set of activities of the process and $E = \emptyset$. (V is instantiated as the log is scanned in the next step.)
2. For each process execution in L, and for each pair of activities u, v such that u terminates before v starts, add the edge (u, v) to E.
3. Remove from E the edges that appear in both directions.
4. Compute the transitive reduction[5] of G.
5. Return (V, E).

Theorem 1. *Given a log of m executions of a given process having n activities, Algorithm 1 computes the minimal conformal graph in $O(n^2 m)$ time.*

Proof. First we show that after step 3, G is a dependency graph. From Lemma 1 we know that the graph after step 2 at least contains an edge corresponding to every dependency. Since the edges we remove in step 3 form cycles of length 2, where there are activities u and v such that u follows v and v follows u, such edges cannot be dependencies.

After step 4, G is the minimal graph with the same transitive closure and, using Lemma 2, the minimal dependency graph.

Lemma 3 shows that this graph is also conformal and, since a conformal graph has to be a dependency graph, it is the minimal conformal graph.

Since $m \gg n$, the second step clearly dominates the running time. The running time of step 4 is $O(|V||E|) = O(n^3)$ [AGU72]. □

---

[5] The transitive reduction of a directed graph G is the smallest subgraph of G that has the same closure as G [AGU72]. A DAG has a unique transitive reduction.

Example 6. Consider the log {*ABCDE*, *ACDBE*, *ACBDE*}. After step 3 of the algorithm, we obtain the first graph of Figure 3 (the dashed edges are the edges that are removed at step 3), from which the next underlying process model graph is obtained with the transitive reduction (step 4).

4 The complete algorithm

We now consider the general case where every execution of an acyclic process does not necessarily include all the activities. The problem is that all dependency graphs are no longer conformal graphs: it is possible to have a dependency graph that does not allow some execution present in the log (Example 5).

The algorithm we give that solves this problem is a modification of Algorithm 1. It makes two passes over the log and uses a heuristic to minimize the number of the edges.

First it computes a dependency graph. As before, we identify those activities which ought to be treated as independent because they appear in reverse order in two separate executions. In addition, to guard against spurious dependencies, we also identify those activity pairs *A,B* that have a path of followings from *A* to *B* as well as from *B* to *A*, and hence are independent. To find such independent activities we find the strongly connected components in the graph of followings. For two activities in the same strongly connected component, there exist paths of followings from the one to the other; consequently, edges between activities in the same strongly connected component are removed.

We must also ensure that the dependency graph is such that it allows all executions present in the log. Having formed a dependency graph as above, we remove all edges that are not required for the execution of the activities in the log. An edge can be removed only if all the executions are consistent with the remaining graph. To derive a fast algorithm, we use the following alternative: for each execution, we identify a minimal set of edges that are required to keep the graph consistent with the execution, and include them in the final graph. Note that we can no longer guarantee that we have obtained a minimal conformal graph. We can now state our algorithm.

Algorithm 2 (General DAG). Given a log *L* of *m* executions of a process, find the dependency graph *G*, assuming there are no cycles in the process graph.

1. Start with the graph $G = (V, E)$, with V being the set of activities of the process and $E = \emptyset$. (V is instantiated as the log is scanned in the next step.)
2. For each process execution in *L*, and for each pair of activities u, v such that u terminates before v starts, add the edge (u, v) to E.
3. Remove from E the edges that appear in both directions.
4. For each strongly connected component of *G*, remove from *E* all edges between vertices in the same strongly connected component.
5. For each process execution in *L*:
   (a) Find the induced subgraph of *G*.
   (b) Compute the transitive reduction of the subgraph.

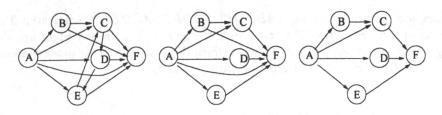

Fig. 4. Example 7

(c) Mark those edges in E that are present in the transitive reduction.

6. Remove the unmarked edges in E.
7. Return (V, E).

Theorem 2. *Given a log of m executions of a given process having n activities, Algorithm 2 computes a conformal graph in $O(mn^3)$ time.*

Proof. After step 3, we are left with a directed graph where each edge path represents a following in L. Step 4 finds cycles in this graph and the set of vertices in each cycle represent independent activities by definition. We thus have a dependency graph for L after step 4. This graph maintains execution completeness as step 2 created a graph that at least allows every execution in L and steps 3-4 do not exclude any of them. Steps 5-6 retain only those edges from this graph that are necessary for at least one execution in L.

The running time is dominated by step 5 ($m \gg n$), whose asymptotic time complexity is $O(mn^3)$. □

Example 7. Consider the log $\{ABCF, ACDF, ADEF, AECF\}$. After step 2 of Algorithm 2, the graph G is the first graph in Figure 4. Step 3 does not find any cycle of length 2. There is one strongly connected component, consisting of vertices C, D, E. After step 4, G is the second graph in Figure 4. Some of the edges are removed in step 6, resulting in the last graph in Figure 4.

5 Finding general directed graphs

If the process model graph can have cycles, the previous algorithms break down. The main problem is that we are going to remove legitimate cycles along with cycles created because two activities are independent and have appeared in different order in different executions. An additional problem is that in the case of a directed graph with cycles the transitive reduction operation does not have a unique solution.

A modification of our original approach works however. The main idea is to treat different appearances of the same activity in an execution as two distinct activities.

A cycle in the graph will result in multiple appearances of the same activity in a single process execution. We use labeling to artificially differentiate the different appearances: for example the first appearance of activity A is labeled

A_1, the second A_2, and so on. Then Algorithm 2 is used on the new execution log.

The graph so computed contains, for each activity, an equivalent set of vertices that correspond to this activity. In fact, the size of the set is equal to the maximum number that the given activity is present in an execution log.

The final step is to merge the vertices of each equivalent set into one vertex. In doing so, we put an edge in the new graph if there exists an edge between two vertices of different equivalent sets of the original graph. The algorithm is given in detail in [AGL97].

6 Noise

A problem we have to consider is noise in the log. This problem can arise because erroneous activities were inserted in the log, or some activities that were executed were not logged, or some activities were reported in out of order time sequence.

We make a slight modification of Algorithm 2 to deal with these kinds of noise. The main change is in step 2 where we add a counter for each edge in E to register how many times this edge appears. Then, we remove all edges with a count below a given threshold T. The rationale is that errors in the logging of activities will happen infrequently. On the other hand, if two activities are independent, then their order of execution is unlikely to be the same in all executions.

One problem here is determining a good value for T. A few extra erroneous executions may change the graph substantially, as the following example illustrates.

Example 8. Assume that the process graph is a chain with vertices A, B, C, D, E. Then there is only one correct execution, namely $ABCDE$. Assume that the log contains $m - k$ correct executions, and k incorrect executions of the form $ADCBE$. If the value of T is set lower than k, then Algorithm 2 will conclude that activities B, C, and D are independent.

Let us assume that activities that must happen in sequence are reported out of sequence with an error rate of ϵ. We assume that $\epsilon < 1/2$. Then, given m executions, the expected number of out of order sequences for a given pair of activities is ϵm. Clearly T must be larger than ϵm. The probability that there are at least T errors, assuming they happen at random, is [CLR90]:

$$P[\text{ more than } T \text{ errors in } m \text{ executions}] = \sum_{i=1}^{T} \binom{m}{i} \epsilon^i (1 - \epsilon)^{n-i} \leq \binom{m}{T} \epsilon^T$$

The use of T implies that if two independent activities have been executed in a given order at least $m - T$ times, a dependency between them will be added. We assume that activities that are independent in the process graph are executed in random order. Then the probability that they were executed in the same order in at least $m - T$ executions is

$$P[\text{ more than } m - T \text{ executions in same order}] \leq \binom{m}{m - T} (1/2)^{(m-T)}$$

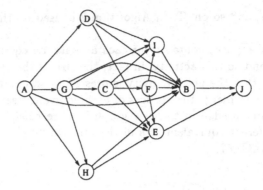

Fig. 5. A synthetic process model graph (Graph10) with 10 activities. Typical executions are *ADBEJ, AGHEJ, ADGHBEJ, AGCFIBEJ.*

Then with probability $\delta \geq 1 - \max\left(\binom{m}{T}\epsilon^T, \binom{m}{m-T}(1/2)^{(m-T)}\right)$, Algorithm 2 finds the correct dependency.

Note that, if T increases, the probability of wrongly reporting an edge decreases, but the probability of adding an edge increases. If ϵ is approximately known, then we can set $\binom{m}{T}\epsilon^T = \binom{m}{m-T}(1/2)^{(m-T)}$, and from there we get $\epsilon^T = (1/2)^{(m-T)}$, and we can obtain the value of T that minimizes the probability that an error occurs.

7 Implementation results

In this section, we present results of applying our algorithm to synthetic datasets as well as logs obtained from a Flowmark installation. Both the synthetic data and the Flowmark logs are lists of event records consisting of the process name, the activity name, the event type, and the timestamp. The experiments were run on a RS/6000 250 workstation.

7.1 Synthetic datasets

To generate a synthetic dataset, we start with a random directed acyclic graph, and using this as a process model graph, log a set of process executions. The order of the activity executions follows the graph dependencies. The START activity is executed first and then all the activities that can be reached directly with one edge are inserted in a list. The next activity to be executed is selected from this list in random order. Once an activity A is logged, it is removed from the list, along with any activity B in the list such that there exists a (B, A) dependency. At the same time A's descendents are added to the list. When the END activity is selected, the process terminates. In this way, not all activities are present in all executions.

Figure 5 gives an example of a random graph of 10 activities (referred to as Graph10) that was used in the experiments. The same graph was generated by Algorithm 2, with 100 random executions consistent with Graph10.

Table 1 summarizes the execution times of the algorithm for graphs of varying number of vertices and with logs having varying number of executions. The physical size of the log was roughly proportional to the number of recorded executions (all executions are not of equal length). For 10,000 executions, the size of the log was 46MB, 62MB, 85MB and 107MB for graphs with 10, 25, 50 and 100 vertices respectively.

Number of	Number of vertices			
executions	10	25	50	100
100	4.6	6.5	9.9	15.9
1000	46.6	64.6	100.4	153.2
10000	393.3	570.6	879.7	1385.1

Table 1. Execution times in seconds (synthetic datasets)

For practical graph sizes, the number of executions in the input is the dominant factor in determining the running time of the algorithm. Table 1 shows that the algorithm is fast and scales linearly with the size of the input for a given graph size. It also scales well with the size of the graph in the range size that we ran experiments.

Number of vertices		10	25	50	100
Edges Present		24	224	1058	4569
Edges found	100	24	172	791	1638
with	1000	24	224	1053	3712
executions	10000	24	224	1076	4301

Table 2. Number of edges in synthesized and original graphs (synthetic datasets)

Table 2 presents the size of the graphs that our algorithm discovered for each of the experiment reported in Table 1. The graphs our algorithm derived in these experiments were good approximations of the original graphs (checked by programmatically comparing the edge-set of the two graphs). When a graph has a large number of vertices, the log must correspondingly contain a large number of executions to capture the structure of the graph. Therefore, the largest graph was not fully found even with a log of 10000 executions. When the number of vertices was small, the original graphs were recovered even with a small number of executions. In the case of 50 vertices, the algorithm eventually found a supergraph of the original graph. As we noted earlier, in the case when every execution of a process does not contain all the activities, the conformal graph for a given log is not unique. We use heuristics to minimize the number of edges in the graph we find.

7.2 Flowmark datasets

For a sanity check, we also experimented with a set of logs from a Flowmark installation. Currently, Flowmark does not log the input and output parameters to the activities. Hence, we could not learn conditions on the edges. The correctness of the the process model graphs mined was verified with the user. In every case, our algorithm was able to recover the underlying process.

Table 3 summarizes the characteristics of the datasets and the execution times ([AGL97] includes the graphs).

Process Name	Number of vertices	Number of edges	Number of executions	Size of the log	Execution time (seconds)
Upload_and_Notify	7	7	134	792KB	11.5
StressSleep	14	23	160	3685KB	111.7
Pend_Block	6	7	121	505KB	6.3
Local_Swap	12	11	24	463KB	5.7
UWI_Pilot	7	7	134	779KB	11.8

Table 3. Experiments with Flowmark datasets

8 Summary

We presented a novel aproach to expand the utility of current workflow systems. The technique allows the user to use existing execution logs to model a given business process as a graph. Since this modeling technique is compatible with workflow systems, the algorithm's use can facilitate the introduction of such systems.

In modeling the process as a graph, we generalize the problem of mining sequential patterns [AS95] [MTV95]. The algorithm is still practical, however, because it computes a single graph that conforms with all process executions.

The algorithm has been implemented and tested with both real and synthetic data. The implementation uses Flowmark's model and log conventions [LA92]. The results obtained from these experiments validated the scalability and usability of the proposed algorithm.

An important and interesting problem for future work is learning the control conditions. The control conditions can be arbitrary Boolean functions of some global process state. To obtain useful information about these functions, additional information about the changes in the global state of the process must be present in the log. One possible approach, discussed in [AGL97], is to make the simplifying assumption that the control conditions are simple Boolean functions of the output of the activity. We can now use a classifier [WK91] to learn the Boolean fuctions.

References

[AGL97] R. Agrawal, D. Gunopulos, and F. Leymann.   Mining Process Models from Workflow Logs.   Research Report RJ 10100 (91916), IBM Almaden Research Center, San Jose, California (available from http://www.almaden.ibm.com/cs/quest), December 1997.

[AGU72] A. V. Aho, M. R. Garey, and J. D. Ullman. The transitive reduction of a directed graph. *SIAM Journal of Computing*, 1(2), 1972.

[AS95]   Rakesh Agrawal and Ramakrishnan Srikant. Mining Sequential Patterns. In *Proc. of the 11th Int'l Conference on Data Engineering*, Taipei, Taiwan, March 1995.

[ASE+96]   P. Attie, M. Singh, E.A. Emerson, A. Sheth, and M. Rusinkiewicz. Scheduling workflows by enforcing intertask dependencies. *Distributed Systems Engineering Journal*, 3(4):222–238, December 1996.

[CCPP96]   F. Casati, S. Ceri, B. Pernici, and G. Pozzi. Workflow evolution. In *Proceedings of ER '96*, Springer Verlag, Cottbus, Germany, October 1996.

[CLR90]   T. Cormen, C. Leiserson, and R. Rivest. *Introduction to Algorithms*. MIT Press, 1990.

[CW95]   Jonathan E. Cook and Alexander L. Wolf. Automating process discovery through event-data analysis. In *Proc. 17th ICSE*, Seattle, Washington, USA, April 1995.

[CW96]   Jonathan E. Cook and Alexander L. Wolf. Discovering models of software processes from event-based data. Research Report Technical Report CU-CS-819-96, Computer Science Dept., Univ. of Colorado, 1996.

[DS93]   U. Dayal and M.-C. Shan. Issues in operation flow management for long-running acivities. *Data Engineering Bulletin*, 16(2):41–44, 1993.

[GHS95]   D. Georgakopoulos, M. Hornick, and A. Sheth. An overview of workflow management: From process modeling to workflow automation infrastructure. *Distributed and Parallel Databases*, 3(2), 1995.

[GR97]   D. Georgakopoulos and Marek Rusinkiewicz. Workflow management — from business process automation to inter-organizational collaboration. In *VLDB-97 Tutorial*, Athens, Greece, August 1997.

[Hol94]   D. Hollinsworth. Workflow reference model. Technical report, Workflow Management Coalition, TC00-1003, December 1994.

[Kle91]   J. Klein. Advanced rule driven transaction management. In *IEEE COMPCON*, 1991.

[LA92]   F. Leymann and W. Altenhuber. Managing business processes as an information resource. *IBM Systems Journal*, (2), 1992.

[MAGK95]   C. Mohan, G. Alonso, R. Gunthor, and M. Kanath. Exotica: A research perspective on workflow management systems. *Data Engineering*, 18(1), March 1995.

[MTV95]   Heikki Mannila, Hannu Toivonen, and A. Inkeri Verkamo. Discovering frequent episodes in sequences. In *Proc. of the 1st Int'l Conference on Knowledge Discovery in Databases and Data Mining*, Montreal, Canada, August 1995.

[RW92]   B. Reinwald and H. Wedekind. Automation of control and data flow in distributed application systems. In *DEXA*, pages 475–481, 1992.

[Sch93]   A. L. Scherr. A new approach to business processes. *IBM Systems Journal*, 32(1), 1993.

[WK91]   Sholom M. Weiss and Casimir A. Kulikowski. *Computer Systems that Learn: Classification and Prediction Methods from Statistics, Neural Nets, Machine Learning, and Expert Systems*. Morgan Kaufman, 1991.

A Scheme to Specify and Implement Ad-Hoc Recovery in Workflow Systems

Jian Tang[1]* and San-Yih Hwang[2]**

[1] Department of Computer Science, Memorial University of Newfoundland
St.John's, Newfoundland, A1B 3X5 Canada
[2] Department of Information Management, National Sun Yat-Sen University
Kaohsiung, 80424 Taiwan

Abstract. Pre-defining a business process can substantially simplify the process design and the implementation of run time support. However, requiring that all the instances of the business process follow a fixed pattern (even if conditions are allowed) does not offer users sufficient flexibility to make changes to the process structures. These changes may be necessary due to the occurrence of exceptions, or other ad-hoc events. Some exceptions/events may be predictable in advance, and therefore can be incorporated into the process definition. However, not all exception/events can be predicted at the process definition time. When this happens, no corresponding exception-specific provision can be incorporated. The design and implementation of the system support for unpredictable exception/event handling is therefore a more complicated issue. In this paper, we study a special case of changing the structure of a business process in the context of unpredictable exception/event, namely, redirecting the control flow at run time in an ad-hoc manner. This phenomenon is termed ad-hoc recovery. We concentrate on two aspects in supporting ad-hoc recovery: the kind of interface that should be used and the increased functionality that must be built into the workflow database. For the latter, we also suggest implementation strategies to maximize the performance.

1 Introduction

The interests in workflow technologies were originated from office automation in early 80's. However, it was not until recently that people started realizing the important roles the workflow technologies play in increasing the productivity for business organizations. In a business environment, it is common that completing a single job requires the execution of many different activities at geographically separated locations. These activities must be executed in certain orders and some activities can be executed only under certain conditions. In other words, the execution of the activities must be coordinated. A workflow, also called a

* This work was supported in part by the Natural Sciences and Engineering Research Council of Canada, individual operating grant OGP0041916.
** This research was sponsored by MOEA and supported by Institute for Information Industry, R.O.C.

business process, is concerned with the coordination of the activities in a business environment.

In many cases, the execution pattern of a business process can be pre-defined. Pre-defining a business process can substantially simplify the process design and the implementation of run time support. The research in this direction results in several proposals for workflow modeling techniques and implementation schemes. For example, The Workflow Management Coalition [16] proposes a workflow reference model which summarizes the main components the business processes normally require in a business environment as well as user interfaces for run time support. The issue of workflow modeling is also studied in works [4, 5, 8, 10, 11, 13]. In [15, 14], the authors propose tools for generating implementation efficiently. In [1, 9, 18], the authors study issues of enforcing intertask dependencies.

A problem of requiring that all the instances of the business process follow a fixed pattern (even if conditions are allowed) is that it does not offer users sufficient flexibility to make changes to the process structures. These changes may be necessary due to the occurrence of exceptions, or other ad-hoc events. Some exceptions/events are predictable in advance, and therefore can be incorporated into the process definition. One example is the conditional structures discussed in [12, 17], whereby depending upon different conditions, different structures can be selected at run time. However, not all exception/events can be predicted at the process definition time. When this happens, no corresponding exception-specific provision can be incorporated. The design and implementation of the system support for unpredictable exception/event handling is therefore a more complicated issue. Different aspects relating to this issue are investigated by several works recently [3, 2, 6].

There are many types of exceptions in a business process. Some of them are already allowed in the commercial systems, e.g., changes of participants assigned to a task; some of them are difficult to achieve, e.g., arbitrary alterations to the process structures. However, there exist types of exceptions that can be implemented. In this paper, we study a special case of changing the structure of a business process in the context of unpredictable exception/event, namely, redirecting the control flow at run time in an ad-hoc manner[3]. This phenomenon is termed *ad-hoc recovery*. Ad-hoc recovery is unpredictable in nature since at the process definition time it is not known when it will occur, what will be the cause, what kind of information users require to make a decision, and where the control flow will be redirected to. We concentrate on two aspects in supporting ad-hoc recovery: the kind of interface that should be used and the increased functionality that must be built into the workflow database. For the latter, we also suggest implementation strategies to maximize the performance. To the best of our knowledge, no other work has addressed this issue systematically.

---

[3] Note that by just redirecting the control flow at run time may not be sufficient to handle an exception. In addition, further actions may have to be taken, e.g., compensation of completed tasks. The kinds of actions to be performed, however, are orthogonal to our work.

The rest of the paper is organized as follows. In Section 2, we present a workflow model, outline failure recovery and introduce ad-hoc recovery. We then describe an architecture of workflow management system that will be used in the later discussions. In Section 3, we discuss in detail how ad-hoc recovery is supported. We describe the role of the interfaces and use examples to show how they are used, and characterize the ad-hoc recovery in terms of the functionalities of the DBMS. In Section 4, we propose implementation schemes. We conclude the paper by summarizing the main results and pointing out the future research directions.

2 Workflow and Workflow Management Systems (WFMS)

2.1 A workflow model

A workflow is an instance of a business process (or simply, process). This instance will achieve a prescribed goal when it terminates successfully. The execution of a workflow involves a number of tasks, each of which may run in a separate processing engine. A task defines some work to be done, and it may be activated more than once in any particular workflow. Each activation generates a task instance, which makes a transition between two workflow states. In general, at the modeling level we are not concerned with the detailed internal structure of a task, except for certain meta-information. Exactly what kind of meta-information is included in the model is application-dependent. In most cases this includes at least the following: task ids, states (not-activated, active, terminated-success, terminated-failed, etc.), instance ids, roles and agents. Depending upon the requirements by business applications, we may also want to include other information such as the starting/ending time of each task instance, as well as the related input/output values. A task is associated with a number of roles, and different tasks may be associated with the same role. The role is a placeholder for the agents that are responsible for the execution of each task. Agents can be either software or human agents.

Tasks may be executed at different (and usually heterogeneous) sites. The possible control flow in the workflow is modeled in terms of the transition, also called ordering, between the activations of the tasks. Each transition is associated with some conditions. These are predicates on workflow states. A transition may or may not fire in a particular workflow, depending upon the truth value of the attached condition. If a transition does not fire, then the task at the sink end will not be executed. The execution of each task may require input data from its preceding tasks and/or the global workflow. It may produce output data to its succeeding tasks or the users of the entire workflow.

In the following, sometimes it is necessary to refer to a workflow in progress. A workflow in progress can be described in terms of *execution dag*, as exemplified in Figure 1.

Each node in the dag denotes a task instance. Since a task may be invoked more than once, different task instances may result from different invocations

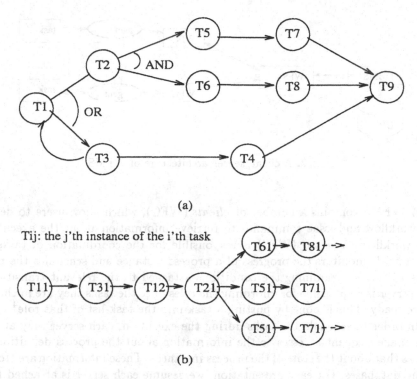

(a)

Tij: the j'th instance of the i'th task

(b)

Fig. 1. (a) The structure of a business process (b) A sample execution dag

of the same task, such as T11, T12 in the diagram. In addition, due to the ad-hoc recovery, the same task instance may appear more than once. For example, after the first execution of T71, the user is not satisfied with the results and requests for the re-execution of T51, as shown in Figure 1(b). The arcs in the dag specify the order that was followed by the task instances. Thus a dag is a condensed version of the execution history for the workflow. Before the start of the workflow, it is empty. Whenever a task instance terminates, it is added to the dag as a leaf node. This expansion continues until the entire workflow terminates. The set of leaf nodes is termed *current stage* of the workflow.

2.2 WFMS architecture

A WFMS is a software tool that enables users to define and instantiate business processes. Defining a business process implies the specification of various components of the model in a particular business environment. During the execution, a WFMS coordinates the execution of the tasks. WFMSs can have different architectures to accommodate different requirements of business applications. However, in many cases a client/server architecture is deemed appropriate. In the following we use a client/server architecture similar to the one suggested in [16]. Figure 2 is an outline of such an architecture.

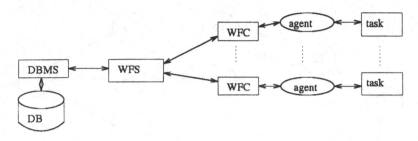

Fig. 2. A client/server architecture of WFMS

A WFMS contains a number of *clients* (WFC), which allow users to define the workflow and issue commands to retrieve information about the execution of a workflow. A server (WFS) is responsible for the coordination of tasks at run time. It monitors the progress of a process instance and schedules the next tasks to run by examining the conditions attached to the relevant transitions. The server is responsible for informing the roles once the tasks they are in charge of are ready. This is done by putting a task into the task-list of that role[4].

In order to schedule the tasks during the execution, each server may at run time make frequent accesses to the information about the process definition as well as that about the state of the process instances. These information are stored in the databases. For easy presentation, we assume each server is attached to a single database.

2.3 Ad hoc recovery

The control flow prescribed in a process definition represents the ideal situations for the business environment. During the real execution, however, based on some unexpected events or whenever he/she feels necessary an agent may initiate an ad-hoc recovery[5] by altering the control 'on the fly'. For example, in a workflow which handles a travel claim, after the applicant fills the travel claim form and passes it to the comptroller's office, the clerk may think that some information is missing or incorrect, and therefore require the claimant redo it. As another example, scientific workflows [19] typically contain tasks which collect experimental data. If after the data being collected the scientists who examine the data find that it is incomplete or not what has been expected, then they may want to repeat the task. This process may repeat for a number of times. These two examples correspond to situations where the control flow must be redirected back. In some cases the control flow may also need to be redirected ahead. For example, in loan application workflow, if the applicant is an important person

---

[4] Multiple servers can be used to enhance reliability/performance. The number of servers used, however, is orthogonal to our discussion.

[5] The term 'recovery' is chosen to mimic the normal meaning of recovery. However, rather than recovery from failure, the term should be understood here as recovery from 'outdated' (prescribed) control flow.

or if the case is urgent, then it is possible that some tasks, such as credit history checking and risk analysis, that are normally executed may be skipped over and the department manager immediately takes control of the case and makes the final decision.

Due to the non-deterministic nature of ad-hoc recovery, it is difficult to predict in advance when it may occur and how. This means that it is in general not feasible to prescribe into the process definition the possible change of control flow resulting from ad-hoc recovery. A direct implication of this is that the workflow must support ad-hoc recoveries only in terms of exception handling. On the other hand, in some situations the user who wishes to initiate an ad-hoc recovery may not have a complete knowledge about the structure of the workflow, or that of every task. Thus it is not always obvious to a user exactly from which tasks the process should be restarted. This implies that simply attaching a traditional procedural-style exception handler in advance may not be sufficient in coping with ad-hoc recoveries[6]. Users may have to play a more active role and/or the system may have to provide users with more assistance. We will discuss this issue in more detail in Section 3.1.

3 Supporting Ad-hoc Recovery

3.1 Interactions between users and WFMS

Users want to initiate an ad-hoc recovery because they are not satisfied with the outcome of the current task instance(s), or because the current situation changes (economically, organizationally, politically, personally, etc.) from that at the time of process definition. In either case, users must tell the WFMS what their restart choices are. There is normally more than one set of tasks to choose from. For example, if task t_1 generates unsatisfactory output, and gets the inputs from t_2 and t_3. The users may want to re-execute t_1 only, or t_2 and t_1, or all three of them. In general, any predecessor from which is originated a data flow path that ends at t_1 is a potential candidate for the restart.

The interactions between users and WFMS can take place in two ways. One is that a user specifies the set of tasks in a manner supported by the WFMS, and then lets the WFMS take over the remaining of the entire ad-hoc recovery. The remaining job includes searching for the correct representations of the tasks specified by the user and then performing the restart procedure. While this method frees users from most of the work, it lacks flexibility. In some workflows, just by referring information at hand a user may be still uncertain what the best choices are for the restart. They may wish to further examine the data associated with the tasks of the initial choices. For example, A user may want to identify first the tasks which are initiated during a high risk period for inputing polluted sample data. Then among the identified tasks s/he may decide to restart those

---

[6] This kind of dynamism is a special case in a more general context often cited as *unstructured workflow* in the literature.

which generate suspicious data, or those which were performed by some agents whom s/he does not trust, or simply those which are randomly chosen.

To allow this kind of flexibility, a multiway hand shake style of interaction is more appropriate. A user specifies a query through a well-defined interface and in terms of the attributes of the tasks. The attributes may include, for example, input/output type or value, date/time, agent name (login name), predecessor level (for example, parents and grandparents respectively have levels 1 and 2), etc. The query can be issued against the WFS database schema that describes all the above information. The WFS database schema, for example, could be similar to the one defined by the WFMC [20]. Upon receiving the response, the user is able to examine the values of some other attributes. This interaction can be repeated a number of times, until the user thinks that s/he can make a decision.

To illustrate, still consider the previous example. Suppose the user intends to examine the tasks initiated between 10am and 1pm in April 1, 1996 and then gets an idea about the agents' names who performed those tasks. Based on the information obtained thereafter s/he will decide the tasks to be chosen for the restart. (For simplicity, we assume each agent is in charge only of one task.) We assume the following operations are contained in the interfaces provided for the user:

- TaskSet gettasks_by_when(TimeDate *start_after*, *start_before*);
- TaskSet gettasks_by_names(StringSet *names*);
- StringSet getnames(TaskSet *tset*);
- restart(TaskSet *tset*);

The user first makes a request through the client program which contains the corresponding invocations (assuming variables have been properly declared):

    names — getnames(gettasks_by_when("10:00,April 1,1996","13:00,April 1,1996"));

Suppose, by examining the results in *names*, the user discovers two names, J. Smith and C. Linda, whom the user thinks might be unreliable. S/he then restarts the workflow from the tasks these two agents are in charge of:

    tasks ← gettasks_by_names({"J. Smith", "C. Linda"});

    restart(*tasks*);

To aid the users in obtaining the knowledge about the kinds of information stored in the system, a browser can be used. More detailed discussion about the structure of a browser is beyond the scope of this paper.

3.2 Additional DBMS functionality

As mentioned before, DBMS is an important component in any workflow system. The information it manages are used by the WFMS to keep track of the ongoing process instances, to schedule the tasks to be executed next, and to perform some other application/system related activities, such as accounting, analysis, simulation, failure recovery, etc.

When the functionality of a WFMS includes the support of ad-hoc recovery, the DBMS must also increase its functionality. Actually, the key role in the ad-hoc recovery is played by the DBMS. This is because redirecting control flow for an ongoing process instance essentially means changing the current state stored in the database for that instance. This is primarily the job of a DBMS. Once the current state has been switched to the other one, the WFMS will do the scheduling as usual, but based on the newly installed state. We assume the DBMS contains a module, ad-hoc recovery manager (AHRM), that is responsible for this job.

Recall that the control flow in ad-hoc recovery may be redirected either ahead or back. If it is redirected ahead, then the current state must be changed to some future states. If it is redirected back, then some previous state must be re-installed as the current state. In the former case, probably there is not much the DBMS can do, except for overwriting immediately the current state with the appropriate future state. This future state must be supplied by the user (since it has not yet been stored anywhere in the database). In the latter case, the DBMS must search on the old states for the one from which the restart can proceed correctly. This is not a simple job, considering the fact that no provision has been previously made to indicate where the desired state might be, and the potentially larger number of old states. Therefore, in the following discussion we discuss the AHRM only in the context of ad-hoc recovery with control flow being redirected back.

3.3 Ad-hoc recovery manager

ad-hoc recovery versus failure recovery In some sense the AHRM is similar to the failure recovery manager (FRM) in a DBMS: both modules restore some previous states. Thus both of them must use log records. However, there are two major differences between the two. Firstly, the FRM can re-install the desired state by using the most recent savepoint (or the start of the uncompleted tasks) as the reference while AHRM does not have such reference. This means that the AHRM must use different mechanism to construct the desired state. Secondly, a failure recovery is a global action which affects all the ongoing process instances. Thus it is usually done in a monolithic action which treats the entire database as a single object. In contrast an ad-hoc recovery can be viewed as a local action which affects individual instances only, namely, those for which the ad-hoc recoveries have been explicitly requested. If more than one process instance has been requested for ad-hoc recovery, then the same procedure has to be repeated for each of them. Thus the overall time overhead may be of a more serious concern than that in failure recovery. We will get to this issue in more detail in Section 4. In the following, we will take a closer look at the structure of failure recovery log, and then illustrate how to modify it to accommodate ad-hoc recovery.

records in failure recovery log We assume three kinds of log records are used in the failure recovery log.

- task data log record: $< T,D, v>$, where T is a 4-tuple $<P,I,t,i>$ where P,I,t,i, respectively, are process id, process instance id, task id, and task instance id, D is a data item pertaining to T (agents' name, starting date/time, etc.), and v a specific value of D.
- task status log record: $< T, u >$ where T has the same form as above, and u is an indicator for the current status of T (e.g, . *not-activated, active*, etc.).
- checkpoint record: CR which contains information to assist in constructing the workflow state at the time this record is created.

Depending upon the requirement of specific workflows, the DBMS may also use other kinds of log records, such as those recording external events, accounting data, simulation results, etc. But the above are the most relevant to our discussion.

Log records are stored in the log following the temporal order of the corresponding operations. When the workflow server fails, all the ongoing process instances are interrupted. Typically, the FRM starts from a log record near the checkpoint and scans the log records forwards to update the database to a state that was generated at the time of failure. It then conducts a backward scan to eliminate the effects of the tasks that are half done. This procedure is very similar to the undo/redo procedures normally used to support the atomicity property of transactions in traditional database systems.

ad-hoc recovery using failure recovery log As alluded to in the previous section, the AHRM may need different log structures for its efficient use. However, to save storage, it is highly desirable for the AHRM to share the same log structure with FRM. This suggests that we should modify the failure recovery log in such a way that the FRM will not be affected while at the same time the functionality of AHRM is supported.

Suppose a user decides to restart the workflow execution from the set of tasks $R = \{r_1, \cdots, r_m\}$. Similar to the operations of the FRM, the AHRM needs to scan the log queue backwards to regenerate the workflow state immediately before the tasks in R are initiated. The problem is: what actions must be taken for each log record during the backward scanning and at which point this scanning should stop.

For a convenient abuse of the symbols, we use r_i to denote also the most recent task instance of r_i at the time when the ad-hoc recovery is initiated. Clearly each r_i is an ancestor of some tasks at the current stage in the execution dag. Let $S = \{s_1, \cdots, s_n\}$ be the set of the descendants of some task instance in R which belong to the current stage. Thus any task at the current stage outside S will not be affected by the ad-hoc recovery. Let $path(r_i, s_j)$ be a path from r_i to s_j in the execution dag. Any task in the path may be repeated after the recovery. On the other hand, if a task is not in the above kind of path for any $r_i \in R$ and $s_j \in S$, then it will not be repeated for sure during the recovery process. In other words, during the backward scanning, for each log record corresponding to a task instance which is not a descendant of any task in R, no action will be taken. For those records which correspond to the descendants of some tasks in

R, all of the values stored in the database for those tasks must be undone. This is necessary since the database state we are trying to reconstruct was originally generated before those tasks were executed. As this backward scanning proceeds, eventually the desired database state will be reconstructed. This is when we have exhausted all the *active* log records for the tasks in R. A log record for a task is active if it is generated after the task is initiated. Not all log records are active. For example, at the beginning of a workflow execution, we may set the status of all the tasks as 'not-activated'. Any log record describing this operation on a task is not active. Clearly, operations described by a non-active log record should not be undone in the backward scan.

We are still left with the problem of how we know if we have exhausted all the active log records for any task in the backward scanning. A straightforward yet inefficient approach is to continue scanning backwards until either the head of the log queue is rearched or a non-active log record is encountered for the task. A better approach is to include a flag in each record which indicates the first record to be generated for a task instance after it is initiated. However, to deal with this flag properly, we need to consider the fact that in ad-hoc recovery some task instances will be initiated multiple times, as illustrated below.

Suppose the desired state has been reconstructed for a process instance. The AHRM will let the WFS rerun that process instance starting from that state, namely the tasks to be executed next are those in R. Note that at this time the backward scanning has stopped at a position somewhere between the beginning and the end points of the log queue. On the rerun, new log records will be generated. A problem is where these log records should be placed. One option is to substitute them for the records for the old run. A problem with this approach is that in some workflows, users may wish to keep the old information for future analysis. Thus completely eliminating the obsolete log records may be unacceptable. Therefore, we adopt the following alternative. The log records for the old run are kept intact in the log, and those generated in the rerun will be appended to the log queue. A question is: when we specify the task instances for the log records for the rerun, should we use a new id, or an identical one to the old run? We adopt the latter. The rationale is that a rerun is in essence aimed at 'repairing' the old run. Thus the rerun of the task instance should (logically) substitute for, not co-exist with, the old one, and therefore is entitled to claim the id of its predecessor. Furthermore, this strategy also makes the query for historical data simple, since different versions of the execution of the same task instance have been explicitly clustered together through the identical task instance id.

As a consequence of the strategy adopted above, the information about a single task instance may be recorded multiple times in the log, i.e., once for the most recent run, and zero or more times for the previous run(s). Those for the more recent run are stored closer toward the end of the log queue. For efficiency as well as correctness reasons we require that the backward scanning procedure stop scanning once it has exhausted the log records for some tasks in R in the most recent run. Thus log records for different runs of the same task instance must be identifiable. This goal is attained by a technique suggested in Section 4.1.

Another issue is that if the user opts not to repeat an actual task in the rerun, or if the task itself is not repeatable, then no new log records will be generated for the task. Instead, the AHRM must simulate the execution of that task by referring to the information stored in the old log records, and restore the necessary attribute values for that task into the database. During this simulation, the old log records should be copied to the new location corresponding to the rerun.

4 Algorithm

4.1 The structure of log records

We adopt a traditional mechanism to identify individual log record, i.e., each log record contains a *log sequence number* (LSN) field. It starts from zero, and incremented by one for the next log record generated. We assume that given an LSN for any record, the AHRM can determine the physical location (usually a disk block address) of that record in a constant amount of time. As illustrated in the previous section, log records for different runs of the same task instances must be identifiable. For this purpose, we include a field, STARTRUN, in each log record. This field takes value of either *true* or *false*. After a task instance has been started, and before it terminates, among all the log records which are generated for it only the one generated first has this field set to *true*. Thus for any task instance, the sequence of all active log records for it can be viewed as a collection of segments. Each segment starts with a record with value of *true* in field STARTRUN, and followed by a sequence of records with value of *false* in this field. We call each of these segments a *run unit* for the corresponding task instance. A diagramatic illustration of run unit is shown in Figure 3[7].

As mentioned before, the AHRM works on per-process instance basis. For each process instance which needs an ad-hoc recovery, the AHRM is concerned only with the log records relating to ('relating to' is interpreted as 'describing a task instance which belongs to') that process instance. Thus most of the log records on the road may be irrelevant. For performance reason, these records should not be scanned. This is done by including a field, NEXTLSN, in each log record. For log record g, if STARTRUN is false, its NEXTLSN field contains the largest LSN of any preceding log record relating to the same task instance; otherwise, it contains the set of the largest LSNs of all the immediate ancestors of the task instance related by g in the execution dag. Thus NEXTLSN fields bind together all the log records relating to a single process instance. In addition, they define a partial order consistent with the execution dag for that process instance.

In the following we use the functional notations to summarize the control information that can be retrieved from each log record g:

---

[7] We assume only one process and use subscripts to identify tasks and task instances. Thus the four tuple notation in Section 3.3 is simplified here.

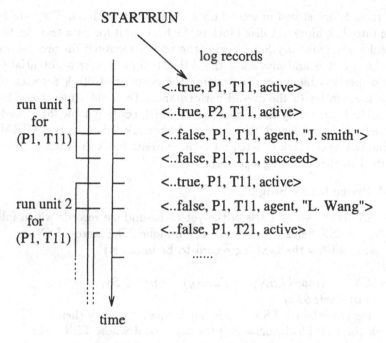

Fig. 3. Run units for task instances

- *Task(g)*: returns an id that uniquely identifies the task instance described by *g*;
- *LSN(g)*: returns the log sequence number of *g*;
- *NextLSN(g)*: returns the values in the NEXTLSN field of *g*;
- *StartRun(g)*: returns *true* iff STARTRUN field of *g* is *true*, which means *g* is the first log record generated in the current run unit for *Task(g)*;

4.2 Algorithm for backward scan

The most work performed in the ad-hoc recovery is to reconstruct the required states for individual process instances. Once this is done, the remaining is straightforward. The workflow server simply resumes the normal execution for those process instances, starting from the newly constructed states. During the execution, log records are appended to the log queue, and at the same time the various fields in the log records are filled with the appropriate values as described above. Thus in the following we will only discuss the algorithm for backward scanning.

Let *P* be the process instance which is requested for ad-hoc recovery. Let *R* be the set of task instances to restart from. Let *S* be the set of all those descendants of the task instances in *R* which belong to the current stage. The AHRM must start the backward scanning from the record that has the largest LSN among all those relating to some task instances in *S*. During the backward scan, for any task instance the first run unit that is scanned must be the most recent one for it.

Log records are stored in secondary storage, such as disks. They are usually grouped into disk blocks. A disk block is the basic unit for data transfer between a disk and a main memory. Since during the ad-hoc recovery, the process instance must be suspended and also since the AHRM iterates over a potentially large number of process instances, minimizing the number of block accesses in each iteration is essential to the overall performance. To avoid unnecessary I/O, we let the AHRM fetch only those disk blocks which contain some log records that are related to P, and ignore those which do not. To this end, the AHRM must determine the next block to fetch once the current block is finished. The detail is described in the following algorithm.

AHRM Procedure - Single

{ *NextLSNs* is the set of LSNs of the yet-to-be-undone records which follow via the NEXTLSN fields the ones already undone. The largest LSN in this set identifies the next log record to be undone.}
1. $Lock(P)$;
2. $NextLSNs \leftarrow \{max\{LSN(g) : Task(g) = t\} : t \in S\}$;
3. $L \leftarrow max(NextLSNs)$;
4. if the log record with LSN $= L$ is not in main memory then
5. fetch the disk block containing the log record whose LSN $= L$;
6. endif;
7. $g \leftarrow$ log record whose LSN is L;
8. undo the operation described by g;
9. $NextLSNs \leftarrow NextLSNs - \{LSN(g)\}$;
10. if $StartRun(g) = false$ then
11. $NextLSNs \leftarrow NextLSNs \cup \{NextLSN(g)\}$;
12. else
13. if $Task(g) \notin R$ then
14.   for each log record q such that $LSN(q) \in NextLSN(g)$ do
15.   if $Task(q)$ is a descendant of some member in R in the execution dag then;
16. $NextLSNs \leftarrow NextLSNs \cup \{LSN(q)\}$;
17.   endif;
18.   endfor;
19. endif;
20. endif;
21. if $NextLSNs = \phi$ then
22. $Unlock(P)$;
23. Exit;
24. endif;
25. go to step 3;

We assume there is a $Lock(P)$ operation which puts a (logical) lock on process instance P. This lock prevents the workflow server from executing any operation relating to P. A matching $Unlock(P)$ operation releases the lock on P. It also signifies the workflow server to resume the normal execution of P. Step 2 initializes *NextLSNs* to the set of LSNs in which each one is the largest for a task instance in S. This step requires the AHRM perform an initial backward scan to obtain these LSNs. In step 12, when $Task(g)$ is not in R, and $NextLSN(g)$ contains the log records of other tasks, it is ensured that a log record in $NextLSN(g)$ is included in $NextLSNs$ only when its pertaining task is a descendant of some member in R. In step 21, an empty $NextLSNs$ signifies that the desired state has been constructed, and hence the end of the backward scan.

The previous algorithm can be modified to handle batched requests, which signifies the case where several process instances are requested for ad-hoc recovery and these requests are made in a time interval much shorter than the duration of each process instance. The modified version is similar to the old one, except that this time the log records to be scanned correspond to a bigger set of tasks, which is the union of all the restart sets by the batched requests.

5 Conclusion

In this paper, we study issues relating to ad-hoc recovery, a special case of workflow applications where users are allowed to make changes to the predefined workflow control structure in an ad-hoc manner. This issue is significant since it provides users with flexibility which are sometimes required to adapt the workflow execution to the exceptions or ad-hoc events. We characterize the ad-hoc recovery by comparing it with failure recovery. We describe the kind of interface that can effectively aid users in making a decision. We discuss the system support in terms of special functionality that must be embedded into the DBMS, and suggest strategies that minimize the overhead.

Our work can be extended in several directions. Firstly, although we propose an interface that enables users to interactively query the execution status of the workflow, this interface is basically a passive tool. Users of the interface may have to know the process flow and the participants in order to determine the set of restart tasks. We are currently investigating the issue of proposing suggestions based on previous processing experiences when exceptions occur. Some machine learning or data mining techniques could be employed in dealing with this problem. Secondly, ad-hoc recoveries may occur much more often than failure recoveries. To speed up the ad-hoc recoveries, it may be benefitial to cluster log records for the same workflow. While this approach may reduce the time for ad-hoc recoveries, it may increase the overhead for both failure recovery and task commit. Detailed evaluations need to be performed. Finally, our algorithm locks the entire workflow while ad-hoc recovery is performed. Thus, even tasks not affected by the roll back cannot proceed during the recovery. Finer lock granularity could be employed to achieve higher availability.

References

1. P.C. Attie, M.P. Singh, A. Sheth, M. Rusinkiewicz: Specifying and Enforcing Intertask Dependencies. Proc. of 19th VLDB Conference, VLDB Endowment. (1993) 134–144.

2. P. Barthelmess, J. Wainer: Workflow Systems: a few Definitions and a few Suggestions. Proc. of ACM Conference on Organizational Computing Systems. (1995) 138–147.
3. R. Blumenthal, G. Nutt: Supporting Unstructured Workflow Activities in the Bramble ICN System. Proc. of ACM Conference on Organizational Computing Systems. (1995) 130–137.
4. P.K. Chrysantis, K. Ramamritham: Synthesis of Extended Transaction Models Using ACTA. ACM Transactions on Database systems. **19** (1994) 450–491.
5. U.Dayal, M. Hsu, R. Ladin: A Transactional Model for Long-Running Activities. Proc. of 17th VLDB Conference, VLDB Endowment. (1991) 113–122.
6. C. Ellis, G. Rozeberg: Dynamic Change Within Workflow Systems. Proc. of ACM Conference on Organizational Computing Systems. (1995) 10–21.
7. A. Elmagarmid: (ed.), Database Transaction Models for Advanced Applications. Morgan-Kaufman Publishers, USA. (1992).
8. A. Elmagarmid, Y. Leu, W. Litwin, M. Rusinkiewicz: A Multidatabase Transaction Model for Interbase. Proc. of the 16th VLDB Conf. (1990).
9. D. Georgakopoulos, M.F. Hornik: Framework for Enforceable Specification of Extented Transaction Models and Transactional Workflows. Intl. Journal of Intelligent and Cooperative Information Systems. (1994).
10. D. Georgakopoulos, M. Hornik, A. Sheth: An Overview of Workflow Management: from Process Modeling to Workflow Automaton Infrastructure. Dist. and Parll. Databases: An International Journal. **3** (1994) 119-153.
11. G. Kappel, P. Lang, S. Rausch-Schott, W. Retschitzegger: Workflow Management Based on Objects, Rules, and Roles. Bulletin of the Technical Committee on Data Engg. **18** (1995) 11–18.
12. N. Krishnakumar, A. Sheth: Managing Heterogeneous Multi-system Tasks to Support Enterprise-wide Operations. Dist. and Parll. Databases: An International Journal. **3** (1995) 1–33.
13. D. McCarthy, S. Sarin: Workflow and Transactions in InConcert. Bulletin of the Technical Committee on Data Engg. **16** (1993). 53–56.
14. M. Singh: Synthesizing Distributed Constrained Events from Transactional Workflow Specifications. Proc. of 12th Intl. Conf. on Data Engg. (1996) 616–623.
15. B. Salzberg, D. Tombroff: DSDT: Durable Scripts Containing Database Transactions. Proc. of 12th Intl. Conf. on Data Engg. (1996) 624–633.
16. Workflow Management Coalition: Workflow Reference Model. (1996).
17. J. Tang, S. Hwang: Coping with Uncertainties in Workflow Applications. Proc. of Intl. Conf. on Information and Knowledge Management. (1996).
18. J. Tang, J. Veijalainen: Enforcing Inter-Task Dependencies in Transactional workflows. Proc of 3rd Intl. Conf. on Cooperative Information Systems. (1995).
19. J. Wainer, M. Weske, G. Vossen, C. Medeiros: Scientific Workflow Systems. Proc. of the NSF Workshop on Workflow and Process Automation in Information Systems. (1996).
20. WorkGroup 1/B: Workflow Management Coalition Interface 1: Process Definition Interchange. The Workflow Management Coalition. (1996).

Exploring Heterogeneous Biological Databases: Tools and Applications *

Anthony S. Kosky, I-Min A. Chen, Victor M. Markowitz, and Ernest Szeto

Bioinformatics Systems Division, Gene Logic Inc.
2001 Center Str, Suite 600, Berkeley, CA 94704
e-mail: [anthony,ichen,vmmarkowitz,szeto]@genelogic.com

Abstract. We present a tool-based strategy for exploring heterogeneous biological databases in the context of the Object-Protocol Model (OPM). Our strategy involves tools for examining the semantics of biological databases; constructing and maintaining OPM views for biological databases; assembling biological databases into an OPM-based multidatabase system, while documenting database schemas and known links between databases; supporting multidatabase queries via uniform OPM interfaces; and assisting scientists in specifying and interpreting multidatabase queries. We describe these tools and discuss some of their scientific applications.

1 Introduction

Exploring data across biological databases entails coping with their distribution, the heterogeneity of their underlying systems, and their semantic heterogeneity. These databases are defined using a variety of data models and notations, such as relational and object-oriented models, and the ASN.1 data exchange notation; they are implemented using different systems, including relational database management systems (DBMSs), and various indexed flat-file systems; they are based on different views of the biological domain; and they contain different and possibly conflicting data.

Strategies for exploring heterogeneous databases range from loose to tight integration of component databases, with distributed or centralized data access [13]. Tight integration of heterogeneous databases entails constructing a *global* schema representing a consistent integrated view of all component databases expressed in a common data model, while loose integration does not require constructing such a global schema.

Constructing a global schema over biological heterogeneous databases is hindered by numerous semantic conflicts between schemas of component databases.

---

* The work presented in this paper was carried out while the authors were affiliated with the Lawrence Berkeley National Laboratory, with support provided by the Office of Health and Environmental Research Program of the Office of Energy Research, U.S. Department of Energy under Contract DE-AC03-76SF00098. This paper has been issued as technical report LBNL-40728.

Often the same concept (e.g., *gene*) is represented in different biological databases using synonyms, alternative terminology, or different data structures. Resolving semantic conflicts among biological databases has been attempted by systems such as IGD [12], but only to a limited extent: these systems detect and resolve only simple schema and data conflicts, such as name and object identification conflicts. A more systematic resolution of such conflicts would require the involvement of numerous groups worldwide,[1] and would be extremely difficult to achieve, if at all possible.

A more feasible approach involves employing multidatabase querying mechanisms in a loosely integrated framework. Such mechanisms support construction of queries over component databases, where a query explicitly refers to the elements of each database involved. Component databases of multidatabase systems can be queried by constructing functions that access the databases in their native format, as done in Kleisli [1], or can be accessed through views in a common data model, as entailed by the strategy we propose. Kleisli is a query system based on the nested relational data model, which is a purely "value-based" model and, as such, does not support any concept of schemas or integrity constraints. This approach makes it relatively simple to add new databases to a multidatabase system, since it is not necessary to convert schemas or construct new views of a database, but does not provide the support or documentation necessary to formulate queries or to interpret their results. Consequently, in order to construct ad hoc multidatabase queries, a programmer must have expert knowledge of each database involved in the query, its semantics and its data model, as well as of CPL, the query language employed by Kleisli.

Providing an efficient, extensible mechanism for evaluating multidatabase queries is not in itself sufficient: in addition it is necessary to provide support for exploring and documenting multiple heterogeneous databases via a uniform model and interface, and to aid non-expert users in formulating meaningful multidatabase queries. Such an approach requires an initial investment of time and effort in developing database views in a common notation and in constructing a directory of information (metadata) needed to assist users in constructing and interpreting multidatabase queries. This initial effort is particularly important for the exploration of biological databases which are not documented in a consistent and comprehensive way [9]: biological database documentation is often incomplete, sometimes hard to access (e.g., hidden in large files), and requires knowledge of the notation of the underlying data management system (e.g., relational, object-oriented, ASN.1 data exchange format).

Our strategy for exploring heterogeneous databases uses the Object-Protocol Model (OPM) [3] as the common data model; takes advantage of a suite of existing OPM tools; and involves developing several additional tools. Each of these tools can be used independently and therefore represents a valuable resource in its own right.

---

[1] According to a recent issue of Nucleic Acids Research (vol 24, no. 1, 1996), there are over 50 important molecular biology databases.

Each database in an OPM-based multidatabase system is associated with a native OPM schema or a retrofitted OPM view. Databases with native OPM schemas are developed using the OPM Database Development tools, that provide facilities for translating OPM schemas into complete database definitions for a variety of commercial DBMSs. Databases developed without the OPM tools can be retrofitted with OPM views using the OPM Retrofitting tools [6].

The OPM Multidatabase tools provide additional facilities for assembling heterogeneous databases into a multidatabase system, together with information on known links between databases; for browsing schemas and metadata for the multidatabase system via Web-based interfaces; and for specifying and evaluating multidatabase queries via uniform OPM query interfaces.

The remainder of this paper is organized as follows. OPM is briefly reviewed in section 2. The construction of OPM views and the structure of the Multidatabase Directory are described in section 3. The multidatabase query system is described in section 4. In section 5 we present the Web interfaces for exploring multidatabase systems. Section 6 presents an application of the OPM Multidatabase tools to a molecular biology multidatabase system. Section 7 contains concluding remarks.

2 The Object Protocol Model

We use the Object Protocol Model (OPM) to provide an abstract and uniform representation of heterogeneous databases. OPM provides extensive schema documentation facilities in the form of descriptions, examples and user-specified properties that can be associated with schema elements. Existing OPM tools provide facilities for developing and accessing databases defined using OPM, for constructing OPM views for existing relational databases and structured files, for representing database schemas using alternative notations, and for querying databases through uniform OPM views. We briefly review below the main features of OPM; details can be found in [3].

OPM is a data model whose object part closely resembles the ODMG standard for object-oriented data models [10]. Objects in OPM are uniquely identified by object identifiers (oids), are qualified by attributes, and are classified into classes. Classes can be organized in subclass-superclass hierarchies and can be classified into *clusters*. In addition to object classes, OPM supports a protocol class construct for modeling scientific experiments. Protocol classes are not discussed in this paper.

Attributes can be *simple* or consist of a *tuple* of simple attributes. An attribute can have a single value, a set of values, or a list of values. If the value class (or domain) of an attribute is a system-provided data type, or a *controlled-value* class of enumerated values or ranges, then the attribute is said to be *primitive*. If an attribute takes values from an object class or a union of object classes, then it is said to be *abstract*.

Figure 1 displays examples of classes involved in the OPM schemas for the Genome Sequence Database (GSDB)[2] and the Genome Database (GDB),[3] representing nucleic acid sequences in GSDB and GDB respectively. For example, attribute confidences of class Sequence is set-valued, while attribute release is single valued; attribute confidences is a tuple attribute consisting of five component attributes, loc_start, loc_end, confidence, multiple_read, and double_stranded; component attribute sp_id of tuple attribute sequence-_pieces of class Sequence is an abstract attribute taking values from class Sequence, while attribute seq_order of the same tuple attribute is a primitive attribute.

OPM supports the specification of *derived attributes* using derivation rules involving arithmetic expressions, aggregate functions (min, max, sum, avg, count), or compositions of attributes and *inverse* attributes.

OPM also supports derived subclasses and derived superclasses. A derived subclass is defined as a subclass of one or more object classes with an optional derivation condition. A derived superclass is defined as a union of two or more object classes.

3   Constructing Biological Multidatabase Systems

Our strategy for exploring heterogeneous biological databases involves (1) constructing OPM views for databases developed with or without OPM; (2) assembling databases within an OPM-based multidatabase system, while documenting the databases and known links between them; and (3) expressing, processing, and interpreting queries over multidatabase systems. In this section we describe the first two stages.

3.1   Constructing OPM Views for Existing Databases

A database designed using OPM can be implemented with a commercial relational DBMS, such as Sybase or Oracle, using the OPM Schema Translator [4]. This tool automatically generates complete definitions for the underlying relational DBMS, including rules and constraints required for maintaining data integrity, while creating a *mapping dictionary* that records the correspondences between the classes and attributes of an OPM schema and the underlying relational tables.

Existing databases implemented as flat files (defined using a parsable notation such as ASN.1) or as relational databases (developed with or without OPM), can be associated with one or more *OPM views* constructed using the OPM Retrofitting tools [6]. The procedure for constructing OPM views for existing databases consists of first automatically generating a *canonical* OPM view from the database definition, where no additional assumptions are made about

---

[2] http://www.ncgr.org/gsdb/
[3] http://gdbwww.gdb.org/gdb/schema.html

the structure of the underlying database, and then iteratively changing or re-fining the OPM view using schema restructuring operations, such as renaming and/or removing classes and attributes, merging and splitting classes, adding or removing subclass relationships, defining derived classes and attributes, and so on. The mapping between OPM constructs and the native database constructs is recorded in a mapping dictionary. Refining an OPM view results in changes to the OPM view definition and corresponding changes in the mapping dictionary, but has no effect on the underlying (relational or flat file) database.

3.2 The Multidatabase Directory

The information core of an OPM-based multidatabase system is a *Multidatabase Directory* which contains metadata on component databases and systems needed by the Multidatabase Query System as well as supporting documentation for exploring and using a multidatabase system. Information in a Multidatabase Directory includes database names, descriptions of the purpose of the databases, information on connections to other related databases in the same multidatabase system, and database schemas or views specified in OPM, as well as information specifically required by the multidatabase query system, discussed in section 4.4. Of particular importance is the information about known links between classes in different databases, including a description of the semantics of the links. From the perspective of a user exploring an OPM based multidatabase system, inter-database links connect classes in distinct databases in the same way that OPM abstract attributes connect classes within a single database.

The (native or retrofitted) OPM schema or view of a database is used as its reference (common) representation in a Multidatabase Directory; in addition, the Directory contains alternative representations for the database schemas using various notations and data models, including the native data model of the database, an Extended Entity-Relationship (EER) model, an abstract, DBMS-independent relational model, and the ASN.1 data exchange notation [11]. A Multidatabase Directory is stored and maintained using structured flat files, with automatically generated HTML versions supporting exploration using Web browsers.

The OPM views of databases in a multidatabase system can be represented using a diagrammatic notation and browsed with a Java based OPM Multidatabase Schema Browser. Figure 1 shows an example of using the OPM Multidatabase Schema Browser for browsing the schemas of GDB and GSDB, where the inter-database links are displayed as abstract OPM attributes and are used for crossing database boundaries (e.g., GSDB_to_GDB_sequence).

4 The Multidatabase Query System

The OPM Multidatabase Query System provides support for retrieving and combining data from multiple heterogeneous databases via queries expressed across the OPM views of the component databases. The main components of the system are shown in figure 2:

504

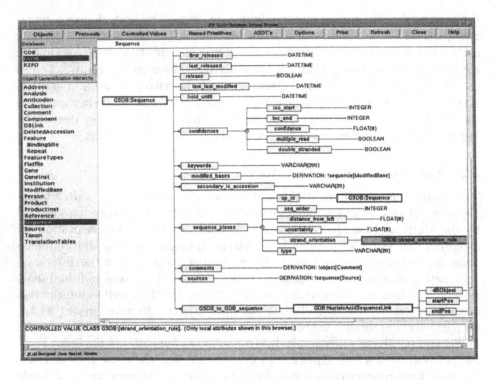

Fig. 1. Browsing Multidatabase Views with the OPM Multidatabase Schema Browser

1. OPM Database Servers provide database specific query translation facilities and a common interface for executing queries for each database involved in the multidatabase system.
2. A central OPM Multidatabase Query Processor interprets OPM multidatabase queries, generates queries for individual databases, performs local data manipulations necessary to combine the data retrieved from individual databases, and provides functionality that is not supported by the underlying DBMSs or file systems.
3. Information on component databases, DBMSs, and inter-database links is recorded in a Multidatabase Directory which is used by the OPM Multidatabase Query Processor in order to translate and plan the execution strategies for queries.
4. Queries can be specified using a Multidatabase Web Query Interface or as textual queries written in the OPM multidatabase query language, OPM*QL.

The Web-based query interfaces do not offer the full expressive power or flexibility of OPM*QL (e.g., for handling aggregates or nested sets), but are considerably easier and more intuitive for non-expert users, are convenient for rapid data exploration, and are sufficiently powerful to express a large class of common queries. OPM*QL provides expert users with the ability to formulate

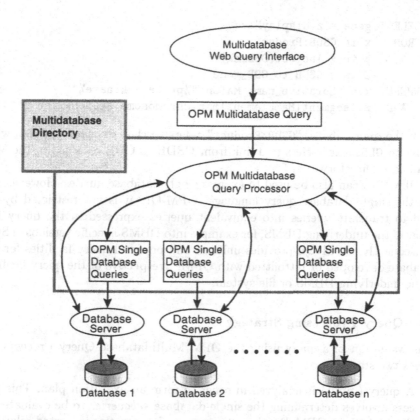

Fig. 2. The Architecture of the OPM Multidatabase Query System

very general queries across multiple heterogeneous databases using a single data model and language. The Multidatabase Web Query Interface will be described in section 5.

4.1 The OPM Multidatabase Query Language

The OPM Multidatabase Query language, OPM*QL, is an object-oriented query language similar to OQL, the ODMG standard for object-oriented query languages [10]. OPM*QL extends the OPM single database query language, OPM-QL [5], with constructs needed for accessing multiple databases and for taking advantage of the additional power offered by the query processing capabilities of the OPM Multidatabase Query Processor. In addition, OPM*QL allows using inter-database links defined in the Multidatabase Directory, in a similar manner to regular abstract attributes. These links hide many of the low-level details involved in formulating multidatabase queries, and simplify the task of finding meaningful connections between objects in distinct databases.

For example, the following OPM*QL query, for finding *protein kinase genes on chromosome 4* is expressed across two databases, GDB and GSDB:

```
SELECT gene = z.displayName
FROM    x in GSDB:Product,
        y in x.!object[DBLink],
        z in y.GSDB_to_GDB_gene
WHERE   x.authorative_name MATCH "%protein kinase%"
  AND   z.!segment[MapElement]map.chromosome.searchAlias = "4";
```

In the query above, "GSDB:Product" refers to class Product of GSDB, while "GSDB_to_GDB_Gene" refers to a link from GSDB to GDB recorded in the Multidatabase Directory.

OPM*QL can also be used to express single database queries. However, unlike the single-database query language, OPM-QL, it is not restricted by the need to translate queries into equivalent queries expressed in the query language of the underlying DBMS, for example into DBMS-specific versions of SQL. Consequently, OPM*QL provides uniform and powerful query facilities for any database developed or retrofitted with OPM, irrespective of the query facilities of the underlying DBMS or file system.

4.2   Query Processing Strategy

The evaluation of a query using the OPM Multidatabase Query Processor involves two stages:

1. A query (input) is analyzed in order to form an execution plan. This process involves determining the single-database *subqueries* to be evaluated by the individual OPM Database Servers, and generating a nested-relational algebra expression that incorporates the single database queries together with those parts of the query that need to be evaluated locally. The nested relational algebra used is similar to that proposed in [2] but with certain modifications to make it better suited to evaluating OPM queries.
2. The nested-relational expression is evaluated, with the embedded single-database OPM queries being passed to the appropriate OPM Database Servers for execution.

Query evaluation follows a "semi-join" approach: remote queries are evaluated in sequence, with the results of each query being used to constrain the next queries. Currently the Multidatabase Query Processor uses the structure of the OPM*QL query in order to determine the order in which subqueries are evaluated. In the future, we plan to develop heuristics for estimating the cost of individual subqueries and the size of their results in determining an optimal evaluation order.

In general, as many of the query conditions as possible are incorporated into the subqueries that are executed remotely. However the evaluation of these subqueries depends both on the underlying DBMS and on the metadata for a particular database. For example, various relational DBMSs support different dialects of SQL, so that the subsets of OPM-QL that can be translated into SQL may differ. Further, for an indexed flat file database, only attributes that have been indexed can be involved in a condition that is used in a subquery. Consequently, each OPM Database Server provides the functions necessary to determine which parts of a subquery must be evaluated locally and which can be passed to a remote database server, and to interpret the results of the remotely executed query.

The individual OPM Database Servers provide results in the format best suited to their underlying DBMS. For example relational DBMSs provide results as flat tables, while object oriented systems can use objects or nested data-structures. Nested data-structures are more efficient in terms of the size of the data-structures that are returned, but interpreting them requires more local computation.

The Multidatabase Query Processor has the ability to compute aggregate and arithmetic functions, as well as general manipulations of nested relational data, and consequently is able to process the same queries over DBMSs with both limited and powerful query facilities.

4.3 The OPM Database and DBMS Servers

An OPM DBMS Server is required for each DBMS or file access system involved in a multidatabase system. An OPM DBMS Server manages all the OPM Database Servers for databases implemented using that DBMS, including creating database servers as they are needed, keeping track of which databases have servers currently in use, and closing down Database Servers that are no longer needed.

The architecture of the Multidatabase System allows new DBMS Servers to be added to or removed from the system dynamically simply by registering the change in the Multidatabase Directory. This approach has a number of advantages, including making it easy to add new DBMSs to a system or update a server to accommodate new versions of a DBMS, and allowing users to tailor the system to their needs by only including servers for DBMSs of interest.

OPM Database Servers handle several tasks, including implementing functions needed to determine what part of an OPM*QL query can be evaluated by the underlying DBMS, and evaluating single database OPM-QL queries issued by the multidatabase query processor.

The OPM Database Servers evaluate queries using the OPM Query Translators [5]. An OPM Query Translator takes queries specified in OPM-QL, and generates equivalent queries expressed in the query language supported by the underlying DBMS or file system. In the case of a relational DBMS, these query translators generate a single SQL query corresponding to the OPM-QL query. For flat file systems such as SRS [7], it may be necessary to generate several queries. The results of single database queries are subsequently structured and returned using OPM specific data structures.

The OPM query translators are driven by an OPM *mapping dictionary* that records the mapping between the elements of an OPM schema or view, such as classes and attributes, and the corresponding elements of the underlying database or file. The content of the mapping dictionary and OPM schema is compiled into a *metadata* file that is dynamically linked into the OPM Database Server for efficiency.

Currently, OPM Database Servers are available for commercial relational DBMSs, such as Sybase and Oracle, and for structured flat-file systems. The relational OPM query translators generate queries in the SQL dialect supported by the underlying DBMS, and employ DBMS-specific C/C++ APIs for database access. Query results are formatted as sets of tuples.

The flat-file OPM Database Servers employ SRS (Sequence Retrieval System), developed at the European Molecular Biology Laboratory (EMBL) [7]. SRS is a system which uses grammars defined in a declarative language to parse and index structured flat files. Query conditions are limited to simple comparisons between indexed attributes and constants, while non-indexed attributes can be retrieved but not used in conditions. Consequently the parts of an OPM*QL query that can be evaluated using SRS are smaller than those that can be evaluated for a relational database, and local processing is needed. Query results from an SRS/flat-file database server are sets of objects which map directly into OPM data-structures.

The interfaces between the OPM Multidatabase Query Processor and the OPM Database Servers are implemented using CORBA based products, which provide a convenient tool for implementing client-server architectures. However CORBA's limitations regarding the data structures that can be passed between applications require extraneous conversions between data structures used in applications and those that can be passed.

4.4 Multidatabase Directory Information for Query Processing

The OPM Multidatabase Directory described in section 3.2 is used to provide the OPM Multidatabase System with information on the DBMSs, databases and inter-database links involved in the system. New DBMSs, databases and inter-database links can be added to a Multidatabase System simply by adding entries to the OPM Multidatabase Directory file, making the system easy to extend and adapt to changing requirements.

For each DBMS, the information required by the Multidatabase System includes the name and location of the OPM DBMS Server, and possibly a description of the DBMS and server.

For each database, the information required by the Multidatabase System includes the name of the database, information necessary for accessing the database (e.g., login name, password and server), and a pointer to the metadata file for the database. The metadata files include schema and mapping file information for the databases.

Inter-database *links* represented in the Multidatabase Directory represent known, meaningful connections between the databases, and are extremely useful in formulating multidatabase queries, while hiding many of the low level details needed for connecting databases. Such links connect classes in (usually) distinct databases. Each link has a name which can be used in OPM multidatabase queries in a similar manner to a regular abstract attribute, except that

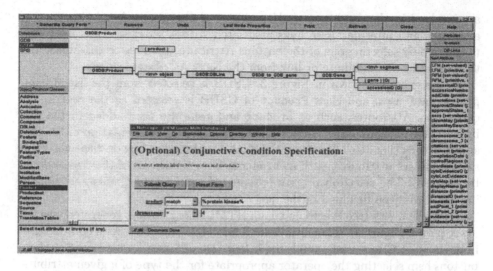

Fig. 3. Query Specification with the OPM Multidatabase Web Query Interface

the domain of the link may be a class in a different database. In addition to
the link name and the class names and database names for the two classes it
connects, the Multidatabase Directory contains the OPM*QL code necessary to
implement a link. This code will often involve several other classes or additional
databases, a number of additional conditions, and possibly some reformatting
and coercions of various values. For documentation and interpretation purposes,
the Multidatabase Directory contains comments and information explaining the
semantics and the significance of links. Examples of such links are given in section 6 .

Links are interpreted in the first stage of query analysis by the OPM Multidatabase Query Processor, when they are simply replaced by the corresponding
OPM*QL code stored in the Multidatabase Directory.

5 The Multidatabase Web Based Query Interfaces

An OPM Multidatabase Web Query interface provides support for constructing
multidatabase queries by selecting databases, classes, and attributes of interest using a graphical user interface, and then dynamically generating HTML
query forms containing the selected attributes, possibly from different classes
and databases. Further query condition specification can be carried out by filling in these forms. Query results are organized in HTML pages with hyperlinks
to related objects and metadata definitions in order to support Web browsing.

In order to specify a query, first a database involved in the multidatabase
system is selected, and the classes of this database are displayed in a Classes list-
box. A query tree is then constructed by first selecting a *root* class in the list-box
and then expanding this tree by recursively selecting classes and attributes that

are involved in the conditions and/or output of the query. Attributes, inverse attributes and inter-database links associated with a selected class, are added to the tree by selecting one of the buttons Attribute, Inverses or DB-Links, and then selecting the attribute or link from the Next Attribute list-box.

In the example shown in Figure 3, GSDB is selected from the list of component databases, and class Product of GSDB is selected as the root of the query tree. Attributes, such as product and gene are then added to the tree by selecting (clicking on) a class in the diagrammatic representation of the tree and then selecting attributes from the Next Attribute list-box on the right-hand side. Primitive attributes, such as product, form the leaves of the tree and can be renamed. The selection process is repeated until all attributes and links of interest have been included in the query tree.

Once the query tree is completed, an HTML query form is generated (see the lower part of Figure 3). This form is used for specifying conditions on attributes in the familiar Query-by-Example mode (e.g., chromosome_number = "4"). Menu buttons help selecting the operator appropriate for the type of a given attribute. For controlled value classes, a list-box displays the set of valid values that can be used in expressing conditions. The query can then be passed to the OPM Multidatabase Query Processor, or the form can be saved as an HTML file that can be customized for subsequent use or inclusion in Web pages.

The two-stage query construction described above leads to the specification of a query in OPM*QL. For example, the query constructed in figure 3, for finding protein kinase genes on chromosome 4, is expressed by the OPM*QL query given in section 4.

The OPM Multidatabase Web Query tool is implemented using a combination of the Java programming language and HTML forms. The tool is schema driven in the sense that the OPM schemas and mapping information for all component databases are loaded once the interface is started. Communication between the Java tools and HTML forms and the Multidatabase Query Processor are implemented using a Common Gateway Interface (CGI) script.

6 An Application

We have employed the OPM Multidatabase tools for constructing several prototype multidatabase systems that involve heterogeneous databases accessed either remotely over the net or via copies located on the same server as the Multidatabase tools. In this section we discuss one of these prototypes, namely a federation of molecular biology databases that includes the Genome Database (GDB), the Genome Sequence Database (GSDB), and GenBank:

GDB is an archival database maintained at Johns Hopkins School of Medicine, in Baltimore [8]. GDB contains information about genomic data, literature references, people and organizations. Genomic data include information on genomic maps (e.g. genes associated with maps), biological functions, and experimental data about maps. The current version, GDB 6, is a native

OPM database: it was designed and implemented using the OPM data model and Database Development tools, and Sybase 11 is used as its underlying DBMS.[4]

GSDB is maintained at the National Center for Genome Resources, in Santa Fe. GSDB contains information mainly about nucleotide sequences and their features, which represent biologically interesting regions on these sequences.[5] GSDB is implemented as a relational database using Sybase 11, and the OPM retrofitting tools have been used to construct an OPM view on top of the relational views provided by GSDB for public access.

GenBank is one of the main international archival genome data repositories, maintained at the National Centre for Biotechnology Information (NCBI). GenBank contains information about nucleotide and protein sequences and supporting bibliographic and biological data.[6] GenBank is implemented as an indexed flat file. The OPM view of GenBank has been built using the OPM flat-file retrofitting tools and is based on the SRS (Sequence Retrieval System) interface to GenBank.

A Multidatabase Directory for this federation has been set up[7] and includes information regarding the component databases and their inter-database links. For example:

Sequences are the main entities recorded in GSDB and GenBank, and are represented by instances of class Sequence in both databases. Sequence data include the actual sequence, sequence length, information on the source (origin) of the sequence, and so on. Sequence information in GDB is represented by objects of class NucleicAcidSequenceLink that contain annotations representing links from primary GDB objects to external sequence databases such as GSDB and GenBank, as well as information regarding the beginning and end points of sequences. Nucleotide sequence references from GDB to GSDB and GenBank are represented by the inter-database links GDB_to_GSDB_sequence and GDB_to_GENBANK_sequence respectively. Evaluating the link GDB_to_GSDB_sequence involves (a) determining which external database is referenced, using attribute externalDB of class NucleicAcidSequenceLink and attribute searchName of class ExternalDB, in the OPM condition

> NucleicAcidSequenceLink.externalDB[ExternalDB]searchName
> = "gsdb"

and (b) finding sequence objects in GSDB related to sequences in GDB using attribute accessionID of class NucleicAcidSequenceLink in a join condition with attribute ic_accession of class Sequence of GSDB:

---

[4] See http://gdbwww.gdb.org/gdb/gdbDataModel.html.

[5] See http://www.ncgr.org/gsdb/schema.html.

[6] See http://www.ncbi.nlm.nih.gov/Web/GenBank/index.html.

[7] http://gizmo.lbl.gov/DM_TOOLS/OPM/MBD/MBD.html

```
GSDB:Sequence.ic_accession
      = GDB:NucleicAcidSequenceLink.accessionID
```

The link from GDB to GenBank sequences is implemented in a similar way. **Genes** are among the main entities recorded in GDB, where they are represented by objects of class **Gene** and are characterized by information that includes the evidence that a genomic region is considered a gene, and links to gene families the gene belongs to. GSDB also has a class **Gene**, but not necessarily representing the same real-word concepts as the GDB **Gene** class; GDB genes are in most cases represented by instances of other GSDB classes, such as **Product** and **Feature**. Gene references between GSDB and GDB are represented by inter-database link GSDB_to_GDB_gene which involves (a) determining which external database is referenced, using attribute **extdb** of class **DBLink** in GSDB in condition DBLink.extdb = "GDB"; and (b) finding genes in GDB related to genes in GSDB using attribute **extid** of class **DBLink** in a join condition with attribute **accessionID** of class **Gene** of GDB:

```
GSDB:DBLink.extid = GDB:Gene.accessionID
```

Some reformatting of accession numbers is also involved in defining this link.

In this prototype multidatabase system, GDB and GSDB are accessed remotely via the net, while GenBank is accessed via a local copy. Examples of queries specified over this system, expressed in OPM*QL or using the OPM Multidatabase Web Query Interface, were given in sections 4 and 5 respectively.[8] Figures 1 and 3 contain examples of using the OPM Multidatabase tools for browsing and querying this system.

7 Concluding Remarks

The existing version of the OPM Multidatabase tools has demonstrated the feasibility and advantage of our tool-based incremental strategy in dealing with heterogeneous databases. Work is under way to improve the Multidatabase Query Processor by developing increasingly efficient query processing strategies, including concurrency and lazy evaluation techniques for evaluating distributed queries, and employing heuristics for estimating the cost of individual subqueries and determining an optimal evaluation order. We also plan to experiment with using secondary storage, rather than main memory, for intermediate results, in order to handle queries involving large amounts of intermediate data, and to allow the results of multidatbase queries to be stored for further querying.

The most difficult problems of querying multiple heterogeneous databases include (i) formulating a query, which involves determining which databases contain relevant data, understanding how data are represented in each of these

---

[8] This prototype multidatabase system is available on the Web at http://gizmo.lbl.gov/jopmDemo/gdbs_mqs.html

databases, and how data in these databases relate to one another; and (ii) interpreting the result of a multidatabase query. The facilities provided by the Multidatabase Directory and the Web based interfaces address the first problem. The second problem has been only partly addressed. We plan to use information in the Multidatabase Directory together with the semantics of the operations underlying multidatabase query processing for interpreting results of queries expressed across multiple databases. For example, information on the semantics of objects in a given class can be used for annotating query results, while information about inconsistent interdatabase links can be used for explaining null query results.

References

1. Buneman, P., Davidson, S., Hart, K., Overton, C., and Wong, L., A Data Transformation System for Biological Data Sources. In *Proc. of the 21st Int. Conference on Very Large Data Bases*, pp. 158-169, 1995.
2. Buneman, P., Naqvi, S., Tannen, V., Wong, L., Principles of Programming with Complex Objects and Collection Types. In *Theoretical Computer Science 149*, pp 3–48, 1995.
3. Chen, I.A., and Markowitz, V.M., An Overview of the Object-Protocol Model (OPM) and OPM Data Management Tools. *Information Systems*, 20(5), pp. 393-418, 1995.
4. Chen, I.A., and Markowitz, V.M., OPM Schema Translator 4, Reference Manual, Technical Report LBL-35582, 1996.
5. Chen, I.A., Kosky, A., Markowitz, V.M., and Szeto, E., The OPM Query Translator, Technical Report LBL-33706, 1996.
6. Chen, I.A., Kosky, A.S., Markowitz, V.M., and Szeto, E., Constructing and Maintaining Scientific Database Views, Proc. of the 9th Conference on Scientific and Statistical Database Management, IEEE Computer Society, pp. 237- 248, 1997.
7. Etzold, T., and Argos, P., SRS, An Indexing and Retrieval Tools for Flat File Data Libraries. *Computer Applications of Biosciences*, **9**, 1, pp. 49-57, 1993. See also http://www.embl-heidelberg.de/srs/srsc.
8. Fasman, K.H., Letovsky, S.I., Cottingham, R.W., and Kingsbury, D.T., Improvements to the GDB Human Genome Data Base. Nucleic Acids Research, Vol. 24, No. 1, pp. 57-63, 1996. See also http://wwwtest.gdb.org/gdb/about.html.
9. Markowitz, V.M., Chen, I.A., Kosky, A.S., and Szeto, E., Facilities for Exploring Molecular Biology Databases on the Web: A Comparative Study. Pacific Symposium on Biocomputing'97, Altman, R.B. & al (eds) World Scientific , 1997.
10. *The Object Database Standard: ODMG-93*, Cattell, R. G. G. (ed), Morgan Kaufmann, 1996.
11. Programmer's Reference. National Center for Biotechnology Information, Bethesda, Maryland, November 1991. See also the ASN.1 homepage at http://www.inria.fr:80/rodeo/personnel/hoschka/asn1.html.
12. Ritter, O. The Integrated Genomic Database. In *Computational Methods in Genome Research* (S. Suhai, ed.), pp. 57-73, Plenum, 1994.
13. Sheth, A.P., and Larson, J.A. Federated Database Systems for Managing Distributed, Heterogeneous, and Autonomous Databases. *ACM Computing Surveys*, 22(3), pp. 183-236, 1990.

Index of Authors

Springer
and the
environment

At Springer we firmly believe that an
international science publisher has a
special obligation to the environment,
and our corporate policies consistently
reflect this conviction.
We also expect our business partners –
paper mills, printers, packaging
manufacturers, etc. – to commit
themselves to using materials and
production processes that do not harm
the environment. The paper in this
book is made from low- or no-chlorine
pulp and is acid free, in conformance
with international standards for paper
permanency.

Springer

Lecture Notes in Computer Science

For information about Vols. 1–1300

please contact your bookseller or Springer-Verlag